FOLLIES
A National Trust Guide

Gwyn Headley
&
Wim Meulenkamp

JONATHAN CAPE
THIRTY-TWO BEDFORD SQUARE, LONDON

First published 1986
Copyright © 1986 by Gwyn Headley
and Wim Meulenkamp

Jonathan Cape Ltd, 32 Bedford Square, London WC1B 3EL

British Library Cataloguing in Publication Data
Headley, Gwyn
Follies : a National Trust guide.
1. Follies (Architecture)—Great Britain—Guide-books
2. Great Britain—Description and travel—1971- —Guide-books
I. Title   II. Meulenkamp, Wim
914.1′04858 DA 660

ISBN 0—224—02105—2

Printed in Great Britain by
Ebenezer Baylis and Son Ltd,
The Trinity Press, Worcester and London

This book is dedicated to Yvonne Seeley
with gratitude, admiration
and love

Contents

Contents

The Heart of England

Eastern Counties

North-West England

North-East England

Scotland

Illustrations

The authors and publishers would like to thank the following for providing photographs: Lucinda Bredin (no. 184), the Rev. L. V. Headley (no. 97), Steve Lang (nos 187, 188), Michael Mansbridge (no. 81), Wim Meulenkamp (nos 51, 67, 86, 98, 102, 105, 145, 147, 172, 174, 175, 176, 178, 179), *The Oban Times* (no. 191), Geert Tomlow (nos 43, 117, 182). All other photographs were taken by Gwyn Headley and Yvonne Seeley. The vignettes for the section headings are taken from (Anon.) *Decorations for Parks and Gardens* (London, 1790) and William Wrighte's *Grotesque Architecture* (London, 1790, *ed. princ.* 1767).

between pages 324 and 325

Illustrations

between pages 452 and 453

between pages 484 and 485

Foreword and Acknowledgments

As some people are devoted to opera, others to racing cars, so am I devoted to follies, ever since seeing Broadway Tower at the age of five. For my birthday the following year I was given Barbara Jones's incomparable *Follies and Grottoes* (2 gns), the first book on the subject, and my enthusiasm has never diminished. A lot of childish scribbling and blurred photographs followed, and the idea for a book started to take shape in the mid-1960s. In 1973 I appealed via a letter in *Country Life* for more information on follies.

This provided little that was new, but four years later it caught the eye of a Dutchman sitting in a dentist's waiting room in Utrecht. Wim Meulenkamp wrote to me to ask if the book had yet been published, as he was writing his doctoral thesis on 'Follies in Britain'. A little overwhelmed by the magnitude of the task I had set myself, while at the same time trying to establish my own PR company, I proposed a collaboration – I would research and write on Wales and England south of the Wash; Wim could do England north of the Wash and Scotland. There was, of course, much mutual rewriting and aid, much deliberation about what to include and exclude, much discussion about our intentions.

The book was conceived as a guide to and inventory of all surviving follies in England, Scotland and Wales. We did not want it to be an academic work, but wherever possible we have tried to give dates and the names of architects, patrons and owners. These have been researched in some depth, so where they differ from accepted opinion it is because new material has come to light to authenticate our attributions. When we suggest names or dates that we cannot justify, we say so in the text.

We have seen the vast majority of follies in this book, but regret that it has simply not been possible to visit every one. The exigencies of one author living in the Netherlands, the other trying to hold down a full-time (and unconnected) job in London — and, to be honest, the sheer expense of the travelling involved — have meant that we had to forgo the pleasure of exploring some of the remoter Scottish islands. Insufficient time and money have also meant that, at least for the time being, we have had to leave out Ireland, both north and south, and there are some magnificent follies there.

What we include or exclude is finally a matter for ourselves. With rare exceptions, we have not included obelisks or those astonishing buildings which on closer inspection turn out to be dovecotes. Yet we included a windmill — the 18th-century power station — because we felt that designing it as a classical Roman rotunda was, to say the least, pretentious. Monuments are trickier; we had to decide whether the builder was more concerned with the building than with the event or person he was trying to commemorate. There is a county by county list of the more interesting obelisks at the back of the book: we should be pleased to learn of others, as we should be to hear of any errors or omissions in the book as a whole.

We write in the introduction of an ideal folly definition. Defining follies is like learning the English language; there are a few rules to establish the framework, but then come a myriad exceptions. We decided early on that churches could never be regarded as follies; there seemed something sacrilegious about the very idea. Then we found the church at Ayot St Lawrence in Hertfordshire — how could we possibly leave out something so obviously designed as an eyecatcher? In catching the follies for this book we have tried to be as comprehensive as possible, and indeed in some thinly follied areas we have cast our net exceedingly wide and included little minnows or borderline follies, to allow visitors or locals the enjoyment of fishing something out. In some cases our researches have drawn a blank — compare, for example, Leicestershire and

Bedfordshire; Leicestershire is twice the size and has half the number of follies. Is this actually the case or are there many more waiting to be discovered?

A note on nomenclature: we have happily disregarded the present controversy on the usage of terms such as sublime, picturesque, romantic (or Romantick) and rococo for describing gardens or garden buildings. Throughout the text we have used the words gothic, Gothick and Gothic; our rule of thumb is that gothic stands for the medieval 'pointed' style — the original; that Gothick denotes the essentially rococo revival of the style as it was popular in the Georgian era; and that Gothic is more or less consistent with the serious-minded Gothic Revival architecture of Victorian times.

In a world of increasing standardisation, it is pleasing to find so much variety remaining in such a simple matter as a place name. There are various spellings for the same place all over the country, and not just out in the sticks either: one of the smartest villages in wealthy Hertfordshire is called Little Berkhamsted in the *Geographia/AA Great Britain Road Atlas*, Little Berkhampstead in *Bartholomew's Gazetteer*, and Little Berkhamstead on road signs. We have used the spellings first from the *Geographia/AA Great Britain Road Atlas*, secondly from the Ordnance Survey 1:50,000 maps, thirdly from *Bartholomew's Survey Gazetteer* of the British Isles (1966 edn).

The book would be three times as long if we had not resorted to architectural terminology to describe various folly features, so to the lay reader we apologise for the lack of a glossary: Any unfamiliar word can usually be found in a good dictionary or in the glossary at the back of a *Buildings of England*.

We should like to thank the owners and the custodians of the seemingly numberless estates over which we have tramped in search of the least impressive part, who for the most part have borne our eccentricities in hunting out their ancestors' eccentricities with patience and good humour.

Many follies and some of the more peculiar structures described here have been built by Britain's aristocracy, a fine body of people when old enough, rich enough and dotty enough. We found it axiomatic on our travels in researching this book that the newer the money, the colder the welcome, resorting in one or two cases (despite impressive National Trust documentation) to offers of violence. So readers should always remember to *ask permission* before venturing on a folly hunt; every building in this book stands on private land except where specifically mentioned, and even the National Trust cannot allow unrestricted access to its follies. Another point to bear in mind is that many of the structures are somewhat rickety, to put it kindly, and there is a strong possibility of being hit by falling masonry. Remember too that many of them were sited to take advantage of a view, rather than for handy ambulance access.

Special help has been given by Denis Perriam, who opened up new avenues of research to us; Joan Plachta, whose constant advice was usually welcome; Mike and Anne-Marie Edwards, for putting up with the sickness of a would-be aerial photographer; June Southworth, for discovering references to follies in the most unlikely journals; Brian Le Messurier, C. J. Bond and Alan Cox, whose enthusiasm and in-depth knowledge of their areas were invaluable. We are also grateful for the assistance of Roger White and of Ben and Angeli Dijkstra, Ulbe Mehrtens, Bianca du Mortier, Anton Nuijten, Geert Tomlow and Bonica Zijlstra. David Sharp travelled the country in the early 1970s doing drawings for this book when only a few hundred words had been written; we cannot trace his drawings, nor tell his widow that the book finally saw the light of day. Thanks are also due to the staff at Jonathan Cape – Liz Calder, who always spots the winners; Tony Colwell for steering it through; Ian Craig, Lynn Boulton and Judy Linard, who made it look like a book and stayed me with flagons; and in particular to Alison Mansbridge, who edited the book with exceptional care and supported her authors with patience, tenacity and determination.

Without the enthusiasm and encouragement of Robin Wright, the Editorial Director of the National Trust, this book would never have been properly started. Sadly, he died in January 1985, just before the manuscript was delivered.

There is obviously not room to thank everyone who told us of unknown follies, who encouraged us along the way or gave us snippets of previously unheard information, but we should like to acknowledge those who have given us specific help in each county.

Above all, this whole thing could never have started if the Rev. and Mrs L. V. Headley had not decided to take the family for a picnic at Broadway Tower in the summer of 1952 . . .

Gwyn Headley
January 1986

ENGLAND: **Avon** V. C. Chamberlain, Isabel Colegate, Pamela Hudson, Mrs D. M. Lewis, Mr and Mrs Martin Sessions-Hodge, Charles Skilton, Sir George White; **Bedfordshire** Alan Cox, A. M. Griffin; **Berkshire** M. C. Bullen; **Buckinghamshire** R. W. Evans, Mrs Joan Rhodes, John Rotheroe, John S. Wilson; **Cambridgeshire** Peter Foster; **Cheshire** John Collins; **Cleveland** J. D. S. Gillis; **Cornwall** Colin Griffin, Brian Le Messurier, Mrs Dorothy Merrett, J. H. Oates, L. W. Robinson; **Cumbria** Denis Perriam; **Derbyshire** Cherry Knott; **Devon** Brian Le Messurier; **Dorset** Miss Cunnington, Kim Duffell, Harriet Huxley, Colin Spooner, A. T. Swindell, John Waite, George Wright; **Durham** Mr B. I. Bagnall, Karl Evans, James Wilson; **East Sussex** Anne Draycott, N. Hutchins; **Essex** A. C. Austin, Norman Dowdy, Mr P. M. Richards, Mr E. White; **Gloucestershire** Basil Barlow, Roger Beacham, Mr G. J. Chilman, Stewart Cypher, James Dawson, Mr J. J. Jefferies, Nicholas Johnson, David Leake, Mrs Lodge, G. A. Pyart, W. J. Phillips, Evelyn Roper, David Ross, Colin Walker; **Hampshire** Paul Atlas, Jonathan Barnes, Krystyna Bilikowski, Roger Brown, Judge Eric McLellan, Sir James and Lady Scott, Charles Wagner; **Hereford & Worcestershire** E. C. Davies, Mr P. H. Gibbons, the late Vere Hodgson; **Hertfordshire** Mrs Marion Cooper, W. A. Dodd, Mary A. Hard, Gordon Higgott, E. V. Parrott; **Humberside** Col. R. A. Alec-Smith, D. C. Gill, Richard Parker, N. L. Smith, Frank Whitmarsh; **Isle of Wight** Mr Baker, S. H. Greenen; **Kent** W. H. Deakin, John de la Rue, Lawrie Hurst, Mr and Mrs W. R. E. Seys, Mr Turner; **Lancashire** David Tattersall; **Leicestershire** Paula Levey; **Lincolnshire** J. L. Allenby, Trevor Hopkins, Mr C. W. Fletcher, M. R. Sellors; **London** John Earle, P. G. Kennedy, Sue Rolfe; **Manchester** D. J. Burns, A. J. Pass; **Norfolk** the Hon. Robin Walpole; **Northamptonshire** Mr Kerrou, Kevin O'Shaughnessy; **Northumberland** J. E. Lodge, J. D. Nichol; **North Yorkshire** Mrs

Elizabeth Savage; **Nottinghamshire** Graham Beaumont; **Oxford-shire** Mr J. O. A. Arkell, Mr J. A. Bateman, Mr C. J. Bond, Mr and Mrs J. Dorman, Mrs M. Rafferty, Reg Wilkinson; **Shropshire** Maj. Clement Hill, J. T. Jones, Michael Law, Miss C. Ryan; **Somerset** Robert Adams, Patricia Reed, Lt-Col. P. Tamlyn; **South Yorkshire** J. C. Harris, G. V. Holliday, D. M. Yorke; **Staffordshire** the Earl of Bradford, John Shryane, A. G. Taylor; **Suffolk** E. E. Barritt, Mrs Birch, Mrs S. Colman, Mrs Aisa de Mille, Miss R. Freeman, Theo H. K. van Thijcklen; **Surrey** Nigel Barker, Lesley Howes; **Tyne & Wear** Jean le Malchanceux; **Warwickshire** Louise Allen-Jones, Mr T. Ashbourne; **West Midlands** H. P. Barnes, Keith Brace, Mr I. S. Hodson, P. Holland, Peter Lyon, Brian Moore, Graham Shaylor, S. Whitehouse, A. A. Wood; **West Sussex** Commander W. M. Phipps-Hornby; **West Yorkshire** M. C. Bradshaw, Mrs J. Mitchell, Arthur Porritt, Colin Spencer, M. Umpleby; **Wiltshire** J. E. J. Chandler, Mr and Mrs C. Corden, G. F. McDonic.

WALES: **Glamorgan** Gareth Jenkins, Caroline Morgan; **Gwent** W. J. Newman; **Gwynedd** G. W. Griffith, D. J. Williams; **Powys** Jane Perkins, Deirdre Rhys-Thomas.

SCOTLAND: **Dumfries & Galloway** Steve Lang; **Grampian** Ron Knox, Mrs Lorna M. Sterling, Arthur Watson; **Highland** Lucinda Bredin; **Lothian** Betty Kirkpatrick; **Strathclyde** Hilary Duguid.

Introduction

What is a folly? Ideally, it should be a big, Gothick, ostentatious, over-ambitious and useless structure, preferably with a wildly improbable local legend attached – but in real life it must be admitted that follies defy even such broad definitions. That's half the pleasure of the things: if they could be categorised and catalogued and pinned down like specimen butterflies we would lose that frisson of excitement and mystery when another unidentified ghostly grey ruin looms up out of a wet wood. The folly must lie in the eye of the beholder.

What about the people who build them? They share with the rest of mankind and several more obscure members of the crow family a deep-seated urge to adorn their property or territory. To pepper your estate with temples is a natural, if expensive, version of the desire to ornament your car with a leopardskin steering-wheel cover, furry dice or an alsatian with brake-light eyes; to erect a mighty tower on the summit of a hill stems from the same impulse that gives rise to the micro world of little red men fishing in ponds in suburban front gardens. The folly builder, then, indulges a natural urge to express eccentricity with all the resources of wealth and imagination he can muster.

Some were, of course, undeniably mad, in the obsessive rather than the psychotic sense, and the most obsessive of them were probably not a pleasant breed; to be so bound up in private gratification is necessarily to ignore the wants and needs of others. On the other hand, there are degrees of madness, ranging from the soft-brained determination of a kitten with a ball of string to the wild, staring unreason of the truly insane. A characterless building can never be a folly; nor can a humourless one — although the humour could be the frivolous gaiety of the simple-minded or the evil chuckle of the psychopath. In this, the most haunted country in the world, it is quite remarkable that out of well over 1,000 follies only one — at Belmont in Lancashire — has acquired a reputation for being haunted. (Why Bull's Tower at Pentlow in Essex has not, we cannot understand; it is without doubt the most minatory building we have ever visited.)

While the word 'folly' is taken to be a derivation of 'foolishness', a study of its etymology and history reveals some other underlying meanings. Its direct ancestor is the Old French *folie, fol* meaning foolishness, and itself deriving from the Latin *follis*, meaning a ball, balloon or bellows. Another ancestor is *feuillée*, from the Latin *foliatus*, or foliage. In the English countryside this came to mean a copse on a hill — hence the great number of Folly Farms, which have nothing to do with our sort of folly – whereas on the Continent it had a more direct reference to building, denoting a hut made from the branches of trees. In 1337 the archives of the town of Alavard forbade the erection of 'foilliatas' without the permission of the authorities, while in England the top of the hill just outside Faringdon in Oxfordshire has always been called 'The Folly', and is marked as such on the earliest Ordnance Survey maps; it wasn't until 1935 that someone decided to build a folly-tower there.

William Beckford used the word 'folly' quite frequently in referring to his building works at Fonthill Abbey in Wiltshire — 'this new piece of abbatial folly' (1812) — and even his constant companion Gregory Franchi used the word in writing to Beckford's son-in-law the Duke of Hamilton – 'new houses, new caprices, new follies, new debts . . . ' (1822). These early uses of the word still had not acquired the nuances it has today.

After some isolated earlier examples, the folly really came into its own in the 18th century, with its heyday between 1730 and 1820. The invention of the English landscape garden brought forth a vast number of garden buildings — exotic, eclectic, some drawn straight from pattern books, others the inspired product of individual aberration. These early garden buildings were frequently rather dull, deriving from the formal classical temples, cascades and grottoes of the average ducal garden of the Italian Renaissance. It was not until the English, striving to achieve an effect quickly and economically, started to use inferior materials, or simply went over the top in quantity or proportions, that these ornamental structures really began to deserve to be called follies. Now the survivors are further enhanced by their antiquity, while the effects of industrial pollution have enormously accelerated the ageing process. The squire who in the mid-18th century built a replica of the Choragic Monument of Lysicrates in his Midlands park had little idea that within 200 years his ornament would look older than the original.

The Rococo of the second and third quarters of the 18th century can be compared to Italian 16th-century Mannerism, particularly in the emphasis that was placed on novelty and oddity. One is reminded of gardens like Bomarzo near Viterbo, built by Pirro Ligorio for Count Orsini (packed with frenzied flights of architectural fancy such as a gigantic gaping stone face, acting as a façade to a shelter, and a Leaning House, deliberately and disturbingly built 20 degrees out of true), or of the miniature Rome, also built by Ligorio, at the Villa d'Este. The influx of Mannerism in England through pattern books such as those compiled by Philibert de l'Orme and Werner Dietterlin towards the end of the 16th century prepared the ground for more than one garden folly.

Robert Morris, a champion of Palladianism, recognised that such ideas were likely to undermine the strict adherence to classical rules, and in his poem 'The Art of Architecture' (1742) he begged the innovators to 'be *Lofty* still':

> Keep up the *Strength*, the *Dignity* and *Force*
> Of *stated Rules*; let those direct your Course.
> New Methods are not easy understood;
> And few will step in an untrodden Road.
> 'Tis better to pursue the Rule that's known,
> Than trust to an Invention of your own.

This was the sort of advice the folly architects ignored. To the delight of their patrons, many of them threw away rules, loftiness and dignity and set about making architecture fun, making buildings to gasp at. A new informality was sweeping the land, and the landscape garden acquired the role of architectural laboratory. As a rule, garden follies were cheaply built, and small enough to be taken down without too much trouble should the result prove unsatisfactory to the client. It was only when they reached unmanageably large proportions that the folly element proper came in.

The circuit of the grander gardens began to resemble a miniature world tour, with architecture from every nation and every period spattered around the grounds. One could take a rest in a Gothick seat or partake of a meal in a sham ruined Banqueting House; or a Gothick Temple could prompt reflections on the state of Liberty in Old England. The Temple of Virtue, in the severest Greek Doric, would remind the promenaders of the democracies of the Ancients, just as a hermitage would recall the purity and innocence of the devotional life of the anchorite. Sometimes a garden would be furnished with a real but usually venal hermit, or with a wooden or papier-maché manikin. A temple, an obelisk or an alcove was dedicated to the memory of a poet, an eminent statesman, a dear departed friend; or to a pig, a horse, a dog. Pagodas, mosques and pyramids conjured up exotic countries and their vices and virtues, giving well travelled visitors a chance to discourse at length on some minutia of life in those fabled lands.

The buildings could take on any form, any style. Egyptian, Chinese, Gothick, Roman, Greek, Indian, Druidical, Grotesque, Rural, Mooresque and Rustic architecture was commandeered to produce temples, obelisks, pagodas, kiosks, screens, mosques, columns, umbrellos, eyecatchers, tents, sham ruins, sham castles, sham churches, sham abbeys, forts, dovecotes, sugar loaves, arches, façades, mausoleums, pyramids, gates, pillars, pavilions, hermitages, bridges, towers, grottoes, seats, cottages, tunnels, caves, byres, kennels, menageries, huts and ice-houses. It was exuberant building, architecture for the sake of itself or architecture by association, which in a few extreme instances manifested itself as an insatiable desire to build, the building mania classified by the phlegmatic French along with *crimes passionnels* as a *folie de bâtir*.

A remarkable number of the great 18th- and early 19th-century architects designed follies or other architectural eccentricities, including such names as Chambers, Soane, Mylne, Archer, Paine, Garrett, Kent, the Adam brothers, Nash, Vanbrugh, Hawksmoor, Carr, Wyatville and Wyatt. Some accepted the commissions reluctantly; others enthusiastically seized the opportunity to experiment in styles they knew would not find general favour in their commercial practices. Their attitudes sometimes bordered on the schizophrenic: Roger Morris (a relative of the architectural poet) turned cautiously to the Gothick late in his career, a choice he presumably felt safe to make only after his reputation had been established. John Soane, on the other hand, actually repudiated his collection of folly designs (*Designs in Architecture*, 1778), and yet he went on building superb follies until the very end, as the lodge at Pell Wall House, Staffordshire, convincingly shows.

Some architects specialised in building follies, notably Sanderson Miller and Thomas Wright. Interestingly, these two were amateur, perhaps dilettante, architects; squires themselves, they could talk on equal terms with their clients and probably understood their problems more readily than could a busy London architect with several commissions to attend to at once. Other architects perhaps better known for their follies than their regular work included John Plaw, John Crunden sr, W. F. Pocock and Henry Flitcroft. With other architects, follies were a profitable sideline and offered a means of experimentation.

For those dedicated followers of fashion who lacked the imagination, the architect or the financial means of other would-be builders, pattern books provided the necessary visual stimulation. These collections of 'blueprints' trickled on to the market *c.*1740; the trickle naturally became a flood, yielding dozens of designs for rural baths, summer or winter hermitages, prospect towers, farm screens, seats and sham ruins in all manner of styles. So much for your common-or-garden folly builder − but to the patron who really wanted to Build, the pattern book was of little use. Relying on his own or his architect's judgment, this last category of patron usually provided the more striking garden follies, employing architects, or at least masons, but keeping a tight rein on the development of the garden and its buildings. Alton Towers in Staffordshire, Hawkstone in Shropshire, Painshill in Surrey and Hackfall in Yorkshire are good examples of owner-controlled designs.

By 1800 the garden folly was on the way out, and in his *Rural Residences* of 1818, despite having included a few good designs for garden follies, John Buonarroti Papworth could write:

> Once, indeed, a style not so consistent had a temporary existence
> with us; then also painted arcades, mock bridges, churches and
> even mock cathedrals, were 'quite in taste': but these were soon
> exploded, and if the imitative powers of art are employed in the
> present day, it is generally in those things only that are ephemeral
> in their nature; and here too the indulgence is not unlimited.

This particular kind of folly had an uneasy afterlife in the suburban
gardens of the professional classes, but these 'bourgeois' productions
were (and are) either ignored or ridiculed by critics.

The kind of folly we label the 'squire folly' is generally quite
different from the garden folly. It is not situated in a landscaped
garden, or at least its reference to the garden is not its most
prominent feature, and it tends to belong more to the late Georgian
period than to the Rococo.

The squire was the most important personage in the village;
wealth and tradition entitled him to judiciary, political and
social power. In the hands of a competent, caring and benevolent
man the system came close to a social ideal, but a weak, vindictive
squire was worse than an extremist dictator. He had his tenants, the
home farm and perhaps a family fortune, enough to maintain a
relatively autarkic economy. He did not have a regular job that paid
a salary, but any squire who sat and stared out of the window (the
18th-century equivalent of watching television all evening) would
soon find himself in penury. The surrounding land was his, and he
was part of it. It was therefore the land – its agricultural
improvement and, if he was interested in the subject, its artistic
beauty – that consumed much of his time. He hunted it, he lived
on it, he fed off it, and his villagers depended on him to provide for
them. It was only natural that an artistically-minded squire would
choose his immediate surroundings for some form of
embellishment.

He would start by adorning his estate with the elements of visual
power, the regalia of his kingship. Towers, obelisks, farm
buildings in the Gothick taste, triumphal arches – all appeared for
his tenants to wonder at and to fantasise upon, to impress his
freeholders with the reserves of money he obviously possessed, and

to display to country peers and visitors from town his taste, his inventiveness and his domination of the area.

Squire follies are usually wildly original, and executed in the rustic, rural or grotesque styles. Good illustrations of these are the undatable follies built by a member of the Messiter family at Barwick Park in Somerset, while although 'Mad' Jack Fuller of Brightling, East Sussex, employed the rising young architect Robert Smirke to build most of his follies, they are essentially Fuller's creations, providing a mirror to his quirky and sometimes disturbed mind. George Durant's follies at Tong in Shropshire, now mostly disappeared, provided even better examples of the squire folly as a sort of architectural Rorschach test.

It is shapes that count in squire follies: pyramids, cones and the cylinders of towers are dominant. The best among them are pure examples of accidental architecture, hurled up with energy and a blithe disregard for correct orders. In the process they inevitably enlarged the vocabulary of building, but even now, because of their provenance, they are treated by art historians with an amused condescension, as cul-de-sacs off the broad avenue of architecture. They were not considered a subject worthy of detailed study.

Because follies are instinctive rather than reasoned, they were seldom used as models. Yet we would do well to remember that the first Greek Revival building in this country was a folly; that the Victorian High Gothic, which influenced architects all over the world, was germinated by the reaction against the increasingly bizarre Gothick favoured by the folly builder; and that one particular configuration – the triangular floor plan – has become the near-exclusive preserve of the folly. Cynics will point out that this is simply because it produces the most inconvenient living-area ever devised by human ingenuity; in its defence we can only say that the fortunate few people we have met who live in triangular houses appear to be unusually happy with their lot – and at least one major modern novel has been written in a triangular house.

Similarly, the garden folly, despite its short but fashionable life, influenced much of the architectural fashion of the 19th century. The first Gothick revival buildings were the garden follies built in the 1720s and 1730s; the first Greek Revival building was Hagley Temple of 1759; the fashion for chinoiserie, things Indian and

Moorish, was introduced with folly pagodas and oriental temples.

The 'druidical' style, being uncomfortably close to home, never went beyond the realm of the folly, but rural, rustic and grotesque styles found their way into cottages, bridges, stations, lodges and the suburban house. The Houses of Parliament, the British Museum and St Pancras Station were not without their predecessors, however humble they might have looked.

The finest, purest folly in the world, it must be said, was French, the Palais Idéal in Hautrives, Drôme, a truly astonishing edifice built singlehandedly by Joseph-Ferdinand Cheval (1836–1924) between 1879 and 1912. He was not a rich man – in fact he was the village postman – but his lust for building overcame such minor considerations as finance. And there were other famous European follies in previous centuries, including the Chevalier de Monville's Maison Colonne, a house in the shape of a gigantic, ruined, fluted column in the Désert de Retz outside Paris, and Ludwig II's fairytale castle in Bavaria, Neuschwanstein – but it was always Britain that overwhelmed with the quantity of follies put up by dedicated eccentrics.

What of the modern British folly? Conditions over the past 40 years have not been conducive to frivolous building, while for years before they had been ludicrously unfashionable. Opinions are changing – advertisements offering small, expensive, glass-fibre follies are beginning to appear in glossy magazines, and it is now distinctly chic to live in or own a folly – but the fashion now is mostly retrogressive, Britain's few post-war follies having nearly all followed the classical path, with a few Gothic bastions here and there. Only in America, where follies are being built with the same fine disregard for architectural rules as characterised the British squire folly, can we find a folly of smoked glass and chrome. Have Britons lost the amiable eccentricity that once made them the puzzle of Europe? We think not. Someone, somewhere must be building a slightly dangerous tower from wine bottles, or an unsuitable fort from breeze blocks. We'd like to meet you.

Gwyn Headley and Wim Meulenkamp
January 1986

The
West Country

Cornwall

They are called emmets in Cornwall, grockles in Devon; they are at once the bane and the salvation of this acre of Britain; they are tourists. Once Cornwall's prosperity lay underground in tin and copper, but the ruins of the wheal engine-houses (wheal is the Cornish name for a mine) stand in mute testimony to the passing of the industry, and now the tripper rules. Only ugly inland towns like Camborne and Redruth remain unscarred by the ubiquitous traveller; more attractive seaside resorts like St Ives even have to go so far as to ban visitors' cars from the town during the season. The real Cornish are difficult to find: many have emigrated, and those who remain distrust the English, a people they hold in scarcely higher regard than they do Devonians. The county looks and sounds Celtic:

> By Tre, Pol and Pen
> Shall ye know the Cornish men

and indeed has more in common with Wales and Brittany than with the rest of England. Its beauty and its romance attract visitors in herds, and it is second only to Ireland as a romantic novelist's choice for a setting, fuelled by tales of insanely brave and arrogant men like Sir Richard Edgcumbe of Cotehele, Sir Richard Grenville of the 'Revenge' or unyielding priests like Bishop Sir Jonathan Trelawny, who, accused by James II of seditious libel, finally achieved immortality through R. S. Hawker's 'Song of the Western Men', which has become the unofficial Cornish national anthem. (Some doubt has been cast on the relevance of Hawker's verse to Sir Jonathan, as the last three lines are thought to have been a popular rallying cry in the 17th century, and referred to an entirely different Trelawny.)

The Rev. Robert Stephen Hawker (1803–75) seems well qualified as an eccentric. At the age of 19 he married a lady of 41, and the marriage lasted happily for 40 years. When his wife died, he remarried the following year and quickly fathered three daughters. His folly, if such it can be called, for it is more of a caprice, is famous: the chimneys of his 1837 vicarage at MORWENSTOW, a secluded hamlet north of Bude, are models of church-towers he particularly liked, apart from the kitchen chimney which is a copy of his mother's tomb. The design for the rest of the vicarage was taken straight from Thomas Frederick Hunt's *Designs for Parsonage Houses* (1827). The model used was 'a Clergyman's house, on a modest scale'. Modern estate agents would describe it as a substantial detached residence.

Just outside Bude is Stamford Hill in STRATTON, where the Civil War battle was fought in 1643. A little oddity marks the spot: a tiny arch one has to stoop to walk through, crowned with a crocketed pinnacle taken from nearby Poughill church-tower. The inscription quaintly records the valour of another romantic Cornishman, Sir Bevil Granville, who defeated the Earl of Stamford's army here. It is strange how the name Stamford always seems to involve fighting.

Most Cornish follies are small; at PORT ISAAC 'The Birdcage' is mentioned as a folly, but in reality is merely an asymmetrical fisherman's cottage just above the harbour. It belongs to the National Trust, but is let privately. The real folly is on National Trust land at Doyden Point by PORTQUIN, a village which probably resembles Port Isaac before the tourists discovered it. The folly is a boxy little two-storey tower, hesitantly castellated, with one Gothic window in each wall and a shallow one-storey extension, also castellated, on the east side. A sad tale comes with it; it was erected to commemorate the loss of the Portquin boat which went down with every man in the village on board – all were drowned, none saved. 'The Huer's House' at NEWQUAY was built for a specific if unusual purpose, so is not a folly – but it is undeniably an eccentric structure. Built of whitewashed rubble, it would not look out of place on a Greek island, with its outside stair climbing one floor at the side of a squat tower. It has diamond-shaped windows and rudimentary castellations, and its function was to serve as a look-out post from which the huer could spot shoals of pilchard and direct the fishing boats accordingly.

The towns of Camborne and REDRUTH are separated by the 816 feet of Carn Brea, not a particularly high hill but one which dominates the surrounding landscape. The summit is topped with an extraordinary monument to the memory of Francis, Lord de Dunstanville and Bassett, erected by the county in 1836. It can be seen for miles around, virtually from all over North Cornwall, although it seems surprisingly small when approached. Again this is deceptive: the tower is big, but the design makes it seem small. Built by Joseph Prior of Gwennap, it is strikingly futuristic, a remarkable work for its date, a tapering hexagonal column rising to the stumpiest cross ever seen surrounding a diamond lozenge. There is a doorway in the plinth where one can enter right into the column, which is circular and hollow, rising up 90 feet. A niche off the entrance passage leads to the staircase, which climbs up inside the wall of the monument to a viewing platform at the top, according to two boys who were sheltering inside from the pelting rain; as the bottom eight feet or so of the stairs had been destroyed, we forbore from making the climb. Carn Brea Castle just along the ridge is a beautifully preserved 18th-century sham castle perched on a crazy jumble of rocks like the chapel at Roche; from underneath it gives the bizarre impression of a straightforward building with aspirations to normality that has been attacked by some frightful disease, the stone warped, moulded and disfigured beyond imagination. It was originally built as a hunting lodge for the Bassetts, and now it is one of Britain's remoter restaurants. A Land Rover would seem to be the most suitable means of getting to it, but once there the diners can feast their eyes on what is probably the finest view in Cornwall. We say probably, because we bumped along there one day in August in driving rain, scraping the bottom of the car on the rocky road not once but a dozen times, only to find it was closed on Mondays — and we couldn't even admire the view because we were standing in a cloud!

Near Halsetown, above ST IVES and Carbis Bay on top of the hill, is the Knill Monument, a strange triangular pyramid with even stranger stories surrounding it. Inscriptions are incused on each side: 'RESURGAM' above a freshly painted coat-of-arms with the punning motto 'NIL DESPERANDU'; 'JOHANNES KNILL 1782'; then on the third side 'I KNOW THAT MY REDEEMER LIVETH'. John Knill, a bachelor, and Mayor of St Ives, excavated a hole in the rock at Mount's Bay which he intended to serve as his mausoleum; sadly he died in London and ended up buried in Holborn, the original plan quite forgotten. Knill had a number of little weaknesses which seem to have afforded him great pleasure and offended no one; his predilection for pubs while in London led him to sample four or five every day before invariably dining at Dolly's Chop House. He made provision in his will for a peculiar ceremony to be performed at the monument, and this still continues after 200 years. Every fifth year on 25 July ten girls, each ten years old and dressed in white, climb up to the monument accompanied by two widows, a clergyman, a fiddler, the Mayor of St Ives and the local Customs and Excise man. There they sing the 100th Psalm, after which the girls dance round the monument for a quarter of an hour to the tune of the fiddler, singing an old song which begins 'Shun the barter of the bay, Hasten upward, come away . . . ' For performing this inexplicable ceremony the young girls, the fiddler and the two widows receive ten shillings each, while the parson, the mayor and the VAT man get £10 each, which they must use to give a dinner party to which they can invite two friends. The unwavering charms of Dolly's Chop House led Knill to refuse every invitation to dine privately during his lifetime. The presence of the Customs man leads one to speculate that he might have been a smuggler, but the reasons for the ritual lie buried with him. Joseph Hocking, Cornwall's truly great bad novelist, set *The Eye of the Triangle*, one of his more atrocious efforts, at the Knill Monument, and he was as fascinated by the rite as we are. 'RESURGAM' means 'I shall rise again'; whether Knill shared the same interpretation of life after death as Mad Jack Fuller, Major Peter Labellière and Sir John Pentillie or not, he at any rate caused something to be done about it. It is merely unfortunate that he isn't inside the monument, with the expected bottle of port, waiting for the Day of Judgment and enjoying the virgins' dance.

The road to PENZANCE from St Ives passes Castle-an-Dinas on

the left, and on the top of the hill is another tiny folly called Roger's Tower. Perched above an escarpment, it looks like a cover for a cheese dish, square with four tiny, round, corner turrets. It was built *c.* 1800 as a prospect belvedere; the views across to St Michael's Mount are superb. Legrice's Folly at Penzance is another minute coastal 'tower', though how a one-storey building gets labelled as a tower puzzles us. It was probably built as another huer's house, the heavy castellations of solid stone giving it a toy fort feeling. The finest thing to see in Penzance is John Foulston's Egyptian House of 1830, in Chapel Street, with a style so fantastic to our eyes nowadays that most people would unhesitatingly regard it as a folly.

In HELSTON, one of the four coinage towns of old stannary Cornwall, the main street is called Coinagehall Street. At the bottom end, opening on to a bowling green, is an elaborate Gothic gateway, erected in 1834 by public subscription to the memory of Humphrey Millet Grylls. The architect was George Wightwick, a Londoner who failed to find sufficient work so moved to Plymouth, where he was inundated with commissions.

The Lander Column in TRURO is a welcome change from the omnipresent commemorative obelisk. It was built in 1834 by Philip Sambell, a deaf and dumb architect, and takes the form of a fine Doric fluted column in granite, crowned with a statue of Richard Lander by N. N. Burnard.

TO HONOUR THE
ENTERPRISE AND SUFFERINGS
OF THE BROTHERS
RICHARD AND JOHN LANDER
NATIVES OF THIS TOWN
AND ESPECIALLY TO
COMMEMORATE THE EARLY
FATE OF RICHARD, EXPLORER
OF THE RIVER NIGER,
BORN 1804 DIED FERNANDO PO 1834

By the popular and therefore very crowded King Harry Ferry is the National Trust estate of TRELISSICK. Described by Pevsner as 'the severest neo-Greek mansion in Cornwall', it nonetheless boasts a delightful piece of whimsy in the garden by the side of the road; a substantial round tower with a conical roof, lucarnes and a circular stair turret also with a conical roof. Peter Robinson was the architect of the house, but the tower is much later, *c.* 1860, and reminiscent of Burges's Castell Coch outside Cardiff. If you have the patience to queue for the ferry, you can reach VERYAN in a matter of minutes. Veryan's claim to fame is its round houses, built, the story goes, at the ends of the village so that if the Devil decided to come prowling round the village he would first be confronted with the round houses which he would circle all night, like the messenger boy with Dunston Pillar in Lincolnshire. The houses are completely circular, with conical thatched roofs surmounted by crosses, and they do stand in pairs like sentries at the entrance to the village. They are said to have been built in the early 19th century for £50 each by Hugh Rowe of Lostwithiel on the orders of Parson Trist, who had a poor regard for Satan's intelligence. Designs published in Worgan's Agricultural Survey of 1811 are almost identical, and were intended for labourers' cottages.

Surprisingly for such a coastal county, grottoes and shell-houses are largely ignored except for the stretch of coast between Gribbin Head and Rame Head. MENABILLY, outside Fowey, was built for the Rashleigh family, and in the landscaped grounds looking out to sea is a tiny dilapidated grotto made entirely from Cornish granite and shells. It was built in the 1780s by Philip Rashleigh from the overstocks of his enormous collection of minerals. The Rashleigh Mausoleum of 1871 at FOWEY is also worth seeing, a great bell-shaped structure overlooking the ruined fort. Eastwards along the coast, picturesque POLPERRO has a house in 'The Warren' with its façade decorated with shells, all done by a Mr Sam Puckey just before the Second World War. The National Trust has a popular and recently restored grotto at Sharrow Point in WHITSAND BAY called Lugger's Cave or Sharrow Grot, excavated in 1784 by James Lugger, an ex-Navy purser who suffered from gout. The cave is 15 feet deep and 7 feet high, with a semi-circular seat at the end, also carved out of the solid rock. When Lugger finished the work after a year, he started to inscribe welcoming verses on the walls:

But, as thou walk'st, should sudden storms arise
Red lightning flash, or thunder shake the skies
To Sharrow's friendly grot in haste retreat
And find safe shelter and a rocky seat.

The warm wet banks of the Tamar valley provide an enchanting setting for lovely houses and narrow Devonian lanes, but this is still Cornwall, where the wild romantic heroes of yesteryear linger on in the memory. None more so than Sir Richard Edgcumbe of COTEHELE, whose literally cliff-hanging lifestyle can only be hinted at in a book like this. He was MP for Tavistock, rebelled against Richard III and consequently was pursued by Sir Henry Trenowth, Richard's feared and loathed Cornish agent. Trenowth drew Edgcumbe's cover at Cotehele and chased him to the cliff's edge, where Edgcumbe threw his hat into the river 70 feet below while he clung to a branch of the overhang. Trenowth looked down to see his adversary's hat floating down the Tamar and assumed Edgcumbe was still underneath it; an assumption he was to regret years later when Edgcumbe became a favourite of Henry VII and had the gory satisfaction of chasing Trenowth off the edge of a cliff into the sea at Bodrugan's Leap. Sir Richard built the Chapel of SS. George and Thomas à Becket on the cliff edge at Cotehele to commemorate his escape, and after restoration in 1620 and 1769 it is still open. It is now owned by the National Trust, but there is a genuine folly at Cotehele which has everything in its favour except for a wonderful story like Sir Richard's. The Prospect Tower, like most follies, has an uncertain history. The local story is that it was built so that the Edgcumbes' servants could signal to Maker Church, 11 miles away near Mount Edgcumbe, when the family was in transit from one house to another. A more likely explanation is that it was built to celebrate the visit of King George III and Queen Charlotte to Cotehele in August 1789; Fanny Burney noted in her diary that the Edgcumbes were 'vastly Excited' by the visit of the Royals and 'were full of the honours done them and told me of the obelisks and arches they meant to construct in commemoration'; there are no arches or obelisks at Cotehele, so perhaps the Prospect Tower is the result. It is a very satisfying tower, about 60 feet high, built of slaty stone with dummy church windows. Architecturally it is similar to a straightforward Perpendicular church-tower from a distance; the ingenuity and *trompe l'oeil* effect reveals itself only as you approach: the building is triangular, and each wall is distinctly concave. A sturdy new wooden staircase was installed in 1980 and three visitors at a time can now climb to the top to admire the view — and yes, Maker Church can be seen.

In far poorer condition is the excellently decayed and really creepy tower on MOUNT ARARAT, a couple of miles to the south. This was built as a mausoleum by Sir James Tillie in 1712, where he intended to be put to rest seated in an upstairs room with his roast and his port, awaiting the Day of Judgment. There is no longer an upstairs room, and the tower is neglected and overgrown, but few things can surpass the delicious thrill of terror we felt when we peered through a stone grill in the tower's wall to see the figure of a man sitting on a chair inside. A fairly long pause to recover our breath, then a second look. Covered in ferns and brambles he may be, but inside is the petrified image of Sir James, sitting on his seat, hands firmly placed on his thighs. The square three-storey tower is surrounded by a wall, and ten steps lead up to the blocked entrance porch. There was probably once a plaque above the doorway, in which is now set the stone grill.

MOUNT EDGCUMBE, the other seat of the Edgcumbe family, overlooks Plymouth Sound and is now a Plymouth park, although administratively still in Cornwall. The folly here is known as the Ruin, and was built in Devon (Cornwall took over Mount Edgcumbe only in 1844). The Ruin was probably built *c.* 1750 by Timothy Brett, and it is a superb example of what a good sham ruin should be. The position overlooking Plymouth and the Sound is spectacular; the ruination is extensive, yet the large traceried window offering the view is high enough from the ground to give a noticeably different perspective. Also in the park are a 14-foot triangular Coade stone monument to Timothy Brett and a little Tuscan temple called Thomson's Seat.

Two final follies in Cornwall. Just north of LISKEARD is the ancient dwelling of Treworgey, where John Connock built a clock-tower in 1730 (the present owner finds it handy as an exotic garden shed). It has three stepped storeys, rather like a pagoda, and the top two storeys are clapboarded — it looks more Kentish than Cornish.

The clock-face has only an hour hand and was made by John Belling of 'Bodmyn' in 1733. A huge pointed arch window takes up almost the whole of the west wall of the ground floor. The clock is in perfect working order and is wound daily; the bell is inscribed 'John Connock His Bell AD 1620', and presumably belonged to an ancestor of the builder.

We couldn't find the last folly. It is in Werrington Park, a beautiful private estate just north of LAUNCESTON, and there is a good picture of it in Barbara Jones's book: a rough stone plinth with a round arched seat set into it, and three Barwick Park-type cones placed above, rising up to a height of about 25 feet. In the photograph it sits on a bare open hillside, presumably staring across at the house, serving as an eyecatcher. The owner gave us detailed instructions, warning us that trees had grown up around it and that it was now in the middle of a wood, but that we couldn't miss it. After an hour and a half stumbling around in the stifling little wood we emerged to admit defeat. 'Funny that,' ruminated the owner, 'my wife couldn't find it when she looked last week.'

Devon

As befits a county which has given us characters as diverse as Sir Francis Drake, Sir Joshua Reynolds and Agatha Christie (and potatoes and smoking, via its son Sir Walter Ralegh), Devon has a fine variety of remote and mysterious follies – not as many as we could have hoped for in such a big county (only Yorkshire and Lincolnshire are bigger), but most of them well worth a visit, and one or two outstanding.

Easily the most bizarre building in Devon is 'The Pack o' Cards' pub in COMBE MARTIN, a long, straggling village running down to the north coast. Photographs cannot prepare one for the shock of delight when it comes suddenly into view; it is much bigger than one anticipates, and at first glance the chimneys seem to be piled on top of each other without any semblance of order, giving an extraordinary, overbalanced feel to the whole structure. In addition the inn has recently been painted a glistering white, so it leaps at the eye. Ann Jellicoe in her *Shell Guide to Devon* describes it as 'a folly said by the literal minded to have windows and chimneys relating to the number of cards in a pack', but Mrs Philips, the present owner, swears this is true. There were originally 52 windows, but many were blocked up to escape Pitt's window tax; there are indeed four main floors, and we certainly counted 13 doors on the lowest. What is less easy to establish is when and why it was built, and for once the familiar old gambling story used as an apologia for several follies throughout Britain (but denied by the owners of Roebuck's Folly in Avon, for example) could have a ring of truth. There is no other good reason to explain why a vernacular building should be designed in this anti-style. The popular tale, written on parchment and framed in the pub, says that the house was built by Squire George Ley, who died in 1716, to celebrate a very handsome gambling win. The actual date of 'The Pack o' Cards' is uncertain; the landlady claims the 17th century, but nearly all pubs in Britain claim to be at least a century older than they are; and even the 18th century of Squire George's lifetime is early for the Venetian windows in the gable ends to appear in vernacular architecture. Less authenticated, alas, is the name: old photographs clearly show it as 'The King's Arms Hotel'. Devon seems keen on card suits as motifs — the International Stores at ASHBURTON has a clapboarded façade where the first and second floors are decorated with patterns of spades, diamonds, hearts and clubs, while near STICKLEPATH on the A30 a cottage has shutters with the suits boldly carved out.

In the early 19th century the Rev. Edward Atkyns Bray of Tavistock felt impelled to improve DARTMOOR's Cowsic (unhappy name!) valley by providing mental as well as visual stimulation to visitors. His intention was to inscribe a treasury of classic poetry on the rocks in the river, and he went so far as to make his selection before realising that the boulders didn't provide a suitably flat surface, and that Dartmoor granite was not the easiest material to work with. Relatively undeterred, he modified his plans: 'As the name alone of Theocritus or of Virgil could not fail to communicate to a poetical mind a train of pleasing associations, I did nothing more, at first, than inscribe upon a few rocks "To Theocritus", "To Virgil", etc. This of itself, in so wild and solitary a scene as Dartmoor, was not without its effect: it seemed to people the desert; at any rate one might exclaim, "The hand of man has been here!" ' Years of water and wild weather have worn away the words; when we were there we could find only 'TO MILTON' and 'TO SHAKESPEARE', although 'TO SPENSER' and 'TO HOMER' are said to remain legible. A bigger but similarly obsessive undertaking was made 100 years later by Mr Whitley of Buckland, who wanted to engrave the Ten Commandments on two tablets on the tor of BUCKLAND BEACON to commemorate the defeat in Parliament of the Revised Prayer Book. He employed Mr W. A. Clement, a stonemason from Exeter, to do the job, which took him from 23 July to 31 August 1928. An interesting sideline here is Mr

Clement's conditions of employment: at night he slept in a cowshed, on wire netting covered in blankets he had to bring himself, while for his food a loaf of bread was left on the roadside wall each Thursday — Mr Whitley appears to have treated him as a 20th-century hermit, even going so far as to nickname him Moses.

Good doggerel can be found at HARTLAND. In the farmyard at Highford Farm is a semi-circular stilted arch set in a giant triangle made of three different types of coloured brick and surmounted by a buzzard. It leads nowhere, serves no purpose, but must have been immensely satisfying to build. A cautious early inscription dates the adjacent dairy to 1886. Ten years later and there's a little bit more confidence on the gate pillars:

OH HOW PEACEFUL THOU ART

O HIGHFORD

JB 1896

Six years later and all reticence disappears:

E ♛ R

JUNE 26TH 1902

KING EDWARD VII CROWNED. BOER WAR ENDED.

I BELIEVE IN CHURCH AND STATE AND ALL OTHER

RELIGIONS THAT DO GOOD AND TO BE PATRIOTIC

TO MY COUNTRY

JAMES BERRIMAN

THE ABOVE BRINGS CIVILISATION TO OUR GREAT

AND MIGHTY NATION

This is inscribed on a gate pier a mile or so to the east of Highford; the piers, each about ten feet high, are capped with pyramids and set in a stuccoed semi-circular wall crudely decorated with plain block pargetting. An iron medallion with a bas-relief of Charles Martell is set into the other pier, above another inscription, also signed James Berriman and dated 1902:

ALPHA THOU ART FIRST I'M SURE

AS OMEGA IS IN THE WEST

AND THOU'LT BE FIRST FOR EVERMORE

NOW SLUMBER ON AND REST.

THIS FIELD WAS ONCE A COMMON MOOR
WHERE GORSE AND RUSH GREW FREE
AND NOW IT GROWS GREEN GRASS ALL O'ER
AS ALL WHO PASS MAY SEE.

Omega in the west? A couple of miles due west we discovered an identical gate (but with the medallion torn out) and the inscription:

OMEGA THOU ART LAST I'M SURE
AS ALPHA IS IN THE EAST
AND THOU'LT BE LAST FOR EVERMORE
TILL ENDLESS AGES CEASE.
WHEN I AM DEAD AND GONE
THESE VERSES WILL REMAIN
TO SHOW WHO WROTE THEREON
BY WORKING OF THE BRAIN.

What can possess a man to immortalise words such as these? Berriman aroused the curiosity and envy of his neighbours by making Highford a model farm — his livestock had better living conditions than many of the local farm labourers.

Hartland also has the ruins of the Pleasure House at 'The Warren' overlooking Hartland Quay, probably a belvedere erected by the Abbott family before 1738, when it first appears on a map. The Hartland peninsula is largely unspoilt because of the tourist magnet of CLOVELLY, the extraordinary picture postcard village which epitomises the West Country. It is the estate village of the Hamlyn family, whose Clovelly Court stands in its park near the village. With magnificent coast and seascapes abounding, the Hamlyns took the advantage of erecting several fanciful summer-houses and ornamental seats, including Miss Woodall's Seat and the prettily named Angel's Wings. The Hobby Drive, a three-mile coastal road often open to the public, is truly in the new wave of romantic landscaping — Sir James Hamlyn, who built it in the early 19th century, deliberately left it as wild as God intended, resisting the then virtually compulsory reshaping of nature, but it must be said the canvas had already been prepared and painted by a greater hand.

Towers are the thing for any coast, but all the good towers in the county are in the south. Carrying on along the north coast there are several small efforts, rather disappointing on the whole. The best has disappeared: Chanter's Folly at Instow was the original for the popular folly story of the merchant building a tower so he could watch for his ships coming safely into harbour, but building it on the wrong side of the hill, so that he couldn't see the sea. It was built in 1880 and demolished in 1952. Tawstock Tower, circular with a higher circular stair turret, was still standing in 1954 but no trace now remains. The tower known as Mortimer's Folly in BRAUNTON is clearly marked on the Ordnance map, but it is possible to pass ten feet from it without noticing, so covered with ivy has it become. It stands, its slaty stones probably held up only by the ivy, in a wood at the edge of a field, totally ruinous, but with the remnants of three storeys still visible from the inside. It was built to celebrate the repeal of the Corn Laws at a time when the views from the now undergrowth-choked hill would have been magnificent. Duty Point Tower at LEE ABBEY outside Lynton perches pugnaciously on the cliff-top, a squat little two-storey belvedere with large windows on the ground floor, a smaller, castellated upper storey and a slightly taller stair turret. It was built *c.* 1850 for the mansion which has finally fulfilled its name; it is now the headquarters of a religious organisation.

On the seafront at quaint, rebuilt LYNMOUTH is the little Rhenish Tower, built in 1860 by General Rawdon to store salt, a purpose for which massive fortifications and two heavily machicolated balconies on different levels were evidently felt to be necessary. A scratched inscription on the tower reminds us tersely of the Lynmouth flood disaster – 'Destroyed August 1952, Rebuilt April 1954'.

At GREAT TORRINGTON is a fine example of that peculiarly English adaptation of Egyptian motifs in producing either a very fat obelisk or a very elongated pyramid – after all, why else should we dream of calling those monstrosities that stride across our countryside 'pylons'? Here it serves, beautifully sited above the ravine of the Torridge, as a Waterloo monument, a pike rather than a tower, 'Erected June 1818 to commemorate the Battle of Waterloo June 1815. Peace to the souls of the heroes ! ! !'

Moretonhampstead, on the edge of Dartmoor, is surrounded by some pleasant little towers and one really spectacular one. There is said to be a mysterious tower shrouded in the trees above WATER, near Manaton, which was used as an observation post during the Second World War, but we were not able to see it. A familiar folly to many must be Rushford Tower near CHAGFORD: few will have seen it in the stone, but it will be well enough known to viewers of the television adaptation of R. F. Delderfield's *Diana*, where the lovers used it as a trysting-place. People who believe what they see on the screen would be surprised by its actual size, because inside the square, unroofed room there isn't enough room to swing a television camera, let alone indulge in a close encounter in front of a production crew. Nevertheless, the BBC have left the little folly with an imposing entrance: a wooden door gnarled with age (courtesy of the paint department) and metalwork held on with Pozidriv screws, a folly door for a real folly. A circular stair turret is attached (complete with solid and climbable stone spiral stair), from the top of which is an excellent view of Castle Drogo.

Despite television fame, Devon's best-known folly must be the superb Haldon Belvedere, or Lawrence Castle, near DODDISCOMBS-LEIGH and high above Dunchideock. It is a proto-folly, triangular, the three big storeys having round, castellated turrets at each corner and Gothick detailing, even down to mighty Gothick venetian windows on the first floor. Years ago we were shown around the building by the Dale brothers, who lived there and angrily refuted any suggestion that the building might be a folly, convincing us more and more with every word that this could stand for all follies. A visit in August 1984 found it closed to the public, whether temporarily or permanently we cannot tell. It is a private house which has remained occupied since shortly after it was built, and the interior has remained intact and original, if a little worn. It is quite remarkable – marble and mahogany and Wedgwood blue and white, faded glories of the past. Sir Robert Palk built it in 1780 in memory of his great friend Major-General Stringer Lawrence, who lived in retirement with the Palk family at Haldon and left all his property, valued at some £50,000, to the Palk children. No expense was spared in the castle's construction, nor need there have been with that size of inheritance.

Pitt House, between Chudleigh and CHUDLEIGH KNIGHTON, was built in 1845 by Sir George Gilbert Scott in the Jacobean style. It seems logical to assume that the folly-tower in the field above the house was conceived at the same time, although it is far from Jacobean. It is a round, castellated, two-storey tower with a gentle batter, like a chess castle. Unusually, the staircase is on the outside, still solid, with a metal handrail, leading up to a little room with a rotting floor and three thin, arched windows. From this room a staircase rose a quarter-circle to the roof, but only the positioning holes in the walls remain. The room at the bottom is used as a cowshed. It is a small tower, an unimportant folly, yet strangely pleasing and memorable in its honest solidity.

At Filham, an IVYBRIDGE village bisected by the new A38, the Manor House appears to have an enchanting sham ruin on the smooth lawn right in front of the house. It proves to be a genuine 15th-century chapel which preceded the Manor House and to which an owner added, in the late 18th century, an octagonal stair turret. The chapel finally collapsed in the 1960s, leaving the stair turret pointing up from the ruined chapel like an index finger from a clenched fist. It is possible to climb it if one has a head for heights; on seeing our faces after our abortive attempt Mrs Hardman, the present owner, took pity on us and provided an enormous dish of wild mushrooms on toast – rare hospitality!

In his remarkable tome *Devon*, W. G. Hoskins complains that the *Dictionary of National Biography* does not devote a single line to John Foulston, 'this most notable of Devon architects'. Yet his fellow countrymen have also done this individualistic architect down: his sterling work in designing from scratch a new civic centre for the newly created borough of DEVONPORT has been left to decay to such an extent that it now merits inclusion in a book on follies. The grand approach to the Greek Revival Town Hall was along Ker Street, with Foulston's great, monumental Doric column set off to the right on a massive plinth. At the right at the top of the street is one of Foulston's set pieces, the Egyptian Library of 1823, now the Odd Fellows Hall. More restrained than his Penzance Egyptian house, its juxtaposition to the classical Greek motifs in the Town Hall and the Doric monument make it if anything more startling in context. The ruination of the street is in the building of municipal dwellings – there is no other word – of a style and quality one would associate more with an early 1950s' suburb in Amiens. A real extravaganza is the clock-tower at nearby H.M.S. Drake, in Portland stone, with columns, pilasters, sprouting balconies, diminishing storeys, carved corbelling, bosses sporting anchors and 'VR', a confectioner's grotesque fantasy. It is magnificent in its own tacky way, but is it Art?

The remaining Devon towers can really be cast as coastal, even though some stand a mile or two inland. TEIGNMOUTH has a jocular little 25-foot sham lighthouse of 1845 at the south end of the promenade, Den Crescent, but nobody knows why. Behind the Singer mansion of Oldway in PAIGNTON, now the council offices and a public park, is Little Oldway Tower, a conventional red, square, castellated tower built as a water-tower for the mansion, but now part of a private house. The most individualistic structure in this part of Devon is not a folly at all; it was built for a specific purpose which it continues to perform. We must admit that seeing it for the first time, on the National Trust headland at Froward Point near KINGSWEAR, we had no idea of its function, nor did we even stop to consider that it might have had one. It is a tall, octagonal tower, 80 feet high, completely hollow, open at the top, no trace of there ever having been floors or a staircase, tapering steeply and evenly from the bottom to the top, the bottom being pierced by eight pointed arches, each about 30 feet high. This is what Isambard Kingdom Brunel would have built had he built a folly. In fact it is a Daymark, erected by the Dart Harbour Commissioners in 1864 as a sort of lightless lighthouse. A lightless lighthouse? Perhaps it is a folly after all.

East of the Exe the towers become more assertive, more folly-like, less Devonian. Right on the edge of the mudflats at LYMPSTONE is Mrs Peters's Clock, an immense structure for a village, with a passing resemblance to St Stephen's Tower, a sort of Little Ben. It was built by Mr Peters in 1885 to show how good his wife was to the poor. It is about 70 feet high, and the riverside fenestration increases with each floor – one, two, three, then the clock. Topping it all is an elongated pyramid with lucarnes. The Landmark Trust has recently restored it for use as a holiday home. The Bicton estate at COLATON RALEIGH is famous for its gardens, and has been for 250 years. They hold a shell-cottage, a hermitage, one of the best proportioned obelisks in Britain and the China

Tower — not remotely Chinese in appearance, since it is the standard Perp-folly church-tower shape plus higher stair turret, but with sufficient detail changes to please the jaded eye. The turret is square, not round or octagonal, and it is attached to the main tower, which is octagonal. The appellation comes from its *raison d'être* — the tower was a birthday present to Lord Rolle from his wife in 1839, and it was used for keeping their porcelain collection.

Bishop Coplestone's tower at OFFWELL on Honiton Hill is a familiar landmark to the south of the town. Again, the family vehemently insist that it was not a folly but a water-tower built to relieve unemployment, and indeed there is a small water-tank at the top of the tower — but if that were its sole purpose, why should it have been necessary to put fireplaces in all the other rooms? In any case, it really is quite absurdly large for its alleged function; a tower that size could provide water for a whole village, and when it was built in the 1830s there was no house near by; the house it now dominates was built in 1847. Stylistically, the 80-foot tower would be more at home in a Lucchesan side street, but a touch of old Italy on a Devon hilltop is indeed a pleasurable sight. Of course the stories are there, the best one being that Edward Coplestone, being Bishop of Llandaff, felt a twinge of remorse about staying in the parish where he was born and brought up and built a tower so that he could keep an eye on his flock in South Wales, 50 miles away as the crow flies. The tower staircase is now rickety, but the owners have been on the roof, by the ingenious method of climbing down from a helicopter! Repairs are under way. At the bottom of the hill on the edge of Honiton is an ochre-coloured, Gothic, castellated cottage shaped like a horseshoe with a single-storey porch bolted on to the front — perhaps a toll-house.

Powderham Belvedere, in the grounds of POWDERHAM CASTLE on the west bank of the Exe, is visible from virtually all along the east bank. At a glance it appears to be a copy of Lawrence Castle, except for its hexagonal corner turrets, but it actually predates its more famous neighbour by some seven years, having been built in 1773 for the 2nd Viscount Courtenay. It is now floorless and completely ruinous, but a curious relic remains in the eastern stair turret — a retractable flagpole. The flagpole was a mighty affair, as high again as the belvedere, so one assumes that, having lost it once or twice in a high wind, this system was devised for reasons of economy.

At ARLINGTON COURT, the National Trust property near Barnstable, the structure known as 'The Obelisk' is actually a rubble cone some 15 feet high, erected to mark the spot where 'a bonfire was lit to commemorate the jubilee of Queen Victoria, June 12 1887'. Traditionally, this was also the site of one of the previous houses at Arlington. More folly-like on the estate are two mighty bridge piers set on either side of the lake and built to support a suspension bridge; planned by Sir John Chichester (it would have led nowhere but over the lake and back again, although it was intended to provide a more impressive western approach to the house) it was, not surprisingly, left uncompleted after his death in 1851.

At HATHERLEIGH, in the middle of the county, is an intriguing folly, a single-storey belvedere built in 1879 to commemorate Colonel Pearce, a local landowner and marksman. It is castellated, with two arches opening to the west, while on the south side a stairway leads up to the flat roof for the view. The arches and the entry to the stairway are highlighted in white brick, giving the little building a faintly lavatorial air. The bottom part is now used as a cowshed, which adds to the illusion.

The 100-foot tall, inscriptionless obelisk at MAMHEAD was built in 1742, supposedly as a navigational aid to sailors. It is eclipsed by the magnificent sham castle stable block, built by the young architect Anthony Salvin in 1829 as a replica of Belsay Castle in Northumberland. The contrast between house and castle is heightened by the house being built of greystone, while the castle is red. It is an extremely large folly, said to be built on the foundations of a genuine medieval castle, with bartizan turrets and a massive gatehouse with sham portcullis. A spiral staircase in one corner of the courtyard leads directly down into the main house, which is now used as a special school. Mamhead's setting is exquisite, with sweeping views along the Exe estuary. No other sham castle in Devon, and few in Britain, can approach this scale and grandeur. Indeed, there is precious little else in this genre in Devon — a sham castle gatehouse at Radford near PLYMSTOCK, and a Gothick, octagonal belvedere known as 'The Castle', little more than an elaborate summer-house, at nearby SALTRAM. However, it has been beautifully restored by the National Trust, with Wedgwood blue and white plasterwork inside. It was built in 1772 to the designs of Stockman, Saltram's head gardener, and an interesting feature is the tunnel opening out into the side of the hill at some distance from the castle, through which servants could enter to prepare food in the basement room. Below the gardens on the banks of the Plym is the Amphitheatre, a mid-18th-century classical façade built across a quarry face. Grotesque faces are carved on the keystones of the arches.

Near Saltram, above the Plymouth suburb of WOODFORD, is a huge and splendid red-brick arch with wings either side, one of which serves as a cottage and the other as a barn. The cottage is called Triumphal Arch Cottage, but it was unoccupied when we visited and we could find no additional information. Perhaps it was built as an eyecatcher for Saltram, as it is close to Boringdon, the old seat of the Parker family before they moved to Saltram.

Castle Hill at FILLEIGH, home of the Fortescues, has a triumphal arch of comparable size, less massive and tripartite this time, the better to serve as an eyecatcher from the house. It is interesting to compare the degrees of economy as practised in both these arches: at Woodford, where the arch faces south and is bathed in strong sunlight, the detail is strongly emphasised with two heavy pilasters either side and a fussy parapet; at Castle Hill, the view from the house to the arch is due south, so it almost always appears in silhouette, needing no detailing but providing a strong argument for a tripartite as opposed to a single arch. It looks unusually clean and well cared-for; the reason is that it is new − it was blown down in a storm in the 1950s and rebuilt in 1961. Aligned directly with the arch and the house at Castle Hill is a sham ruin on the top of the opposite hill, which we have not been able to see. A smaller arch, more a folly gatehouse, stands on a ridge in a field overlooking the river Taw between ASHFORD and Barnstaple as an eyecatcher to Upcott House; the single arch has castellated towers on either side, one now losing its castellations. There is a re-created arch at Watermouth Castle near BERRYNARBOR, now a holiday centre; castellated and pinnacled, it opens into part of the famous gardens and is notable for being built with pieces (one dated 1525) from the 16th-century porch of Umberleigh House, demolished in the 19th century.

The final arches are very different. Quite the opposite of eyecatchers, they take a bit of searching out as they are buried in a typical Devon sunken lane. The lane used to run from Dousland to Sheepstor until 1895, when the Meavy valley was drowned by the waters of the BURRATOR RESERVOIR. George Shillibeer, of the Plymouth County Water Works, rescued the door arch-stones from the farmhouses in the catchment area and incorporated them into two arches, built in 1928 and 1934, spanning the narrow and disused old Sheepstor road. Two huge millstones are built into the wall either side of the first arch, and the keystone is dated 1668; through the arch the road has been converted into a serpentine walk by building fern-covered cairns alternately either side against the old banks. The second arch, at the bottom, is built with stones dated 1637 and 1633, taken from Longstone Manor House, as was the arch itself, one of the original doorways.

Grottoes were popular in Devon, but never reached the heights of artistic decoration obtained elsewhere. None is particularly memorable, with the possible exception of the grotto at Tapeley, near WESTLEIGH on the A39 north of Bideford. The house and gardens are often open to the public, and the strange little grotto by the well preserved ice-house is a curiosity well worth seeing. More a shell-house than a grotto, it is a small grey circular building with two pointed arch entrances and four diamond windows picked out with a red-brick surround. The roof is steeply sloping, single pitched, as if a child had sliced a diagonal through a Smartie tube. The entrances are barred by chicken wire, but one can peer inside to admire the well preserved but uninspired decoration. Endsleigh Cottage, near MILTON ABBOT, now an hotel, was built for the Dowager Duchess of Bedford in 1810 by Sir Jeffry Wyatville, and the grounds were landscaped by Repton, so the grotto is of a higher quality, as might be expected. It serves as the focal point of a yew walk, above the valley of the young Tamar. Another quondam hotel, now council offices, had a good grotto (now all but vanished) – Knowle Grange in the delightful seaside town of SIDMOUTH.

There is a grotto – we think it is a grotto, but we have not been able to get inside to see it – in the grounds of the Bishop's Palace in

EXETER, remarkably forgotten and unknown for a city centre folly; even the Bishop could not tell us anything about it. There is a small grotto at Maidencombe in BABBACOMBE BAY, and in the garden of Spring Lodge at Oxton House near KENTON, just north of Mamhead, is an arch in a rock cliff opening into a tiny bare room now handily used as a garden shed. One window and a curious arrangement of latticed strips by the door let in light.

The derelict estate of Oldstone at BLACKAWTON has the perfect folly atmosphere. There is something ineffably weird and remote about still visible remains standing mutely among the activities of a bustling, modern farm, written over the old pleasure gardens like a palimpsest. The magnificently ruined house stands in a valley, protected from the barbarians by a fine fort strategically placed by the old main drive, now a cow path. The cattle graze unconcernedly round its ivy-covered ramparts; it was all a sham really so it cannot be blamed for not protecting such a fine house. Directly behind the sham fort is the shell-house, a very large and elaborate affair, despite the presence of a giant plastic sheet in front of the building held down with old car tyres and covering a pile of manure. The shell-house has a central rectangular room, still decorated with stones and bones and shells, entered through an archway. Wings either side have archways into roofless rooms from which all the decoration has now disappeared. Back between the old house and the farmhouse, the path leads under a dry bridge across a field into a wood; here the path drops down to the three brackish, overgrown ornamental lakes, beside which stand a grotto, an arch, and a hermitage. We found the grotto, now in a perilous condition, but the arch and the hermitage remained hidden. Oldstone is in peak folly condition, a vision perhaps of life in the future with mankind eking out a living amidst the mouldering magnificence of a once glorious past.

There are several unexplained buildings in Devon: a Pleasure Tower at Hawkmoor Hospital and the Hall Pleasure House above the village of HARFORD. Both are just piles of rubble now (the Hall Pleasure House is marked on the current Ordnance map as 'Cairn', but was clearly marked by its old name on older maps). Scobitor Round House, above WIDECOMBE IN THE MOOR, is a circular one-roomed building with a slightly domed roof and random fenestration.

The really fascinating part of its construction is the presence of nine massive granite beams radiating from the top of the central pillar. They are far too heavy for the sole purpose of supporting the modest roof; another reason has to be sought. It has been speculated that the house was intended as a beacon, but although the views across Dartmoor are spectacular, the only village it can be seen from is Widecombe. Perhaps the intention was to provide a firm base for another storey or two; certainly the random pattern of windows seems to have been chosen to frame superlative views. A belvedere, then.

SHOBROOKE PARK, near Crediton, was demolished after a fire in 1947, but high on an eastern hill remains a huge walled and covered seat for drinking in wonderful views over Dartmoor. It is semi-circular, flanked either side by columns with ball finials and covered by a half dome. The low surrounding wall had a ball on each of its six piers, but every one of these has been knocked off by vandals.

Some strange houses round off this beautiful county, few stranger than the sibling houses in EXMOUTH, 'A La Ronde' and 'Point In View'. 'A La Ronde' is famous throughout the country and a magnet for tourists. It was built in 1798 by the cousins Jane and Mary Parminter, the exterior allegedly inspired by the church of San Vitale in Ravenna, although the similarities are difficult to detect. The name is in fact misleading,' for the building has 16 sides rather than being round. Inside, the octagonal hall is 60 feet high, surrounded at the top by the Shell Gallery, a grotto with a view, and the collections and handiwork of the Parminter cousins. 'A La Ronde' has only once been owned by a man (the Misses Parminter were not interested in men) – it is the most feminine house we know, and if that conjures up pictures of pink frills and chintz then you misunderstand our meaning. We strongly recommend a visit; there is nothing like this anywhere in Europe . . . except perhaps a little way up the road, where the more inquisitive visitor will discover 'Point In View', built in 1811 by the Misses Parminter as a little chapel surrounded by four almshouses, strictly reserved for single women. Awkward little pointed windows rob it of the charm which typifies 'A La Ronde', but as a curiosity it should be seen.

One Devon house became a folly because of its situation; the final Devon folly became a house for similar reasons. Prinsep's Folly on GIDLEIGH TOR was built in 1846, but the builder, Thomas Levett Prinsep, died before he could move in. The house was demolished before 1850 for reasons that remain unclear. Prinsep's intention was to blend the house in with the rocks of the tor, and to that end he chose the most difficult site he could. Some portions of the wall can still be made out, as well as a small, octagonal, roofless tower just by the summit of the hill. In BIDEFORD, a folly in the old grounds of Wooda was built in 1848 by a Mr G. Richards, the partner of Mr Abbott, an iron-foundry master who lived at Wooda. It is a very Victorian, Gothic, little two-storey belvedere, with a good view over the town and the Torridge. In 1981 the then owner applied for planning permission to demolish it as it had become dangerous; the permission was refused and it is now an unusual and appealing home for a proud young family.

Wessex

Avon

Wessex is an ancient kingdom of Britain that lacks immediate physical identity, a clearly defined border, such as a mountain range or a major river, and, except for Somerset, a distinct dialect. But Wessex lives on as an area, even manifesting itself in an eccentric nationalism – some may say parochialism – as well as an uncommonly fierce pride.

On the other side of the river from the pretty town of Bradford-on-Avon is the small village of MIDFORD, where stands a private house of *c.* 1775 called Midford Castle. It is much better known as Roebuck's Folly, from a story the present owners say is completely untrue, as it first surfaced in a magazine over 100 years after the house was built. Nevertheless, it is so plausible it bears repeating. The house is trefoil in plan, and the porch on the east side completes its uncanny resemblance from above to the Ace of Clubs. Why should anybody build a house in the shape of the Ace of Clubs?

The story goes that Henry Woolhouse Disney Roebuck, an inveterate gambler, staked £100,000 on the turn of a card. The correct card – the ace of clubs – was duly turned up, and young Roebuck went off to build a folly to commemorate his mighty success. Sadly for the story, a design for a building very similar to Roebuck's Folly appeared in *The Builder's Magazine* in 1775, by an architect called John Carter, so Carter is generally credited with the building. The Rev. John Collinson, in his *History and Antiquities of the County of Somerset* (1790), referred to it with admirable self-restraint as a 'singular construction'; had he known of Carter's predilection for surrounding himself with young female acolytes dressed in boys' clothing, he might have had something more forceful to say.

In the grounds of the castle stands, just, 'The Priory', a real folly but no match for the calculated eccentricity of the main house. As one might expect, it was built as a gambling den. Its design is attributed to the Knight of Glin. Pevsner dismisses it as a summer-house, but in its ruinous state it has acquired a sort of overgrown charm and mystery. Collinson, still thinking the best, described it as having 'a commodious tea-room with offices beneath'. A rustic hermitage which stood at the top of this steeply sloping site has disappeared.

BATH sometimes wears its beauty a little self-consciously. Its site, its stone, its sudden discovery as a fashionable spa-town at a time when English architecture was at its most elegant, have combined to make it a fortunate city. The 18th century belonged to Bath; in modern terms it was a Gstaad or Mustique. One of its most elegant inhabitants was Ralph Allen, who augmented his fortune as a quarrymaster by an income of £12,000 per annum through revising the postal system. A little of that huge fortune was spent on building what is now one of the best loved and best known follies in Britain — Ralph Allen's Sham Castle. Set high on the slope of Bathwick Hill (you reach it by taking the road to Bath Golf Club), this perfect example of an eyecatcher looks proudly down on once glittering Bath. When it was built, alone on its hillside, it was sited so as to be seen from Allen's town-house in Old Lilliput Alley. Now, with new houses springing up all along the hill, it is difficult to pick out the sham from the town, so at night the City of Bath, which was given the castle in 1921, proudly flood-lights it.

It is not a big building, but it is remarkably well done. The design has always been attributed to Sanderson Miller, and indeed he drew up plans for a sham castle for Allen in 1755, but the actual building is now known to have been designed and built in 1762 by Richard Jones, Allen's clerk of works. Allen was evidently not easy to get on with from an architect's point of view; he dismissed John Wood the Elder from his villa Prior Park and let Jones finish the job. Jones responded by providing a magnificent copy of a Palladian bridge, and although he might not have been an architect of great original talent, his eye for mass and effect gave us one of our most successful follies.

The 'castle' is two-dimensional, Disneyesque; two 'round' towers are in fact semi-circular, the smaller square towers at either end of the façade offset the bulk of the central gatehouse and the whole edifice, with its blank windows and blank arrowslits, looks blindly out over Bath. No more than 40 feet high and 100 feet long, its cardboard frivolity and excellent state of preservation give it the air of a recently abandoned film set.

Pinch's Folly in Bathwick Street is a baroque gateway leading nowhere. The story goes that it was built in 1853 by a builder's merchant called William Pinch, who wanted to stop coal-carts making a short cut into his yard, but from its style it looks to be the re-erection of an entrance gateway from a long forgotten house.

Bath's other great folly builder was the extraordinary William Beckford of Fonthill Abbey notoriety. Shortly before Fonthill collapsed, he came to live in Bath at 20 Lansdown Crescent, driven from his Gothick fantasy by relative poverty and scandal. Compared with Fonthill his new home was like a terraced house in Hackney as against Buckingham Palace, but he did manage to acquire a good sized garden. Although not very wide, it stretched over a mile in length, all the way out of Bath to the village of LANSDOWN, and for the end of it the impoverished sybarite built himself a 154-foot tower. Unlike Fonthill, this one did not collapse, and it is the finest surviving example of Beckford's work. It was built by his friend H. E. Goodridge in 1825–6, and begins as a very plain, straightforward square tower for about two-thirds of its height, its severity offset by the house, now converted into a mortuary chapel, at its foot. Then comes an overhanging parapet, and above that three plain glazed windows on each side. To top it all, Beckford and Goodridge allowed full rein to their imaginations and built a replica of the Lysicrates Monument in Athens, a favourite theme for folly builders. The columns here are of cast iron, and have a bluish tinge against the rust-red background of the rest of the lantern. At dusk, when the lights are on in the tower, the effect is quite chilling. The tower, open to the public in the summer, is now part of the cemetery at its foot; both Beckford and Goodridge are buried there.

Heading north past the Lansdowne Racecourse, one comes to a small stone monument in a field on the right. This is not a folly but a war memorial to commemorate the Battle of Lansdown in 1643 and the Royalist leader Sir Bevil Grenville. As you approach WICK, you suddenly come across the enormous columns at the gateway to Tracy Park, now a country club. At the south entrance they are circular, brick-built, with Doric capitals and grossly over-proportioned cornices apparently capable of holding the mightiest of arches, instead of thin air. At the north the columns are square, more like gate piers; they are the same over-stated size, but this time the cornices are embellished with masonic symbols.

DODINGTON HOUSE has a fine cascade designed by 'Capability' Brown in 1764, complete with a castellated tower. Somehow, although undeniably impressive, it is not as pleasing as the rotunda-like Bath Lodge to the south, designed by James Wyatt in 1802. The follies in the great park of BADMINTON are mainly by Thomas Wright, and although the ivy-shrouded Ragged Castle is a triumph of rustic romanticism, some of the others have a pattern-book feel about them, as though the Duke of Beaufort had been told that he should embellish his park and, at a loss to know what to do, had handed the commission over to Wright with orders to get on with it. The lodges are decorated: two have battlemented or pyramidal roofed turrets at each corner; another has Gothic windows and overhanging eaves; Bath Lodge is in the classical style; and Castle Barn has two massive towers, either side of a screen wall with a crow-stepped gable in the centre, now obscured by a prefabricated Atcost barn. The Root House is the splendid exception of course – thatched, riddled with worm, but still eerily standing, solitary in the deer-park – a superb hermitage showing the mysterious Wright at the height of his powers. The buildings were all erected between 1748 and 1756: for a thatched building made out of unworked roots and lumps of diseased trees still to be standing after two and a quarter centuries is an achievement in itself.

Lord Edward Somerset, one of Wellington's major-generals, had a long and distinguished military career in Europe, as befitted a son of the Duke of Beaufort. He died in 1842 at the age of 66, and shortly afterwards work started on the distantly beautiful tower at HAWKESBURY, designed by Lewis Vulliamy, one of the more

fashionable early Victorian architects. He was said, in his mastery
of the Gothic, to have been 'far in advance of his contemporaries',
so it is a puzzle why the style of the tower, and particularly the
ornate stonework on the roof, seems more Indian than anything
else, since neither Vulliamy nor Somerset had any connection with
India. As if to excuse this heathen decoration, the top of the tower
is surmounted by a large cross. This is a rarity among follies: it is
easily accessible, in superb condition, and for a small fee payable at
the towerkeeper's cottage one can climb it. The view, as expected,
is extensive; the wind on the day we visited was phenomenal. 'I
reckon you'll be blowed away when you get up the top there,' said
the towerman cheerily. The marble slab inside the doorway records
the valiant derring-do of Lord Somerset, and a damp but
comfortably solid spiral staircase leads up to a balcony. Here the
wind made it nearly impossible to stand, but there was not a hint
of movement from the tower. Vulliamy's talent and careful
maintenance have ensured its survival.

Lord Ducie, whose activities at Woodchester and North Nibley
are followed in the Gloucestershire chapter, commissioned Samuel
Sanders Teulon to design him a new house at Tortworth, a Viollet-
le-Duc derived fantasia. When the house became Leyhill Open
Prison, the word 'WELCOME' over the archway was removed. The
remains of a Ducie-inspired tower are hidden in the undergrowth
of Priest Wood by CROMHALL, a mile to the south. Further south,
on the M5, to the west of Junction 17, can be seen the Hollywood
Park Tower, now standing on land owned by Bristol Zoo in
COMPTON GREENFIELD. The tall tower is square with chamfered
corners, battlemented, and with a taller stair turret. Buttressed at
the base and with a relatively small clock-face, it resembles a
church-tower without a church. It was built for Sir John Davis
some time between 1848 and 1854, and although the architect's
original drawings still exist, they are unfortunately unsigned. Sir
George White, the last private owner, believes it might have been
the work of Francis Niblett, the church architect, who was active in
this area at the time. Davis had purchased the estate, then called
Holly Hill, in 1839, but did not retire there from the Governorship
of Hong Kong until 1848. Sir Stanley White, Sir George's
grandfather, said that Sir John either won or was given the clock,

and had to build a tower to put it in. In the early years of aviation it was used by the Whites as a landmark to fly around, and when the flag was being lowered even the Graf Zeppelin used to dip its nose in salute as it cruised by.

A short way off the M5 in HENBURY lies Blaise Hamlet, the picturesque yet eminently practical model village designed by John Nash in 1811 for the retired estate workers of a Quaker, the banker John Scandrett Harford. There was already a folly on the estate, a triangular castle on the hilltop built in 1766 for a previous owner, Thomas Farr, by Robert Mylne, at a cost of £3,000. It differs from the standard run of triangular folly-towers in having a circular core with three slightly taller round turrets on the corners. Today it looks crisp and clean, mantled with a carefully controlled amount of ivy and looked after by Bristol City Museum. The entrance doorway is blocked up with matching stone.

The outskirts of Bristol are tawdry. Like New Jersey, what beauty once lived in the landscape has been erased by indiscriminate ribbon development and indifferent planning regulations. The Kingswood Trailer Park at WARMLEY is not a pretty site. Row upon row of mobile homes stand hopelessly on a patch of scrubby, unhealthy looking land. In this unpromising locale the sudden appearance of a colossal statue of Neptune towering above the caravans and surrounded with a halo of ivy comes as a real shock. The lady living in the mobile home closest to the statue was eager to explain. 'That's King Neptune, that is, he used to have a tripod but now they've taken it away and I'm glad because it used to be ever so scary at night. And a crown, but it's all covered up with ivy.' His right or reason to be there was unquestioned. The trailer park is the bed of a drained lake, once the major feature of the estate of William Champion, a Quaker zinc and copper smelter. Neptune stood in the middle of the lake proudly and economically, being built of furnace slag (the merits of this unusual building material are described below). His cement face has fallen away, and now that his trident has been stripped from him, it is difficult to make out his shape, except for his thunderous thighs. He is five times taller than the caravans surrounding him, and his calves alone are too big for a man to encircle one with both arms. Champion's boat-house remains, bridging the carefully tamed stream which is all that is left of his lake. Built, along with the rest of the estate, in the 1760s, when Champion was employing over 2,000 people in his works, it has the typical folly battlements, and once again was built of spelter slag. It has been converted with the utmost lack of understanding into a house, the black slag painted white, the white corner-stones black, so that the building looks like a negative. Compressed around the bottom of the towerlet is a modern timber-clad house totally unsympathetic to the good Quaker's architectural intentions. What will happen to the remnants of the estate, now that the Council has moved its offices from Champion's mansion, is anybody's guess.

A folly converted into a pub is a mixed blessing: on the one hand its preservation is ensured and you can get a drink; on the other it loses the mystique of the true folly as the design departments of the breweries are irresistibly tempted to turn the whole thing into a pub on 'ye olde medieval' theme, with age-blackened plastic beams and other fitments as remote from historical accuracy as the original building was. 'The Castle Inn' at Radway in Worcestershire is an important folly because it was one of Sanderson Miller's earliest works; 'The Ship On Shore' in Sheerness was originally built as an alehouse and has become a folly; but BRISLINGTON's 'Black Castle' is perhaps the strangest of them all. To begin with, it is much larger, more obtrusive, more bizarre than the others. Then again, it is built out of this extraordinary spelter slag, a type of purplish-black stone which looks as if it has been boiled. These cut blocks of the slag left from copper smelting, being strong, light and impermeable, make an excellent building material.

'The Black Castle' sits in confused perplexity in the middle of an industrial estate on the outskirts of Bristol, surrounded by cars, lorries and cash-and-carries. William Reeve, another Quaker copper smelter, built it as the stables to his house at Arnos Court in the 1760s. Incongruous though this black and white castle looks in its present surroundings, it was so out of place in rural Brislington in the 18th century that the startled Horace Walpole called it 'The Devil's Cathedral', a name by which, together with Arnos Castle, it is still known. It is a famous folly, and yet, and yet . . . it was built for a purpose, it has been in continuous use for well over 200 years, it was remarkably cheap to build, because the material used in its construction was free, an otherwise useless by-product, and there is no sign of the fabric deteriorating. None of the classic parameters used to describe a folly applies in this case, although it is indisputably a folly. It is thought to have been built for Reeve in about 1760 by James Bridges; however, it does have striking similarities to Ralph Allen's Sham Castle in Bath, which was conceived by Sanderson Miller in 1755 but actually designed and built by Richard Jones in 1762. Which influenced which?

Mr Reeve built several other little 'conceits' on his estate, now bisected by the A4. The best of these was the Bath-house, now safely preserved at Sir Clough Williams-Ellis's home for distressed gentlebuildings, Portmeirion. The elaborate gateway still gets its daily shaking from the A4 juggernauts, and still stands bravely up to it; it adjoins Junction Road, which leads to the Black Castle, and to passing travellers no doubt looks authentically medieval.

On Brandon Hill, in the heart of BRISTOL, the 105-foot Cabot Tower is a pink stone manifestation of Victorian confidence and assertiveness. Designed by W. V. Gough, who was also responsible for the inappropriate Port of Bristol Authority building, it was built in 1897–8, at a time when architects were not afraid of decoration. Like St Pancras Station, the Cabot Tower has enough detail to keep the eye occupied for some considerable time; but its primary function was to look from, not at. As a municipal building in a public park it is carefully maintained, and usually open to the public for a small fee. Cabot was the Venetian who set off from Bristol to discover America in 1497, and his city's somewhat belated monument to him reflects the population's civic pride, as much as pride in their most famous adopted son.

Thomas Goldney was another Bristol merchant of high repute and, if we can judge by what he has left us, a rare and elegant taste. His follies – just on the folly side of garden ornament – are small, well preserved, elegant, carefully looked after and quite enchanting. Goldney House is now a hall of residence for Bristol University, and the grounds are not open to the public. The natural site offered an obvious opportunity; the garden runs along an escarpment overlooking the Avon Gorge at Clifton, with all the panoramic benefits that suggests. At one end is a castellated circular summer-house built in 1757, unusually enough in the Jacobean style. It

1 Bomarzo, near Viterbo, Italy

2 The Palais Idéal du Facteur Cheval at Hautrives, Drôme, France

3   Carn Brea Castle, Redruth

4 Church towers as chimneys on the roof of R. S. Hawker's vicarage at Morwenstow

5 The Knill Monument, St Ives

6 The clock-tower, Treworgey

7   The triangular sham church tower at Cotehele

stands above a carefully manicured bastion, running 30 yards beyond the end of the garden, guarding the sympathetically designed students' quarters. Back along the terrace walk from the summer-house is the most remarkable statue of an ancient Greek God playing baseball in the shadow of the small folly-tower. It has three storeys above a low entrance room, with extremely narrow Gothic windows on each storey, an open arch on the second storey and a porthole window at the top. Castellations and pinnacles complete an architecturally unimportant but oddly fascinating little tower, built to hold the water-tank which fed the cascade. At around 40 feet high, it is smaller than the trees that surround it. Hard by the tower is the celebrated Goldney's Grotto, started in 1737, finished in 1764, and one of the best preserved and most remarkable of 18th-century grottoes. We have not been able to see inside this because it is kept locked, but from all accounts it is spectacular, the walls lined with the most fantastic shells and mineral formations, and an extraordinary cascade. It is possible, when the entrance is locked, to go down a Stygian passage on the right of the entrance (the passage on the left is a dead end) and venture along it as far as your courage will take you. In our case, without a torch, it was not very far.

In LONG ASHTON there is a remarkably ugly house built by someone who knew exactly what he wanted and was quite prepared to sacrifice his aesthetic sensibilities to achieve it. Now called 'The Bungalow', but previously known as 'The Observatory', it is square and flat-roofed like the base of a wedding cake. Plonked in the centre of one side, the entrance porch sticks out and is capped with a pyramidal roof. On either side, perched on the corners, are round window rooms with absurd conical roofs which don't even reach the ground-floor roof level. A 360° glazed lantern with a dome and a weathervane caps the structure. A foolish building indeed, the lantern being necessary to bring some light into the middle of the house as the walls are too long and the windows too small to allow a square house to be lit naturally. It looks like an over-ambitious pre-fab.

From a house-folly to a folly-house. Walton Castle in CLEVEDON was built by John Poulett (a Puritan cavalier who hence lived in more interesting times than most) between 1614 and 1620, when he was MP for Somerset. The castle was ostensibly a hunting-stand, but it is so conspicuously sited on a hilltop looking out over the mouth of the Severn and across to South Wales that it is difficult to imagine the site was not chosen with the view in mind – or with an eye to his escapades 20 years later with King and Parliament. Collinson described the castle as 'octangular', which it certainly is: an octagonal curtain wall with round towerlets at each corner encloses an octagonal keep with an octagonal stair turret. By 1791 it was derelict; the roof and floors had fallen in and the bailey was used as a dairy by a local farmer. Despite its exposed position, the structure remained, and remained controversial, meriting Pevsner's description in 1957 as 'remarkable as a piece of ornamental planning', and Barbara Jones's 'not very exciting' in 1974. Now Walton Castle has been completely rebuilt as a luxury home, a very desirable residence indeed, turned from crumbling shell into a unique and unusual house.

WORLE observatory was built in the most economical way – by adapting an existing tower, in this case a windmill. But to observe or be observed? Faced with white stucco and prominently castellated, it can be seen from all over Weston-super-Mare. It was converted in the early 19th century, and given an onion dome roof, 'to make it look like Brighton Pavilion' says the present owner, who looks after it lovingly. He re-roofed it, with a flat roof, a couple of years ago, the dome having collapsed many years before, and the police are now installing a radio transmitter.

A hill shaped like a submarine shelters the village of BANWELL from the south, a long, dank, overgrown ridge diving down to the M5. In 1780 two local men discovered a large cave while prospecting for lead; no lead being found, they closed it up again. It was reopened in 1824, and the bones of several prehistoric animals were found, some unidentifiable. The Bishop of Bath and Wells at the time was a keen palaeontologist, and in order to pursue his interest more closely he soon built a small house, a fashionable *cottage orné*, at Banwell. An interest in bones leads naturally to a keener sense of mystery and drama, and Bishop Law built a dramatic garden. The site was perfect, a high, sunbathed, south-facing ridge; but the Bishop made his garden on the damp north side, with the moss and the slugs. The paths are now heavily overgrown with skeletal, light-starved plants whose fronds brush wetly against your face as you slide on the greasy steps that lead inconsequentially away up the hill. Low stone walls border the paths; unnatural shapes can dimly be made out through the bony overgrowth; and suddenly, in classic folly fashion, a tiny alcove appears. It is difficult to imagine it could ever have been intended as a seat, as it is perpetually damp. Directly above is a little building covered in tiny pebbles, roofless and very derelict, with three arches facing west, built for meditation and tranquillity. By a trick of the land, the noise of the motorway is particularly intrusive here. The gloomy paths intertwine, climbing and descending the hill randomly. One descends more steeply than the others, becoming steps and spiralling down, down into a tunnel, barred by a rotting but still functional wooden door. Is this the entrance to the bone cave? It is very dark and very wet, and a powerful stench of decaying vegetation is everywhere. The slugs are plentiful, huge and juicy. This is the end. There is nowhere else to go.

Up on the backbone of Banwell Hill, the sun is shining. It has been for hours. There isn't a cloud in the sky. The Stygian pathways fall behind, and the ridgeway ride passes through two 10-foot gate piers near a large, ugly water-tank. The piers are made of tufa, ossified rock, and large blocks of it line the path at regular intervals up to the Monument, a folly-tower, octagonal, three-storeyed, and decaying rapidly. Once it had a parapet and a spire, but now their remains lie on the ground at the bottom of the tower, and the drum that supported the spire stands naked like the fuse on a banger. The stairs, strangely, are still intact — at least, it was possible in 1983 to climb to the second storey and look at branches instead of a view, because the trees have overtopped the tower. The monument (to what?) is architecturally quite different from anything else on the Bishop's estate. It is squat, assertive, outward-looking, while the garden is introspective and quiet. It was finished in 1840, when the Bishop was 79, suffering from a 'gradual decay of mind and body' and no longer active in the diocese. It seems probable, therefore, that it was built by his son, Henry Law, rector of Weston-super-Mare, who assisted him with the gardens from the start.

The inscriptions and exhortations that once graced the gardens (they were intended to be open to the public) have now almost all disappeared; one remains, difficult to read in the afternoon sun, on the Druids' Temple at the foot of the hill (built by real druids say the locals):

> Here, where once Druids trod in times of yore
> And stain'd their altars with a victim's gore,
> Here, now, the Christian ransomed from above
> Adores a God of mercy and of love.

It is a low, roofed shelter, semi-circular, with five pointed arches, pebblestone facing, a circular wooden table inside and a little pebble pyramid on the top.

Leaving Banwell on the A371, the most extraordinary sight unfolds in front of you at the top of the rise outside the village. A full-blown Gothic castle, immaculately kept, with portcullis, gate-tower, pinnacles, castellations, crenellations, towers – a child's full-size toy fort. It was actually built as a house in 1845 by Joseph and Amelia Sampson, but within 10 years they went off to rebuild Banwell Abbey. The castle has been continuously occupied ever since, and is described as 'very comfortably arranged' by the present owner, but the obvious handicap of living in such an extraordinary edifice is summed up by a notice on the gatehouse which reads:

> BANWELL CASTLE
> Built in the nineteenth century and
> of no historic interest. Kindly observe
> that this Englishman's castle is his home,
> and do not intrude.

HUNSTRETE HOUSE, off the A368, is now an elegant and expensive country-house hotel. In a cornfield to the north stands a plain wall pierced by five round-headed arches; this is all that is left of an enormous mansion planned by the owners of Hunstrete in the 18th century. The money ran out before the first rooms were properly finished, and the arches stand in a golden field as an awful warning against profligacy.

Dorset

Dorset is a broad sweep of a county, a county of seascapes and landscapes, of prospects and sonorous village names — Ryme Intrinseca, Whitchurch Canonicorum, Cerne Abbas, Wooton Fitzpaine, Child Okeford, Gussage All Saints — leavened with villages of a lesser euphony — Gribb, Droop, Throop, Stony Knapps and Piddletrenthide. Wool and Beer make their appearance; the traveller in Dorset will be more distracted by the village names than by the profusion of follies.

The scarcity of Dorset follies is no bad thing. It gives us time to appreciate fully that in terms of quality Dorset outranks every other county. In one small area we can find three of the best follies in the whole of England, as well as a folly group by one of the last insatiable builders which, taken as a whole, is one of the most sustained and imaginative urban improvement schemes of the Victorian era. Magnificent though these few are, there is a distinct lack of variety, despite six major obelisks and five superb towers. Dorset enjoys its panoramas, and additional ornamentation does not seem to have been popular. One good eyecatcher and one little sham ruin complete the scene. It is almost as if the 18th century gracefully skirted the county.

The landscape garden, the *raison d'être* for so many follies, never achieved the level of importance in Dorset that it did in the rest of the country; perhaps because the natural beauty of the county needed little enhancement. The lack of squire follies in 18th-century Dorset is noticeable: the majority of squire follies were built to be seen; in Dorset the fashion was to build follies to see from. The earliest recorded folly still existing in Britain is generally agreed to be Freston Tower in Suffolk, beautifully sited with a still lovely view on the banks of the Orwell. It was built in 1549, but ten years earlier John Leland, visiting MELBURY SAMPFORD in Dorset, wrote, 'Mr. Strangeguayse hath now a late much buildid at Mylbyri quadrato, avauncing the inner part of the house with a loftie and fresch tower'. The 'fresch tower' is now nearing its 450th anniversary, which makes it the earliest surviving building intended solely for pleasure — a prospect tower — in the country. Because it is part of a house, it is difficult to take in isolation, but had the house been demolished and the tower left, as has been suggested happened at Freston, Dorset could well have boasted Britain's first folly.

Who built the unique Rock Arch at ENCOMBE? The Scott family, who still live at Encombe, refer to it as a grotto, which is not strictly accurate. Huge blocks of stone have been laid higgledy-piggledy at the end of the lake, and the road to the dairy passes over the top. The interior is devoid of any decoration at all, relying for its effect on the massiveness of the stone. Two passages lead through it from north to south, joined at the southern end by a lateral passage which opens to the south halfway along its length. At that point a rough seat is hewn out of the rock, looking out over a marshy grove of saplings. It is said that the sea could once be seen from here, but this seems unlikely. The puzzle is whether this remarkable structure, quite unlike a grotto, was by the gifted amateur architect John Pitt, who built Encombe House for himself in 1734, or by a member of the Scott family. Hutchins's *History of Dorset* dated it to the first half of the 19th century; Pevsner points out the existence of a painting of the Rock Arch with tricorn-hatted gentlemen, which would seem to place it some 60 years earlier. Pitt's work on Encombe House would appear to commit him to pure classicist architecture; the most likely begetter of the Rock Arch would be his son William Morton Pitt, who sold to the Scotts.

George Burt of SWANAGE was a great folly character. Bursting with Victorian civic pride and supplied with the means to do something about it, Mr Burt set about improving Swanage in every way he could. He would, one imagines, have regarded himself as economical as far as his buildings were concerned; nearly every one of them originated in London before he bore them home to Swanage. In his time he gave the town a clock-tower (with no clock), two massive Ionic columns, a 40-ton globe, a castle, a new façade to the Town Hall, an archway from Hyde Park Corner, two headless statues of Charles I (or II), a Chinese pavilion complete with dragons, assorted iron columns from Billingsgate, floor tiles from the Houses of Parliament, and probably much more. He managed most of this through his uncle's firm, John Mowlem, still flourishing today. In the Victorian era, Mowlem's did a considerable amount of construction, and consequently demolition, in London, and Burt was never slow to appropriate items he felt could enhance Swanage.

The magnificent clock-tower, now in the grounds of the Grosvenor Hotel, originally stood on London Bridge, where it had been erected in 1854 as the Wellington Testimonial Clock-Tower. With its blank clock windows staring blindly out over the Channel it stands as a testimony to Burt's Folly rather than Wellington's Glory. Two Ionic columns stand forlornly in the hotel car park. The statues, the Chinese Pavilion, the archway and the iron columns are all to be found in the garden of Purbeck House in the High Street, now a convent.

Out on Durlston Head to the south of the town we find Burt's finest and most original efforts. No removals here; this is all original, and very impressive it is too. Durlston Castle was a commercial venture and, though fanciful, it was built as a restaurant (and remains one today), so cannot be regarded as a folly. But Burt's enthusiasm had to find some outlet. Suspicions are aroused with the three pillars marked 'DURLSTON HEAD CASTLE', the third one 'ABOVE SEA 215 FT'. All along the side of the castle on the path down to the sea are educational inscriptions on geographical and astronomical detail; we learn that the time in Swanage is 8 minutes before the time in Greenwich, that the longest day in Hamburg lasts 19 hours, that when it is 5.54 in Calcutta it is 7.04 in New York. To help orientate the holidaymaker a relief map of the district at a scale of one inch to one mile (carved in stone) is provided. All this goes a little way to prepare us for the Large Globe. It is surprisingly big; a diameter of 10 feet sounds small enough until you get close. It weighs 40 tons and appears, unlike the earth, to be a perfect globe. Surrounding it are plaques with pious, educational and exhortatory inscriptions incised on every available space, but by far the most touching inscription in the whole collection is to be found on the two stones at the entrance, where Burt, fearing the attentions of like-minded souls, requested 'Persons Anxious To Write Their Names Will Please Do So On This Stone Only'. And, to the credit of Swanage and its visitors, they have honoured George Burt's wishes.

Near Swanage are two enchanting follies, Creech Grange Arch and Clavel Tower. The first, a National Trust property, stands solid, proud and well cared-for on the ridge between Creech and Steeple, while the second crumbles, forgotten and desolate, on the headland above KIMMERIDGE BAY. Clavel Tower was built in 1820 by the Rev. John Richards, who took the name Clavell when he inherited the Smedmore estate in 1817. (Why the tower has one 'L' and its builder two is not certain.) Richards/Clavell was a reclusive man, but he evidently enjoyed his views in comfort: there was a fireplace on each floor of his derelict tower. It was built as solidly as could be expected, from stucco-covered stone with brick surrounds on the doors and windows, but years of neglect and the biting Dorset winter have taxed the presumption of building on such an exposed site. Clavell enjoyed his tower for 13 years until he died intestate in 1833. A will was discovered which made the estate over to his steward and his housekeeper, but two years later it turned out that the will was a forgery, and the greedy servants paid their penalties. Denis Bond's folly, Creech Grange Arch, is entirely different. Massive, but not physically large, it crouches at the top of CREECH HILL, grey, lichen-covered stone in the sunshine. It is one of the earliest eyecatchers in the country, dated to 1746. The arch is simple, elegant and has to be seen from the back; it presents itself permanently in silhouette when seen from the house below. It is reminiscent of Vanbrugh's work, but there is no record of the architect. The Bond family, which gave London's fashionable Bond Street its name, made over the eyecatcher to the National Trust in 1942.

A fast straight road from the bottom of Creech Hill leads us into Wareham and out of the Isle of Purbeck. To the north lies the village of Morden. CHARBOROUGH PARK, the seat of the Drax family, is large, impressive, and private; it was so made by altering the course of the main Dorchester–Wimborne road so that it travels in a semi-circle around the park's northern perimeter, instead of through the middle as it did until 1841, when J. S. W. S. Erle Drax had the road closed to the public. He was sued for the reopening of the road by a Dorchester man, who lost, and the triumphant Drax had a plaque erected to commemorate his victory (prudently, he placed it on the park side of his entrance lodge so it couldn't be seen from the new road). The old road must have passed close to the foot of Charborough Park Tower, one of the finest folly-towers in Britain.

The approach to the tower from the house is grand: a long, wide, grassy avenue flanked by monolithic plinths — empty, of course; what real folly builder would dream of putting statues on bare plinths? — leads directly to a balustraded bridge crossing nothing in particular, then up a flight of steps to the tower. It has been likened to a factory chimney, but we think it one of the most perfect of folly-towers. Gothic (of course), it appears to have five storeys, octagonal, with buttresses rising two storeys (a pinnacle fell off in 1973 and has not been replaced). Inside the tower, we can see at once it has been loved and protected, yet from the outside there is a perceptible southward list. A plaque on the ground floor records its history:

> This tower was built by Edward Drax, Esquire, in the year 1790, during the short time he was the possessor of Charborough. It was struck by lightning on the 29th of November 1838, which so damaged it that it became necessary to take down the greater part. It was rebuilt in 1839 by John Samuel Wanley Sawbridge Erle Drax Esquire who carried it forty feet higher than it was originally built making the present height upwards of one hundred feet.

A grotesque bearded head (Edward Drax?) greets the visitor on the banister rail at the foot of the stairs. For a folly, the staircase is superb. Most prospect towers were thrown up in such a hurry that a permanent staircase was very much a secondary consideration, and the cheapest option was usually chosen, if indeed the stairs were remembered at all. At Charborough the Draxes were building for posterity, and they have left their heirs an excellent example of a geometrical open-well staircase, stone built with iron balustrades supporting a wooden rail. What makes it exceptional is that whereas the open string is naturally a geometrical spiral, the wall string has had to follow the octagonal exterior of the tower. The unknown architect handled the problem with confidence, and the result makes the stairs easy and comfortable to climb. The prospect room at the top gives panoramic views over four counties, and from the roof the views and the wind are literally breathtaking. This is always assumed to be the tower in Thomas Hardy's novel *Two on a Tower*.

Safely down again, one views the folly with a new sense of respect, for its style, quality and condition put it a rank above most other follies. It has 28 blank windows, with prominent hood-moulds and label-stops showing faces of bears, grimacing prelates, monkeys and devils, and only five real windows. A Drax family legend says that a white stag in the deer-park presages the birth of an heir to Charborough. Let us hope that white stags appear frequently enough to ensure the survival of this magnificent folly.

A few miles to the north stands a folly-tower of a very different sort. There is nothing like a good folly to produce a certain inexplicable frisson of fear, and not many are as chilling as HORTON TOWER — Sturt's Folly — even when approached at noon on a hot summer's day. Few unsupervised people expect buildings to talk to them, but this one positively exudes silence. It stands in an open field, easily accessible on foot from the road, solitary, massive and unusually ugly. Horton is built of red brick and is seven-storeyed and hexagonal, with three domed, round towers reaching two-thirds of the way up its 140 feet. Regrettably, there is no horrific story to go with it; no one even knows when it was built. The difficulty in dating it is that everyone in the family seems to have been called Humphrey Sturt. Because of its three massive corner turrets, Horton gives the impression of being triangular; the only other triangular buildings in the county are the ruined North Lodges to derelict Lulworth Castle near COOMBE KEYNES, built in 1785 as eyecatchers by Thomas Weld. Thomas Archer has been suggested as the architect for the tower; he at least was conversant with triangular buildings, and lived about 15 miles away. The Humphrey who built Sturt's Folly intended to use it as an observatory. However, he is supposed to have tired of star-gazing, and used it instead to watch deer on Cranborne Chase. Originally there was supposed to have been a spire (on an observatory?) but that has long gone, as have the floors and roof. Traces of white plaster remain in one of the three smaller towers; no trace of the staircase can be found. Edward Gibbon visited Humphrey Sturt in May 1762 and saw 'an artificial piece of water of two hundred acres and an elegant turret 140 feet high; but such is the nature of the man that he keeps his place in no order, sells his fish, and makes a granary of his turret'. Could this have been the Sturt that built the tower? This one inherited Crichel House in 1765 and embarked on a massive building programme there. The Horton lake has now gone, and a local farmer uses the walls of the tower as a slurry tip. *Plus ça change*.

Two final Dorset towers used to be in Hampshire until BOURNEMOUTH was handed over in the county boundary reorganisation. One is a small, heavily castellated and machicolated red-brick tower skulking among the trees at the top of the Upper Gardens, looking like a late Victorian water-tower; it has never been a water-tower and no one seems to know why it is there. The other *is* a water-tower, big, square and with bartizan turrets at each corner, standing in Seafield Gardens in Southbourne.

As the Bonds of Creech Grange gave their name to Bond Street, so the Shaftesburys of WIMBORNE ST GILES gave their name to Shaftesbury Avenue. St Giles' House, the ancestral home of the Earls of Shaftesbury, is now abandoned and derelict, although there were signs in early 1983 of restoration work. The park is dank and overgrown. At one time it contained a grotto, a large gazebo, an Ionic temple and a sham gateway, but a recent search failed to find the gazebo or the temple. The grotto, a particularly fine example, is well protected against the vandals who would have the idiot drive to seek it out, but the gateway close to the house is a more obvious target. It is a very satisfying folly in all but siting; two sturdy, round, castellated, two-storey towers with vermiculated banding flank an arched gateway no more than six feet wide, leading imposingly to a ditch. The structure is solid and the casement windows remain, but neglect proceeds. It seems to be the work of the 3rd Earl, in about 1754.

Another Dorset folly on the edge of a wood is the sham chapel at MILTON ABBAS, now a school. It was built by the Earl of Dorchester, who had demolished the old market town because it interfered with his views. The desire to build a sham chapel in the woods when you already have one of the largest parish churches in the county and have razed the local town can only be described as bizarre, especially when there was already a genuine ruined Norman chapel, St Catherine's, in the grounds. A design for the sham, by an unknown hand, survives in the RIBA drawings collection.

Out of the woods, Dorset is a county of panoramas, and the finest view in the whole county is to be had from Black Down near PORTESHAM. Appropriately enough, Hardy's Monument crowns the ridge, for Hardy is the best-loved name in Wessex, a writer whose love of Dorset pervades every line he wrote. It is to be regretted that a more dignified memorial than a 70-foot sink plunger could not have been chosen for Dorset's greatest man of letters, and it would be difficult to imagine a colder or more exposed place. It was winter when we visited. We were numb with cold when we read the inscription above the locked steel door, only to find it had no connection with Thomas Hardy at all. This delightfully ugly chimney designed by A. D. Troyte was built when Hardy was four years old, and erected by public subscription in 1844 to commemorate 'Admiral Sir Thomas Masterman Hardy Bart, CCB, Flag Captain to Lord Nelson on HMS Victory at the Battle of Trafalgar'. So it's the Hardy of 'Kiss me, Hardy' fame. Sir Frederick Treves saw factory chimneys all over the county, for this, as well as Charborough, reminded him of one; but this time he was more to the point. The monument has also been compared to a chess-piece, a peppermill, a candlestick telephone and, most accurate of all, a factory chimney with a crinoline. Nevertheless it survives, having been under the care of the National Trust since 1900, one of their earliest properties.

Somerset

Some say Somerset, the most beautifully named of counties, evoking apples and the onset of autumn, is the loveliest English county. Its scenery is magnificent, but its architectural jewel was Bath, torn out to make the new county of Avon. Although coastal, it does not come to mind as a seafaring county. Bristol was the nearest major port, and it was always separate, a county in its own right, so the choice of a lighthouse as a pattern for a folly is reassuringly inappropriate. At KILMERSDON, in Ammerdown Park, the Eddystone stands safe from the pounding of the surf, the crash of the waves and the lonely sea mists — it is, as the seagull flies, 27 miles inland. Quite why the Ammerdown Park Column should have been a replica of the Eddystone Lighthouse is not clear; the designer was Joseph Jopling, an architect not noted for his marine work, and it was erected to commemorate 'the genius, the energy and the brilliant talents' of Thomas Samuel Joliffe. A long inscription testifies to the 'profound affection' of the anonymous descendant who caused the column to be built (in fact Lord Hylton), and in order that the point should not be missed the same inscription is repeated in full in Latin and in French on the north and east sides. The 150-foot column was finished on 6 June 1853. Let's imagine it. A sunny, warm day. The glistening new tower stands surrounded by its low curlicued walls, its lantern tower sparkling in the sunlight. An apt inscription graces the lantern top, below the lightning conductor. Coade stone animals guard the four points of the compass on the plinth. The entrance door opens into a cool square room with chamfered corners and marbled walls; the tower extends its foot into this room, so to climb the stone spiral

49

staircase one enters through another doorway to the stair tower, an unusual and pleasing device. The staircase, regularly lit by ten tiny portholes, winds up to a splendid view from the glass lantern at the top. Doubtless there is gaiety and celebration, and much gasping at the view – but one heart is black with envy.

A Mr Turner, whose lands abut the Joliffe estate, went home determined to outdo the Ammerdown Column. For a while he succeeded, as his square Italianate tower at 180 feet topped Ammerdown by some 30 feet. But it was not to last: it was very soon declared unsafe, and a large proportion of it had to come down. Then, true to folly tradition, it was bought by Lord Hylton and finally pulled down completely in 1969.

Still standing, but looking very dilapidated, is another tall square Italianate tower at EAST CRANMORE, about six miles south. This was built in 1862–5 by W. H. Wyatt for Sir Richard Horner Paget. Cranmore Tower peers above the trees to the north of the A361, deceptively close to the road, since the climb, up a green lane in the hamlet of Dean, is invigorating but takes an hour to get there and back. From a short distance, the tower looks well preserved; only right up close does its dereliction become apparent. It is much bigger than expected, at least 100 feet tall, and the facing stones on the east side have sheared off in bulk, leaving huge areas of exposed fabric from the base to just under the top. Still roofed, the top of the tower looks deceptively solid from a distance. Inside, the greater part of the wooden staircase survives. It was very sturdily built, and only total neglect allowed it to decay to this extent. To have climbed it as it was when we saw it would need a degree of stupidity we thankfully do not possess. In 1984 a Glastonbury farmer bought the folly with the intention of restoring it and opening it to the public, at the same time building himself a four-bedroomed house at the base. The local newspaper gleefully seized on this and headlined it 'MR BEATON'S FOLLY'. It remains a good, creepy folly – a totally unnecessary building.

Even prisoners succumb to the county's charms and show their thanks. On the left-hand side of the A39 at WEST HORRINGTON, about two and a half miles before Wells and opposite a tall television mast, is an extraordinary structure built into a low wall. Four square shingled columns rise eight feet to support a rusticated pediment, on top of which stands a statue of Romulus and Remus suckling the she-wolf. It is a very small folly, but its siting and accessibility make it somehow memorable. The sculptor who made it was called Gaetano Celestra, a Roman prisoner of war who was not, as one might imagine, from the 3rd century but from the Second World War.

In Yorkshire there is a column to Admiral Keppel, court-martialled after the battle of Ushant. In Somerset there is a column to the memory of Admiral Sir Samuel Hood, who falsified his ship's log and testified against Keppel. Hood's monument was built nearly 50 years after Keppel's, in 1831, by William Beckford's protégé H. E. Goodridge. It stands in BUTLEIGH WOOD, south of Street. Once there was a way up to the top, from where there would have been remarkable views to Glastonbury Tor, but now the entrance has been traditionally blocked up. On our visit we could dimly make out the shape of a galleon's stern at the top of the column. We were above cloud level, and visibility was poor. The galleon's stern is said by those who have seen the monument on clearer days to be merely a stone shield, but we prefer, for an admiral's sake, to see it in the mist.

Cock Hill, a National Trust property on the road from Street to Bridgwater, overlooks Sedgemoor, the site of the last battle fought on British soil, in 1685, between Monmouth and·James II. Near CHILTON POLDEN, on the north side of the hill and set slightly below the road, is an immaculately kept sham church originally built for the antiquarian William Stradling as a house in 1840. Still a private house, its only drawback is its proximity to the main road. On a clear day the view is spectacular; you can see across smoky Bridgwater and the motorway to − if you look in the right direction − a village called Goathurst, nine miles away as the crow flies. The road to Goathurst passes KNOWLE HALL on the right. On the crest of the park, now a school, is a small eyecatcher sham castle façade, one wall thick, built by the Greenhill family when they lived at the hall.

The big house at GOATHURST is called Halswell. It is not a beautiful building, but it is large and rambling, and from the hill above it gives the impression more of a small village than a private house. The fabric is dilapidated and neglected, and the owner has

divided the house into flats; the estate hums with life as the old
house dies. The residents of Halswell are attached to its ugliness, its
amorphousness and, certainly not least, its exquisite setting. They
deeply regret the landlord's indifference to its maintenance and they
share a delight and interest in the remarkable profusion of garden
ornaments scattered around the estate. There is no building that on
its own would really qualify as a folly, but the sustained building
over a period of years, the stories that have built up around them
and the stifled, overgrown atmosphere of the estate make Halswell
a major folly group.

'What chiefly attracts the notice and attention of strangers are the
decorated grounds,' wrote Arthur Young in 1768, and he lists the
following structures that are still to be found – a Doric Rotunda, a
temple to Robin Hood, the cascade with bridge, bench and tablet,
and an Ionic Portico. Also still extant but not mentioned by Young
are a grotto, a stepped pyramid and an unusual bell-roofed
dovecote. Most of these were built by Sir Charles Tynte, or
Kemeys-Tynte. The Doric Rotunda stands hidden in an overgrown
wood to the east of the house, apparently covering an ice-house,
still elegant, still intact, but recently robbed of the lead from the
domed roof: decay is inevitable. Robin Hood's Temple, a
wonderful name for a disappointing building, is slowly collapsing
at the top of the hill above the house. What remains is a plain
oblong with a ridiculous, 1930s, Bletchley-style central chimneypot,
and two ogival windows flanking a ruined circular or semi-circular
prospect room. The views are magnificent, looking across the
Bristol Channel to South Wales; it was obviously intended as a
dining room with a view. The right-hand window is blanked off
and the room behind seems to have been a kitchen. The element of
surprise, so beloved of folly-builders, seems to have prompted the
thinking behind Robin Hood's Temple. The approach was
evidently intended to be made from the back through the woods
and up to the great door covered with rustic bark. Arthur Young,
who was also an agriculturalist, wrote about the new plantations to
the south of the house, 'from a dark part of which you enter
through a door into a temple dedicated to Robin Hood, upon
which a most noble prospect breaks upon the beholder.'

By contrast the cascade, some way over to the west, is still impressive. Five lakes at different levels start from a weird array of alcoves at the highest level, under a rock-carved inscription:

When Israel's wandering Sons the Desert trod
The melting Rock obeyed the Prophet's Rod.
Forth gushed the Stream, the tribe their thirst allayed
Forgetful of their God, they rose and played.
Ye happier swains for whom these waters flow
Oh may your Hearts with grateful Ardours flow.
Lo! here a Fountain streams at his command
Not o'er a barren, but a Fruitful land
Where Nature's choicest gifts the valleys fill
And smiling Plenty gladdens every Hill.

At the second cascade, crossing the lake, is an ornate bridge with two statues, one with an absurd false chin, and a new retaining wall which looks as if it was bought off the shelf at the local garden centre. By the bottom lake is the Ionic Temple, built in 1767 and attributed to Robert Adam, now roofless and appropriated by cows as a makeshift shed. Confusion sets in here, as Pevsner maintains that this temple has been re-erected in Sir Clough Williams-Ellis's Portmeirion; but here it is, and Sir Clough denied having taken any building from Halswell. The Adam attribution comes from Colvin, but John Johnson the Elder is listed as having designed a Temple of Pan for Sir Charles Kemeys in 1788. There is no trace of this building, unless it has been confused with the Ionic Temple. Young describes it as an 'Ionic Portico' in 1768, so as it was started the previous year he probably saw it in a half-built state. One of Halswell's present-day residents called it the Temple of the Virgins, while it has also been referred to as the Temple of Harmony. Could there be three names for the same building? If so, then Johnson's design was never constructed.

More confusion arises over the dating of the stepped pyramid by the side of the house. It is not easily overlooked, and therefore cannot have been built before Young's visit in 1768. The inscription on the side is now too badly worn to be legible, but it is said to have been written by Alexander Pope, who died in 1744. The lines on the tablet at the head of the cascade are in Pope's metre, but lack his style. The impetus of the Egyptian revival would place the pyramid at *c.* 1770, and if we ascribe it to Sir Charles's group we can only marvel at his eclecticism – Greek, Gothic, Egyptian and Rococo within one park. The pyramid was built as a wellhead, and now serves as a water-tank.

At the back of the house there is a very large dovecote with a remarkable bell roof in an excellent state of repair – unlike the grotto in the wood near the rotunda, which is now so overgrown that it is impossible to see it properly. Once there were plaques, inscriptions and memorials affixed – one, discovered lying in the undergrowth, reads 'JIM. DIED DECEMBER 30TH 1903. HE WAS FAITHFUL TILL DEATH', and others commemorated a favourite canary and a chicken – but these have now disappeared. One memorial that does still exist is a sarcophagus for a stallion which died winning a wager for its owner. Until recently it survived in a nearby field; then a tractor knocked it over and the farmer removed it to his garden in North Newton. He had the inscription let into the floor of the changing room for his swimming pool.

Halswell Park lacks only a good prospect tower to make it one of the finest folly groups in southern England. A polygonal hermitage and a Druids' Temple have completely vanished, but enough remains to satisfy nearly every taste. How much will remain for how long is much more of a worry; the owner's lack of interest and the already fragile structure of the follies can only hasten their demise. It would be a pity to lose them. Halswell is unique.

There is another removal at WIVELISCOMBE, where Viscount Boyd was fortunate enough to secure a 25-foot pinnacle from Westminster Abbey and have it re-erected in his garden. In the grounds of Hestercombe House at CHEDDON FITZPAINE are two small 18th-century temples, one Doric tetrastyle and the other a semi-circular brick recess with a round-headed rusticated arch.

Getting lost in the Quantock or Brandon Hills in mid-summer without a timetable must be close to heaven. Good places to get lost near are Cothelstone, Elworthy, Combe Florey and Crowcombe. Two have the sort of views you seem to get only in Somerset, one has a patently false legend, and the last is an enchanting period piece, an already ruined chapel moved painstakingly to where the ruins would look better. COTHELSTONE is the strangest of the four, with two tiny follies no more than 100 yards apart on a ridge overlooking the vale of Taunton Deane, one an astonishing half-headless figure with half an upraised arm perched on top of an alcove seat positioned for contemplating the view. No one seems to know what it was supposed to represent. The other is breathtakingly beautiful, by accident rather than by design, for the beacon tower that stood here has now collapsed to a paltry 10 or 15 feet in two piles of masonry, overshadowed by a well-shaped Scots pine. 'Capability' Brown could not have contrived a better landscape.

Winter's Folly in COMBE FLOREY was used by Henry VIII to imprison one of his more recalcitrant wives. The truth behind this legend, sadly, is more prosaic, but still vaguely unsatisfactory. Winter's Folly was built in the late 18th century as a keeper's cottage, probably by John Francis Gwyn, the grandson of 'Rotchester's Gwine'; but why build a cottage five storeys high and make it look, as Jeboult said in 1873, like 'a very debased attempt to represent a church tower'? The building is in fact quite ugly, except for the colour of the red stone used in parts of its construction. Above the front door is an arched window with a trefoil on a wooden batten, but the rest of the fenestration is utilitarian cottage casement. It was obviously used as a house; there is a large fireplace on the ground floor, plastering on the walls and remnants of room partitions on the first and second floors and part of a staircase. The top three storeys are rendered, and the top two show no sign inside of ever having had floors. Why build so high? By the time Mr Jeboult visited, 'the tenants seemed ignorant for what purpose this unseemly tower was erected'. His exasperation shines through bright and clear. A brick on the ground marked 'W. Thomas and Co. Wellington' would date the tower in the first half of the 19th century, so now, even more confused by dates, let us leave Combe Florey and go to Crowcombe.

On private land behind CROWCOMBE COURT is a part sham, part genuine ruined castle of sandstone and ironstone. The genuine gothic fragments were taken in the late 18th century from the demolished chapel of Halsway Manor, just up the combe. It owes its continued existence rather more to the binding of undergrowth than of mortar. Now the estate has been parcelled off, and its future is uncertain.

The last of the Quantock Quartet is another sham church-tower, this time on Forestry Commission land at ELWORTHY, and blessed with views to equal those from Hardy's Monument in Dorset. To be geographically accurate, Willett's Tower is on the Brendon Hills, but it doesn't have the Exmoor mood. It is visible from miles around, clearly marked on the maps and impossible to find once you start walking. The folly is built of the local slaty stone, with red mortar and red brick trimmings which give the whole tower a red sandstone appearance. It looks like a cardboard church-tower – an effort to bring Glastonbury to Elworthy – and was built in 1820 by a Mr Belmerton, probably as an eyecatcher to be seen from Willetts. The wooden staircase inside was probably installed later, to take advantage of the view or to look out for forest fires.

North-west and south-east of this comfortable group lie Dunster and Wellington. DUNSTER is very much an estate village, quaintly pretty with the castle, a National Trust property, perched above, guarding it against the encroachment of the brashly successful holiday town of Minehead. The most obvious landmark in the village, however, is the folly-tower on Conygar Hill. It is low, squat, hollow and circular and was built *c.* 1770 by Luttrell purely as an eyecatcher. As a piece of architecture it is unexceptional; as an eyecatcher it is magnificently successful, visible from miles around. At the foot of Conygar Hill nestles the village, and as we come down St George's Street looking for an easy way to get across to the tower there is a delightful *jardin imaginaire* behind Spears Cross Hotel. On a steep bank above the lawn are at least 25 model houses, the majority half-timbered, with two churches of wildly differing scales and a rather token representation of a castle. The overall effect is delightfully surprising, the more so because no real attempt has been made to verisimilitude. St Audries School at WEST QUANTOXHEAD, east of Dunster, has a little shell grotto by the chapel, but it is always kept locked.

Leaping south-east to the Black Down Hills which separate Devon from Somerset, the Wellington Monument at WRANGWAY is familiar to travellers on the M5. This huge obelisk, designed by Thomas Lea Junior in 1817, dominates the surrounding landscape. It is difficult for us nowadays to realise the adulation given to Wellington at that time. He was a Kennedy, a Beatle, a Botham, a Che Guevara all rolled into one, and he seemed to be well aware of it. He allowed the burghers of Wellington to record the memory of his spectacular military exploits by building this 175-foot obelisk, now preserved by the National Trust, and embellished with a spiral staircase leading to a tiny chamber at the top. On a clear and preferably windless day the view alone is worth the journey.

The hills and views of central and west Somerset diminish to the south-east into a flat fertile plain, relieved occasionally by peculiar island-like lumps in a green and yellow sea. At one time nearly the whole area was water or marshland, and mumps such as Glastonbury Tor were genuine islands. As a child spending holidays in Somerset, I remember feeling a little cheated that St Michael's church-tower on Glastonbury Tor was not a folly. It had all the necessary attributes, except that it was genuine. Luckily, and unbeknown to me, 10 miles and 200 years away someone else felt the same way. Although Burrow Mump at BURROW BRIDGE lacks the grandeur and sheer size of Glastonbury Tor, it rises just as abruptly out of the flat surrounding countryside, and it has the same stepped ridges encircling the hill, in Glastonbury, it is said, gouged out by the tail of the dragon defeated by King Gwyn long before recorded time. It seems they had a second bout at Burrow Mump. But Burrow Mump, unlike Glastonbury, didn't have a tower, an irresistible challenge to an 18th-century Englishman. There had been a church here, in the province of Athelney Abbey, but it was destroyed in 1655 when Royalist troops held it as a fortress. Like Glastonbury, it was dedicated to St Michael. Work started on repairs in 1724, but they were never completed, although the ruined parts were carefully accentuated and capped. Major A. G. Barrett gave it to the National Trust in 1946, as a memorial to the men and women of Somerset who died in the Second World War.

No trace remains of the great monastery of ATHELNEY half a mile away across Stan Moor. A farmhouse now occupies the site, together with a peculiar squat memorial signposted 'TO KING ALFRED'S MONUMENT'. Pevsner describes it precisely: 'a short plain truncated obelisk of no architectural merit'. It was erected in 1807 by John Slade, a local farmer (and Lord of the Manor of North Atherton), to commemorate King Alfred fleeing past the spot in 807. From the little monument we can see Burrow Mump Sham

Church and, to the south on a ridge, a tall, elegant tower — one of the best known follies in Somerset.

Burton Pynsent Steeple at CURRY RIVEL is a deservedly famous folly. It is large, it crumbles, it has a suitably spectacular setting, its purpose was properly pointless, and it has an amusing story attached to it. A Tuscan column with the obligatory drum and urn on top, it was built in 1765 by 'Capability' Brown to the instructions of Sir William Pitt, whom Sir William Pynsent so admired that he left him his estate. Pitt, who never met his benefactor, returned the compliment by leaving us this 140-foot column with a rather barbed inscription: 'Sacred to the memory of Sir William Pynsent. Hoc saltem Fungam inani munere.' Barbara Jones wrote that in the 1940s a cow twice managed to climb the spiral staircase to the top, and was shooed down backwards (how did the cowherd ever get past her?). The third time, as in all good rural legends, she got to the top and fell off the parapet. The door was then blocked up. Nowadays it is as much for our protection as for the cows': the masonry at the top of the tower is jutting out dangerously, and urgent work needs to be carried out to preserve this wonderful, archetypal folly column.

In ILCHESTER there is a boring structure to the west of the bridge in the middle of the town. It is called 'The Bell Tower', but it has no bells, nor is it a tower. A real tower, one that can be seen for miles, is superbly placed on the top of the conical St Michael's Hill at MONTACUTE, a National Trust property. It was built in 1760 on the site of the first Montacute Castle — and never did a hill live up to its name more acutely. Don't take what looks to be the quickest way up unless you have crampons. Skirt round the wood at the bottom of the steepest part of the hill and you will discover a track leading up to the flat hilltop and the tower. Here comes the first surprise: the tower is remarkably small for such a visible object, scarcely 40 feet high. It is circular with a conical roof, not unlike an Irish round-tower, but with peculiar fin-like protrusions at the top. Above the doorway is a Greek inscription with the date 1760. Then comes the second surprise: the doorway is not blocked up, the stairs are intact, and you may freely ascend to the top of the tower, 52 steps bringing you to a little room with four barred window-holes giving a view spanning, on the right day, Devon, Wales,

Shaftesbury, Lyme Regis, 80 churches and a 300-mile circle. The mystery of the strange protrusions is solved; they are the remnants of an external staircase, now thankfully inaccessible, to the flat roof where once there stood a flagpole as tall as the tower itself.

A very different folly can be found on the outskirts of YEOVIL, at Brympton. Brympton D'Evercy house is built of Ham stone, and it is difficult to imagine any more beautiful building material when looking at Brympton in the late afternoon sun. In the garden on the west front is a peculiar, useless little building, put up in 1723 from older assorted parts: an archway, a tiny belfry. It looks at once like a lych-gate, a dovecote and a summer-house, but appears so natural in its setting, so at peace with its environment, that it could not be bettered. Known as 'The Alcove', its function as a shelter seems purposeless when the house is only 20 yards away. The clock-face, a Victorian addition, faces south, and so cannot be seen from the house. Like most good follies, it is beautiful, useless and pleasurable.

Somerset's greatest folly achievement is the group at Barwick Park, a mile south of Yeovil. They are as fine as any in the country, and for enigma they cannot be surpassed. Not large or obtrusive, they impale themselves upon the memory by their pointlessness, and the mystery is increased when research fails to discover much about their history. The four follies are the Obelisk, the Fish-Tower, the Cone and Jack the Treacle Eater, as well as a damp, eerie grotto, morbid rather than contemplative. The most reasonable explanation for their existence is that they were built by George Messiter in the 1820s 'to relieve unemployment in Yeovil', but Barbara Jones dates them some 50 years earlier, having seen two paintings of *c.* 1770 in which two of them appear. It is impossible to date them by their architecture, for they have no architecture. Even the normally conventional obelisk is here transformed into something widely different – instead of the solid, worthy municipal structure familiar to us all, it has metamorphosed into a neurotic stiletto, a tall, beastly thin, crazily tilting rubbly object, as far removed from an urban obelisk as a javelin is from a caber. Just over a mile to the north is the Fish Tower, again in the same rubble, a plain, unadorned, thin tower about 50 feet high with a carved drum top. There used to be an iron cage with a fish weathervane (hence the name), but that has now disappeared. The inside is hollow, wide enough and rocky enough to climb up if the folly is upon one. There are holes for the light.

The Cone is astonishing. Tall (about 70 feet) and slender, with a ball finial, it stands on a tripod; three Gothic arches face north, east and south out of the circular base, and the west wall is solid. There are nine layers of square holes rising to the top of the cone, as if in a dovecote, but this was never a dovecote. There are traces of what may have been a wooden roof above the arches. Jones describes it to perfection: 'a highly functional structure designed for no function that has yet materialised'. It looks as if it should work.

Due east of the Cone is Jack the Treacle Eater, the most bizarre in name and shape. The by now familiar rubble style makes a coarse, shouldered arch about 30 feet high, but here the rubble is massive enough to climb. On top of the arch is a smooth round towerlet with a conical roof, and perched at the very top is Jack himself, a statuette of Mercury. The towerlet seems to have had a door, long ago blocked (but perhaps it was a sham door), with what looks like a short flight of steps leading to it up the shoulder of the arch. Access to the steps can be gained only by climbing the vertical wall of the arch. Perhaps this led to the now famous legend of Jack the Treacle Eater, who lived in the towerlet, trained on treacle and ran messages to London for the Messiter family. Only someone as agile as he could live in such a dwelling. For the true story we can only fall back on speculation. The Greeks used statues of Hermes as boundary markers, and the Barwick Park follies are said to mark the boundaries of the old Messiter estate. The Romans used statues of Mercury as garden ornaments. Treacle originally meant an antidote to the bites of wild beasts, and the statue of Jack (Mercury, Hermes) carried a wand or caduceus, which was supposed to have healing or narcotic effects – our heads are spinning and we are no nearer the truth. The most fanciful stories can be devised with so rich and remote a source, and there are few follies so calculated to stir the imagination as these. The legends at Barwick should be fostered; the truth may prove to be too prosaic.

Wiltshire

Of the four Wessex counties, Wiltshire is perhaps the bleakest, with little to offer the traveller in search of scenery. The M4 cuts the head of the county off from the rest, leaving Swindon, born like Atlanta as a railway marshalling yard, soulless and vacant, an artificial city. There is only one curiosity worth seeing north of the motorway, and that is not a folly. WANBOROUGH CHURCH, like Ormskirk in Lancashire, has both a tower and a steeple, but here they are at opposite ends of the nave. The strangest thing about it is that no legend has grown up in explanation. South of the motorway the county wastes away to the sparse treelessness of the Marlborough Downs and Salisbury Plain, beloved of Ancient Britons, flying saucers and the British Army, and punctuated only by Savernake Forest and the pretty Vale of Pewsey. Despite the county's initially unprepossessing appearance to an outsider, its people's pride is strong. Europe's most important prehistoric monuments are to be found in Wiltshire, and it is said that its very barrenness was due to the intensive agriculture carried on here in prehistoric times.

Leave the motorway. The A4 is a much finer road, and you don't get the eerie radio silences encountered driving through Wiltshire on the M4. At Hungerford in Berkshire, detour south on the A338 and see how the trees and copses fall away as you come into naked Wiltshire. As the hills rise in front of you, you will discover the hamlet of WEXCOMBE, and the local pride, perhaps inherited from the Beaker People, asserts itself. 'We was the first village in Wiltshire to have our own pumped water,' declared a farmer, and the local pride and joy is the village waterworks, a reservoir on the top of Grafton Hill with a tiny pumping station in front, adorned with a pineapple roof. The 'Gift' of Dr William Corrin Finch is still in working order, though nowadays the village water comes from the mains. Why the pineapple roof? 'Because the doctor liked pineapples,' answered the farmer, obviously perplexed that anyone should find it the least bit strange. 'It's used in car rallies and the like – find a pineapple in Wiltshire and that sort of thing.' The inscription above the door of the tiny tower is in gothic capitals, probably the most illegible script devised by man, and records that Wexcombe Waterworks were built in 1899. The little red-brick pineapple tower is enchanting.

Heading back to the A4 we pass the famous and ancient SAVERNAKE FOREST where in 1781 Thomas Bruce, Earl of Ailesbury, erected a tall column by way of thanks to his uncle for leaving him his title and estates. If it is possible for a sycophant to disclose himself through one inscription, then Bruce succeeds:

> This Column was erected by Thomas Bruce, Earl of Ailesbury, as a testimony of gratitude to his ever honoured uncle Charles, Earl of Ailesbury and Elgin, who left to him these estates, and procured for him the Barony of Tottenham, and of loyalty to his most gracious sovereign George the Third, who unsolicited conferred upon him the honour of an earldom, but above all of piety to God, first, highest, best, whose blessing consecrateth every gift, and fixeth its true value. MDCCLXXXI.

It must be rare to find an inscription irritating, but 100 feet of Ionic column towering over the unsolicited earl's pious beliefs and his reverential trust in the proper order of things (1. Uncle Charles 2. George III 3. God) cannot be anything but annoying. The column itself is satisfying: perched on a monumental plinth, it is crowned by an urn, covered in lichen and splendidly sited on a low rise at the end of the avenue, over a mile long, running from Tottenham House. Still in excellent condition, it is solidly built in an attractive dusky red stone. On the north side of the plinth the servile Bruce had another tablet inscribed:

> In commemoration of a signal instance of Heaven's protecting providence over these kingdoms in the year 1789 by restoring to

perfect health from a long and afflicting disorder their excellent and beloved sovereign George The Third.

King George had spent most of the previous year in a strait-jacket out of harm's way, and despite the stony ministrations of the Earl of Ailesbury, it was not long before he returned to it permanently. But perhaps the saddest thing about the Ailesbury column is that it wasn't originally Bruce's; he bought it second hand. It had originally been erected in 1760, at La Trappe House in Hammersmith, by George Bubb Dodington in memory of his wife, and was moved to Savernake 20 years later. The octagonal summer-house in the forest now used as a cattlefood store was one of two designed for Bruce's uncle by Richard Boyle, Lord Burlington, together with a banqueting hall which was demolished in 1824.

The Marquess of Lansdowne was partly responsible for a really primitive statue which sits with a shopping basket on a column at the top of WICK HILL, north-west of Calne. It commemorates one Maud Heath, a market trader who left money in her will when she died in 1474 to build a causeway over the often flooded land between Wick Hill and Chippenham Clift. In 1698 pillars in her honour were erected at the start and finish of the causeway, and in 1838 came this column, erected by the Marquess of Lansdowne and W. L. Bowles, Bremhill's vicar, and bearing the inscription:

> Thou who dost pause on this aerial height
> Where MAUD HEATH's Pathway winds in shade or light
> Christian wayfarer, in this world of strife
> Be still and ponder on the Path of Life.

Bowles's poetry could have been better — he was a friend of Wordsworth and Lamb, and corresponded with many of the leading literary figures of the time. An enthusiastic amateur of all artistic things, he may well have perpetrated the statue too. He was a frequent guest at the Marquess's Bowood House.

BOWOOD, just beyond Calne, is open to the public in the summer. It is a place of pilgrimage for the folly hunter because the great cascade was designed by the Hon. Charles Hamilton, who created the famous gardens at Painshill in Surrey. His work at Bowood owes much to the influence of Poussin and other romantic landscape painters. The major work is the Cascade, far more impressive than his own at Painshill, largely because it still works; but there was also a grotto by the Lanes of Tisbury — as at Painshill, but virtually non-existent nowadays — a still extant Doric temple and a superb mausoleum, kept in immaculate condition, by Robert Adam. The towering asymmetrical Italianate gate lodge known as the Golden Gate was designed for the Marquess in 1834 by Sir Charles Barry at his Barrymost. It took four years to complete.

We are in Cotswold Wiltshire now; the land has softened and mellowed, the stone is more honeyed. At Bowden Hill, on a back road to Lacock, two gatehouses stand glowering across the road at each other, one the Tudor gateway to SPYE PARK HOUSE, the other an eyecatcher, an upstart, a gateway to BOWDEN PARK halfway down the hill, hinting perhaps of ancient rivalries. There is a grotto in Bowden Park which we have not seen. But the Spye Park gateway is not all it seems: although genuinely Tudor, it was erected here after the estate it originally graced, Old Bromham House, was destroyed by the Roundheads in 1645. The Boynton family moved in style — when they bought Spye Park they brought their gatehouse with them. SANDRIDGE TOWER, south on the A3102, is a castellated tower made into a house. No names, no dates. Down Bowden Hill is the National Trust's LACOCK, famous almost as much for its beauty as for being the birthplace of William Henry Fox Talbot, the inventor of the photographic negative. There are two Tuscan columns in the grounds, topped with a sphinx, and the Gothick gateway to the Abbey is by Sanderson Miller. The village, wholly owned by the National Trust, must be seen.

CORSHAM COURT as we see it today was built in 1844–9 by Thomas Bellamy for Lord Methuen. Bellamy was a student under David Laing, who specialised in building picturesque villages and *cottages ornés*, which may explain the extraordinary edifice behind the stables, an enormous crinkle-crankle wall, about 60 feet high and 100 feet long. Evidently intended to convey an ecclesiastical air, this monstrosity was built with stones from Chippenham Abbey, including some of the window tracery. If it was meant to disguise the stables it fails magnificently; so blatant an object in this setting cries out to be investigated. Solidly, massively, and very carefully built with Gothick chimneys perched on the top apparently as afterthoughts, it is large enough to conceal small rooms in its base, which probably came in handy as hen-houses. Details such as the Gothick window tracery are far more prominent on the north side of the wall, showing it was intended to be seen from the house. If not Bellamy, then Repton may have been responsible for this magnificent folly.

A very different sort of folly stands on the escarpment at MONKTON FARLEIGH, a Wiltshire cliff hanging out over the county of Avon with magnificent views of Bath. Mr Wade Brown, who leased the manor of Monkton Farleigh in 1842, built this unexceptional tower in 1848 for 'surveying' purposes. Mr Brown had little time to waste on architectural niceties; his tower is devoid of decoration. It is square, faintly Italianate, windowless and tapering up to the top room, which is lit by four round-arched windows with balustrades underneath. The entrance is of course blocked up, but above the door is a plaque:

W 1848 B
E
C 1907 H

We have not discovered who CH was, nor what happened in 1907. Wade Brown died in 1851, leaving a village school where he had personally taught the girls. He insisted his pupils should dress in red cloaks, blue gowns, white aprons and collars, and this evidently had a deleterious effect on their descendants: several of the present-day inhabitants of the village seem to be tenpence in the shilling and menacing to boot.

Near Trowbridge are two splendid and heavily castellated lodge-houses to the now demolished ROOD ASHTON HOUSE, built in 1808 by Jeffry Wyatt. Part of a wing remains, as at Fonthill, and it has been rehabilitated as a house. The lodges have all the right castellations and machicolations: Castle Lodge is asymmetric, with a bartizan turret, and Rood Ashton Lodge is built as a long, straight façade, rising to a twin-turreted archway. On the other side of Trowbridge, at TROWLE COMMON, is Longscroft Farm, the disconsolate survivor of an abandoned project, a tall, spindly, L-shaped house on the A363 originally erected in connection with the abortive plan to link Widbrook and Trowle by a branch of the Kennet and Avon Canal.

We went down to DEVIZES because we had heard that there were two folly castles. Devizes Castle was originally a Norman motte and bailey fortification around which the town grew up. It fell into disrepair, was slighted by Cromwell and by 1842 had virtually disappeared. Then William Beckford's protégé H. E. Goodridge 'rescued' it by building a Gothic fantasia full of louring walls and forbidding battlements which has now been robbed of its grimness by being turned into flats. Shane's Castle sounded promising, but turned out to be a castellated toll cottage built by George Wyatt in 1812 on the junction of the A361 and the A342. The Wyatts liked Devizes: the Market Cross, a tall, open neo-Gothic spire, was put up in 1814 by Benjamin Dean Wyatt, possibly from an earlier design by James Wyatt, and paid for by Lord Sidmouth. An inscription on the building records the fate of Ruth Pierce of Potterne, who in 1753 had come with some other women to buy corn in the market. When it came to collecting the money, Ruth told the others that she had already paid, swearing that she might drop dead if she hadn't. She died instantly.

South-east of Devizes is ETCHILHAMPTON HILL, on top of which is the Lydeway Monument, an iron-tailed lion dating from 1768, sitting on a pedestal to commemorate a road improvement scheme. To the south is Salisbury Plain, folly-free until we get to WILTON. Wilton House is open to the public, but the Old Schoolhouse in the grounds is not. It was built in 1838 using the façade of the old grotto, which had been built in the 17th century by Isaac de Caus and was therefore one of the earliest in the country. The façade is formal, rigid in its rustication; the Italian style was still the correct approach and the eccentric, eerie, English grotto was 100 years away. The Triumphal Arch of 1757 by Chambers was originally built on the hill to the south of the house, but was moved to the entrance court around 1800.

There is a grotto called 'The Diamond' in the grounds of AMESBURY ABBEY, where everyone says John Gay wrote *The Beggar's Opera*. Why not believe it? This would mean the grotto would have been built before 1732, and therefore the ubiquitous Jos. Lane of Tisbury could not have crafted it. Wilbury House at

NEWTON TONEY has two grottoes, perhaps designed by the owner-architect of the house, the egregious William Benson (1682–1754). Talented Benson undoubtedly was, but he was also a conniving, self-seeking sycophant, who wheedled his way into the lucrative governmental position of Surveyor of the Works, displacing Sir Christopher Wren, the previous incumbent. He held the post for 15 months while he and his collaborator Colen Campbell milked it for what they could get. In 1719 he was forced to resign, having made more out of the job in one year than Wren made in 40, as Hawksmoor remarked. He sold Wilbury House in 1734 to Henry Hoare of Stourhead, so it is possible that Hoare built the grotto — but Tower Hill to the south used to be crowned by a circular brick structure known as Benson's Folly, now demolished. If Benson built that, then he could well have built the grotto, which would make him one of our earliest folly builders. One grotto is buried in a mound below an octagonal Gothick summer-house, while the other, larger, and almost certainly earlier one is in the wood between the house and the main road. There is also a column to commemorate Queen Victoria's Jubilee of 1897.

In and around Salisbury are the three oldest buildings in this chapter. Are they follies? Certainly one has been accepted as such since before follies were called follies — the National Trust's Pepperbox, or Eyre's Folly, on Pepperbox Hill at WHITEPARISH. It is hexagonal and brick built, with a pyramidal roof and three low storeys; all the little windows are bricked in. At ground level it originally stood on open arches; these too have been filled in. Built by Giles Eyre in 1606, it is generally regarded as one of the earliest follies in the country. The story — there has to be a story to justify such ancient folly — is that Eyre was envious of the tall towers of the bizarre Longford Castle (which we will discuss in a moment) and built the tower on high ground so he could overlook Sir Thomas Gorges's strange creation. The epitaph on Eyre's tomb in Whiteparish church describes him as a man 'much oppressed by Publick Power'. If there is a saner reason for the existence of this sensible little tower (it has no folly atmosphere), it may logically have been built as a hunting stand.

Longford Castle, near ODSTOCK, was built as a house in the late 16th century and has remained continuously inhabited for 400 years. It can scarcely be counted as a folly, yet its unusual triangular plan is shared in Britain only by the contemporary Triangular Lodge at Rushton in Northants and the rash of 18th-century folly-towers germinated by Henry Flitcroft with Fort Belvedere at Windsor Great Park. Unquestionably the builder, Sir Thomas Gorges, was a cerfifiable eccentric, but tantalisingly little is known about him. There are stories of a Swedish wife pining for her triangular castle back home and Longford being built on the booty from a Spanish galleon; and it is true that there is a triangular castle at Gripsholm in Sweden, dating from 1537, and that a Sir Ferdinando Gorges was a contemporary naval commander who was probably a relation, but further than that we cannot go. The building with its symbol of the Holy Trinity in the central courtyard should be regarded in the same light as Rushton: an affirmation of faith in the Trinity.

James Wyatt removed an elegant 15th-century porch from SALISBURY Cathedral during his restoration work in 1791, and it was re-erected in the grounds of Wyndham House, now the Council House, in Bourne Hill. The garden is now a public park abutting the Council House, and the little porch with its polygonal roof acts as a secular archway over one of the shady paths.

The Larmer Gardens in TOLLARD ROYAL on the Dorset border are surrounded by a double-thickness, barbed–wire-topped, ten-foot-tall steel fence, more suitable for a chemical warfare research establishment than a pleasure garden laid out for the 'recreation of the people in the neighbouring towns and villages', as was General A. H. Lane Fox Pitt-Rivers's intention in 1880. The grounds were open to the public free every day, a band played on Sundays, crockery and cutlery were loaned free of charge to picnickers (but alcohol was forbidden), and six 'quarters' — Indian-style picnic houses — were available to parties. A wooden theatre was built in the classical Corinthian style in 1895. We have not been able to get in to see all this.

West of Wilton are the two great parks of Stourhead and Fonthill; on our way we are detained briefly by an arch at COMPTON CHAMBERLAYNE and a grotto at WARDOUR CASTLE. The arch, right on the side of the A30, leads to a scrubby sapling covered hill, showing

8 One of the Sheepstor arches
near Burrator Reservoir

9 Haldon Belvedere, or
Lawrence Castle,
Doddiscombsleigh

15   The Ten Commandments on Buckland Beacon

22 Ralph Allen's sham castle, Bath

23 The Black Castle, Brislington

no trace of a drive to Compton Park, the house of the Penruddocks.
A small plaque reads:

CP

FHP

1858

The embattled arch is flanked by two square towers of different
sizes.

The grotto at Old Wardour Castle was built by Josiah Lane of
Tisbury, the most famous grotto builder of them all. It may be
thought that it was his work here and at Fonthill which drew him
to the attention of a wider circle of clients than could be found
within two miles of Tisbury, but both these grottoes would seem
to have been made towards the end of his life and rank among his
last commissions, after his successes throughout the rest of the
country. A grotto builder is not without honour, save in his own
county.

The garden at STOURHEAD is the jewel in the National Trust's
crown. Of all the great 18th-century gardens — Hawkstone,
Hackfall, Studley Royal, Stowe, Painshill, 'The Leasowes', among
many — Stourhead alone has maintained a continuity over 200
years, maturing slowly under the English summer sun, lying
dormant in the changeable English winter. It is the *premier grand cru*
of English gardens, owned by the same family, the bankers Hoare,
from 1715 to 1947. Henry Hoare II began the garden as we see it
today in 1740, by damming the head of the river Stour to create a
romantic serpentine lake. He employed Henry Flitcroft, who had
designed Benjamin Hoare's Boreham House, Essex, in 1727, to
provide some garden buildings. Flitcroft's first essays in folly
architecture were classical, and the formality of his temples
contrasted sharply with the new informality in garden design
pioneered by Kent and Bridgman and enthusiastically maintained
by gifted amateurs like Hamilton, Shenstone and Hoare, before
reverting to professionals with Brown and Repton.

The National Trust's guidebook goes into much greater detail
than we have room for here, so a short catalogue of the interesting
buildings will suffice. The first, chronologically, was the grotto of

1740, perhaps by Hoare himself, looking across the lake to St Peter's Church and the Tuscan Temple of Flora (originally the Temple of Ceres) by Flitcroft in 1744. Then came the obelisk of 1748, possibly by Francis Cartwright, to the memory of Hoare's father, then Flitcroft's Pantheon, or Temple of Hercules, from 1754, domed and with a Corinthian portico, unnaturally white in the naturally green and brown landscape. Flitcroft's last garden building was the Temple of Apollo, or the Temple of the Sun, based on the Temple at Baalbec, finished in 1767 — but as this was taking shape he designed a real no-nonsense folly up west on a hill straddling the Somerset border.

Alfred's Tower is one of the finest triangular folly towers in the country, designed by the man who gave us Wentworth Woodhouse's Hoober Stand and Fort Belvedere in Windsor Great Park, the first triangular folly-tower. Alfred's Tower, a 160-foot high expanse of sheer, windowless brick, was unashamedly built for the view from the top — the ten tiny stair-turret windows do no more than illuminate the steps. Designed in 1765, it was completed in 1772 on the spot where, as the plaque above the door tells us, 'Alfred the Great AD 870 On this summit erected his standard against Danish invaders.' Above the plaque is a large niche holding a statue of King Alfred. Lighter coloured brickwork in one of the angle turrets show where a de Havilland Mosquito flew into the tower during the war. Henry Hoare had the idea of the tower in 1762 after reading about Alfred in Voltaire's *Histoire générale*; initially, he wanted to build a replica of St Mark's Tower in Venice.

A little way away is St Peter's Pump, a 15th-century conduit removed from Bristol in 1768 and re-erected on a grotto base over the spring in Six Wells Bottom, a grassy, marshy valley descending towards the house. There is another removal right at the head of the lake — the 1373 Bristol High Cross, given to Henry Hoare in 1780. It punctuates the view of the lake and the Pantheon to perfection.

If we treat a garden as important as Stourhead in an apparently desultory fashion, it is because there is already such a wealth of accurate and accessible information about the place that little or no amplification is needed in a work of this nature. FONTHILL is different: it is private and there is no guide-book, although the interested student will find a very wide range of literature on the subject. Stourhead is romantic fact — it exists; Fonthill is romantic fiction — it doesn't.

Fonthill was the classic folly, 'the most prodigious romantic folly in England' as Pevsner described it. But there is virtually nothing to see. Gone is the vast Gothick house by Wyatt, gone is the 276-foot high tower; but what captured the imagination more than either of these was the vision of the spire, towering to an incredible 450 feet, overtopping the spire at Salisbury Cathedral — the tallest in Britain — by nearly 50 feet. The water-colour by Charles Wild depicting it was based on a design by James Wyatt, but luckily the spire was never built: the tower which was to have supported it would have collapsed much sooner. Beckford's father followed the fashion of his day by employing Josiah Lane to build him a grotto, and it is said that he also built a folly-tower on Stop's Hill, the start of young William's fascination with towers. The story of Fonthill and its houses is long and complicated; we need be concerned only with the Fonthill of William Beckford.

Beckford was a child of his era: born in 1760, he fervently embraced Romanticism in all its forms. In addition to his early talents as a writer and his remarkable looks, he was by all accounts the richest young man in England, having inherited a vast fortune from the family's West Indian sugar-cane plantations. As such he was the natural prey for every marriageable young woman in the country, but his sensational affair with William Courtenay, then a twelve-year-old boy but later to become the Earl of Devon, soon put a stop to all that. He was married off in 1783 to Lady Margaret Gordon, and they had two daughters before she died three years later. In that year, 1786, he published *Vathek*, a seminal Gothic novel, now almost unreadable but which influenced writers as diverse as Byron and Disraeli. The hero of the novel lived alone in a mighty tower, master of all he surveyed and possessed of an evil eye which could strike people dead with terror. Unlike other romantic writers, Beckford had the means to indulge his fantasies. He began by surrounding his estate with a 12-mile long, 12-foot high wall, behind which he could live in 'despotic seclusion' (at the time he divided his life between France, Portugal and Fonthill Splendens, the house built by his father, with a public road running in front of it which even his wealth and influence could not close). Having secured the services of the fashionable but slapdash James Wyatt because of his undoubted skill with the Gothick touch, Beckford could write, or contemplate, or entertain his catamites. largely as the means of translating his ideas into stone. The original intention was to build a Ruined Convent on top of the hill, where Beckford could write, or contemplate, or entertain his calamities. Wyatt, of course, had ideas of his own, including the dumpy spire which appears in J. M. W. Turner's 1799 water-colour of Fonthill. This spire collapsed in 1800. Wyatt was also enthusiastic about compo, a form of ornamental stucco or plaster, in which he encased the Abbey. This lasted six years in the English climate before it deteriorated so severely that it had to be stripped off.

Legends grew up about the place: that it was a den of vice and perversity (true); that it was possible to drive a coach-and-six to the top of the tower (false); that building went on throughout day and night — partly true. Beckford wrote to his friend and companion Gregory Franchi in 1808:

> It's really stupendous, the spectacle here at night — the number of people at work, lit up by the lads [sic]; the innumerable torches suspended everywhere, the immense and endless spaces, the gulph below; above, the gigantic spider's web of scaffolding — especially when, standing under the finished and numberless arches of the galleries, I listen to the reverberating voices in the stillness of the night and see immense buckets of plaster and water ascending, as if they were drawn up from the bowels of a mine, amid shouts from subterranean depths, oaths from Hell itself, and chanting from Pandemonium or the synagogue.

Beckford's relationship with Wyatt, whom he nicknamed 'Bagasse' (slang for the worthless residue left after refining sugar-cane), veered from adoration to exasperation, and his lamentations have a familiar ring to anyone who has ever tried to get building work done. On the actual design, Beckford was unstinting: 'Wyatt merits and, I am sure, will receive the highest praise', but as Wyatt's interest in the actual execution of his design diminished, so Beckford's frustration increased. In 1808 he expressed a desire to strangle him, and thereafter much time was spent in trying to catch

Wyatt and bring him back down to Fonthill to finish the job. Sometimes everything became too much, and he vented his spleen not only on Wyatt but on architecture itself:

> Would to God that he had never been born and that the Turks, Moors and Arabs had been not merely circumcised but castrated before inventing their pointed saracenic-gothic architecture — the cause of my ruin. The devil take them.

But when Wyatt did eventually come, he was transformed from the 'stupid, lazy Mr. Wyatt':

> He works with a brio, a zeal, an energy, a faith that would move the largest mountain in the Alps . . . He is all ardour and zeal as never before . . . My dear, angelic, most p-p-p-p-perfect Bagasse is killing himself with work: every hour, every moment, he adds some new beauty.

Full of admiration for Wyatt's work though Beckford was, he was less enthusiastic about his company — 'Certainly if I could be bored, it would be in his company. Ah my God, how slow, silent and null he is!'

Beckford's criticisms were not without foundation — unlike Wyatt's tower. During the 16 years that Wyatt sporadically worked on Fonthill there were rumblings of discontent about the quality of his construction, rumblings that were echoed elsewhere, for example at Blithfield Hall in Staffordshire, where the notorious compo cement made another appearance through the courtesy of his brother Benjamin. It seems to have been forgotten that the building was originally intended to be a sham. In 1814 Franchi wrote to the Marquess of Douglas, Beckford's son-in-law, that 'almost all that the villainous Bagasse built has been dismantled (to forestall finding ourselves buried in its rotten ruins)'. However, the magnificent central tower remained, and it was still standing when Beckford's creditors finally caught up with him and he was forced to sell his beloved uninhabitable Fonthill in 1822. It was bought for £330,000 ('very advantageously,' admitted Beckford) by John Farquhar, an unkempt and eccentric gunpowder millionaire who enjoyed being mistaken for a beggar in the street.

On the night of 21 December 1825 the massive foundationless

tower could stand no more. It collapsed, watched by only one man, into a pile of rubble, and brought much but not all of the rest of the Abbey down with it. Farquhar died of apoplexy the following year; the subsequent disappearance of the rest of Fonthill Abbey was due to the Marquess of Westminster, who used the ruins as a quarry for his house (demolished in 1955) much as Beckford used Fonthill Splendens as a quarry for his Abbey. All that remains of Fonthill Abbey today is the Oratory, the Sanctuary and the Lancaster Tower, amalgamated to form a small private house. Meanwhile Beckford was building another tower at Lansdown, north of Bath — which still stands. He must have the last word: 'Some people drink to forget their unhappiness. I do not drink, I build. And it ruins me.'

Southern
England

Hampshire

Hampshire is a big, quiet county with much to boast about but little need to. Two factors have led to its relative peace, inasmuch as any southern English county can be called peaceful: it is buffered from London by Surrey and reasonably poor communications; and it has protected itself from tourists by achieving an almost completely urban, industrial and military coastline. The miles of golden sands so beloved of trippers did once exist in the county, but then Bournemouth was cunningly shifted into Dorset, which caters for that sort of person. What remains as a result is a large county with picturesque villages apparently all set in parkland and very few tourists; here nature anticipated 'Capability' Brown.

Real Hampshire is to be found in the villages and small towns. Alton, Petersfield, New Alresford and Lyndhurst are all far more typical of the county than Andover, Aldershot, Basingstoke, Farnborough and Portsmouth. Winchester, the first capital of England, is like all capitals a law unto itself, while Southampton, which gave its name to the county, took advantage of its superb natural deep-water port and eagerly embraced commerce. The Army and the Navy have both chosen Hampshire as their headquarters, with the result that the county is packed with retired generals and admirals, while Farnborough and aircraft are indissolubly linked.

But while these towns and fighting men are in Hampshire, they are not part of Hampshire. There is a reserve in the county which Chesterton would have approved as being quintessentially English. Overlords may come and go but the rural Hampshire Hog ambles on his way, watching his rulers' antics with patience, condescension

77

and occasional bafflement, as when sudden orders were given to run up a little frippery of a building here, an obelisk there, all to no apparent purpose. The final outcome has yet to be decided, for here, far more than in any other English county, the joy of folly building has not died. Since 1973 two follies have been planned and built, and an already lovely garden has been enhanced still further through the addition of a monumental column (already making its bow on the Ordnance map as MON.), a grotto and other garden ornaments.

Hampshire's new folly builders have worked independently of each other, deliberately conceiving and building follies they are proud to call by that name. A purist may argue that structures built with forethought and a regard to the expenses involved cannot properly be called follies, and constitute a deliberately retrograde step. While it is true that none of the new Hampshire follies breaks architectural ground, both the fact that they are a conscious harking back, an appendix to architecture, and their very uselessness (though deliberate) demand their inclusion. Jonathan Barnes, a pupil barrister then living at his parents' house in MEDSTEAD, was the first. Jonathan's Folly, a small circular castellated tower in the traditional Hampshire style of brick surrounds and flint infill, was built, as Barnes freely admits, because he wanted a folly in the garden. A short flight of steps leads up to an open entrance into the one room, from which a ladder leads up to a flat roof some 20 feet above the ground. It is small but memorable; a little slate plaque at the top of the steps reads 'M.J.B. 1973' and at a glance it already seems to have aged ten years for every one. A villager attending a fête in the grounds sought out Barnes's father to exclaim that although he'd lived in Medstead for over 50 years he'd never known there was a castle in the village before.

West Green House near HARTLEY WINTNEY is a National Trust property and the home of Lord McAlpine. Since 1974 McAlpine has been adding garden buildings at the rate of about one a year, using the services of Quinlan Terry, perhaps the last unashamedly classical architect working in Britain today. Most are elaborate accessories — terms, vases, urns etc. — but the irresistible urge to inscribe has overcome McAlpine from time to time. At the north end of the garden is an exotic rope-ringed rusticated column, about

50 feet high and surmounted with a device which resembles the top of an elaborately turned chess-piece.

HOC

MONVMENTVM

MAGNO PRETIO

QVOD ALITER IN

MANVS PVBLICAN

ORVM QVANDOQVE

CECIDISSET

AEDIFICATVM EST

ANNO MCMLXXVI R.A.MCA

The inscription can roughly be translated as 'this monument was built with a great deal of money which otherwise some day would have been given into the hands of the public revenue'. In 1979 a classical triumphal arch was planned, flanked by two Ionic columns and female acroteria and topped with a squat obelisk bearing a plaque dedicating the arch to the 'first lady Prime Minister of Great Britain', and then, underneath on the frieze, proclaiming 'Vivat Regina'.

Terry with McAlpine has produced some remarkably fine work, notably the *trompe l'oeil* Nymphaeum, curving inwards like a Borromini church façade until one gets quite close, when all is revealed as a sham, a flat façade cleverly painted. A smoke-house, heavily influenced by West Wycombe, an elaborate eyecatcher complete with the Ghost of West Green, a Doric Lodge, a shell grotto, a birdcage, Chinese cowsheds, an island gazebo and more go to make up this 20th-century folly garden, which continues to grow.

Folly-building is enjoying something of a renaissance, perhaps led by the efforts made in Hampshire. At the time of writing there are still some people around with more money than they really know what to do with, and the advent of fibreglass has enabled small to medium size garden ornaments to be thrown up quickly and (relatively) cheaply to achieve an immediate effect. A temple at the end of the garden erected by next Saturday has good conversational value at the next dinner party, but the nouveaux folly builders as a whole lack the panache and variety of their forefathers, eschewing Gothic, Chinese and rustic architecture for a simple and severe classic line. The Greek temple can seldom have been as popular.

The traditional way still lingers: in 1981 Adrian Bird, a Liphook architect, won planning permission to build a 40-foot tower in Rectory Lane, BRAMSHOTT, submitting the application as an honest-to-goodness folly. He was quoted as saying that it had long been one of his ambitions to build a folly, and the local paper commented drily that 'he must be one of the few people who have had experience of doing so, gained when he worked for Lambeth Council.'

Hampshire has its share of older follies. The Vyne at SHERBORNE ST JOHN, one of the most famous houses in the county, has a beautiful brick garden pavilion by John Webb, dating from the mid-17th century. It is round and domed with cruciform doorways, looking like a debased Roman church. The lodges to the north and south of the house follow a similar pattern, but date from a century later, and indeed the National Trust now uses the pavilion's memorable shape to symbolise the property. The north lodge has a curious addition, best described as an oriel chimney.

King John's Hunting Lodge near ODIHAM is immaculately tended, the mystery of the folly all but gone, but still an extraordinary home — brick, two storeys surmounted by wildly exaggerated Jacobean gables every bit as tall as the main body of the house itself. Although a National Trust property, it is not open to the public. It was built in the 18th century as an eyecatcher to Dogmersfield Park. Apart from this one superb example eyecatchers did not appear to win popularity in Hampshire. The Grange at NORTHINGTON, the magnificent Grecian mansion designed by William Wilkins in 1804, has a small lodge eyecatcher, made up to look like a fierce little Pekinese of a castle, with battlements topping its mighty two storeys and an octagonal stair turret. The Grange itself had much more of the air of the folly about it when we first saw it in 1969, a great gaunt Grecian ruin, derelict and abandoned. It has now been restored by the Department of the Environment.

Another Grange, another eyecatcher, this time at PETERSFIELD, where Grange Farm House was given a rusticated flint frontage so it could be an object of beauty from Petersfield House. The folly has long survived the house, which was demolished in 1793. The last individual eyecatcher in the country is the Dower House in WARNFORD, prettified to catch the eye of the passing traveller, built of flint and unbonded brick as a summer-house rather than a dower-house. As in Petersfield the great house in the park has disappeared, leaving the folly behind. Warnford also has a flint grotto running through an earth bank.

Hampshire's finest folly — the biggest, the most impressive, the oddest — is unquestionably Peterson's Tower at SWAY. Andrew Thomas Turton Peterson was born in Yorkshire in 1813 and died in London in 1906. In the intervening 93 years he ran away to sea, became a lawyer, went to India, made a fortune, retired to Hampshire, became a Spiritualist, and built Peterson's Tower. Even if it isn't quite the tallest folly in the country, its 218 feet and 13 storeys make it spectacular by any standards. Add to that its undeniable ugliness, the stories about the ghost of Christopher Wren, the half-remembered stories of the New Forest Shakers, mutterings about 'Judge' Peterson being buried at the top of the tower, and its total unsuitability for the New Forest or indeed anywhere else, and one begins to realise how compelling this wonderful folly is.

When Peterson, an irascible but soft-hearted radical, retired he found two things to occupy his interests. One was a Mrs Girling, who arrived in the area with her religious troupe known as the New Forest Shakers. The other was a very real concern for the plight of the unemployed in the locality. The first started his interest in Spiritualism; the second stirred his conscience. He brought back from India an interest in concrete as a building material, and finding a ready source of labour in Hampshire he set to work to build additions and improvements to his estate at Drum Duan, all to his own design and using concrete. Here he met opposition: as a radical he was concerned about improving the lot of his fellow man; as a rich man he could pay his men far more than they could have earned elsewhere in the district, which aroused the wrath of all the other local employers. Peterson was at pains to stress that he never employed someone who was not genuinely jobless, but the suspicions remained. As the work he had employed his men to do neared completion, Peterson began to worry about their future. But salvation was at hand in the shape of Mrs Girling. By an extraordinary stroke of luck she was able to introduce him to Sir Christopher Wren (via a medium) and he was delighted to discover that Sir Christopher was as keen on concrete as he was. Together they planned the tower, and if the finished design does not recall Wren's work as vividly as one might have hoped, one can only assume that his powers had faltered a little after 200 years or so.

Work started in 1879, employing 40 men and no scaffolding. The tower rose gradually, to be completed only in 1885. It was the first major building in Britain to be built from concrete, and although its continued existence owes not a little to the efforts of Paul Atlas, the present owner, it remains a triumphant vindication of Peterson's beliefs. The estate at Drum Duan became known as Arnewood Towers. Peterson put two concrete slabs in the basement of the tower. When his wife discovered their true purpose she flatly refused to have anything to do with them, declaring she wanted a good Christian burial like everyone else. So perhaps Peterson was thwarted in an original attempt to build a mausoleum. The rooms were never furnished, and although he apparently intended to install electric lights — the very latest thing — Trinity House forbade him, saying it would be a danger to shipping. They also forbade plans to install illuminated clock-faces in the circular holes just below the second cornice.

Peterson's life in India may well have persuaded him that the Indian tower cremation and subsequent interment of the ashes was the cleanest means of disposing of the dead; in any case he had his final wish granted. He was cremated at Woking and his ashes were placed on the concrete table in the tower.

All but one of the other Hampshire towers are insignificant affairs compared to Peterson's folly. ROCKBOURNE, in a spur of the county surrounded by Dorset and Wiltshire, has a monument erected by the East India Company in honour of Sir Eyre Coote, the Indian Army general who died in 1783. Henry Bankes wrote the inscription, and the monument consists of a regulation 100-foot column on a plinth, with a viewing platform and an urn on top. Needless to say, it cannot be climbed. At SHAWFORD, on the Itchen between Winchester and Southampton, behind the Bridge Inn, is a small brick and flint belvedere; and a two-storey tower called — for no good reason — Cromwell's Tower stands in the grounds of Shawford Park by the mill stream. Probably dating from the mid-18th century, it has a tile roof, flint walls and no history. A similar tower, this time three storeys high and a century newer, is Hopton Tower in the grounds of Folly House in HAMBLEDON, the home of cricket. The Gardener's Tower at Rotherfield Park in EAST TISTED is very different; this is a massive sham castle in the style of Radway and its imitators, but built very late, towards the end of the 19th century. It is also much too close to the main house, separated from it only by the stable road. A great, square, heavily machicolated tower was originally used for hanging game; this abuts a taller, round, three-storeyed tower which provided the living quarters, and an even taller round stair turret. Nearby, the laundry chimney is executed in the same style, with the addition of a conical roof. The Gardener's Tower has now been converted into a luxurious house.

Minley Manor at HAWLEY on the Surrey border has a little 19th-century summer-house with a thatched roof and a pebble floor, as well as a gazebo neatly topping the water-tower, a pragmatic late Victorian compromise, built by Arthur Castings in 1898. The only comparable folly to Peterson's, however, is Luttrell's Tower at EAGLEHURST near Fawley. Not strictly a tower, it is described by Pevsner as a 'super-folly', and it was built regardless of expense as a genuine high-class smugglers' hideout. It consists of three storeys with a very much taller stair turret looking out to sea; the rooms are finely decorated, with exquisite fireplaces, including one in the cellar giving on to an underground passage which still leads directly to the beach. It is quite obvious that this was a smugglers' den, and if one wonders how Temple Simon Luttrell, the owner, got away with such blatancy, the answer is that he did his smuggling for the Prince Regent. In 1793 he was arrested in Boulogne and imprisoned in Paris for two years, where he was exhibited to the *citoyens* as the brother of the English King. He died in Paris in 1803, but the wonderful folly he left can now be enjoyed by everyone, as it is let out as a holiday home by the Landmark Trust.

Up Southampton Water from Luttrell's Tower is HYTHE, surprisingly screened from the massive refinery at Fawley and still retaining some village atmosphere. Forest Lodge, on the road in from Fawley, had an early 19th-century Chinese garden with bridge, pagoda, observatory tower and boat-house, but although remnants are still said to be visible, everything of interest has disappeared. Knightons, on the sea-front, was the home of the eccentric Charles Kelsall, who put up nine terms of great men and a round clock-tower with a triple cross on top, explaining in a Latin inscription that it stood for Catholicism, Protestantism and Reformation.

Hampshire cannot boast folly groups or gardens to compare with Stowe or Stourhead, but a few estates have more than the traditional solitary Greek temple to offer. Walhampton House in the parish of BOLDRE has a fine grotto, a marble arch and a mount view, all said to have been built in the 1780s for Admiral Sir Harry Burrard Neale. The grotto — above ground in a brick summer-house — is decorated with shell, glass and marble-chip representations of lions, dragons, lizards, butterflies and so on, said to stand for the names of the ships on which the Admiral served (missing are a centaur and a roebuck, the names of ships we know he did serve on), but as Sir Harry would have been 15 years old in 1780 this is fanciful, and the grotto was almost certainly built by his uncle Sir Harry Burrard. An obelisk was erected to the admiral's memory in 1840, at Mount Pleasant, after he had served as MP for Lymington for 40 years. The Marble Arch in the middle of the garden is Venetian, built of ashlar stone; this also, we would guess, is by the uncle.

The Hermitage at GOSPORT is a Victorian seaside villa, probably built for another naval officer, which has in its garden a collection of brick-built oddities of no known provenance. Arches are the most common, each with a niche holding a cross. Another, more eclectic selection of monuments can be found on the other side of the harbour in PORTSMOUTH's Victoria Park. They commemorate naval men, officers and exploits, so cannot be classed as follies, but they do demonstrate a remarkable motley of style in a very small area. Pre-eminent is a tiny Chinese temple complete with a solid stone pagoda roof supported by four brown marble columns enclosing a Chinese bell captured by *HMS Orlando* at the turn of the century. 'PERPETUAL FELICITY ACHIEVED' reads the inscription on the pediment, and the plinth carries a translation of the inscription on the bell:

COME PLEASANT WEATHER AND GENTLE RAIN
THE EMPIRE HAPPY, AT PEACE AGAIN.

As one enters the park there is a grey obelisk, a pink obelisk, a pink column surmounted by a lion, another pink column topped with a ball, another, larger, grey obelisk, a fountain and then the temple. Mention must be made here of the extraordinary Nelson Monument on the downs above PORTCHESTER, designed by John Thomas Groves in 1807, a mighty obelisk-like structure 120 feet high with an incused panel running the height of the structure from the tapering plinth, topped with a little hollow arch in which, virtually out of sight from the ground, sits a tiny bust of Nelson. Groves was a little known architect whose best work was the pierced obelisk at Garbally, Co. Galway.

Hartley Wintney, Havant, Highclere, Hursley and Hurstbourne Priors all have garden ornaments which verge on the folly, one in particular being splendidly inexplicable. We have already dealt with the new follies at Hartley Wintney; at HAVANT's Leigh Park we come across another dedicated builder, Sir George Staunton. Sir George was fluent in Chinese and wrote extensively on China. In 1832 he commissioned Lewis Vulliamy to design him a library to stand separately from the house to hold his great collection of Chinese writings, including his own publications such as *An Inquiry into the proper Mode of rendering the word God in translating the Sacred Scriptures into the Chinese Language*. Vulliamy provided him with an octagonal building of one and a half storeys, with arched windows, which now makes a pleasing ruin. Sir George was proud of his ancestors, writing a biography of his father, an Irish diplomat, and erecting the Staunton Memorial, a hexagonal garden grotto-house with tablets inside commemorating members of the Staunton family (Sir George himself was a bachelor). 'The Beacon', a circular domed temple with eight Doric columns, stands in open farmland above the old estate, and Staunton's final offering lies in Havant Thicket, now barely recognisable but once a monument to George Canning.

HIGHCLERE is the seat of the Earls of Carnarvon, and the largest house in Hampshire. The estate has several useless buildings, but our favourite is unquestionably Heaven's Gate, an eyecatcher placed on the top of Sidown Hill, with a central round-headed arch and two smaller side ones, the whole pleasingly overbalanced by a massive tympanum flanked with curtain walls sweeping up to the pediment. Somehow, as it stands forlornly in its rubbly dereliction amid the uncontrolled undergrowth, it is immediately appealing, crying out to be loved. It has no particular feature apart from its excessive size – 60 feet by 100 feet – but it is a very desirable building. It was first built in 1731, perhaps designed by Henry Herbert, Earl of Pembroke, for his brother Robert, but in 1739 it collapsed. An eyewitness, the Rev. J. Milles, wrote, 'We had not been there above half an hour before we saw it cleave from ye foundations and it fell with such a noise yt was heard at three or four miles distant.' Long ago there were tea-rooms and a seat for admiring the view, but these have disappeared. The re-erected arch now stands on firmer foundations, but the fabric is in such poor condition that it cannot survive for many more years, and another delightful folly will have been lost.

A more favoured folly at Highclere is Jackdaw's Castle, a wonderful name for an unexceptional Greek temple, which has been listed Grade One, probably because it was built in 1743 with Corinthian columns which came from Berkeley House in Piccadilly, designed by John May and accidentally burnt down in 1733. The Ionic Rotunda has been attributed to Sir William Chambers, but it was 'improved' by Sir Charles Barry in 1838, who added the drum, the urns and altered the dome. The Lake House by Milford Lake was built as a serene fishing pavilion, and has been variously attributed to the Earl of Pembroke, William Kent and Barry. Barry may well have reworked it, but the interior is by Kent, and the probability is that Pembroke originally designed it.

Grotto Lodge, by Ashworth, on the track that runs to Heaven's Gate at the top of the hill, is a strange little flint-and-stone dressed building with seemingly nothing to link it with a grotto. It consists of two round towers connected by a short, battlemented curtain wall. The larger tower is three-storeyed, naked without its battlements, with a ludicrous little octagonal battlemented chimney placed in the centre of the flat roof. The smaller tower is two-storeyed, with a conical roof topped with a ball finial. Cruciform arrowslits and tiny roundheaded windows complete the picture. The Ordnance map explains the name: opposite is Grotto Copse, where the nine daughters of the Rev. Thomas Lisle of Crux Easton built a long vanished grotto.

Cranbury Park at HURSLEY holds creeping Chandler's Ford at bay. In the grounds is 'The Castle', built in 1770 from remnants of the north transept of Netley Abbey by Thomas Dummer, the owner. Other pieces left include the remains of two grottoes, a shell grotto in a steep bank and Wordsworth's Grotto, built over a spring. A tablet bears the inscription:

Written by Wordsworth
on visiting this spring.
'Gentle Reader view in Me
An Emblem of true Charity
Who, while my Bounty I bestow
Am neither heard nor seen to flow
For every Drop of Water given
Repaid by fresh Supplies from Heav'n.'

George Dance built the Dairy, a colonnaded garden-house, and there is also a sundial alleged to have been designed by Sir Isaac Newton.

HURSTBOURNE PARK is the final Hampshire estate to see; here is the splendidly inexplicable object we referred to earlier. A small, armless, leaden statue of a Roman Emperor stands on the dome of a curious rectangular structure with four projecting arches opening into blank, knapped–flint lined niches. The whole appears from a distance to be built of drystone, crudely positioned. The statue is said to be George III, but it was obviously added long after this enigmatic building was erected. Thomas Archer designed a new house here for the 1st Earl of Portsmouth, and a painting shows a sham castle and a cascade as well, but it is thought that the work was never started. Certainly this folly could never have come from the same hand that designed the pavilion at Wrest Park in Bedfordshire. Andover Lodge, or 'The Bee House', on the road from Whitchurch to Hurstbourne Priors, is referred to as a folly, but even to our over–enthusiastic eyes it appears to be little more than a house with wilful detailing.

At the west end of NETHER WALLOP church is a 15-foot pyramid built as a mausoleum for Dr Francis Douce, who endowed a school in the village on the provision that his pyramid be looked after; but Hampshire's best pyramid is the delightful 30-footer on FARLEY MOUNT, between Winchester and King's Somborne. It has three blank porches and one open; inside the pyramid one can shelter from the remarkably cold wind that blows up along these Hampshire downs, and discover the wonderful reason for the pyramid's erection on the tablet inside:

UNDERNEATH LIES BURIED

A HORSE

THE PROPERTY OF

PAULET ST. JOHN ESQ

THAT IN THE MONTH

OF SEPTEMBER 1733 LEAPED

INTO A CHALK PIT TWENTYFIVE

FEET DEEP A FOXHUNTING

WITH HIS MASTER ON HIS BACK

AND IN OCTOBER 1734 HE WON THE

HUNTERS PLATE ON WORTHY DOWNS

AND WAS RODE BY HIS OWNER

AND ENTERED IN THE NAME OF

'BEWARE CHALK PIT'.

There really is nothing more that need be said.

At nearby HOUGHTON the lodge gate to Houghton Lodge (confusing but true, Houghton Lodge itself being a large, comfortable house in the *cottage orné* style, attributed to John Nash) is a flint-built sham ruin. A Gothic doorway leads into a grotto with arches giving on to a shaded drive to the house.

As with every county, there are little architectural scraps insignificant in themselves but worth a look if one happens to be in the relevant village. MOTTISFONT ABBEY and STRATFIELD SAYE have rustic summer-houses, the one at Stratfield being built to celebrate a visit by Queen Victoria; AVINGTON HOUSE has a Doric temple pavilion now converted into a flat; there is a pathetic little druids' circle on the north side of the A272 between Bramdean and the

WEST MEON HUT, built by a Col. Greenwood in the 19th century to mourn a favourite horse. Studwell Lodge in DROXFORD has a tunnel joining the upper garden to the lower garden, a favourite early 19th-century romantic device. At about the same time a row of Gothic cottages was being built to provide an eyecatcher to HEADLEY PARK.

A folly definition that merely includes useless buildings would have to ignore one of Hampshire's most extraordinary edifices, Massey's Folly in FARRINGDON. The locals called it Massey's Folly from the day work started, even though for more than a century this crazy structure has served as village school, church hall and general meeting place. Farringdon is a small village divided into two parts, Lower Farringdon on the A32, and Upper Farringdon half a mile east up the hill. In 1870 the rector, the Rev. Thomas Hackett Massey, decided to build in Upper Farringdon. What he decided to build is still not certain, but what he left us was a very positive statement about something. For a start it is big, wildly out of scale with anything else in the village, more suited to St Pancras than Farringdon; and secondly it is red – very red. The village is predominantly thatch and whitewash; Massey's Folly is built of scarlet brick and off-the-peg Victorian terracotta panels. It has towers, battlements, ridge irons – a Chas. Addams delight. So what was it for? Two favourite stories are that it was intended to be tea-rooms for when the London–Portsmouth line arrived at Farringdon (in fact the line eventually ran to the west even of Lower Farringdon), or that it was supposed to be a theological college, which could have accounted for the 17 bedrooms it ended up with. Once we dispel any speculation about its purpose, however (there was none; Massey had the *folie de bâtir*), we are left with the folly of the construction. The rector and his bricklayer (whose name is unfortunately lost) built the whole thing themselves, without any other help. Mind you, it took them 30 years because Massey would periodically demolish parts of it that no longer appealed to him, and would add others seemingly, and probably genuinely, at random. During his 62 years as rector of the parish his congregation diminished as his folly grew; not because of any unspoken condemnation of his eccentricity but because of the unrelieved diet of hellfire and damnation preached at them Sunday after Sunday. Finally he was ranting at only two members of his parish, his faithful bricklayer and his washerwoman, the rest of the faithful having decamped to nearby Chawton Church. The Reverend Mr Massey died in 1939, one of Hampshire's great eccentrics.

Isle of Wight

The Isle of Wight is a distillation of the beauty of the English countryside: picture-book villages, chocolate-box scenery, and the disadvantages that the obviously picturesque attracts — trippers. After a strenuous hike up one of the more isolated hills on the island to visit a National Trust property, we were greeted at the top by an elderly lady with a stick, self-appointed guardian of the tor, who enquired coldly, 'You do realise you have come up by an animal path? The proper path runs around there. Please to keep to it on your way down.' Suitably chastened, we hung around, taking surreptitious photographs of an inoffensive column, then crept back down the hill, following the designated human animal path. The folly in question was Hoy's Monument at CHALE, on the north spur of St Catherine's Down, erected to commemorate the visit of His Imperial Majesty Alexander I, Emperor of All the Russias, to Great Britain in the year 1814 and in memory of many happy years' residence in his dominions by Michael Hoy of 'The Hermitage' (a suitable name) nearby. The plaque has now gone, and has been replaced by a small plastic label with the relevant details. On the south side of the pillar is another plaque, added in 1857 by Lt William Henry Dawes, in memory of the fallen at the battles of Alma and Inkerman in the Russian Crimea. The monument itself is a plain unadorned column, 72 feet high, surmounted with a ball, and commanding magnificent views over the island.

Views are inescapable in the Isle of Wight. With the rolling scenery of Southern England, but entirely surrounded by the sea, it cannot fail to stir the sight. Little hills suddenly open out magnificent land and sea prospects to all sides, and it seems surprising that more prospect towers weren't erected. There is only one; at the far east end of the promenade at RYDE, after the road finishes and the walk continues into the seaside pine-woods, stands a little castellated prospect tower at sea level, right at the water's edge, giving in an island of superb viewpoints only the view across the flat sea to military Portsmouth. Appley Tower was part of the Appley estate, and the coat-of-arms remains above the first-floor entrance, with a lapwing surmounted with the motto, 'VOULOIR EST POUVOIR'. Designed by Thomas Hellyer, the tower is heavily castellated, round, three-storeyed, with a splayed base and an oriel window looking out to sea.

The south coast of the Isle of Wight is falling into the sea. We followed the signs from BLACKGANG to a house called South View, down a rutted road to the entrance-gate piers (or, rather, pier, for the right-hand one has fallen down the cliff, leaving the left balancing unsteadily on the edge) above the sea. Naturally the drive disappears down the cliff, but on the left along the remaining road is the smallest rotunda ever built, a minute Temple to Shakespeare on a little bluff in the woods. Six fluted columns support a modillion cornice, the whole edifice being just large enough to admit one person inside. On the road below is a little spring head with an indecipherable inscription from *The Two Gentlemen of Verona* around it, while a tablet in the temple which had lines from *Cymbeline* has now completely disappeared. This charming, tiny temple was built in 1864 by Thomas Letts of Letts' Diaries.

Talk of the Salt Cellar and the Pepper Pot on Niton Down, just above Blackgang, leads the enthusiastic folly-hunter up a stiff climb to discover a genuine 14th-century lighthouse called St Catherine's Tower which, with its splayed foot buttresses and pyramidal roof, looks uncannily like a medieval rocket. It is octagonal outside and square within, and is known locally as the Pepper Pot. In 1785 Trinity House started to build a new lighthouse here 150 yards away, but the attempt was abandoned when it was discovered that the top was perpetually shrouded in mist. The derelict tower was inevitably christened the Salt Cellar, and it stood unused for nearly 200 years until the MoD built a radar station in it after the war.

The western half of the island has little in the way of follies; the great, high, granite cross on Tennyson Down above TOTLAND, commemorating the poet, makes a fine objective for a walk from the chalk pit by the 'High Down Inn' — the views over the island and north towards Hampshire are spectacular — while in complete contrast Billingham Manor, near KINGSTON, lies in serenity in a fold of the downs, secluded in its walled garden, complete with an odd little thatched gazebo topped with a dovecote and a weathervane, now tumbling gently down. The only real folly in this part of the county is the temple at Swainston. On a slope just south of the B3401 between CALBOURNE and Carisbrooke, hidden in trees and undergrowth at the edge of a wood, is a Greek Doric temple, forgotten and abandoned but magnificent in decay. As Revival temples go, it is quite large and actually served as a labourer's cottage for many years; but now the dwelling has collapsed leaving only three or four walls, a staircase leading to the sky, and the mighty portico. Surrounded by undergrowth as it is, it is almost impossible to photograph, but the temple has atmosphere. It was built in the late 18th century for Sir John Barrington, perhaps by William Pordern who was remodelling Swainston at the time, as a belvedere over the Solent and as an eyecatcher from the house. Now the trees have grown up around it and the temple stands forgotten.

The last stop in England's smallest county is EAST COWES. In Cambridge Road, just off the Promenade, is a rarity in England, a *jardin imaginaire* in a style more popular in France. In 1916 Frederick Attrill, then 78, began to decorate the outside of his modest semi-detached villa with shells. When he died ten years later the house had become a tourist attraction, covered on front, side and back with a myriad shells, plates, mosaics, fragments of porcelain, figurines — anything he could lay his hands on. Much has disappeared in the 60 years since then, but the East Cowes shell-house is still a sight to be seen. Attrill worked at Osborne House, Queen Victoria's much-loved seaside palace, where a number of odd buildings — not follies, but worth a look — dot the grounds. A Swiss Chalet was imported as a playhouse for the royal children, and proved so popular that another was built to house their anthropological and archaeological collections. The children themselves built Albert Barracks with their own hands, even making the bricks themselves. They were also allowed a thatched toolshed, while the Queen herself had an alcove to see the sea from, and a boating- cum tea-house with a central two-storey tower, now a private residence. Osborne House is open in the summer months for an admission charge, rather like the island itself.

Kent

The Garden of England is a wonderfully evocative appellation, and
one that Kent still, perhaps surprisingly, deserves: half the orchards
in England are to be found here. London has swallowed a good part
of the north-west of the county, and several follies built in rural
Kent are described in the London chapter. There is still a good
variety evenly scattered – some genuine eccentricity, a good folly
group, and a real mystery!

Two roads leave London almost in parallel: the A2 to Dover and
the A20 to Folkestone. Our tour of Kent starts on these roads,
roughly following the coastline round to Dungeness, then inland to
the warm white villages of the Weald. Travellers to Folkestone in
the 18th century would often find FARNINGHAM, 20 miles from
London, a convenient coaching-stop, and its neat prosperity dates
from that time. Luckily the A20 bypassed the village early in this
motor century, and now the M20 bypasses the A20 and Farningham
can settle back into welcomed obscurity, its architecture intact. The
Darent flows through the village, and north-east of the bridge is a
peculiar screen crossing the river, looking like the remains of an
older bridge. It was probably built for a mundane purpose such as a
cattle-trap or to protect the ford before the road bridge was built in
1773, but the local builder couldn't resist tarting it up a little: three
segmented arches in red brick and flint, rusticated, with brick and
flint piers at the ends and pointed brick cutwaters, a smart sham
bridge. The Mill House in Farningham has three octagonal turrets
in the grounds, flint and brick again, one with a ball finial, one plain
and one crenellated, standing in a row, with a summer-house on
the right. The summer-house has an inside wall lined with

cockleshells, and underneath the buildings are two chambers dug out from the hillside, with brick-arched entrances set in a flint wall. Was this to be the start of an ambitious grotto? One chamber has a small cistern dated 1790; it has been suggested they were used to store grain for the mill. If that is the case, the three turrets and the shell-lined summer-house were certainly surplus to requirements — and, as a local said, 'It's always been called "The Folly", I don't know why.'

The depressingly anonymous agglomeration known as Medway, which includes Rochester, Chatham and Gillingham, is grey and ugly, a landscape of pylons, mudflats, mean urban housing crouching round the Royal Dockyards, the reason for Chatham's existence. One of the most famous follies in Britain was here in GILLINGHAM, the Jezreel Temple of the Flying Roll, a remarkably advanced building which was never finished after the sect, led by an ex-Indian army corporal, ran out of cash in the 1880s. Sadly, the great gaunt shell was demolished in the 1960s. Gillingham's contribution to folly architecture is, as might be expected, municipal. England had been at peace with Japan for hundreds of years before the clock-tower/fountain/memorial was constructed in 1934 to honour a native of Gillingham who went to Japan in 1600 and became the Shogun's adviser. The clock-tower was expensively built out of solid blocks of Portland stone and designed by J. L. Redfern, Gillingham's Borough Engineer, in a curious mixture of styles ranging from Egyptian to London Underground, but this fraternal memorial was not enough to prevent the yellow hordes sweeping into Singapore less than a decade later. Reading the inscription, we can see where the inspiration for James Clavell's successful series of Shogun novels came from:

WILLIAM ADAMS

BORN GILLINGHAM A.D. 1564

DIED JAPAN A.D. 1620

William Adams, after service in the English Fleet of Queen Elizabeth, embarked with a Dutch Trading Expedition which left Texel, Holland in 1598. Cast ashore off the coast of Japan in 1600, he was taken into the service of the Japanese Shogun and became his Adviser. He constructed for the Shogun two vessels of European design and instructed his adopted countrymen in gunnery, geography, mathematics and the like and engaged on their behalf in foreign trading. A monument erected in Yokosuka perpetuates his memory and his work for the Japanese nation.

A Japanese translation of the plaque is mounted next to it.

Some people may love the scenery of the Isle of Sheppey, but most find it frankly boring. Even in sunlight it has a sort of hopeless utilitarianism which one can imagine permeating the very souls of the inhabitants. Preconceptions such as these are dealt a mortal body-blow when we come across a building like the Grotto at the 'Ship on Shore' public house in SHEERNESS. It is sheer fun, built in a genuine spirit of serendipity with whatever building materials came easily to hand, which for the most part meant concrete. In 1830 a ship carrying barrels of cement was wrecked on the north shore. Naturally the barrels leaked, water got in and the cement set hard in barrel-shaped blocks. A local farmer, spying his opportunity, carted the barrel blocks away and built this gorgeous little grotto, piling the barrels six high and filling in the gaps with rubble, flint and burr bricks, shaping the whole to form a sweeping parapet with a succession of curves. The building is L-shaped with three arches facing the pub car-park and two arches facing the road, now planked in and forming the windows and doors. At the moment it is used as the games arcade for the pub, and local youths bleep and buzz and gobble on Pac-Man and Donkey Kong, stolidly oblivious of their surroundings.

Inland Kent is far more attractive than the coast. Fifteen miles from Sheerness is THROWLEY, south of Faversham — it could be on a different continent. This is the perceived image of rural England, with soft rolling hills, wooded glades and the distant, summery sound of leather on willow. Here is Belmont Park, reconstructed in 1787–92 by Samuel Wyatt for George Harris, the first of a long line of distinguished public servants, who was ennobled in 1815. The Harrises were punctilious to a man, correct, reserved, polite, hard-working and honourable — one of them even captained England at cricket in the days when they used to win — but somewhere in the family (perhaps in George's wife Ann) was an exuberant sense of frivolity that manifested itself behind the house in an enclosed garden in a wonderful grotto, constructed with enormous ammonites, tufa and 70 sarsen stones, with one upright stone at the entrance. The Coronation Walk leads from the house to the cricket field, and at the end of the avenue is a sham chapel made of flint, part Gothic and part Indian, a curious but suitable mixture of styles as Harris's chosen title was Baron Harris of Seringapatam and Mysore. If the name of the avenue refers to the coronation of George IV, this would propose a realistic date of 1820 for the sham chapel.

Clearly marked on the Ordnance Survey map at Holly Hill, north of DUNKIRK on the A2, is a tower. Barbara Jones described it as 'A dumpy little hexagonal tower two storeys high, made of flint dressed with stone, and the inside of brick; there is an iron spiral staircase running up to a small hexagonal turret on the roof'. Traces remain of a carefully landscaped wood, with walks and rhododendrons and arbours, but two attempts to find the tower have failed.

Dane John, a linguistic corruption of *donjon*, is the name of a curious mound in the centre of CANTERBURY, now part of a public park. Perhaps it seems surprising that in this closely studied patch of land its original function has not been discovered, but various theories for its existence include a Roman burial mound and a defensive fortification. The park used to be private, but since the 15th century the citizens of Canterbury ignored the ownership and took it for their own, and it is said that an alderman who tried to reverse the practice literally lost his head at the hands of the said citizens — a rather strong reaction. In 1790, with this memory in mind, another alderman, James Simmons, spent £1,500 to slice the top off the mound; and in 1803 a pillar was erected 'by voluntary subscription' as a mark of gratitude. The monument is a whitestone tapering column topped with an urn, standing on a big square pedestal with a niche and further inscriptions in each recording various improvements made to the gardens at various times throughout the 19th century.

The Isle of Thanet, no longer an island since the Minster and the Chislet Marshes silted up hundreds of years ago, is still reachable only by crossing water, but of this the modern traveller is unaware as he crosses the Stour or the tiny but enjoyably named Wantsum. It seems an unlikely spot for follies, but they abound here, and they rank among the best — certainly the most mysterious — in Britain. Quex Park at BIRCHINGTON is the home of the Powell-Cotton Game Museum, a fascinating if gruesome collection occasionally open to the public. In the grounds is a large copse with an unbelievable sight — a white Eiffel Tower poking out above the treetops. This is the Waterloo Tower, built in 1819 as a bell-tower and mausoleum, and now one of the most famous follies in a county famous for them. It is completely ringed by trees and is difficult to picture properly. Four-storeyed, square and built of red brick, it is castellated in cast iron and has four octagonal corner turrets, but the most remarkable thing, the beauty which transcends workaday architecture and can make a folly into an object to be remembered for a lifetime, is the spire. The simplest way to describe it is as like the Eiffel Tower but more graceful, more ethereal; it is made of cast iron painted white, with each of its four convex bowed legs (not concave like Eiffel's) firmly planted on a corner turret. John Newman says it was inspired by the tower of Faversham church, but the similarity is in concept rather than execution. The architect is unknown, but William Pocock, the author of *Architectural Designs for Rustic Cottages, Picturesque Dwellings, Villas, etc. with appropriate scenery*, did some unspecified work at Quex between 1806 and 1809 and may have been called back after the reprint of his book in 1819; if so, the Waterloo Tower is his masterpiece. It is listed Grade II by the Department of the Environment, but the spire is said to be a later addition. It was certainly planned from the start: J. A. Parnell wrote in *The Gothic Traveller*, 'Mr Powell will have a lofty spire on his Tower thirds of Cast Iron and to be sprung from four quarter circle arches — then it will be a noble seamark being only one mile from that briny fluid'. The base of the tower comprises two single-storey rooms making up the mausoleum, with the inscription 'This tower was restored and the mausoleum was dedicated to the memory of Henry Horace Powell Cotton by his son 1896'. The whole edifice is in remarkably good condition; apparently the local bellringers use the 12-bell carillon regularly. A smaller brown-brick tower in the same park is called the Gun Tower, and was built in 1812 to mount a gun to signal out to sea. Circular this time, it is again of four storeys, with circular and round-headed windows.

MARGATE has the greatest folly mystery in Kent. In 1835 a

schoolmaster called Newlove and his two sons were digging out a disused well on Dane Hill when they broke into a passage leading to an underground chamber. They found torches, entered, and were dumbfounded by what they saw. Carved out of the solid chalk was a passage leading to an oblong chamber, then two semi-circular passages opening out into a central domed room. The walls were packed with tiny shells of every sort: it has been calculated that there are 28 different varieties, most of them foreign, covering an incredible 2,000 square yards of wall in the most wonderful mosaic patterns. Investigation showed that the cement with which the shells were stuck to the walls contained fish-oil and crushed shells, a method frequently used by the Romans. (Portland cement came into common use only after the Napoleonic wars, after the great grotto builders had finished.) The extraordinary patterns made by the shells included abstract geometrical designs favoured by Indian, Phoenician, Greek, Egyptian and Roman civilisations from over 2,000 years ago, as well as floral patterns more at home in 18th-century England. Small anomalies were ignored; in popular imagination it became a Mithraic Temple, or a Phoenician shrine to the moon goddess Tanit (Tanit = Thanet?), since several of the patterns show the sun, moon and stars. However, there are traces of modern bricks used in the building of one of the gothic-shaped arches; it seems unlikely that if the grotto had been built 2,000 years ago it would have survived undiscovered — and even more unlikely that the Phoenicians would have used 18th-century bricks. All the evidence would seem to point to the end of the 18th century, but the amount of work it must have taken, and the time — Scott's grotto in Ware took 30 years to build and is spartan in its comparative simplicity — and money, would surely never have passed unnoticed by the citizens of Margate. And yet, and yet . . .

The only really rich man in the area at the right time was Henry, Lord Holland, and he was busy building his own follies a mile or two away at KINGSGATE on the North Foreland. The superbly named Hackemdown Tower, the Arx Ruohim, the actual King's Gate, Kingsgate Castle, the Whitfield Tower — these are the remnants of a once extensive collection of publicly funded follies, although the public was not aware of that fact at the time. Henry Fox, an able, treacherous, self-seeking man, was appointed

24 Goldney House Tower, Bristol

25   Somerset Monument, Hawkesbury

26   George Burt's clock-tower, Swanage

27   Long Ashton Observatory

28   Roebuck's Folly, Midford

35   Romulus and Remus on the A39 near West Horrington

Paymaster-General after a stormy political career during which George II had asked him to form a government. By the time he was forced out of office it was alleged that over a quarter of a million pounds had found its way into his pockets. The poet Thomas Gray was one of his fiercest critics, for example, in a poem entitled 'Impromptu, suggested by a View, in 1766, of the Seat and Ruins of a Deceased [sic] nobleman at Kingsgate, Kent':

> Old, and abandon'd by each venal friend,
> Here Holland form'd the pious resolution
> To smuggle a few years, and strive to mend
> A broken character and constitution.

Holland's building works at Kingsgate were said to be an attempt to re-create Tully's Formian Villa; how close he came is best left to the imagination. Most of Holland House has been demolished, although a small part remains staring out to sea, converted into terraced houses. The biggest folly still standing is Kingsgate Castle, but this has been radically changed. Originally it was built as stables for the house in the style of an Edwardian Welsh castle, but the skill of Edward's master masons was lacking and it soon collapsed, leaving only a large, round tower. What one sees today is the Castle Keep Hotel, a 19th-century reconstruction by Lord Avebury built around a quadrangle on the cliff edge, grey against the white of Holland House. Across Joss Bay is a pub called 'The Captain Digby', crenellated, not a folly, but mentioned because it was built specifically to put up 18th-century visitors who came to see the follies. Then it was called 'The Bede House', and was apparently a house of some licentiousness; at any rate half of it fell into the sea during a storm or an exceptionally good party, and what remained was rebuilt and renamed 'The Noble Captain Digby' (after Lord Holland's nephew and drinking companion) in 1809. The Arx Ruohim, or Neptune's Temple, was a small-scale copy of one of Henry VIII's renowned concentric forts such as Deal or Camber. There was a red-brick tower in the middle, faced with chalk, and a statue of Neptune together with an inscription which claimed the monument had been erected by Vortigern in the year 448. Most of it has collapsed; only the ten-foot high plinth remains.

The Whitfield Tower on Northdown Hill, the highest point in

Thanet, is another rebuilding. It collapsed in 1818, but by then had become a useful landmark for sailors, so Trinity House re-erected it. With a square base, two octagonal upper storeys and an onion-shaped ball finial, it was built 'To the memory of Robert Whitfield Esquire. The ornament and under Thomas Wynne Esquire, the adorner of Kingsgate.' Whitfield had sold his land at Kingsgate to Holland, then acted as his agent and builder. As everything he built collapsed within a few years, he must have been a man of singular personal charm to have had a client build him such a memorial. Up until 1683 Kingsgate had been known as St Bartholomew's Gate, but after King Charles II landed here the name was changed. To commemorate the event Lord Holland built an arch, the King's Gate, at the gap in the cliff where the King landed, and covered it with suitable inscriptions in Latin and even Saxon characters explaining the reason for the change of name as from 30 June 1683. A stone eagle, crowned plaques, entwined 'C's, a 'Y', 'God Bless Bath'lem's Gate' complete the picture, and inevitably the arch collapsed in a gale in 1819. It was re-erected (the residents are proud of their notorious follies) in the grounds of Port Regis School.

The final Holland folly still standing, Hackemdown Tower, is also in the school grounds. In the 1760s Lord Holland excavated a barrow on his estate and assumed by the quantity of bones he found inside that he had discovered the site of an ancient battle between the Saxons and the Danes. Accordingly he built this flint tower, circular and castellated, set in the middle of a circular wall which repeats the tower's style and castellations. It used to be set on a base of ogee arches on Doric columns, but these have been removed. A clock was added later, and the Latin inscription roughly translated means, 'To the shades of the departed and in memory of the Danes and Saxons who were killed here while fighting for the possession of Britain (soldiers think everything their own), the Britons having been cruelly and perfidiously expelled, this was put up by Henry Holland. History does not record the names of the leaders or the result of the action. It happened *c.* 850 and that it happened here seems true from the quantity of bones buried in this and the nearby tumulus.'

With the huge amounts of money at his disposal and his enjoyment in creating monuments purporting to come from ancient times, Henry Holland would seem to be the likely begetter of the Margate grotto. The lack of documentation blurs the issue, but the lack of a better candidate points to him or his wife who, as the daughter of the Duke of Richmond, grew up with a shell grotto at Goodwood House.

There is nothing else down the coast until the Belvedere at WALDERSHARE PARK near Eythorne, inland from Dover. The Belvedere was built for Sir Robert Furnese in 1725–7 at a cost of £1,703 7s 4d by the most fashionable architect of the period, the Earl of Burlington, and its design seems to have been based on one of the mausoleums at Palmyra. Built unassumingly of red brick, it was nevertheless conceived on a grand scale — three storeys, Palladian, 60 feet tall in a double-cube plan, with boarded-up Venetian windows on the first floor, which was once used as a music room. Now rather sad and derelict, it was not one of Burlington's more graceful works — in fact, he never completed it — and it now sits, embarrassed, by the edge of a wood like the fat stupid kid in every classroom who always sits next to the radiator. The Georgian Group is concerned by its current condition and an inquiry is being held into how best to restore it, although the cost already looks to be in the region of £250,000. Nearer Dover, at KEARSNEY ABBEY, is an elegant little sham ruin built from genuine medieval fragments, probably in the early 19th century, with two pointed window openings which appear to be genuine. One stone used in its construction is dated 1609. The pretty walled garden is generally open to the public.

Temple Cottage, a castellated square house with a cupola at Newington, north of Folkestone, need not detain us as we head west towards the silted-up Cinque Port of New Romney and the best meal in Kent. From the Blue Dolphins Hotel, a tower raises itself laboriously from the distant shoreline and we ask what it could be. 'It's not a folly,' says my host knowledgeably, 'it's a water-tower. A bloke built it at the end of the last century, only he found that the water he pumped up into it was always brackish, so it was never used. Somebody turned it into a house, but it's supposed to be haunted.' Wonderful. We rushed down to the chilly LITTLESTONE coast, and the tower is as ugly and as municipal as one would expect a Victorian water-tower to be — big, six-storey, red-brick, white-banded and immaculately preserved despite the biting wind from the Channel. Was the story true? There was nobody around to confirm or deny it. A more remote function was served by an inexplicable blank wall down the road at GREATSTONE. A huge concrete bow, 25 feet high and 200 feet long, sits forlornly on the flat, marshy sands; there is no reason for it to be there, and no reason for it not to be. It would take an inspired guess to divine the reason for its existence, even with the knowledge of its date of construction – 1928. Its local name begins to hint at its purpose, which turns out to be the sole sad justification for its redundant life. The 'Listening Post', officially 'The Greatstone-on-Sea Listening Device', was the concrete manifestation of a civil defence idea to pinpoint enemy aircraft or airships by acoustic reflection. Needless to say it didn't work. So there it stays, now a listed structure, puzzling curious inmates of the neighbouring holiday camp.

In TENTERDEN, once a seaport, are two early 16th-century gazebos in the grounds of Hales Place in Oaks Road; built of red brick, octagonal in shape, they are now roofless, with castellated parapets and Tuscan columns by the doors. Towards ROLVENDEN is a gnome garden to make other gnome gardeners creep home in shame, but after that nothing until TONBRIDGE, where there is a small grotto in the grounds of a house called 'The Cedars' in Bordyke, probably dating from the late 18th century. Bordyke is otherwise known as the A26, leading to Hadlow and the best known folly in Kent.

Samuel Bagshaw's *History, Gazetteer and Directory of the County of Kent* (1847) describes HADLOW CASTLE as 'a superb mansion, recently erected, and a fine example of architectural embellishments. An octagonal tower at the east end rises ninety feet high, built partly with stone and partly with brick, cemented, from which the level nature of the country can be seen at a great distance. This tower exhibits a unique specimen of diversity and beauty; another short tower decorated with pinnacles, rises from the body of the building, to which costly appendages are constantly being added.' The castle, or May's Folly, can be seen from miles around, and its silhouette is familiar to every traveller in the area. It was built in 1838–48 by the architect George Ledwell Taylor for the rich squire Walter Barton May, and has been the source of several good folly stories: (1) May's wife left him and he wanted her to be reminded of him wherever she went in the county; (2) May wanted to see the ships in the Thames but forgot the downs were in the way; (3) May had a rivalry with William Beckford and wanted to out-Fonthill Fonthill (the tower does in fact bear a remarkable resemblance to the Fonthill tower which fell in 1822); (4) he wanted to be entombed above ground so that an old prophecy that the property would pass out of the family when he was buried would never come true. Strangely enough, May's wife did leave him, and he built a 39-foot top turret after her departure. The tower is spectacular, its present height of 170 feet making it one of the tallest follies in the country, and it has been converted into a luxurious if inconvenient house. In 1981 it was offered for sale for £175,000; two years later the price had tumbled to £125,000; in October 1985 it was back up to £135,000. May's actual house, Hadlow Castle, has long been demolished and the tower, originally an afterthought, has outlasted it and assumed its name. By any standards, it is an excellent piece of Gothic architecture, phallic in the extreme (it is interesting to note that the architect Taylor was four times married, and had eleven children by his first wife; perhaps there is something in it).

Along the road to Maidstone is MEREWORTH CASTLE, which has a fine but deteriorating triumphal arch of 1723 on a wooded hill to the south; the arch has the same feel as the much bigger Heaven's Gate in Hampshire but is not as appealing. It is loosely based on Titus's Arch in Rome, and the designer may have been Colen Campbell.

Unless one particularly wants to see a Greek rotunda in MAIDSTONE's Mote Park, built by S. Nelson in 1801, one should move on to visit KNOLE at Sevenoaks, more a village than a house. In its huge park is a little octagonal Gothick building of 1761, known as 'The Birdhouse', now a gamekeeper's cottage; next to it stands a sham ruin built about the same time with pieces acquired from Otford Palace. It was in 'The Birdhouse' that Lord Amherst kept the pheasants that now bear his name, which he brought back from China where he had been ambassador.

Knockholt, on the London borders, was the site of Vavasseur's Folly, which was demolished during the Second World War. We mention it out of the hundreds of demolished follies we have had to ignore because of its dual function as belvedere tower and communal house chimney — the only existing example of this kind we have been able to discover is at Osmaston in Derbyshire. Kent's final folly is the belvedere at Squerryes Court, WESTERHAM. Frustratingly little is known about this roofless, ruinous building, romantically associated with Henry VIII and Anne Boleyn, but it was obviously built in the 18th century as a prospect tower or hunting lodge. Oddly enough, it is built of rubble masonry instead of the ubiquitous north Kent flint and brick, which shows it to have been designed as a building of some consequence. It had two floors and a basement — there are still remnants of plasterwork — but apart from being built by the Warde family, its history is a blank.

Surrey

Imagine you are standing beside a tall wall. It encloses a kitchen garden, eight acres of kitchen garden, the sort of self-sufficiency that would satisfy a Sainsbury. On the other side of the dirt road is a scrubby wood, derelict, ramshackle and overgrown. In the wood is a strangely formless holly tree. You duck under the branches; it has a hollow centre. In the middle of the encircling holly tree, like something out of a Rupert Bear story, is a door. There is nothing else above ground, just the tree and a door. You go through the door and find yourself walking down a ramp, a spiral going down into the earth. There is very little light. What little there is illuminates, on your right, an empty, circular room lit from above by glass pavement lights let into the floor of the wood. Windows roughly cut into the wall allow you to look into the room as you walk down the ramp. Eventually there is a door from the ramp into the room. The room is cold and damp, faintly repellent. The ramp continues down. It gets darker. The sloping floor gives way to steps. The steps carry on down. There is now no light at all. You have a torch. You *need* a torch. You can pick out the shape of another room beneath the round one. You are now about 40 feet down inside the earth. It is musty. Make your way through another doorway and suddenly the torch is shining into emptiness; you are in a room so large that the beam will not touch the other side. Walk carefully across the rough floor. Don't look in the niches; nothing pleasant lives in them. Walk over to the other end of the chamber, where you can see a pinprick of light. There are more steps, steps down to a boat — yes, a boat, moored in this flooded tunnel 50 feet below ground level. Embark. Cast off. Walk the boat down the tunnel to the point of light a mile? a hundred yards? away. It gets brighter.

You come out on to a lake, a warm, comfortable, capable sort of a lake. In the middle of the water is an oblong island, quite small, with a low wall surrounding it. There is a statue in the water just offshore. Row across to the island. It lies about 50 yards from the lakeside and is big enough to take a dance band, if only there were somewhere to dance.

There is somewhere to dance. There is an underwater ballroom, domed, and built of iron and glass so you can watch the fish dance around you as you dance. Climb down the stairs to a room directly below the floor of the island; light and airy, nothing to worry about. Down some more steps, through a short tunnel, and you're in the glass ballroom. It isn't very big, but it's big enough and it is completely underwater. You can dance underwater by yourself: not even the Joneses could keep up with this. A lancet arched submarine tunnel leads 100 feet back to dry land and reality.

All this is true. This fantastical place exists — not in crazy California or in sensual Samarkand but in stolid, suburban Surrey. It was built at the turn of the century by Whitaker Wright, a financier and self-made millionaire who spent one and a quarter million pounds — who can guess what that would be worth today? — to improve his estate at WITLEY PARK, south-west of Godalming. He built four lakes, moved a couple of inconvenient hills, planted a forest or two, imported treasures from all over the world, including the head of a dolphin in bronze so big that when they were hauling it up to the estate from Southampton it got stuck under a bridge and they had to lower the road, and then erected a very ordinary, undistinguished house, now demolished, to overlook the lake with the underwater ballroom. (Wright's demise was as sensational as his follies. Sentenced to seven years' imprisonment for fraud, he committed suicide by swallowing cyanide before he could be taken from the Old Bailey.)

After that we can fairly expect any other follies in the county to be something of an anti-climax, but Surrey is full of surprises. Whitaker Wright's work is indubitably the most awesome, but there are wonderful gardens, towers and sham ruins to be found all over this much maligned county. The outsider's general attitude is that Surrey was long ago concreted over to make a car-park, but although it has a very high population density there are still some rural, if not remote, spots to be discovered. Surrey does have a splendid quantity of folly-towers, far more than one would expect from a county of such unremarkable hills, and at COBHAM it also has the renascent glories of Painshill.

In 1738 the Hon. Charles Hamilton, the ninth and youngest son of the Earl of Abercorn, returned from his European grand tour with a love of romantic landscape painting and a head full of ideas. He bought a 31-year lease on 200 acres of land near Cobham Bridge, formerly part of a deer-park belonging to Henry VIII, and set about re-creating in reality the romantic ruined landscapes popularised by Poussin, Rosa and Giovanni Panini. To prepare his canvas, Hamilton first burnt the existing heather, then planted turnips which he fed to sheep, then sowed grass over the entire estate. This done, he proceeded to achieve one of the triumphs of 18th-century English landscape gardening. The park at Painshill was lauded by all Hamilton's contemporaries, by people as diverse as Walpole and Wesley; the amateur had succeeded beyond the expectations of professionals, from Kent to Brown. For 35 years Charles Hamilton lovingly created the finest garden in England from unpromising material – Walpole commented, 'he has really made a fine place out of a most cursed hill' – until at the age of 71, crippled by debts and arthritis, he was forced to sell. All the walks, the vistas, the lakes, follies, canals and bridges, were left to moulder away, until after 200 years they had all but disappeared. But help has come from an unexpected source: over the last decade Elmbridge Council has purchased 158 acres of the original estate, and a charity called the Painshill Park Trust has been set up to attempt to preserve what is left and where possible to re-create Painshill as it was in Hamilton's day. Many of the follies of course are now beyond redemption, but some of the choicest items are undergoing complete restoration. The Gothick Tent or Temple is perhaps the best known of these; it now looks brand new, perhaps a little too white and pristine. Nevertheless it remains a beautiful building, small, octagonal and pinnacled with ogee arches below quatrefoil windows. It has been attributed to Batty Langley, but there is no real evidence for the claim and it is more reasonable to suppose that Hamilton acted as his own architect. Walpole was less enthusiastic: 'In all Gothic designs, they should be made something that was of that time, a part of a church, a castle, a convent or a mansion. The Goths never built summer-houses or temples in a garden. This of Mr Hamilton's stands on the brow of a hill – there an imitation of a fort or watch-tower would have been proper.'

The centrepiece of the garden is the artificial lake, 19 acres of it, which Hamilton constructed *c.* 1760 at some height above the level of the river Mole and fed through an elaborate system of locks and waterwheels. Batty Langley, who died in 1751, had been advertising his services to provide 'Engines for raising Water in any Quantity, to any height required, for the service of Noblemen's Seats, Cities, Towns &c.', so the possibility that he was earlier called in to advise cannot be discounted. The remarkable thing is that the artificial lake has now become natural; the horse-wheel that Hamilton used to pump up water from the Mole and its later replacement, a massive cast-iron Bramah wheel of the 1820s, are now redundant, for the lake sustains itself through rainfall and surface drainage. As well as the tent Hamilton built a superb grotto, severely damaged by soldiers billeted at Painshill during the war, a hermitage (one of the very few which actually had a live hermit!), a Roman mausoleum, arches, a Turkish tent, designed by Henry Keene, a ruined abbey, a Temple of Bacchus based on the Maison Carrée at Nîmes and a tall, red-brick prospect tower which is one of England's most visible follies, overlooking the busy A3. The grotto was intact until shortly after the war, when its roof collapsed after the lead had been stolen. Enough remains to inspire a real sense of awe at the care and dedication that went into the construction. The ruined abbey is surprisingly large, and looks more like an early industrial building than an ecclesiastical one. The house itself was designed for Hamilton in 1774 by Richard Jupp, the architect of Severndroog Castle, but Hamilton had to sell the estate the following year, so it was built for his successor, Benjamin Hopkins, in 1778. It is an enormous relief to folly lovers – and all admirers of the English landscape garden – that this unique park is being restored with the same degree of dedication as Hamilton himself must have lavished on his garden – other ghost gardens such as Enville, Hawkstone and Hackfall would indeed be fortunate to be rescued with equal affection and scholarship. It is intended that the park will be open to the public, as it was in Hamilton's day.

Hamilton as an amateur concentrated on his own garden and did little advisory work; unlike his contemporary William Shenstone of 'The Leasowes', who was consulted about several Midlands gardens, Hamilton's only outside commissions appear to have been at Bowood House in Wiltshire and St Anne's Hill in CHERTSEY, which left other Surrey estates free for the professionals. Charles James Fox's St Anne's Hill has recently lost a Temple of Friendship, a derelict tea-house grotto built after Hamilton's death, in 1794, and an octagonal gazebo of the same date which is now in the grounds of a house called Southwood. The M3 thunders by underneath; all hopes of tranquillity have gone.

Another famous amateur, Sanderson Miller, designed a Gothick greenhouse at Chart Park in Dorking for Henry Talbot. William Kent worked at Addlestone, Richmond, Oatlands and CLAREMONT, where Charles Bridgeman and 'Capability' Brown also worked. Claremont, just three miles away from Painshill, was the only estate that came near to rivalling it for breadth of imagination, yet even with the help of the three greatest names in the greatest period of English landscape gardening, the work of the single dedicated amateur was judged to be the better. How satisfying for the English love of the non-professional.

Nevertheless, and despite having suffered nearly as many changes of ownership as Painshill, Claremont is a splendid estate. Sir John Vanbrugh was the first owner in 1708; he sold it to the Duke of Newcastle, who sold it to Clive of India; it was then bought by the nation as a wedding present for Princess Charlotte and Prince Leopold, who lent it to Queen Victoria when he became King of Belgium; she in turn lent it to the King and Queen of France. Then it passed into the hands of the Forestry Commission. Queen Victoria bought it for her son Leopold; when his wife the Duchess of Albany died in 1922 the government confiscated the estate, as it would have passed to Queen Victoria's grandson, the Duke of Coburg, who was considered an enemy alien. Instead it was bought by a director of Cunard; finally, in 1931, it became a girls' school, which it has remained ever since. The National Trust acquired 50 acres of the estate in 1949.

The most remarkable item to concern us at Claremont is the Belvedere, perhaps the first true folly, deliberately built for pleasure. Vanbrugh had sold the estate to Thomas Pelham (later the Duke of Newcastle) in 1714, but Pelham called him in to enlarge the house and to build the Belvedere in 1717. It is typically Vanbrughian in design, a massive square central section with four taller square towers at each corner, very large and gloomy for a building intended to be light-hearted, partly because of the grey-brown brick chosen for its construction, which is relieved only by Vanbrugh's banding and red brickwork over the round arched windows, and partly because of its enclosure by heavy, dark trees. Originally it was whitewashed. Several years ago the Belvedere was derelict but still solid; we hear now that a restoration programme has taken place and that it once more conveys an air of gaiety. It is as difficult to imagine this as it is that a politician such as Pelham commissioned such a piece voluntarily; more likely, Vanbrugh had already designed it and determined its site, then persuaded Pelham to pay. The stir caused by the Belvedere must have pleased the dour Pelham, for he went on to commission William Kent to build some other little follies in the grounds, including a Bowling Green House and a Temple on an island in Bridgeman's lake. The temple survives, as does a grotto, but the other buildings have gone. A 19th-century obelisk to commemorate Clive, Prince Leopold and Princess Charlotte also survives, as does a Gothic Retreat, designed by J. W. Hiort and John Papworth in 1816 for the Princess and converted into a chapel after her death a year later.

With Kew and Richmond now in Greater London, the only estates left in Surrey that concern us here are Woburn Park at ADDLESTONE, Albury Park at SHERE, and Busbridge at GODALMING. The grotto at Oatlands Park in Weybridge, which cost £40,000 to build in the mid-18th century, was demolished in 1948 by the local council and the Ministry of Works. It was said to be the finest grotto in Britain. All that remains at Woburn Park, once the site of Philip Southcote's experimental, landscaped *ferme ornée* of 1735, are two brick arches by Kent and a grotto. Albury Park has 17th-century terraced gardens laid out by the diarist and gardener John Evelyn in 1655 for the Duke of Norfolk. There are no follies as such, but there is an empty grotto dated 1676, and the famous 500-foot tunnel or 'crypta' Evelyn made through the sandstone hill. The Norfolks have been great folly patrons over the years, and this seems to have been the family's first venture into landscape amelioration; a younger brother, Charles Howard, also had tunnels at Deepdene in Dorking, but these disappeared long ago.

Busbridge Hall was remodelled in 1775 for General Sir Robert Barker by John Crunden. The house was demolished in 1906, but the early 19th-century gardens remained; the estate was split into two and the gardens went with Busbridge Lakes, a house converted from the old stable block. It is hard to believe we are in Surrey, because here are four succeeding lakes bordered by louring red cliffs, still managing to convey the impression we are a thousand miles from civilisation. The cliffs, though small, are packed close to the lakes, thereby giving a feeling of much greater size. As we have seen, this Surrey sandstone is easily worked, so there is a profusion of tunnels, caves and grottoes here. A Hermit's Cave, with pointed doorway and round windows on either side, houses an ice-house and a pillared chamber. A shell and bottle-glass grotto below a crumbling Doric temple carries the date 1810 and the initials of the builder, Henry Hare Townshend. There are two rustic bridges over the lakes, and there were other temples and a tower, but these have now gone. Still remaining are a stuccoed Gothic boat-house and the Ghost Walk, a splendid path up to the top of the cliff through gruesome fanged arches. Townshend died in 1824; his son Chauncey, unsurprisingly after growing up in this romantic environment, became a poet.

Sham ruins and real ruins go together to improve the Surrey landscape; at PEPER HAROW (pronounced Peeper Harra) A. W. N. Pugin designed a sham chapel and some farm buildings at Oxenford Grange as eyecatchers to Peper Harow Mansion in 1841–8. There is a beautiful barn with a steeply pitched roof looking like a sunken cathedral, and the arch lodge has a stubby tower over a non-existent road. The present owners tell us that the sham ruined chapel is real, only the window tracery being false, but the siting is uncannily perfect for the big house. Some of the walling is genuinely medieval, from the old Waverley Abbey estate, but clearly it has been tastefully rearranged. The real folly on the estate is the Bonville Fount, also by Pugin, but this has been heavily vandalised, and the owners are worried about its future. They are proud that the man who designed the Houses of Parliament designed their farmhouse, and the buildings are beautifully cared for, the sham chapel set inside an enclosing wall and a carefully tended garden.

Another rearrangement of genuine medieval architecture took place at REIGATE in 1777. After the Civil War, the Parliamentarians demolished Reigate Castle. They left sufficient rubble for a mock medieval gatehouse to be built, and in case of confusion the builder, Richard Barnes, announced the deception with two plaques, one in Latin and one in English explaining that in 1777 he had erected the gateway at his own expense:

TO

SAVE THE MEMORY

OF

WILLIAM EARL WARREN

WHO IN OLD DAYS DWELT HERE

AND WAS

A LOYAL CHAMPION OF OUR LIBERTIES

FROM PERISHING

LIKE HIS OWN CASTLE

BY THE RAVAGES OF TIME

The oldest rearranged ruins in the county are at VIRGINIA WATER. This again is an artificial lake, made for the Duke of Cumberland (the Butcher of Culloden) by Thomas Sandby in 1765. The clay and sand dam he built collapsed in 1768, earning him the nickname of Tommy Sandbank, but it was soon rebuilt in more durable materials. Sandby designed the grottoes and sham ruins at the head of the lake in 1785; strictly speaking these are in Berkshire but as they are part of Virginia Water we include them here. These are by no means as well known as the old ruins, the Leptis Magna columns by the lakeside bridged by the A329, a gift to England from the Bey of Tripoli, and re-erected here by Sir Jeffry Wyatville for George IV in 1826. Some of the columns stand in triplets retaining their architraves, some are broken, some lie on the ground, all carefully organised to give the best effect. There are triumphal archways — everything, in fact, that the lover of the romantic could desire, but somehow all seeming cold and clinical, an emotionless folly put up out of ostentatious conformity. The most exciting building hereabouts is Fort Belvedere, built in 1750 as Shrubs Hill Tower by Henry Flitcroft for the Duke of Cumberland. Once again Surrey can boast a first: this is the first triangular folly-tower in the country, the begetter of many, and probably for many of us the triangular Gothick tower on a hill is the archetypal folly image. Flitcroft's Hoober Stand in South Yorkshire dates from 1748, but it is a completely different style of triangular building; it has had no successors and therefore remains unique, but Shrubs Hill spawned a country of similar towers – Hiorne's Tower, Lawrence Castle, Powderham Belvedere, Broadway Tower, Paxton's Tower, to name a few. The belvedere was castellated and adapted as a house by Wyatville in 1828-9, and in the 1930s it became the Duke of Windsor's favourite residence up until his abdication.

CLANDON PARK, east of Guildford, is a National Trust property with a simple flint and brick grotto, Kentian in style although the grounds were landscaped by Brown, and elevated above the ordinary by a charming and elegant statue of the Three Graces. There is also a surprisingly late circular Ionic Temple of 1838, built for the 3rd Earl of Onslow by the father-and-son partnership of William and Henry William Inwood. Coincidentally, these two both died in March 1843, one in bed, the other on board a ship which sank in the Bay of Biscay. The chief joy of Clandon, however, is the genuine 18th-century Maori House, painted red and grey, in the garden right by the house. This was shipped over by the 4th Earl, who had been Governor of New Zealand and who liked the country so much that he gave his younger son a Maori name, Huia.

It is tempting to include Waynflete Tower, the gatehouse to ESHER PLACE, in a list of Surrey follies. It looks like a folly but it was a genuine 15th-century gatehouse, minding its own business for 250 years until William Kent came along and Gothicised it for the Hon. Henry Pelham, younger brother of the Duke of Newcastle at Claremont. What we see now owes rather more to Kent's romantic imagination than to the 15th century, like Stafford Castle or Castell

Coch. So in it goes. Pelham was in the right frame of mind in any case: in the 1730s he built the Travellers' Rest in the High Street, a sort of grotto bus shelter, and also a garden temple for Esher Place which is now in the back garden of No. 36 Pelham's Walk. Both could logically be attributed to Kent. EPSOM, which is close but almost impossible to reach from here by road, very suitably has a tomb to a horse in the grounds of Durdans in Woodcote Road. Nearby in Stoke Wood, PRINCE'S COVERTS, just outside Oxshott, is Jessop's Well, the pitiful 18th-century pump-house remnants of a spa which was going to turn a Mr Jessop into a millionaire; the rival attractions of Epsom overwhelmed the enterprise. Another well-head, dated 1886 and with iron guard rails like tusks or post horns, is in SHERE High Street.

Surrey has several oddities which border on follydom. The strangest of these is undoubtedly GATTON Town Hall, which we dismissed almost out of hand when we first heard about it because of its name, reasoning that a town hall, however bizarre, could not really be classed as a folly. We were wrong. Gatton was not a town, nor was it a village. It consisted of a church and one house, and yet this borough was represented in Westminster for nearly 400 years by two members of parliament. Naturally enough the borough was abolished in the 1832 Reform Act, as the third rottenest in the country. In 1765 the owner of Gatton Park erected a Greek temple with iron columns in the park, behind a large urn on which was inscribed:

> Stat ductis Sortibus Urna
> Salus populi Suprema Lex Esto
> Comitium Gattoniense MDCCLXV
> H M Dolus Malus Abesto

Pevsner translates this:

> When the lots have been drawn, the urn remains
> Let the well-being of the people be the supreme law
> The place of the assembly of Gatton 1765
> Let evil deception be absent.

Cynicism or crass stupidity? Sometimes one wonders. Still, with 200 years' hindsight Gatton Town Hall can be seen as an attractive joke, despite the intrusion of modern school buildings close by.

WOTTON, the home of John Evelyn, has the enchantingly named, but ruined, Tortoise House, where apparently visitors could take tea and watch the antics of terrapins in the pool. This strange building has a four-bayed Ionic portico with an open gallery above, sheltered by a plain tiled pitched roof. It may have been built by the architect Francis Edwards, who worked at Wotton between 1830 and 1853 for W. J. Evelyn. Going back 200 years, John Evelyn's cousin George designed and built the Doric temple in the gardens; since the result did not meet with Evelyn's full approval, he had an artificial hill thrown up behind, which half buried the temple at its base. This is one of the first garden temples in the country. Wotton also has a 19th-century grotto and a mausoleum.

Two final oddities worth noticing before we look at the astonishing number of towers in the county are the Gothick summer-house of 1754, solidly placed in the middle of the mound that used to be Starborough Castle, near LINGFIELD, and the 1765 windmill on REIGATE HEATH, which for some unknown reason was converted into a chapel in 1880.

Surrey has a lot of towers, probably more than any other county, which seems strange in an area where the land never rises above 965 feet without human aid. Admittedly, few of Surrey's towers are good follies. The biggest, the best and the most famous is Hull's Tower on the highest point in south-east England, the 965 feet high LEITH HILL, owned by the National Trust. The tower was built in 1765, plain and square, and the altruistic Mr Hull placed a plaque over the door, proclaiming in Latin that it had been built for Mr Hull's pleasure and for the pleasure of anyone else who wanted to take in the wonderful views from the top. After he died, this privilege was abused and the tower was severely vandalised, so the interior was filled with concrete rubble to prevent access. When in 1864 W. J. Evelyn of Wotton Hall decided to open it up again, it was discovered that the rubble had set so hard it was impossible to remove, so a new octagonal stair turret was built on the side, incidentally raising the height at the top to 1,000 feet above sea level — the magic mountain in English terms. The view was remarkable: with a telescope it was possible to see the English Channel to the south and Dunstable Downs 50 miles to the north. But once again it was vandalised, and had to be blocked up. Rumour spread that Hull was buried upside down at the bottom of the tower, so that when the Day of Judgment came and the whole world was turned upside down he would be on his feet to meet his Maker, a story we have come across before and will encounter again on the slopes of Box Hill. Recently it was decided once again to open up the tower, this time attacking the solidified rubble with pneumatic drills. It was during this drilling in October 1984 that a National Trust workman broke through the bottom of the tower to discover Hull's tomb . . .

The tower on BOX HILL, again on National Trust land, is a much more modest affair, a round flint building with no doorway built as a Waterloo monument by Thomas Broadwood, the piano maker. Nearby, at the bottom of a 100-foot shaft, is the grave of Major Peter Labellière, who was buried head first because at the Day of Judgment . . .

Whitehill Folly is an anonymous flint tower in War Coppice Road, which runs along a ridge called Arthur's Seat south of CATERHAM. It must have been built for the view, around the turn of the last century. Naturally it has castellations. Willey Farm in CHALDON has a fine 19th-century water-tower, also of flint and brick; and at Westcroft Park outside CHOBHAM is a magnificent bell-tower, a folly only in that the tower was needed to fulfil a life-long ambition: H. O. Serpell, a biscuit manufacturer from Plymouth, loved the sound of church bells as a child and determined that one day, if he could, he would have his own peal. Biscuits showed him the way to his fortune, and in 1910 he treated himself to a carillon of 25 bells, the largest weighing a quarter of a ton, which he placed in a half-timbered tower in his garden. We have not had an opportunity to ask the neighbours how they feel about it.

Being in line between London and Portsmouth, Surrey has a number of semaphore towers set up in 1821 to replace the wooden towers of the Napoleonic wars. One, in Telegraph Lane, CLAYGATE, has been converted into a three-storey house; a taller one at CHATLEY HEATH, just by Painshill, is five-storeyed and octagonal; and the last is on Pewley Hill in GUILDFORD.

Tower Hill Cottage in DORKING is a mystery. The cottage has evidently been added on to the flint and brick folly-tower dated

1828. The tower should have been built as an eyecatcher to Deepdene, but the owner of Deepdene at that time, Thomas Hope, was too pedantic and classically inclined to permit a vernacular building of no breeding on his estate. There was said to be a small round folly-tower of 1840 in the trees north of the church at MERSTHAM, but it turned out to be a dovecote. NUTFIELD, east of Redhill, has a small folly-tower in the grounds of the Ewell House Country Hotel, and Surrey's final towers are the garish watch-tower built by Frederick Barnes in 1860 at Foxwarren Park in COBHAM, in the full joyous flush of Victorian architectural exuberance, and the tessellated tower built by the Earl of Lovelace at EAST HORSLEY in 1858, banded with plaques successively depicting stars, horns and grenades. The round tower stands at the end of the former drive to the house, now unused because the elaborate and extraordinary tunnels through which it passes are said to be unsafe.

East Sussex

'Sussex-by-the-Sea!' proclaimed the Southern Railway's holiday posters in the 1930s, with a degree of accuracy rarely found in advertising. You can't be more than 25 miles from the coast wherever you go in East Sussex, and the whole county has a slightly raffish holiday air, a far cry from 'kiss-me-quick' resorts in the North like Blackpool and Bridlington, but nonetheless with a slightly forced gaiety, leavened by the grim-faced commuters hurrying up to dirty London from healthy Brighton. Hove, Brighton, Eastbourne, Bexhill, Hastings — no other county can claim so many nationally-known resorts on so short a coastline, and the truth is that, facing south as it does, Sussex does get more than the average amount of sunshine for an English county.

Oddly enough, the Sussex climate has not generally attracted the folly builder. Perhaps it has always been too cheerful, lacking the proper grave melancholia so admired in the 18th century. Since the sundering of Sussex, two-thirds of the county's follies have ended up in the western part, and East Sussex has a few pleasant, desultory towers, a little grotto, the egregious Mad Jack Fuller's follies, and of course the Royal Pavilion at Brighton.

'It's as if St Paul's had come down to the sea and pupped,' commented Sydney Smith on seeing the cascade of domes, pinnacles, towerlets, arcades, minarets and every imaginable motif of oriental architecture which make up BRIGHTON PAVILION. Completed in 1821, it is as much an expression of royal whimsy as of the talent of the favourite royal architect, John Nash. Nash was the third architect to work on the Pavilion; the original building had been put up as long ago as 1786 by Henry Holland (not the eponymous folly-building lord) for the Prince of Wales as the Marine Pavilion; stables, a tennis court and other outbuildings were added in the early 19th century by William Porden; and finally the whole structure was completely remodelled from 1815 by Nash in the oriental style. The place is literally a palace; is it a folly as well? The arguments against say that it was built for a purpose (albeit a frivolous one but there is a long precedent for that); that it was never built without a true reckoning of the cost; that it was properly finished; that it was well constructed by a master architect; and that it has been perfectly maintained. The arguments for merely point out the incongruity of Xanadu-by-Sea, the sheer stark shock of its shape on the skyline. Who is to decide? One can scarcely be objective about this. Public opinion at the time was far more clear-cut, as is shown by this excerpt from an 1820 satire by William Hone, entitled *The Joss and his Folly*, which, besides showing an amusing liberty of expression unthinkable today even by *Private Eye* standards, is particularly interesting for giving us a very early usage of the word 'folly' in the context of architecture:

> The queerest of all the queer sights
>   I've set sight on; —
> Is, the *what d'ye-call-'t thing*, here,
>   THE FOLLY at Brighton
> The outside — huge teapots,
>   all drill'd round with holes,
> Relieved by extinguishers,
>   sticking on poles:
> The inside — all tea-things,
>   and dragons, and bells,
> The show rooms — all show,
>   the sleeping rooms — cells.
> But the *grand* Curiosity
>   's not to be seen —
> The owner himself —
>   an old fat MANDARIN;
> A patron of painters
>   who copy designs,

That grocers and tea-dealers
 hang up for signs:
Hence teaboard-taste artists
 gain rewards and distinction,
Hence his title of 'Teapot'
 shall last to extinction.

After the Pavilion, the other architectural eccentricities in the town pale into insignificance. In the central court of a block of modern flats at Carn Court on the Queen's Park Estate is an anonymous monument, a square porch-like structure with Ionic corner columns and a tiled roof topped with a spike, probably a remnant from some long forgotten estate. HOVE has a scrap of a modern folly, a sham chapel wall complete with window tracery in the garden of a house on the corner of Dyke Road and Porthall Road, near Booth's Bird Museum.

There can be no doubt about Mad Jack Fuller's follies at BRIGHTLING and DALLINGTON, however. John Fuller (1757–1834) was a true British eccentric. Having inherited a fortune at an early age, he not unexpectedly became wilful and autocratic, but these unpleasant traits were redeemed to a great extent by his fierce defence of his county, tenants and constituents. Hilaire Belloc, himself obsessed by Sussex, wrote that 'this man Fuller deserves to be famous and to be called, so to speak, the very demigod of my county, for he spent all his money in a roaring way, and lived in his time like an immortal being conscious of what was worth man's while during his little passage through the daylight'. At a time when indigents were accustomed to demanding alms from the servants of great houses (and most households set aside an allowance for this), Fuller issued orders that any able-bodied man who came begging should be given work, and paid justly for his labours. As a result, the massive miles-long wall round Brightling Park came into existence, an actual example of the 'built to relieve unemployment' story attached to so many follies. But this was not enough for Fuller. He was the stuff of which legends are made – swearing at the Speaker of the House of Commons, thundering down from London in a carriage with footmen and coachmen armed to the teeth with pistols and drawn swords (how he trusted his fellow man!), refusing a peerage ('I was born Jack Fuller and Jack Fuller I'll die'), drinking three bottles of port a day and indulging in impossible wagers. He seems to have found solace in folly building after becoming disillusioned with politics on 27 February 1810, when he insulted the Speaker and had to be forcibly removed by the Serjeant-at-Arms. The abolitionist William Wilberforce referred to the incident as 'the interlude of that mad bull Fuller'.

Possibly the earliest of the Brightling buildings is a small Gothick seat in a plantation in the park. It dates from 1803 (so before the Commons débâcle) and bears the trademark 'COADE SEALY LONDON'. Also in the park is a brick pillar with a cast-iron vignette on top: a cannon, flame and anchor, a monument to the iron foundries that provided the source of the family's wealth. Another pillar, said to have been a companion piece marking the site of the grave of Mad Jack's favourite horse, has disappeared. The Rotunda Temple of about 1810, by Smirke, is a strict garden ornament. Fuller was reputed to have held bawdy parties in it. This sounds possible from the man who had Susan Thrale, the daughter of Dr Johnson's friend, followed around by harlots from Tunbridge Wells when she refused to marry him.

Brightling Church is also worth a visit. One wall holds a bust of Fuller by Henry Rouw. On the other walls are plaques com-memorating two of Fuller's cronies: the forgotten composer William Shield, who died in Brightling in 1829, and Dr Primrose Blair, 'formerly physician to His Majesty's fleet in the West Indies', who died in 1819. The barrel-organ was a gift of Fuller's, as was the peal of bells named after Wellington's battles.

Fuller's most famous wager gives us probably the best folly story in Britain. One evening at Rose Hill, as Brightling Park used to be known, he was dining with friends and boasting of the view to be seen from his dining-room window: 'You can see the spire of Dallington Church,' he declaimed, and several guests, knowing the lie of the land – the village of Dallington lies in a fold of the downs, although it is only a mile or so from Brightling – rose to challenge him. Fuller accepted all bets. The following morning the curtains were drawn and Jack Fuller gazed out over the rolling woods and fields, across the downs to the sea in the invisible distance, and over the little ridge which completely hid the village and church of Dallington from view. No spire. Fuller would nowadays be known in pop psychological terms as a Right Man, a character unable in his own mind to make a mistake or to be contradicted. No spire? He built one. When the punters came to collect their money they were taken to the dining-room window, and there, unmistakably, was the cone-shaped spire of Dallington in the middle distance. Nowadays the folly is called the Sugar Loaf, and at one stage it was converted into a two-storey cottage for a farmworker. A fascinating footnote was added to the story by an article in the *Manchester Guardian* in 1961, reporting the restoration of the Sugar Loaf. The builders found that the original structure consisted of 'nothing more than stones held together by mud', which suggests that the Sugar Loaf had indeed been put up in a hurry.

The Needle is a rather dumpy, dilapidated banded obelisk on top of Brightling Down, 646 feet above sea level. There is no record of why Fuller built it, other than the fact that obelisks were fashionable. In 1985 a row blew up over proposed repairs to it, which would cost an estimated £26,000. The East Sussex County Council narrowly voted to contribute £6,800, with one member objecting strongly to spending part of the money available for historic buildings on 'a pile of bricks' – follies still have their detractors. A more sensible objection came from a gentleman who pointed out that if public money were to be spent to restore it, then the public should be granted access. The restoration was carried out.

The Observatory is a different matter; designed by Sir Robert Smirke, it seemed to have been a genuine attempt at a scientific laboratory, as in retrospect Smirke's other commission at Brightling may have been – Fuller's pyramid mausoleum. Nowadays it's not just the cranks who believe in the ability of the pyramid shape to preserve things – sharpening razor-blades and the like – but then the theory was unknown. Or was it? The story runs that Fuller is seated fully dressed on an iron chair in the centre of the pyramid, with a bottle of port and a roast chicken on the table in front of him, awaiting the Resurrection. Just in case the Devil came first to claim his own, the floor of the pyramid was strewn with broken glass to cut his hooves!

The pyramid was built in 1811. The story goes that Fuller got permission for his unusual mausoleum from the Rev. Mr Hayley on condition that he would arrange to have his pub 'The Green Man' moved from its position directly opposite the church. The pub is now in a converted barn in an awkward corner of the village and is called 'The Fuller's Arms'. The story may be true, but it is not substantiated by the parish register. On 15 November 1810 Hayley made a marginal note:

> Be it remembered that John Fuller Esq. of Rose-hill at the beginning of the present year applied for permission to erect a mausoleum in Brightling Churchyard and to lay open the south side of the said Churchyard by removing the old Post and rail fence and erecting a stone-wall: and when he had fixed upon the site for erecting his Edifice he inquired of me as Incumbent of the Living what would satisfy me for the ground it was to stand on: my reply was that as he would be at considerable expense in erecting the Wall would be a good improvement I should not demand any Fee for the other Building. The Wall is now finished and John Fuller Esq. has added hereto a couple of substantial stone pillars & an iron gate way.

By the time his pyramid was finished, Fuller had the famous ninth verse of Gray's 'Elegy Written in a Country Churchyard' inscribed in the mausoleum's interior:

> The boast of heraldry, the pomp of pow'r
> And all that beauty, all that wealth e'er gave,
> Awaits alike th'inevitable hour,
> The paths of glory lead but to the grave.

Rather melancholy – but it was not in Fuller's nature to sulk for long.

Fuller's last folly is a little 25-foot Hermit's Tower in the trees, with a view opening out over Robertsbridge on to Bodiam Castle, now a National Trust property, which Mad Jack restored at his own expense. The idea of the Hermit's Tower was obviously to house a hermit, but despite assiduous advertising Fuller failed to find one to fit the bill. The requirements were a little excessive: no shaving, no washing, no cutting of hair or nails, no conversation with any outsider for a period of seven years, after which the happy hermit would be made a Gentleman. No takers.

Fuller died in 1834. His obituary in the *Gentleman's Magazine* noted that 'Mr Fuller was distinguished through life by much eccentricity' — a fitting epitaph.

Five miles east of Brightling is HEATHFIELD, where the 55-foot Gibraltar Tower, when we first saw it in 1968, was looking very sorry for itself. It was built in 1792 by Francis Newbery to commemorate the exploits of Brigadier-General George Augustus Elliot at the siege of Gibraltar between 1779 and 1783. The walls inside the tower were decorated with pictures of the siege. General Elliot was later created Baron Heathfield. The three-storey circular tower features in a Turner landscape in the Tate, and in the 1970s it was refurbished to a high standard to form the centrepiece of a new theme park, which opened with a flourish and closed shortly afterwards. In nearby Cade Street is a little monument marking the site of the assassination of the rebel Jack Cade by Alexander Iden in 1450:

> This is the success of all rebels
> and this fortune chanceth ever to traitors.

On Saxonbury Hill in ERIDGE PARK, eight miles north of Heathfield, the Marquess of Abergavenny built a fine Camelotian tower in 1820 to mark the highest point on his estate. It has long been one of our favourite follies; it is said to have the most magnificent views but we have never had the courage to climb it. Saxonbury Tower is very dilapidated and the stone spiral staircase has been knocked away at the bottom to deter foolhardy climbers; it now starts about eight feet from the ground. It is still possible for those with nerves of steel to get to the top. Rhododendrons and broad-leaved trees cluster round the base of the tower and flank overgrown rides, making it one of the most delightfully situated follies. A squatter, fatter, castellated round tower stands solidly on a ridge at FIRLE, near Lewes, built by Lord Cage in 1822 as a gamekeeper's cottage and signal tower, so the gamekeeper could signal with flags to his men on the estate and communicate by telegraph with the keeper at Plashett Park, Ringmer, five miles away. Also at RINGMER is a little octagonal gazebo at Willingham House, surmounting a tiny shell grotto.

STANMER HOUSE, west of Lewes, has a Coade stone monument erected in 1775 to commemorate Lady Pelham's father. It takes the form of an urn on a triangular plinth, resting on three tortoises, and it must have come from a pattern book — there are three others like it around the country.

West Sussex

There are few follies in West Sussex, but almost all are fine ones, scattered along the western slopes of the South Downs like vineyards.

In the middle of a sweep of ARUNDEL parkland stands the 11th Duke of Norfolk's southern folly. Nowhere near as well known as his Greystoke follies in Cumbria, it nevertheless plays its role admirably. Triangular — yes; castellated towers — yes; knapped flint — yes; falling to pieces — yes. It is a regulation folly which now serves to warn visitors of shooting on the nearby rifle-ranges. In 1787, the formidably eccentric Duke had Francis Hiorne, the architect applying for the position of rebuilding the ruined Arundel Castle, build this tower as a 'specimen'. The Duke was satisfied with the result, but before Hiorne could carry out his work on the Castle he died, two years later, aged 45. The tower now stands derelict in the park, made smaller by the flat pasture surrounding it. In front stands a little plinth with an urn, a plaque relating its history, purpose and reason.

The Nore Folly at SLINDON is one of the few marked on the Ordnance map purely as 'The Folly'; most are euphemistically labelled 'Tower' or 'Mon.'. And a truer folly never was: it looks like no other building anywhere and could never conceivably have served any useful purpose. It has been likened to a railway arch or tunnel entrance, but the resemblance is passing. The National Trust are proud of this one: the quirks of its builder have been meticulously restored with new cement and shining new flints, and it gleams in the sun on the edge of its copse. Behind it was once a thatched luncheon room, where the Earl and Countess of Newburgh presumably refreshed themselves and their guests while shooting – how did they explain the rest of the building? Slindon was the family seat of the Countess, formerly Barbara Kemp; it seems most likely that Nore Folly was built between 1749 and 1786, while she was married to the 3rd Earl. The name Nore is puzzling: there is a sandbank by that name in the Thames a little way out from Sheerness; and Charles Radclyffe, the Earl of Newburgh's roaring Jacobite father, was captured in the North Sea by the frigate *Sheerness* and taken past the Nore Bank on his way to execution in the Tower in 1746 – an extremely tenuous connection – or it may be an old Sussex dialect word meaning slope or bank.

GOODWOOD is famous for its racecourse, the most beautifully sited sportsfield in Britain (even more so than Pontypool), but its shell grotto would be world famous if the public could see it. A description cannot do it justice, and it is sensibly closed to visitors in order to ensure its preservation. The shell-work was all done in the 1740s by Sarah, Duchess of Richmond, and her daughters. In 1739 Captain Knowles of *HMS Diamond* had brought in a shipload of shells for the Dukes of Richmond and Bedford, and over the years many more were contributed from collections made all over the world, particularly the West Indies. The mystery grotto at Margate may have its antecedents here, as one of the Duchess's daughters married Lord Holland (see the description in the Kent chapter).

Further along on the edge of the Downs, at LORDINGTON by the Hampshire border, is the magnificent Racton Tower, or Racton Monument as it is marked on the map. The present owner doesn't want the public to get too close; quite right too – it is horrifyingly unsafe. The tower lurks in a small wood, surrounded by concrete fence posts, rabbit wire and barbed wire on the top – one expects man-traps but vandals have helpfully removed most of the fencing. Inside the building is large, louring, and very ruined. Again, it is triangular, but it differs from the popular triangular folly plan as seen at Arundel and other places. The two-storey bottom section is three-sided, with three circular corner towers. Above the centre section rises a gently tapering, three-storeyed round tower to a height of about 80 feet. The corner towers have the remains of smaller turrets on top; the whole building is hollow, roofless and floorless. It was built by the 3rd Lord Halifax in 1771, with £10,000 of the money his father had left. Stanstead (or Stansted) House, the family home, also has an 18th-century Ionic temple in the grounds, called Lumley Seat, after the 1st Earl's father-in-law. Halifax had employed Henry Keene to design the spire of Westbourne Church in 1770, but the elevation of the tower, dated 1772 and entitled 'A View of Stanstead Castle, near Emsworth', was drawn by his son Theodosius Keene, who was then aged 18. The drawing shows a quite splendid building, with castellations on the base and corner towers, castellations on the little corner turrets, quatrefoil windows in the central round tower (now sightless circles), more castellations round the top of the tower and a conical roof surmounted by a lantern, with the Union Flag flying boldly from the flagpole. Was this huge folly really designed by an 18-year-old? Colvin ascribes it to him, but young Keene's father was himself busy two years later designing a folly five miles north, at UPPARK, for Sir Matthew Fetherstonhaugh.

This was the Vandalian Tower, now almost totally destroyed (by vandals?), but sufficient remains on its magnificent hill site to gladden us. All that is left are five or six tall piers for arches or Gothick windows; the original shape cannot be discerned. Sir Matthew commissioned it to celebrate the coming of age of his son Harry, and to mark the founding of Vandalia, a new American colony — but young Harry stayed home and partied with a dissolute set which included the gorgeous 18-year-old Emma Hart, whose 'giddy ways' (she kept getting pregnant by other men) upset Fetherstonhaugh so much that he threw her out; she went on to become Lady Hamilton, Nelson's mistress, and one of the most famous women of the age. The estate is now in the care of the National Trust.

Inside the wall that encircles PETWORTH stands a tall, plain, stone-built square tower with a much taller octagonal stair turret known as the Upperton Monument. It has now been converted into a luxurious house, with magnificent Turneresque views across the park to Petworth House. Curiously, the garden for the monument is on the other side of the road, enclosed by a high wall. Petworth Park itself has a Doric temple and an Ionic rotunda. In a valley half a mile to the west is PITSHILL House, a beautiful Georgian house facing the side of a hill, ignoring the vista which opens out to the south. The Ordnance map marks a belvedere here, a square, three-storey tower with a taller pyramidal-roofed stair turret, the whole pierced at the bottom by an arch, perhaps built by the Mitford family. It is exceptionally hard to find.

Seen from the road, the Deer Tower in Shillinglee Park, north-east of NORTHCHAPEL on the Surrey border, looks unpromising: a squat, ugly box partly screened by trees, hardly worthy of the appellation 'tower' bestowed upon it by the Ordnance map. But if you walk along the bridleway, across bleak Sussex downland, it assumes a more promising shape. A castellated brick box is stuck on the front of a cardboardy, ur-castle keep, square with a round tower at each corner, colour-washed buff. It is set in a nicely wooded little garden, a dream house for imaginative children. Like so many follies, it was built to serve two roles, and presumably filled neither of them very well. One was to be a look-out tower for the deer-keeper – not really tall enough, despite having four floors; another was to be an eyecatcher from Shillinglee Park House – not pretty or spectacular enough. Now the trees have grown up around the Deer Tower the roles have been reversed: the gutted Shillinglee House makes a splendid eyecatcher, but all that can be seen of the tower from the house is a clump of trees on the horizon.

East of Stane Street the follies are less fine but still amusing. The most famous railway-tunnel entrance in Britain is at CLAYTON, on the London–Brighton line, where the keeper's cottage above the line is straddled by two mighty machicolated towers built in 1840 but reminiscent of Sanderson Miller at his most whimsical. HICKSTEAD, famous for show jumping, has a large sham castle summer-house at Hickstead Place which may predate follies – it seems as if it could have been built for a purpose long forgotten.

Four small towers and a house unique in England complete the West Sussex picture. The best of the towers is the Toat Monument north of PULBOROUGH; it stands in a hedge bordering an apple orchard, and although it is four storeys high and embattled it remains a very small tower, perhaps 40 feet, erected in 1827 to the memory of Samuel Drinkald who was killed when he was thrown from his horse on this spot in 1823. The now demolished 106-foot Holmbush Tower was built singlehandedly by a Mr Summer during the Crimean War for the Victorian Gothic mansion of Holmbush on Beacon Hill at COLGATE — some summer-house towers and a fine stag's gate remain — and there is a remarkable octagonal water-tower north of STEYNING at a house called Wappingthorn, built by Maxwell Ayrton in 1928 and benefiting from the addition of a summer-house on top. The style could best be described as Helter Skelter. At Michelgrove, a farm hidden in a fold of the downs above PATCHING, is a strange tower dovecote and a Gothic arched wall with a small tower at one end, the remnants of a house demolished by the Duke of Norfolk in 1845.

CASTLE GORING on the outskirts of Worthing is extraordinary; the only similar building we can think of is Castle Ward at Downpatrick in Northern Ireland. The entrance front is good strong castle Gothick: massive frowning turrets, heavy castellations and cross arrowslits. But on the garden side is a pleasant pedimented classical façade, seven bays with Ionic pilasters. The ensemble was designed — if that's the word — in 1791 by John Biagio Rebecca for Sir Bysshe Shelley, grandfather of Percy. Shelley it was who was responsible for the schizophrenic layout of the house: not only is one side Gothic and the other classical, but the rooms inside change style halfway through; the staircase is on the opposite side of the house to the main rooms; there is no entrance hall, no corridors; the porch prevents any light reaching the ground-floor rooms — and so on. This frightful mish-mash took 34 years to build, by which time Sir Bysshe was dead, never having lived in it. The locals fondly refer to it as the Rat's Castle.

39   Jack the Treacle Eater, Barwick Park, Yeovil

40   Ammerdown Park lighthouse, Kilmersdon

41   Stepped pyramid, Goathurst   42   Willett's Tower, Elworthy

43   All that remains of the mightiest folly in Britain – Beckford's Fonthill Abbey

44   An admission ticket to the sale of Fonthill Abbey, 1823

THIS · TICKET · WILL · ADMIT · THREE · VISITORS · DURING · THE · VIEW · AND · IS · NOT · TRANSFERABLE ·

FONTHILL
ABBEY
1823

VISITORS

52   Corsham Court folly wall

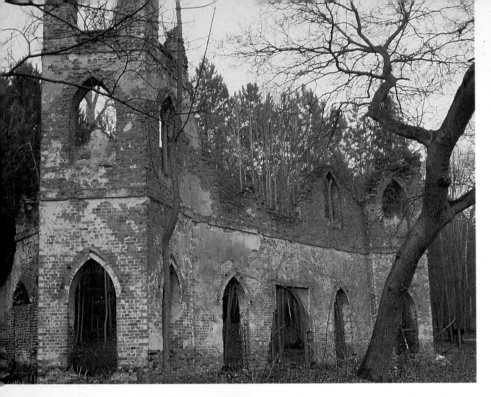

53 The sham cathedral at Painshill Park, Cobham

54 The remains of the Painshill Park grotto

Wales and the
Welsh Borders

Clwyd

Wales lacks follies. The inhabitants were in general too busy surviving to concern themselves unduly with outshining their neighbours by building sham ruined castles; there were plenty of real ones around anyway. But despite the scarcity of the squire folly, Wales has some notable achievements in the field, in particular the first folly to be recorded as such. In the 13th century, Hubert de Burgh began to build a castle on the Welsh/English border. He was, however, building in ignorance or defiance of an agreement Henry III had recently made with one of the Welsh courts not to permit military building in the borders, and as soon as the authorities heard of the building down it came, the clerk dutifully recording it as 'Hubertus Stultitiam', or Hubert's Folly.

The Principality is not famous for its indigenous architecture. Blessed with large supplies of impermeable slate to keep out the soft, wet weather, the country roofed itself in grey from north to south. Pink and blue slates were eschewed as being too frivolous. Practicality was the key note and, the economy being largely agrarian at the height of folly fashion, surplus income was directed towards new stock, or cowsheds, or walling, rather than towards architectural conceits. Nevertheless, there were some to transcend the survival ethos and build just for the sake of building.

First impressions make Clwyd the least attractive of the Welsh counties. Escape from the coast and flat, industrial-estate Flintshire, however, and a different land hesitantly reveals itself, as beautiful in its own way as more famous tourist centres and with the benefit of far fewer people.

Compared with English counties there are few follies here;

compared with Powys there are plenty. Easily the biggest and most impressive is the gigantic Gwrych Castle outside ABERGELE. This is a folly designed to impress by sheer bulk; it was built as a private house for Lloyd Bamford Hesketh, who designed it himself. Work started in 1814, but the foundation stone was not actually laid until 1819, and thereafter it is only fair to say that work meandered along. A massive marble staircase leading, in best folly tradition, nowhere was installed in the 1870s, and it is still unclear in the 1980s whether the house has actually been finished. At any rate, building has stopped and it is presently serving as an amusement park. Hesketh called upon many architects to assist him in his grand design, including Charles Busby, Thomas Rickman and Edward Welch; the core of the house is built in the unremarkable, over-castellated Gothic popular at the time, but what makes it a cast-in-bronze folly is that from the road one can scarcely pick out the actual house from the immense curtain walls running for hundreds of yards along the steep hillside, containing a total of 18 towers. All this is sham: the walls are blind façades fronting nothing.

North of Denbigh on the A5382 is the site of one of the most famous folly stories in Wales, although there is little of the folly about the building that inspired it. A Mr Lloyd had an estate at Foxhall, by HENLLAN, when in 1592 the local MP, Mr Panton, decided that he was going to build a grander, newer mansion close by — much too close for the liking of Mr Lloyd — and call it Foxhall Newydd (New Foxhall). Lloyd predicted financial disaster for Mr Panton; and when disaster duly struck he bought the nearly finished mansion and, in the orgasmic *schadenfreude* of which all true Welshmen are secretly capable, stripped the roofs and the furnishings, leaving the walls to stand in testimony to Panton's folly. The ruin is remarkably beautiful, reminiscent of Lyveden New Bield, standing in a cherry orchard behind the prosperous working farm of Foxhall.

In the centre of DENBIGH, near the ruins of the castle, stands some walling consisting almost solely of arches. They constitute Leicester's Folly, the beginnings of a cathedral that was paid for by Robert Dudley, Earl of Leicester. Nothing came of it, the ruins were left to themselves, and the epithet stuck. Near the A543 towards the south-west, about halfway to GROES, is Dr Johnson's Monument, a Grecian urn. The monument was erected by Mr Myddleton, the owner of Gwaenynog, to commemorate Johnson's visiting this spot. Johnson immediately commented on this gesture in a letter to Mrs Thrale that Mr Myddleton's efforts looked like 'an intention to bury me alive . . . '. Nearby is a cottage known, of course, as Dr Johnson's Cottage, carrying over the door some verses extolling 'this humble shed'.

Near the Brigidine Convent on the A543 leaving Denbigh is a castellated wall concealing a farm from the road, but after Gwrych façade walls have to be rather special, so instead head south-east towards Ruthin. Castell Gyrn at LLANBEDR DYFFRYN CLWYD has another remarkable story, this time of co-operation between two parties normally seen at loggerheads: the county planning officer and the householder. John Taylor, an architect, wanted to build a house with a beautiful view of the Clwydian range and Snowdonia, but the planning authorities felt that a conventional building would be scenically detrimental. To general astonishment they proposed that only a building 'which punctuated the landscape in the manner of an 18th-century folly' would be permissible, and Mr Taylor joyously responded by building a four-storey castellated tower. Unlike most follies it has solar heating and double glazing fitted as standard — after all, it was built in 1977.

The tallest mountain in the Clwydian range is MOEL FAMAU, 'Mother of bare hills', a little further north from Gyrn. A superb, exhilarating long walk brings one in sight of a cairn marked on the map as Jubilee Tower; seen closer to, the cairn becomes an immense pile of rubble, all that remains of a gigantic three-decker Egyptian tower constructed in 1810–19 to commemorate George III's Jubilee. The architect was Thomas Harrison, who also designed Lord Hill's column in Shrewsbury and the Marquess of Anglesey's column at Llanfair PG, both of which are still standing, while the Jubilee Tower isn't: the contractor Thomas Penson had an argument with Harrison and refused to finish the building. It was blown down in 1862; in 1970 the rubble was cleared up and four concrete staircases were built up to the 30-foot plinth, which had remained relatively intact, to provide a viewing platform comparable with Castell Gyrn.

NERCWYS HALL south of Mold was heavily Gothicised in 1813–20 by Benjamin Gummow for Miss Gifford; he added wings, an archway, an orangery, a porch and apparently a sham castle. Much of this has now been demolished; we did not see the sham castle. Nor have we seen Sir Watkin's Tower, 1,843 feet up on the top of Cyrn-y-brain above PEN-Y-STRYT, but this is merely laziness on our part as the undoubtedly splendid walk would have taken us about three hours, which we didn't have. The tower is marked on the 1981 Ordnance map as a ruin, so traces almost certainly remain. Sir Watkin was of course a Williams-Wynn, the great family who owned much of North Wales, and their family seat was Wynnstay, at RUABON, now a school.

The house at Wynnstay is well documented architecturally, but there is no attribution for Sir Watkin's Tower. The succession of Sir Watkins were all enthusiastic builders, and among others they consulted Francis Smith, 'Capability' Brown, James Gandon and Benjamin Gummow. There are several interesting buildings left in the park, including a dairy by Brown, a large, fluted, Doric column tower, and Nant-y-Belan Tower. The column, about 75 feet high, was built in 1790 by James Wyatt in memory of Sir Watkin Williams-Wynn the fourth; it is topped by an urn with rams' heads at each compass point above a viewing platform, and there are seven little windows for the spiral stairway. Yobs have been up it recently, to spray graffiti at the top, but the entrance is now blocked up. There was no question of relieving unemployment at Wynnstay Park – the labour force consisted of French prisoners of war.

Nant-y-Belan tower still exists – just. One man we spoke to said it was demolished and all you could see were its foundations. If you walk along the track to it south of the house, past Penynant, you come across the foundations of something just before running out of parkland. Don't give up; cross the field and go into the woods beyond, even further along the ridge, and you'll find the remnants of the tower teetering on the edge of a precipice, marked very correctly on the map as a ruin. Half at least has already collapsed down the ravine, and now there is hardly anything left; it is very derelict and certainly beyond salvation. One part of the back wall still reaches its original height of about 35 to 40 feet. A man working on the estate reminisced:

> When I was a kid, it used to have plaques all the way round the walls recording the names of the people in the Charge of the Light Brigade. You could get inside and there were two huge oak doors and in the middle of the floor there was a huge eagle crouched over with a cup on its back and my friends and I — we were kids, mind — my friends and I went underneath and we found a room underneath and there was a big fireplace in the room and when you lit a fire in the fireplace the smoke came out of the rams' heads round the top of the tower. You should have seen it 30 years ago, it was wonderful then. The other monument in the park [the column] is a monument to something, the Wynns or something, they were all eagles or rams you know, but now they've blocked it up because the stairs were falling down inside.

The eagle remained on site until fairly recently, when the children of our generation threw it down the ravine and shattered it. The tower was designed by Sir Jeffry Wyatville in 1806 to commemorate the brother officers of the 5th baronet who were killed in the Irish rising of 1798 — not the Charge of the Light Brigade. We failed to find a final folly: there is also said to be a castellated tower above Cefn Bychan celebrating the victory at Waterloo.

James Wyatt also worked in the area a few miles away at Acton Park, on the outskirts of WREXHAM. The house he designed for Sir Foster Cunliffe has now been demolished, but the great Doric screen put up as the entrance to the park, attributed to Moel Famau's Thomas Harrison, remains to overwhelm the pedestrian housing estate surrounding it. Further along the same road is the remarkable, enchanting village of MARFORD. About 14 or 15 houses, right in the middle of the A483 with traffic thundering through, have been built in an uncompromisingly picturesque Gothick, with ogee windows everywhere, everything black and white — even the pub. They were built in 1805 by George Boscawen as the estate village to Trevalyn Hall. Turner painted Marford Mill but ignored the village, which must have been even more picturesque then, when all the roofs were thatched.

HAWARDEN has a genuine castle, improved in 1866 but otherwise real. It was a 13th-century English border castle in the park of an 18th-century country house and, following a precedent nobly set by Charles Grey of Colchester, the antiquary Sir Stephen Glynne restored the castle sufficiently for it to make an excellent garden ornament. Sadly, the cost of restoration proved too much, and he had to sell the estate to his brother-in-law Gladstone.

The final folly in Flintshire is Dry Bridge Lodge at MOSTYN. This fascinating building serves as a bridge, an archway, a house, a tunnel and an eyecatcher — one of the most economical buildings we have come across. It is a two-storey castellated house with an archway through the middle, straddling the drive to Mostyn Hall. The drive to Mostyn Hall from Whitford itself crosses the minor road from Mostyn to Tre-Mostyn, and the wide arch is built on this bridge, making it more of a tunnel. It is very pretty and quite unexpected.

Dyfed

Dyfed is compiled from Carmarthenshire, Pembrokeshire and Cardiganshire. The variety is immense, with the deep-water oil terminal at Milford Haven, Llanelli's rugby fervour and massive tinplate works (hence 'Sospan Fach'), the academic calm of Lampeter and Aberystwyth, as well as Britain's smallest city — St David's, with a population of 1,638. Again there are few follies, but the size and story of Paxton's Tower at LLANARTHNEY goes some way to compensate for the rest.

Sir William Paxton was a Londoner who made his fortune in India. Evidently the sort of man who needed to be a big fish, he set about looking for a small pond and found it in Carmarthenshire. The next step was to get elected to Parliament as member for the county, and here he made a miscalculation. He made the assumption that the voters of Carmarthenshire could be bought. The men of the county accepted Paxton's prodigious hospitality with enthusiasm, and then went out to vote for his rival, as they had intended to do all along. The story of the Great Election of 1802 — *Y Lecsiwn Fawr* — has passed into folk history, along with an uncannily precise account of Paxton's expenditure: £15,690 4s 2d on 11,070 breakfasts, 36,901 dinners, 684 suppers, 25,275 gallons of ale, 11,068 bottles of whisky, 8,879 bottles of porter, 460 bottles of sherry and 509 bottles of cider, as well as 18 guineas for Milk Punch and £786 for campaign favours and bunting — the equivalent today of about £388,000. The Tory Sir James Hamlyn Williams was the victor, winning 1,217 votes to Paxton's 1,100, and the announcement was greeted with vicious fighting between the rival factions, the Reds for the Tories and the Blues for the Whigs — yes, that way round. Once the initial emotions had calmed down, it is said that the Reds took to jeering that Paxton had overspent himself. In order to disprove them he built this mighty folly-tower on the hills above Llanarthney on the Tywi valley.

Paxton's Tower is now owned by the National Trust, who have recently restored it from its ramshackle state. It is a wonderful, grumbling, massive proto-folly, triangular with round corner turrets springing from hexagonal bases. On top is a hexagonal turret, and the whole affair is lightly castellated. The entrance arches at ground level are big enough to drive a carriage through; there was once a dining room on the first floor. Plaques above the first-floor windows in Welsh, English and Latin commemorated the ostensible reason for the tower's construction:

> To the invincible commander Viscount Nelson, in commemoration of deeds before the walls of Copenhagen, and on the shores of Spain; of the Empire everywhere maintained by him over the seas; and of the death which is the fulness of his own glory, though ultimately for his own country and for Europe, conquering, he died. This tower was erected by William Paxton.

It was designed by Samuel Pepys Cockerell and built in 1811.

No other folly in Dyfed can compare with Paxton's; it is among the finest in the country. The column tower on the A485 north of LAMPETER, however, Derry Ormond Tower, is an excellent example of its type. It takes its name from the Derry Ormond estate on which it was built, and was erected to commemorate the battle of Waterloo. There are said to be 365 steps inside to the top, but the entrance has been blocked up since before living memory. The tower was probably designed by Samuel Cockerell's more famous son, C. R. Cockerell, who built Derry Ormond mansion for John Jones in 1824 as well as St David's College in Lampeter. Built of slate-coloured stone, the tall, crumbling column stands high and exposed and is now eroding badly. The railings round the top have fallen and even the plinth is sagging; urgent work needs to be done to rescue this Lampeter landmark.

In 1847 a 78-foot obelisk was erected in Carmarthen to the memory of General Sir Thomas Picton, a local man who was a hero of the Peninsular Wars and who was killed leading his division to victory at Waterloo. In 1984 the district council decided it was unsafe, found it would cost £90,000 to repair it, and ordered it to be taken down. The protest from General Picton's regiment was such that they eventually decided to dismantle the top half only, number the stones, and store them until such time as there would be enough money to reconstruct it. Picton's commander-in-chief is commemorated by the Wellington Monument in ABERYSTWYTH, built on the top of Pen Dinas, the 413-foot hill south of the town. Major Richards of Bryn Eithen Hall in Llanfarian, now a folk museum, built it in the form of an up-ended cannon, but never managed to finish it properly. A John Nash folly here, a triangular Gothic castellated tower for Sir Uvedale Price, was demolished in 1895.

Tourists usually manage a quick scurry up the picturesque Vale of Rheidol on British Rail's last remaining steam-train service as far as the remarkable DEVIL'S BRIDGE, but otherwise Aberystwyth's hinterland is empty. The Devil's Bridge itself retains an air of mystery; one of the unique curiosities of Britain, it consists of three bridges riding piggyback over the river Mynach. Historians say that the bottom bridge was built by monks in the 11th century, but everybody else knows that Pont-y-gwr-drwg (literally the Bridge of the Bad Man) was built by Old Nick himself. Above that is an 18th-century stone bridge, and above that an iron bridge of 1901. To the south is the Ystwyth valley, and it was here in 1783 that Thomas Johnes conceived the finest flowering of the Gothick revival in Wales. Hafod Uchtryd was the bleak, untended estate Johnes inherited from his father and, having been brought up in comparative luxury in Croft Castle in Herefordshire, he was expected to be yet another absentee landlord. But Johnes was a romantic; he secretly married a girl from Dolaucothi, by the Ogofau gold-mines, and they decided to turn Hafod into their ideal home. Their ideals were in the school of the picturesque, influenced by and influencing their friends John Nash, Richard Payne Knight and Sir Uvedale Price. In 1786–8, with the architect Thomas Baldwin, they created the finest Gothick mansion in the country; it was destroyed by fire on 13 March 1807, rebuilt, then left to sit in almost forgotten splendour for 133 years until John Piper rediscovered it in an article for the *Architectural Review* in June 1940. A spate of appreciations followed, culminating in a book, *Peacocks in Paradise*, by Elisabeth Inglis-Jones. In the wake of this acclaim the house was blown up in 1958 to make way for a caravan site.

All that remains of Johnes's Xanadu in Wales is an obelisk to the memory of the 5th Duke of Bedford, built in 1803 and designed by W. F. Pocock, and Johnes's Arch, a very Welsh-looking arch over the B4574 two miles south-east of Devil's Bridge. Two massive drystone-style piers support a spindly arch, built in 1810 to commemorate George III's Jubilee. Once there were three such arches; this is the only survivor.

As we go south towards Tenby something seems amiss; instead of the familiar Pontrhydygroes and Llanfihangel-y-pennant we get alien names such as Yerbeston, Saundersfoot, Lydstep and Sunny Hill. This is Little-England-beyond-Wales; like Gower, it was settled centuries ago by English speakers coming in from the sea. Little Welsh is spoken here, but some names retain their pre-invasion origins — PENALLY, for example, outside Tenby. On the cliff-top was a domed Temple of the Winds, but as the area is now a Ministry of Defence firing range with forbidden access, it may well have proved to be too tempting a target: we have not seen it.

North again, and we return to Wales proper. CILWENDEG is just outside Boncath on the B4332, and in the woods near the house is a pretty shell-house, dressed with quartz and built by John Jones in the late 18th century. It used to have a roof lit with coloured glass, but that collapsed and was replaced by a pitched one. Much of the decoration has now disappeared, but a knucklebone and horsetooth floor remains. Still at Cilwendeg, the Pigeon House is a massive three-bayed building in eyecatcher style, built 'AD 1835' by Morgan Jones, absurdly large for a dovecote, standing at the end of what was once an ornamental lake and is now a farm pond. It is screened at the front by an extraordinary display of six-foot tall railings carved from slate.

If we leave Dyfed on the A40 we pass one final curiosity, the Mail Coach Pillar between Llandovery and PENTRE-BACH, almost on the Powys border. The road here skirts a wooded precipice above the river Gwydderig, and in a lay-by on the west side of the road is an awful warning of the perils of drunken driving, a small obelisk on a plinth with a cautionary inscription describing in wonderful detail the accident that inspired its erection. In 1835

Dyfed

Edward Jenkins was driving the Gloucester and Carmarthen mail coach. He was intoxicated:

AND DROVE THE MAIL ON THE WRONG
SIDE OF THE ROAD AND GOING AT
A FULL SPEED OR GALLOP MET A
CART AND PERMITTED THE LEADER
TO TURN SHORT ROUND TO THE RIGHT
HAND & WENT DOWN OVER THE
PRECIPICE 121 FEET WHERE AT THE
BOTTOM NEAR THE RIVER CAME
AGAINST AN ASH TREE WHEN THE
COACH WAS DASHED INTO
SEVERAL PIECES.

On the next side of the pillar is a rather prim and self-satisfied comment:

I HAVE HEARD SAY WHERE THERE IS
A WILL THERE IS A WAY ONE PERSON
CANNOT ASSIST MANY, BUT MANY CAN
ASSIST A FEW AS THIS PILLAR WILL
SHEW WHICH WAS SUGGESTED
DESIGNED AND ERECTED BY J. BULL
INSPECTOR OF MAILCOACHES, WITH
THE AID OF THIRTEEN POUNDS
SIXTEEN SHILLINGS AND SIXPENCE
RECEIVED BY HIM FROM FORTY ONE
SUBSCRIBERS IN THE YEAR 1841.

Glamorgan

The old principality of Morganwg is now municipally divided into three counties: South Glamorgan, Mid Glàmorgan and West Glamorgan. However, Glamorgan it remains, easily the most densely populated area of Wales, the bedrock of Welsh prosperity, the most savagely hit in times of recession, and offering the archetypal Welsh image of rainwashed, grey-slate terraced houses scarring once beautiful valleys and populated by a short, dark race whose concept of heaven is a singing rugby team. Like all assumptions, this has scant basis in fact, being an amalgam of 50-year-old English prejudices and fear. What is undeniable is that Glamorgan's mineral wealth is not matched by its architectural glory. The 18th- and 19th-century coal- and steel-masters were far more intent on stripping the country than on constructing fancies and conceits. It is not surprising that these three counties should provide a total of nine follies between them, most of them belonging to the rural (and Anglicised) Gower, west of Swansea.

But we start with the Marquess of Bute's work at Cardiff and Tongwynlais, because Cardiff is the capital of the country and the Butes built it. CARDIFF is brash, ugly, exciting, confident in its status to such an extent that it doesn't feel like a British provincial city. It has all the manners and charm of an American state capital, which in a way it resembles. Two hundred years ago Cardiff barely existed. The population in 1804 was less than 2,000; in 1871 it was 50,000 and it doubled in size in the next ten years. Now, well over a quarter of a million live there, and the city's growth was due in the most part to the efforts of one man, the 2nd Marquess of Bute, who built the docks that turned Cardiff into the largest coal port in the world; his son, the 3rd Marquess, built follies.

This is not to diminish the achievements of John Crichton-Stuart, the 3rd Marquess of Bute. He was a remarkable man. Tall, dark, handsome, uncontrollably rich, gifted with a formidable intellect, he had a passion for language and literature, for building and the Scriptures. Cardiff Castle had been built in 1080, but its only claim to fame was that William the Conqueror's eldest son spent the last 30 years of his life there. Henry Holland and 'Capability' Brown had been employed in 1777 by Lord Mount Stuart to rebuild it in the fashionable Gothick style, but the 18-year-old Bute decided to turn it into a palace, and employed William Burges, one of the greatest — certainly the most individualistic — of all Victorian architects, to help him. Over the next 16 years Burges added a mighty tower, state apartments and a succession of galleries and rooms running along the west side of the castle walls. The original keep itself was relegated to little more than a picturesque garden feature, a genuine 'sham' castle on a mound in the garden. Lavishly decorated both inside and out – even the statues and shields in niches on the tower walls are gaily painted – the whole ensemble is more French than Welsh. Although Burges was renowned for his knowledge of French gothic, Bute's scholarship was no less, and at this time he converted from Presbyterianism to Roman Catholicism. The sensuous, sumptuous grandeur of the castle design is likely to have been the product of the enthusiasms of both men.

In 1871 Bute and Burges embarked on a new project, the 'restoration' of Castell Coch, a 13th-century ruin on a hillside at TONGWYNLAIS, five miles north of Cardiff. Little remained of the original castle, but this did not deter Burges, who produced plans the following year showing a sort of miniature Azay-le-Rideau, complete with conical roofs on the three towers. Despite his acknowledged scholarship, there was little doubt that the original Castell Coch did not remotely resemble the proposed plans drawn up by Burges. Bute, however, was delighted, and work started in 1875. The end result is magnificent by any standards. The building is now looked after by the Department of the Environment, and is kept, as one would expect, in superb condition. It is a compact, tight, neat little castlet, and this, more than anything — more than the fanciful reconstruction, more than the enormous expense, more than the extravagant decoration — is what made it a folly. The banqueting hall and the large drawing room are designed to cater for a large number of guests, but the only sleeping accommodation is the Lord's bedroom and the Lady's bedroom. The castle was obviously unusable, and Bute very seldom visited it.

Another four miles up the road brings us to GLYNTAFF, just outside Pontypridd, and to perhaps the most eccentric figure in Welsh history. In 1838 Dr William Price of Llantrisant — druid, chartist, pioneer of cremation, who fathered three children when in his 80s, called his first-born Iesu Grist and cremated him in a barrel of vaseline when he died of convulsions, who wore a fox-skin cap and a green tunic edged in scarlet and embroidered with druidical symbols when treating his patients, who went barefoot by preference — in 1838 this Dr Price decided to build a Druidical Temple of Harmony at Glyntaff, the site, so he thought, of an ancient burial ground of the Druids. He collected £137 17s 11d from his fervent supporters and started his Temple by building two squat, white stuccoed towers to flank the gateway, which was aligned directly with the Rocking Stone on Pontypridd Common. Unfortunately Lady Llanover got to hear about this ambitious project, and as she owned the land she not unnaturally made strenuous objections. Dr Price managed to finish the towers and the money before he was stopped, went back to Llantrisant and became a Chartist. The towers remain, now part of a safe, non-druidical housing estate which accepts cremation as a matter of course.

Now drive up the Rhondda Valley, not because there are follies there, but to see what coalmining has done to and for Wales. If you turn right at Treorchy, you can head for Cymmer and NEATH through the Michaelston Forest, and guess at what this part of Wales used to look like. At Neath turn right for Tonna, then right again up a small road on the outskirts of the town. About a mile along the road on the left you will glimpse the Ivy Tower, superbly sited overlooking industrial Neath. Little ivy remains; obviously someone is prepared to look after it. The building remains enigmatic — some say a belvedere, some say a dance-hall with stained-glass windows, but the big fireplace in the basement suggests another dining-room-with-a-view, Kymin style. It is circular, castellated, rubbly, only one storey plus basement, with inordinately large Gothic pointed windows surmounted by blind quatrefoils. Perhaps the story of the stained-glass is true, and the view would have been enjoyed from a flat wooden roof behind the castellations.

An old tinplate works at ABERDULAIS has one of the most baffling edifices in this area. The National Trust came across an ornamental Victorian aqueduct while restoring the works, the cradle of industry in South Wales. The site archaeologist was forced to class it as a folly, as it seemed to be purposeless; a folly on an industrial site is a very rare creature. Back down to Neath, and on to JERSEY MARINE along the B4290, where the pitiful remnants of a 19th-century pleasure park huddle hopelessly round a pub. There's a plain but oddly attractive little four-storey tower, hexagonal and with elongated castellations round the parapet, which apparently started life as a camera obscura and is now roofless and floorless. Next to the pub is a pretty (private) flower and kitchen garden which has at one end the crested back wall of an 1878 racquets court. The sound of vanished laughter haunts these light-hearted confections long after the heart has left them.

Swansea is a much maligned city. Yes, it is industrial, disfigured by bombs and business, by inept or corrupt planning, but the hand of man cannot completely disguise the God-given beauty of its position — built on seven hills overlooking the majestically sweeping bay, the fairest city site in Britain. Behind the bay from the strangely named village of Mumbles is Swansea's playground, the lovely Gower peninsula, offering the city dweller secluded coves and beaches, quiet country lanes, wild walks and follies. For the benefit of any locals who may read this, we would advise visitors that the quiet, secluded beaches can be found only in January and February; for the rest of the year Gower is one big traffic jam.

The bay road turns off towards Gower at BLACK PILL, before one gets to Mumbles, and just by the turn-off is a small, low cottage with castellated ends, looking for all the world like an eyecatcher lodge. Surrounded by bungalows and garages, it looks more out of place in its modern setting than it must have done when it was an estate cottage for Clyne Park, the home of the coal-mining Vyvyans. The house itself is now a college, but the park — a landscaped ravine and stunningly beautiful when the rhododendrons are out — is public, and conceals an extraordinary little structure, consisting of a stone spiral staircase with an iron railing wrapped round a thin column, little more than a newel post, huddled among some trees at the bottom of the valley. It can hardly be a look-out: the site is totally wrong, as even without the surrounding trees there would be no view. Again, it is only some 15 feet high. It is inexplicable but pleasing. At the top of the gardens is an octagonal summer-house looking out over Swansea Bay, and a thin, rubbly, castellated clock-tower up by the house completes this little group of Clyne Park follies — small, undistinguished but oddly memorable.

At the far end of the Gower, a disappointing and elusive fake stone circle stands in the old grounds behind Stouthall Park at REYNOLDSTON, right by the road going up to the village, but small, boring and hidden behind a hedge. On the other side of the road is a much more interesting object: a tomb in the middle of the field with a tree growing through it, the grave of a favourite horse.

Near KITTLE, the A4118 passes the elegant Kilvrough Manor, and on the opposite hill to the house is a drystone-walled enclosure with a tiny tower tacked on one corner. Gymkhanas are sometimes held in the field, but the style of the tower does not prepare us for the splendour of the next folly west, the remarkable PENRICE WALL. The design is similar, but the difference in scale works triumphantly, for here is over 200 feet of sham ruin, with towers and battlements and a gate (not to scale), and more gymkhanas behind, and even an occupied house incorporated in the façade. It looks real — it looks as if Cromwell slighted it — but the whole crazy structure was built in 1780 for Thomas Talbot of Penrice Castle, a real 13th-century castle at the bottom of the valley, by Anthony Keck.

Gwent

Monmouthshire was a county administered jointly by Wales and England until the county changes of 1972, when its name was changed to Gwent and it became firmly Welsh. If you should happen to be in MONMOUTH, the old county town, on one of those rare days that always appear in tourist brochures but so seldom in real life, when the air is so clear it sparkles and the sky is as blue as a sapphire, then cancel all other plans and take the Forest of Dean road out of town, following the National Trust signs to 'The Kymin'.

At the top of the steep little hill, less than 1,000 feet high, one of the most sensational views in the British Isles unrolls over the undulating hills of Gwent. It looks like nothing so much as a map of Tolkien's Shire, with patchwork fields and copses lying contentedly under the sun for as far as the eye can see. And right on top of the hill is a building Bilbo Baggins would have been proud to call home: a round, castellated, whitewashed, two-storey tower with a little mast, and the Welsh flag and the National Trust flag fluttering in the breeze. 'It's not a folly,' said the occupant indignantly. 'Don't make the mistake of calling it a folly. How can it be a folly when it was built for a purpose?' This is true, but as its purpose was to serve as a dining room for a group of gentlemen to dine in once a week, it can hardly be regarded as an essential structure. The Round House was built in 1794 by a Monmouth dining club headed by Philip Hardwick, but in proper Welsh tradition the area of the Kymin, which they had landscaped the year before, remained open to the public. Its popularity was immediate, and the Kymin became the smartest recreation area in Monmouthshire. A bowling green and racquets court were built, stables, another dining room (given by the Duke of Beaufort), a summer-house, the Naval Temple, and Mr Swinnerton's Beaulieu Walk, which ran north of the Round House as a high hedged promenade with 'windows' cut into the hedge at intervals to show different aspects of the view. The Kymin's finest hour came in 1802, when Lord Nelson visited Monmouth with Lady Hamilton. It is said that his boat was spotted sailing down the Wye and that he was recognised through the telescope mounted on top of the Round House. A warning gun was fired from the Naval Temple, and by the time Nelson's party moored at the quay, the Mayor and Corporation were there to greet him. The Admiral was so impressed that he returned three weeks later and had breakfast at the Round House, where he thought the view one of the finest he had ever seen. The glory faded; even during Philip Hardwick's lifetime the pleasure gardens were overgrown, and by the mid-19th century the site was derelict. Eventually it was bought by the people of Monmouth, and in 1902 it was presented to the National Trust as one of its earliest properties. The Round House and the Naval Temple, restored and refurbished, still remain to grace this beautiful hill. The Naval Temple, a curious structure rather like a rustic summer-house, is topped with a stepped roof, an arch and a figure of Britannia, commissioned by the National Trust and installed in 1979. A plaque on the wall commemorates its erection in 1800:

TO PERPETUATE THE NAMES OF THOSE

NOBLE ADMIRALS

WHO DISTINGUISHED THEMSELVES BY THEIR

GLORIOUS VICTORIES FOR ENGLAND

IN THE LAST AND PRESENT WARS

The names of British admirals and the dates of their famous victories are carved around the frieze, and the building was dedicated to the Duchess of Beaufort, daughter of Admiral Boscawen. It was opened to the public on 20 June 1801. The architect's name is not known for sure, but the National Library of Wales holds two unexecuted designs for the Temple by T. Fidler, dated 1798. Fidler may have been successful in his third attempt.

On the road to Abergavenny, near LLANGATTOCK NIGH USK, stands a contemporary but very different folly, Clytha Castle. Clytha, like the Naval Temple, is a memorial, but in a very different mood. The memory here is so touching, so pathetic, so genuine, and the building itself so ghostly and remote, that it goes straight for the emotional jugular. It is impossible to stand in front of Clytha and read the inscription without feeling that this, in spirit, is the Taj Mahal of Wales:

> This Building was erected in the Year 1790 by
> WILLIAM JONES of Clytha Houſe Eſq
> Fourth son of JOHN JONES
> of Lanarth Court Monmouthſhire Eſq and
> Huſband of ELIZABETH the laſt ſurviving Child
> of Sir WILLIAM MORGAN of Tredegar KB
> and Grand-Daughter of the moſt Noble WILLIAM
> Second Duke of Devonſhire
> It was undertaken for the purpose of relieving a mind
> ſincerely afflicted by the loſs of a moſt excellent Wife
> whoſe Remains were depoſited
> in Lanarth Church Yard A.D: 1787
> and to the Memory of whoſe virtues
> this Tablet is dedicated.

William Jones, like Shah Jahan, needs no more eloquent testimony to his loss and grief. As a lesser soul might find solace in spirits, so Jones found solace in stone. The building he left us is pure magic; derivative yet wildly original, it is a late fling of Strawberry Hill Gothick, to a pattern which is its own master. Built in an L-shape, it consists of three towers joined by two curtain walls. The first tower is oval and hollow, joined by the north-facing curtain wall to the square centre-block tower. This in turn is joined to the south, round tower, two-storeyed, but with only the ground floor habitable. The most remarkable feature of the building is the aptly named north curtain wall, which sweeps like a battlemented theatre curtain up to a coronated pinnacle; there is nothing else like it in folly architecture − or, for that matter, in the real world. Jones's architect was John Nash, who designed the castle in much the same mood that produced the Royal Pavilion at Brighton, Blaise Hamlet and the now-demolished Hafod. J. C. Loudon dismissed it as 'gaudy and affectedly uncommon', but time has weathered its initial assault on the landscape, and now the Landmark Trust has bought Clytha, refurbished it and lets it out for villa holidays with a difference.

At first glance PONTYPOOL may not have much to recommend it, except the international fame of its rugby club. A pilgrimage to the hallowed turf will come as a surprise to the stranger, for Pontypool Park, where terrible deeds were wrought on hapless visiting teams by the fearsome Pontypool Front Row, is one of the most beautiful sports grounds in Britain. It is sylvan, arcadian even, and the reason for this is that the pitch was laid out in the park of the Hanbury family, now a municipal garden. Yet within the ordered regimentation of a council park there exists a fantastic survival — one of the best preserved grottoes in the country, built by the Hanburys in 1836. It is kept locked, but it may be seen on application to the park-keeper.

For all its English influence, there are no more follies in Gwent, apart from one bog standard folly-tower built in 1807 with the traditional view of seven counties. This stands at KEMEYS COMMANDER, off the A449, and is now a private house, with sightseers actively discouraged. The standardisation of tower design among folly builders is a surprise one never quite comes to terms with. Towers are either wildly eccentric or stultifyingly predictable, and Kemeys falls into the latter category. Imagine a plain Perpendicular church-tower, stripped of ornament and delicacy, rectangular, with an octagonal stair turret at one corner, higher than the main tower. This is the unenterprising model for too many of our less distinguished follies, a fashion which seems to have been started by Sanderson Miller of all people, with his Edgehill Tower, now the Castle Inn at Radway.

Gwynedd

From this stunningly beautiful corner of the country comes the finest, most elaborate, imaginative and sustained piece of folly work in Great Britain — the village of PORTMEIRION. The genius of one man built it; its worldwide fame will preserve it.

To describe Sir Clough Williams-Ellis as a gentleman-architect is to convey a slightly dismissive attitude to his work. He described himself, in the title of his autobiography, as an 'architect errant', yet his power and individualism (see his works at Stowe and at Bishop's Stortford College) have not been justly celebrated, purely because he had the fortune to be able to pursue matters of greater interest to him. This imaginative, fertile man, inventive and derivative at the same time, created the greatest folly in Britain, inspired by the Italian fishing village of Portofino. It was his dream and his vision that created this extraordinary fantasy town on the little peninsula between the estuaries of the Glaslyn and the Dwyryd. The dream had been with him all his life; initially he had wanted to buy an island and express his architectural thoughts there. Unusually for a folly builder, commonsense prevailed, and when an uncle offered to sell him the Aberia peninsula he realised at once that this was the ideal site for his ideas. This part of North Wales has its own micro-climate (we have sunbathed in Portmeirion in January with the temperature nudging the 70s), and the estate when he bought it was already covered with exotic plants. With pure Welsh practicality the first thing Sir Clough did was to open the existing house as an hotel and invite influential friends to come and stay. The food, as he admitted, was terrible, but the natural beauty of the renamed Portmeirion peninsula so captivated the guests that word quickly spread and the hotel became a fashionable success.

This enabled Sir Clough to embark seriously on an un-programmed expansion, quickly building the major features of the village, such as the campanile and the dome, like an artist delineating a scene with a few brush-strokes before filling in the detail. From 1926 to the end of his long and fruitful life he added continuously to the village, his 'home for fallen buildings' as he called it. There are columns, a shell grotto (with a very low roof, the top of which doubles as the Belvedere Outlook), arches, fountains, statues, paths, the Gloriette, steps, cottages, balconies, cobbles, gateways and every other imaginable form of explorable architecture. Colour too — not content with the grey-washed Merioneth stone and slate, Sir Clough picked a Mediterranean paint pot and poured its rainbow colours over the village. S. J. Perelman summed it all up: 'It's Ruritania!' It is a jewel in a magnificent setting, a gem partly inspired by medieval Tuscan hill towns and partly by Portofino, as Sir Clough wrote: 'How should I *not* have fallen for Portofino? Indeed its image remained with me as an almost perfect example of the man-made adornment and use of an exquisite site . . . ' But Portmeirion today is so much more than Portofino today. The very random variety of the village is its own cohesiveness, whereas Portofino's undisputed beauty has been masked by its obtrusive commercialism, the overpainted face of a beauty long past her prime.

Plas Brondanw, a mile or two away in the parish of LLANFROTHEN, is the family home of the Williams-Ellises. It is over 500 years old, and the proud boast of the family is that the house has never been bought or sold. To Brondanw the young Lieutenant Clough Williams-Ellis brought his bride, Amabel Strachey, whose reaction to the wedding present given by his fellow officers is not recorded. Sir Clough recounts the incident in his autobiography with glee:

COMMANDING OFFICER: Ah! I have been asked by your brother officers of the Welsh Guards to present you with this cheque on their behalf and my own as our wedding present. I don't want you just to blue it on night-clubs or any such nonsense, but to have some lasting memento of our regard. I suggest it should take the form of a silver salver, engraved with our signatures, which would be the usual thing and in order.

LT WILLIAMS-ELLIS: Thank you very much, Sir. That would indeed be delightful. But it so happens that we already have a certain amount of family silver that just lies at the bank or stored away as we have small hope of using it. So might we perhaps choose something else?

C.O.: Why, yes, of course, but what — because I should like to know.

LT W-E.: Well, Sir, what I should really like would be a ruin.

C.O.: A . . . WHAT?

LT W-E.: A ruin — as an outlook tower. You see, Sir, there happens to be a rocky eminence close above my home on which I have always felt there should be a tower of some sort as a fitting crown and as a superb view-point commanding wonderful panoramas from the summit of Snowdon to the sea.

C.O.: Well, if you want a ruin, I suppose you had better have a ruin — though it's an odd sort of wedding present, I must say.

And that is how 'The Watchtower' at Plas Brondanw came to be built, although of course there are now locals who will swear it was put up by Owain Glyndwr.

At RHIWLAS near Bala is a mausoleum built by a horse. An unlikely story, but one that has given pleasure to generations of Bala schoolchildren, because the inscription clearly states:

> I bless the good horse Bendigo
> Who built this tomb for me.

Bendigo, of course, was a famous racehorse owned by the Thelwall Prices; his winnings paid for the mausoleum.

The only other candidate for follydom in old Merionethshire are the arches and gateways at Nannau, the ancient seat of the Vaughan family in LLANFACHRETH, above Dolgellau. At the entrance to Maes-y-Bryner, a farm on the Nannau estate, a small arch joining piers pierced either side with window-slits carries a crudely carved plaque reading:

> THIS Arch was finished
> The Day
> Good KING GEORGE IIIrd
> Died

There is a very good entrance gate to Nannau on the road from Dolgellau to Llanfachreth. Now heavily overgrown, the drive to the house used to go through it to Maes-y-Bryner, through the folly arch and thence to the main house, now a restaurant. Sir Robert Williames Vaughan (1768–1843), who ruled the surrounding countryside with benevolent autocracy for over 50 years, was a progressive estate manager who carried out many improvements to roads, buildings and farming methods. He built five carriageways radiating from Nannau like the spokes of a wheel, and put up another arch at the entrance to one of these, known locally as 'Y Garreg Fawr' (The Great Rock) because of the huge flat stone that spans the road. It is said to have been brought from Harlech, 20 miles away, and of course the reason for it being built was to give employment after the Napoleonic Wars.

In what used to be Caernarvonshire there is a particularly beautiful battlemented folly-tower at DOLBENMAEN on the Bryncir estate. It is square with chamfered corners, steps at the front and a driveway leading up to it in a curving sweep. There are six storeys, with an intact staircase most of the way up set between the outer and inner walls – which seems strange in a half-ruined building. The date, 1821, is on the keystone above the arched Gothic entrance doors. Window tracery remains in the upper three storeys. The situation, like almost everywhere in this glorious county, is very fine. The tower was built by Joseph Huddart, who 'had great schemes for converting the Bryncir demesne into a paradise in the wilderness – a gentleman's country seat worthy of the name,' and whose inheritance from his father, who had patented a new kind of rope for sailors, enabled him to put his schemes into practice. In his will, he stipulated that whoever inherited Bryncir had to build new additions to the house, but unfortunately the income from the patent rope diminished as the years passed, whereas the codicil remained, so that new wings were perpetually being built as old ones crumbled away through lack of money to maintain them. The house is now in ruins and the estate has been bought by the London Borough of Hillingdon. Sir Clough Williams-Ellis appears on the scene once more: in the mid-1930s he offered Bryncir Tower (then presumably in somewhat better repair) as a home to Bertrand Russell – but got exceedingly short shrift!

Further north, in the park of GLYNLLIFON College on the road to Caernarvon, is Williamsbourg Fort, a standard octagonal battlemented folly-tower, sides battered for the first storey, vertical for the second storey, and with an external stair turret rising one level higher — but no stairs. There is a solid floor on the second storey, but no roof; the lower room has a little fireplace, slate seats, slate windowsills, and a plaque above the door reading 'Williamsbourg Fort'. There is a little circular viewing point in front with a slate floor, rather nicely made, and a little chamber under the viewpoint has 'Magazine' inscribed above the door. A short tunnel leads from the little fort to the house. All this sounds like a pleasant if rather unexceptional folly-tower; few realise that it was our first line of defence against an anticipated French invasion in the 1770s. Sir Thomas Wynn's predilection for toy forts and private armies soon grew to unmanageable proportions. Between 1773 and 1776 he created Fort Belan and extended Fort Williamsbourg into the real thing: Belan guarded the western approaches to the Menai Straits and was even provided with a dock and all the necessary equipment for maintaining a man o'war, while the area behind the first folly was extended to make a formidable redoubt. Fort Belan cost him over £30,000 to build, and at the same time he had over 400 paid volunteers in his private regiment, the Royal Carnarvon Grenadiers. King George III, himself none too stable in matters of the mind, gratefully created him Baron Newborough in recognition of his patriotism; this achieved, and having mortgaged himself irretrievably to fund this mighty military project, Lord Newborough became deranged and decamped to Italy, where he married the 13-year-old daughter of a village constable.

Outside LLANFAIR P.G. in Anglesey, beloved of car dealers for some reason and the town with the longest name in Britain (oh, all right then — Llanfairpwllgwyngyllgogerychwyrndrobwll-llantysiliogogogoch: 'St Mary's Church in the hollow of the white hazel near to the rapid whirlpool of Llandysilio of the red cave'), is the Marquess of Anglesey's Column, erected in 1816. He was a brave soldier whose claim to immortality reposes in the response made by Wellington to his strangled cry at Waterloo: 'By God sir, I've lost me leg!' 'By God sir, so you have!' Overlooking the Menai Strait, the fluted Tuscan column is 91 feet high; inside, a spiral staircase of 115 steps climbs to the open parapet surrounding the pedestal on which stands the statue of the Marquess. The sculptor was Mathew Noble, but the statue was not raised until Rear-Admiral Lord Clarence Paget supervised the operation on 24 November 1860. The inscription on the base of the column reads:

> The Inhabitants of the counties of Anglesey and Caernarvon have erected this column in grateful commemoration of the distinguished military achievements of their countryman Henry William Marquess of Anglesey the leader of the British cavalry in Spain throughout the arduous campaign of 1807 and the second-in-command of the armies confederated against France at the memorable Battle of Waterloo on the 16th June 1815.

Waterloo was on the 18th, but never mind.

From the top of the tower one can see the Nelson Monument, almost in the water just by the Britannia Bridge, with an oblivious slogan facing out over the Menai Straits reading, 'ENGLAND EXPECTS THAT EVERY MAN WILL DO HIS DUTY'. On the plinth is a large statue of Nelson, by the aforementioned Clarence Paget, Sculptor, 1873. On the west side it says, 'FELL AT TRAFALGAR 1805'; on the east it repeats in Welsh, 'ALADDWYN YN TRAFALGAR 1805'. The letters are incused in the slate and infilled with a strange yellow stone – mauve slate with bright yellow lettering gives a pleasingly odd effect. A small entrance lobby and a metal ladder with 13 rungs lead up to a little viewing platform at the base of the statue, about 15 feet high. Admiral Paget wanted to prove that a large monument or statue could be made out of local raw materials instead of marble, so Nelson was chosen as an apt subject for the experiment.

Anglesey's only other folly has almost completely disappeared. At Bull Bay, north of AMLWCH, a sea-bathing establishment was built by a Mr Fowler at the turn of the century. It was still operating between the wars, but despite the attractions of changing-rooms and a sweeping great entrance, Mr Fowler's potential customers found they could get just as wet without paying him a fee. All that remains is part of the enclosing wall and the circular, whitewashed, cone-topped turrets at either side of the old entrance, opposite a pub.

South of LLANRWST, in a garden in the beautiful Conwy valley,

the Maenan Tower commands the most amazing position overlooking the whole of the valley and the mountains beyond. A lady
at the house said it was at least 15th-century, if not before, but it
looked a little more modern to us, perhaps Georgian. Within the
last 20 years it has been rebuilt and restored by Lady Aberconwy. It
has red brick in it — unusual for this part of the country — and a
modern (flat) roof and stairs. On the first floor there is a circular
room with elaborate cane furniture and a carpet, a round window
and four tall arched windows. A spiral staircase climbs up the
outside, while on the ground floor is a circular paved area up five
steps with a large white statue of Bacchus in the middle. Inside the
circular base area there are two carved wooden goats' heads with
little plinths on the top and also an elaborate stag's head coat rack.
'We call it "The Tower",' said the lady of the house, but nobody
knew who built it.

Powys

When the time came in the 1930s for the editor of Ward Lock's famous Red Guides to retire, having worked on the series of county guides since its inception in the late 19th century, he sent to the warehouse for the sales figures for every guide published over the 40 years he had edited them. As this was in the age before computers, the answer came back the same morning. He studied them carefully before making his farewells to the Board of Directors. Upon being asked why he had chosen to retire to Radnorshire, he answered that it was because the sales figures for that particular guide were so few that he doubted if anyone ever visited the place, so his privacy would be assured.

Radnorshire, Brecknockshire and Montgomeryshire now make up the wild, empty and beautiful new county of Powys. It is almost completely rural, the largest town being Brecon with a population of less than 8,000 – but in length it stretches the equivalent of the distance from Oxford to Derby. With over a million and a quarter acres and a population less than that of Newport in neighbouring Gwent, the average density is ten acres per person, and as may be expected this sparse population has produced virtually no follies; a few monuments are worthy of note.

Admiral Rodney's Pillar at CRIGGION in the far north of the county is a Doric column superbly sited 1,186 feet up on Briedden Hill, to commemorate Admiral Rodney's victory at Domenica in 1781. The best monument in the county is at NEW RADNOR, which was once a county borough but is now little more than a village. It is a 77-foot high Victorian fantasy, the Albert Memorial of Wales, a gabled Gothic chess-piece designed by John Gibbs who built the equally overblown Tatton Sykes monument in Humberside. It was built in 1864 to commemorate Sir George Cornewall Lewis, a gifted classical scholar who became Palmerston's first Chancellor of the Exchequer: 'cold as a fish but good humoured,' as a contemporary described him.

A modern monument to Sir Harry Llewellyn's famous horse Foxhunter stands high up on the Brecon Beacons, and apart from the Victorian clock-towers in almost every market town commemorating every royal or patriotic event, that is all there is of folly interest in Powys. At CERI there are some pretty black-and-white Gothic cottages, but they were built as dwelling places from the start and do not qualify to be included here. However, the clock-towers in this part of the country are indeed exceptionally good, the ones at KNIGHTON (1872, by the Haddon brothers) and MACHYNLLETH (1873, by Henry Kennedy) being particularly noteworthy. The Forge at Machynlleth has an appropriate horseshoe-shaped entrance arch, a concept taken up with enthusiasm by America in the early years of the motor age when every filling station seemed to be designed in the shape of an oil drum, petrol pump, doughnut or whatever — a form of architecture by association.

Gloucestershire

Gloucestershire is a richly varied county with three distinct faces — the Forest of Dean, the Vales and the Cotswolds. Each has its own charm, but the Cotswolds probably offer the most quintessentially English picture to the visitor. The astonishing Cotswold stone has much to do with this; it is the colour of baking bread and, just as everyone loves the smell of baking bread, so everyone loves the sight of Cotswold stone. The colour is surprisingly varied, from the grey-white of the south to the ochre of the north, caused by the presence of iron ores in the oolitic limestone. The abundance of wood in Gloucestershire meant that the stone was scarcely used as a building material until Tudor times, and so we find surprisingly few Gloucestershire follies taking advantage of its natural warmth.

The Vale of Berkeley and the Vale of Gloucester are the central low-lying lands bordering the mouth of the Severn, Britain's longest river. The soil is fertile and suitable for growing towns and motorways. The Forest of Dean is a place apart, beautiful countryside dotted with ugly little towns and peopled by small, round-faced folk with fuzzy hair — one might guess at hobbits. The other inhabitants of Gloucestershire look on the Foresters with a mixture of awe and contempt; the area is the butt of local jokes of the Irish, Polack or Gotham variety.

The Wye Valley, which separates Wales from the Forest of Dean, is beautiful. Across the river from Chepstow and its great grand castle is TUTSHILL, with the ruined shell of a rubble look-out tower on top of the hill overlooking the castle and river. It is listed only Grade III because no one knows what it was, whether it was used as

60   The towers at Rotherfield Park, East Tisted

61   Water-tower, Littlestone-on-Sea

62   Heaven's Gate, Highclere

63   The Nore Folly, Slindon

64   Ionick clashes with Gothick at the schizophrenic Rat's Castle,
Castle Goring

a prospect tower or for military purposes. 'Tut', as in Tutshill, means watch-tower in the local dialect, so the owner argues that it must have had a military significance — but there is a fireplace, and would the builder have been that concerned about the comfort of a mere sentry?

Along the road to Parson's Allotment in Tidenham Chase a tall standing stone has been raised to commemorate Queen Victoria's Jubilee (the citizens of the county are punctilious in observing royal jubilees), but the Forest of Dean's most unexpected pleasure is to be found in the town of COLEFORD, dominated by a big Beecham's factory to the south. Coleford is neither particularly beautiful nor ancient, the oldest house being 17th-century, but in Newland Street is a 19th-century Gothic sham castle like a pink fairy armadillo, now a dentist's surgery called 'The Rock House'. It has no certain provenance, but speculation leads us to guess that the architect might have been the Rev. Henry Poole, Vicar of Coleford from 1818. He was passionately fond of building, and designed churches at Coleford, Parkend, Bream and Berry Hill.

At RUARDEAN the Bishop's Wood valley is bisected by the Hereford/Gloucestershire border, and forestry roads, wide and red, further divide the valley. Here and there are echoes of a grander past — a South Lodge on the main road with a coat of arms, the remains of what might have been an ice-house, two overgrown lakes — but the memory of what used to be has been excised from local minds, all except for The Oldest Inhabitant: 'Yes, there used to be a big house here, but it must have been demolished oh, over 80 years ago — before I was born!' It was owned by Sir George Bellew, whose crest with three bees was on the lodge wall, and previously by a Major Macalman, who achieved much success with a racehorse named Isinglass. In fact the house here was built for John Partridge by Sir Jeffry Wyatville in 1820, in the Gothic style, and burnt down in 1873. The most tangible relic is, amazingly, a splendidly preserved folly-tower, perhaps somewhat pedestrian in its architecture, certainly a copy of previous, more innovative designers' work and thus dated to the late 18th century — it must have been built before Wyatville's house. The standard folly-tower pattern — octagonal, battlemented, with a taller stair turret — has been converted into a house, with modern windows, and an extension, hesitantly castellated to blend in when seen from the Ruardean road, added at the back.

The *Companion Guide to the Shakespeare Country* describes DRYBROOK as 'probably the most consistently horrible village in the Forest'. The Euroclydon Hotel, somewhat uncommercially named after a cold, vindictive east wind, is a residential hotel for elderly people, built on a hill above the town. It is a large black and white building, unremarkable except for a five-storey square tower erupting from the south side, adorned with a wrought-iron balcony looking north over the roof of the house. A mine-owner, J. B. Brain, built it in 1876, in order to keep a watchful eye on his workers, so the story goes; now it is used as a loft for the hotel owner's doves.

Away from the Forest of Dean and on to the Vale of Berkeley, and we could be entering a different country. The scenery is uninspiring, but the villages are prettier. Frampton Court in FRAMPTON ON SEVERN boasts the finest garden pavilion in Gloucestershire, and one of the finest in Britain: the Orangery. It· is a stunning, virtuoso display of Gothick by the Bristol architect William Halfpenny – two two-storey octagons linked by an entrance bay, an octagon on top, everything castellated and pinnacled, every façade lit by a beautiful, ogee-framed, honeycomb-paned window, and a cupola to crown it all – but the windows are its chief glory. It stands at the end of an ornamental canal in the grounds of the big house of the Cliffords and is, according to the local publican, often let to visiting Americans.

In the grounds of BERKELEY CASTLE is Park Lodge, which contains the stables, kennels and estate offices, and which was violently fortified with black and white stone in the early 19th century, so that it cannot be missed from the house. It is a nine-bay building, with a central arch crowned with castellations. There is a castellated cottage on the B4066 coming in to Berkeley, and in the village is the root hut called the Temple of Vaccus, where Edward Jenner carried out the first vaccinations against smallpox. It is said to have been designed by Thomas Wright.

Gloucestershire's tallest tower monument is S. S. Teulon's Tyndale Monument, 111 feet high on Nibley Knoll above NORTH NIBLEY and visible for miles around. With the excuse, as good as any, that William Tyndale had been born in North Nibley 382 years before, and the existence of a perfect site for a tower, clearly visible from Lord Ducie's new estate in Tortworth, it was opened by Lord Ducie on 6 November 1866, a tall, tapering belvedere tower with a pyramidal roof:

IN GRATEFUL REMEMBRANCE OF
WILLIAM TYNDALE
TRANSLATOR OF THE ENGLISH BIBLE
WHO FIRST CAUSED THE NEW TESTAMENT
TO BE PRINTED IN THE MOTHER TONGUE
OF HIS COUNTRYMEN
BORN NEAR THIS SPOT HE SUFFERED
MARTYRDOM AT VILVORDE IN
FLANDERS ON OCT 6TH 1536.

Also in attendance on that inaugural day was the vicar of North Nibley, the Rev. David Edwards, whom we shall come across again in Stancombe Park. Biographical information in the 16th century being what it is, there is a strong suspicion that the William Tyndale of North Nibley was not the same as the William Tyndale 'born on the borders of Wales' who translated the Bible, in which case the monument is pure folly. This is one of those rare towers that can be climbed – the key can be obtained from a house in the village, and the address is given on a notice-board at the beginning of the path to the tower. To help spot distant landmarks, there is a topograph near the tower, erected to commemorate Queen Elizabeth's 1977 Jubilee.

STANCOMBE PARK in Stinchcombe is just north of North Nibley. Too recent to be a legend, the story of the Vicar's Secret Garden smacks of rumour and the Sunday papers. In the mid-19th century Miss Purnell, who owned Stancombe Park, married the Rev. David Edwards, vicar of North Nibley. He set about building a romantic garden far from the house where, so the local story goes, he could have assignations with the gypsy woman who was his one true love without being observed. It is difficult to see how he could have managed this, as the garden would have been constantly filled with workmen building paths, cascades, grottoes, temples, water-works and all the other impedimenta deemed essential to the creation of a mood. However, the mood he eventually achieved was romantic in the extreme; any gypsy with fire in her blood would have capitulated immediately. The house is a jewel. It looks earlier than 1840 but is actually later: the 1840 house was burnt down and mostly rebuilt in 1880. The site is magnificent, at the head of one of the most beautiful naturally landscaped valleys in England. An iron-fenced path winds gently downhill below the immaculate main garden, looking high and over the valley to the Tyndale Monument, and down to a small lake in the valley with an island reached by a Chinese bridge. As the path gives way to steps, so the mood changes from serenity to mystery; we are aware of the sound of rushing water, the air becomes humid, the atmosphere torrid — even in March! Massive replanting is going on; the owners are justifiably proud of their remarkable garden. Suddenly the path becomes paths — there are stone flagged paths everywhere, a multiple-choice garden. The main one goes into a tunnel under the old drive, emerges briefly into the light giving enough time for a huge white stone dog to startle visitors, then plunges into blackness again, a seeming cul-de-sac but for a pinpoint light at the end. The light looks out over the lake, and here the path divides, the left leading round under a pergola-covered lakeside walk, the right to another underground junction, where a straight path leads to what is the most memorable part of the garden, a small square court with a plain urn in the centre and a doorway on each side, one a whalebone arch, one a Cretan doorway with curved lintel, and the third an extraordinary affair like a keyhole or an Egyptian ankh — straight out of *The Story of the Amulet*. The sense of mystery is dispelled only by the traffic on the B4060 right behind the hedge — we are a long way here from the house. The flawless hedges flank a narrow path leading from the keyhole gateway round the foot of the lake and past a massive whale's skull to the Temple, a small golden-stoned Tuscan eyecatcher/summer-house ignorant of the punctiliousness of true classical architecture but freely using its motifs to make a warm and welcoming building. At the end of the Temple walk are two little leaded glass summer-houses, like Tweedledum and Tweedledee, guarding the corner.

Could this all have been built by a love-lorn vicar? The folly garden may be remote and invisible from the house, but it is right next to the main road and is flanked by servants' cottages; moreover, the old main drive to the house runs right over the garden and is used as a landscape feature. The present owner's theory is that the garden predated the Rev. Mr Edwards, and was built by persons unknown in about 1820, who learnt the motifs from soldiers who had served in the Egyptian campaigns in the Napoleonic Wars. Stancombe is one of the most satisfying gardens in the country and, although private, it is often open to the public in the summer months. Don't miss it.

There is a sprinkling of interesting follies around STROUD, in itself another disappointing Gloucestershire town. The site at the junction of two valleys is ideal, but as all too often in England it has been spoilt by unprepossessing commercial and speculative building. Directly above the town to the south is Rodborough Fort, a massive sham castle on the scale of Bladon Castle in Derbyshire, on the edge of Rodborough Common. It was built in 1761 as an eyecatcher by Captain Hawker, and rebuilt as a house in 1870, a typical folly of pedestrian imagination: square towers with heavy battlements, a taller stair turret, cross arrowslits, big, noticeable but somehow oddly unsatisfying. Rodborough Fort changed hands twice in the 1980s and in 1985 was for sale with nine acres for £250,000.

Rodborough, Amberley, Inchbrook and Nailsworth are all strung along the valley and hillside south from Stroud like a conpagation. The AMBERLEY Eyecatcher, a house called 'The Gateways' in St Chloe, was built by the wonderfully named Sir George Onesipherous Paul, who died in 1820, as an eyecatcher to Rodborough Manor, which burnt down in 1906. Two round towers with Gothic windows are joined by a battlemented arch, now filled in. The architect was probably Anthony Teck, although the whole structure looks Sanderson Millerish. The best view of it comes from the A46 below, but it is difficult to see on a sunny morning as it hides against the hillside.

Woodchester Park Tower, in the Inchbrook valley, is all that was built of a huge mansion planned for William Leigh in 1846. It would seem that if ever a house deserved to be called a folly, this one does — but we have not been able to get into the park to see it. Leigh demolished Spring Park, Lord Ducie's house, where Thomas

Cubitt and Anthony Salvin had been working only six years previously, on A. W. N. Pugin's advice, but jibbed at paying the price Pugin proposed for the new house. He therefore employed Benjamin Bucknall, a local man, and for 15 years the house slowly took shape. The reason for the leisurely speed of building is unclear, but it would appear to be linked with Mr Leigh's parsimony. A datestone on the tower reads 1858; shortly after that time work stopped, and the mansion was never finished. It is magnificently built, in the style of Viollet-le-Duc, using solid stone throughout, even for baths and drainpipes. A garden temple from the 1730s was moved to Bodnant in Gwynedd in 1938.

North of Stroud is PAINSWICK, a sleek, wealthy little town. The M5 has taken much of the holiday traffic away, but the A46 running through the town remains a busy road. Painswick House is to the north-west; built in the 1730s, it was originally called Buenos Ayres. Bishop Pococke visited in 1757:

> Mr Hyett built an house of hewn stone, in a fine situation, and made a very pretty garden; before it is a court with statues and sphynxes, and beyond that a lawn for the grand entrance; the garden is on an hanging ground from the house in the vale, and on a rising ground on the other side and at the end; all are cut into walks through wood and adorn'd with water and buildings.

Some of the buildings still remain. There is a classical seat with rustificated columns, a rather uninspired Gothic alcove with proof that hooliganism is hereditary — graffiti read 'B. Perrott 1952' and, elsewhere, 'Gary Perrott 1973' — a rustic alcove by a bathing pool, and two pavilions, the Red House and the Eagle House. The garden, which became derelict after the war and is now undergoing extensive replanting and refurbishment, is convincingly attributed to Thomas Robins, who also built a castellated stable-barn with quatrefoil and diocletian windows out of the beautiful honey-coloured Cotswold stone (which he then painted red) on the other side of the Painswick valley. No longer red, it now stands opposite Greenhouse Court, but it was originally the stable to Pan's Lodge, a vanished pleasure-house of Hyett's.

At nearby BISLEY there is an 18th-century gazebo at Over Court, and in the grounds of Nether Lypiatt Manor is a small obelisk in the woods to the memory of a horse which died in 1721:

> My name is Wag, who rolled the green
> The oldest horse that ever was seen,
> My age it numbered forty-two
> I served my Master just and true.

The plaque is a replacement engraved on metal in 1938; the graffiti on the obelisk are old and extensive – '1802 W. HUXFORD, G. L. WYATT 1828' – they carved rather than scratched in those days. The manor house itself is exquisite; the quintessential small English country house, utterly desirable, perfectly proportioned and of a manageable size. It was built in 1702–5 by an unknown architect.

Still in the Stroud area, along the road to Cirencester, is a house called 'The Grove' in CHALFORD. In the steep, terraced grounds are a grotto and a summer-house with three mighty ogees under a curved pediment, and in the garden of Wickham Grange is an early 19th-century gazebo. The Golden Valley of the Frome is aptly named in Chalford's case: the autumnal trees in the valley make a display worthy of New England, and the golden stone reflects what people have to pay to live in this village of steep hills and steep prices.

All roads lead to CIRENCESTER, the ancient Roman capital of Corinium. The park laid out by the Earl of Bathurst stretches from the middle of town for five miles into the countryside. The house itself acts as the straight arc of a huge yew-circle hedge, as tall as the house, a device repeated by the Ten Rides rond-point in Oakley Wood. Lord Bathurst was the patron of Alexander Pope, and Pope's influence is everywhere. He helped Bathurst plan, plant and develop the park with an almost proprietorial enthusiasm, even going so far as to call it 'my bower'. What interests us most here is Alfred's Hall, the first 'romantick' folly in England. Originally built in 1721, it was enlarged in 1732 with pieces taken from Sapperton Manor. It is big, and the interior is wainscoted, with a large carved chimneypiece; sadly, part of the folly has recently collapsed and this sham ruin, which has lasted over 260 years, is now in danger of becoming a real one. So successful was the then unique asymmetric design that a contemporary antiquarian is said to have mistaken the 12-year-old building as dating from King Arthur's time. Despite the recent collapse, it was carefully made, unlike many of its successors; Bathurst, who lived to be 91, was determined to build to last. Consequently, virtually every embellishment he made to the park survives today, despite the open access granted to the townspeople. The Hexagon is exactly what it says: three heavily rusticated open arches and three blind arches, set on a plinth; Pope's Seat is a little rusticated arch with seats in niches either side of a pedimented gateway; the Round House and the Square House are both cottages with castellated towers added; Ivy Lodge was an eyecatcher folly converted into a house with a square central tower and crow's-foot gables at either end of the screen walls — one is merely a façade, decorated with sham windows. The Horse Guards are two Ionic alcoves three-quarters of a mile before the Ten Rides rond-point, and the final Bathurst buildings are Queen Anne's Column, built in 1741 with a statue of Queen Anne on the top, and an obelisk on the edge of the Bull Ring. A word of warning to people who stroll up to the park gates in Cirencester: it will take you two and a half hours' brisk walking to get to Alfred's Hall and back. We know from bitter experience.

BARNSLEY PARK is off the A433 out of Cirencester; the house was built from 1720 by an unknown architect who did a magnificent job, giving us one of the most beautiful houses in the county — but there are no follies, only the name Pepper Pot which led us here in hope, and which turned out to be an octagonal lodge by Nash. Barnsley House, however, the old rectory built for the same Bourchier family that owned the Park, has two delightful garden buildings, an elegant Gothick alcove and a Doric Temple, built in 1787 and removed from Fairford Park in 1962. The garden is open to the public on Wednesdays and Sundays in summer. It is difficult to pin down what makes the village of Barnsley so satisfying, until the total absence of overhead wires, telephone cable and street furniture is pointed out. All necessary services are buried underground or hidden behind houses, an example we wish could be followed everywhere.

Just south of Cirencester are the villages of Coates and Siddington. The Round House at SIDDINGTON is castellated and looks like a converted 18th-century windmill, although the occupier swears it never was but instead was built by a Dutchman. Why that should serve as an explanation we can't imagine. The Thames Head Stone at COATES was a statue of Neptune which sat in a meadow to mark the source of the Thames. It was put there by the Thames Water Authority in 1958 and removed 15 years later because of vandalism. Nowadays there is nothing to see, not even in the 'Thames Head' pub nearby.

Gloucestershire has a number of inscriptionless columns which commemorate some forgotten event or person. At FAIRFORD PARK a comprehensive school stands on the site of the 17th-century mansion, demolished in the 1950s. An elegant but short 18th-century column, perhaps by Sir John Soane, who carried out some alterations to the house in 1789, stands in a field to the north. STAUNTON on the Worcestershire border has some Ionic columns set up in a garden on the B4208, and below SELSEY, south-west of Stroud, is an Ionic column on a plinth standing anonymously in a field under the fantastic Stanley Park.

LOWER SWELL, near Stow-on-the-Wold, was another village with aspirations to become a spa, after a chalybeate spring was discovered. A cottage at the east end was built in 1807 as the Spa Cottage; it is probably surprisingly large inside, but from the outside the central section is tiny. As in a child's drawing of a house, the front door is in the middle with a window either side, and two more windows on the next floor. The door is surmounted by a solid stone-carved canopy, and the windows with their large diamond-patterned paning have Gothick ogee surrounds. The parapet frieze is ornately carved, and the dormer windows have concave gables, giving the cottage an oriental flavour. The double windows in the side extensions have attractive shell fanlights; the only thing against this charming cottage is that it stands right by the main road. It is supposed that the materials used in its construction were overs from Sezincote.

Was Samuel Cockerell the architect here as well as at SEZINCOTE? Sezincote must be recognised as his masterpiece; built for his brother Sir Charles Cockerell in 1805 in the 'Hindoo' style, it still impresses today because it comes as such a surprise, rather like a Cotswold Brighton Pavilion. In ruins, it would unhesitatingly be described as a folly; as a sturdy, well cared-for and very private country house it can only be described as an eccentricity.

Lord Redesdale found fame through his garden. A man as talented as he could have reached the top in any of his chosen fields, but it is for his arboretum and his Japanese gardens that he will best be remembered. As a diplomat he spent four years in Japan, coming away with an admiration for the country which he had a chance to put into reality when a cousin died, leaving him his estate and his fortune. The garden at BATSFORD PARK, near Moreton-in-Marsh, reflects Redesdale's enthusiasm for trees and for Japan, with scattered Buddhas and a pretty red and white tea-house temple, set on a knoll in the arboretum.

Going up to the far north of the county, a modern folly has been built outside CHIPPING CAMPDEN: in the 1960s Sir Gordon Russell built a small-scale sham castle at Kingcomb in the garden designed by Geoffrey Jellicoe. Back in the 18th century: on Lidcombe Hill above STANWAY stands a pyramid built by Robert Tracy in 1750 to commemorate his father. The beautiful Tudor manor house of the Tracys sits peacefully in the valley, guarded by its remarkable gatehouse, but the pyramid is even more remarkable, probably the largest in the British Isles, 60 feet high and standing on an open arched base, forming the centrepiece of the cascades and water gardens which tumbled down the hill. The high-level canal no longer exists; as the owner of Stancombe Park remarked, playing around with waterworks is the quickest way to go bankrupt.

WINCHCOMBE, on the road to Cheltenham, was once the county town of the long forgotten Winchcombshire; then it was the second most important town in Gloucestershire; then it became the centre of Britain's tobacco plantations. A remarkable history lies behind this little town, now with a population of only 4,000. Bleby House in Abbey Terrace has a small, early 18th-century grotto in the garden sloping down to the Isbourne, one of the few grottoes which may have been inspired by religious rather than fashionable sentiments, since Winchcombe was the shrine of St Kenelm, and the grotto is said to have been built on the spot where he died.

There is a fine Gothick house on Cleeve Hill as we come into Cheltenham, but there is nothing grand now left to see in Gloucestershire. The Grotto Tea Gardens at PRESTBURY a mile along the road were the height of fashion in the late 18th and early 19th centuries, but towards the mid-19th century they acquired a liquor licence and quickly became disreputable and licentious. Local opinion put a stop to these activities when the Grotto was demolished in the 1860s. Not completely though – a diligent search in the undergrowth can reveal a five-foot plinth for a lamp, the sad remnant of forgotten fun.

Hereford and Worcester

These two counties do not merge naturally. They have distinct identities and separate interests, yet in the name of bureaucracy they have been forced reluctantly together in an arranged marriage, in an attempt at an artificial homogeneity of beef and apples. Still, the new county does have a remarkable variety of follies, and it needs only a good 18th-century grotto to make this a microcosm of folly types from the earliest times to the present.

Worcestershire is bisected by the M5; Herefordshire is innocent of motorways. Communication between the two halves does not follow any logical or historical pattern, so it will be simplest to discuss the county's follies according to type, and let the traveller make up his own mind in which order he can best see them.

We start with towers, and with the one that started this book. BROADWAY Tower is right on the Gloucestershire border, on top of Broadway Hill at a height of exactly 1,000 feet, which to British schoolchildren of the 1950s made it a mountain. In 1952 the Headley family visited it, and the photograph shows Richard, Joanna and Shân Headley walking away having seen the old tower, leaving five-year-old Gwyn absolutely captivated by this extraordinary building which didn't seem to do anything or to be used for anything. Buildings were where people lived or worked or worshipped, and Broadway Tower wasn't any of those. It was very confusing for a five-year-old, and parents explaining that the building was called a folly and didn't have any purpose other than to look pretty was no sort of an explanation, especially when it was so honestly ugly. This brief digression explains how one of us at least got swept up into folly mania at an early age; from then on car trips always had to have a 'folly hunt' included, or there was hell to pay. The tower itself was finished in 1800 by the Earl of Coventry of Croome Court, of which more later. The story behind the tower is a mixture of sense and showmanship: when Broadway Hill was first proposed as a site for a tower to be seen from Croome Court, which is 15 miles away as the crow flies, the Countess of Coventry suggested that a beacon be lit on the hill to ensure it could indeed be seen from Croome. When this had been done to her satisfaction, she called on all the local gentry to ensure the beacon could also be seen from their estates!

BREDON HILL, the same height as Broadway, is much nearer Croome, and this lends a touch of authenticity to the story of the Countess's night-time dash around her neighbours, for it is just as suitable a site for a folly-tower as Broadway. But perhaps Mr Parson of Kemerton Court had beaten the Coventrys to it, for his little square tower built inside a 2,000-year-old hill fort also dates from the late 18th century, and could even have influenced the building of Broadway, which outshines it in every respect. Worcestershire's most bizarre folly-tower, however, is surely the clock-tower at ABBERLEY, an extraordinary piece of Scottish Baronial architecture set among the apple orchards, completely out of proportion and an eyecatcher for miles around. The top of the tower takes up half its height, if that makes sense (the building doesn't make any sense, so why should we?), which means that instead of bursting out into over-florid decoration and then stopping once the object has been reached, as clock-towers are expected to do, this pinnacled pike carries on for the same height again, sprouting gargoyles, turrets, and tiny lucarnes. Because of this imbalance the tower looks gigantic when seen from the road; the mind assumes that such a mighty head must be carried by an equally massive body, and expects at least 150 feet of tower trunk underneath. It comes as quite a shock to see how small it actually is. The foundation stone was laid on 4 May 1883 by John Joseph Jones and his wife Sarah Amelia (Amy). It was designed by J. P. St Aubyn, a Victorian church architect, and built as a bell-tower in memory of Jones's father. On the entrance front above an oriel window and just below a clock-face is a sundial — a good example of Victorian belt and braces. There is a much less impressive clock-tower in WHITCHURCH, to the memory of John Leech and his sisters: square, red-brick, with a pyramidal roof and an inscription, 'REDEEM THE TIME'. An unheeded warning?

Sleepy ROUS LENCH, dozing with its brother villages Ab, Atch, Church and Sheriff's in the south midland sun, has nodded off again after the shock of having Dr W. K. W. Chafy as its squarson for 40 years round the turn of the century. He built the village school, an extraordinary multi-coloured Victorian brick building banded like an armadillo; two remarkable half-timbered postboxes with steeply pitched tiled roofs, one in Rous and the other in Radford, a mile away (both the size of bus-shelters); and a beautiful Italianate 60-foot red-brick tower, heavily machicolated, at the top of his topiary garden, with two white ceramic plaques on the first floor — Dr Chafy and his son?

Herefordshire has one of the loveliest eyecatchers in the country at SHOBDON, a spidery edifice standing at the end of a long, wide grass walk up the hill. Unusually for an eyecatcher, it is three-dimensional, with the two side arches set back from the central arch and joined to it by curtain walls with doorways. The columns and arches are decorated with cable mouldings and chevrons, remarkably ornate for mid-18th-century folly work, and also extremely weathered. The tympana above the side doorways are barely discernible through weathering, suggesting a date much earlier than 1752, when it was set up — and indeed the whole structure is a picturesque re-erection of pieces of the original Norman church at Shobdon, which was demolished by Lord Bateman when he built the existing church. This may be regarded as 18th-century vandalism — the only Norman church in Britain comparable to Shobdon was Kilpeck, south-west of Hereford — but he replaced it with a unique creation, a Gothick-rococo symphony in pale blue and white. The architect is unknown, although it is attributed to Richard Bentley, a member of Walpole's 'Committee of Taste'.

Two great gardens in Worcestershire overshadow anything else in the county, CROOME D'ABITOT and HAGLEY PARK. Both are linked by the dilettante genius of Sanderson Miller. Croome Court is credited to 'Capability' Brown, who was not renowned as an architect, but it appears Brown followed Miller's sketches: in 1752 the Earl of Coventry wrote to Miller, 'it will be ungrateful not to acknowledge you the primary Author'. Miller designed the house at Hagley, in similar four-square vein, for Lord Lyttelton in 1754, but earlier he had produced his masterpiece in sham ruins, the Ruinated Castle at Hagley. This was the very one that prompted Walpole to write his famous comment, 'There is a ruined castle built by Miller that would get him his freedom even of Strawberry; it has the true rust of the Baron's Wars' — a generous compliment seeing that Walpole had proposed that George Lyttelton should use John Chute, the architect of Strawberry Hill. Lyttelton wrote in his accounts book, 'In the year 1747 I built the Castle and also the Cottage. In 1748 I built the Rotundo and in 1749 the half octogon seat and made the "Haha" over against it. Mr Miller, architect of the Castle. Mr John Pitt of the Rotundo and Octogon. Sir Thomas Lyttelton paid William Hitchcox for Building the Rotundo in Hagley Park the sum of £151.' William Hitchcox was, of course, Miller's action man, the one who executed his schemes. John Pitt was the gentleman-architect who designed his own house at Encombe in Dorset, including the famous Rock Arch.

Hagley seems to have been a breeding ground for new talent. After Miller's successful sham castle it seemed every estate in the country had to have one, and Lyttelton followed it up in 1758 with an even more influential building, the Temple of Theseus. He wrote to Mrs Montagu that James Stuart was 'going to embellish one of the Hills with a true Attick building, a Portico of six Pillars, which will make a fine object to my new house, and command a most beautiful view of the country'. This Doric hexastyle temple was the first work by 'Athenian' Stuart after his return from Greece with Nicholas Revett, and is the first Greek Revival building in Britain. As such, its importance is undeniable, and it is interesting to speculate on how many architectural styles or revivals first saw the light of day as follies or garden buildings. In spite of Lyttelton's enthusiasms, both parties seem to have regarded the building as something of an experiment, as Stuart's payment for the design was only £20. The estate also has a thin obelisk and a rather amusing statue of Frederick, Prince of Wales, dressed as a Roman Emperor, perched on top of a tall, thin column. As it was a gift from the Prince, a friend of Lyttelton's, its erection was inevitable.

Surprisingly, with Sanderson Miller and 'Capability' Brown on hand, Croome Court's garden buildings were largely the work of Robert Adam. The house was sold by the Coventrys in 1948, became a Catholic school, then was bought by the Hare Krishna sect who in 1985 put it up for sale at £750,000. Most of the follies had been sadly neglected, but the Krishnas undertook a careful maintenance programme, and looked after them well. The round-domed Panorama Tower, built by Adam in 1766, still has the eyecatching effect originally intended. It looks like a professional version of Clavel's Tower at Kimmeridge in Dorset. Adam was also responsible for the temple near the church, similar to Stuart's at Hagley. Corinthian columns were used for the summer-house by the lake, and another rotunda, open this time, has a dome coffered on the interior. There is also a dry bridge, a grotto, a park seat with Tuscan columns and a Gothick ruin on the other side of the motorway. Many of the buildings, including Sanderson Miller's tremendous eyecatcher at DEFFORD, Dunstall Castle, can be seen from the M5, which cuts through Brown's carefully landscaped park. Dunstall is Miller out of El Greco, two tall, thin, round towers joined by an impossibly elongated archway – no rust here, simply decay.

Miller is also said to have influenced the design of the Gothic gateway at Croft Castle, a National Trust property near MORTIMER'S CROSS in Herefordshire, but to our eyes it looks too clean and finished. CLENT GROVE, near Hagley, also has a sham ruin attributed to Miller, a two-towered real ruin now, in the grounds of a children's home, but nothing is really known of it and it seems unlikely that he would consent to copying his favourite formula so close to one of his major patron's estates.

No other estate in the county can compare follywise with Hagley and Croome. The most impressive ruin in the county, however, is undoubtedly Witley Court at GREAT WITLEY. The gigantic house was partly burnt down in 1937, but since then has been allowed to decay until all that remains is a shell. The church, a magnificent example of English rococo, remains intact, but what concerns us here are the astonishing fountains by the Scottish brothers James and William Forsyth. Inspired by Bernini's fountains in Rome, they outclass them in size and silence. Facing the east front is the Flora Fountain, an impressive enough work, but the Perseus

Fountain on the south side is truly staggering. The sculpture is said to be the largest in the British Isles, and one can well believe it. It rises 26 feet above the long-vanished water level, and when it was playing the thunder of its waters could be heard all over the estate. Underneath is a high-domed chamber big enough to hold 50 people, reached by a tunnel running the whole length of the grounds from the house, off which other tunnels, containing the pipes and pressure-boxes, run. Will these fountains ever play again? The last garden to be seen is at SPETCHLEY PARK, just outside Worcester, a haven for horticulturists, with a well-stocked garden centre and the sweetest smelling jasmine we have ever encountered. Just across a little canal from a lawn of rare fritillaries is a little summer-house built of bark and boles, knotted roots and chevroned twigs. It exudes peace, but the garden separates the M5 and the Birmingham–Bristol railway, so the buzz of traffic drowns the hum of bees.

Two and a half miles north-east of LEDBURY is the site of Hope End. It was demolished in 1867 and its Victorian successor was burnt down in 1911, but the stables to the first house still remain – and what stables! If it weren't for the utter Englishness of the surrounding countryside, one would imagine one had stumbled on the crumbling *fata Morgana* of an Emir's palace. Hope End was built in 1810–15 by the landscape gardener and publicist J. C. Loudon for Edward Moulton-Barrett, who declared, 'if I thought that there was another such [house] in England I would pull it down'. There wasn't. Of course Brighton Pavilion and Sezincote were being planned or built at the same time, but although Hope End was in the same Indo-Mooresque style, and much smaller, its stark individuality ('coarsely designed,' thought Colvin) set it apart from the others. Elizabeth Barrett Browning remembered her childhood home as 'crowded with minarets & domes, & crowned with metal spires & crescents, to the provocation (as people used to observe) of every lightening of heaven'. The stable block itself, now converted into a house, is common enough, except for the tall oriental columns on the corners, but the gateway-cum-clocktower looks thoroughly Moorish, even if the four pinnacles surrounding its dome have gone, as well as the clock and bell, which now find themselves in Jamaica. The nine-year-old Elizabeth wrote a poem about the clock. The stableyard wall has seven squat columns, also oriental in design, and near the stable block is a minaret topped with a crescent, very much like the one in Knutsford, Cheshire.

There are as many, if not more, rock hermitages in this county as there are in Derbyshire, although here they all seem to have been used as everyday living quarters at some stage in their histories. Astley, Downton, Southstone, Stourport and Wolverley all have troglodyte dwellings; the façade of Redstone Rock at STOURPORT mimics Petra in having a Borromini-like recess with two columns at what would be the first-floor level above the entrance — carved, or through natural erosion? The Rock Hermitage at DOWNTON is in the grounds of Richard Payne Knight's Downton Castle, and as the path to it leads through a suitably creepy tunnel and hugs the cliff-side above the picturesque river, it is a reasonable assumption that nature was aided here, perhaps with the ultimate but unfulfilled intention of creating a grotto. Payne Knight's library was built as a detached tower, almost a folly in itself.

The only outbreak of chinoiserie in the county seemed to be a peculiar little sheet-metal pagoda in front of the failed spa at TENBURY WELLS, but this has now lost its covering and stands naked with an octagonal brick base and traditional English joinery above to support the tiny water-tanks and the metal cladding. But in 1975 a Chinese Kiosk was built in ROSS-ON-WYE to join the Gothic bits and pieces left by John Kyrle, the 'Man of Ross', who died in 1724 and is still remembered as the town's great benefactor. This brings us to two final 20th-century follies in Hereford and Worcester: at DINMORE MANOR, Richard Hollins Murray built what must surely be the first grotto to use chicken-wire for its basic structure. Mr Murray invented the cat's-eye road stud in 1924, and bought Dinmore Manor, once the Commandery of the Knights Hospitaller of St John of Jerusalem, in 1927. Conscious of the religious history of the foundation he had acquired, Murray started to build cloisters and added stained-glass liberally throughout. An octagonal court was built at the junction of the two cloisters, and, as he wrote:

From this court on the western side is a room with a large Gothic-shaped window which has been glazed with coloured glass depicting an Eastern landscape, the horizon on the window having been measured to coincide with the true horizon beyond. A grotto effect has been reproduced, the roof being formed with concrete pressed through stout fine mesh wirework and coloured with various earth colours. Two small pools are within, and the effect of the reflection of the window on the lower pool is very pleasing.

The final folly is actually called 'The Folly', and was built at Gatley Park, near LEINTHALL EARLS, in 1964. The architect was Raymond Erith, who deliberately harked back to 18th-century models to build this very odd house. It is circular, three-storeyed, with a domed roof and central chimneypot. Arched ground-floor windows are flanked by low wings looking more like buttresses, the whole making a decidedly unusual effect, like an old-fashioned beehive or a jelly mould.

Shropshire

Shropshire is a large, sparsely populated and rather beautiful county which has remained surprisingly unspoilt. A wealth of half-timbered building, lovely scenery which presages the savage grandeur of Wales and an almost entirely rural aspect make it difficult to realise that this was the first industrial area in the world. Shrewsbury, with a population of only 60,000, was by far the largest town in the county until recently, when they welded Wellington, Oakengates, Dawley and some other townships together to create the inchoate but well-named Telford. The climate for follies in Shropshire must have been as appropriate as a damp warm cellar is for mushrooms − good countryside with rolling hills, lots of money coming in at the prime time for folly-building − so it's surprising that there aren't more. However, what there is is varied, perhaps more so than anywhere else in the country, and the follies are generally of a high standard, even if their preservation leaves almost everything to be desired. Unlike many other counties, Shropshire did not stop thinking as soon as someone came up with the idea of an obelisk.

Easily the most coherent group of follies in the county exists at Hawkstone Park; it is also one of the best preserved British parks in the sublime picturesque vein. The sum total of atmosphere, follies and landscape provides an unforgettable experience. The best approach would be to take the road leading from Hodnet to Weston. Just before leaving the A442 there is a splendid view on the left of the ruinated columns in the gardens of HODNET HALL. They were acquired from the demolished Apsley House and were put up as recently as 1970, a good piece of neo-classicism before plunging into HAWKSTONE PARK.

A couple of hundred yards from the village of Weston there is a building looking like a fortress, trefoil-shaped, with a terrace in front which may be used for installing batteries of cannon. Of course, it's all just for fun. 'The Citadel' was built somewhere between 1780 and 1800, with additions in 1825, and was used to house the steward of the Hill family, the owners of Hawkstone. Apparently the design was taken directly from the Hill coat-of-arms. Many of the park's attractions were completed in the 1780s by Sir Rowland Hill. After that Sir Richard Hill took over, and building went on well into the 1850s.

Hawkstone cannot be visited without the services of a guide, to be contacted through the Hawkstone Park Hotel, now mainly visited for the golf course which winds its way through the park. It started, however, as the Hawkstone Inn, built *c.* 1800 to accommodate the growing numbers of sightseers. Hawkstone in a way can be said to be the inspiration for Longleat, Woburn and all the other stately homes which attract visitors; one could pay for a day out at Hawkstone nearly 200 years ago. Without the guide one is liable to lose one's way or even fall into an unexpected crevasse, as several people have done these last few years. The guide is Mr J. T. Jones, in his sprightly 70s, and the last of four generations of Jones guides at Hawkstone.

He led us through the park, up the very steep hill and down the valley — to be repeated an exhausting three times. The first stop is the Red Castle, approached through junglish paths, a beauty of a folly. Normally people mistake 18th-century towers for the well-worn remains of some medieval burgh. This time it is the other way round, for the castle is real, 13th-century. Its natural defences and unassailable position must have made an attack on it sheer hell. So is the walk up there, if one is too eager and makes a dash for it. The tower, built out of the solid rock, was topped up in the 18th century to improve the scenery, but all this has come down again. They don't build like they used to.

At the foot of the hill is a large opening through which one enters the rock and peers down the Giant's Well, again cut out of solid rock. Sublimity has taken over at this point, and is likely to stay on our tour. Nearby is the Lion's Den, a neat gorge which ends with the den itself, a half-circular opening. Now the bars have been broken away and the huge sculpted head of the fearsome lion lies meekly at your feet. It was possibly sculpted by John Nelson, who also provided the statue on top of the column and two sphinxes for the park. The vandalisation of much of Hawkstone appears to date from the Second World War, when the park was turned into a P.O.W. camp.

The second large rock is called Grotto Hill; its apertures and Eyecatcher Arch are admirably viewed from Castle Hill. The Grotto is stupendous. Tunnel, chambers and galleries whirl and twirl on top of the hill. Conflicting claims are made as to who excavated it: Roman miners and/or early Brits, or the Hills, that is to say their labourers. On our visit Mr Jones had forgotten the torch, and we were advised, on entering an innocent enough looking hole, just to follow him and keep in touch with the wall. Ten yards later it was impossible to turn back as all the light had gone. This went on for a very long 90 yards; meanwhile we were pathetically groping the wall and claustrophobia had set in. At last a little light fell on our white hair and we entered the part of the grotto that is decidedly 18th-century.

A thorough job has been done on the grotto-room: shells, minerals, roof, stained-glass – all has been destroyed, apparently by two cyclists who were refused refreshments at the hotel. Their delirium might be understandable if they had cycled up the hill. The 1807 *Description of Hawkstone* aptly remarks that the grotto is 'without any thing of that diminutive or formal decoration and petitesse, by which Grottoes are usually rendered more like artificial baby-houses, than grand natural and romantic caverns'. The stained-glass represented 'The Four Seasons' and a 'Philosopher at his Studies', done by a Mrs Peirson. A pity that such things are always the first to go.

A rhododendron-lined path will see one safely down again, near the remains of the Victorian Gingerbread Hall or Temple of Patience, a thatched hut backed by the rock, where in olden days Martha Higginson sold ginger-beer and gingerbread to hungry and thirsty tourists. Then it is uphill again, via a sublime underpass made in 1853 to the column. But first, covered in undergrowth, the scanty relics of the Hermitage. Reports of a hermit living here around 1800 seem to be false, but at this point on the tour the guide would leave his group and enter the hermitage through a secret back door. Whilst the visitors were peering into the hut, discerning the dim outline of a bearded hermit, with skull on the table in front of him, the guide would work some levers. The papier maché hermit's eyes could roll at will, he would rise to greet the people at his door, and his mouth would mimic words spoken by the guide. The manikin fell apart scores of years ago.

Much was made of the hermit's existence: at the coming-of-age party of Lord Hill in 1851, as the clock struck twelve, the then guide entered the ballroom dressed as the hermit. Presumably he delivered some wise and well-meant eulogy. From the site of the hermitage one can walk towards the White Tower, which is of course red. It is very difficult to reach, and the little octagon is a disappointment. Really, it is meant to be seen from a distance.

The path leads on to the Obelisk, which is in fact a column. Upon this stout Doric fabric stood the statue of another Sir Rowland Hill, who was the first Protestant Lord Mayor of London. Only his feet now remain where they should; the rest of his body came down some years ago. Anyone left with enough breath can climb the 112-foot high column and gulp the equally breathtaking views. Take care: the railings round the top of the column have gone as well. Despite being listed Grade I, it is in a seriously dilapidated condition.

The building of the column in 1795 seems to have served for giving much-needed employment to locals, who were also put to work digging the enormous stretch of Hawkstone Lake. A Dutch scene on the lakeshore, consisting of a Dutch house called Neptune's Whim inappropriately decorated with Swiss landscapes, a whalebone arch and a windmill in the Dutch style, has gone. It would have made an interesting change from the semi-Chinese, Italianate and Druidical landscapes normally encountered in parks. The whole set was meant to remind one of a Ruysdael painting. Also gone are a Tahitian hut, Murad Bey's tent (brought over from Egypt in 1801 as a trophy by Colonel Hill), and a fortified vineyard, while the Gothick Menagerie is a virtual ruin. Yet there remains enough of the Hawkstone follies, and above all the landscape, to be able to enjoy the risk of falling off columns and precipices, getting stuck in tunnels or even being hit by killer golfballs.

Off the A49, just before entering HADNALL, is the Waterloo Windmill. If it cannot be found, don't ask! People will take a long, hard look at you when windmills are mentioned. It was built for General Lord Hill on the estate of the now demolished Hardwick Grange, where he lived. The house was built *c.* 1820 by Thomas Harrison, and the folly is probably of the same date and by the same architect. Harrison was something of a family architect to the Hills: the Citadel at Hawkstone was altered by him, and he also worked on the Hill column in Shrewsbury. He seems to have specialised in memorials; the obelisk at Moel Famau, the column at Llanfair P.G. and the Memorial Arch at Holyhead were all his work. Waterloo Windmill of course commemorated Lord Hill's deeds on the battlefield; it is supposed to be a replica of the Waterloo headquarters, and its arrowslits and Gothicised windows, however unlikely in a field HQ, assure one that it is not just another converted windmill. The surrounding woods were planted in order to indicate the position of the armies at the start of the battle. The story sounds very *déja entendu*: a similar story is told about the woodlands at Woodford, Northamptonshire. It could, however, represent a so-called battle-garden (or in this instance a battle-park), an arrangement of earthworks and/or plantations to resemble in miniature the location of a famous battle. A good example has recently come to light at Kilwarlin, County Down, which re-creates the battle of Thermopylae during the Graeco-Turkish wars of the 1820s.

Near UFFINGTON, north-east of Shrewsbury, the scant ruins of Haughmond Castle squat in the middle of an ancient hill fort on top of Haughmond Hill. The folly originally consisted of two embattled round towers with a screen wall, but in 1931 the *Shrewsbury Chronicle* reported that one of the towers and part of the wall had collapsed. Although nearby Haughmond Abbey belonged to the Hill family, the tower folly is said to have been built for John Corbet of Sundorne Hall, a flag being hoisted whenever Corbet was hunting in the Shifnal country. From 1778 onwards Corbet hunted in Warwickshire, where he eventually became Master of

Hounds. This, and the fact that Robert Mylne carried out alterations at Sundorne Hall in 1774, would seem to give us the likely date and architect for Haughmond Castle.

Reaching SHREWSBURY, we come across Hill connections again. The huge column with its statue of General Hill really does catch one's eye — as it should: at 133 feet 6 inches it is said to be the tallest Doric column in the world. The stone records Hill's 18 battles, but also his 'benevolent and paternal care' for both foes and countrymen. The Salopians seem to have been happy to provide funds to build the column, and toasted a hearty 'Hills of Shropshire; may they last as long as the Shropshire hills' to it. The statue itself is made from the mysterious and seemingly everlasting Coade artificial stone, ensuring General Hill's position on his perch for a good time to come.

Still in Shrewsbury, 'The Quarry', a park by the river, consists of folly odds and ends: architectural fragments, statues, a summer-house and a removal folly, the Gateway of the Shoemaker's Arbour. Its date is 1679; exactly 200 years later it was taken from Kingsland and re-erected here in the Dingle, the park's main area. There is also an obelisk with Gothic decorations, transported from the station square where it had been placed in 1874. In the grounds of Shrewsbury Castle, on the mound, is Laura's Tower. Between 1787 and 1790 Sir William Pulteney engaged the young Scotsman Thomas Telford to make the castle habitable again, and for decoration he contrived this octagonal red sandstone tower, on the site of the medieval tower, and named it after Pulteney's wife. Through Pulteney's influence Telford acquired the position of Surveyor of Public Works for Shropshire, and so an illustrious career was started by building a folly!

A few miles east of Shrewsbury lies Attingham Park, a superb Humphrey Repton creation. The approach is from the village of ATCHAM, which is still graced by some remains of a projected model village by John Nash. There is an ice-house and an 18th-century wooden bee-house in the park, but the follies consist of two cottages flanking a side entrance to Attingham: a churchy edifice called Western Lodge, probably by Nash, and a very half-hearted attempt at an Eyecatcher Lodge, made by attaching a narrow façade with an elongated cross for a window to the projecting part of the lodge. The rest of the house is untouched. Both buildings can be dated *c.* 1800. South of Atcham is PITCHFORD HALL, probably the finest half-timbered house in the county, with a remarkable tree-house which deserves mention both because of its age — it was put up in the 17th century and embellished around 1760 — and because it illustrates one of the sources of the word folly: *feuillée*, or a hut made out of tree-branches. It is 11 feet up in a lime tree, with the wood painted in a brick pattern, a proper door, three windows and the whole embellished by Gothick details. Even the interior has been decorated with Chippendale Gothick plaster-work. Fortunately its importance has been recognised, and it is listed Grade I.

To get to the prettier village of ACTON BURNELL, one has only to drive down the road from Pitchford, crossing the old Roman Watling Street West. There is a beehive-shaped grotto room here set upon the hill, with its 18th-century decorations still intact. The lady of the manor must have spent her idle hours in here, season after season patterning quaint little shellwork vases, faces and flowers on the walls. At one point she was presented with some Delftware tiles, and they line the lower part of the room.

The fires have now all died down at IRONBRIDGE, the much publicised Cradle of the Industrial Revolution. But its Gates of Hell, the furnaces, the foundaries and the warehouses, where work never stopped, like some Moloch machine needing fuel day and night, are well preserved by turning Coalbrookdale into a string of museum areas. In the middle of it, near the world's first all-iron bridge, squats the Severn Warehouse, built in the 1840s for the Coalbrookdale Company. Minerals were offloaded from the boats moored here and entered the warehouse by carts. The grooves for the rails can still be seen on the wharf. Some whim of the owners saw to it that the building was castellated, and two hilarious towerettes were put up in front, flanking a Gothic apse. As in Germany, industrialists often compared themselves to medieval barons. Minstrels on the battlements could have provided the Music while you Work, but apparently bad taste didn't stretch that far. It is now the Visitor Centre for the valley's museum complex.

Downstream, past Bridgnorth, the village of QUATFORD has two follies to show for itself, both built by the same man. The red-brick, castellated watch-tower is as picturesquely sited as Quatford Castle, a sham, built as a home for John Smalman in 1829–30. Smalman was a local builder, and in Colvin's words he had 'pretentions to gentility, and claimed descent from the Smalmans of Wilderhope . . . ' (whoever they may have been). What does a builder who claims gentility do? He builds himself a castle. He also rebuilt the village itself, thus earning the admiration of George Griffiths, who dedicated his poem 'The English Village' to him. Smalman was something of a poetaster himself, writing verse of a 'somewhat eccentric character'. He sounds the man to have built more follies, but none has come to light.

Mr Benjamin Flounder of Ludlow decided to build himself a tower on top of CALLOW HILL, east of Winstantow, marking the boundary between four different estates. One morning in 1838, he drives up from Ludlow in a carriage-and-four. The scaffolding has just been removed. His dilettante's eye does not notice the inauthenticity of his castellations. He opens the door, which bears his initials and the date of construction, and climbs the staircase. On the parapet he is met by his steward and the head mason. 'Fine view. Fine view indeed. But — what's this?' His two companions notice Mr Flounder's face turning purple. There's a hill obstructing the view towards his own estate! Mr Flounder works himself into one of his tantrums. 'I won't have it! Take it down!' The steward is worried about the extra cash that will have to be found for the demolition of this silly and already preposterously expensive project. Suddenly he points to the north. There, in the hazy distance, a silvery stretch of water can be seen. 'Look, sir — the Mersey!' And Flounder decides to keep the costly tower and use it for observing the ships going in and out of port. He must have had sensational eyesight: the Mersey is over 60 miles away as the crow flies.

Near WESTON RHYN, on the north-western edge of Shropshire, some slabs of stone are standing about in a field trying hard to pretend they are part of an ancient stone circle. In fact, they were put up by a Major West in 1830–40 to be seen from the nearby Quinta House. Why are there never runic Bovril advertisements on these sham Stonehenges, waiting for touring professors from Leipzig or Wroclaw to decipher them? Perhaps the Quinta Circle was another example of squires trying to alleviate unemployment by devising labour-intensive projects.

The home of Little Nell in *The Old Curiosity Shop* stood hard by a church porch, and the church porch Dickens is supposed to have based it on is TONG. 'There are few parishes in England that bear more marks of the ownership of a family than Tong does of the Durants,' stated G. H. Boden's *History of Tong Church, College and Castle* (c.1910). Today we have to change the verbs in the above sentence to 'have been', 'bore' and 'did'. Few folly groups can have suffered so many casualties.

The first George Durant amassed his wealth in 1762, 'at the plunder of Havana', and part of the village is still called Tong Havana. He chose to retire to Tong, bought the medieval castle (originally built overnight by Merlin the magician for Hengist) from the Vernon family and had it altered into a spectacular piece of Gothick-Moorish fantasy by 'Capability' Brown. It was pulled down in 1954. The second George, happily for us, was mad. During his reign pillars and urns were strewn about Bishop's Wood, a hermit called Carolus was installed in a cave, a round house was built in the village, and a circular dovecote in the park. All this sounds like the common-or-garden insanity of so many folly builders, but the best was yet to come: George II developed mottomania. The wheelwright's shop in Tong Norton was fitted out with the shape of a coffin and the words 'In Mortate Lucrum' (In Death is Gain); a well on the estate received a plaque which read 'Adam's Ale, Licensed to be Drunk on the Premises, 1838'; a coal-house was inscribed 'Mausoleum'. Gates and walls held a special interest for Durant. He started with the old entrance near the church, carving crosses and X's into the still existing wall, and 'Beati Qui Durant' on the iron fence posts. He was just beginning. Two jaw-bones of a whale spanned the drive to the castle, inscribed 'Death The Gate Of Life' and 'A Haven After So Many Storms', and near the castle was an elaborate gateway with pillars, upon each of which 'an Aeolian Harp denotes sweet music to unappreciative animals' (the animals in question presumably being the hounds in the nearby kennels). If the Aeolian harps actually functioned, the dogs must have been driven berserk by the ceaseless, vacant harmonies. Here again there was a plaque, with a poem that began

'Harp of the North! that mould'ring long has hung . . . ' No wonder he called one of his sons Ossian.

Durant could not be satisfied with so few gates. He had another built, with an adjoining cottage called Convent Lodge. The lodge still stands. The gate piers in front must have been the most bizarre pillars this side of the Channel — very fruity, with lots of flowers and vegetation, a pineapple (the folly-builder's favourite fruit) topping the lot. The Gothic niches showed the east and west views of the castle, the whole set off by thick stone ropes and tassels. The iron gates themselves came from the Coalbrookdale Works, and the whole astounding, unique, irreplaceable flight of fancy was torn down a couple of years ago to facilitate works traffic for the M54.

The lodge appears to have suffered from deliberate neglect. It doesn't seem particularly remarkable until one has a closer look; there are queer patterns on the walls and a plaque which reads:

No more to Chiefs and Ladies bright
The harp of Tara swells
The Chord alone that breaks at night
Its tale of ruin tells.

Ruins indeed! From the lodge a stretch of wall leads into a small valley. One plunges in the exuberant growth of grass and nettle, holding the camera high. The jungle closes in. It's worth the trouble. Large butterflies, crowns, shields, crosses and other emblems are hewn out of the wall. It is very slippery indeed underfoot. Eventually the dingle is reached. There's the brook, spanned by a small stone bridge. Carolus the Hermit could have resided here; the grounds look promising enough.

Returning along the wall, past Gothic seats, one discovers the lower part of the Pulpit, which is settled on the wall and is almost totally overgrown. Eight years ago the Pulpit was in perfect condition; it must have been destroyed deliberately. According to the *History of Tong*, Tara again was featured here:

The harp that once through Tara's halls
The soul of music shed
Now hangs as mute on Tara's walls
As if that soul had fled.

Judging from an old photograph, the Pulpit appears to be a copy of the medieval refectory pulpit in the grounds of Shrewsbury Abbey. The references to Tara, the legendary court of the Irish kings with their bards, were taken from Thomas Moore's *Irish Melodies*, published in parts between 1807 and 1835.

Another example of the Tong mottomania is the Egyptian Aviary, still going strong and cared for, at nearby Vauxhall Farm. It is an elongated pyramidal shape, set on a rectangular base, advertising its use by the egg-like openings in the top. The motto here is 'AB OVO', still visible under the openings. Most of the other mottoes are no longer to be seen — the brick has weathered badly — but a list of them reads as follows:

EGYPTIAN AVIARY 1842
LIVE AND LET LIVE
TRIAL BY JURY
SCRAT BEFORE YOU PECK
TEACH YOUR GRANNY
CAN YOU SMELL
GIVE EVERY DOG HIS DUE
HONESTY IS THE BEST POLICY
TRANSPORTATION
BETTER COME OUT OF THE WAY LOVE

Mr Wynne, the farmer, told us that each centre brick on the pyramid was carved to represent a local area. The only one still distinguishable — and that very faintly — is a lizard representing the copse on the hill opposite, which is in the shape of a lizard. Hence the name of the neighbouring village over the border in Stafford-shire, Weston-under-Lizard.

The pyramid spawned another, similar, building also designed for Durant. It is about two miles away, in a cottage garden at Bishop's Wood in Staffordshire, but as it belongs with Durant's follies we will mention it here. This time Durant built a pyramid for pigs, smaller than the Vauxhall Farm pyramid so that the poor pigs must have been cramped for space and thus belying the inscription: 'TO PLEASE THE PIGS'. Hard by is a Tudor-Gothic stable, also none too large, with the text 'RANDZ DE VACHE', which sounds uncannily like a bastardisation of 'cow-ranch'.

Even towards the end of his life George Durant indulged his peculiar sense of fun. On 19 September 1839 a Water Tournament was held on the now drained Tong Lake. A cannon shot gave the champions, standing in small boats and armed with jousting lances, their signal to start, and the winner received a gold purse from the Queen of Love and Beauty. The tournament was in all probability a mockery of the famous tournament held by Lord Eglinton scarcely a month earlier. This 'great event' was ridiculed, especially as festivities had been dampened by a steady downpour.

One of the buildings was destroyed the very night Durant died, in 1844. Boden tells the story: 'Mr Durant had a monument erected on Tong Knoll to commemorate his victory in a law suit against his wife. [Presumably this was his first wife and mother of his children, Maria Eld of Leighford. In 1830 he married again, this time to Celeste Lefeore or Lavefue — Boden and the epitaph in Tong church disagree.] It caused great annoyance to his sons, who on the very night their Father died took two barrels of gun powder, and blew up the whole structure, the report being heard many miles away.'

Durant's ice-house escaped destruction by kin, time or motorway planners, and found a loving home at the Avoncroft Museum of Building in Worcestershire. On first sight the follies at Tong present a riddle as to what Durant might have intended with his buildings, decorations and mottoes. Their only reason for existence appears to be their owner's eccentricity, but one wonders whether there may be something deeper to Tong — an iconographic programme, in a rather perverse manner, mocking religion, chivalry and nobility (the Durants were nouveaux riches, and their closest neighbours were the Earls of Bradford at Weston Park) — maybe also a celebration of death and decay.

Suddenly it starts to get grim, the obsession with harps, walls, ruins and crosses; the fear and hatred of the children who destroyed mad George's gloating monument on that night of death. Where do jokes end? Where does madness begin?

London,
the Thames Valley
and the Chilterns

Bedfordshire

Unsung, unfashionable Bedfordshire! A small, crowded county nervously squeezed away from London by its more confident and urbane neighbours, it is difficult to assign an identity. It is a county without castles; its largest town is undeniably frightful and lacks a proper river, which all towns need for their souls. It is hard to think of anything other than trucks, bricks and Bunyan to go with Bedfordshire. Yet it is not at all a bad place to be. Once away from unlovely Luton, the brickworks and the M1, rural Bedfordshire takes on a quiet attractiveness which is all the more enhanced by being unexpected, rather like a 1950s' movie starlet taking off her glasses so that our lantern-jawed hero can gasp, 'But Miss Bedford – you're beautiful!'

Not Luton. LUTON is the cuckoo in the Bedfordshire nest. Easily the largest town, bursting through the bottom of the county like an overweight fledgling, it has the rare merit of being wholly undistinguished. As Pevsner, always the first with a kind word, writes, 'it is a town of very little architectural interest . . . it is no good pretending that a perambulation is possible'. In only two cases has Luton's imagination been untethered – in 1900 and 1901, when the Luton Water Company built two massive water-towers, one on Hart Hill and the other on West Hill. We know water-towers should not be admitted as follies, but these two are so joyfully bizarre that even the most pedantic would unbend to include them. The West Hill tower, designed by Henry Hare in 1901, was described by Pevsner as 'One of the most enjoyable buildings of Luton. Decidedly Arts and Crafts and resourcefully handled'. Hart Hill's tower is decidedly eclectic: as Alan Cox of the

County Planning Department put it, 'It is difficult to say whether its style owes more to a French Gothic Château or a Chinese pagoda'.

In the 1960s an attempt was made to join the towns of Leighton Buzzard and Linslade under the name of Leighton Linslade. It failed as far as the public was concerned; Leighton Buzzard is a deeply pleasing name, one that is satisfying to repeat quietly to oneself, but it is LINSLADE that has the follies. One is an early example of the popular Victorian hobby of castellating railway tunnels: the north entrance of Linslade Tunnel has two towers, arrow slits, battlements — everything a good railway tunnel could desire. Not as elaborate or as famous as Clayton Tunnel at Hassocks in Sussex, it is particularly interesting because it must be the first example of its kind, having been built in 1838. The other is a late example of its kind, a gazebo built at the end of the 19th century. Gazebos had been in declining popularity in the previous century, and few were subsequently built, but at 'The Lodge' in Bossington Lane this pleasing sample can be found. It is a plain, two-storeyed, castellated building with an external staircase, but its particular attraction is a finely carved stone fountain on the west side, with bullrushes and a spouting fish.

Just north of Leighton Buzzard, in the village of HEATH AND REACH, is one of Bedfordshire's multi-purpose buildings. It sits on the village green looking like a concertinaed church, but is in fact a combined well-house and clock-tower, allegedly erected by public subscription — but as Baroness Angela Burdett-Coutts turns out to have been involved the extent of the public's contribution would appear to have been minimal. We will be seeing her philanthropic efforts again in London's Victoria Park and Holly Village, and this extraordinary little structure, while not as ostentatiously expensive as her London offerings, clearly bears the stamp of her determined charity. Plaques on the building admit only to Baroness Burdett-Coutts having shared the cost of the clock with Baroness de Rothschild, while a Mr Branton presented the pumping equipment in memory of a Mr William Abraham — but somehow everything points to the Baroness as the onlie begetter.

Across the A5 from Heath and Reach is WOBURN ABBEY, perhaps the most famous stately home in Britain. The magnificent abbey and park together provide the best that Bedfordshire has to offer. The trippers assuredly do not visit Woburn to see its follies, the finest group in Bedfordshire, but they do pay for their survival. Woburn's follies are enjoyable and accessible, if not in the grand manner. They follow style and fashion rather than mania, and were largely the work of two brothers, the 5th and 6th Dukes of Bedford. At least ten buildings could be mentioned, but as descriptions abound in guide-books and all are easily visited we will content ourselves here by describing only the major follies.

At Woburn there can be found a Chinese Dairy, a Chinese Temple, a pavilion, a Temple of the Graces by Wyatville, a very early grotto (1630, by the French architect Isaac de Caus), the Thornery, a log cabin, columns from a ruined gateway in a wood, a sample mock Tudor house from the 1878 Paris Exhibition (now a posh restaurant) and a round ice-house with dome and battlements, built in 1788 by Henry Holland. The most important buildings are the Chinese Dairy and the Thornery. The former was built by Holland again, probably around 1794, and with its covered gallery running alongside the lake it recalls Le Hameau at Versailles. Built of scarlet-painted wood, it is exquisitely picturesque. There are decorations, etched and painted glass with flowers, birds and butterflies all around. No Chinese milkmaids; no room for cows even – but the building is fun and immensely cheerful. Not that the Thornery is depressing. It seems to have been built as a thatched luncheon box by Humphrey Repton in 1808, and again the flower and bird motifs appear, this time round the dome and as murals, painted by Augustine Agilo. If the idea of a thatched dome strikes one as bizarre, the execution is even stranger. Inside, the building has two rooms, one up, one down, the upper, painted room being octagonal with a domed ceiling, and the lower, white-tiled room tunnel vaulted. Outside, nothing could be more different: the building is square with four steeply pitched gables and a verandah similar to the church at Roxton, also built in 1808. The least peculiarity of this Hansel and Gretel house is its name; it is surrounded by hawthorns.

Outside the north-west corner of the park, in the prettily named village of APSLEY GUISE, a quaint and ancient house known as the Henry VII Lodge turns out to be another commission for Repton from the Duke. A student of architecture might put it down to the end of the 15th century, perfectly preserved, but it was actually built in 1811 by Humphrey and his son John Adey Repton as a deliberate attempt to re-create a 15th-century house from known details. It is a true mongrel of a building. Repton wrote, 'The hint of the lower storey was taken from Eltham Palace, the hints for the brick-nogging from a house at King's Lynn, for the arches at the top of the narrow panels from a house near Kelvedon, for the barge-boarding from a house near Bury St Edmunds, for the pinnacles from a house near Shrewsbury, for the oriel from Norwich, and for the chimneys from Wolterton Manor House, Barsham, Norfolk.'

The little bridge in the grounds of FLITWICK MANOR is a charming conceit – a grassy arch spanning grass, one side classical, one side Gothic, with a pebble grotto area beneath. Nothing is known of its history; we can date it to the end of the 18th century, but no nearer. Just up the road from Flitwick is AMPTHILL, a small, not particularly distinguished town without any obvious attractions or notable sights. To the west of the town stands an all but forgotten cross which achieved sudden fame in 1982 as the climax to a treasure hunt. Catherine's Cross was erected in 1773 by James Essex for the 2nd Earl of Upper Ossory (an Irish title – his seat was Ampthill Park) on the site of the long vanished Ampthill Castle, where Catherine of Aragon stayed while the fate of her marriage to Henry VIII was being decided. Horace Walpole, that indefatigable traveller, composed an ode for the base of the cross which is still just legible:

> In days of old, here Ampthill's towers were seen
> The mournful refuge of an injured queen;
> Here flowed her pure but unavailing tears
> Here blinding zeal sustained her sinking years.
> Yet Freedom hence her radiant banner waved
> And love avenged a realm by priests enslaved;
> From Catherine's wrongs a Nation's bliss was spread
> And Luther's light from Henry's lawless bed.

In Walpole's and Ossory's eyes, at least, good came out of injustice. The progress of the design and subsequent erection of the cross is traced in Walpole's correspondence with the Rev. Mr Cole:

> June 22nd 1771 — I promised to Lord Ossory to erect a Cross to [Catherine's] memory . . . ; October 12th — Lord Ossory is charmed with Mr Essex's Cross [and Walpole sent Mr Cole the poem for the inscription]; July 12th 1774 — I have lately been at Ampthill, and saw Queen Catherine's Cross . . . Lord Ossory is quite satisfied . . . and designs Mr Essex a present of some guineas.

A hundred yards away over the flat top of Ampthill's castle mound stands another cross, at first glance identical — same size, same shape — but in fact different in almost every detail. This second cross was put up as a war memorial in 1920 by the Duke of Bedford, to commemorate the 707 men trained at Ampthill camp who died in the First World War. It is not easy to understand why the Duke chose to make his cross so similar and yet so different.

At noon on the spring solstice the shadow of Catherine's Cross touches the spot where the artist Kit Williams buried the golden hare that was to be the bait for millions of readers of *Masquerade*, his fabulously successful picture-book cum treasure-hunt. His publishers should seize the opportunity of erecting another monument on the spot.

In Dunstable Street, back in the town, stands a strange, triangular, two-storey building just in front of a new supermarket. Here, says local legend, Catherine of Aragon used to teach pillow lacemaking to the women of Ampthill — but as she died 200 years before the gazebo was built another legend falters. The house it served is now demolished, and the quaint little building's survival as the Gazebo Flower Kiosk has to be applauded.

Before the Russells (the family name of the Dukes of Bedford) came to pre-eminence in the mid-1700s, the leading family in Bedfordshire was the Greys of WREST PARK, near Silsoe. As early as 1295 Reginald de Grey was lord of the manor of Flitton-cum-Silsoe, and the Greys were in possession for the next 622 years. Henry Grey, the 12th Earl of Kent, was created Duke of Kent in 1710, at the time that Thomas Archer was building for him the magnificent pavilion in the grounds of Wrest Park. It was an early work by Archer, who trained under Vanbrugh, and it is such an arresting building that it has been accepted by the architectural establishment in its own right, conveniently ignoring its pre-eminent claim — being huge, useless, ostentatious and wildly expensive — to be a folly. It is undeniably magnificent, the finest individual building in Bedfordshire, built to a complicated plan based on Borromini's S. Ivo della Sapienza in Rome. In 1773 Walpole, having no taste for the 'old-fashioned manner', had only one word for it — 'frightful'. Wrest Park is a rarity among English gardens in that it has remained formal, despite the attentions of 'Capability' Brown, who worked here for three years. Archer's pavilion stands at the end of a formal canal called the Long Water, half a mile from the house (which, incidentally, was designed and built by Earl de Grey himself, first President of the Institute of British Architects). The garden is packed with buildings, all verging on the folly without, as at Woburn, sufficient individuality to stand alone. There is a splendid bath-house, designed in 1770 by Edward Stevens, together with a bridge, the Bowling Green House, designed for the Duke by Batty Langley in 1735, two half houses encouragingly called the West Half House and the East Half House, and a bizarre Tuscan column which commemorates the work done on the gardens:

> These Gardens were begun in the year 1706 by the Duke of Kent, who continued to beautify them until the year 1740; the work was again carried on by Philip Earl of Hardwicke and Jemima, Marchioness de Grey, with the professional assistance of Lancelot Brown Esq. 1758–60.

No trace remains of the hermitage Brown is supposed to have built, but another column on Cain Hill commemorates Jemima again — she inherited Wrest in 1740 from her grandfather, the Duke — and was erected in 1831 by Earl de Grey. The final touch to the gardens is the Chinese Bridge of 1874, which was supposed to give to the landscape a willow-pattern atmosphere. An energetically inventive mind is required to make the connection. The curiosities will surely be preserved, as the grounds are in the care of English Heritage. The most surprising thing is that Archer's Pavilion is not a Grade I listed building.

In the park at SOUTHILL stands an exquisite white-brick fishing pavilion, modestly set back a little way from the lake. It is small — one room — with tetrastyle pedimented Tuscan porticos at the front and back. On either side, red-brick arcades run away from the pavilion, leading to large arches standing on the east and west; there is a cottage on the east side as well. It was probably designed by Henry Holland and built posthumously in 1807, and is currently (1983) being carefully restored. Originally it was built on a spur of land between two lakes; now, across the greensward, across the lake, it stares intently at the big house, so directly that one is driven to the map to see if it is part of a greater plan. And, satisfyingly, an avenue running south of the house does line up the fishing temple with the church at Meppershall, four and a half miles away, while two miles due north, on the identical orientation, is the parish church of Northill. There is a contentment in working out ley lines on a map; there is a quite different and sometimes alarming gratification in pacing one out on the ground. These old straight tracks do seem to have something other-worldly about them.

Between Southill and Northill is OLD WARDEN, famous as the home of the Shuttleworth Collection of vintage aeroplanes. Right behind the aerodrome is another extraordinary survival — an enchanting, complex and hidden garden of less than eight acres. It is known as the Swiss Garden, and is now administered by Bedfordshire County Council, who open it to the public whenever practicable. The Swiss Garden was first laid out in the early 19th century by Lord Ongley as a romantic adjunct to his Old Warden Park estate. With ponds, winding paths, bridges, terraces and islands it had all the right qualifications for the role, and to this foundation the Ongleys added a Swiss Cottage, a grotto, a thatched tree-shelter, a fernery, a wellhead, a chapel, an Indian kiosk and several other small conceits. The Swiss Cottage itself is a thatched 'umbrello' with extensive fretworking; it is said that the name of the garden derives not from a general Swiss style but from the Swiss mistress of one of the Lords Ongley. The grotto and fernery were built *c.* 1830, and while the grotto is fairly unexceptional the fernery is an interesting example of an early cast-iron glasshouse in the style of Paxton and the Crystal Palace. It predated Paxton by several years, being built by Barwell & Hagger at the Eagle Foundry, Northampton in 1830–3. Joseph Shuttleworth bought the estate from Lord Ongley in 1872 and continued to improve the garden. He still found time to build the Queen Anne's Summerhouse in 1875, now severely damaged by fire and vandals. It is a square brick building with corner turrets and balustrades, attributed to Henry Clutton, who designed Old Warden Park for the Shuttleworths. After the Second World War the Swiss Garden fell into decay, and only in 1976 was the decline halted, when the council took over the lease with the aid of the Historic Buildings Council. The garden is beautiful, unspoilt and as yet relatively undiscovered – another plus point for Bedfordshire.

At the corner of a wood south of BUSHMEAD PRIORY stands a minute tower, three storeys high, with a pyramidal roof, battlemented corner turrets, and one room per floor. Once it was supposed to be an observatory, then a gamekeeper's lodge; now it is a tiny house called 'The Grotto', which refers to the remnants of a shell grotto stuck to its northern side. It was built by the Gery family when the Priory was rebuilt as a private house in the 18th century.

Just past GREAT BARFORD on the road from Bedford to the A1, on the right-hand side, is a gateway, now unusable because the level of the road has been raised. It is unremarkable in itself, but ten yards further on an almost identical gateway has been re-created in brick relief on the otherwise blank wall. It was never used, never filled in – why was it constructed? The only reasonable explanation was that it was built as a simple eyecatcher to be seen from Barford House on the other side of the road. Trees and traffic now conspire to keep this little oddity from fulfilling its original, if mysterious, purpose. Another extraordinary building can be found a mile down the road in ROXTON. Congregational churches are usually somewhat severe architecturally; if any style in particular is favoured, then classical Greek is the choice. What a surprise therefore to find a congregational church – any church for that matter – built in the style of a thatched Gothic rustic *cottage orné*. (The only other thatched church we have come across is at Little Stretton in Shropshire.) Roxton Church was built by Charles Metcalf, the local squire, because he was bored with travelling six miles to his nearest congregational chapel. It is T-shaped, with massive overhanging eaves forming a verandah right round the building and supported, visually at least, by gnarled and weathered tree-trunks. The main body of the T is the delightful little church, while the cross-bar houses a utility room on the north side and a Sunday school on the south. The Metcalf family used to use this part as a summer-house, hence the fantastic and somewhat too secular entrance.

Right on the borders of the county are two final fripperies worth mentioning: between PERTENHALL and Kimbolton on the Cambridge-shire border, in the grounds of Woodend House, is a small garden-house, hexagonal and with a hexagonal lantern, probably built in the 1850s; while on the opposite side of the county, at TURVEY on the Buckinghamshire border, an odd couple live on an island in the Great Ouse. 'Jonah and his wife', the locals have dubbed them, despite the fact that Jonah's 'wife' sports an all too obvious beard. Jonah originally came from Ashridge House in Hertfordshire, which was demolished in 1802. The squire of Turvey found him in a stonemason's yard and installed him on the island in 1844, where he waited patiently for 109 years until his wife joined him in 1953. The wife was found as a headless female torso built into the side of a barn along with several assorted heads. Despite the female body, a bearded head was felt to be the most suitable, so s/he went to join Jonah on the island. The people of Bedfordshire are not as conformist as they would have you believe.

Berkshire

Until Oxfordshire swallowed nearly a third of the county in 1974, Berkshire, or the Royal County of Berkshire to give it its full and unique title, looked like a mirror image of the map of Austria. Nothing remotely resembles Austria on the ground, however; the nearest Berkshire gets to an alp is Walbury Hill on the Wiltshire/Hampshire border, at a trifling 974 feet. But as Austria is divided into alpine and lowlands, so Berkshire is divided into Commuterland and Otherland. Reading, the county town, is the pivot and the border dividing the two, half an hour from London by train and straddling the wild west and the stockbrokers' splendour of the less than mysterious east. Strangely, Berkshire is the only shire county not to have derived its name from the quondam county town.

For our purposes, the biggest surprise about the county is the scarcity of follies. Follies are the playthings of the rich or eccentric, and Berkshire, although undeniably rich, gives the impression that eccentricity is not an admired trait. The nurturing of a good crop of follies requires a generous sprinkling of large estates, and these Berkshire lacks. Perhaps the old lords were made nervous by the proximity of the monarch. The Royal County is so honoured because of urbane Windsor, frowning across the river at squat and urban Slough, indisputably unfit for humans but the second largest town in the county since it was acquired from Buckinghamshire in the reorganisation. What were the planners thinking of when they swapped all those towns around?

Certainly not WINDSOR. The private gardens of the Castle show that Royalty were just as susceptible to the whims and the fashions of the day, for here is an 18th-century grotto and a Gothick sham ruin. The grotto is cut out of chalk and lined with flint and pebbles rather than the shells and crystals of flashier neighbours. One part, the central octagon, used to be covered in mirrors, but these have fallen and broken, and only the bare brick remains. At Frogmore the Gothick Ruin is said to have been designed by James Wyatt for Queen Charlotte as an elaborate summer-house. The window tracery is of a higher quality than in most sham ruins, and in the right season it ranks among the prettiest anywhere, enveloped as it is in an ancient wisteria.

The people of the county guard their privacy carefully. Even a police station we passed had a sign reading POLICE NOTICE − NO TURNING on its forecourt. It's the sort of county that given half a chance would impose a toll to keep out the riff-raff, and as such it attracts the sort of riff-raff who have acquired sufficient money to be allowed in.

Berkshire's few follies seem to have a preference for water: half of them are on or by the Thames. Travelling upstream from Slough to Windsor, the river is studded with a remarkable number of tiny islands, known to Tamesians as eyots. MONKEY ISLAND by Bray is now an hotel, its past tranquillity lost for ever to the M4 thundering over the river 400 yards away. In the 18th century it must have been idyllic. Charles Spencer, Duke of Marlborough, thought so when he bought the island. There was an octagonal fishing lodge built from the most massive blocks of cut stone − at least they looked like stone until the young duke tapped them and discovered to his delight that they were blocks of wood carved to look like stone. The lodge has spawned, and now it is crushed in the middle of the hotel which at least has made an attempt along one wall of the bar to reproduce the massive woodstone blocks. The domed ceiling of the lodge was decorated with paintings of monkeys indulging in river sports by Andien de Clermont, who specialised in 'singerie'. It has been speculated that the name of the island derives from these paintings, but the probability is that it is a tautologous corruption of 'monk's eyot'. The Duke built a pavilion to go with the lodge. Originally it was one room standing on an arcade, a pleasant belvedere, but the hotel bedrooms are linked to it, the arcading has been filled in and it now forms the conference room of the hotel.

Further upstream, near REMENHAM, is an even more peaceful fishing lodge, this time in classical Grecian style by James Wyatt, dating from 1771. A little cottage on Temple Island (the name had to postdate the building) has a three-light bay crowned with a rotunda of Tuscan columns all painted white, supporting a shallow dome. It is surrounded by a small arboretum, spectacular in its autumn foliage. Built as an eyecatcher to Fawley Court, over on the other side of the river in Buckinghamshire (in fact on the borders of Buckinghamshire, Berkshire and Oxfordshire), its serenity is disturbed only by the stertorous breathing of scullers powering their way up and down from Henley. Oh — and of course a six-lane motorway, which now appears to be under construction across the river, missing the temple by 50 yards.

At Remenham itself, down a bumpy track off the Marlow–Henley road, we see the top of a church spire sitting on a plinth in a meadow. About 30 feet high, it does nothing and says nothing, but Fuller Maitland, who erected it here in 1837, has done us a good turn by preserving it. The spire is elegantly fluted and has a small carved figure on the tilting top. Job? A monkey? It turns out to be the spire of London's St Bride's church, in the City. A little further along, the track leads into the rear entrance of Park Place School (PRIVATE), once the residence of Field Marshal Henry Seymour Conway. In the tangled wood on the right lies a small ruined edifice — a tower, say some; an ice-house, say others. It proves to be an ice-house. The entrance to the cellar has been opened up, and a beautifully made circular brick room can be seen, with a domed brick roof and matching floor, now silted up — like a large squashed sleeping-pill. It's worth seeing if you're looking for the spire, but be careful, for the cellar roof — hidden under the mound — is none too safe.

Conway was soldier, statesman, cousin and closest friend of Horace Walpole, the man who personified the 18th century. The Field Marshal was the epitome of the English fighting man: brave, upright, honourable, courteous, dashingly handsome, beautifully spoken, but, as William Hunt pointed out, 'he was a better soldier than he was a general, a better general than he was a statesman'. With his tremendous presence, genuine popularity and Walpole's sustained assistance, success and great office were inevitable. It is, however, unlikely that a simple manly soldier would have been greatly concerned about the amelioration of his estate with architectural conceits and fripperies, and we suspect that the 'improvement' of Park Place and the surrounding area owed not a little to Cousin Horace.

At TEMPLE COMBE, just down the road (PRIVATE − KEEP OUT), stands a Druids' Circle, complete with burial chamber. This is not a folly as Ilton Stonehenge is; the small stone circle is as real as Hetty Pegler's Tump. It is included here because of its situation; discovered in Jersey in 1785, it was given to General Conway (as he then was) by the people of the island, of which he was Governor. The French inscription shows that Conway inspired a very real respect among his people. The old house at Temple Combe has long gone, and with it, one assumes, much of the atmosphere. Now the lawns are carefully tended, clumps of daffodils grow among the monoliths and a modern, circular house of yellowstone and glass sits blindly by.

More Conwayana − an obelisk, a large but uninteresting grotto at the head of HAPPY VALLEY, and at the bottom of the valley, bearing the A321, Conway's Cyclopic Bridge, a remarkable piece of work which used stones from 14 different countries. It resembles, and is probably contemporary with, the Rock Arch at Encombe in Dorset, and, coincidentally, both were probably designed by Pitts. Thomas Pitt, Lord Camelford, built Conway's bridge in 1763, and work was well in progress when Walpole wrote to George Montague on 7 October that year, after a visit to Park Place: 'The works of Park-place go on bravely; the cottage will be very pretty and the bridge sublime, composed of loose rocks, that will appear to have been tumbled together there; the very wreck of the deluge. One stone is of fourteen hundredweight. It will be worth a hundred of Palladio's bridges, that are only fit to be used in an opera.'

Still following the Thames upstream, we pass through Reading, which has nothing much to offer but traffic jams (and a wonderful war memorial in the shape of a lion in Forbury Gardens), and reach PURLEY. Purley Hall is said by locals to have been the residence of the impeached Governor General of India, Warren Hastings − except that he lived in Gloucestershire. Facing the house on the shores of a lake (PRIVATE — KEEP OUT — GUARD DOGS) is a little flint and brick pavilion painted, on the inside, in a virulent Datsun ochre.

ERECTED, ACCORDING TO TRADITION,
TO COMMEMORATE
THE BATTLE OF CULLODEN
1746
RESTORED 1913.
H.C.W.

On the pediment is a magnificent grotesque face, with blackstone pebbles for eyes and an expression of such salacious malignity that one feels quite benevolently disposed towards it.

The river will shortly be swallowed up by Oxfordshire, but one short stretch remains with a curiosity rather than a folly; the folly has gone. At BASILDON, we can see one of the magnificent fountains that once graced Whitaker Wright's Witley Park in Surrey (there is another at York House in Twickenham); now it spouts in the company of others in the grounds of the Child-Beale Wildlife Trust, a sort of open farm with rare breeds of cattle, llamas and little bits of sculpture dotted throughout the grounds. In addition a pavilion, most of which came from Bowood in Wiltshire, was erected in 1956 by the owner, Gilbert Child-Beale, in memory of his parents. Nearby there is a monkey orchestra in stone, echoing de Clermont's work on Monkey Island. But are these follies? The real folly at Basildon was the famous grotto at Basildon Park, long gone, but commemorated by Lady Fane's fine house, which is still known as 'The Grotto'. At the end of the west drive from the house stands the perfect eyecatcher, a curvaceous gabled house squarely facing the drive gates, perhaps by John Buonarotti Papworth; but the drive dips down into a wooded valley and nothing can be seen from either house or eyecatcher.

A large part of old Berkshire, as well as the Thames, here disappears into Oxfordshire, so we turn inland to ASHAMPSTEAD. This is Berkshire before the commuters and weekenders and fat cats discovered it, a peaceful, pretty, remote village on a low hill, built around a crossroads. Two miles south of Abergavenny in Gwent is a mountain with the peculiar name of Blorenge, and here

in Ashampstead, 80 miles away, is Blorenge House. In the garden
is a small, brick, castellated tower, two-storeyed, with a substantial
flight of steps leading up to the first floor. In fact there seem to be
more steps than tower, which can be explained by the fact that it
was built *c.* 1830 by Isaac Septimus Nullis, a local preacher, as
somewhere to practise his sermons. From his personal and private
brick pulpit he could harangue and rant at the cows incuriously
grazing in the meadow below. Blorenge House also has a rather
wonderful coach-house, with stepped gable roof and ornamentation
added by the present owners – panels depicting the four seasons
and a madonna-style figure which appears to have been made out
of the brown leathery stuff they sell in supermarkets for dogs to
chew in place of slippers.

In the parish of WINTERBOURNE, bisected by the M4, is one of
Berkshire's best follies, the Hop Castle. It is now derelict and
vandalised, and as a result the owners are loth – no, refuse – to let
anybody near it. This is the folly which has attracted virtually all
the folly stories in the county. The stories are, as usual, without
foundation – or are they? The Hop Castle is still remote and
inaccessible, a perfect breeding ground for legend, despite a busy
motorway less than 600 yards away. King John liked to hunt round
Newbury way – therefore it's King John's Hunting Lodge; and
Bad King John used to keep his wife Queen Isabella locked in the
coal cellar; *and* there's a secret passage running from the castle to
the 'Blue Boar Inn' on North Heath. Unfortunately for legend,
King John was lurking in the area many many years before the Hop
Castle appeared. There is no trace of it on a local map dated 1761,
and the likelihood is that it was built by John Elwes of Marcham
near Abingdon, MP for Berkshire from 1771 to 1784, who
succeeded to his uncle's estate in 1763, changing his name (from
Meggot, presumably not unwillingly) in order to do so. He was
renowned for his miserliness and for keeping the best pack of
foxhounds in Berkshire, so the castle was almost certainly built as a
hunting lodge. But why the tunnel? For here, as rarely among folly
stories, the legend is the truth. There *is* (or rather was) a tunnel
which ran from the Hop Castle to the nearby Penclose Farm;
within living memory there were people who remembered
exploring it as children. Now it has caved in completely, but its

course can still be traced as a shallow indentation running across the fields. And what about the tunnel to the Blue Boar? A few years ago a neighbouring farmer was ploughing the field up by the main road near the pub when his tractor fell into the field; the ground he was working on collapsed into a ditch. Did the covered ditch lead to the Hop Castle?

The building itself is quite substantial. It is made from brick and flint and bones, with an octagonal first-floor room and four smaller rooms leading off it. The ground floor contains what could have been a kitchen, a wine cellar (or Queen Isabella's coal cellar?) and three more rooms. The halls and staircase are covered with shells and pebbles. The central octagon has an ogival roof, while the side wings are terminated with hop finials, which give this attractive folly its name.

The concrete river back to London takes us to a hamlet half-way between Newbury and Hungerford, and called, logically, HALFWAY. Known and loved by all users of the old Bath Road, Halfway House is a white, square, castellated toll-house with four corner turrets, so striking and solid that it looks like a giant pastille burner rather than a utilitarian turnpike building. It ought to be a pub — but we have recently heard that it may have been demolished.

Back to the freeway, or rather the M4, and just before Junction 12 (the Theale exit), heading to London, there is a small folly-tower alone in a field on the left. This is a plain, red-brick, castellated, hollow, round tower, and that's about all one can say of it. The only point of interest is that it must, by its very position, be the most frequently seen folly in Britain. Pedestrian though it is, it grew on us after a while, and now every journey down the motorway is punctuated by yells of 'There it is!' when SULHAM TOWER hoves into view. Tittenhurst Park in SUNNINGHILL, near Ascot, is the home of the ex-Beatle Ringo Starr, and in the grounds he has a folly which he wanted to turn into a video studio — the local council first refused (rightly) to give him a grant, but then refused to allow him permission for 'change of use'. One can scarcely imagine the planning meeting where it was decided that 'this building is used as a folly and no other usage can be permitted'.

Berkshire's grandest folly is unquestionably the Grotto at ASCOT
PLACE. Indeed, it is difficult to think of a finer grotto in Britain, and
the Department of the Environment has listed it Grade I, together
with Kent's Margate Grotto. It is intact, beautiful and unvandalised,
and for once the county's PRIVATE — KEEP OUT — NO ENTRY greeting
to all visitors is justified, for this is protecting something more
fragile and more valuable than privacy. What astonishes the visitor
most is the preservation of the grotto — here is the real thing, the
incarnation of all those pitiful shards of shells and feldspar seen as
remnants in old forgotten gardens. Here everything is pristine and
elegant, yet not institutionally precise. It is still a private, homely —
albeit a very grand home — garden.

There are three other pieces in the grounds of Ascot Place, so
immaculately preserved that in any other context they would
deserve a couple of pages each. Very closely packed together, in an
autumnal garden to the north-west of the house, are a Gothic seat, a
rotunda temple and a dry bridge, all in a remarkable state of
preservation — even the stonework shows no signs of crumbling. It
is as if they were built 20 years ago rather than 200. The Gothic Seat
has four clustered columns separating three four-centred arches,
topped with crocketed pinnacles and delicate frieze tracery. Facing
the seat at the end of a short avenue is a giant urn with snake
handles. The Rotunda with its Corinthian columns is no more than
30 yards away, an echo of how Halswell in Somerset must have
looked. Facing it is the Dry Bridge, a tunnel joining two gardens
with the bas-relief head of a woman over the entrance on the west
and two monkeys over the east entrance. A serene and peaceful
garden, and a fitting private close to Berkshire.

Buckinghamshire

The best follies in the Home Counties are to be found in Buckinghamshire. From the gardens at Stowe, which have more follies than most counties, to the dubious delights of West Wycombe, Buckinghamshire's follies are rich in style, variety and quantity. Buckinghamshire itself is otherwise a county without an assertive character, probably because it lacks a clearly defined centre. The town of Buckingham has a population of just over 5,000 while Aylesbury, now the county town, is still small with 40,000. Slough was the largest and least typical of Buckinghamshire's towns, but in the reorganisation it sidled over to Berkshire; Milton Keynes in the north, with its projected population of 250,000, looks like being more than its replacement. Despite its newness, MILTON KEYNES has already provided us with eccentricities – at Bradwell, circumscribed by roundabouts and dual carriageways, is a scene of rural felicity with four Friesian cows and two calves gambolling around them. They gambol in permanence, for they are made of ferro-concrete and placed in a field among housing estates in order to de-urbanise the area.

The only other town of any size is now High Wycombe, which means that the county is endowed with more than its normal share of parks, and a plentiful supply of follies. South Buckinghamshire is stockbroker land, the Chalfonts, Gerrards Cross, Beaconsfield, solidly Tory, London commuters, the greenback belt. Yet there are 18 follies south of Amersham, and that's on the London Underground line.

Fashion, style, appearance have always been important to the Buckinghamshire mind, more so than in neighbouring Berkshire where Money is the sole criterion. In the 16th century the county was swept by a mania for building moats, so that now there are more moated houses in Buckinghamshire than in any other county in England. For our purposes it is interesting to see that the classic folly story of a man building himself a house so grandiose that he bankrupts himself in the process occurs six times in Great Britain, and no fewer than three of those are in Buckinghamshire. The best known is Hamlet Seabrook at Ivinghoe, where Roger Seabrook set out to build 'the greatest house on earth', but there is nothing to see there and the story turns out just to be a story, to have no substance. There is plenty of substance however at Claydon House, a National Trust property at MIDDLE CLAYDON, and at LITTLE HORWOOD MANOR. Ralph, Earl Verney, a true blue Tory, inherited Claydon House in 1752 and set about toppling Stowe, which was a Whig stronghold, from its pre-eminence as the social, cultural and political centre of the county. He clearly felt the answer lay in bricks and mortar, and he began to add wings to the house. The additions were gigantic: the final straw was a ballroom which took up an entire wing and bankrupted him at the same time. Verney died in 1791; his additions were demolished the following year and we are left with an unpretentious country house with startlingly opulent interiors. Little Horwood Manor is a much later example, built in 1938 in the style of Lutyens. Construction stopped abruptly when the builder went bankrupt.

Towers, columns, obelisks and other aerial projections did not particularly appeal to the Buckinghamshire landowner. The restrained Englishness of the county landscape does not lend itself easily to vistas, except where man assisted nature as at Stowe and West Wycombe. Outside the great gardens there are surprisingly few towers, given the variety of other styles and formats. No lonely tower squats on a raging hill, abandoned, derelict and menacing; Buckinghamshire towers are tamed and ordered.

Medmenham Abbey has a deliberately ruined 18th-century tower, but as Sir Francis Dashwood was probably involved we will couple it with West Wycombe. Neath Hill in MILTON KEYNES has a surprising touch of chinoiserie in a shopping centre clock-tower built only ten years ago, but the only true folly-tower in the whole county is the 'Tudor' gatehouse called 'The Keep', probably built at the turn of the 18th century by Humphrey Repton, at BULSTRODE PARK, Gerrards Cross.

Two pillars grace the county. One was built by Disraeli at HUGHENDEN, his country house, in memory of his father Isaac d'Israeli. It is a 50-foot high pink granite pillar designed by E. B. Lamb, a High Victorian architect who in Pevsner's estimation rivalled S. S. Teulon. The other, taller at 68 feet and more traditional, is a Doric column surmounted by a statue by J. F. C. Rossi to the memory of:

SIR EDWARD COKE

1552–1634

FIRST LORD CHIEF JUSTICE OF ENGLAND

It was built by James Wyatt in 1800, and now stands on the golf course at the white wedding-cake house of Stoke Park in STOKE POGES.

Eyecatchers are uncommon in Buckinghamshire, but an early example was built in 1719 at Grange Farm in North Crawley, near Newport Pagnell, to answer the view from the newly built CHICHELEY HALL. It is now being restored, but lacks all fancy, being only a two-storey, five-bay, blank frontage. The Hall also has a dovecote with an ogee roof, and at ASTWOOD, just down the road towards Bedford, a tall octagonal dovecote has been converted into a smart house. The real eyecatcher in Buckinghamshire far outstrips these miscellania; it is so big, and so complicated, that its role as an eyecatcher must have been sublimated in the mania for building. On top of a small hill above the Thames Valley, at BOURNE END, sits Hedsor Priory, a large, well chimneyed house with the parish church huddled slightly below it. In 1970 another small hill to the north had strangely regular vegetation on its crown, which on closer inspection turned out to be Lord Boston's Folly. Ten years later, we found the submerging ivy and creepers had been cut away, and the true extent of the building was revealed. It is surprisingly large – not in height, for the tallest tower is only about 40 feet, but in area – and seems to wander all over the summit of the hill, constantly revealing new aspects as one walks around it. There are three asymmetrically placed towers, one square, one circular and one hexagonal, plus the front half of another hexagonal tower, a piece of wall standing buttressed in cramped isolation between the round tower and the hexagon. Somehow it looks as if once it could all have had a purpose – but no, the romanticism of the setting and the absurd little castellations on all the towers, the careful flint and brick construction place it firmly as a building for contemplation and enjoyment. Lord Boston did a fine job but, despite its size, his folly remains a mystery apart from an alleged dedication to George III and a suspicion that Sir William Chambers, who worked for Boston, may have helped in the design. No stories appear to have grown up around it, people living half a mile away are unaware of its existence, and little is known of Lord Boston himself. A blue-chip folly.

Much more is known about Lord Cobham, probably the most prolific folly builder of all time. A list of the architects and designers he employed sounds like a roll-call of the country's greatest 18th-century artists: Bridgeman, Brown, Gibbs, Kent, Leoni, Vanbrugh . . . but the architect he employed to build his gaol in BUCKINGHAM is unknown. The most likely attribution is James Gibbs, who was working at Stowe in 1748 when the gaol was built. How can a gaol be a folly? Well, Lord Cobham built it as a speculative venture, Buckingham having lost the County Assizes to Aylesbury before the mid-18th century. There was no point in having a courthouse when there was no gaol to put people in afterwards (or before), argued the Tories, so Cobham, a staunch Whig, built one, complete with medieval towers, crenellations and battlements. A hundred years later, George Gilbert Scott, the controversial Buckinghamshire-born Victorian church architect, added a semi-circular gaoler's house to the front, in the same design. Alas, despite all this pomp and show, Aylesbury still retained the County Assizes.

AYLESBURY itself cannot boast anything as grand as little Buckingham's castle gaol, but at Green End House in Rickfords Hill a printer, Elliott Viney of Hazell Watson & Viney, took a fancy to the 15th-century rose window from the parish church and had it erected in his garden. The fortress-like new county offices which dominate the centre of the town are locally known as Fred's Folly, after the county architect F. B. Pooley, who built them in 1966.

Another mock castle is crumbling nearby: halfway between Aylesbury and Thame on the A418 is DINTON CASTLE, built by Sir John Vanhatten in 1769 for his collection of fossils. It is not certain whether he intended his collection to be housed in or to form part of the building – ruined, roofless and floorless, it appears to be largely built with ammonites, trilobites, pterosaurs, for all we know, and other fossils. WOTTON UNDERWOOD, ten miles west of Aylesbury off the A41, has a bridge of 1758 designed by Sanderson Miller. Its most unusual possession is a Turkish temple – the Chinese pavilion that used to accompany it is now in County Kildare.

FAWLEY COURT outside Henley-on-Thames, now the Divine Mercy College for the Marian Fathers, has a vista over to Temple Island, described in the chapter on Berkshire; but in the grounds there is another sham ruin with a genuine church window. The ruin is big, built of flint with brick highlights and surrounds again; real enterprise has been shown in the construction of a circular room with a flint and knucklebone dome, tiled on the outside and with a spike on the top. The floor is tiled with a swastika pattern from the time when swastikas meant good luck, and the whole eclectic structure confidently melds its differing styles. It was designed by John Cooke Freeman before 1752. A heavily rusticated flint and plaster covered bridge and a dairy with a real Norman doorway are also in the grounds.

Flint and brick were the predominant building materials in the southern part of the county, not just for the follies. Tufa, limestone and shells were rare materials in landlocked Buckinghamshire, which may explain the paucity of grottoes. Even the larger estates seem to have eschewed the form, which is peculiar when neighbouring counties can all boast fine examples. Woodrow High House at PENN STREET has an octagonal domed grotto built of black and white pebbles; LANGLEY PARK outside Slough has a grotto wall in a conservatory; and there is said to be a grotto at Chequers, near ELLESBOROUGH, but not surprisingly we haven't been able to see it.

Temples and pagodas thrive in this county. Perhaps Stowe and West Wycombe propagated the idea throughout the shire like spores from a mushroom, for alongside the romantic Revett-style temples and 19th-century pagodas comes the real thing, as implacably rich religious sects discover Buckinghamshire to be an English nirvana. At Willen in MILTON KEYNES Japanese Buddhists erected a Peace Pagoda in the early 1970s, solid inside, and no doubt admired by the locals in the same way that the little iron pagoda from the 1851 Great Exhibition was admired when it was re-erected at the National Trust's CLIVEDEN, now an hotel. At WESTON UNDERWOOD in the far north of the county is a garden which used to belong to the Throckmortons of long-demolished Weston Manor. Still called 'The Wilderness', it has a Gothick temple, a Gothick alcove and other bits and pieces where poor mad William Cowper found solace. The pedestals which once held busts and urns remained; then the garden became part of the Flamingo Tropical Bird Gardens and Zoo; now it is derelict again. Cowper's alcove is set a little way up the slight hill, hexagonal and surprisingly tall, with a splendid panorama of the English countryside, which here has scarcely changed since his day. His poem 'The Task', a diatribe against graffiti, is here inscribed, and we are told that:

WILLIAM COWPER LIVED IN OLNEY AND WESTON UNDERWOOD
BETWEEN 1783–1795. MANY OF HIS WORKS, INCLUDING THE TASK,
WERE WRITTEN DURING THIS TIME, PROBABLY IN THE ALCOVE.
THE ALCOVE, ERECTED BY THE THROCKMORTON FAMILY IN
1753, NOW FORMS PART OF THE BUCKS COUNTY COUNCIL
GREEN BELT ESTATE.

Alcoves for poets seemed to find favour in Buckinghamshire; at Stoke Court, STOKE POGES is another Gothick arch with a niche for a seat, built out of the same rubbly conglomerate, but this time for Thomas Gray. Gray himself is commemorated by a massive Wyatt-designed sarcophagus placed not in the churchyard, as tradition dictates, but in a field nearby where it could the more easily be seen from Stoke Park:

HARD BY YON WOOD NOW SMILING AS IN SCORN
MUTTERING HIS WAYWARD FANCIES HE WOULD ROVE
NOW DROOPING WOFUL-WAN LIKE ONE FORLORN
OR CRAZED WITH CARE, OR CROSSED IN HOPELESS LOVE.

Humphrey Repton is said to have organised the siting. It is now owned by the National Trust.

Folly Farm outside HADDENHAM is yet another misleading name – no folly can be found – but in Haddenham itself is a weirdly decorated cottage, 'The Bone House' in the High Street, dated 1807. This is vernacular architecture at its most vernacular: not for this village dweller the marble columns and dressed stone of the squires. The cottage was built with whatever came readily to hand, and the most plentiful commodity in 1807 would appear to have been dead sheep. Knuckle-bones are formed into patterns to make faces, animals, tools, hearts, diamonds and the proud date, but the artist, with rare modesty, forbore to write his name in bones. Smaller structures, not designed as living quarters, dot the estates of the county. DORNEY, cut off from the rest of the county by the M4, has a hermitage which may once have served as a lodge to Dorney Court, flint and stone like many buildings in the area, with a small octagonal central tower, not wildly exciting in itself but with splendid rubble pillars on the garden side, and the bottle bottoms Buckinghamshire builders seemed to enjoy using to delineate floor levels. GREAT MISSENDEN has a Gothic summer-house at its abbey, probably built by a millionaire Holborn ironmonger, James Oldham.

The extraordinary Victorian architect William Burges was at work in the county, at GAYHURST to the north of Milton Keynes, where he constructed a circular outdoor lavatory for the menservants of Lord Carrington. It is now a private house known as 'The Dog House' – do the owners know they are living in an old khazi? Elsewhere at Gayhurst is a tunnel running from one abandoned garden to another under the main road, with a splendid pointed arch entrance surmounted by the Carrington crest.

Such an eminent 20th-century architect as Sir Edwin Lutyens could scarcely be accused of perpetrating follies, yet at TYRINGHAM HOUSE near Gayhurst the two pavilions the Königs ordered him to inflict upon Sir John Soane's grand design come perilously close. Identified as a bathing pavilion and a music-room-cum-chapel, the two domed temples – for that is what they are – stand awkward and ill-at-ease in their environment, even 60 years after they were built. Up the road, in FILGRAVE, Lutyens's Coronation Clock-

Tower commemorates the coronations of George VI and Elizabeth II. Lutyens used motifs he had tried and enjoyed in the past — the tower top with its diminishing stages has bisecting arches in halfhearted imitation of his great war memorial at Thièpval. It is obviously much too big for Filgrave, and is now used as a bus-shelter.

In the mid-19th century Buckinghamshire took on a new role as the promised land when it was discovered by the Rothschilds. Mayer Rothschild bought Mentmore in 1850, and he was closely followed by brother Lionel (Halton, 1851), brother Anthony (Aston Clinton, 1851) and, a generation later, Nathan (Ascott, 1874) and Ferdinand (Waddesdon, 1874). The Rothschilds, being in the main a pragmatic banking family, tended not to go in for fripperies in the park, preferring to lavish vast sums of money on their actual houses. But in all families there are exceptions, as Sir Anthony Rothschild discovered when he was bitten in his park by a large cassowary belonging to his son Alfred. Poor Alfred was banished to build Halton, which he finished in 1888, and where he took great delight in driving round in a carriage pulled by two zebras. Yet the only Rothschild building to approach follyship, if one discounts the sheer opulence of the château-cum-railway-station baronial magnificence of Waddesdon, is the Swiss Chalet at ASTON CLINTON, the only relic from Sir Anthony's time now that the great house has been demolished. At WADDESDON, now a National Trust property, a French landscape gardener named Lainé was employed to design the park, and among the incidentals he produced a little rock grotto and a delightful aviary. This· is nearly a match for the astonishing aviary at DROPMORE, perhaps built for Lady Grenville *c*. 1806 by C. H. Tatham. Tatham had a taste for designing ornamental metalwork, and was paid £10,000 for working at Dropmore over three years, so this fantastic parrot-coloured edifice may well be attributable to him. It is built of red-painted iron with green chinoiserie tiles, surmounted with domes, enhanced with wings and bays, an aviary fit for an eagle.

Before we cover the great folly groups of the county, there are a couple of miscellaneous curiosities which are worth seeing if you happen to be near. IVER, now in imminent danger of being engulfed by the Great Wen, used to boast a pretty house called Richings

Park, which had in its grounds cascades, an ice-house and a bridge. Traces remain of these, as they remain of the house, but only the real enthusiast will be able to make much sense of them. A little further north, at CHALFONT ST GILES, a castellated arch shelters a column topped by a globe. It was built by Sir Hugh Palliser in the late 18th century to commemorate Captain Cook. The house before it is called 'The Vache', which of course makes us think of dairies again. There is a thatched dairy — square, with pyramidal roof and overhanging eaves once presumably supported by rustic wooden columns — at Brookend Farm in BURNHAM, where the carved oak lodge prepares us for greater things at Hall Barn; and the ruins of a flint dairy at COLESHILL, south of Amersham.

The Hall Barn estate is just outside BEACONSFIELD, the tip neatly sliced off by the M40. The house is small and tall; Colen Campbell worked here, and in the grounds are an obelisk with ball finial and finely detailed carving of agricultural implements, as well as a large and elegant three-bay Doric covered seat, the remains of a grotto and a Temple to Venus. But the Oak Lodge north of the M40 is the prize: a remarkable house completely covered on two sides with elaborately carved black oak. From ground to roof it is decorated with patterns, portraits, mottoes, scenes, crests and fruit, so richly that the fabric would seem in danger of collapsing without the support given at the front by the carved, Borromini-style coiled pillars. Among the bas-relief portraits is one of Edmund Waller, poet and quondam owner of Hall Barn, and above the ram's-head crest of Lord Burnham, the present owner, is his motto, 'OF OLD I HOLD'. As the carvings on this unique building (the one by Brookend Farm pales to insignificance) decay, they are replaced by superb modern carvings from Colin Mantrip, who has been working on the building for the last ten years.

Coming down from the Chilterns into Aylesbury, the first village is STOKE MANDEVILLE, with its famous hospital. Moat Farm (one of hundreds in the county) here belonged to John Hampden, whose objection to paying the 20 shillings levied from him in ship-tax was one of the contributing factors to the Civil War; much less serious is the front fence of little Elm Cottage, which has been devised out of agricultural implements to make peacocks and other fantasias. Skirting Aylesbury to the south, we reach LOWER

HARTWELL (there is no Upper Hartwell) and Hartwell House, with an obelisk and statues of George III and Frederick Prince of Wales. The folly here is the Egyptian Spring, a well-head designed by Joseph Bonomi Junior in 1851, a severely plain little structure distinguished only by a line of hieroglyphs running along the lintel. A castellated and domed round tower with quatrefoil windows stands near the ruined Gothick church – real, not sham – and there are scattered bits and pieces throughout the grounds, pieces of older houses and churches incorporated into the park walls, and a façaded dry bridge under the drive.

Before moving to West Wycombe the egregious Sir Francis Dashwood lived at MEDMENHAM ABBEY on the banks of the Thames. He leased the place from 1752, and founded there the notorious Hell Fire Club, originally called the Order of St Francis of Medmenham, about which the stories are too widely circulated to bear repetition here. There is little indication that many follies were built at Medmenham, and the pleasantly sited ruined Abbey tower adjoining the house looks genuine enough, although it is credited to Dashwood and dated *c.* 1755. Long after Dashwood's time Medmenham came again into the public eye, with a minor event commemorated by a minor but pretty monument, a plinth with a tiny sloping tiled roof and a plaque celebrating the successful action brought by the 1st Viscount Devonport to make Medmenham Ferry public, in 1899. There is no longer a ferry.

When Sir Francis moved on to WEST WYCOMBE, his previously sublimated urge to build broke out. The National Trust now owns West Wycombe, and a Sir Francis Dashwood still lives in the house, which is surrounded by a number and variety of follies which would be unequalled in any county that did not also contain Stowe. Visible from miles around is the golden ball on the church-tower which Sir Francis added to the existing 14th-century church between 1761 and 1763. It is reached by ladder from the roof of the tower, and is big enough to hold six people. Of course, stories of black magic rites abounded, and were never convincingly denied. Below the church is the Mausoleum, a mighty hexagonal roofless monument built by John Bastard for Sir Francis in 1763–5 with £500 provided from the will of Lord Melcombe. The design was inspired by Constantine's Arch in Rome. Not so the entrance to the

Hell Fire Caves. This is real folly stuff — gloomy, sinister, amateur and threatening, despite the large numbers of visitors going in to see the waxworks and recorded commentaries that sanitise the caves themselves. The façade is knapped flint, with pointed and broken arches rising on top of each other like shark's teeth. Inside is a salute to our American cousins: most of the exhibits concern Benjamin Franklin, who once stayed at West Wycombe, and there is virtually nothing about the lascivious and immeasurably more interesting John Wilkes, a frequent visitor. At the bottom of the hill is the Pedestal, a plain column with a ball on top built to mark distances and the completion of Sir Francis's new road:

FROM THE UNIVERSITY MILES XXII
FROM THE CITY MILES XXX
FROM THE COUNTY TOWN MILES XV
SIR F. DASHWOOD DERAE CHRISTIANAE MDCCLII

The park is on the south side of the road. It is said that the trees were originally planted in patterns of great vulgarity but that Repton scrubbed it all up when he worked here. The temples are what remain, several of them designed by Nicholas Revett. The Temple of Venus, an Ionic rotunda with dome and ball finial set on a mound above a flint tunnel archway flanked by pyramids, was painstakingly restored in 1984. The others are the Temple of the Four Winds, Daphne's Temple, Flora's Temple, the Temple of Bacchus, a Music Temple on the island, and another small temple. There are also an exedra, a cascade and a triumphal arch. Wilkes mentions a 'lewd temple', probably demolished by Repton. Many of the estate cottages are built in brick and flint, the commonest local building material, and those visible from the house usually have some monstrous flint excrescence grafted on. In the case of St Crispin's Cottage the addition is a beautifully proportioned and well worked church-tower with quatrefoil windows and fretted belfry window, the equal as a sham-church eyecatcher of Suffolk's Tattingstone Wonder.

And so to STOWE. There are more follies in a smaller area at Stowe than there are anywhere else in the world, and anyone with any interest in the subject should make a pilgrimage there. The mansion now houses a public school, but the grounds, 221 acres of which were covenanted to the National Trust by the school in 1968, are often open to the public during the holidays, and work is continually going on to maintain the follies in reasonable condition. It is a long and expensive task which deserves support from the widest possible quarters. Partly for that reason, and partly from sheer fear at the enormity of the subject, we will not discuss the buildings at Stowe in depth here. The essential book is *Stowe: a Guide to the Gardens*, written by Laurence Whistler, Michael Gibbon and George Clarke, first published in 1956 with revised editions every decade. It is published anonymously, but is printed by E. N. Hillier & Sons Ltd of Buckingham. This 40-page booklet concisely covers the history of Stowe and discusses each folly in turn. We will simply list the still extant buildings, single out a few favourites and summarise the chronology.

ARCHES
> The Corinthian Arch, designed by Thomas Pitt, 1765
> The Doric Arch, erected 1768

PAVILIONS
> Oxford Lodge, by William Kent, re-erected 1760
> Boycott Pavilions, by James Gibbs, 1728
> Lake Pavilions, by Sir John Vanbrugh, 1717

BRIDGES
> Oxford Bridge
> Shell Bridge, by Kent, *c.*1742
> Palladian Bridge, by Lord Pembroke, *c.*1740

OBELISKS, TOWERS, COLUMNS
> Wolfe Obelisk, 1760
> Grenville Column, 1747
> Cobham Monument, by Gibbs, 1747
> Bourbon Tower, by Gibbs, *c.*1740

TEMPLES
> Ancient Virtue, by Kent, 1734
> British Worthies, by Kent, 1735
> Gothic, by Gibbs, 1741
> Friendship, by Gibbs, 1739
> Rotondo, by Vanbrugh, 1721

Venus, by Kent, 1732
Concord and Victory, by Lord Temple, 1747
Queen's, by Gibbs, 1744

MONUMENTS

Captain Cook, 1778
Congreve, by Kent, 1736
Queen Caroline, 1732

OTHERS

Seasons' Fountain, 19th-century
Fane of Pastoral Poetry, by Gibbs
Gothic Umbrello near the obelisk
Pebble Alcove, by Kent
Cascade
Menagerie (now the school shop), 1780
Hermitage, by Kent
Grotto, 1741
Dido's Cave
Stowe Castle, by Gibbs, 1740 (outside the grounds)

Gibbs's triangular Gothic Temple is doubtless the most striking building at Stowe. It is ugly (even to aficionados), a hideous rusty-brown colour, big, intrusive and wonderful. All it has to recommend it is its solidity and leering self-confidence. It predates Flitcroft's triangular follies, but Gibbs could have been influenced by Thomas Archer's now demolished triangular rectory at Deptford, built in 1724.

The bulging Bourbon Tower is some way from the main gardens, but its dumpiness and its decrepitude are immensely appealing. Originally a keeper's lodge, it was renamed after a visit by exiled French royalty in 1808. The Cobham Monument is a tall column with a domed cupola; once there were stairs to the top, but naturally the doorway is now sealed. The Grenville column is an extremely rare example in Britain of the freestanding *columna rostrata*, a column decorated with prows of ships, jutting like beaks out of its shaft, looking more like a totem pole than a classical architectural motif. William Kent's buildings are grandiose garden ornaments rather than follies; nevertheless, the Temple of British Worthies rewards close study. Perhaps the finest of Kent's buildings

65   Sham ruin, Peper Harow

69   Wappingthorne helter-skelter, Steyning

70   New Foxhalls, Henllan

71   A house in the village of Marford

is the Temple of Ancient Virtue, an elegant domed rotunda with an Ionic colonnade, a reinterpretation of the Temple of the Sibyl at Tivoli.

Stowe was the seat of Sir Richard Temple, Viscount Cobham, a general and the leader of Whig society in Buckinghamshire. His garden was more than a pleasance, it was also a political statement – for example, the Temple of Ancient Virtue was adjoined by the now vanished Temple of Modern Virtue, deliberately built ruined as a sharp comment on the policies of Walpole. The remarkable works at Stowe began when Cobham appointed the unknown Charles Bridgeman to design the grounds. Bridgeman was the catalyst for the revolution in landscape design, the father of the natural line of succession of William Kent, 'Capability' Brown, Humphrey Repton and J. C. Loudon. The ha-ha was his innovation, and he was the first to abandon rigid formality in garden design. Cobham played safer but no less brilliantly with his architect, choosing Vanbrugh, like himself an old soldier, but then at the height of his architectural fame. Vanbrugh was succeeded by James Gibbs, Giacomo Leoni and William Kent, who followed Bridgeman as garden designer (as he did at Rousham in Oxfordshire, on a much smaller scale), and finally, in 1741, the 24-year-old Lancelot Brown, later to be nicknamed 'Capability', was appointed head gardener. With such a galaxy of stars, it is not surprising that Stowe has probably the most important position in English garden history.

Hertfordshire

It's strange how Londoners of all sorts and types agree on one point — that foreigners (to put it as politely as possible) begin at Calais in the south and Watford in the north. Why the whole of Hertfordshire should thus arbitrarily be dismissed as containing a race of lesser beings while Kent and even Dover are granted equal status to London can only be explained by the fact that while Kent is the Garden of England, no Londoner goes to Hertfordshire unless he has to. To bring in beer, Kent was famed for its hops (labour intensive) and Hertfordshire for its malt (labour hardly needed). As a holiday centre it has very little to offer. As a place to live it has plenty, so Londoners reserve for Hertfordians that special contempt all city-dwellers reserve for their country brethren. It doesn't seem to worry the natives overmuch; they are aware of the existence of the metropolis, but far from awed by it, preferring to keep their obstinate independence. Pragmatic and sensible, the Victorian Hertfordians were as unlikely to put modesty skirts on table legs as their descendants are to change what must be one of the two most unfortunate village names in the British Isles — Nasty. The other contender, Ugley, is only ten miles away, across the Essex border.

Central Planning (Londoners all) dictated that no one should be allowed to traverse Hertfordshire laterally without immense difficulty, to which end the A414 was constructed, probably the most tortuous cross-country route ever devised. The three major roads, the M1, A1, and A10, all head north to quit the county as rapidly as possible, so internal travel is virtually restricted to north/south routes. This makes touring downright difficult, particularly in the eastern half, where one only seems to be able to get to Puckeridge, an utterly insignificant village signposted from all over Britain. But there is one overriding advantage – the remarkable feeling of isolation and remoteness one gets in the Hertfordshire countryside between the main traffic arteries. It is hard to believe that London is so close, except that its orange glow fills the night sky and makes star-gazing impossible. This remoteness also preserves the follies, but to recommend a particular route to see them would be impracticable for this reason. Better by far to select the five top-ranking follies in the county, show other examples of that style and then present other oddities as they come.

Hertfordshire is short on grottoes. There used to be one at St Paul's Waldenbury, but it was long ago replaced by a garden pavilion. There is an excellent grotto in WARE, adjoining 28 Scott's Road, although the dank bedraggled entrance does not promise much. It was started in 1734 by Samuel Scott, a Quaker linen-draper, and finished in the summer of 1773 at a purported cost of £10,000 – a phenomenal sum – by his son John Scott, a popular contemporary poet, and his brother-in-law Charles Frogley. It is difficult to see how it could have cost so much, as the grotto is not large and is, as befits a Quaker grotto, somewhat austerely decorated. The layout is quite complicated though, and the various little caverns and chambers are endowed with portentous names – two Committee Rooms, the Robing Room, the Consultation Room, the Refreshment Room and the Council Chamber. The Robing Room, furthest from the entrance, is 70 feet into the hillside and 34 feet from the surface, but the air inside is surprisingly fresh and dry.

Dr Johnson, a friend of Scott who usually had little time for grottoes or follies, called the grotto 'a fairy palace', so perhaps he appreciated the austerity, or perhaps it was never properly finished. Scott obtained his shells from a Mr Turner in Exeter and there are some splendid conches, but restraint is everywhere. Now it is owned by the local council, who are doing an excellent job of restoration, and looked after by the Ware Society, who will show visitors round by appointment.

Towers too are scarce in Hertfordshire, but just the other side of Hertford, in the variously spelt village of LITTLE BERKHAMSTED, is Stratton's Observatory, probably the best known folly in the

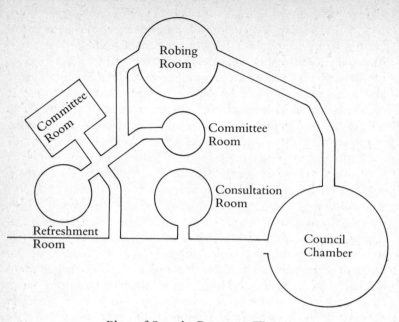

Plan of Scott's Grotto at Ware

county and now beautifully converted into a private house. It is a
rare example of a Georgian tower, and one glance is sufficient to see
why: the cool elegance of Georgian architecture, so much admired
nowadays, fails dismally on the vertical plane. Stratton's Observatory
is a round, battlemented, brick tower set on an octagonal base, and
the fenestration differs on each storey – square, arched gallery,
round, portrait. The whole edifice looks like a Soane scribble of
four unequal parts, the least successful being the blind arcading
punctuated by the gallery and round windows, looking like early
industrial architecture. But like 'Just William', its ugliness is
endearing, and when we learn that it was built in 1789 by Admiral
Sir John Stratton, we immediately forget about the 'observatory'
name and assume that he wanted to be able to see his ships in the
Thames from it. The tower is 92 feet high, 346 feet above sea level
and 17 miles from the Thames. Might the story for once have been

true? It is mathematically possible, especially with the powerful telescopes all admirals appear to have . . .

Other Hertfordshire towers include a late 18th-century pavilion tower at 'The Vineyard' in the Home Park at HATFIELD HOUSE, and a squat little two-storey affair called Charter Tower in Gadebridge Park, HEMEL HEMPSTEAD, near St Mary's Church. It is in fact a porch, removed here from a long-demolished Elizabethan house.

Hertfordshire's final tower is a column, which may seem like a contradiction, but a column can act as a tower while a tower cannot act as a column. If you are confused, there's worse to come. We define a tower as a free-standing structure, taller than it is wide, that was designed to be climbed, whereas a column, whose original function was to serve as a structural support, cannot be climbed. Therefore Nelson's Column in Trafalgar Square is just a column whereas the Monument in the City, also a column, is at the same time a tower. The Hertfordshire column/tower that concerns us here is the Bridgewater Monument built at ASHRIDGE, 'in honour of Francis Third Duke of Bridgewater, "Father of Inland Navigation". 1832'. It is a National Trust monument, a Doric column by Wyatville topped with a copper urn, sometimes open to the public (172 steps and a fine view) and a focal point for motorists for miles around. It is not a folly for solitude. Ashridge is always packed with picnicking families, screaming children, giggling girls and pimply youth — the 3rd Duke would have been appalled. By all accounts an unpleasant piece of work — fat, stupid and a misogynist to boot — his sobriquet was given because he constructed the first completely artificial waterway, in order to carry his coal from his Lancashire mines to his docks in Manchester. One can sense his reluctance to commission non-essential works such as landscaping, so it was not until after his death in 1803 that Repton was employed at Ashridge; the flower garden was laid out in 1815 for the 7th Earl of Bridgewater and there is a grotto built from huge boulders as well as a Gothic conduit, attributed to Wyatville.

The most outstanding eyecatcher in Hertfordshire is a church, and although time and again we have vowed that churches, being built for a good purpose, have no place in a book on follies, time and again we come across an exception that begs for inclusion. The

New Church at AYOT ST LAWRENCE merits its position here through style, substance and story. Sir Lyonel Lyde, the lord of the manor, decided to pull down the old 13th-century church of St Lawrence and replace it with something more harmonious. In 1778 he commissioned Nicholas Revett of West Wycombe and Shugborough fame to design him a startling modern church in the Grecian style Revett and 'Athenian' Stuart had so successfully popularised. The Bishop of Lincoln, in whose diocese Ayot St Lawrence then was, came to hear of the demolition and promptly suspended further work, leaving us in the 20th century with a picturesquely ruined church traditionally sited opposite the village pub. Meanwhile, across the fields to the west of the manor house, Revett's temple was taking shape, a Doric portico with two colonnaded wings terminating in two small pavilions, one either side. The east front, facing the house, was stuccoed; the back was left as plain brick. There is no shadow of a doubt that the primary function of the new church was to serve as an eyecatcher from the house: for a country church to be built in the Grecian style was revolutionary, and is still rare today, but not as revolutionary as it was to turn the church the wrong way round, so that the altar is at the west end rather than the east, in order for it not to interfere with the Grand Design. Beyond the church's outrageously fashionable design for its time, beyond the Bishop's ban, beyond the eyecatcher façade, lies perhaps the true reason for Sir Lyonel, a traditionalist in every other way, to build such a revolutionary church. The pavilions at the end of each colonnaded wing running north and south from the main body of the church contain respectively the sarcophagi of Sir Lyonel and his wife, whose marriage was apparently less than blissful. 'Since the Church united us in life,' rumbled Sir Lyonel, 'she can make amends by separating us in death.'

There are two outstanding folly arches in Hertfordshire; one was moved there and one was left there. The one that was left is known as the BROOKMANS PARK Folly Arch, although when it was built it had nothing to do with Brookmans Park. Once there was a village called North Mymms, and in that village was an estate called Gobions, once the seat of Sir Thomas More's family. Around 1730 the owner was Sir Jeremy Sambrook, and he employed James Gibbs to build him a mock-medieval castellated gateway. A hundred years later the owner of Brookmans, another North Mymms estate, demolished Gobions to enlarge his park, and in 1891 Brookmans itself was burnt down. Brookmans Park then became a nice middle-class housing estate, and through all this the Folly Arch (change and decay in all around I see) abided in peace. There is a story, a long way from being disproved, that a farthing was placed beneath each brick. Another story has the arch commemorating a visit by Elizabeth I — 150 years earlier? Particularly interesting as one of the first sham medieval follies, its design is reminiscent of Vanbrugh's Claremont belvedere. One striking touch that makes the Gibbs attribution probable is the different treatment given to either side of the arch. Flanked by two square, castellated, three-storey towers, the side facing the road is straightforwardly presented, with brick quoins and a brick keystone. But the park side has a massive Gibbs surround, somewhat uncertainly handled, as the whole structure — battlements, mouldings, windows — is brick built.

The other Hertfordshire arch is even earlier, although it has graced the county for only around 100 years. Driven from town by traffic congestion, this arch made its home in rural (as it was then) WALTHAM CROSS. Now a highway roars past a couple of hundred yards away, and there is again talk of removing the arch back to London. For this is the famous Temple Bar, one of the old entrances to the City of London, now enjoying a tranquil retirement in a Hertfordshire wood. The architect is popularly supposed to have been the great Sir Christopher Wren, although there is no conclusive evidence for the attribution; it was actually built by Joshua Marshall and Thomas Knight, both master masons, and as Marshall was a monumental sculptor as well as a contractor, it is quite possible that he designed the building. Originally erected in Fleet Street in 1672, by the busy 1870s the archway was hopelessly in the way of traffic, so Sir Henry Meux and his actress wife Susie had it dismantled and re-erected on their Theobalds Park estate in 1878, presumably for a conversation piece at their lavish parties. The parties may have spilled over into the park, because the arch is fitted with a primitive central-heating system and an additional wing is dated 1889. We are thankful that it has been preserved, for despite being roofless and vandalised it is not beyond restoration. Now it is one of Hertfordshire's best surprises; to walk down a woodland bridleway and suddenly (it really can't be seen until one is very near) come across Temple Bar — grand, overstated, baroque and quintessentially urban — is a highly enjoyable experience; it is much bigger and more solid than one expects, despite its poor condition. This building has been listed Grade I by the Department of the Environment, but few seem to care. In early 1984 a media fuss started about a proposal to resite the Bar in the shadow of St Paul's, where it would be dwarfed into insignificance, but at the time of writing nothing has been resolved and the arch continues to moulder quietly away in its rural resting place.

Wren, typical Londoner that he was, is the attributed architect of only one house in Hertfordshire — Tring Park — and that has been altered almost beyond recognition. We thought that the genius of Britain's most famous architect had passed Hertfordshire by entirely. Not quite: since 1975 when Hertfordshire acquired SOUTH MIMMS it also acquired some more of Wren's work. As Forest Hill in South-East London has the spire of Wren's City church of St Antholin, so Clare Hall Sanatorium had bits of St Antholin's built into its wall and gate after the church was demolished in 1874.

In the garden of a house in Prospect Road, ST ALBANS, is a sturdy but top-heavy classical arch dated 1773, placed on to a Victorian back, with a dovecote in the roof. Quite how it came to be there no one knows. It was obviously part of a now vanished house, but for the moment it holds its secret.

'The Lordship' in BENINGTON is a large house built next to Benington Castle, which was destroyed by King John in 1213, but which fired the imagination of George Proctor, the 19th-century owner of 'The Lordship', so much that he embarked on a full-scale romanticisation of the remaining ruins, and his house as well, employing a gardener called Pulham as architect. In 1832 they added a huge gatehouse, which overbalances the scale of both the house and the original ruins. Incorporated into the gateway are a shrine to Buddha and a Trojan inscribed stone.

Protected from Watford by the M1, Wall Hall College at ALDENHAM is an oasis in steadily encroaching suburbia. At the beginning of the 19th century, George Thellusson, son of one of the richest men in England, built a house at Wall Hall to which he grandly added a Gothick façade. He sold the estate in 1812 to Admiral Pole who, not to be outdone, constructed a ruined abbey, decorated his park with other Gothick trivia and renamed it Aldenham Abbey.

Another scrap of a sham ruin was built by the novelist Lord Bulwer-Lytton, author of *The Last Days of Pompeii*, at KNEBWORTH. The rather mannered house and park constitute a fine example of High Victoriana, so for Lord Lytton to erect the ruins of 'Queen Anne's Chapel', as he called his folly, must have been a conscious looking back to an earlier, more romantic era. Perhaps he was poking fun at himself, as trendy people deliberately put gnomes in their gardens, because in his novel *Pelham* he described a London garden with 'a pretty parterre here, and a Chinese pagoda there; an Oak-tree in one corner, and a mushroom bed in the other; and above all, a Gothic ruin opposite the bay-window! You may traverse the whole in a stride; it is the four quarters of the globe in a mole-hill.'

The Japanese influence in architecture and garden design has not been extensive in this country. There is Lord Redesdale's garden at Batsford in Gloucestershire, and Hertfordshire has the remarkable garden-house in COTTERED. In 1984, when the owners were trying to move, the house was valued at £150,000 and the garden — it *is* a garden, not a park — at £600,000. The garden was laid out over 28 years, from 1905, by Herbert Goode, a porcelain importer, and while it is the exotic plants that make it so valuable, Goode also built a mini-mountain complete with waterfalls, cascades and a Japanese tea-house made out of rare woods.

A dairy is a difficult building to romanticise, yet there are instances from all over the country — Woburn, Blaise etc. — where a dairy has been chosen to make a particular architectural statement. The fashion probably started in France, with Marie Antoinette's dairy at Le Hameau, her immaculately conceived model hamlet at Versailles, and Hertfordshire has three dairies that have been specially treated. The earliest is at NEWGATE STREET, south of Little Berkhamsted, and is a Doric temple to Ponsbourne House, built in the early 19th century. The other two are quite extraordinary. The Node Dairy at DRIVER'S END was built in 1927 by an American,

Maurice Chesterton, and although it was built as a working model dairy it is so fantastic in concept and execution that it has to be included here. The main building is essentially a circular wall enclosing a circular courtyard, the diameter of the courtyard being the same as the turning circle of a 1926 Foden milk lorry. Vehicles enter the courtyard through an arch set in a massive gable, repeated at the rear, and four wings one room deep jut out from the circle. From the air the thing must look like an OXO advertisement. The roof, which contains the second storey, is extremely steeply pitched. A mock Germanic medieval tower disguises a silo, but the really staggering thing about it is that it is entirely thatched – even the tower! It is said to have been the biggest thatched roof in the world at the time, and as we cannot imagine why anyone should wish to build a bigger, we suppose it still is. Now it is elegantly maintained and used as an up-market fitted bedroom showroom. The idea was copied four years later at ABBOT'S LANGLEY, for Ovaltine, who managed to cram half-timbering into the design but didn't go so far as to thatch everything in sight – only everything that could be seen from the main London–Birmingham railway, thus purveying an image of wholesome country goodness to train travellers for over 50 years. An inspired piece of advertising.

At the end of the A414's mad scurry in all directions through the county is the tiny village of GILSTON, just north of Harlow. Gilston Park was built in 1852, and in the garden is an apparently authentic Elizabethan porch dated 1583, which Pevsner says came from the previous house on the site, New Place. But the jingoistic inscription around the bust of Elizabeth I is remarkably legible and unworn:

FEAR. GOD. OBAYE. THE. RIAL. QUEEN.
Spaines Rod; Romes Rvine; Netherlandes Reliefe; Earthes joy,
England's gemme, World's Wonder, Natvres Chieffe.

As there is no record of the existence of this little porch before it appeared on a John Buckler drawing of 1830, we suspect it could be a 'Piltdown porch', a clever sham built by the owner of New Place in the 1820s. A little way east along the A414, at STANSTEAD ABBOTS, is the turning to Hunsdon, then Briggens Home Farm, which was gothicised with ogee windows to provide an eyecatcher from Briggens. On the south side of the road, rotting in the woods, is a splendid water-tower with an octagonal clapboarded 'house' disguising the tank, rather like a modest House in the Clouds. In Hunsdon itself is a small sham Gothic ruin in the garden of Longcroft, probably built for the Rev. Mr Calvert in 1832 as a garden ornament to his rectory, now Hunsdonbury.

Serenity is not a word that outsiders immediately think of in association with Hertfordshire, but we leave the county with two of the most peaceful and beautiful corners in all Britain. ST PAUL'S WALDENBURY has been the home of the Bowes Lyon family for over 250 years – the Queen Mother was born here – and their tranquil garden, occasionally open to the public, is studded with pavilions and temples; none would qualify individually as a folly, but when taken together they contribute the essential whimsy and unexpected beauty that make the English garden admired throughout the world. The gardens were remodelled in the 1950s by Geoffrey Jellicoe, the planner of Hemel Hempstead New Town, and as late as 1961 a 'new' temple was added: 'IN 1773 THIS TEMPLE WAS DESIGNED BY SIR WILLIAM CHAMBERS ARCHITECT AND WAS REMOVED FROM DANSON PARK KENT AND REERECTED 1961' (the inscription runs round three inside walls of the temple on the skirting-board). A large circular plaque on the back wall repeats the date, with the initials of David Bowes Lyon, one-time President of the Royal Horticultural Society. The Doric temple occupies a picturesque position on the shore of the little lake, facing another removal, a temple by Jeffry Wyatt from Copped Hall on the Essex/Hertfordshire border. The vistas in the garden are beautifully devised, one of them ingeniously incorporating the low tower of All Saints, the parish church. A hidden glade has a terraced theatre and another small temple, and finally there is an octagonal pavilion dated 1735, called, somewhat obscurely, 'The Organ House'. There is no longer a grotto and there appears never to have been a pyramid, as mentioned by both Barbara Jones and Pevsner.

The most beautiful spot in Hertfordshire is the New River at GREAT AMWELL – and if that sounds too sweeping, go and see it. The little village has a number of attractions for the folly-hunter, including a modern unroofed rotunda in a garden apparently unattached to any house and an avenue composed of different types of concrete lamp-posts, put up by a retired lamp-post manufacturer. The Mylne family, nine generations of architects, made Amwell. Robert Mylne was architect to the New River Company, and also built Blackfriars Bridge. A column from the bridge stands in the garden of Flint House, built by Robert's son William in 1842–4. Robert Mylne's crowning achievement in our eyes is the elysian plot at the end of the hill, below the church. It is dark, shaded, but not gloomy. A small dam in the river has created a tiny lake, no more than a pond, with two manicured, lushly turfed islets. One has a weeping willow, with a white Coade stone urn as a monument to Sir Hugh Myddelton, who constructed the New River in 1609 to bring water to the capital.

> From the Spring at Chadwell 2 miles west and from this source of Amwell the Acqueduct meanders for the space of XL miles conveying health, pleasure, and convenience to the metropolis of Great Britain . . . an immortal work since man cannot more nearly imitate the Deity than by bestowing health. This Monument was dedicated by Robert Mylne, architect, Engineer in 1800.

On the same islet is the Source stone, inscribed:

> O'erhung with shrubs, that fringe the chalky rock
> A little fount purr'd forth its gurgling rill.

The second, smaller islet has a yew tree and another monument to Myddelton, dated 1818, with lines from John Scott's poem 'Amwell':

> AMWELL, perpetual be thy stream
> Nor e'er thy spring be less
> which thousands drink who never dream
> whence flow the streams they bless.

The islets are linked by delicate little bridges, and the whole ensemble is so peaceful, so calm, that if sublimity can be found within an hour of London, it is here.

Greater London

An astonishing number of follies and architectural curiosities survive within the boundaries of Greater London — whimsical houses, over-elaborate monuments, grottoes, towers, arches — London has more follies to the square mile than anywhere else in the country. The quantity is unexpected; the quality is not. Few of them would excite much comment outside their urban environment, but their very survival, the tenacity of a useless scrap of brick and mortar holding out against the inexorable growth of the biggest urban sprawl in Europe, makes them worth recording.

London's follies and allied structures can be divided neatly into two types — the pampered and the ignored. The pampered ones are well known, sometimes even loved; the ignored have no known history, and unless they happen to be lived in or otherwise used neglect and vandalism accelerate the deterioration. Many are lived in, or were built as individualistic houses, a cry for identity in a uniform street. The housing shortage in London, as in all big cities, usually means that if a building can be lived in it will be.

So, as London consists more of houses than anything else, let's start with houses. In the 1980s a revolting new fashion for 'customising' one's house with artificial stone cladding sprang up like a rash on the terraced streets of the suburbs. These multi-coloured excrescences jar horribly with their brick or stuccoed neighbours and, apart from the honest and understandable desire to differentiate one's house from those of one's neighbours, we are at a loss to see why people should want to do this. It is unsightly, expensive, useless and can be potentially dangerous — but that is a reasonable description of a folly. Why not go the whole hog, as the nearly forgotten architect Ernest Trobridge did in Kingsbury, NW9, after the First World War? Encouraged and financed by the success of a prefabricated house he had exhibited at the Ideal Home Exhibition in 1920, Trobridge bought ten acres of Kingsbury and set about building his own ideals of popular housing. Being a concrete human being rather than an abstract architect, he designed houses that were and still are highly popular with their inhabitants, despite (or perhaps because of) looking like medieval castles with mighty battlements, arrowslits, moats and machicolations. Those were just the flats. The individual houses were variations on the Anne Hathaway's Cottage theme, mostly thatched, with low ceilings, the southern English dream-house. Start at the corner of BUCK LANE and Highfield Avenue to immerse yourself in Trobridgeshire.

Numbers 73 and 75 BELVEDERE ROAD, SE19, have glazed brick prospect-towers added to make a show among their neighbours, while 84 PHIPPS BRIDGE ROAD, SW19, is a real folly, a flint and stone sham castle grafted on the end of a row of terraced houses. The folly predates the terrace, and may well have been built *c.* 1788 as a lodge gatehouse by John Ewart for his house Morden Hall.

Public houses have good reason for bedecking themselves in architectural splendour — anything that sets them apart from their neighbours must do something for trade — but, perhaps surprisingly, few London pubs have chosen to do so. The best known is of course 'THE SWISS COTTAGE', which has given its name to a district and to an underground station. Way north in New Southgate is a pub called 'The Turrets' in FRIERN BARNET ROAD, N11, an unremarkable building except for the two spidery-thin, conical-roofed bartizan turrets flanking the façade giving on to Station Road. A crudely lettered plaque reads 'AD 1887 WWW'. Crocker's Folly in ABERDEEN PLACE, NW8, was more properly known as 'The Crown Hotel', and at first glance it looks like an elaborate Victorian pub with little of the folly about it. A closer look reveals the almost Byzantine elaboration of the pub's decoration, especially its interiors, and its sheer size, surely unnecessary when catering for a small catchment area. The story when it comes is truly satisfying and the perfect material from which follies are made. Frank Crocker knew — just *knew* — that the terminus for the new railway was going to be in Aberdeen Place, so in 1898 he speculated with all his available cash to build an emporium that would be an irresistible magnet for thirsty travellers alighting from the trains. As work progressed on his gin palace, so work progressed on the railway, and Mr Crocker watched in horror as the navvies dug relentlessly past his pride and joy to finish up at Marylebone. Even if the story isn't totally true — and who is to say it isn't? — we are still left with a glorious, enormous Victorian pub in a quiet backwater, now properly rechristened 'Crocker's'.

We come across the Swiss influence again at HAMPTON COURT, where Huck's Chalet on Hampton Court Road was built in 1899 as the offices of a marine engineering company. The building is in fact genuine, imported from Switzerland and re-erected here on the banks of the Thames — inappropriate but, as with pubs, a good advertisement for the company.

Away from the classical vocabulary of architecture, the adoption of another nation's vernacular style to build a house, pub or office would seem to be a peculiarly British weakness. It would be difficult to envisage a row of semi-detached villas in Peking, so why does it seem any less strange that a pagoda house should be built just off Blackheath? As with Swiss Cottage, the pagoda was sufficiently unusual to lend its name to the area, and the road this particular one is in is called PAGODA GARDENS, SE3. The house itself is Chinese only in the exaggerated upswing of the eaves and the peculiar horns at each end of the roof; apart from this, its most obvious feature is an enormous, oval, *oeil-de-boeuf* window on the second floor. As we were struggling to take a photograph over the high wall that surrounds the house, legs flailing in mid-air and lenses dangling either side of the wall, two children walked past and muttered 'Perverts'. The finest Chinoiserie in London is Sir William Chambers's Pagoda at Kew, which we will come to later, but there is an excellent and amusing Siamese petrol station on the WICKHAM ROAD roundabout in Beckenham, quite startling with its double eaves and upswung ridge culminating in a tiny pagoda. It is in excellent condition, well looked after by Texaco, and was built as a garage in the 1930s. On the banks of the Thames in BATTERSEA PARK, halfway between the Chelsea and Albert Bridges, is a gross, alien intruder — another Peace Pagoda, like the one at Willen in

Milton Keynes, and built by the same Japanese Buddhist sect of Nipponzan Myohoji. This one is the height of an 11-storey office block, set in the middle of the only wooded river-bank in town. It was finished in the summer of 1985, to the astonishment of Londoners, who never dreamed that such a folly could be granted planning permission in a London park.

The least expected ornamental architecture to be found in London must be Russian, but there is an *izba* in the garden of a house in THE VALE, SW3: an *izba* is a Russian peasant's thatched hut, with pink or whitewashed walls, and how this one found its way from the Ukraine to unrevolutionary Chelsea is a mystery.

The *cottage orné* is too common on country estates to merit a mention unless interpreted in a particularly eccentric fashion, but an almost forgotten example in North London is a different matter; in WOODSIDE PARK, on Wood Green High Road, N22, stands a round house with central chimney, little and deserted, pathetically guarding the park which, when we saw it, appeared to be being dug up and built over by the Council.

There are strange houses to be found all over big cities – sometimes they aren't even houses. Nos. 22–4 LEINSTER GARDENS, W2, look to all appearances like the grand stuccoed town-houses terraced on either side of them – but there are no curtains at the windows; in fact there are no windows. The two are mere façades to stop an unsightly gap where the Circle Line runs between the houses. One of the most eccentric houses in London is the 'Coach House' in FITZGERALD AVENUE, SW14, a hotch-potch of red brick, Ionic pillars and turrets, assembled seemingly at random from discarded elements of older buildings. The lintel above the door is dated 1696, but the overall structure would appear to be mid-Victorian.

Gothic houses abound in London, but some transcend the acceptable face of Gothicism. 'The Logs' in HAMPSTEAD LANE, Hampstead Heath, came to national prominence in the autumn of 1984 when it was announced that the pop singer Boy George had bought it for half a million pounds, but the deal fell through as soon as it became public knowledge. The media pounced on Pevsner's description of it as 'a formidable atrocity' and headlines gleefully announced 'BOY GEORGE BUYS A FOLLY'. In fact it is a large, grey-brick Victorian mansion, built in 1868 by J. S. Nightingale, simply a rather florid expression of 19th-century Gothic. Far more follylike is the Gothic house in LANGFORD PLACE, NW8, a sharp, crouching little house more at home in a Chas. Addams cartoon than in St John's Wood. Its most startling feature is a bay-window like a scarab beetle, and its oddity is set off by the sober town-houses that surround it. HOLLY VILLAGE in NW5, off Swain's Lane, is a model estate built in 1865 by the philanthropic Baroness Angela Burdett-Coutts, who also carried on her good building works in Hackney's Victoria Park and the village of Heath and Reach in Bedfordshire. Holly Village is the jewel in her crown — a tiara of tiny Gothic cottages sprinkled round an enclosed green, like refugees from Highgate Cemetery over the road. The architect was H. A. Darbishire, and the intention was to provide a pleasant living environment for the Baroness's staff, along the lines of Blaise Hamlet in Avon. Where Blaise succeeds through its tranquillity and serenity, Holly Village exudes gloom and despair; the lightheartedness intended by some Victorian Gothic architects does not seem to have been passed down to us.

The true folly — and here we include such items as towers, commemorative obelisks, grottoes and shams — found in London is a delightful puzzle. Is it the palimpsest of some half-forgotten vanished country estate, years before cheap housing made its indelible mark on the landscape? Is it a more recent effort at townscaping? Has it 'always been there'? The Grotto Cottage in STAMFORD BROOK ROAD, W6, is one such example. An ordinary little house has been given an excellent grotto façade — by its owner, or by someone who wanted a little eyecatcher to see from a bigger house? The discovery of Gothic stables in nearby RYLETT ROAD points to the latter explanation: before the 'ideal' suburb of Bedford Park was built in the 1870s the estate belonged to the Dukes of Bedford.

Grottoes are the most fragile, the most susceptible to damage of all these buildings, so it is remarkable that any have survived. Fortunately one of the earliest and most important in Britain remains intact. Alexander Pope started the fashion that swept the 18th century, and although his villa was demolished in 1807 and the gardens have been built over, his celebrated grotto remains in

GROTTO ROAD, Twickenham. Frankly, it is a disappointment, a garden ornament better read about from contemporary accounts than visited in the 20th century. Pope was the acknowledged King of Twickenham, and when in 1718 he dared to reject the previous formality of garden design and embrace the natural look, the beau monde followed. Grottoes and gardens sprang up imitatively all over Twickenham and spread to the rest of the country in succeeding years. The Countess of Suffolk at Marble Hill, Horace Walpole (the successor to Pope's crown) at Strawberry Hill, James Johnstone at Orleans House — all followed the lead set by Pope, though of course Walpole was to extend the boundaries of fashion beyond anything Pope dreamed of. But Pope's grotto was the catalyst, and Twickenham was the retort. The Countess of Suffolk had two grottoes at MARBLE HILL PARK; one has disappeared and the other has only just been rediscovered, and is being excavated by the GLC's Historic Buildings Division. It was first mentioned in a letter to the Countess from George Grenville in 1742, in which he 'sends his compliments to the inhabitants of the Grotto which, I hope, goes on prosperously'. A 1767 description of the grounds notes that 'there is an Ally of flowering shrubs, which leads with an easy Descent down to a very fine Grotto; there is also a smaller Grotto, from whence there is a fine view of Richmond-hill'.

Before we look at Twickenham's other delights, it may be as well to see how grottoes have fared in the rest of London. Up river from Twickenham at HAMPTON COURT HOUSE, now a children's home, is a grotto dating from 1769, said to have been built by the mysterious Thomas Wright to simulate the firmament and now being restored. On the other side of Hampton Court Road, opposite Garrick's house, is the Shakespeare Temple, an octagonal building with a Greek portico, built for Garrick by L. F. Roubiliac to hold his sculpture of Shakespeare. It is connected to the house by a Popish grotto-passage under the road.

The grotto at the National Trust's Osterley Park in ISLEWORTH is actually inside the house under the staircase; the rest of the house is more interesting. The park itself has two summer-houses designed by Robert Adam in 1780, but again and again one is distracted by the sight and sound of the M4 carving through the exact centre of the huge park, an incredible piece of planning.

Carshalton House and Carshalton Park at SUTTON both have grottoes, perhaps, the relics of some forgotten 18th-century rivalry. Carshalton House is now a girls' school, and at the head of the dry lake in the grounds is a five-bayed grotto façade screening a series of blocked up rooms and passages. It was probably built for Thomas Walpole in the 1770s. The park is on the site of Carshalton Place, demolished over 50 years ago, but the grotto remains, larger than the grotto at the school but more susceptible to the attentions of hooligans.

Grotto Passage in Marylebone, off Paddington Street, W1, commemorates a long vanished grotto built as a commercial undertaking by John Castle in 1738. It appears to have been enormous, built on one and a half acres of land, offering wining, dining and entertainment for an admission charge of half-a-crown – a stupendous sum in those days. Castle died in 1757, and the Royal Grotto, as it had become known, was demolished shortly afterwards. Castle also built Sir Robert Walpole's vanished grotto in Chelsea. Viscount Castlemain's WANSTEAD PARK in E11 was one of the 18th century's most fashionable houses; demolished in 1824, it is now an unkempt public park, but the mighty grotto head remains on the lake shore, carefully protected from the attentions of vandals by a fearsome and highly visible steel fence. It has been attributed to Kent, but only on the grounds that he decorated the ceiling of the Great Hall there in 1721.

And so back to Twickenham, and its most important building. Too well described elsewhere to need a full description here, but unfortunately not open to the public, STRAWBERRY HILL was the first significant house wholeheartedly to embrace the Gothick style, and coming from such a society figure and arbiter of taste as Horace Walpole, its repercussions were felt as far away as Northumberland and for 100 years. Walpole's Committee of Taste and the brilliant designers and architects he surrounded himself with combined to produce the epitome of light-hearted gothicism. In later, less sure hands the style took on a barbarity more appropriate to the marauding hordes who unknowingly lent their name to this most delicate style of architecture – in general the Goths preferred demolition to construction, as Walpole himself admitted. Walpole's Gothick was a joyous affair, architecture from the heart rather than accurate historical re-creation of the fine medieval ecclesiastical architecture which formed the inspiration for the Committee of Taste.

Here it may be as well to reiterate our definitions of Gothic and Gothick. For the purposes of this book — and in real life — we work on the belief that gothic was essentially a medieval style of architecture prevalent in the 12th and 13th centuries; Gothick was the revival of certain elements of that style — notably the pointed and the ogee arch — which lasted for about 100 years from 1720; and the Gothic Revival was a more serious, academic and austere architecture which led into the Victorian age and the flamboyant excesses that are gradually returning to favour. Strawberry Hill is indisputably Gothick.

In 1747 Walpole wrote to his cousin General Conway, 'Strawberry Hill is a little plaything-house that I got out of Mrs Chenevix's shop, and is the prettiest bauble you ever saw. It is set in enamelled meadows, with filigree hedges.' Obviously delighted with his lease, he lost little time in organising his friends to help him improve the house. William Robinson made the first alterations to Strawberry Hill in 1748, closely followed by John Chute of 'The Vyne' in Hampshire, who was largely responsible for the elevation. Walpole purchased the house in 1749, and in 1751 Richard Bentley, another member of the Committee of Taste, started to design the hall, the chimneypieces, the stairs and much else until 1761, when he had a spat with Walpole. Bentley was a prolific designer of follies, some of which were and some of which were not built. Among the latter we must regret the Triangular Chinese Building he designed for Lord Holland in Thanet, and among the former most of his architectural essays have now collapsed. Strawberry Hill remains his major work. Later, in 1766–7, Walpole called in Robert Adam to do a Gothick ceiling and chimneypiece. Ever a pioneer, Walpole anticipated a more learned approach to Gothicism, and in 1776 employed James Essex, who designed a gateway and the Beauclerk Tower and who was probably the most accurate gothic architect at the time, having studied it as an antiquary. Walpole's final commission before he died was given to James Wyatt for the Offices in 1790.

The prestige and influence of those who worked at Strawberry

Hill was immense, but the house, although the inspiration for many follies, cannot remotely be considered one. Walpole, who positively advocated ornamental building, had little time on his estate for follies. There were indeed garden buildings, but these were the expected ornamentation of the time: a shell-seat, an ornamental bridge, a rustic cottage — nothing particularly exciting and they have now disappeared. The one survival is the sham Chapel in the Woods, a tiny building designed by John Chute in 1772 and built by Thomas Gayfere in 1774 to hold Walpole's collection of stained glass. As Strawberry Hill is now an RC college, a chapel not a chapel was held to be a bad thing, so it was restored and consecrated after nearly 200 secular years.

In the grounds of York House, now the TWICKENHAM council offices, is a gigantic Italian fountain, far too large for its site, picked up by Prince Ratan Tata in 1906 from the effects of the suicide Whitaker Wright of Witley Court, who hadn't even unpacked it. (The egregious Wright and his extraordinary follies are described in the Surrey chapter.) London has very few fountains of any note, but there are one or two amusing drinking-fountains — a far more practical idea. On the way to Wanstead Park, on the corner of GEORGE GREEN, E11, is a tiny Rumpelstiltskin of a Jubilee fountain, while its Brobdingnagian equivalent towers in Hackney's VICTORIA PARK. The latter was built by Baroness Angela Burdett-Coutts in charitable mood as a gift to the impoverished East-Enders; made of porphyry and marble, and complete with clock, it cost a whopping £8,000. The clock has stopped at ten past one and the water has long been turned off, but the edifice is still too awesomely grand to deface.

Outside Victoria Station, in GROSVENOR GARDENS, are two little shell-houses rather improbably built by the French Government after the First World War to house gardeners' tools for looking after the triangular garden dedicated to Marshal Foch. This practice of disguising urban toolsheds cannot be praised too highly: it has given us one of London's best known follies, the half-timbered Tudor mini-manor house in the middle of SOHO SQUARE, built in 1876 and attributed by Pevsner to S. J. Thacker. It does not, as has been suggested, hide a ventilating shaft. There is a lesser known toolshed *orné* in LINCOLNS INN FIELDS.

The folly-towers of London are more common than might be expected. Any large, dangerous structure is more likely to disappear here than in some remote corner of the country, so the preservation of those that remain seems assured. The majority date from the 19th century, but the earliest and the best is Severndroog Castle, built in 1784 in what is now CASTLEWOOD PARK, on Shooters Hill, SE18.

This Building was Erected MDCCLXXXIV by the Repreſentative
of the late
Sᵖ· WILLIAM JAMES Bart.
To commemorate that Gallant Officer's Atchievements in the
EAST INDIES
during his command of the Company's Marine Forces in thoſe Seas
And in a particular manner to Record the Conqueſt of
The CASTLE of SEVERNDROOG off the COAST of MALABAR
which fell to his ſuperior Valour and able Conduct
on the 2ⁿᵈ Day of April MDCCLV

The tower is a beauty — a classic, triangular, brick folly-tower with hexagonal corner turrets, all in superb condition — gently Gothick, but above all Georgian in its elegance and refinement. Apart from letting the trees grow up around, so preventing its use as a belvedere, the GLC who now own it look after their charge with love and care. Their flag flutters proudly from the battlements. Let us hope the tower's future caretakers do as good a job. As befitted a Company building, the tower was designed by the Company's Surveyor, Richard Jupp, who had designed Painshill House in Surrey for the Hon. Charles Hamilton the previous year, but who was otherwise an architect of little originality. The 'Representative' was in fact Sir James's widow. The massive water-tower nearby, which can be seen 14 miles away in North London, was built in 1910.

There is an earlier 18th-century tower in CARSHALTON near the grotto in Carshalton House; this was built as a water-pump to maintain the level of the lake, but it is so massively ornate that it is certainly worthy of mention. Called the Water House, it was built *c.* 1720 in a grandiose Vanbrughian style. It would appear that the architect was Henry Joynes, who used to work for Vanbrugh.

The Oxo Tower is a familiar landmark to most Londoners, sited in a prominent position overlooking the Thames on the SOUTH BANK. We are not certain quite why public imagination has classed it as a folly, but there it is. We see it as a permanent advertisement, a clever ploy by the directors of Oxo and their architect Albert Moore. When plans for the five-storey tower on top of the Oxo warehouse in Coin Street were submitted in 1928, the London County Council objected on the grounds that advertisements could not be placed over a certain height; the architect successfully argued that it was not an advertisement, but that the windows in the tower just happened to be in the shape of 'O's and 'X's. The plans were allowed through, and now there is another struggle going on – to prevent its demolition.

Apart from the 20th-century Oxo Tower, London's eligible towers are 19th-century. A wonderful survival lingers on in CLOCK TOWER PLACE, N7, the old clock-tower and carillon of the Caledonian Metropolitan Cattle Market. This tall, Italianate whitestone tower by J. B. Bunning, with open arched buttresses at the base, was the centrepiece of one of London's busiest markets, closed since 1939. It was built in 1855 on the site of the 17th-century Copenhagen Tea House, and now stands just to the south of a housing estate, towering over the new buildings but now silently guarding an empty playing-field, all that remains of the market.

As well as the water-tower on Shooters Hill and the Water House in Carshalton, there are two other water-towers particularly worth seeing, one in Croydon and one in Southall. Both are remarkable because of their prominence and because, their primary function finished, they owe their survival to public acclaim. The 100-foot high Norman tower in Croydon was built in 1867 by Baldwin Latham and was decommissioned in 1971. Perched on the top of Park Hill – in WATERTOWER ROAD, naturally – it is such a familiar Croydon landmark that its existence after it ceased to be functional was never seriously threatened. The resurrection of the SOUTHALL water-tower is little short of miraculous. A familiar sight to Paddington commuters, it long ago became surplus to the requirements of the neighbouring gasworks. Luckily its bizarre appearance – hexagonal, with mighty machicolations, angle turrets and a great spindly stair turret — resulted in its being listed Grade II, and eventually a housing cooperative bought the shell for £38,000 in 1978. £1,100,000 later there were 37 flats inside the old hulk; the first inhabitants moved in in 1984.

MARKHOUSE ROAD, E17, has an engaging curiosity, built with faith and passion. A land lighthouse is quite useless, of course, in landlocked Walthamstow — but 'I am the Light of the World' was taken literally by the builder of this remarkable folly, perhaps Captain King, who laid the keystone in 1892. It was built as a United Methodist Free Church, and such it remains to this day, proudly labelled 'THE LIGHTHOUSE'. The logic cannot be faulted; as a beacon to save lost souls, the tower has an undeniable presence, but to come across this memorable edifice bursting out of even-terraced East London, with its carefully delineated ramp staircase and steeply pitched tiled roof surmounted by a large glass lantern, is quite enough to make anybody gasp and stretch one's eyes.

There is a mystery tower in Tottenham's LORDSHIP LANE, N17, at Bruce Castle — red-brick, battlemented, blind-arched and hollow. Pevsner puts it as 16th-century, but it would appear to be far later, early 19th-century at the earliest. At 21 feet in diameter and 30 feet high, it is too short to be a prospect-tower (anyway, there could never have been a prospect) and too austere to be a summer-house. There is a small window at the top of one of the arches, and one blank quatrefoil; a good and accessible enigma. Down the road in Hackney ('Britain's Poorest Borough', as it delights in telling its long-suffering residents) is an astonishing survival, a genuine squire's burnt brick folly-tower and arch covered in ivy and jutting into the parking area of a block of council flats. It was built in the 1840s by Arthur Craven as a prospect-tower for his house Craven Lodge, set in 70 acres on Clapton Common, the highest point in Hackney. The block of flats, built in 1957, was named TOWER COURT after it.

St Michael's Convent is north of STREATHAM COMMON; originally Park Hill House, it was built for William Leaf, a rich draper. The grounds were ornamented like a country estate in miniature, with a Doric temple, a rustic seat, and a sunken rockery garden which winds the width of the estate to a small octagonal folly-tower with gateway, all built by John Papworth in 1835 — and they all survive, cherished and preserved by the Sisters of the Congregation of the Poor Servants of the Mother of God. Not far away is Honor Oak, one of those London areas like Stroud Green which everyone has heard of but no one can quite place, where the owners of 23 LIPHOOK CRESCENT, SE23, have the great good fortune to have inherited a folly in their garden, a splendid 19th-century octagonal brick and stone tower. It was built on the top of the hill as a prospect-tower for Tewkesbury Lodge in Honor Oak Road, and survived when the house was demolished in the 1930s. The views over London from here are quite amazing. Far to the north of the river, in QUAKER'S WALK, N21, an architect has carefully converted an old Victorian water-tower into his home, with a glass wall at the top to take advantage of the southerly views.

One final tower, really huge this time, freestanding and far too grandiose for its simple purpose as a carillon, is almost unknown to Londoners despite being in the middle of South Kensington. At 280 feet, the Collcutt Tower easily outstrips folly giants such as the 218-foot Peterson's Tower in Hampshire or the 253 feet of Wainhouse's Tower in Halifax, but hidden among the buildings of Imperial College in IMPERIAL INSTITUTE ROAD it is almost ignored. True, there was a successful campaign to save it from demolition about 20 years ago, but since then it has been keeping a low profile, if such a thing can be said about the tallest folly in Britain. It was designed by Thomas Edward Collcutt as part of the Imperial Institute exhibition centre in 1886, and was saved when the Institute was demolished to make way for the new Imperial College buildings. The tower now stands alone in its glory, which we suspect was Collcutt's intention all along – he was particularly fond of towers in his early years, as seen by his design for Wakefield Town Hall in West Yorkshire.

Most of the estates that ringed London are now little more than memories perpetuated in street names: Tottenham Court, Stapleton Hall. Some were large enough or held out by virtue of the owner's position or wealth against the encroaching houses for long enough to become public parks, and it is in these few areas that we find oases for follies. GUNNERSBURY PARK, for example, has a rather distinguished pedigree. Princess Amelia, the second daughter of George II, started it, rivalling Kew, yet she never went for the

Chinese and Moorish quirks across the river. Amelia's follies were classical and Gothick, but most have disappeared, leaving only the Doric Temple/Dairy facing the Round Pond, whose builder is said to be William Chambers. Princess Amelia's Bath House suggests another survival, but the building appears to be of a later date. The Bath House, a Gothick pavilion with battlements, corner pinnacles and putti carved in the lintels, is near Gunnersbury House (now a museum) and is half hidden by municipal planting. Through the barred windows one can just make out the actual bath room and the remains of a shell-room. Right in the middle of the park is 'The Farm', plain but ornamented with Batty Langley-style windows.

In the 19th century, Gunnersbury Park was divided into three parts. Nathan Meyer Rothschild bought the largest section in 1835 and started building stables in the north-eastern corner, hard against the property of a certain Thomas Farmer. Rothschild's grandiose stables dominated Farmer's carefully conceived garden, so Farmer re-employed the architect W. F. Pocock, who had built lodges and gates to his estate in 1834, to erect a Gothick screen to conceal Rothschild's obtrusive white stable range. Farmer was so pleased with the result that after Pocock's death in 1849 he employed his son William to carry on building the ruins, tall mouldering arches like the remains of some once great abbey. The ruins themselves have become ruinous, particularly the tower, which has been made safe by being cut to such a low height that only a few steps can be climbed to a low parapet. There is some good sham Anglo-Saxon detailing. Rothschild was not to be outdone by his tiresome neighbour. In 1861 he acquired the southern part of the park, and where the M4 now flows he built castellated lodges, still surviving under the flyover. An old claypit was transformed into Potomac Pond, with matching rockery and boat-house. From the boat-house a boarded-up and castellated octagonal tower rises with all the required details (brackets in the form of heads of medieval kings) in the required places, so the whole effect is convincingly old.

On 5 July 1761 Horace Walpole wrote to the Earl of Strafford, 'We begin to perceive the tower of Kew from Montpellier-row; in a fortnight we will see it in Yorkshire.' Montpelier Row is two miles from the Pagoda in KEW GARDENS, which remains one of the great landmarks of South London. It was designed by Sir William Chambers for Augusta, Dowager Princess of Wales, and a plaque inside describes it further:

> It is 163 feet High and has Ten Storeys, the lowest being 26 ft in Diameter and 18 ft High. Above this each storey decreases by One foot in Diameter and one in height from the next Storey below.
>
> The Building was formerly rather more spectacular in appearance than it is at the present day, each Angle of the Roof was decorated with a Guardian Dragon. These Dragons were covered with a film of Multi-Coloured Glass which produced a dazzling reflection.
>
> Each Roof was covered in Sheets of Varnished Iron in varing Hues. The Decoration at the top being gilded.

The Pagoda is still a spectacular sight — it must have been magnificent. There were also bells on each roof angle, 80 of them, so in a breeze the whole building would have harmonised with itself in gentle tones reminiscent of the chink of porcelain teacups, which was presumably one of its few functions. It is not open to the public because the staircase, which takes up most of the interior space, is only wide enough to allow one person to ascend or descend at a time. But Kew, besides being the finest park in the London area, has other delights to offer the folly-hunter. Of course it is not really a park at all but a botanic garden which is open to the public, and the variety of trees alone makes it worth a visit, but we are concerned here primarily with useless buildings. The dowager Princess allowed Chambers free rein, and in rapid succession he produced a Mosque, a Gothic Cathedral, the Alhambra (these **three** inspired by J. H. Muntz, an associate member of Walpole's Committee of Taste), the Temple of Aeolus, the Temple of Arethusa, the Temple of Bellona, the Temple of Victory, the Temple of Pan, the Temple of Solitude, the Temple of the Sun, the Temple of Peace, the Ruined Arch and probably the Queen's Cottage, as well as several galleries and a theatre. Lewis Goupy, the fan painter, added another Chinese building, the House of Confucius, and for George IV Sir Jeffry Wyatville built the Pantheon in 1837. Ten years later, Decimus Burton supplied a folly with a function: the Italian campanile, the only building in the gardens that can be seen from the Kew Road, is a disguised chimney for the heating beneath the Palm House.

Much of this has disappeared. We are left with Chambers's Ruined Arch, marking the division between the Botanic Garden and the Park, which was built in 1760 out of Act of Parliament brick, the result of an attempt to standardise the size of building materials (Walpole commented acidly that this showed that 'a solecism may be committed even in architecture'); and the Pantheon, or King William's Temple, which survives on a mound in the park with Chambers's Temples of Aeolus, Arethusa and Bellona.

North London has no folly estate to speak of. There is an attractive sham bridge at KENWOOD on Hampstead Heath, wood painted white, but otherwise the nearest is CHISWICK HOUSE, like Strawberry Hill the home of a trend-setter in style, design and architecture, Lord Burlington. The house and its grounds now lie between the pincers of two major roads, the A316 and the A4; although its survival is ensured, its serenity has gone for ever. Not that Burlington searched for serenity. His 1725 house was as shocking in its time as the international style, or neo-Brutalism, was in this century, an uncompromising architectural statement, an essay in Palladianism. Of course it was hopeless for living in, and Burlington remained in his Jacobean mansion, using the villa as an art gallery and a place to entertain. When the 4th Duke of Devonshire acquired the property, he demolished the old house and had Wyatt add two large wings to the little villa. These were finally demolished in 1952 and the house we now see is as Burlington intended it. Before starting work on the house, however, he had begun the garden with the help of first Bridgeman and then Kent. It is this garden that opened the way for the great flood of creativity in English landscape design, a true break with the past, and although to modern eyes it may look episodic and indecisive it gives that impression only because it was the first attempt at a new look for landscape. The grounds, maintained by the Council, are crammed with statues, the centrepiece being the *exedra* by Kent. There were obelisks, a grotto seat, a cascade, columns, busts, terms, a temple, a rustic house − all packed so closely together that they could not be described separately. Many still exist, and still more have been replaced or rebuilt by the enlightened Council.

We are left with a ragbag of unclassifiable buildings, oddities that survive through a planning oversight at the bottom end of the scale or national pride at the top. The Albert Memorial, at KENSINGTON GORE, comes in the second category; the finest flowering of Victorian Gothic, it cost £150,000 and took 12 years to build, using materials of biblical sonority − agate, onyx, jasper, cornelian, crystal, marble and granite. The architect Giles Gilbert Scott regarded it as his masterpiece and would no doubt have been horrified by the derisive attitude of Londoners towards it a couple of generations later, when it was vilified as a hideous monstrosity. In our own lifetime, public opinion has gradually shifted so that more people now approve than disapprove, but there are still those who find it an eyesore of the first magnitude. Lovers of trivia will be interested to learn that the book lying open on Albert's lap is the Catalogue for the 1851 Great Exhibition.

Another bizarre memorial is in the Roman Catholic cemetery at MORTLAKE, in North Worple Way. This is a stone tent to the memory of the explorer Sir Richard Burton, who died in 1890. The mausoleum was designed by his wife, and the star and crescent frieze around the tent is incongruously surmounted by a cross.

Sham churches are not suited to London. Walpole had his Chapel in the Woods, and the only others that fall within the county of Greater London are captured from a previously rural existence. Harts Hospital in WOODFORD GREEN, on the Essex border, is said to contain a sham ruined abbey in the grounds, but the hospital was closed at the time of writing and we have not seen it. Much more solid and pleasing is Tooke's Folly in PINNER HILL ROAD, Harrow. We drove straight past this at first, thinking it was a real chapel, then came slowly to the realisation that real chapels don't stand in farmyards, and came back. There was the tower, and there was the nave, but the roof of the nave had Velux windows, looking far too up-to-date. An indecipherable plaque on the tower would appear to read, 'THE TOWER OF A. W. TOOKE'; the date 1862 can be seen. The owner told us that this was not Tooke's Folly − that name was given to his mansion of 1864, a huge baronial Belgian château-tower properly known as Woodhall Towers, now demolished. Arthur William Tooke was the son of the first President of the Society of Arts, but other than that seems not to have distinguished himself in any way, apart from his fine 'chapel'. The sham chapel used to be the stables to Woodhall Towers (and served as a tolerable eyecatcher into the bargain, despite being built two years before the house); the present owner wanted to make it habitable but the Council refused permission, saying it couldn't be a house as it hadn't got a garden. So it became an office.

Nearby, in DUCK'S HILL ROAD in Northwood, is a little rotunda nearly overhanging the road, incongruous in leafy suburbia. From the outside it is an unremarkable garden gazebo, colonnaded on the garden side, walled to the road. Its joy is in the wooden domed interior, finely carved with 20 ribs culminating in a huge central boss of diminishing circles. The ribs spring from 20 carved faces of saints, kings and angels, all different. The rotunda was originally part of the grounds of Northwood Hall, built in the mid-19th century by Daniel Norton, a timber merchant from Uxbridge. Northwood Hall is now Denville Hall, a home for retired actors, and the grounds have been parcelled off to make large, and interesting, gardens for the neighbours. Another London rotunda is a very different affair; this one is gigantic and far from being a garden ornament. It is in Woolwich, off REPOSITORY ROAD, SE18, and it houses the Museum of Artillery. John Nash built it originally in St James's Park, for the Year of Peace in 1814, as a mock tent; like Crystal Palace it was too huge to ignore, and it was re-erected here in 1819. It is unmistakable with its huge concave roof sweeping up to the lantern at the top, the entire structure being nearly all roof supported only by a low, yellow-brick wall. This is not circular as we expected, but polygonal, although we failed to agree on the number of angles. This wonderful, eyecatching building deserves to be better known. Surprisingly, it seems not to have given rise to any legends.

East London, carefully ignored by almost every tourist and every guide-book, has its share of curiosities. We have already read of the remarkable survival of a 19th-century folly-tower in Hackney; there is a large lancet arch flanked by taller buttresses at the entrance to MEATH GARDENS, E2, freshly painted in white with the shield bearing the inscription 'V. P. C. 1845'. What it guarded we do not know, nor why it remains intact between the scrubby little recreation grounds and the dismal council flats. A newer housing estate in BALLANCE ROAD, E9, has an interesting oddity — the complete text of Lewis Carroll's 'How doth the little crocodile' set in a paving-stone in the walkway between Ballance Road and Hassett Road.

On a fine day, the driver who glances down LINSCOTT ROAD, E5, while motoring along the Lower Clapton Road runs the risk of being severely distracted from the job in hand — at the end of yet another East London mean street towers the Acropolis, glowing in the sun. In fact it is the enormous 13-bayed shell of the London Orphan Asylum, designed by the 23-year-old architect William Inman in 1821. Later it became a Salvation Army Congress Hall; now only the façade remains, a massive four-column portico flanked either side by open distyle colonnades four columns long. Set on a hill in the country this would make the finest eyecatcher in Britain; lost in the back streets of London it has become a golden, forgotten folly.

Not far from Linscott Road is the Stoke Newington Pumping Station in GREEN LANES, N4. In its own way this is just as spectacular as the London Orphan Asylum, but it has a claim to be excluded from folly consideration as it was designed as a working building and remains so to this day. However, its architecture is so outlandish that it forces its way into the book. Set between Clissold Park and a row of self-righteous mock Tudor houses, an enormous, grim castle thrusts turrets of varying shapes and sizes indiscriminately into the air. There is a different design of tower at each corner of this heavily buttressed building; the architect, William Chadwell Mylne, secure in the knowledge that he had already served 43 years as surveyor to the water company and that they couldn't sack him now, allowed his imagination to run riot. It is a splendid, eyestopping building, tremendously sited even today, high on a mound dominating Green Lanes. Mylne's son Robert was the last of this remarkable family to practise architecture (nine generations of architects, beginning in Dundee in the 16th century) and Mylnes feature elsewhere in these pages.

Returning to the centre of London — Charing Cross is the point from which distances are measured, but TRAFALGAR SQUARE is close enough — the curious globular lights on either side of the square in line with Nelson's Column are interesting in two ways: first, for the theory that, like a diamond, a lamp globe with 40 facets would cast a more brilliant light than a regular globe (it didn't; that's why there are only two); and secondly for the fact that the pedestal on which the east light stands is Britain's smallest police station — room for one copper and a telephone, to keep an unnoticed eye on demonstrations and disturbances in the square.

There must be many more follies and architectural oddities to be found in London — we were surprised by how many merited serious consideration, and new candidates came forward regularly. Many great buildings have of course been lost. We would like to have seen Grant's Folly in Prince of Wales Terrace, SW7, a house built in 1872 at a cost of £300,000. In order to make himself a seven-acre garden, Alfred Grant, company promoter and MP for Kidderminster, demolished Jennings Rents, the homes of 1,200 people, and rehoused them in Notting Hill. The job completed, Grant gave a party — but he never moved in and the house was demolished within ten years, in 1882. Another delight would have been England's answer to the Eiffel Tower in Wembley. The building reached 100 feet, about a tenth of the intended way, before interest was lost, and the rusting hulk stood there forlornly for a number of years until it was demolished after the First World War to make way for Wembley Stadium. In 1904 there was a 300-foot Ferris wheel near what is now Chelsea's football ground; it was never intended to be a permanent structure, but the sheer size was awe-inspiring. Go and see the Collcutt Tower in South Kensington and try to picture a wheel of which the diameter was 20 feet taller! Crystal Palace would have been a delight — but at least there are still dinosaurs to be seen in CRYSTAL PALACE PARK. Not of flesh and blood, but bronze and paint, they are lifesize and lifelike, built in 1854 by B. W. Hawkins and Professor R. Owen. North of the Thames, the Regent's Park Colosseum was an enormous art gallery built by Thomas Hornor to display his bird's-eye views of London, complete with the first passenger lift in the city; but the money ran out, the building wasn't finished, and Hornor fled the country,

72 Derry Ormond Tower,
Lampeter

73 Penrice Wall, Gower

80   Ivy Tower, Neath

81   Clytha Castle

82-3 The Naval Temple and the Round House on the Kymin, Monmouth

84   The grotto made with chicken wire at Dinmore Manor

leaving behind him vast crowds of visitors who paid a fortune to
gawp at Hornor's Folly.

There are many more tales of grandiose schemes that ganged
agley, and they are excellently documented in Felix Barker's
essential book *London As It Might Have Been*; though we may regret
the city we could have had, the one we have inherited has
something for everyone.

Oxfordshire

Part Cotswold, part Chiltern – Oxfordshire seems to have a little of everything in its makeup. Is it the southernmost midland county or the northernmost southern county? There is an equal uncertainty about its follies, which follow no particular trends, although the best in the county are both eyecatchers.

In 1974 Oxfordshire acquired one of the most famous folly-towers in Britain, when the town of FARINGDON was transferred from Berkshire. Lord Berners' Folly, as it was known from the start, is the last major folly-tower to have been built. It was completed in 1935 despite strenuous local opposition, the 14th Lord Berners, a talented musician, being a good deal too obviously unmarried for the fulminating generals and admirals who lived in the region. When the Council met to decide whether to grant planning permission – a factor that never troubled the original folly builders – one furious old salt bellowed that it would totally destroy the view from his house. When counsel for Lord Berners pointed out that the proposed tower could only possibly be seen from the Admiral's house with a telescope, the sailor retorted that being an admiral he only ever looked at the view through a telescope. Nevertheless, Lord Berners won his battle, and the 140-foot tower, designed by Trenwith Wills and Lord Gerald Wellesley, later the 7th Duke of Wellington, was finally built. Much amusement was caused by an old soldier contemptuously referring to it as 'Lord Berners' monstrous erection'. The building provided diary editors and social pages with their bread and butter during 1935, and the culmination was a grand party and firework display on the 5th of November and the release of hundreds of doves dyed red, white and blue. Alas, the tower itself is plain rather than ugly. Apparently it was originally colourwashed cream, but no trace remains. Gaunt ribbed bricks rear up 120 feet with two tiny wood-framed windows, devoid of ornament, one on each side. At the top is a smaller square belvedere room with three arched windows on each side. The local lads must have had very powerful catapults to have broken every pane of glass in these. On the top, an octagonal pinnacled room, with elongated oblong windows which remain unscathed, stands as the only decoration on the mouldering pile. Although it is only 50 years old it already appears ruinous and derelict. The mortar has fallen from between the bricks, the glass has gone and, worst of all, the entrance was firmly and finally blocked up 15 years ago. Inside, apparently, is a rotting wooden staircase, another example of the limited funds available to folly builders, but for those brave enough to get to the top, the Bristol Channel could be seen on a clear day. There was also a note from Lord Berners which read 'Members of the public committing suicide from this tower do so at their own risk'. The first building to greet one in Faringdon is a pub called 'The Folly', but this was so called long before 1935: the clump of trees (*feuillée*) on the hill was planted in the 18th century by Henry Pye, the half-remembered Poet Laureate, who wrote a poem, 'Faringdon Hill', about the site, which has been known as Faringdon Folly for at least 200 years.

That is the only tower in Oxfordshire. The building called 'The Tower' in WOOLSTONE, in the Vale of the White Horse, is only a three-storey house with fanciful brickwork, and 'A. N. 1877' picked out boldly on one gable end, 'W. N.' but no date on the other.

At WROXTON ABBEY there is an obelisk commemorating a visit by the Prince of Wales in 1739, as well as a classical temple and a dovecote trying to look like an ancient Gothick tower, but the real joy to be discovered here is the beautiful 1750 Sanderson Miller eyecatcher on a hill a mile away, south of Drayton. Trees have now grown up, concealing the eyecatcher from the Abbey, but like all Miller's work it is equally enjoyable close to. This was his country: his estate of Radway is only a few miles away, and he knew the land and its stone. To see Wroxton Eyecatcher on an autumn evening with the sun slanting across the golden field on to its golden stone is to be captivated by this extraordinary cul-de-sac of architecture, in which buildings made with no thought for posterity have somehow survived and given untold pleasure to succeeding generations. It is a simple, symmetrical folly, a central stepped arch flanked by two slender towers, but its stone and its situation make it memorable. Miller worked on Wroxton Abbey for the Earl of Guilford, producing a now demolished Gothick temple and a new tower for the 14th-century church. We must always remember that Miller was an *amateur* architect; when Horace Walpole visited he commented, 'the tower is in a good plain Gothic style, and was once, they tell you, still more beautiful, but Mr Miller, who designed it, unluckily once in his life happened to think rather of beauty than of water-tables, and so it fell down the first winter.' Walpole described also the Chinoiserie – the first recorded Chinoiserie – with which Wroxton's park was decorated: 'There are several paltry Chinese buildings and bridges, which have the merit or demerit of being the progenitors of a very numerous race all over the kingdom; at least they were of the very first.' Unfortunately, not a trace remains.

Miller's great predecessor William Kent produced Oxfordshire's other notable eyecatcher for General Sir James Dormer of ROUSHAM HOUSE. Starting in 1738, Kent remodelled the house and landscaped the relatively small garden nestled in a bend in the Cherwell to such effect that it became a blueprint for succeeding landscape architects, and is generally regarded as his masterpiece. His paths, walks and cascades overlaid the Charles Bridgeman designed garden of 20 years earlier and remain substantially unaltered to this day. Kent's stroke of genius lay in opening up vistas outside the garden to involve the surrounding landscape. Aware that a view needed to be answered, he erected two structures to catch the eye – one, the transformation of an old mill into 'The Chapel of the Mill', complete with flying buttresses, stepped gables, pinnacles and a quatrefoil window; the other, a straightforward eyecatcher, the first ever built, standing a mile to the north on a hill to the east of the village of Steeple Aston, a large tripartite arch, buttressed, with blank side wings and a curved pinnacled top. Close to, the basic structure is seen to be severely rectangular, the curved top seeming to be a later infill; there is no record to show if this was Kent's original intention, although the eyecatcher was intended to be a triumphal arch celebrating General Dormer's victories in Spain. There is no need to list all the temples, terraces and statues in the garden itself, but mention must be made of the elegant Arcade and the cascades in Venus Vale which echo, perhaps unconsciously, the eyecatcher. In front of the bottom cascade is a memorial inscription to Ringwood, 'an OTTER-HOUND of extraordinary Sagacity', with an exhortation to local otters ('Tyrant of the Cherwell's Flood') not to pollute his tomb.

Shotover House at WHEATLEY, on the outskirts of Oxford, can also boast the survival of a nearly complete early 18th-century garden. Rousham has the first eyecatcher; it is very likely that the Gothic Temple at Shotover is the first Gothick revival garden building in Britain. Once again the credit goes to Kent, the building in the past having been variously attributed to Vanbrugh, Hawksmoor, Gibbs and Townesend, but recently Kent's own drawings for it have been discovered and sold to the United States. As a model it could scarcely be bettered; despite Walpole's acid comments on Kent's ability with the Gothick touch, this first Gothick folly has almost all the requirements. It is large, gabled, battlemented, pinnacled, turreted, mysterious, enigmatic and old. In Bickham's bird's-eye view of Shotover dated 1750 it appears well settled into its environment, squarely facing the house along the formal east–west axis. General James Tyrrell commissioned Kent in 1734 to improve his landscape, and here the first tentative steps away from the formal garden and towards a more picturesque appearance were taken. Instead of rigid straight lines, rectangular canals and formal ponds, Kent laid out serpentine paths in the woods between an obelisk and an octagonal domed temple which he built on an artificial mound. The reduced circumstances of later proprietors of Shotover have largely been responsible for the preservation of these gardens in the face of rapidly changing fashion.

The other great estates in the county are less appealing to the folly-hunter. BLENHEIM is gigantic, its conception and scale such that they preclude follies: the spirit of the place is national rather than personal. Hawksmoor's 130-foot Column of Victory, the closest contender, is the product of a committee rather than the caprice of a single mind. There were possibilities in such buildings as the Temple of Diana, the Temple of Health (built, prematurely, to celebrate George III's recovery from lunacy), the Swiss Chalet, the Shepherd's Cot, and especially the Springlock Boulder, a massive boulder blocking a path which moved aside when a hidden lever was pulled, but the whole estate was generally too worthy and serious to trifle with architectural eccentricities; it impresses by size rather than surprise. BUCKLAND is built on a much more human scale but lacks any real follies, although there is a pleasant rotunda, probably built by Romaine Walker in 1910, which contains a memorial plinth and urn to the 20th-century Knights of Kerry. It is most famous for its ice-house, the finest in Oxfordshire, with grotto overtones, but there is particular pleasure to be had in comparing the solemnity of the big house with the architect's own description of himself when applying for membership to Liverpool's Ugly Face Clubbe four years earlier, in 1751: 'A stone colour'd complexion, a dimple in his Attic storey. The Pillasters of his face fluted. Tortoise-ey'd, a prominent nose. Wild grin, and face altogether resembling a badger, and finer tho' smaller than Sir Christopher Wren or Inigo Jones's.' Sadly, John Wood does not seem to have been commissioned to design any follies; a man with such a self-deprecating sense of humour would have enjoyed a stone joke

Beneath an ivy-covered stump on the side of a hill at NUNEHAM COURTENAY is an old wooden seat with a plaque on top reading:

Thiſ Tree
Waſ planted by one Barbra Wyatt who waſ ſo much
attached to it that at the removal of the Village of
Nuneham Courtney ſhe earneſtly entreated
that ſhe might remain in her olde habitation
her requeſt waſ complied with and her Cottage not
pulled down till after her death. Anno 1760.

and then the back of the seat below has a 36-line poem painted on it which ends:

Hear this ye great, whose proud poſſeſsions spread
O'er earth's rich surface to no space confin'd
Ye learn'd in arts in men in manners read
Who boast as wide as empire o'er the mind

With reverence visit her august domain
To her unletter'd memory bow the knee:
She found that happineſs you seek in vain
Bless'd with a cottage and a single tree.

If the rhythm and metre of this poem seem familiar, it is not surprising: it has been proved to most people's satisfaction that Nuneham Courtenay is the Sweet Auburn of Oliver Goldsmith's *Deserted Village*. The poem itself is by another forgotten Poet Laureate, William Whitehead. Simon, 1st Earl of Harcourt, demolished the village of Nuneham Courtenay in 1760 to create a magnificent park and landscape; we visited the park one beautiful spring morning and it would not be easy to disagree with Horace Walpole's assertion that the landscape is the most beautiful in the world, a quite remarkably lovely scene, with daffodils and cherry blossom clothing the hill sloping softly down to the Thames from the church — or, rather, the eyecatcher basilica — which Harcourt designed with 'Athenian' Stuart and built in 1764. The 2nd Earl, Harcourt's republican son, mellowed with age and employed 'Capability' Brown in 1778. He designed a Gothick tower which was never built, because in 1787 Harcourt acquired the magnificently ornate Carfax Conduit, which originally stood in Oxford's High Street, and erected it on the tower's chosen site as an eyecatcher. This splendid building, excellently preserved, stands on a high ridge overlooking the Thames and its former home. It is square, with an ornate carved parapet with 'O N', for Otho Nicholson, the builder of the conduit, repeated all round, and is topped by an even more elaborately carved octagonal turret supported on four legs, with carved figures in niches, on the columns and on the top of the little dome. The grotto at Nuneham has now disappeared, but a bark temple remains in the later stages of decay, and it is possible to discover here and there fragments of former glories of these urn-bestrewn gardens. The house is now a conference centre, so the park will be cared for as a facility for delegates.

DITCHLEY PARK near Charlbury was laid out by James Gibbs in the 1720s and reworked by Brown in 1770. William Kent worked inside the house rather than in the garden, although Lodge Farm, built as an eyecatcher to the south, has some qualities of his strained Gothick. The façade facing the house has three arches in the centre, formerly open but now filled with door and windows – Gothick traceried windows in the side wings and five quatrefoil windows on the first floor. A barn to the west also has arches and quatrefoils. There are two temples in the park itself: a Tuscan temple originally built by the lake but moved nearer the house in 1930, and a round Ionic temple built by Stiff Leadbetter in 1760 but which has also been attributed to Henry Holland. There is a three-arched stone grotto at the head of the lake. Another much finer grotto is in the grounds of Crowsley Park at SHIPLAKE, now largely a wireless transmitting station but still retaining an excitingly gloomy yew walk to a hollow in the woods, where the flint façade of the grotto looms, like an ogre's mouth. Inside it is plain and friendly, a vaulted roof with *oeil-de-boeuf* centre and ribs running down to the corners, terminating in smiling faces. The four niches either side may once have held busts, but nothing now remains, not even a shell. Surprisingly, it is warmer inside than out. The owner credits the building to the Earl of Uxbridge and Lord Dungannon, two dissolute members of Dashwood's Hell Fire Club; West Wycombe is only about ten miles away.

Oxfordshire's most bizarre building is the French Gothic mansion of Friar Park, set in 42 acres of grounds behind the Town Hall in HENLEY-ON-THAMES. It is now the home of ex-Beatle George Harrison, and as visitors are not allowed in this description has had to be assembled from other books and a dash of hearsay. It was built in 1896 by a solicitor, Sir Frank Crisp, and his architect, M. Clarke Edwards. Crisp gave full rein to his fantasies not only in the house but also in the park, constructing a range of sham Swiss Alps (complete with china chamois), underground caverns and lakes lit by electricity. There were several caves: the Blue Grotto, the Ice Grotto, the Vine Grotto, the Large Cave, the Wishing-Well Cave, the Skeleton Cave, the Gnome Cave and the Illusion Cave. All these were decorated and electrified in such a way that the visitor passing through them could be treated to a display of conjuring tricks from a Victorian Disneyland. Electricity was still very much a novelty at the time, and to see a crocodile with flashing eyes was genuinely shocking. There was an artificial underground rainbow, faces not your own staring back at you from sunken pools, a skeleton that jumped out at you – all the fun of the fair. In the house all the bells and light switches were model friars: the noses were turned to switch on the lights. Lady Ottoline Morrell, who visited in 1905, couldn't decide whether Sir Frank was 'colossally simple and really thought these vulgar and monstrous jokes beautiful and amusing'. Gradually the monstrous jokes fell into decay; up until 1969 when George Harrison bought it, the Order of St John Bosco used it as a Roman Catholic school and presumably had little interest in maintaining jokes at the expense of friars, or in perpetuating models of walled-up friars in the caverns. However, it is rumoured that the ex-Beatle has spent one and a quarter million pounds renovating the garden with its amazing private fun-fair; it would be wonderful to see it.

Much better known than the Lodge Farm at Ditchley is Strattenborough Castle Farm near COLESHILL, right on the Wiltshire border outside Watchfield, a splendid sham façade dated 1792 on the back of an otherwise unremarkable farmhouse. About 14 years ago the owner was claiming it to be a genuine castle dating from the 11th century and refurbished in the 18th, but now this claim has been relinquished. The stone front is charming, with its mock windows, turrets and battlements, but the most convincing part is the brick infill, without which the western wall of the front would crumble away to ruin — intentional or otherwise? The two main walls are high and level with it; the remains of the battlements can be seen on the top. Incorporated in a barn wall are the remains of a massive round-arched window, and underneath, set into the wall, is the carved figure of a man on a horse, which looks early medieval. Coleshill Park lies a mile away across the valley; from the famous house that stood there until 1952 Strattenborough must have seemed a vanquished rival in picturesque decay. South of Witney the quaintly named Fish House Mill at COKETHORPE also received the eyecatcher façade treatment to make a viewpoint from Cokethorpe Park. The square mill-house was battlemented and ornamented with heavily crocketed pinnacles in the centre and at the corners of each wall, and Tudor windows. It is three storeys high and carries a datestone of 1723 which, as Jennifer Sherwood points out, is too early for this treatment. It is much more likely to have been modified later in the 18th century: the tower includes masonry taken from Stanton Harcourt manor, which was demolished *c.* 1750.

The ruined Abbey cloisters at ABINGDON deceive many visitors and probably one or two of the residents. Easily accessible in a public park behind the Council offices, they are large, elaborate and fraudulent. Parts of the extensive ruin are indeed medieval, genuine fragments of the dissolved Abbey, but in about 1860 a Mr Trendall gathered them all together and built this fine fake abutting the wall of his garden in Abbey House. Abingdon's own glory is a little faded: it used to be the county town of Berkshire, but now it ranks only as the third largest town in Oxfordshire, and even the famous MG is no longer made here.

At MAPLEDURHAM HOUSE, hidden in the woods, is a little statue on a grossly over-elaborate plinth; it is hard to decide whether the statue was intended to decorate the plinth, which looks like a chimneypiece without a house, or vice versa. It is known as Old Palm, and on Christmas Eve the statue climbs down and passes through the village spreading good cheer. In the north wall of the kitchen garden is an ornamental arch, originally part of a mid-18th-century summer-house.

The other follies in the county are scraps — little conceits for the most part, with the mighty exception of Mr Bliss's Tweed Mill, with which we shall end this chapter.

Druids seem never to have caught the Oxford imagination to any great degree. There are sham stone circles at STONOR PARK and across the road from Ipsden House in the surprisingly bleak village of IPSDEN, but neither has stones more than two or three feet high. The Ipsden one was built in 1827, and in the same year, in a field a little way to the north, near a dissenters' chapel, a small pyramidal monument was erected to John Reade, who died in India. The parish of Ipsden also incorporates STOKE ROW, a very much more suburban settlement, neat, tidy, and safe, which has one of the more curious gifts to be offered to this country by a foreigner. Known as the Maharajah's Well, its oriental design and cosy English situation appear incongruous to modern eyes. Things were very different in 1863 however; at that time Stoke Row was 'a number of cottages scattered around a melancholy common' on the chalk Chilterns, and the water supply was sporadic, with empty claypits being used as reservoirs. Edward Reade of Ipsden House, Lieutenant Governor of the Indian North-Western Provinces, was friendly with the Maharajah of Benares and pointed out to him the similarity between the Chilterns and a part of his estate, as well as the similar suffering caused by the lack of water. The Maharajah endowed a charitable trust to supply a well at Stoke Row, and the unusual maroon, gold and blue wellhead was erected above a 368-foot deep borehole. The well was used up until the Second World War; it is still beautifully painted and maintained and could still be used for drawing water if required. On the road from here to Nettlebed is a tiny, easily overlooked curiosity by the side of the B481 at HIGHMOOR – a model country-house/castle no more than two feet high, built, so the inscription tells us, by '343 ENGNRS US ARMY 1942'. Why?

In HOLTON PARK near Shotover is a curious octagonal ditched earthworks, said by some to be a Civil War battery emplacement and by others to be the site of a long vanished folly, Holton Park being a Gothic house of 1815. The long barrow in HENLEY DEER PARK was a pure practical joke, to be enjoyed fully only long after the practitioner had died. In 1932 a Colonel North excavated the mound, expecting to find evidence of a Bronze Age burial; instead, he discovered an urn and a tiled chamber of chalk blocks containing a Latin inscription etched on a piece of glass to the effect that 'This mound was built by John Freeman of Fawley Court, 1731'.

The Folly at Woodcote sounded promising, but it turned out to be a house called 'The Folly' on a housing estate with a narrow enclosed avenue running back towards a plinth which once held a statue. The village of MIDDLETON STONEY has a small 1815 Gothic lodge and a barn dating from the same time, to which strips have been applied to the gable end to form a large traceried blank arch. The extremely ancient National Trust property of GREYS COURT in Rotherfield Greys has a delightful 20th-century addition to the garden – a full-moon gate; this one is complemented by a Chinese wooden bridge over a ha-ha and a turf maze dedicated by the Archbishop of Canterbury.

Folly Bridge in OXFORD is famous, but not for being a folly; the nearest thing to a folly to creep into that architectural paradise is Cauldwell's Castle next to the bridge. It is a castellated house with statues set in niches, built in 1849 by Joseph Cauldwell, an eccentric accountant, who wanted the house built as a castle to withstand attacks made by rioting undergraduates, a perpetual fear of his. As is so often the case, it was Cauldwell who proved to be the aggressor, shooting and severely wounding a student who had tried to make off with one of his brass cannons. Also in the town is an early 18th-century domed garden-house behind 16 St Giles' Street, formerly known as 'The Judge's Lodging House'. Oxford could, however, have had the biggest folly in the world. In 1975 John Madden, an undergraduate, submitted plans for a 450-foot pyramid to be built in Christ Church Meadow. The submission was properly drawn up and presented: it was necessary to freeze the Thames over for seven and a half years in order to excavate the 100-foot deep foundations; then a further sixteen and a half years and eighteen million tons of stone from Headington Quarry were needed to build the thing. Labour was no problem − there was to be compulsory secondment of second-year undergraduates − but the question of finance was delicately avoided. The intention was that the pyramid should serve as Mr Madden's mausoleum, and his application got as far as the City Planning Committee, where it was defeated by the narrowest of margins − five votes to four − after the city engineer pointed out that street lights would have to be kept on all day because the sheer bulk of the monument would keep the city in perpetual darkness.

Which finally brings us to Bliss & Sons' Tweed Mill in CHIPPING NORTON, a fine example to start or finish arguments about how follies should be defined. This was a factory, built in 1872 and operating continuously until it closed in 1982. By most standards this excludes it from candidacy. But the driver who on leaving Chipping Norton and seeing the mill for the first time doesn't narrowly avoid driving off the road in shock is blind to the delights of architecture. It was designed by the Lancashire architect George Woodhouse in the style of a French château, with balustraded parapets punctuated by graceful urns, apparently to blend in with the non-industrial countryside; but the imposition of a gigantic Tuscan factory chimney erupting out of the domed bay front to twice the height of the building is shattering in its effect. One can only stop and gape at such obtrusive camouflage. Listed Grade II*, the building was up for sale in 1983 for £175,000.

The Heart of
England

Cheshire

Cheshire has a fair number of follies, though most turn out to be the result of Tutankhamun's curse — obelisks. Usually where one finds obelisks, one also finds columns, but this phenomenon Cheshire has ignored. Antiquity is represented by one or two fake stone circles and a good number of sham ruins. There is no full-blown folly estate, however, no folly garden or squire's collection of stone eccentricities. Knutsford makes a late but charming urban exception.

Cheshire's two stone circles are both in the care of the National Trust: a 19th-century one on a neolithic site on ALDERLEY EDGE and the other below the main runway of Manchester Airport at Norcliffe Hall, near the village of STYAL. The latter owes its existence to the antiquarian pursuits of Robert Hyde Greg. The Gregs owned the cotton mills in the village, and young Robert took to accompanying his father on commercial trips that covered Europe and a fair part of the Middle East. He wrote monographs on *Cyclopean, Pelasgic and Etruscan Remains* and *Remarks on the Site of Troy*, but when his studies reached prehistory he went for the real thing and built himself a stonehenge at home.

In American terms, KNUTSFORD is a 'quaint old town'. Its comfortably prosperous inhabitants look on it as a convenient place from which to commute to Manchester: an Arab's eye would be caught by a rare sight in commuterland — the Drury Lane Minaret. No loudspeakers are visible on the parapet, so one surmises that followers of the True Faith in suburban Cheshire are called to their morning devotions by a real live muezzin. Richard Harding Watt, the man who decided at the turn of the century to adorn Knutsford with a minaret, was a wealthy and eccentric glovemaker. He used professional architects like W. Longforth for the practical side of building, but otherwise kept a tight rein over his scenic and architectural improvements. The minaret served as a water-tower to a laundry and was modelled on an actual example from Damascus. A row of galleried cottages alongside culminates in the Ruskin Rooms, a bizarre recreation hall in assertive but unadopted Art Nouveau style with extraordinary towerlets capped with realistic, oversized, upside-down acorn cups. The total ensemble would be more at home in Mostar than Cheshire. Mr Watt also built several unorthodox houses in Legh Road, his own 1907 Old Croft among them. Knutsford's other high spot is King Street, where Watt's King's Coffee House (galleried again) jars magnificently against the soaring whitestone pile of the Gaskell Memorial Tower, joyously out of keeping with everything else in the town. Taken by itself, it is a well-handled if whimsical example of Glaswegian Art Nouveau, started in 1907 with stones from Manchester's demolished St Peter's Church and Royal Infirmary. Mrs Gaskell, one of the few Victorian novelists still read today, is commemorated by a bust, a plaque and a list of her works.

Just outside Knutsford is TATTON PARK, a National Trust property. Tatton Hall's formal garden is the site of a mysterious two-storeyed towerette, the Sheep-stealer's Tower. A rotunda nearby is one of the many British copies of the Choragic Monument of Lysicrates. This one was built by William Cole III of Chester and appears to be his first building, as it was erected in 1820 when he was only 20 years old. A more recent addition is the Japanese Garden where, on a small island in Golden Brook, stands a Shinto Temple imported, along with several workmen, in 1910. This particular period appears to have been quite rich in Japanese architectural imports: the Japanese Gateway in Kew Gardens was brought over to England in 1912 and a garden in The Hague, Holland, was designed in 1895–6 with professional advice from the Japanese Embassy, and consecrated by a Buddhist monk. Japan in Cheshire is not as remarkable as it sounds, when one takes into account the various exploits of the then owner of Tatton Hall, Maurice, 4th Lord Egerton. He was an adventurer who prospected for gold in the Yukon (one would have thought he already had enough), lived in the Gobi Desert for a while and took his aviator's certificate the same year the Shinto Temple was erected. Egerton's astounding collection of big-game trophies (of course he was a Great White Hunter as well) is permanently exhibited in the specially built Tenants' Hall.

DISLEY is bisected by the county border, and strictly speaking the eyecatcher to Wybersley Hall is in Greater Manchester. The eyecatcher is a farm near Windlehurst which has been made agreeable by a castellated façade with tall, arched windows. Definitely in Cheshire is Woodbank Garden, which has a 19th-century brick belvedere tower, four storeys high with an iron-railed top balcony. Just south is Lyme Park, now owned by the National Trust, and previously home to the Legh family for 600 years. The original Hall was Elizabethan, and so was 'The Cage', a huge hunting box with four rusticated towers and a central square block with balustrading on top, giving a prospect over the extensive deer-park. In 1726 Giacomo Leoni palladianised the exterior, adding the towers. At one stage in its history it appears to have been used as a lock-up, hence its name. In the late 19th century it found new employment as a shepherd's house. The Lantern in Lantern Wood (the Leghs liked to keep nomenclature simple) was originally a part of the 16th-century Hall. It was taken down by Samuel Wyatt in the last quarter of the 18th century, refurbished and re-erected in the wood. Its design is rather plain — three storeys with a pyramid roof and an archway running through the base — but as a focal point it is highly effective. ADLINGTON HALL, another ancient Legh property, also has a deer-park. The Hall stands on the site of a hunting lodge, and in the old park is a sham castle dating from about 1760. There is also a prettily decorated shell-room and a rotunda.

BOLLINGTON, to the south, has a medieval European equivalent to the Knutsford minaret: a chimney, built in 1840 for William Clayton and decked out like some robber baron's tower. But the most famous folly in these parts is White Nancy, on the top of Kerridge Hill, visible from miles around. It is in the shape of a small, domed sugar-loaf, topped with a small ball, frequently whitewashed, always an eyecatcher. It was built in 1817 by Colonel Gaskell of North End Farm as a Waterloo monument.

Its rival as the most famous folly in Cheshire is on the

Staffordshire border near Biddulph. The National Trust property of MOW COP, or Mole Cop as it used to be known, has on its summit a small, round, machicolated tower with attached arch, running off into a rubbly wall. It is the prototype sham ruin, copied nearly everywhere, and of course it was one of the first, built in 1754 for Randle Wilbraham as an eyecatcher to nearby Rode Hall. In 1807 the site became a place of pilgrimage for Methodists when the first open-air camp meeting was held here, followed by a larger meeting in 1812 when Primitive Methodism was founded. On the centenary of the first assembly over 70,000 people climbed the hill; many more have since followed the same path, some out of religious fervour, others simply to enjoy the spectacular view.

COMBERMERE ABBEY, also in the south of Cheshire, has another Gothic eyecatcher in Brankelow Folly. The derivation of the name is not known, but it appears to have served as a keeper's cottage with attached kennels and the essential pinnacles and battlements required by all keepers. It was built before 1828, probably by two Irish architects called Morrison: the owner of the estate, Stapleton Cotton, Viscount Combermere, was Commander-in-Chief in Ireland in 1822–5 and he may well have brought the Morrisons back with him when his tour of duty ended. The final eyecatcher is Mickerdale Cottage at HARTHILL, built in the mid-19th century for Robert Barbour. The actual cottage is connected to a cowshed by a Gothic arcade, the whole being typical but late medievalising.

Tilstone Hall Folly at TILSTONE FEARNALL is an enigma: is it a folly, or the genuine ruin of a Jacobean gatehouse? It looks like a folly – two ruined two-storey towers built around an archway – but if it were genuine, would that make it a sham folly? Certainly it seems to have been left to decay picturesquely. Another difficult-to-assign building is the heavily battlemented toll-tower at SANDIWAY on the A54; lacking the porcelain prettiness of the four-square castellated toll-booth at Halfway in Berkshire, its fortifications seem unnecessary for such an inoffensive 19th-century working building.

The eyecatching qualities of the genuine ruins of Halton Castle near RUNCORN were helped along by James Wyatt in the 1770s. In order to improve the skyline towards Norton Priory, modern bits and pieces were added on diverse, strategically placed sites, thereby creating yet another sham ruin for Cheshire.

Derbyshire

Most counties have a characteristic type of folly. Derbyshire's would be the Rock Hermitage, were it not for the fact that they are well-intentioned, honest to goodness hermits' caves — although most were added to in the 18th century. There is the series of caves at FOREMARK: the Anchorage Church, extended by the local squire. The medieval hermitage at DALE was enlarged by Sir Robert Burdett, father of Francis Burdett the radical politician, and used as a meeting place for convivial evenings, rather like a dampened down Hell Fire Club. BIRCHOVER has natural caves that were 'improved' by the vicar Thomas Eyre in 1717; he also built the local chapel. The Rowter Rocks at Birchover, with their rocking stone, have not unexpectedly been associated with the druids; hence the Druids' Inn at the foot of the hill.

Derbyshire's follies proper are mainly grouped in two patches: one runs down Derwentdale from Chatsworth; the other forms a crescent south of Derby itself. The heart of Derwentdale is MATLOCK, a damp delight with its Petrifying Well, Lovers' Walk, Wishing Stone, Venetian Nights, Dioramas — all the trappings of a spa that saw its great days when Victoria was queen. There are two follies here, plus a report of a three-arched grotto façade standing neglected in a car-park behind a Matlock Bath hotel. We couldn't find it.

The Heights of Abraham, above the town on the west bank, are so called because they reminded a visiting old soldier of the Québecois battlefield, and after a walk to the Victoria Tower one begins to appreciate the stamina Wolfe's men must have had. Walking up this hill is bad enough; storming it must have been highly unpleasant – but here we are recompensed by a view that can even be improved by climbing the tower itself. There is no special feature to distinguish this tall, round, roughstone tower; again, it was built to relieve unemployment among local miners and stonemasons. Perhaps Victoria's visit to Matlock in 1832 inspired the choice of name; however, John Petchell, who then owned the Heights of Abraham, didn't build it until 1844. It is nicely echoed by the round turrets of two large houses on the south slope of the Heights.

On a hazy day Riber Castle, between Matlock Bath and Matlock proper, offers a view that will find its equal only in Switzerland. Nervous drivers should think hard before attempting the road up to the castle. A small castellated lodge of blackened stone prefigures the main building, then the castle itself appears, crouching on a crag, dominating the skyline for miles around, the guardian of centuries. In fact it was built in 1862–8 by John Smedley, a mill-owner who made a considerable fortune. He took unusual care of his workers, providing them with rainproof capes and boots, sleeping places and a religious service at the start of each day, dispensing Fearn's Family Pills to those taken ill, and even paying sickness benefit to those workers too ill to get to work if this particular medicament failed. Smedley was converted to Methodism and Hydrotherapy, and he brought his huge enthusiasms to both creeds, building six chapels and buying an already existing hydro in Matlock. He enlarged it considerably and made it an enormous success, ensuring the town's prosperity. Riber Castle cost him £60,000, but he lived to enjoy it for only six years. His original plan was to build a 225-foot tower on the hilltop, but he abandoned the idea when he discovered the telescopes he intended to order wouldn't fit the tower. Later the castle became a school, but by the 1930s it was derelict, and the shell now houses a small fauna reserve and wildlife park.

The A6 from Matlock to Buxton passes several follies, the first of which is near TWO DALES. Beside a minor road returning to Matlock is Sydnope Stand, a castellated eyecatcher to Sydnope Hall, screening a little cottage and built of a beautifully dressed dark stone. It is dated 1865, and looks as if it will stand for ever. The B5057 swings round off the A6 to STANTON MOOR, where a square, sturdy, roughstone tower commemorates the Reform Bill of 1832. It is exactly right in its setting — bleak, with only a few arrowslits for ornament. An inscription reads 'Earl Grey 1832' and the builder was probably Lt Col. Thornhill of Stanton Hall. Returning to the A6 we are just a few miles from Chatsworth, but perversely we will return there later and first visit BUXTON — another spa, another tower. Here is Solomon's Temple, or Grin Low Tower. Although on a similar site to the Reform Tower, this structure is anything but grim. A round tower, made of different hues of roughstone, its treatment is such that it has a very smooth appearance. This was built in 1896 on the site of an earlier building by Solomon Mycock, who economically ran a public subscription to build the tower and relieve unemployment. The mounds around the tower are Bronze Age barrows.

A small by-road west of Chapel-en-le-Frith leads to the National Trust property of ECCLES PIKE and a folly in the making. One of the lanes ascending the hill has a crenellated gateway, two turrets connected by two arches, one of which has been knocked down by a lorry, unintentionally creating a picturesque sham ruin. Time and ivy will accord it its folly status.

South of Matlock straggles the village of HOPTON. For generations the Gell family have been the owners of Hopton Hall, in the grounds of which stands a tower with two doors and no windows, linked to a crinkle-crankle wall. It was probably built by Sir Philip Gell, an active and enthusiastic builder, in 1790. Barbara Jones tells an amusing story of how Gell's Tower came to have no windows. Sir Philip was impatient to get to London, so when the builders came to him for instructions he replied with exasperation, 'Oh for God's sake go on building,' which they did; when he returned and saw the results of their handiwork he managed, with great equanimity, to accept the situation, muttering, 'Nothing to do now but put a roof on it.' The family Gell was interesting and varied. Admiral John Gell died of apoplexy in 1806, probably on hearing that his cousin William Gell had been knighted at the age of 26. Sir William loved bright colours and gay conversation, died a bachelor and left all his papers to his great friend Craven. He lived in Italy for a time, and thus may have dreamed up the name 'Via Gellia' rather grandly given to one of Sir Philip's road-building projects, now more prosaically known as the A5012. The trade name 'Viyella' is a bastardisation of Via Gellia, as this cotton cloth was first made on Sir Philip's road.

The most visible tower in these parts is a huge lighthouse called CRICH Stand, on the road to Ripley, 70 miles from the nearest sea. It was built as a war memorial in 1923 so cannot be classed as a folly. But why a lighthouse, and why so far from the sea? Crich also boasts the National Tramway Museum, and the National Tramway Museum boasts the façade of the Derby Assembly Rooms. The story behind this modern removal is the same as for all removals and it is encouraging to hear. The Assembly Rooms in Derby was an attractive but not specially distinguished building dated 1755. Unfortunately its builders had not anticipated that 200 or so years later it would be dreadfully in the way of a new building development in the heart of Derby, and as the building meanwhile had gone and got itself listed as being of architectural importance, it couldn't be demolished. So, regrettably, there was a fire, and the building was declared unsafe and demolished. But the façade, like a bedraggled black phoenix, has been triumphantly re-erected at Crich, in the old quarry among the old trams, and it now forms the entrance to the museum.

South-east of Ripley, in CODNOR PARK, stands a tall Doric column on a plinth — the Jessop memorial, a monument to William Jessop, engineer and founder of the Butterley Iron Works. The column looks and is unsafe, and one can no longer climb the spiral staircase. It was built in 1815, the year after Jessop died. This prepares us for the crescent loop of follies running south of Derby, and just south-east of the county town is ELVASTON CASTLE. One of its lodges introduces the visitor to the Sino-Mooresque-quasi-Gothick — yes, it's unique — style of Elvaston's famous Moorish Temple. As so often with Moorish temples, tents or kiosks, this is interchangeable with a Chinese temple. Its large-windowed, bulbous forms are roofed by a curved baldachin, the whole undignified mix a fitting tribute to the confusion of styles of the mid-19th century and the mild eccentricity of its builder, the Earl of Harrington. As Lord Petersham he invented the eponymous overcoat, owned 365 snuff-boxes, refused to appear in daylight, employed 90 gardeners, and devoted most of his life to litigation and temperance reform.

William Barron of Edinburgh was employed to build the Temple and the other conceits, including some rather good grot-work by the lake, and was under strict instructions from the Earl not to let *hoi polloi* in: 'If the Queen comes, Barron, show her round, but admit no-one else.' Now *hoi polloi* have the run of the park: it was acquired by the Derbyshire County Council and opened to the public at the beginning of the 1970s.

Westward, along the A5132, turning off towards Melbourne, is SWARKESTONE Stand. It has been called a summer-house, balcony field, jousting tower, bull ring and banqueting house. Nobody seems to know exactly what it is, but there is a record of a local mason, Richard Shepherd, being paid £111 12s 4d in 1630–2 for the building of the 'Bowl-alley House'. The flat arena in front of the Stand could well have been a bowling green, or a pall-mall alley, but whatever it was it was obviously built for recreation and entertainment. It is two-towered, with a cardboardy silhouette of battlements, and has ogee arches.

Bladon Castle is enormous. It lours over the village of NEWTON SOLNEY like the cape of Dracula, running the whole length of the ridge between the village and Burton. Battlements, towers, unscalable walls frown down at the cowed population – but it's all harmless really, because Bladon is basically just a wall. It was designed and built by Sir Jeffry Wyatville for Abraham Hoskins (so it is sometimes known as Hoskins' Folly) and finished – as far as it could be called finished – in 1805. This is the only example in Britain that we have discovered of a double folly. First, it was built solely as an eyecatcher – a folly – by Hoskins, but it was so big, so egregious, that there was no way the populace was going to stand such ostentation and let it pass as a mere whim; wagging tongues forced Hoskins to move into his folly to justify its being built. Secondly, having moved in, he discovered a basic flaw – there was no water. No well, no stream, no problem for an uninhabited eyecatcher, but a major snag for a house and home. So having made his folly habitable, Hoskins endured two seasons of having his water yoked a mile and a half up the hill in buckets before he cracked and made his getaway. Part of Bladon is inhabited now by a farmer and his wife; a simple electric pump has solved the water problem.

Further west along the Staffordshire border is SUDBURY, owned by the National Trust, with its eyecatcher deerfold. It first appears on a map of 1751, but tradition says it was built for the Vernons in 1723, which stylistically is very early. The corner towers look a little like Thomas Wright's work, but the entrances and quatrefoil windows resemble the designs for a banqueting house at Wallingford, Northumberland, attributed to 'Capability' Brown, although Wright worked there as well. The deerfold is as simple as it is effective, a good piece of Gothick. The four towers are connected by crenellated walls, while the façade to the house has been given a tall gateway which may have been added later.

Up to Ashbourne on the A515, and just outside the town on the Derby road is OSMASTON Garden Centre, built in the kitchen garden of Osmaston House which was demolished in 1966. The house was built for the industrialist Francis Wright in 1849, and since Mr Wright loved novelty, H. J. Stevens, the architect, provided him with a real wonder — a house with no chimneys. The idea was that the place should be heated by hot-air ducts, the used air to be exhausted through a single chimney set in the kitchen garden above the house. Mr Wright was delighted. When preliminary calculations proved that in order to make the system halfway workable the exhaust chimney needed to be at least 150 feet high, he took the opportunity to make the chimney double up as a belvedere tower, and equipped it with a spiral staircase. Now the big, square, Italianate tower dominates the garden centre, having outlived the house as well as its usefulness long ago: a photograph of Osmaston taken at the turn of the century shows the rooftops packed with chimneys.

Just north of Derby is QUARNDON, a village that once had hopes of becoming a spa. After a small Gothic building had been erected to protect the newly discovered spring with its wealth-giving properties, a rather insignificant earthquake opened up a cleft which promptly swallowed the source again. The machicolated bath-house was undamaged and remains as a tiny, sad monument to frustrated ambition.

Past Chesterfield with its crooked spire is RENISHAW, home of the tumultuous Sitwells. Osbert Sitwell tells us in his autobiography that it was the then owner, Sir Sitwell Sitwell himself, who sketched out on a piece of paper the design for the Gothick entrance to the park. However, since both its pinnacles and battlements are in exactly the same style as the house, which was enlarged and Gothicised between 1793 and 1808 by Joseph Badger, a local man, it would appear that Badger put the professional touches to the arch to keep it in line with the overall style. By the mid-19th century the house itself was considered to be a folly. An owner of the time, Colonel Herbert Hely-Hutchinson, actually commented, 'By whom, or by how many, Renishaw was built, it is a folly.' Later, Sir George Sitwell was let loose on both house and garden, and he started well by stencilling all his white cattle with a blue willow-pattern design. He brought 4,000 unemployed over from Scarborough to dig the lake, and was forever planning follies on the estate. Sadly, only a few were built, but the ruins of an aviary linger on, hopefully described as 'the Gothic Temple'.

Now for CHATSWORTH, large, beautiful and rewarding for all, but with only a grotto to show for the heroic period of 18th-century folly building (the others date from the 16th and the 19th centuries). There is, however, one remarkable building which has been all but ignored by architectural historians.

The Hunting Tower to the north-east of the house is a four-square, four-storey tower with round corner turrets, each capped with a little dome (afterthoughts?) so that it looks like an early observatory. It was built by Bess of Hardwick, and it was unquestionably intended to be a prospect tower – the fenestration alone proves that. Bess was fond of windows (remember 'Hardwick Hall, more glass than wall'), and this stand has 36, at the third count, large, attractive, mullioned and leaded. Barbara Jones, that most enthusiastic of writers, dismisses it as 'carefully preserved and dull'; Pevsner notes it but does not single it out for praise; other writers pass it by as an ordinary gazebo. But this tower is probably the most important folly in Derbyshire, for it is over 400 years old. Only Freston Tower in Suffolk is earlier, and there is a suspicion that Freston was originally part of a long-demolished house, which would make the Hunting Tower the oldest free-standing, purpose-built folly-tower in Britain. It is in remarkably good condition for a tower built in 1582, and it is beautifully sited.

Queen Mary's Bower is a structure looking like the foundations of a house, surrounded by a moat. It was in fact a walled-in garden in which Queen Mary is said to have walked during her five periods of captivity at Chatsworth. The bower was reconstructed by Wyatville in the early 19th century. In the south-east corner of the garden is a neat grotto overlooking a sheet of water. This was built under the direction of the Duchess Georgiana in the last quarter of the 18th century. It contained a collection of minerals found by White Watson, a Bakewell geologist. The round rustic hut on top of the grotto arch must date from the same period — at least it should, as hut and grot balance each other perfectly.

The majority of follies at Chatsworth date from the time William Cavendish, 6th Duke of Devonshire, began to take an active interest in the gardens. It all started with the village of Edensor at the estate gates, built in 1839–45 by Joseph Paxton and John Robertson, who specialised in cottage and villa architecture. Robertson appears to have been inspired by the popular work of P. F. Robinson, *Rural Architecture; or a Series of Designs for Ornamental Cottages* (1823), and the village was populated by the homeless inhabitants of the old Edensor, which was razed because it interfered with the view from Chatsworth. New Edensor was smaller, so the surplus villagers were billeted in nearby Beeley and Pilsley.

The result of this feudal autocracy is a very picturesque village with rather large houses in the rustic, Swiss and Gothic styles. Set apart, several of the buildings might count as follies: there are watertower-like outcrops and miniature castles, together creating a never-never-land of rural felicity, despite having been built during the Chartist troubles. The cottage style spread into the park, with a Swiss cottage of 1839 and a beautifully decorated Russian cottage, now used as a gamekeeper's house (the Russian, or Muscovite, style is a rarity in Britain, but was used quite extensively in Germany) and probably built in anticipation of a visit by Tsar Nicholas in 1843. The Duke of Devonshire had been on a mission to see the Tsar in 1826, spending £50,000 of his own money on the journey. The two Emperor Lakes were made in honour of the expected visit but, although the Tsar met the Duke in London, he never came to Chatsworth.

One folly in the grounds of Chatsworth came directly from

Germany: the aqueduct of ruined arches serving as a cascade, built, like the Swiss cottage, in 1839. Cavendish had seen a similar aqueduct in the folly garden of Schloss Wilhelmshöhe near Kassel. Ruined aqueducts are a staple ingredient of German folly pattern-books, this one looking remarkably like a design in Grohmann's *Ideen-magazin* of 1796–1810. In the north-east corner of the garden is a Moorish summer-house, small but elegant, with two plaques, one reading:

> Won from the brow of yonder Headlong Hill,
> Through grassy channels, see, the sparkling rill
> O'er the chafed pebbles, in its murmuring flow
> Sheds freshness on the thirsty valley below,
> Quickening the ground till trees of every zone
> In Chatsworth's soil, and clime, forget their own.
> H. L. sept. MDCCCXXXIX

A very rare and whimsical object stands in the middle of the garden, reminding one of the practical jokes to be encountered in Italian mannerist gardens. Set in an area dominated by huge boulders forming tunnel passages and artificial rocks is the Willow Fountain, a metal construction imitating a weeping willow to perfection, the drooping branches simulated by jets of water. A pipe made up to look like a gnarled old log provides the water supply. A 'heathen' pedestal is nearby. The fountain is supposed to be a replica of one standing in the gardens at the time of the 1st Duke of Devonshire, who had the famous cascade built.

Leicestershire

Leicestershire is fox-hunting country, home of the Quorn and the Belvoir. The landscape favours the sport, being flat or gently rolling. The county now incorporates Rutland, long famous for being the smallest county in England and which has been flooded to provide water for Leicestershire; a few follies balance gaily along the abyss of decay, neglect and vandalism on the scant acreage remaining. The rest of the county's follies are mainly to be found north and north-east of Leicester.

BELVOIR CASTLE (pronounced Beaver in a deliberate attempt to mislead foreigners) is situated in the northern tip of the county by the Lincolnshire border. In the summer it is the scene of 'olde medieval' jousting contests, as sham as the castle itself, which is an early 19th-century job by James Wyatt and an amateur architect, the Rev. Mr Thoroton. Near the castle is a grotto of rough stone, conical, with pointed arches and a rustic hut placed carefully on top. Wyatt added a Gothic dairy in 1810. The follies were probably the result of the Duchess of Rutland's enthusiasm for matters architectural, and the castle itself seems to have been as much her creation as it was the architect's; she also landscaped the park, painted 'in the manner of Claude', and was described by Mrs Arbuthnot as 'a woman of genius and talent mixed up with a great deal of vanity and folly'. She died young, in 1825, and was buried in the Norman Mausoleum, built by Benjamin Dean Wyatt.

There are minor grottoes at SCRAPTOFT, near Leicester, with scanty remains of shell decorations, and at BURTON ON THE WOLDS, which has another shell grotto combined with a dairy in the Gothick 'chapel' of Burton Hall. The house was built in 1790 and the chapel must date from the same period. Garendon Park is a little west of LOUGHBOROUGH, within sound of the M1. From 1729 to 1737, when he died, the estate was owned by Sir Ambrose Phillips, whose travels in Italy won him membership of the Society of Dilettanti. Like the Shugborough monuments by James 'Athenian' Stuart, the buildings at Garendon are reproductions of what their designer, or rather their copier, had seen on his travels. The circular Temple of Venus is a copy of the Temple of Vesta, and the Triumphal Arch an imitation of the Arch of Titus, both in Rome. The drawing for the arch is in the RIBA collection, inscribed by Phillips: 'A Design of My invention for a Gate for a Park'. Sir Ambrose's other creations include a classical summer-house and an 80-foot obelisk. While lacking the insanity to be found in the true folly, the garden buildings at Garendon deserve inclusion through their builder's dramatic appropriation of known classical motifs as his own invention. The Gothic gatehouse on the drive towards Hathern came a century later, and is the work of William Railton, a Leicestershire architect.

Old John, to the south of Garendon, is an eyecatcher in BRADGATE PARK, a well-designed prototypical sham ruin built in 1786 on a low hilltop. The story connected with it is rather good and consequently probably untrue: Old John was a miller in the employment of the 5th Earl of Stamford who was killed when a flagpole, stupidly the centrepiece of a bonfire to mark the coming of age of the Earl's eldest son, inevitably toppled and brained him. The folly was subsequently erected on the spot in memory of the unlucky servant. Old John's mill was said to have been sited here, and the ruined arch attached to the castellated round tower does give the passing impression of an old mill, though its provenance is far more likely to derive from Randle Wilbraham's 1754 folly on Mow Cop in Cheshire, 40 miles away as the crow flies. John Hope, a Cheshire architect who had worked for Wilbraham, also worked for the Earl on his Enville estate in Staffordshire; it is not impossible that he was the author of both follies.

The delightful gardens of Whatton House, just off the M1 near LONG WHATTON, are late Victorian and Edwardian, although work was still carried out in the Great Depression to relieve unemployment. The follies are minor but lighthearted. Even 'The Bogey Hole', a small grot, can scare only the over-impressionable. The Chinese garden holds the usual ephemera of the Edwardian Chinese or Japanese garden — bronze lions, birds, monks and urns, Buddhist shrines and umbrellos — and near the entrance to the gardens is the main feature, an elaborate seat with a jagged roof and a jumble of neo-renaissance and neo-gothic detailing.

MEASHAM is a large bustling village just south of Ashby-de-la-Zouch, a solid, no-nonsense, down-to-earth sort of place — which makes the 13 Gothic cathedrals built in the garden of Mr Bill Talbot decidedly unusual. Actually, any Gothic cathedral in one's front garden often leads to un-neighbourly speculation on one's motives, but Mr Talbot is unabashed. He *likes* building Gothic cathedrals (he mixes the cement himself) and as long as they don't harm anybody else he doesn't see why he shouldn't go on building them. The almshouses at RAVENSTONE, between Measham and Coalville, date from 1711. There should be nothing of the folly in an almshouse, but when the place was enlarged in 1784 two identical bow-fronted pavilions were added, one for the master's house and one for the chapel. For some reason (perhaps the window tax?) virtually every window in the chapel by the road is false. They have been cleverly picked out in white and grey so the effect is realistic enough — why couldn't they have been real in the first place? Another sham, or perhaps just lack of influence, can be seen at BARSBY, between Leicester and Melton Mowbray. Godson's Folly was originally intended as a mortuary chapel but nobody got around to consecrating it, so now it serves well as a small if gloomy house.

CLIPSHAM, just off the A1 in old Rutland, allegedly had a modern folly built by a Mr Wheatley, but when we visited we met Mr Wheatley's builder, who says it is planned but not yet built. An excellent folly in Rutland, the Hermitage Sanctuary of the Hermit Finch, was destroyed by children setting fire to it in 1965, and another sad loss in this rapidly diminishing category of naïve wooden buildings is the collapse of the Bark Temple at EXTON. Other follies remain on the estate, probably dating from 1811 when Sir Gerard Noel-Noel's house was built. Sir Gerard's architect, John Linnell Bond, is known to have designed a Moorish room in Southampton Castle, and as the Bark Temple has, or had, prominent Moorish features Bond could well have been the designer. Exton is a folly park, the buildings ranging from a stupendous, pinnacled, octagonal dovecote rising from a polygonal cattle-shed and a game larder built as a circular temple with a thatched roof to the Gothick gimmickry of Fort Henry. This is a splendid lakeside pavilion, crenellated and enhanced with ogee windows, the building trailing off into short stretches of wall. The Bark Temple stood right behind; it could and should be re-erected. But what hope can there be for a forgotten, collapsed and rotting wooden pavilion when a whole village was drowned in the making of Rutland Water?

The reservoir may still have provided us with a new folly. In the 1963 *Shell Guide to Rutland*, W. G. Hoskins wrote of NORMANTON Church that 'the little white church seems to float alone in a large, denuded park'. It now seems to float quite literally: in order to preserve the church with its 1826 tower by Thomas Cundy as a monument when the area was flooded to make Rutland Water, the first few yards of the church were filled in and a small island created round the part still sticking out of the water. The result is eyecatching indeed and the effect on a misty day quite spectacular, with part of the church and the pineapple-topped tower rising eerily from the lake.

Northamptonshire

In this shoemakers' county the follies are far from pedestrian. There are relatively few, but while Sir Thomas Tresham's buildings at Rushton and Lyveden may not be the oldest British follies, his Triangular Lodge of 1597 has a strong claim to be the purest in the country. With Tresham, building loses all pretence of function; it is a means of expressing an idea, an obsession.

The mind that thought up these remarkable structures can perhaps best be explained in terms of family history. The Tresham family seems to have had a standing order of bad luck. Sir Thomas's great-great-grandfather got himself murdered in 1450 by some servants in what appears to have been a politically motivated attack. His son Thomas, robbed and wounded on the above occasion, was beheaded 21 years later after the battle of Tewkesbury. Sir Thomas's grandfather threw in his lot with Queen Mary, but unusually died of natural causes. As his son predeceased him, Sir Thomas inherited directly from his grandfather. His son Francis was deeply implicated in the Gunpowder Plot, ending up with his head stuck on a pole in Northampton. The tumultuous family died out in the mid-17th century, apparently the only way to stop the Tresham curse.

Sir Thomas Tresham himself spent the best part of his life in gaol. Nominally brought up in the Church of England — it was a criminal offence not to be — he became a recusant at the age of 15, and for the rest of his life, though fiercely loyal to the Crown as head of state, waged an unyielding battle against the religious intolerance of that time. Roman Catholicism was the passion of the Treshams; Sir Thomas transmuted that passion into stone. Fuller,

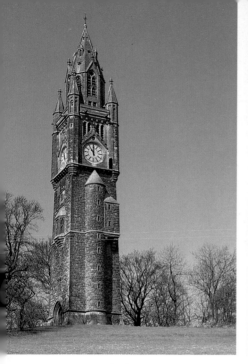

94   One of E. F. Trobridge's castle houses in Kingsbury, London NW9

95   Severndroog Castle, Castlewood Park, London SE18

96   'The Rotunda', Woolwich, London SE18

97 Richard, Joanna and Shân Headley leaving Broadway Tower in 1952 –
and Gwyn, silent upon a peak in Darien

98 The Gothic warehouse at Ironbridge

99 The root-house, Spetchley

103   Stoke Newington pumping station, Green Lanes, London N4

in his *Worthies of England*, found it 'hard to say whether greater [Tresham's] delight, or skill in building, though more forward in beginning than finishing his fabricks'. Tresham's fortune was considerably depredated by fines for his resolute recusancy, and for hiding the Jesuit Edmund Campion in 1581, the year of Campion's execution, he was sentenced to seven years' imprisonment, first at Fleet Prison, then under house arrest at Hoxton Hall, and finally at Ely Prison. Here, on the walls of his cell, he worked out the mottoes, emblems and symbols that were to result in his magnum opus, the Rushton Triangular Lodge.

Before working on the Triangular Lodge, Tresham had begun the Market House at Rothwell. This was started in 1578, but, whether through gaol sentences or the excitement of a new project, he never got around to completing it and it was not roofed until the 19th century. The Rothwell building was only a precursor to the lodge in so far as its walls were used as a gallery for a large number of Tresham coats-of-arms. In the year 1593, the date he later put on the Lodge, Tresham took the firm intention to build his monument to the Trinity in the grounds of RUSHTON HALL, north-west of Kettering. Work started on the Triangular Lodge − originally known as the Warryners Lodge, presumably because the rabbit-keeper lived there − the following year. The Tyrell family were engaged as masons, while a man called Parriss was employed on much of the fancy work. John Thorpe has been credited as the architect, largely because he was certainly involved in the building of Rushton Hall in 1595 and because one of the few buildings confidently to have been ascribed to him is the triangular Longford Castle in Wiltshire. However, as Thorpe has been credited as the architect of almost every house of any importance in Britain at this time, including the magnificent, perpetually ruined Kirby Hall at DEENE, it is more likely that the strong-minded and obsessive builder Tresham was his own architect.

The format is quite simple − as soon as one overcomes the initial shock of seeing what is unquestionably the oddest building of its period in the country. The brick building has three sides, each measuring 33 feet; three storeys; three gables on each side; and a total of nine gargoyles. In addition, the exterior is littered with trefoils, three to a row, and the crowning (solitary) central chimney has, inevitably, three sides. All this stands for the Trinity, but Tresham himself also comes into it: above the door (only one door) and below the Tresham coat-of-arms is a text reading:

TRES . TESTI

MONIVM . DANT

This is a biblical quotation (I John, 5:7): 'For there are three that bear record [in heaven]'. The 'TRES' stands for Tresham as well, a wordplay quite acceptable to Elizabethans. Biblical quotations are carried on as a frieze along the outside walls of the lodge; each text consisting of 33 letters. They can be interpreted to reflect on the persecution of Catholics in England:

QVIS . SEPARABIT . NOS . A . CHARITATE . CHRISTI

CONSIDERAVI . OPERA . TUA . DOMINE . ET . EXPAVI

APERIATVR . TERRA . ET . GERMINET . SALVATORUM

'Who will part us from the love of Christ?' 'I have looked on thy works Lord and am afraid.' 'Let the earth open and bring forth a saviour.' There are still more mottoes on the walls, gables and chimney, together with some singular ciphers that have been attributed to a presumed interest in the Cabbala and Black Magic. However, the ciphers also prove to be biblical in content. Above the door, for example, is the number 5555. If one puts the date of the Creation at 3962 BC (as more than one 16th-century cleric did), the date turns out to be 1593 AD. The other numbers, 3098 and 3509, are important Old Testament dates: the Deluge and the Call of Abraham.

Lyveden New Bield (New Building), a National Trust property set in the surprisingly remote, rolling Northamptonshire hills between BRIGSTOCK and Oundle, is much larger than the Triangular Lodge. The first reaction is one of astonishment. Expecting a ruin, one discovers an unfinished building, and the two are very different. As it comes into sight over the crest of the hill the New Bield looks immaculate, apart from not having roofs or windows, as if it has just been built and is even now awaiting completion. In the silence it seems as though a 16th-century bank holiday is taking place, as though tomorrow the builders will be back at work with the hammering of nails, the rasp of the saws and the creak of the winches. But work has stopped here for nearly 400 years. Apart from its condition and situation, this seems no different from the normal run of Elizabethan country houses, but closer examination shows that the New Bield is Rushton's logical heir. Lyveden was started in 1594, and is represented, along with hundreds of other houses, in John Thorpe's famous book of plans and elevations now at the Soane museum. For a long time Lyveden was ascribed to Thorpe: anything was possible from an architect who based the ground plan of his own house on his initials. But the actual builder of Lyveden was Robert Stickells; and there is a drawing in the British Museum of the lantern that was intended to top the house. This was not executed; there was never a roof on the New Bield, although around 1750 plans were made to Palladianise the unfinished shell.

Lyveden New Bield is planned in the shape of a Greek cross, each wing ending in a bay window, and set in the remains of a garden constructed at the same time as the house, doubtless a part of Tresham's emblematical|intentions. Lyveden's symbolical content is that of the Passion and the Mater Dolorosa. There are inscriptions and emblems of the Passion to confirm this. The number symbolism is that of three, five, seven and nine. The bay windows are five-sided and five feet long; each wing has a frieze inscription of 81 letters (9 × 9; 3 × 3 × 3 × 3); and the emblems of the Passion are sevenfold. Three and nine signify, as we have seen, the Trinity; five is the Five Wounds on the hands, feet and side of Christ; seven stands for the Seven Sorrows of Our Lady, the Seven Instruments of the Passion, the Seven Stations of the Cross, the Seven Last Words of Christ, the Seven Gifts of the Holy Ghost and, the personal touch, Tresham's seven-year stretch.

At HOLDENBY, north-west of Northampton, are two lonely arches standing forlorn in a field, the survivors of a gigantic house that ended its life here in 1651. Were they just forgotten or were they even then considered to be of value as agreeable objects? The Holdenby Arches are twins, one standing behind the other and each consisting of the actual arch flanked by two arms, of which the upper part has been brick infilled, the lower containing niches. On top of the arches is some uncertain scrollwork with a label and the date 1583. Messrs I. Davis and C. Wright have each scratched their signatures in the sandstone with accompanying dates — 1850 and 1868. Even graffiti become interesting with age. The Holdenby House that now stands here is about a quarter of a mile from the arches, and has a similar style entrance arch, though dated 1659. It is said that the present house is merely part of the north side of the north-west courtyard, and that the old house extended all the way to the arches.

There are two Boughtons in Northamptonshire, each consisting of a Boughton Park and a Boughton House. We concern ourselves with the House at GEDDINGTON and the Park near NORTHAMPTON. Boughton House was built in the latter half of the 17th century, and is often referred to as a miniature Versailles. Its builder, the 1st Duke of Montagu, had served as Ambassador to the French Court. John Montagu, the 2nd Duke (c. 1688–1749), apparently tried to improve upon this: in order to link Montagu House, his London residence, with Boughton, he proposed a 70-mile avenue of elms to run in a straight line between the two. The plan did not take root, though several elm avenues did, and survive in the immediate vicinity. Montagu thoroughly enjoyed an innocent bit of fun, as his mother-in-law implies in a letter: '[His] talents lie in things natural to boys of fifteen, and he is about two and fifty. To get people into his gardens and wet them with squirts, to invite people to his country house and put things in their beds to make them itch, and twenty other such pretty fancies.'

Montagu kept a portable folly in the garden in his London house: a Chinese tent, that most elusive of garden ornaments. A Chinese (or Turkish, or Moorish) tent can mean anything from a real tent (General Hill brought one over from Arabia to Hawkstone in Shropshire) up to a pagoda or mosque — hardly portable. Britain is still dotted with molehills called Tent Hill. The Montagu tent is one of the rare survivors. It was eventually transported from London to Boughton and there, on special days, it rests on the lawn. It is made of oilskin and is 12-sided with a curved roof. The interior is painted with fiery dragons that start to show some craquelure, nevertheless making it the sort of tent Genghis Khan would have coveted. Even its provenance has been established: it comes from a workshop in no less exotic a place than Knightsbridge. The house itself has a Chinese staircase which, together with the tent, makes the Duke an early China fancier, although the tent itself may have been bought by the 2nd Duke. Sir William Chambers's *Designs for Chinese Buildings* (1757) made pseudo-Chinese edifices fashionable:

> The trav'ler with amazement sees
> A temple, Gothic, or Chinese,
> With many a bell, and tawdry rag on
> And crested with a sprawling dragon . . .
> (Lloyd's *Poetical Works*, 1774, i. 45)

The Duke seems also to have been one of the first to embrace the castellated style of farm building, although most of his commissioned designs or those prepared by himself as an amateur architect have come to nothing.

Boughton Park, north of Northampton, has a confusing number of follies built under William Wentworth, 2nd Earl of Strafford (1722–91). Like Montagu, Wentworth was a dilettante in architecture, usually a guarantee of first-class follies. Wentworth, however, was not entirely original. Several of the Boughton buildings closely resemble those at Wentworth Castle in South Yorkshire, built by his father Thomas. The 1764 obelisk, south of the house, is definitely one of the younger Wentworth's creations. The Hawking Tower, along the A508, is essentially a copy of Steeple Lodge at Wentworth Castle, and serves as the park's main entrance lodge. Built in or before 1755, it is three storeys high with ogee and quatrefoiled windows and an outer staircase. Nearby are two similar castellated archways, one leading from the village into the park, the other into the kitchen garden. The castle style is carried on in the park, although the 1770 Newpark Barn has been decastellated. Bunker's Hill Farm, inscribed 'S 1776', retains its castellations, with quatrefoils in the façade facing the house. Strafford was a friend of General Howe, who led the attack on Bunker's Hill in the American War of Independence.

Towards Moulton is another cluster of Boughton follies. Holly Lodge, a pretty, castellated house adorned with putti, is the centrepiece. A tall clock-tower, dating from *c.* 1861, rises to the back of the lodge. Two other follies belong to the same period as Newpark Barn: one of them has been christened 'The Spectacles';

the other remains nameless. Both consist of an arch between slender, castellated turrets. Again, these follies have a common ancestor at Wentworth Castle — the archway of the sham Stainborough Castle there.

The follies at FINEDON near Wellingborough are redolent of the tragic story of the village's last squire, William Mackworth-Dolben, who lived to see all three of his sons die. The Volta Tower was dedicated to the memory of a son who was lost when the ship *Volta* sank in September 1863. The memorial consisted of a circular tower with crosses round the parapet, stuck against a farmhouse. But there was further tragedy to come: some 30 years ago it collapsed, killing the owner. Mackworth-Dolben decorated a substantial part of the village. Thingdon Cottage, the Vicarage, a school or two and Finedon Hall are all more or less in his particular style, but best of all is Exmill Cottage. A more modern house has been attached to the truncated 'ex-mill', which with its castellations and finials makes a convincing piece of medievalism. Finedon, the scene of much sublimated anguish, still shows itself as an elaborate *memento mori*.

Between Finedon and Woodford, on the A510 to Thrapston, is the Wellington Tower. Short, fat and circular, with a railing round the central chimneystack, it carries a large cruciform plaque under a round window reading: 'PANORAMA WATERLOO VICTORY June 18 AD 1815'. The tower was built by Charles Arbuthnot, MP and Secretary to the Treasury, whose friend Wellington pointed out the local landmarks that reminded him of Waterloo from the top of the tower. Others maintain that the Iron Duke pointed them out with his feet firmly on the ground, the tower being built afterwards to commemorate the occasion.

The follies at CASTLE ASHBY tread the narrow line between garden buildings and true follies. 'Capability' Brown, who worked here in the 1760s, let himself go only when the mood took him. No such mood took him here, for his buildings are classical: a temple-fronted dairy and an aviary/menagerie which has now been turned into a house, with a central dome resting on Doric pillars and two end bays with Soane-like windows. Pretty, but no follies. Knucklebone Lodge and Nevitt's Lodge are better, though too late. Both are of the Victorian rustic brand, Knucklebone Lodge owing its name to the knucklebones that pattern the floor. Later than these two are the buildings by Sir Matthew Digby Wyatt, among them a water-tower of 1867–8 in the hybrid style peculiar to the era, and a screen of nine bays in the Renaissance style, a favourite motif of his. The lettered balustrade of the house itself, though, remains Castle Ashby's main attraction.

The HORTON HALL Menagerie, some miles to the south-east, has been saved from destruction and now makes a delightful private house. It is one of the few Thomas Wright buildings to survive, resembling the Castle Ashby menagerie, although here the façade is much broader. The heavy rustication shows a singular vermicelli pattern. The second folly at Horton is 'The Arches', a triumphal arch acting both as an eyecatcher and a lodge. The likely builders were Thomas Wright or Daniel Garrett – if Wright, then he could have been inspired by the arch at Shugborough in Staffordshire, where he also worked. Near 'The Arches' is a later classical garden temple.

On the other side of the M1, below Daventry, is a little group of three follies within easy reach of each other. A sham ruin 19th-century dovecote – tiny, ivy-clad, complete with towerette – sits on an islet in the lake at NEWNHAM HALL (dovecotes and windmills are often Gothicised, as only a few battlements are usually needed to transform them into convincing medieval castles).

The Lantern House, also called Fawsley Lodge, on the A361 at BADBY, is a smallish octagonal lodge to the Tudor Fawsley Hall. Recently it has been restored and extended with help from the County and Daventry District councils. Looking towards the same Hall is a group of castellated cottages at PRESTON CAPES, two on each side of a battlemented arch. They were designed by Lady Knightley, the wife of Sir Charles Knightley, possibly with the help of Thomas Cundy, who made some alterations at the Hall in 1815–16. The Lantern House may also be Cundy's.

Nottinghamshire

Nottinghamshire means Sherwood Forest, Robin Hood, the Trip to Jerusalem, the prettiest girls and the tallest men, D. H. Lawrence, pits, tobacco and the once so fashionable Dukeries. It's a great county for digging in; Dukes and Aldermen alike have tried their hand. The miners are sometimes still at it.

There are three ducal follies. One of these is simply called Duke's Folly and is on the Edwinstone road towards CLIPSTONE. Archway House, to use its more prosaic name, is a Gothic, buttressed building erected by the 4th Duke of Portland in 1844 as, for some obscure reason, a copy of the Worksop Priory Gatehouse. A lighthearted element is added by statues in niches of Maid Marion, Robin Hood and his Merry Men, and the cause of their rebellion, Richard Lionheart. In fact Duke's Folly is only two miles from the ruins of the royal hunting lodge or King John's Palace, as it is called locally. Evidently the 4th Duke preferred to throw in his lot with the buccaneers of the forest. The lodge is now divided into two houses, and in 1984 the families living there were appealing for £10,000 to prevent the roof collapsing.

Another ducal folly stands a little north of Nottingham, at BESTWOOD. The Pumping Station is typical of those genuine working buildings like Mr Bliss's Tweed Mill in Chipping Norton, Oxfordshire, and the Green Lanes Pumping Station in North London, which are architecturally so over-dramatic for their mundane function that they have to be classed as follies. In the early 1870s the Duke of St Albans granted a permit for the 150-foot water-tower to be built on his land on condition that the architect, J. Witham, made Bestwood ornamental rather than starkly functional. In tune with the times, a classico-gothic skin was grafted on to the tower. Pevsner dismisses it as 'a tall, tasteless tower', but it is immaculately preserved and cared for, surrounded by manicured lawns. It will be many years before it completes the folly cycle, gracefully bowing its balconied head and collapsing overnight in approved Beckfordian manner.

Bestwood can be visited by appointment, but not so the third, last and finest of Nottingham's ducal follies: WELBECK. The 5th Duke of Portland's underground (and above ground) mansion has now been taken over by the army as a sixth-form college, and the only way to visit it is to exert considerable influence in the upper echelons of the Ministry of Defence. Those who have been there say, sadly, that the legend is greater than the reality. The man behind it all is the prime motive for a visit. William John Cavendish Bentinck-Scott, 5th Duke of Portland, was an eccentric of the first order, in a country which prides itself on its eccentrics. He refused the Order of the Garter because it would have entailed presenting himself at Court. No member of his staff was allowed to acknowledge his presence if he were surprised in one of his nocturnal forays. Withdrawing into just five of the hundreds of rooms in Welbeck Abbey, he communicated with the outside world (which included his servants) by means of a letterbox. He was in the habit of wearing several coats at the same time, and of assuming a number of dismally ineffectual disguises; he was said to be disfigured, which perhaps accounted for many of his less lucid actions. The better to keep his own company, he had a string of underground rooms dug at Welbeck; this subterranean refuge consisted of three libraries and a chapel, which was later converted into a ballroom-cum-picture gallery — a strange choice for a man with such a horror of socialising. Periodically, the Duke had stacks of paintings burnt because he didn't like them. It seems to have been his only really unpleasant characteristic.

All his underground rooms were painted pink, and they opened into the Rose Corridor, a conservatory. The burrow was not a true tunnel, however, being constructed on the cut and cover method, light coming in from the glass roofs at ground level. Food was supplied by a small railway, and that was another of the Duke's little foibles — the train. Even a reclusive Duke has to emerge occasionally, so in order to get to London unobserved he had another tunnel dug which took him and his private railway carriage the three miles to Worksop station where he could be coupled up to the London train. Needless to say, a vast workforce was needed to answer Portland's demands. All accounts of Welbeck mention the 15,000 men who, before they started the day's work, were each equipped with a donkey and an umbrella. The scene must have been picturesque, if noisy.

The Duke of Portland may have been an awkward man, but at least he was compassionate towards his servants and workers and a generous giver to charity. Not so the 5th Lord Byron, the Wicked Lord, who was at least as mad, bad and dangerous as his heir the poet. On his NEWSTEAD ABBEY estate, now a public park, Byron, still in his 20s, built Folly Castle, where he presumably held orgies in Hell Fire Club style. The building became so disreputable that it was later torn down. Probably at the same time, 1749, two Gothick facades were erected, confronting each other across the lake. These sham forts took part in mock naval battles with a 20-gun boat on the lake manned by Byron's luckless servants. The forts are mere façades, and thin façades at that. The corner towers are on the same level as the embattled walls, with only those towers flanking the blocked entrance gate rising above the remainder of the building. In 1765 Byron killed his cousin William Chaworth in an after-dinner scuffle. Being a peer, he was not convicted, but public disapproval thereafter virtually confined him to Newstead, where he became more and more of a recluse, living in only a small part of the house and letting the rest fall into disrepair. Many of the rooms were used as stables, while the woodlands were deforested, apparently in an attempt to irritate his family. Byron died in the scullery which, being the only dry room in the house, had for some time been his bedroom.

Façade architecture is also in evidence at Castle Mill, LINBY, a couple of miles south of Newstead. Castle Mill should be part of Papplewick rather than Linby, as it originally belonged to the Hon. Frederick Montagu's property there. The mill was built before 1785, because in that year James Watt installed the first cotton-spinning steam engine here. The vile working conditions of that period are attested by the churchyard's full quota of children's graves: we counted 163, dead from starvation, exhaustion, and the occasional accident. The mill, now converted into flats, looks a little more pleasant than it used to, but it is impossible to look at this folly without being reminded of how grimly appropriate its whimsical militaristic architecture was, a dungeon for children with a toy castle façade. Only the front towards Papplewick has been embellished, with corner towers, pointed windows and door, and quatrefoils sprinkled in between.

Papplewick Hall itself was built *c.*1787. Robert Adam has been tentatively put forward as the architect, although Samuel Stretton, a local man, may have been involved. Stretton made a speciality of designing industrial buildings so Castle Mill may be his, however tempting it may be to ascribe a Gothick folly to the affected, elderly Scotsman. Thomas Gray and William Mason were cronies of Montagu in Cambridge, and he honoured them by erecting an urn and a Tuscan tempietto to their respective memories in the grounds of Papplewick. Mason, whose ecclesiastical career had been considerably furthered by Montagu, wrote part of his longwinded but contemporaneously influential poem 'The English Garden' at Papplewick; the question is whether he inspired Castle Mill, or Castle Mill inspired his famous lines:

> Let every structure needful for a farm
> Arise in castle semblance!

Further down the social scale we find Alderman Herbert of NOTTINGHAM who *c.*1856 drove a tunnel from the cellars of his house in Rope Walk to facilitate entry to his garden on the other side of the street. This was probably only an excuse, as the tunnel itself seems to have captured most of Herbert's interest. A series of figures was hewn out of the stone — the Lion's Den, with Daniel flung in between the lions, his body twisted in an oddly expressionistic way, doubtless a result of the sculptor's ineptitude, and along the same biblical path, an Egyptian Temple, with sphinxes substituted for the lions. The figures of some pre-Christian druids are to be found, but alas no Buddhas or Aztec Sun Gods. Also in Nottingham is a mid-Victorian pagoda of little consequence with some aviaries at the Arboretum in Waverly Street, a sort of provincial Kew Gardens. Radford Folly in Radford

Street, often mentioned, has long disappeared; in the last stages of its life it was little more than an octagonal post where the Radford Tea Gardens used to be.

North-west of Nottingham, in the shadow of the M1, is the village of NUTHALL, where until 1929 Thomas Wright's glorious Nuthall Temple stood – not a temple, but a magnificent Palladian house. All that remains is a Gothick summer-house by Wright. The M1 skirts Nottingham to the west; 2,000 years ago the Romans skirted to the east with the Foss Way, now the A46 running from Leicester to Newark. In the village of SCARRINGTON, just off the old Roman road, a blacksmith got into the habit of throwing discarded horseshoes on one spot, until by 1978 the spot had reached a height of 18 feet and a millwright had to be called in to straighten the dangerously leaning edifice.

Further along the Foss Way is ELSTON. Elston Towers is a house that, like Bladon Castle in neighbouring Leicestershire, has been a folly from the start, setting itself aside from lesser dwellings. It is called Middleton's Folly because of the enormous outlay Robert Middleton made on his house: Elston Towers was built in 1872–4 at a cost of over £30,000. Mr Middleton indulged in a peculiar hobby – preaching. He performed in strange attire, the oddity of which was heightened by his circular frame, and being able to afford his indulgences he also built himself a chapel to seat 300, although locals privately doubted that he would be able to fill it. A small building connecting the chapel to a cellar is said to have been used by Middleton so that he 'never needed to sit through the sermon without a cosy nip', which of course is plainly illogical if he was the preacher. Another feature at Elston is the bell-tower connected to the mansion, famed for being able to perform 28 different tunes, ranging from 'There's no luck about the house on washing day' to an array of more conventional hymns. Middleton's house-warming party went on for several days and the whole village was invited to take part in the consumption of six sheep and an enormous bullock. Small wonder the party was gatecrashed by people from as far afield as Newark and Grantham in Lincolnshire. In the 1960s Elston Towers enjoyed a modest degree of fame as one of Britain's more important bluebottle breeding establishments, a fitting pinnacle of achievement for a folly.

To end with the largest estates in the Dukeries: THORESBY has a charming 1807 model village called Budby. Budby Castle is a castellated folly in the village, apparently synonymous with Castle William, designed by John Carr *c.*1789. On the estate are several Gothick farmhouses of which at least one was built by P. F. Robinson, the best known early Victorian cottage and farm architect.

After Welbeck and Thoresby we must mention CLUMBER PARK, a National Trust property, as the third member in the Dukeries triumvirate. The house has vanished, leaving a splendid Victorian church and nearly 4,000 rolling acres of woodland and lakes. But the expected follies have all disappeared or, Robin Hood-like, have secretly melted into the undergrowth. All we are offered is two classical temples, a grotto and a Palladian bridge.

Staffordshire

Staffordshire stands in the mind's eye for the Black Country and the Potteries, but these are just patches of soot on a largely rural map. The county will eventually become a sort of open-air museum of the way things were before the Great Depression of the 1990s set in. It has its fair share of follies, with some good garden ones at Shugborough, Enville and Alton Towers.

Just west of Stafford, in the grounds of SEIGHFORD HALL, is an 18th-century gamekeeper's cottage, quite pretty with stepped gables. It has been built on to a 14th-century tower from the former Ranton Abbey, giving the effect of a converted Norman church. Oakley Folly, probably built by the Chetwodes of nearby Oakley Hall, is another 'church' of this kind, here concealing a barn and now in a dilapidated state, standing north of Hales, near the B5415 leading to MUCKLESTONE. IPSTONES, north-east of Stoke-on-Trent, has a construction that turns the concept of sham churches inside out: John Sneyd of Belmont Hall built the village church in 1790, but shortly afterwards had a serious disagreement with his incumbent which led to his building his own church at the gates of the Hall. Like good Christians they resolved the matter fairly quickly and the half-finished church was converted for use as a cottage.

Northwards along the Shropshire border is WILLOUGHBRIDGE, another of England's many failed spas. This one became fashionable as early as the last quarter of the 17th century, when Lady Gerard erected a house called Willoughbridge Wells in order to take advantage of the warm springs here. On the lake's edge stands a small and simple bath-house, a reminder of thwarted ambitions.

The hunting lodge of some hundred or so years earlier, set on a hill, points to an earlier interest taken by the Gerards in this particular spot.

The ancient town of STAFFORD, though a little dull, is a good starting point for a folly hunt as it sits smack in the middle of the county. It boasts only one folly — Stafford Castle, dominating at the side of the motorway. Sir George Jerningham, later Lord Stafford, wanted to build himself a Gothic mansion on the foundations of the ruined medieval castle. His nephew Edward, who had practised by building a chapel in the grounds of Sir George's Norfolk estate, was put in charge of the project. In five years, two towers and one storey of the new castle were erected, but by 1815 the whole fabric had started to give way and the site was abandoned. Slowly the rest of the structure crumbled away and some years ago parts of it were demolished. The remains of the ill-fated rebuilding still make a rather sublime skyline, not unlike Riber Castle in neighbouring Derbyshire.

The area north of Wolverhampton, comprising Brewood, Somerford, Chillington Hall, Weston Park, Gailey and Shareshill, is still remarkably unspoilt. BREWOOD is a small market town and serves as the area's natural heart. On the corner of Market Place is Speedwell Castle — a town house, but what a town house! Its ogival windows and doorway offer sufficient exuberance for it to count as a folly on the strength of its decoration alone. To top this, a garden gnome stands above the doorway, flowerpot in hand. The interior of this Gothick extravaganza has a Chippendale staircase in the Chinese manner, and, a local story says, the whole was built from the winnings of the Duke of Bolton's aptly named racehorse Speedwell. We do not know who the architect was, but there are similar Batty Langley-type styles to be seen at the Gothick House at Coleshill, Warwickshire, and at SOMERFORD GRANGE, not far from Brewood, with its eyecatcher façade on the banks of the river Penk, facing Somerford Hall.

Eyecatcher façades abound in the park of Chillington Hall, near CODSALL. 'Capability' Brown and James Paine worked here for Thomas Giffard around 1770, and one of them must have designed the Grecian Temple, the Ionic Temple (hiding a cottage from view) or the Gothick Temple, although the Grecian Temple, listed Grade

I, has been attributed to Soane in the 1780s. The fourth temple, called 'The White House', built as early as 1724 by Francis Smith, has a classical façade with Tuscan columns and serves as an eyecatcher from across the lake. The rest of the house stands outside the park and is used simply as a farmhouse.

Before tackling Chillington, the Brown-Paine duo collaborated a few miles away at Weston Park, WESTON-UNDER-LIZARD, Paine building in 1765–70 a Temple of Diana and a Roman Bridge. In addition, Weston had a Swiss cottage, an observatory, an unmarked obelisk, a sprinkling of boat-houses and a later prospect tower, which visually connects Weston with Tong in Shropshire. The Earls of Bradford, who own Weston to this day, probably regarded loopy George Durant of Tong as very nouveau, but there is an indication that the siting of the tower was carefully chosen to allow a view of both Weston and Tong. It is a straightforward, basic-pattern, square folly-tower built from red sandstone quarried at Weston, battlemented and flanked by a slender octagonal stair turret. Its one eccentricity is a plaque dated 1631, referring probably to a fireplace, not the decidedly 19th-century tower. Our guess for an architect would be Thomas Rickman, who worked at Weston in 1830–1. Of the other follies at Weston, only the observatory (now used for parties and conferences) and obelisk remain.

On the A5 near GAILEY, beside the Staffordshire and Worcester-shire Canal, stands the Round House, a squat tower which served as the lock-keeper's cottage. It is battlemented and rather dull apart from a picturesque arrangement of chimney pots. Another of these lock-keeper's cottages, octagonal this time, is at 'The Bratch' near WOMBOURN, and at Wombourn itself sits a battered, roofless Gothic tower in the grounds of Bearnett House – no date, no architect.

South of SHARESHILL, next to the M54, stands the hexagonal embattled Portobello Tower, commemorating Admiral Vernon's capture of the Spanish fort of Porto Bello in 1739. The Vernons of Hilton Park belonged to a distant branch of the Admiral's family, but they must have decided to go with the jingoism that led to medals being struck in Vernon's honour, pubs named after him and several villages being renamed Portobello; there is even a Portobello, now part of Wolverhampton, some four miles away from Hilton.

Richard Trubshaw worked for the Vernons at Hilton in 1743 (in fact, he appears to have been the family architect since 1734), so he was probably responsible for the design.

A few miles west of Stafford lies the National Trust property of SHUGBOROUGH, the home of the Ansons, Earls of Lichfield, for over 350 years. It is well cared for, much visited and the follies in the garden (as opposed to those in the park) tend to look almost too spick and span.

Two men were responsible for the Shugborough follies: Thomas Anson (1695–1773), a founder member of the Society of Dilettanti, widely travelled (from the Pyrenees to the Holy Land) and ready, by the 1740s, to settle down and display a little of his expensively acquired good taste; and his younger brother George, who went to sea at the age of 13 and was given command of six ships in 1740. He returned after a four-year voyage having circumnavigated the world, sacked settlements, sunk ships and captured the most glittering of all prizes, the treasure-laden *Acapulco* galleon. The booty amounted to some £500,000, and a large proportion of it remained with Admiral Anson.

Thomas seems to have been subsidised quite handsomely by his famous brother. He became MP for Lichfield in 1747 and in the same year work started on converting the house. Two tower-like pavilions were added by the elusive Thomas Wright, designer of some of the best follies in Britain and Ireland, and he may also have done some of the garden work around the house. The Shepherd's Monument, to the north of the house, closely resembles one of Wright's *Six Original Designs for Arbours* (1755). The centrepiece, now removed, was a Scheemakers bas-relief of Poussin's 'Et In Arcadia Ego', which, with the Ansons' sudden fortune, uncannily echoes the legend of Rennes-le-Château, the Holy Grail and the enormous riches that came to the guardians of its secret. The enigmatic inscription has never been deciphered, only adding to the mystery:

O. U. O. S. V. A. V. V

D.   M.

A twisted arch encloses the vacant spot, and this is set into an alcove with abundant classical detail, resting on two stout Doric pillars.

The Ruins, assembled from fragments of several buildings, among them the Bishop's Palace at Lichfield, give a view from the west front of the house. In the 1740s they were more extensive, and incorporated a Gothick dovecote. Nowadays they look faintly ridiculous: too small to impress; too large to ignore. Two arches attempt to sink dramatically into the earth, weighed down with the Piranesian dust of centuries past, but the immaculately tended turf surrounding them belies the illusion. The statue of a philosopher sits amid the ruins, stoically contemplating these absurdities. A ruined colonnade across the river Sow has disappeared. William Gilpin, in his *Observations Relative Chiefly to Picturesque Beauty Made in the Year 1772*, was not impressed by his visit to Shugborough, and was moved to comment:

> It is not every man, who can build a house, that can execute a ruin. To give the stone it's mouldering appearance — to make the widening chink run naturally through all the joints — to mutilate the ornaments — to peel the facing from the internal structure – to shew how correspondent parts have once united; tho now the chasm runs wide between them — and to scatter heaps of ruin around with negligence and ease; are great efforts of art; much too delicate for the hand of a common workman; and what we very rarely see performed.
>
> Besides, after all, that art can bestow, you must put your ruin at last into the hands of nature to adorn, and perfect it. If the mosses, and lychens grow unkindly on your walls — if the streaming weather-stains have produced no variety of tints — if the ivy refuses to mantle over your buttress; or to creep among the ornaments of your Gothic window — if the ash, cannot be brought to hang from the cleft; or long, spiry grass to wave over the shattered battlement — your ruin will be still incomplete — you may as well write over the gate, Built in the year 1772. Deception there can be none.

Thomas Wright may have had something to do with the actual building of the Chinese House in 1747, one of the first pieces of Chinoiserie in Britain. It was copied from a design by Sir Percy

Brett, Anson's First Lieutenant on the *Centurion*, and inspired by architecture seen in Canton. The pavilion is surprisingly simple, almost classical, with fretwork windows and rococo-chinoiserie inside. An afterthought in the shape of a small pagoda of 1752 has gone. The pavilion is linked by an iron bridge, dating from 1813, to a small island, on which the Cat's Monument presents something of an enigma. On a bulky plinth stands a large urn, around the base of which are four rams' heads, perhaps representing the herd of Corsican goats Thomas introduced at Shugborough. On top of the urn a cat curls its tail. The plinth bears a Coade stone tablet with a heraldic device in bas-relief. The structure may be intended as a whimsical memorial to nothing in particular, or may commemorate the cat that accompanied the Admiral on his trip round the world, or it could be a memorial for the last of a breed of Persian cats that died at Shugborough soon after 1768. We can date the monument to this time, as artificial stone began to be used in 1767 and Mrs Coade started her famous firm in 1769.

A Doric Temple in the garden links up with the second stage of development at Shugborough. It is attributed to James 'Athenian' Stuart in the 1760s. Stuart — painter, architect, and also a member of the Society of Dilettanti — had been sent by the Society together with the gentleman architect Nicholas Revett on a 'fact-finding' trip to Greece. The results of this journey were published in four volumes of *Antiquities of Athens*, a seminal work, which precipitated the Greek Revival. George, Lord Anson, had seen to it that Stuart was appointed Surveyor of Greenwich Hospital, which brought him £200 per annum. Naturally, Stuart would have been delighted to return this favour when some years later he was asked to design several buildings for the Admiral's brother.

It is usually taken for granted that the Greek Revival buildings in the park were financed with Thomas Anson's inheritance, left by the Admiral when he died in 1762, but the Triumphal Arch was started a year before, as is shown by an estimate for its building by John Hooper, Mason, dated November 1761, for £284 14s 1d.

The arch is in Shugborough Park, which for the following ten years was to be the nursery for the Greek Revival in Britain. Designs from the store of drawings made by Stuart and Revett in Athens were taken and constructed, and both the Tower of the

Winds and the Lanthorn of Demosthenes found their way into numerous British gardens. The Triumphal Arch, a copy of Hadrian's Arch in Athens, manages in turn to look menacing and lighthearted, serious and frivolous, as it stands on a slope south of the house like a solitary tree. After the death of Admiral Anson the arch was decorated with statues, busts and medallions by Peter Scheemakers, commemorating Lord and Lady Anson. If the earth moves as you contemplate this magnificent structure you are not, alas, participating in some supernatural awakening of your artistic sensibilities, but merely standing on top of the tunnel which carries the London–Stafford main line. This also explains the film of black soot disfiguring the marble. The train leaves the tunnel through a medieval fortress to rival Hassocks and Linslade, turrets and all, built in 1847 by Livock.

The second of Stuart's Greek toys, the Lanthorn of Demosthenes (its more precise name being the Choragic or Lysicrates Monument), can be seen in one form or another, on its own or topping columns and towers, at Holkham in Norfolk, Lansdown Tower in Avon, the Burns Monument in Alloway, Tatton Park in Cheshire, and at Staffordshire's Alton Towers. It has become, like the Tower of the Winds or the Sybil Temple at Tivoli, a stock pattern in European architecture. The Lanthorn is a slightly simplified version of the real thing: a tallish drum with nice detailing and an elaborate trophy above. Originally this consisted of a metal tripod and a Wedgwood bowl, but these disappeared long ago and were replaced by fibreglass replicas in 1965, setting an honourable precedent for the use of fibreglass in modern follies. The Lanthorn is just the right size to have been used as an arcadian convenience, but this is scatalogical speculation.

The Temple of the Winds was built in 1764–5 by Charles Cope Trubshaw after a design by Stuart (he was beaten to it by his partner Revett, who built a Temple of the Winds at West Wycombe in 1759). It is hexagonal, with two porticos and a half-round bulge attached to it that mirror Wright's additions to the house. In 1805 it was converted into a dairy by Samuel Wyatt for Lady Anson. Like the other two Greek edifices in the park, the tower is well sited, although Gilpin found there was 'something rather absurd in adorning a plain field with a triumphal arch; or with the lanthern of Demosthenes, restored to all it's splendor. A polished jewel, set in lead is ridiculous. But above all, the temple of the winds, seated in a pool, instead of being placed on a hill, is ill-stationed.'

We leave Shugborough with a picture of the world as seen by the Anson brothers. The house itself is full of mementoes of the Admiral's voyages, of Chinoiserie and classical details, of paintings of the park, the gardens and the buildings (the best are by Nicholas Dall). The buildings reflect the brothers' travels in China, Greece and Egypt (an obelisk on Brocton Hill fell down in the early 19th century); their social and political aspirations; and of course the Admiral's vast wealth. The estate is a remarkable example of autobiography expressed in terms of architecture. But what can that inscription mean?

About two miles north-west of Shugborough is TIXALL, which has a small octagonal building with an ogee roof aptly named Bottle Lodge. It mirrors the corner towers of the over-large Tixall Gatehouse, a late 16th-century structure now restored to its former magnificence by the Landmark Trust. Needless to say, the gatehouse lacks a house to lead to; it was rebuilt umpteen times before finally being demolished early this century. Tixall village itself has some curiosities: an obelisk of 1776 doubles as a milestone, and there is an octagonal Tuscan temple of the same period, rescued from the rapidly dilapidating park at nearby Ingestre.

Three miles south of Shugborough is BROCTON HALL, built in 1801 for Sir George Chetwynd, Bt. There is a borderline folly, an octagonal Gothic dovecote in the garden, and also a neat little ruin consisting of two genuine medieval arches, said to have come from the Priory of St Thomas, but perhaps also the relic of an earlier Brocton Hall.

Another removal stands amidst the rural solitude of 18th-century Batchacre Hall, near ADBASTON. Now a farm, it was once the seat of the Whitworth family, the bachelor politician Richard Whitworth being the last of the line and justifiably tinged with more than a streak of eccentricity. In the woods to the south of the Hall stands the Porch, which had been taken from Gerard's Bromley Hall of 1584. Nearer to the house is a small look-out tower, while according to 18th-century paintings in the house there was also an island in a vanished lake defended by a mock fort equipped with cannon.

A few country lanes down to the Shropshire border, just above Newport, is FORTON. Something stands next to the A519; what it is no one knows, but the word 'folly' could have been invented to describe it: conical, and built of red sandstone (from the quarry in Weston Park?), it is known as the Sutton Monument, or simply the Monument, but to what, where or whom is unknown. If anything, it brings to mind Indian architecture as brought to Britain by way of the Daniell cousins' drawings. A pleasingly inexplicable structure, it may have started life as a mill, later being truncated and turned into a folly. Nearby Aqualate Hall, at MERETOWN, has a Repton park, some quaint lodges and 'The Castle', a gabled, red-bricked house with a fortified garden, probably by John Nash and thus another instance of a Repton–Nash collaboration, as at Attingham Park in Shropshire.

Following the border northwards one comes to Pell Wall House, near HALES. This was built by John Soane in 1822–8 for his friend Purney Sillitoe. In 1778 the architectural publisher John Taylor had published Soane's *Designs in Architecture*, a work devoted to garden buildings and, according to a letter from Soane, '. . . intended to form a set of designs to please the different tastes in Architecture and to render the work generally useful and immediately calculated for execution . . .'. In essence, it consisted of a weird collection of projected follies, and when Soane in later years came to regard himself as a great architect he disassociated himself from the book. Nevertheless, Taylor published a reprint in 1790, and Soane, despite himself, never really lost his taste for the outré, as we can see from the contents of the Soane Museum and the fact that at Pell Wall, the last substantial commission he undertook, is a lodge very much in the vein of his *Designs*. At the entrance to the north drive stands this tiny, recently restored triangular lodge, executed in a vague Egypto–classical style. It is the sort of folly to take home and cuddle, proof that a folly builder, however grand, ultimately cannot deny himself.

Ten years after Soane's Last Fling, in 1839, Thomas Trubshaw, grandson of the Trubshaw who acted as master mason for the building of Shugborough's Tower of the Winds, built the Goat Lodge at Blithfield Hall, ALMASTON. Pevsner describes it as 'crazily overdecorated', with goats' heads and ornamental chimneys. The Trubshaw family's contribution to the appearance of Staffordshire was substantial, at least four generations working as architects, engineers or masons. Thomas's father, James, won fame as a bridge builder, achieving feats even Telford considered impossible. And, as an aside, the actor David Niven had a great admiration for the clan, ensuring that a Trubshaw appeared in every one of his films. Thomas, a talented architect who died young, designed several garden buildings and churches, the churches, in Colvin's words, 'possessing a perverse originality'. The lodge commemorates the herd of wild goats given to Sir William Bagot of Blithfield by Richard II, which still roams Bagot's Park. His descendant, another William Bagot, employed Wyatts as well as Trubshaws, and nearly resorted to law when he accused Charles Wyatt of supplying faulty cement for Gothicising the Hall. With hindsight, the Wyatts seem to have been pretty fly – remember they built the famous self-destructing Fonthill Abbey, even though they had the help of a Trubshaw,. the 16-year-old James. The Trubshaws and the Wyatts raised families by courtesy of Blithfield Hall; the original hall was built by Thomas's great-great-grandfather Richard and a cluster of Wyatts appears to have been involved with building there from the 1760s up to the 1820s. Innocently or racily, we cannot decide which, rooms at the newly decorated Hall were given names such as 'Paradise' and 'Quality Cockloft'.

SANDON HALL lies due west of Blithfield. Dudley Ryder, the 1st Earl of Harrowby, managed to become engaged, although as a bystander, in some of the political violence that marked the turn of the 18th century. In 1798 he was one of William Pitt's seconds in his duel with Tierney. In 1820 the Cabinet was to have been assassinated by the Cato Street conspirators at a dinner to be held at Harrowby's London House. In between these dates, in 1812, the Prime Minister, Spencer Perceval was murdered and Harrowby felt sufficiently moved to erect a Gothic alcove in the Sandon Hall park, the Perceval Shrine. Six years earlier he had commemorated William Pitt, who had considerably furthered Harrowby's career, by erecting a 75-foot Doric column with an urn on top. But the best folly at Sandon owes its existence to the 4th Earl, and is simply called Lord Harrowby's Folly. Normally this would be regarded as a neo-renaissance pavilion, common enough to merit a passing mention as a garden ornament, but a folly it is, because it is actually the top cupola of Sir Charles Barry's Trentham House, built between 1834 and 1849, and demolished in 1912. Harrowby bought the topmost fragment for £100 and re-erected it stone by stone at Sandon.

Although TRENTHAM HALL has been pulled down, its follies remain. The Duke of Sutherland owned Trentham, and a Sutherland Monument, one of many in the country, was erected here three years after his death in 1833. The design was provided by local architect Charles Winks, and the bronze statue of the Duke on top is said to be by Chantrey. Of quite another order is the Mausoleum on the A51 leading past the estate. It was built in 1807–8 by C. H. Tatham, an architect proficient in near-follies such as lodges, ornamental cottages, gates, mausoleums and sundry garden buildings. For Trentham he designed a thoroughly Egyptian greenhouse, apparently never built. The Egyptian influence in the mausoleum was much diluted. The building is square with corner pylons and a second storey topped by what can only be described as a drooping cross made out of stone lotus flowers. The lodges and gates across the road are also by Tatham.

James Bateman bought a farmhouse at BIDDULPH in 1842 and immediately started the activities that made him famous: between 1842 and 1869, when he had to sell the place, he created one of the most remarkable gardens of the Victorian era. Biddulph Grange, now an orthopaedic hospital, is first and foremost a garden, with buildings taking a secondary role. Yet the whole concept cannot be called anything other than Folly. The sales catalogue of Biddulph gives some impression of the gardens:

> The prevailing idea in the arrangements of the grounds . . . is that of a division into classes of Countries, each with its distinctive Plants and their appropriate Soils, and by a clever arrangement of the Surface into Undulations, Rocky Summits, and Watery Dells, Climates and their Horticultural Results are shewn. A clever adaptation of Back-Grounds and Vistas, Yew,

Holly and Beech Hedges, artificially designed Tunnels, Rocks, Caves, Mounds, Masses of Roots and Trunks and other 'Material' arranged in 'skilful disorder' and 'picturesque shape' have been some of the means to bring about their present excellence.

Enough to whet anyone's appetite! The countries represented are China, Egypt and Italy, the last by the Italian Garden which unfortunately has no particularly striking features. China has pavilions, bridges, grotto tunnels and gates, all delightful, but at least one bridge was later given a simplified pattern, and the enchanting small dragons from the roof of the Pagoda Pavilion have apparently taken wing and flown off towards Stoke. Egypt is represented by yew pyramids and obelisks, stone sphinxes and more gates. Bateman made the most of his few acres.

Although James Bateman appears to have designed most of the gardens himself or with the help of one Waterhouse Hawkins, Edward Cooke R.A., a marine painter, was responsible for many of the architectural features, also designing several of the village buildings. Biddulph also boasts Britain's only metaphysical folly, the Great Wellingtonia Avenue, 'which is a straight walk nearly three-quarters of a Mile long, planted for a considerable length with very healthy and well-grown Wellingtonia Gigantea, Deodars, Chesnuts and Australian Pines, and presenting, through its ascending character and the diminishing Perspective, the curious effect of an upright Obelisk'. Clearly Messrs Bateman, Hawkins and Cooke gained enormous pleasure in planning their representation of the world in an otherwise forlorn corner of north Staffordshire.

Here on the Cheshire border, in the colliery town of KIDSGROVE, is a Georgian round tower — no story, no history, although the County Planning Department describes it as an ex-mill. Someone must have wanted it once. Much more recently, in the early 1930s, someone built a mock castle with a copper spire in the hamlet of ECTON, near the curiously named National Trust property of Ape's Tor in the Manifold Valley. The B5053 leads from here down to the already mentioned cottage/church of John Sneyd at Ipstones. The Sneyd family also owned Basford Hall, near CHEDDLETON, north-west of Ipstones towards Leek. 'The bathhouse' here is a rather elaborate, picturesque sham castle, built in 1841. Barbara Jones writes of a 'swimming bath, waterwheel, underground passages, living room and kitchen' which all add to its mystique. At the other end of the Manifold valley is ILAM, now a National Trust property and once the inspiration for Johnson's Happy Valley (the philosopher in *Rasselas* is called Imlac, a name reminiscent of the place). The village centres on a tall Gothic cross, erected in 1840 in memory of the wife of Jesse Watts-Russell, who built the model village. The small, two-storeyed, pyramid-roofed tower in the grounds of Ilam Hall seems, however, to be of a later date, mid to late Victorian.

At the other end of the county is Drayton Bassett. The manor, built by Prime Minister Peel's father, a textile millionaire, has now been demolished. A few garden ornaments remain, but the best survival is the small footbridge crossing the canal at FAZELEY. Two white, round, castellated towers conceal the spiral staircases which lead on to the bridge, like the footbridges connecting platforms at country stations. On top of Borrowcop Hill in LICHFIELD, whence came the stone for the building of Lichfield Cathedral, stands the Observation Pavilion, double arches all round its four brick-built sides. The date for this remarkable structure is 1756 and it must have been put up by a local landowner who wished to enjoy the view.

Another, but very different, tower stands due north at TUTBURY, in the middle of the picturesque medieval ruins of Tutbury Castle. This round sandstone building, known as Julius's Tower, is not another medieval relic; it was built *c.* 1775 by the 4th Lord Vernon. It is pure folly. Why should anyone wish to build a romantic, ruined, sham tower in the middle of a romantic, ruined, real castle?

ALTON TOWERS lives up to its name. Towers, temples and pagodas spring up from the Churnet Valley's rocky earth like mushrooms, popping up above the woods to give a craggy skyline. Like Shugborough, Alton is the work of two men. Charles Talbot, the Roman Catholic 15th Earl of Shrewsbury, started the whole thing *c.* 1811. He was a single-minded man, set on running his own show alone. J. C. Loudon wrote in his *Encyclopaedia of Cottage, Farm and Villa Architecture* (1833):

Though he consulted almost every artist, ourselves among the number, he seems only to have done so for the purpose of avoiding whatever an artist might recommend . . . His own ideas or the variations of a plan that he had procured were transformed to paper by an artist or clerk of the works whom he kept on purpose; and often, as we were informed by Mr Lunn, the gardener there in 1826, were marked out on the grounds with his own hands. The result, speaking of Alton as it was at the time of the late Earl's death and as we saw it shortly before (October 1826) was one of the most singular anomalies to be met with among the country residences of Britain, or perhaps of any part of the world.

And artists there were: James Wyatt; Loudon himself; J. B. Papworth in 1818–22 for some bridges (including one sham) as well as for Grecian and Gothick temples; Thomas Allason for the landscaping and some of the buildings; and Robert Abraham. Abraham appears to have been the very man the Earl looked for, his reputation resting, according to Howard Colvin, 'on reliability rather than originality as a designer'. This architectural yes-man was responsible for the faintly Moorish conservatories. Around 1814 he built what is often termed the Chinese Temple, but is in fact a well designed although slightly old-fashioned wood and iron tower in the Gothic style. His masterpiece is the three-storeyed pagoda, still spouting a 70-foot jet of water, which was completed in 1827, the year of the Earl's death. It was called the Duck Tower and its prototype was the To-Ho Pagoda in Canton, which was illustrated in Chambers's *Designs of Chinese Buildings* (1757).

Several structures with no architect's name ascribed to them survive at Alton and were almost certainly put up by the 15th Earl. The first two are garden ornaments, the Druid's Sideboard, a child-like stack of boulders, and the Corkscrew Fountain, a weird and literally twisted edifice. The Flag Tower, at some distance from the other follies, is exactly what one has by now come to expect of towers: several storeys high, with turrets and battlements, simple and effective. It was built before 1830. The Ingestre Courtyard may date from the same period; it is a façade, only to be seen from across the lake, two squat towers on the corners and a battlemented wall connecting them, with a fortified entrance in the middle. It gives the impression of a medieval fort. Being accustomed to shams, we were prepared for the emptiness that undoubtedly lay behind it, but once inside the contrast between the small utilitarian farm buildings (renovated and turned into bars and toilets) and the exterior remains striking. Alton Towers is now one of the biggest Disneyland-type 'theme parks' operating in Britain, and the Ingestre Courtyard is shown on the guide map as 'Numerous Toilets'.

On Charles Talbot's death in 1827 his nephew inherited. Anybody in his right mind wouldn't have dared carry on where the previous owner left off, but John Talbot, the 16th Earl, with the help of Pugin, finished work on the house, which grew into a web of towers, turrets, chapels and cloisters, making it quite obvious why the suffix of Alton was originally Abbey, not Towers. In the gardens the new Earl erected a Choragic Monument (*vide* Shugborough) to his predecessor, complete with the legend 'He made the desert smile' — 'grin' might have been a better word. Another of his additions was the Harper's or Swiss Cottage, unremarkable but cosy, built *c.*1835 by Thomas Fradgley, and predictably the home of a blind Welsh harpist who would strum for his supper by entertaining visitors.

Near the village of Alton, John Talbot brought Transylvania to Staffordshire. Not content to have finished Alton Towers, he set to work, again with the aid of Pugin, on Alton Castle, a variation on the Dracula theme. (Pugin also built St John's Hospital, a 'hospitium', for the rabidly Catholic Earl.) After the castle was finished in 1852 there was nothing left to do, so John Talbot took to his bed and died. The Shrewsburys sold the estate to a private company in 1924, and the gardens were opened to the public. Now Alton Towers Amusement Park is advertised on television as far away as London, one of the few British versions of Six Flags or Knott's Berry Farm and all the other American pre-packaged days out. The loop-the-loop big dippers and all the other modern paraphernalia are sensibly kept at arm's length from the park, and there is something very touching about the determined faces of the families who, before abandoning themselves to the raucous gaiety of the sinfully enticing amusements, resolutely march through

History and Culture in the frightful old house and incomprehensible gardens. Perhaps at a later point in time a new Piranesi will produce holograms of the ruins of Alton's Aerial Cable Cars, Scenic Railway, Aquarium, Fun House and Planetarium.

North-west of Alton Towers is OKEOVER HALL, built for Leak Okeover by Joseph Sanders in 1745–8. Two garden temples date from this period: the Temple of Pomona, goddess of fruit, and nearby a building of Useful Intent, the Necessary House, a classical closet in harmony with the Pomona temple. Camouflaged garden lavatories appear to have been as popular as they were useful, though survivals are rare. The folly toilet was the subject of serious consideration; John Plaw, for example, published the design of a rustic 'Wood Pile House' in his *Ferme Ornée* of 1795. This 'convenience in a park or plantation where the walks and rides are extensive' was realised at Mistley Thorn in Essex and Wootton Court, Kent, while German and Dutch pattern books show a relatively high number of conveniences disguised as rustic huts, sham ruins or even rather daringly as Gothick chapels. The French appear to have been deficient in this respect.

During the course of our researches for this book we were unable to visit ENVILLE. A pity, the more so as Enville remains, although a well known garden, a relatively uninvestigated one. It is part of the triumvirate formed by 'The Leasowes', Hagley and Enville (or Enfield). 'The Leasowes' was the property of gentleman-poet William Shenstone; Hagley and Enville were owned by Lords Lyttleton and Stamford. Shenstone lived his life in relative poverty, and the grounds of 'The Leasowes' were ornamented with both Taste and the Nearly Always Empty Purse in mind. But Shenstone's Taste was much admired, and he began to advise the two lords. In both their parks he could take a swing at the grandiose without any personal financial risk. So 'The Leasowes', to adapt a Sidney Smith image, came down to Hagley and Enville and pupped, the offspring being conceived on a somewhat larger scale than their parent.

Enville's buildings appear to exist not so much in brick and mortar as in ethereal lists of labels, the names of the follies being lost, or interchanged, or new ones invented along the way. There is one particularly important 18th-century source: Joseph Heeley's

Letters on the Beauty of Hagley, Envil and The Leasowes (1777) sums up 'a small dusky antique building' above the cascade; a boat-house, octagonal, with a 'curious sliding window . . . adorned with painted glass in whimsical groups of grotesque figures'; a rotondo; a Gothick Shepherd's Lodge; a chapel dedicated to Shenstone; a thatched cottage; a Gothick arch; and an 'exceedingly well designed' Gothick Billiard Room, housing a billiard table, an organ, and the busts of Homer and Cicero. Nomenclature after Heeley collapsed; the Billiard Room, for example, has been called the Greenhouse, the Summer-house and the Museum. Out of the hotchpotch of descriptions emerge several buildings which appear to have survived to the present day. The continued existence of a few of these is assured, but other follies may by now be in a ruinous state, or even completely destroyed.

To begin with the more ephemeral structures: Osvald Sirén, in his *China and the Gardens of Europe*, publishes a photograph of what he terms 'The Hermitage' (obviously the building Pevsner called a 'Hermit's House'), a makeshift, octagonal, bark-covered hut with stained-glass windows – Heeley's original thatched cottage? Barbara Jones saw Ralph's Bastion, dated 1753, and Samson's Cave, which she thought might be Shenstone's Chapel, although the chapel, while unexpectedly simple, is decidedly not so grubby as to merit being described as a cave. The octagonal Gothick boat-house described by Heeley has gone, crushed by a falling tree some years ago, but the Chinese Pavilion – missed by Sirén, mentioned by Pevsner (as a Pagoda) and seen by Jones – still stands, buried in a wood; it is probably the Chinese House mentioned by Sanderson Miller when he visited the gardens on 13 June 1750. Also gone are a Doric Seat, a Gothicised farmhouse and the fabulous conservatory with its onion domes.

Recently restored is the Eyecatcher, a weakly designed assemblage of three Gothick arches, the central one with a portcullis. Urgently needing repair is the beautiful Museum, thought to have been designed by Sanderson Miller, although Timothy Mowl has convincingly argued a case for the Gothicist Henry Keene as architect, and Roger White believes Miller's design to have been altered in execution by T. F. Pritchard of Shrewsbury. The Greenhouse, often confused with the Billiard Room, was designed by Miller and disappeared only a few years after it was built. In a letter dated 15 March 1750, to William Jago, Shenstone noted that 'Lord Stamford is now building a Gothic green-house by Mr Miller's direction, and intends to build castles, and God-knows-what'. Mowl infers that Shenstone, who didn't like either the gentleman-architect or his work, later had Stamford dismiss Miller. Whoever the architect was, the Museum is a splendid building. The roof has collapsed, but the façade still stands, showing Langleyesque treatment of the three ogival arches, with three rose windows thrown in for good measure.

Enville is one of the many British gardens that deserve to be Painshilled — replanted, restored and reopened. Its buildings are important enough to merit a preservation order, whether they are by Miller, Keene, Shenstone or an unknown architect. There is a beauty in decay, a wistfulness that vanishes when the decay dissolves into disappearance, but how does one freeze an emotion in time? Either the gardens are restored, with new paint and new glass and tame little garden buildings, everything in its proper place; or they are left as they are now, rotting, defeated, crumbling, mysterious and romantic, to be no more than a memory in 50 years. Who is to choose?

Warwickshire

Of all the shire counties, Warwickshire has probably the fewest follies. Even allowing for the annexation of the new county of West Midlands, leaving it a largely rural area, there are no more than ten sites worth mentioning – which is remarkable when one considers this was the home county of Sanderson Miller, one of the most influential folly builders in Britain.

Miller was born in 1716 at Radway Grange under the lee of EDGE HILL, the son of a prosperous Banbury businessman. At 21 he inherited a substantial fortune which enabled him to lead the life of gentleman-architect. He was a trend-setter rather than a technician; his charm, sociability and avant-garde taste won him fashionable friends and commissions which were drawn up as often as not by his master mason William Hitchcox. The combination of Miller's ideas and romantic imagination was unbeatable; to have him design you a castle stained, in Walpole's famous phrase, with 'the true rust of the Barons' Wars' was to be in the height of fashion. He had started to Gothicise the Grange six years before Walpole thought of doing the same to Strawberry Hill, and the previous year (1743) had built a picturesque thatched cottage on the side of Edge Hill which attracted favourable comment from Dean Swift. He completed his first major folly in 1747. Edge Hill Tower was sensationally well received by society for its positioning and its apparent authenticity; built on the spot where Charles I raised his standard before the indecisive battle (commemorated by two monuments on the plain below), it commanded a magnificent sweep of a view to the north-west, while architecturally it appears to have been based on Guy's Tower at Warwick Castle, with thin,

104   Angela Burdett-Coutts's drinking fountain in Victoria Park, London E9

105   The tower at Gunnersbury Park, London W3

106   Castle House, Phipps Bridge Road, London SW19

110   Blorenge House Tower, Ashampstead

114 Temple Bar, Theobalds Park, Waltham Cross

115 A rustic doorway to the Congregational Chapel, Roxton

116 Lord Cobham's gaol, Buckingham

120   The sham ruin at Fawley

121 The church at Nuneham Courtenay

almost fragile castellations surmounting stumpy little machico-lations. The tower is octagonal and judged by the standard of other folly-towers appears commonplace — which is rather like criticising Beethoven's Fifth for being hackneyed. Richard Pococke, that insatiable traveller, described it: 'A very noble Round tower which is entire, to which there is an ascent as by a ruine, and there is a very fine octagon Gothic room in it, with four windows and four niches, and some old painted glass in the windows.'

Edge Hill Tower is a seminal folly by a master folly builder; Sanderson Miller was to originate a style of ruined castle which in its various forms was to be imitated the length and breadth of Britain. An indication of how Miller's contemporaries reacted to his style is given in Richard Jago's 1767 poem 'Edge Hill, or the Rural Prospect delineated and moralised':

> Thanks Miller! to thy Paths
> That ease our winding steps! Thanks to the fount,
> The trees, the flowers, imparting to the sense
> Fragrance, or dulcet sound of murmuring rill,
> And stilling ev'ry tumult in the breast!
> And oft the stately wood, and oft the broken arch,
> Or mould'ring wall, well taught to counterfeit
> The waste of time, to solemn thought excite,
> And crown with graceful pomp a shaggy hill.

The folly is now a pub called the 'Castle Inn'.

Whether he tired of improving his own estate or found more enjoyment in new challenges we do not know, but Miller built nothing else at Radway except perhaps the little arched grotto. The slender, elegant obelisk at the foot of the hill was not his.

Passing through ARLESCOTE on the way to Farnborough Park, we found four elegant ogival-roofed Elizabethan pavilions terminating the garden walls of Arlescote Manor House, but the real hidden jewel in this part of the world is FARNBOROUGH PARK itself, a National Trust property with a terrace walk laid against the gentle rise of the hill like a fringed tablecloth. With earth and evergreen shrubs a rampart defence has been created, a broad grassy walk sweeping up at the back. The view is to the west, with the gap between Edge Hill and Bitham Hill opening out to Stratford in the plain distance. We pass a little tetrastyle temple seat with worn composite columns before reaching the gem, an oval two-storeyed temple, open at the bottom with Tuscan columns and at the back a comfortably rising, if crude, open staircase. This is visually entirely out of keeping with the rest of the building, and leads to a tiny parquet-floored first-floor oval room decorated in Wedgwood blue and white rococo plasterwork, miraculously still intact. The view is very beautiful from here. At the end of the grass walk is a tall obelisk of 1751, with a faded inscription reading, 'REERECTED 1828'. Farnborough Park displays English landscape garden architecture at its most elegant. To have the place to oneself on a warm, clear, sunny spring morning is to experience the real beauty of the English countryside.

North-west of Farnborough Park the ridge of the Burton Hills culminates at the BURTON DASSETT Country Park, a warren of wind-blown, close-cropped, hassocky turf dropping away to the Itchen plain below. If a good folly is all you seek, then it's hardly worth paying the car-parking charge to see the Beacon, a squat little round tower with corbels and a dumpy cone roof. The story is that it was built hundreds of years ago by the wicked Baron Blenknap, who would signal from it to other equally wicked barons for help if his serfs looked like revolting — but the tower looks awfully like a windmill adapted to provide a modest but highly visible eyecatcher.

South-west of Southam is the village of CHESTERTON, where the famous windmill arouses more argument about what constitutes a folly than any other building included in this book. Built in 1632, it has traditionally been attributed to Inigo Jones, but modern opinion holds it unlikely that the great man would have stooped to designing a windmill, especially for a mere baronet, and tends to favour the baronet himself, Sir Edward Peyto, or his architect John Stone. Nevertheless, it was evidently inspired by Inigo Jones's classical style, and this circular domed building standing on six open arches is high, mighty and solitary in its splendour. The design is sufficiently eyecatching, so utterly unlike any other windmill in the country, for many people to question whether it was originally designed as such, and to ask, with Pevsner, 'Was it an observatory, or else a gazebo, or a "standing"?' To us, it seemed to have been an honest attempt at a working mill, but Sir Edward, a staunch royalist obviously strongly influenced by the King's favourite architect, could not resist the temptation to classicise. One wonders what the dusty miller, hauling sacks up the ladder which provided the only access to the perspiring wheel-room, thought of his employer's need to prettify the building.

CHARLECOTE PARK, a National Trust property on the road to Stratford-upon-Avon, contains many pieces of furniture and ceramics bought by George Hammond Lucy at William Beckford's 1823 sale at Fonthill. The seemingly genuine Jacobean gate at the west entrance was built by John Gibson in 1865. One field north of STRATFORD-UPON-AVON is the pretty little three-storey Clopton House Tower, octagonal, heavily battlemented, with a higher spiral stair turret. It has been carefully converted into a private house, and a new section has been added in the same grey stone brick and with the same battlements, a perfect match. The owners love it − despite the husband's having fallen off the top of the stair turret one Christmas while stringing lights around it (he managed, just, to cling to the icy battlements of the main tower some 50 feet above the ground until his cries for help were finally answered). It was designed as a belvedere for Clopton House, a lovely 17th-century building now sadly abandoned and decaying, and was built by Charles Thomas Warde in 1844, as the 'smallest castle or grandest cottage in England'.

On the far west border of Warwickshire outside ALCESTER is Ragley Hall, seat of the Marquess of Hertford. Unlike other landed gentry, the Seymours seem not to have succumbed to the fatal fascination of follies, although they bowed sufficiently to fashion to allow 'Capability' Brown to do the gardens in 1758. It took the Prince Regent, visiting Ragley in the early 1800s and playing billiards with his host, to look out of the window and suggest, 'My dear Lord Hertford, your view would be improved by a Castle,' for Oversley Castle to be built on top of a hill a mile and a half away, above the village of Wixford. Such suggestions were seldom ignored. Originally just a plain castellated square tower, it has since been added to, and now a large white 1920s'-style private house surrounds the original folly completely.

Down in the south of the county are two odd little structures that are certainly worth seeing if one is in the neighbourhood − though whether they are both follies is debatable. At IDLICOTE, a tiny hill-top village in scenery more reminiscent of the Wiltshire plains than of Warwickshire, is a charming 18th-century dovecote-cum-water-tower, octagonal, castellated, with ogival windows and spirelet roof.

COMPTON WYNYATES is often said to be the most typically English house in the country; it is certainly one of the most beautiful. On a hill to the south is an elongated, slightly hipped pyramid capped with a ball finial which we would unhesitatingly describe as a folly, except that Compton Pike is authoritatively said to be a beacon site dating from the 16th century, for the Armada warnings. It is strange to see the use of the word 'pike' as a sharp or pointed structure this far south; in Lancashire and Yorkshire the word is often used to describe a pointed hill or the folly built on its summit.

Warwickshire's final folly is actually called 'The Folly', although it is less like one than any of the others we have looked at here. It is a house, built by Thomas Webb in 1779 in the village of HALFORD near Shipton-on-Stour, and originally consisted of twin five-storey octagonal towers built, so the story goes, so that Webb could see Stow-on-the-Wold — but for what reason we are not told. The upper two storeys were taken down at the end of the last century, and today it looks like a comfortable but unremarkable home.

West Midlands

When the new metropolitan counties were created only London and Manchester retained their individual identities. Once upon a time London was in Middlesex; now Middlesex has been obliterated by London. Once Manchester was in Lancashire; now two urban agglomerations, Merseyside and Greater Manchester, have been carved out of that county. Birmingham was in Warwickshire, but now the second largest city in the British Isles has to be content with being part of the anonymously named County of West Midlands. It seems unfair on poor old Birmingham — and why pick on Birmingham? It shares its fate with Coventry, West Bromwich, Walsall, Wolverhampton, towns with just as much right to the autonomy that Birmingham should have, and, in the case of Coventry, rather more. Coventry was a cathedral city when Birmingham was a hamlet; Lady Godiva had probably never heard of the place.

Birmingham is ugly, architecturally undistinguished; there's nowhere decent to eat, the beer is pretty poor and the place constantly undersells itself. From the time of Jane Austen — 'One has no great hopes from Birmingham. I always say there is something direful in the sound' — to the present day, when a Birmingham publisher produced a 1984 guide-book imploringly titled *Birmingham is* not *a boring city*, the town has silently suffered the opprobrium of outsiders. It isn't the butt of jokes, like Wigan; it is simply ignored. The people of Birmingham are like Chesterton's 'Silent People': 'For we are the people of England, and we have not spoken yet.' They lack the sheer number of the Londoners, the cosmopolitan flair of Liverpudlians, the brash radical capitalism of

Mancunians. Quietly (boasting is alien to them) they go about their businesses, uncomplainingly eat their noisome food, and just as discreetly they bank their profits – wherever they are in the world.

Such a mentality is not really conducive to building follies. There are only eight candidates in the county, and the best is the most central – Perrot's Folly in EDGBASTON. This remarkable survival, a six-storeyed, 96-foot tower, octagonal, red-brick, with a circular stair turret, was built in 1758 by John Perrot on his country estate. Perrot lived at the Lodge in Rotton Park and was said to have built the tower for the view, or so that his daughter Catherine could watch the hare-coursing in Smethwick (why a 96-foot tower?), or to entertain friends. However, a booklet on the Birmingham and Midland Institute Edgbaston Observatory tells a more tragic story – that John Perrot built the monument so that he would be able to see from the top St Philip's Churchyard in Belbroughton, where his lady love lay buried. Unsentimentally, it has to be said that the only direction that can't be seen from the top of the tower is towards Belbroughton: the stair turret is in the way. By 1922 the old oak stairs had become rotten, and were replaced by concrete. Now the old monument in Waterworks Road is surrounded by little houses cuddling up to its base; it is also a listed building in an excellent state of repair, because for the last century the B. & M. I. have been using it as a meteorological observatory, for which purpose it is admirably suited.

A little distance away in George Road is a Tudor Gothic pavilion, described rather misleadingly as a bothy. Built *c.*1830 of red and blue brick, the polygonal four-windowed building forms an attractive composition with a castellated wall joining it to a coach-house. LIFFORD HALL in King's Norton has an earlier example, an 18th-century castellated watch-tower at the end of a battlemented wall.

In the history of the picturesque, the most important contribution in the West Midlands area was that made by William Shenstone at 'The Leasowes' in HALESOWEN. The publication in 1777 of Joseph Heeley's collection of letters on the beauties of 'The Leasowes' and the two other gardens Shenstone designed, Enville and Hagley, brought national fame to the gentleman poet among the cognoscenti, and 60 years later Hugh Miller could still write, 'It is thus not to a minor poet that I have devoted a chapter or two, but to a rural poem . . . that cannot be printed, and that exists nowhere in duplicate.' Now, sadly, there is little left to see of the triumph of taste over nature, the rural poem; a century ago a writer bemoaned the ruining of the area's tranquillity by the noise and bustle of a new canal, and the arrival of the M5 on the doorstep has finally destroyed every last echo of Shenstone's peace. 'The Leasowes' started as a grazing farm and is now a golf course, but the Dudley Metropolitan Borough are fully aware of the historical importance of the estate and now provide visitors with an informative and detailed guide to it, together with markers showing where Shenstone placed his urns, seats, temples and cascades, all carefully sited to take maximum advantage of the viewpoints. Shenstone's poetry has now been consigned to the backwaters of English literature, but there will always be a deep respect in our hearts at least for a great landscape gardener who could also find time to coin the word floccinaucinihilipilification.

Walsall and Sutton Coldfield both make a small offering to the folly-hunter. Highgate Road in WALSALL boasts Skidmore's Observatory, originally built as a windmill in the early 19th century; after it ceased work in the 1860s it stood derelict for over 60 years until the new owner added the upper third to the tower and crenellated it suitably for use as an observatory. In SUTTON COLDFIELD a little tetrastyle Ionic garden pavilion was removed from Old Moor Hall and re-erected in the grounds of Ashfurlong Hall, on the Tamworth road.

COVENTRY holds the final, slightly puzzling piece in this West Midlands jigsaw: a 19th-century gazebo, an octagonal, arcaded sandstone building on a plinth, topped with a flat roof, looking like a rather disreputable bandstand for a string duet. Why should anyone want to build a gazebo in the London Road Cemetery?

Eastern
Counties

Cambridgeshire

At present there is only one folly of national importance in the whole of Cambridgeshire, even after Huntingdon and Peterborough were added in the county shuffle. This makes it the most barren ground in Britain for the folly-hunter in follies per capita, but there is hope yet, since the architect Peter Foster, the bell-wether with Quinlan Terry of the 20th-century folly revival, lives in the county.

Foster's works in Cambridgeshire are confined at the moment to his own garden at Hemingford Grey and Lord de Ramsey's at ABBOTS RIPTON, but an increasing number of commissions are coming in, even from as far afield as Somerset. The majority cannot in the truest sense of the word be classified as follies, being elaborate garden structures and ornaments, but one or two take a delicate, trellised step across the border. Take, for example, a wooden Gothic temple built entirely of trelliswork in the centre of Lord de Ramsey's herbaceous borders. Traditional British gardening would dictate that trellis should be used as a framework for climbing plants, but this one is innocent of creepers, allowing the mind to provide the infill. Foster chose the wood from which it was built for its quality when weathered, but the crockets on the gables have weathered differently — they turn out to be fibreglass, as do the massive urns surmounting the gate piers at the end of the path. Fibreglass mouldings are as much a feature of the 20th-century folly as Coade stone was of the late 18th and early 19th centuries. On the wall of the house are three trellised alcoves, but here again the eye deceives, for the trellis is flat and only the ingenious curvature of the slats gives the impression of depth. There is a Chinese bridge (looking not at all Chinese, but the original design was too expensive to build) with a white latticed aviary nearby, and a small grotto fountain on the wall at the end of the stream, a tributary of the Nene. Through the colonnaded indoor swimming pool, the conservatory has a Moorish temple looming at one end — again all sham, painted and jigsawed plywood fixed to the road wall. A number of structures were designed but remain unbuilt, including a 'medieval' fibreglass jousting tent complete with struts and stays. The most substantial building is the Fishing Temple, a few hundred yards out of the garden on the shores of the lake. The flat fenland would not be an inspiration to most of us, but with the help of his faithful gardener of over 20 years and Peter Foster's follies, Lord de Ramsey has created a remarkable garden. 'I can't paint,' he is quoted as saying, 'I can't compose music, I'm not sure that I can write — but I *can* garden.'

Foster's own follies at HEMINGFORD GREY are more modest, since he had a smaller area in which to work, but there is a delightful temple, built with his own hands 20 years ago and not quite finished yet; a Pompeiian Grotto, which sounds marvellous and is, even if it is only three feet high; and columns and urns everywhere. Some years ago he designed a three-piece column mould, elegant, fluted and with the correct degree of entasis, and discovered that making columns was immensely enjoyable. They have since sprung up all over his garden, and friends have borrowed the moulds and passed them round the country. Soon there could be columns of the Foster order in every English county.

Apart from a Gothicised flint house in King's Lynn Road in WISBECH, now used as an office, and a little grotto in the gardens of the National Trust's Peckover House in the same town, there is nothing else worth mentioning in the north, east or south of the county. CAMBRIDGE itself has but two candidates, neither particularly worthy of inclusion. There is supposed to be a Gothic window arch flanked by two eight-foot towers at Laundry Farm, but we have never discovered where Laundry Farm is, so we can't verify it. Hobson's Conduit, like Oxford's far grander Carfax Conduit, was built for a specific purpose, but when it became redundant it was moved: not, like Carfax, to grace an exquisite landscape (at Nuneham Courtenay), but from Market Hill to a humbler site on the corner of Lensfield Road and Trumpington Road. Hexagonal, with niches and topped with a cupola, it was endowed in perpetuity by the will of Thomas Hobson, who achieved a sort of immortality by allegedly being the first person to rent out horses, a kind of 17th-century Godfrey Davis. Unlike that worthy organisation, Hobson made his clients take the first mount they were offered — hence 'Hobson's Choice'.

On the A1 at NORMAN CROSS stands a plain column about 20 feet high, built in 1914 to commemorate:

ONE THOUSAND SEVEN HUNDRED & SEVENTY
SOLDIERS AND SAILORS
NATIVES OR ALLIES OF FRANCE
TAKEN PRISONERS OF WAR DURING THE
REPUBLICAN AND NAPOLEONIC WARS
WITH GREAT BRITAIN A.D. 1793–1814
WHO DIED IN THE MILITARY DEPOT
AT NORMAN CROSS, WHICH FORMERLY
STOOD NEAR THIS SPOT, 1797–1814
DVLCE . ET . DECORVM . EST . PRO . PATRIA . MORI

On the Bedfordshire border is the hamlet of GAMLINGAY CINQUES, with a charmingly named folly — the Full Moon Gate. The name is the most attractive thing about the folly, which stands rather forlornly in a hedge at the side of a public footpath dividing two fields in the village. No road leads up to or from it, and it is getting more difficult to tell that it once was a gate. It was built in 1712 by Sir George Downing, and originally there were two large rusticated brick piers flanking a large lunette, which gave rise to the name. Now it is ruinous, rubbly and overgrown, standing about 20 feet high. The magic has all but disappeared.

Outside Peterborough, the Milton Park estate at CASTOR has all the necessary ingredients for a folly estate, but never quite makes it. The garden was designed by Repton in 1791, and the various garden buildings include the tetrastyle Corinthian temple by Chambers built in 1774–6, an orangery, and the elegant Gothic Lodge near the entrance by the motorway roundabout, built by William Wilkins in 1800. But the best, or rather the most folly-like, piece of work on the estate is the Kennels, also attributed to Chambers and built in 1767 as a sham medieval gatehouse. It has now been painstakingly restored – a good squat tower with a gigantic buttress, a curtain wall with arrowslits and a Gothick arched door, terminating in a round cone-topped tower. There is also a rusticated dairy and another Gothick lodge near Ferry House, but somehow all this energetic building lacks the required lunacy; it is too studied.

STAMFORD is in Lincolnshire, but Burghley House and its park, the great house of the town, are now in Cambridgeshire. 'Capability' Brown was at work here, and his Bath House of 1756 is one of the first Jacobean revival buildings in the country – so early in fact that we question whether it was a revival or a hangover. He also produced a gamekeeper's lodge, another dairy and a Gothick greenhouse. Brown also worked at MADINGLEY HALL, now part of Cambridge University, where all that remains of his landscaping is a small serpentine lake with a sham bridge at the end.

This brings us to Cambridgeshire's best folly, the sham ruin at the National Trust's WIMPOLE HALL. It was commissioned in 1749 by the then Lord Chancellor, the Earl of Hardwicke, from Sanderson Miller, one of his early ventures outside the Midlands, although it appears not to have been built until 1772. Again, 'Capability' Brown seems to have been involved; either he or James Essex was actually responsible for overseeing the construction, which may well have taken place during one of Miller's periodic bouts of insanity. The Lord Chancellor dealt with Miller through an intermediary, Sir George Lyttelton, and his purpose was clearly spelt out:

> As the back view will be immediately closed by the wood there is no regard to be had to it, nor to the left side, but only to the front and right side as you look from the house. As my Lord desires it merely as an object he would have no staircase or leads in any of the towers, but merely the walls so built as to have the appearance of a ruined castle.

The tower was in fact built with floors, stairs and roof, but the overall plan was followed. The structure is huge, and the eye is of course immediately caught by the massive four-storey tower, but joining it are some 200 feet of curtain wall, pierced with doorways and arches (including one with a Gothick window above) and terminated at either end with two more towers. Many years ago, long before Wimpole became a National Trust property, it was into one of these towers, pitch black inside, that we pushed through the brambles and bracken and choking undergrowth that effectively concealed the enormous size of the folly. Nervous because of the plethora of 'NO TRESPASSING' signs (we couldn't find anyone to ask permission), we entered cautiously, hoping not to be caught. As Gwyn walked into the room a white, staring face silently and suddenly rose up at him, draining the intruder of strength, confidence and the ability to think logically. The sound of a man screaming on a hot summer's afternoon in the country could have been unnerving to his partner, sunning herself on the edge of the field, having seen enough of the folly as she wanted to. But no. 'Frightened of a barn owl,' she observed dispassionately, as she watched the equally terrified bird shoot silently past. The undergrowth and, one assumes, the owl have now all been cleared away; in the winter of 1980 the Trust had scaffolding up all round the folly and its preservation as a ruin is now assured.

Essex

Essex is a schizophrenic county, urban yet rural, industrial yet also a holiday centre. Places like Southend and Clacton have long been a playground for London's East-Enders, but the county also caters for the more refined tripper with Frinton and Brightlingsea. The western end, where it abuts London, is a seemingly endless factoryscape; the road through East London, through Dagenham and Rainham and out to Grays Thurrock and Tilbury would be an easy winner for the Most Depressing Drive In Britain competition.

Rural Essex is a delight, but the beauty of villages such as Finchingfield and Dedham has been their own worst enemy, causing coachloads of tourists to descend on their inadequate resources all summer long. There are many other beauty spots, less well known, where the voice of the tourist is seldom heard; one such is ALRESFORD, reached through unprepossessing roads bordering the mud flats of the river Colne, south-east of Colchester. 'The Quarters' at Alresford is a Chinese fishing temple, built in 1772 (according to a builder's mark found on the roof) by Richard Woods, a landscape gardener. It is a pity that Woods's work is not better known, for he created here one of the most tranquil scenes to be found in the English countryside, and 'The Quarters', standing on the shore of its little lake at sunset, is one of England's most beautiful artificial compositions. Woods was commissioned by Colonel Rebow to build the Chinese Temple at a cost of £343 13s 6d, and it seems probable that work actually started in 1765. In 1816 Colonel Rebow's successor, General Isaac Rebow, commissioned John Constable to paint the temple; the picture, now in the National Gallery of Victoria in Melbourne, shows the verandah of the cottage jutting out over the water to provide a fishing platform; nowadays it stands a few feet back from the water's edge. The delight of the building is the roof, a double-curved, concave, copper-covered affair which to an untutored Western eye appears Chinese without there being any architectural precedent for its being so.

No other house in Essex can rival 'The Quarters' in allure, but there are several buildings more strange and wonderful. Cinder Hall at LITTLE WALDEN is a house variously described as Gothic, Tudor and Georgian, built of flint and red brick with turrets, castellations and burnt cinders for added decoration, a gallimaufry of styles. Recently a modern extension in the same eclectic style and materials has been added, tripling the size of the house. The addition has been handled sympathetically and intelligently, and the result is brilliantly successful. Some buildings are not all they seem, such as the wonderfully medieval Moot Hall in Albany Garden West, CLACTON, which turns out not to be medieval at all but merely a re-assembly of 15th-century timbers taken from a barn at Hawstead in Suffolk. Stone Hall, just north of the A120 to the west of GREAT DUNMOW, was built in the mid-18th century as a *cottage orné* by the Maynards of the now demolished Easton Lodge; remote, romanesque (unusual in folly architecture), with two turrets, conical roof and mullioned 14th-century windows taken from the local church, it has been converted into a desirable residence. Copped Hall at EPPING is another stately home that has disappeared; only the shell remains, but it seems at first glance to be entire, a pleasing, chilling *trompe l'oeil*. It was designed for John Conyers in 1753 by John Sanderson, who also designed a renaissance garden pavilion which was built only in 1895, when the architect C. E. Kempe followed Sanderson's original designs for the pavilion and the arcade walls. The house was burnt down in 1917; the pavilion and the walls remain. Hylands Park outside CHELMSFORD has a Gothic cottage which may have been designed by J. B. Papworth, but the objects that link Epping with Chelmsford and with Colchester are three mighty water-towers.

EPPING's tower is in the High Street and is tall, ivy-covered and square, built of red brick with a thin, circular stair turret and whitestone castellations. The one at CHELMSFORD was built in 1888, also in red brick. The most popular, however, is the 105-foot tower at COLCHESTER, the only water-tower in our experience to have acquired a nickname. 'Jumbo' is what the townspeople call it, because it was built in 1882, the year Barnum & Bailey's famous circus elephant first hit the headlines. Unlike the others it has a pyramid roof, capped with a lantern. Colchester lays claim to being the oldest town in England, and it could almost claim to have the largest folly, in the garden of Hollytrees. Hollytrees is the best 18th-century house in Colchester, and is now the town museum. Charles Grey, MP, the owner, incorporated in his garden the vast bulk of Colchester Castle keep, the largest keep in the British Isles, to provide, as Pevsner so excellently put it, 'a somewhat Brobdingnagian garden ornament'. Not satisfied with the sheer size of the keep, in 1747 Grey added a circular domed and buttressed summer-house on top of the walls and erected nearby, with total disregard for any attempt at architectural harmony, a small Tuscan tempietto. To the east he built a massive pedimented archway with stones taken from the castle. It would seem likely that he was assisted in these undertakings by James Deane, the Colchester architect who had already worked at Hollytrees. In the garden of 'The Minories', also in the High Street, is an octagonal summer-house with a mighty castellated brick façade, originally built in 1745 at East Hill House but moved here when Thomas Boggis built the new house in 1776. Berechurch Hall two miles south has now been demolished, and the little folly we were told was in the grounds can no longer be found.

The water-towers were included here largely because of their style, size, central locations . . . and above all because one is called Jumbo. Essex has a number of folly-towers of a more traditional sort. All are eclipsed by Bull's Tower in PENTLOW, a rather attractive, unostentatious Victorian brick tower in a rectory garden. When we called we tugged on the old bell-pull and far away in the depths of the house a rusty bell finally tolled. No one answered. When we stepped back we saw that every window of the house had a white cat sitting in it looking out at us. Nervously we made our way across the ramshackle lawn to the tower. It is 70 feet high, banded with diapered cross-and-diamond bricking, with the date, 1859, prominently set above the door. Above that is a narrow window, and then further up the initials 'AC'i', also picked out in dark blue brick. We cannot find out what this could stand for. A plaque records, 'This tower was erected by the Rev. Edward Bull, M.A., in memory of his parents on a spot they loved so well.' It is also the most frightening building we have ever been halfway up. Only long after we had got away from it, tyres squealing, overcome by inexplicable terror, did we sit down and try to rationalise the fear. A little research made it worse. We discovered that the Rev. Mr Bull left Pentlow to become rector at another village four miles away and built himself a new rectory there in 1865; his Borley Rectory, which burnt down mysteriously in 1941, took only a few years to establish itself as the most haunted house in England. Old photographs of Borley show it to be similar in style to the rectory at Pentlow.

Nothing in Essex equals Pentlow for atmosphere — we haven't been back since 1974 — and no other tower in the county compares with it as a folly. Bateman's Folly on the front at BRIGHTLINGSEA is too insignificant, a 25-foot, gently leaning, two-storey tower used for rigging practice, said to have been built by Mr Bateman as a freelance lighthouse. HEYBRIDGE Towers is an Italianate house built in 1873 for E. H. Bentall, MP, of the Heybridge Iron Works; he built not one but two castellated concrete towers in his garden.

LAYER MARNEY Tower is one of the glories of Essex. It is a medieval skyscraper eight storeys high, built in 1520, and apparently complies perfectly with the dictionary definition of a folly. It was intended to be the gatehouse to a magnificent, vast residence for the Marney family, but the first Lord Marney died in 1523 and his heir followed him only two years later, so the mansion was never built. Why, then, is it not a folly? First, the tower was designed to impress, a prime motive in building many follies, but built at a time when the ruling classes were more impressed by displays of military might than by artistic skill. Secondly, it is unlikely that the Marneys had not carefully budgeted the cost of their new house; the problem was that they assumed the continuation of the line and hence the continuation of the family income. When that stopped, so did the building. So there it stands, confused in the shallow Essex countryside, a harbinger of a building that never arrived.

The MISTLEY towers are similar in story; they were originally part of Mistley Church, one of the few churches designed by Robert Adam. The church was originally built in 1735, and Adam was called in by the grossly corrupt politician Richard Rigby to remodel it in 1776. He added identical classical towers at either end of the nave, each one square with eight supporting Tuscan columns and topped with a tall domed cupola with Ionic pilasters. This made for a strange but eyecatching church which became even stranger in 1870 when the nave was demolished because of dry rot, leaving the towers facing each other like two queens on a chess board. The intention was to use the towers as mausoleums, but in the event the highest they aspired to was temporary service as the village morgue. The Ten Commandments and fragments of Richard Rigby Senior's will can still be seen in the east tower: 'Richard Rigby Esq by his will dated August 8th 1730 charged a portion of his estate at Mistley to the value of six chauldrons of coal . . . '. The towers, surrounded by warehouses, are now kept locked, but the key can be obtained from the address given on the notice board during reasonable hours.

Rigby Junior was out for all he could get. Through connivance, making and breaking alliances, conviviality, treachery and under-handedness he finally achieved his ambition, which was to become Paymaster General, a lode worked with equal corruption by his one-time mentor Henry Fox. He died in 1788, leaving (as his best known epitaph) 'near half a million of public money'. Some of that was spent on Gothick and Chinese temples and bridges in Mistley Hall — even Horace Walpole designed a Sino-Indian room for him in 1750 — but all has now gone, except for two Adam lodges. Mrs Birch of Brantham Glebe, just over the river in Suffolk, wanted to buy one of the lodges and re-erect it in her garden with her modern obelisks and temple, but the Georgian Group stepped in to prevent the sale and, presumably, thereby condemned the building to death, as it is now derelict and fading fast. Rigby's other ideas for Mistley included launching the village as a spa, but like so many spa enterprises it came to nothing, and the only trace we have left is a stone swan, also by Adam, gazing at its reflection on the circular basin in the centre of the village.

Robert Adam did some of the interior decoration at Weald Hall in SOUTH WEALD outside Brentwood. The house was pulled down in 1951, and the architect of the belvedere tower, now in the Country Park overlooking the M25, is unknown. RAYLEIGH, fast becoming a suburb of Southend, had the sails of the old town mill removed and then the top battlemented, pointless but pretty. Essex seems to have been fated with spas: a good spring was discovered at HOCKLEY, just next to Rayleigh, in 1838, and an attempt was made to capitalise on this in 1842 by James Lockyer, who built a heavy and inappropriate pump room alien to the rest of the village which then suffered the same fate as Mistley. The redundant pump room lingers on, and most locals are ignorant of its original purpose.

Essex is surprisingly short on columns and obelisks. Colne Park in COLNE ENGAINE has a column surmounted by an urn of 1790, its only claim to fame being that it was designed by Sir John Soane for Philip Hills. There are no grottoes left at all – the closest we can get is the pretty shell-house in HATFIELD GREAT PARK outside Bishop's Stortford, built in 1759 by Laetitia Houblon on the shore of the artificial lake – but there is a fine catacomb at HIGH BEACH in Epping Forest. It is said to have been built using stones from Chelmsford Jail in the 1860s; the entrance is normal enough, through a circular colonnade, but as you penetrate the earth the architecture goes awry: the columns supporting the ceiling are massive at the top and fragile at the bottom, reminiscent of Knossos; the floor is deliberately uneven; and there is a terrible sense of impending collapse. A subterranean folly to make one think.

Most of the large Essex estates have been broken up or have disappeared, some swallowed by ever encroaching London, some just abandoned and decaying. Fortunately one of the finest remains intact, though a shadow of its former self. AUDLEY END at Saffron Walden was one of the largest houses ever built in Britain, designed by the Earl of Northampton and Bernard Janssen for Thomas Howard, the Lord of the Treasury, and built in 1603–16. When James I saw it he commented, 'it is too much for a King, but it might do very well for a Lord Treasurer,' and indeed shortly afterwards Howard was a guest at the Tower of London, accused of defrauding the King of £240,000. The house itself was the size of a small town, and in 1707 Vanbrugh was called in to demolish the major part of it. What remains is of course still magnificent, but the works in the park are what concern us here. 'Capability' Brown landscaped it in 1763, and Robert Adam was appointed to design a bridge that same year, going on to design the Temple of Victory on Ring Hill (1772), a circular Ionic temple to commemorate victory in the Seven Years' War, and a Palladian bridge with a summer-house on it by the cascade in 1782–3. The Springwood Column of 1774, Doric and surmounted by an urn, was dedicated to Lady Portsmouth. All these were commissioned by Lord Braybrooke. The only piece not by Adam is the Temple of Concord, rectangular with unfluted Corinthian columns, designed by Robert William Brettingham in 1790 as yet another premature celebration of George III's recovery from madness. Audley End is clean, well preserved, safe and slightly antiseptic; the park's embellishments are too sane to deserve full folly status.

Be that as it may, there is no comparable group left in the county. There is a small island temple on the pond at Hill Hall in THEYDON GARNON, once a women's prison, and a rotunda of 1780 at Warlies Park at UPSHIRE, close by. Now a Dr Barnardo's home, Warlies also has two obelisks, one marking the spot where Boudicca took her fatal draught of poison, the other marking the spot where she died, almost exactly a mile away. It is a continual source of wonder to us how people could be so confident of a historical site as to erect something as permanent as an obelisk – there are two at Naseby to commemorate the battle, but far apart.

The gatehouse at Beckingham Hall in TOLLESHUNT MAJOR dates from 1546, and again seems to presage a grand house which was never built. It is thin, mad and pinnacled, and is invariably compared with the Erwarton Hall gatehouse in Suffolk. THORNDON HALL, south of Brentwood, is now a golf course and Country Park, the house built by James Paine in 1764 for Lord Petre having burnt out in 1878. The shell has recently been converted into flats. 'Capability' Brown landscaped the grounds from 1766, and Samuel Wyatt designed Hatch Farm in 1777, a neo-classical, red-brick building with centre gate, colonnades and two-storey end pavilions; also on the estate are a mausoleum and Chantry Chapel by Pugin.

There are scraps of follies to be found in every county: usually too insignificant to get a mention in type, they lack provenance, authority or protection, so when their time comes they pass and are forgotten with the rest. Essex has its share; time forbids further researches than to list some that may be threatened in the future, and hope local readers will be interested enough to look further into the backgrounds of these defenceless buildings. For example, SAFFRON WALDEN has a castellated laundry (once the Railway Mission), a folly in the garden of Elm Grove, one in the garden of a house called 'The Folly' in Abbey Lane, and a circular 18th-century temple in Bridge End Garden. None merits a detailed description, but they have all brought somebody pleasure. FINGRINGHOE HALL, south of Colchester, has a bear-pit, a rare survival from more barbarous days. We have already lost the folly garden at Matching Green, a front garden packed with concrete effigies of animals and people, poured by a cantankerous old man who was the son of the village blacksmith. Decaying and overgrown, they were still there in 1973, but they have since been destroyed. At BELCHAMP WALTER HALL is a tiny ivy-covered folly gateway. Some would include SOUTHEND Pier, the longest in the world and prone to collapse, but regrettably piers are out of our scope, and anyway a full restoration programme started in 1984. CHELMSFORD's 1814 domed circular Doric conduit must be safe now; it survived a relocation in 1939 from the High Street to Admiral's Park so it must have municipal protection. One lost forever is the hermitage at Whitleys on the hill outside BAYTHORN END, well known enough in its day to have been the subject of a popular engraving. There was another hermitage on the lake at BRAXTED PARK, to the west of Witham, an 18th-century ice-house crowned with a summer-house where a hermit is said to have lived for a year and a day.

Right on the county border with Suffolk, just by Sudbury, in a ploughed field north of MIDDLETON church, is a small, sweet, unexceptional little folly called the Middleton Arch. About 15 feet high, and built of brick, flint and bits of Lavenham church, it bears an inscription which initially seems puzzling: 'PLANTED BY OLIVER RAYMOND . LLB . RECTOR . OF . THIS . PARISH . IX . NOV. MDCCCXLI . THE . DAY . OF . HRH . THE . PRINCES . BIRTH' — but the inscription refers to the great avenue of oak trees the royalist rector planted; the arch merely served the ancillary purpose of announcing the avenue. Now, in the interests of improving agriculture (and despite a preservation order), most of the mighty oaks are gone, and the commemorative arch with its incongruous carvings of De Vere mullets is a lonely loyalist testimony.

Thankfully, follies are still being built in Essex. Sir Frederick Gibberd, one of the very few modern-day architects with the courage to practise what he preached (he designed most of HARLOW and chose to make his home there), enjoyed building landscapes in his relatively small garden, relishing the challenge of constricted space. He added summer-houses, statuary and a log fortress, ostensibly for his grandchildren to play in, but perhaps we know better. And just as we started with a Chinese fishing temple, so we can end with one, for the architect Peter Foster received a commission to build one in Essex in 1984 – but the client has requested anonymity.

Lincolnshire

Not just Skegness but the whole of Lincolnshire is *so* bracing —
which is advertising talk for a remorseless east wind that scythes
through as many layers of clothes as you care to put on. The
winters are even worse. Flat counties usually seem to deter follies,
but there is a fair number here, mostly in the slightly warmer west,
as well as several monuments and obelisks and bits and pieces
attempting to be sham ruins. Now and again a really remarkable
folly, a building of national significance, appears. — like 'The
Jungle', described at the end of the chapter.

BROCKLESBY is the northernmost settlement in the new Lincolnshire. 'Capability' Brown undertook the new layout of the park in
1771; the grotto and the root-house would seem to be earlier. The
grot, tufa-coated with one room and a tunnel, serves as focal point
for the root-house, and vice versa. The root-house has an entrance
like a whalebone arch and is built from rough stones and branches.
A hermit is alleged to have lived here, but the plain brick back of
the hut establishes it as pure ornament; genuine hermitages can
normally be stalked from all four sides. Away from the wilderness
is Arabella Aufrere's Temple, possibly by Brown. Sophia Aufrere,
who died aged 33, is buried in James Wyatt's stunningly beautiful
mausoleum of 1794, which also holds a full-length figure of her by
Nollekens; perhaps Wyatt was also responsible for the Holgate
Monument near the Orangery, another Coade stone sculpture of an
urn on a triangle supported by three tortoises. There are three
similar monuments in Britain and Ireland; this one was erected by
the 1st Earl of Yarborough to the memory of George Holgate of
Melton, who died in 1785, 'a tenant and friend, who as a mark of

gratitude bequeathed to him a small estate at Cadney . . . '. Also in the park is a dry bridge, the result of the draining of the lake.

Newsham Lodge on the edge of the estate is a Georgian cottage attempting to look like a medieval relic; the Tenants and Friends of the 2nd Lord Yarborough erected a Memorial Arch in the grounds in 1865; but the best known Yarborough folly is five miles away, near CAISTOR. Pelham's Pillar, more tower than pillar, being square with a lantern top and ogee roof, was erected to commemorate Lord Yarborough's Brocklesby Plantation; an inscription above the doorway, guarded by two lions couchant, tells us that he 'commenced planting 1787 and between that year and 1828 placed on his property 12,552,700 Trees'. The monument, designed by Edward James Willson, cost nearly £2,400 and was visited by Prince Albert on its completion. The tower is always locked, but a key can be obtained during reasonable hours from Keeper's Cottage, Pillar Lodge.

The market town of LOUTH, to the south-east, has no fewer than three 19th-century follies. The top of the church spire, which came down around 1844, now stands appropriately in the vicarage garden, where a hermitage used to stand before the vicarage was built in 1832. Another religious removal is at 'The Priory', a Gothic house built by local architect and antiquarian Thomas Espin in 1818. Scraps from the 12th-century Abbey were pieced together to make the sham ruin in the garden, probably by Espin himself. When he died in 1822 he was buried in his Gothic mausoleum near the ruin. Broadbank House had until recently a peculiar shellwork screen of 1859. Castellations, Gothic windows and turrets made up the folly; the whole was decorated with shells and fleurs-de-lis. A little north of Louth, near Little Grimsby, is Brackenborough Hall with another ruined sham ruin, this one built about 1850 by a Mr Fotherby, out of several different Gothic leftovers.

Outside Market Rasen, famous for its racehorses, stands Castle Tealby Farm, on the Viking Way footpath. Here a stone stockade has been decorated with battlements and turrets to imitate a castle, perhaps for the now demolished Bayons Manor, described by the county's Property Services Department as having 'good claims to have been the most ambitious and thorough-going Romantic Folly of them all. It had towers, barbican, inner and outer bailey and keep' – so would these feeble little castellations at TEALBY even have been noticed?

Sir Cecil Wray, a much ridiculed 18th-century politician, was once the owner of Eastgate House in Lincoln. Irritated by the noise from a smithy opposite, he built a new house at FILLINGHAM, nine miles north of the county town on Ermine Street, which he called Summer Castle from his wife's name, Esther Summers. It is in the Gothick style, and was possibly built in 1760 by John Carr. In the park is the so-called Manor House, according to Pevsner a 17th-century cottage later 'done up with pointed lights' and serving as an eyecatcher. Summer Castle was given two Gothick archways, whether from Eastgate House or not we are not told. One could be seen from Ermine Street (the A15) before it collapsed several years ago; the other, somewhat larger, still stands by the side of the B1398 – two square towers guarding the arch in between, with triangular lodges. More recent removal follies can be found 25 miles away at ASHBY PUERORUM, where the garden of Holbeck Manor contains pieces from Denton Manor and an arch from Eastgate House.

If on a winter's night a traveller in the 18th century dared to venture up Ermine Street towards Lincoln without protection, he ran a greater risk of getting into trouble than a 20th-century stroller in the seamier streets of London. Footpads – bucolic muggers – were scarcely the romantic figures of legend; it was all too easy to get lost on the featureless heaths of Lincolnshire, and if one of them took a fancy into his head to make a little extra on the side then it was all over for the traveller. Sir Francis Dashwood of West Wycombe and Hell Fire Club fame owned an estate at Nocton, seven miles south-east of Lincoln, and in an unusual gesture of public-spiritedness paid for a Land Lighthouse to be built, to guide travellers safely across the heath. The inscription testifies to the tower's use: 'COLUMNAM HANC UTILITATI PUBLICAE D.D.D. F.DASHWOOD M.DCC.LI'. The 92-foot tall DUNSTON Pillar, as it is known, guided travellers safely for over 50 years. One young messenger boy was given strict instructions to keep the light to his right as he journeyed to Lincoln; he was found the following morning a mile away from the pillar, having walked round it in circles all night. It was also widely believed that the fire that lit the beacon came directly from hell (although no one ever quite summed up the courage to propose the theory directly to the mercurial Sir Francis), so after his death the beacon apparatus was removed and replaced by a Coade stone statue of George III by Joseph Panzetti. It was the King's Golden Jubilee, and a mason named John Willson was employed to put the statue in place. His tomb in nearby Harmston churchyard refers obliquely to the subsequent accident:

> He who erected the noble King
> Is here now laid by Death's sharp sting.

George III stood there for the best part of a century and a half, until the Second World War, when he and the top 60 feet of the tower were demolished as a hazard to the RAF. The top half of his torso can still be seen in Lincoln Castle, and the truncated pillar has since served as a chicken coop and bicycle shed, dominating the garden of its very proud owner.

COLEBY HALL, two miles to the west, has a Temple of Romulus and Remus built in 1762 by William Chambers for his friend Thomas Scrope. Not to be outdone, Scrope designed himself an expedient Temple to Pitt. All nice and neat, but the real folly is the gateway, which was copied stone for stone from a ruined Roman arch in Lincoln which Scrope had tried to prevent being demolished. Perhaps the imitation was built to advertise the worthy cause, or to provide a record once the original had finally disappeared. Lincolnshire, famous for poachers, has a peculiar interest in commemorating unusual anniversaries. At BOULTHAM, just outside Lincoln, a neglected column in the grounds of the now demolished Hartsholme Hall was erected in 1902 to commemorate the establishment of the Lincoln Waterworks in 1846. At SOMERBY HALL, near Caistor, a 1770 pillar crowned with an urn marks 29 years of happy marriage between Edward and Ann Weston.

Not long ago Grantham was voted the most boring town in England, a title it had probably come close to winning for years. At any rate, local squires seemed to find solace and amusement in folly building. Near Harlaxton is DENTON MANOR where an old porch makes an agreeable object in the park. Near the lake is a grotto on a hillock. The room behind the cyclopean arch is decorated with shells and fossils, and inside a barely legible text reads:

Approach you then with cautious steps
To where the streamlet creeps
Or Ah! too rudely you may wake
Some guardian nymph that sleeps.

This appears to be a rendering of the 'Huius Nympha loci', but differing from Pope's translation in the grotto at Stourhead.

BELTON HOUSE, just north of Grantham and recently acquired by the National Trust, has one of the county's most spectacular follies, the Bellmount Tower. Set on a hill, it was designed by the little known landscapist William Emes in 1750 as a hunting lodge, using motifs from as many different architectural orders as he could muster. A roundheaded arch pierces the bottom half of the tower, so it looks more like an overbalanced arch than a tower, topped with blind Venetian windows, obelisks at the side and curious angled windows set in the corners of the stepped side buttresses. At the top a four-angled roof slopes up to a flat balustraded level, once presumably accessible; now the balustrading hangs tiredly over the edge of the roof and the whole structure is in poor condition – dilapidated rather than ruinous. A less successful marriage of styles is difficult to conceive. Another of Lincolnshire's sham ruins made from medieval pieces is nearer the house, and may possibly be by one of the Wyatts, as James Wyatt and Jeffry Wyatville worked at Belton for the 1st Earl of Brownlow in 1776 and 1810. The village has an obelisk that serves as a pump, probably by Salvin, who built the pretty estate village in the overblown Harlaxton style in 1828–39.

Europe's most bizarre bus shelter must be the Egyptian Gate to the Villa Borghese in Rome, but LONDONTHORPE, just behind the Bellmount Tower, tries hard. The 19th-century builder of the Londonthorpe bus shelter did not understand the classical vocabulary of architecture (with Bellmount nearby anything was possible), but he must have leafed through some books and picked out the elements he liked. The shelter is in the form of a heavily rusticated arch, with liberal use of keystones. There is a horse on the roof. It must have started life as something more dignified.

MARSTON HALL to the north-west is the site of a precious folly: a summer-house in the garden, which started life as an 18th-century gazebo, was restored in 1962 for Henry Thorold by John Partridge.

Pevsner records that Christopher Blackie made the pinnacles and Barbara Jones did the murals. Jones's painted birds are inside, but it is the exterior that gives it away — it looks a little too crisp, the thin façade with its crenellations and fantasy pinnacles, yet it remains an object to be coveted.

After the famous BOSTON Stump, the town's Freemasons' Hall must rate as its most important sight. This gaudy temple was built in 1860–3 in the Egyptian style popular with freemasons. The idea was taken from an early 19th-century French book on Egyptian temples. Its most prominent feature is the portico with two columns in antis and hieroglyphic inscriptions giving the dates of building, emulating a similar device of 1856 on the entrance to Antwerp Zoo.

GREATFORD, near Stamford in the underbelly of the county, has several weird ornaments decorating the village. They are all the work of Major C. C. L. Fitzwilliam, who was also responsible for the famous roof garden on top of the old Derry & Toms department store in Kensington. The items in themselves are negligible, but cumulatively they are effective and amusing. Obelisks, huge crowns, statues, seats, mushrooms, tiny houses and Gothic bric-à-brac are all scattered throughout the village, not only in the Major's garden, as if the Gnomic rising had taken place. North at SWINSTEAD is a two-storey, three-bayed pavilion of 1725 with small flanking towers set on a hill above Grimsthorpe Castle, convincingly attributed to Vanbrugh. Heading back north to Lincoln, the A15 dog-legs through the village of ASWARBY, where a pale imitation of the Virginia Water Leptis Magna columns ornament a roadside garden; enough to puzzle a passing motorist but not enough to stop him. In SLEAFORD, along the path leading from Northgate to Westgate House, is a wall into which have been built a number of perpendicular windows complete with tracery. They do not come from the demolished Sleaford Castle, nor from the church's restoration in 1883 (or 1853), which left little for contemplation. Their provenance remains a mystery, though the remover is thought to have been one Charles Kirk.

Past Dunston Pillar again, a road turns off to BRANSTON, where a Mr Lovely built a strange house called Stonefield with wonderful gates. On top of gate piers made out of rubble and decorated with masks lurk monkeys that look as if they were used on the set of 'The Hunchback of Notre Dame'. They don't do anything, they just look at you. Unusually, Pevsner tells us the story: 'There'll be a good monkey [mortgage] in that house,' said one local. 'I'll show them where the monkeys will be,' says Mr Lovely. There are also a couple of Lovely houses in Silver Street.

GATE BURTON is almost in Nottinghamshire. The 'Shatoo' here is a temple designed by John Platt for Thomas Hutton in 1748, the fascinating name perhaps a Lincolnshire rendering of 'château'. We have left Lincolnshire's best folly till last, the extraordinary house called 'The Jungle' at EAGLE, south-west of Lincoln by the Nottinghamshire border. Set in the middle of nowhere, this sham ruined castle façade looks uninhabitable, but in the 1820s there was a perfectly normal house at the back where Samuel Russell Collett was able to live. He kept a zoo around his Gothic bungalow, with kangaroos, goldfish, buffalo, American deer and pheasants – hence 'The Jungle'. The façade is unbelievable, with its jagged outlines, burnt brick, creeper and rusticated stone, and yet this well-proportioned sham was obviously carefully thought out. It is now – well, it always has been – a private house, and in 1976 it was completely rebuilt to a luxurious standard as an extremely large modern house, retaining Collett's incredible façade.

Norfolk

The finest folly in Norfolk is unquestionably the Chapel at CRIMPLESHAM HALL, a remarkable edifice which bears little relationship to any chapel built by anyone other than the Brothers Grimm. A tall, spidery bell-tower is the most prominent feature, and at first glance that is all there appears to be; but a closer inspection reveals a rather substantial building, so encrusted in ivy and creeper that it is hard to make out the overall shape. It is not known whether it was built as a ruin or whether the undergrowth has acted as architect, but the general effect at the moment is near perfection. Any further botanical encroachment and the structure will be threatened; any less and it will lose much of its brooding mystery. Three masses of ivy mark the roofless walls of the main building, dominated at the back by a large traceried window. An entrance porch, also assembled from medieval fragments, stands to one side. Behind the bell-tower is the much shorter main tower with one room per floor, that on the first storey being remarkable for the mosaic on the floor which is made from horses' teeth. The staircase is now blocked up, but the owners assure us that the floor is still there, and showed us a photograph of it. A bell still swings precariously in its wooden cage at the top of the bell-tower, but it is no longer rung, for safety's sake. The tower, capped with a pointed roof, looks romantically Germanic; any moment one expects Rapunzel to appear at the top and let down her golden hair . . .

After Crimplesham, which we would guess was built in the early 19th century — certainly before the existing house — the other Norfolk follies seem tamer, although there are some fine examples. We arrived just too late to see the Reffley Temple in South

122　The roof of a former gents' urinal, now a private house, at Gayhurst

123　Concrete cows at Bradwell, rural Milton Keynes

124 Lord Boston's Folly at Hedsor Priory, Bourne End

125 Engraving of Flitcroft's Fort Belvedere by M. A. Rocker after P. Sandby, c.1752

126   The Gothick Temple, Stowe

127   Scott's Grotto, Ware

128   Chambers's temple at St Paul's Walden

129 The Node Dairy, Driver's End
130 The church at Ayot St Lawrence

131 Brookmans Park folly arch

132 Stratton's Observatory, Little Berkhamsted

133 Wroxton eyecatcher

134   Rousham eyecatcher, Steeple Aston

135   US Army model house, Highmoor

136 Mr Bliss's Tweed Mill, Chipping Norton

137 Mrs Gaskell's Tower, Knutsford

138 Riber Castle, Matlock

139   Bladon Castle, Abraham Hoskins's massive folly at Newton Solney

140   The deercote at Sudbury

Wootton, outside King's Lynn, with its sphinxes and obelisks all set on what once may have been a little moated island, but an eight-year-old boy remembered it well: 'Kids wrecked the building so they came and knocked it down and took all the other things away.' All there is left to see is the tiny round chalybeate spring with a central socket – perhaps for the obelisk? 'The Folly' at Sandringham, which aroused great hopes, turned out to be just the name of a house, while the follies at Hillington Hall mentioned in the Shell guide turn out never to have existed, except for a garden alcove with a crow-stepped gable. 'The only folly round here is my house!' said the owner, proudly standing outside his immaculate home.

So we made our way to HOLKHAM HALL, the seat of the Earls of Leicester, near Wells-next-the-Sea. There are no real follies here, just monumental scale. The Leicester Monument, the house, the obelisk and the Triumphal Arch are all exactly aligned over a distance of 2·8 miles. The road itself is straight only between the arch and the obelisk, a distance of over 1·6 miles, and curiously there is a Roman road less than half a mile away. The Leicester Monument is a 120-foot Corinthian column using cows' heads for the helices, a neat touch by the designer W. J. Donthorne, as Thomas William Coke, Earl of Leicester (1754–1842), can lay strong claim to being called the father of modern agriculture. Coke of Norfolk, as this prodigious man liked to be known, had an interesting married life. His wife died in 1800, and 22 years later his god-daughter proposed to him, which enabled him to go on to sire five children after the age of 70; there was a 52-year age difference between his eldest and his youngest child. His Monument has four extensions from the plinth, which are labelled 'BREEDING IN ALL ITS BRANCHES', 'LIVE AND LET LIVE', 'SMALL IN SIZE BUT GREAT IN VALUE' and 'THE IMPROVEMENT OF AGRICULTURE', with statues of cows, sheep and agricultural implements, in case anyone missed the point. On three sides of the plinth are elaborate friezes; on the fourth (north) side a lengthy and fulsome inscription. Near the obelisk, inscriptionless and allegedly erected in 1729 before the building of the house, is the Temple, supposed to have been designed by William Kent but erected, with alterations, by Matthew Brettingham senior some time after 1734. It is not a successful design: the grandeur of the Tuscan portico is lessened by the wings either side with their lean-to roofs and the rather hesitant dome on a drum with Diocletian windows. Neither is the Triumphal Arch a triumph of architecture, the central arch carrying more masonry above it than one might reasonably expect, probably so that it could clearly be seen from the obelisk.

Within ten miles of BLICKLING HALL there are eight follies, one of the most concentrated areas in the country. Unfortunately none is what one might call a classic, although they all have their own distinctive charm. Blickling itself is one of the best loved National Trust properties, the first major house to be made over under the Country House Scheme, meaning that the Trust owns the house and opens it to the public, while the family is allowed to remain in occupation, thus ensuring the building's preservation as a home rather than a museum. The finest pyramid in England can be found here; it is the mausoleum of John, 2nd Earl of Buckinghamshire, and his two wives. Built by Joseph Bonomi in 1794, it has weathered exceptionally well, and even the massive entrance porch and the side windows seem to harmonise with the regularity and superb workmanship of the 45-foot pyramid. In the gardens themselves, the three-bay Tuscan temple is probably by Thomas Ivory of Norwich, while the Racecourse Stand, a square, two-storey, castellated red-brick Gothic building with a much higher circular stair turret, some way from the Hall, is unattributed. It is now a private house, and on the hot summer's morning when we visited it it was actually living up to its name: 'And a clear round for Spellbinder ridden by Laura Buxton' echoed from the field in front of the Stand as the gymkhana sweated its way through the day.

HEYDON HALL has an obelisk and a tower clearly marked on the Ordnance map, but the tower is so tiny among the encircling trees that it is very difficult to spot. When it is found it seems hardly worth the effort, since it is the smallest, plainest type of look-out tower, octagonal, brick with flint infill, and only about 40 feet high. The trees tower over it. Just over two miles further north is Mannington Hall, near SAXTHORPE, with its beautifully tended gardens, open to the public in the summer. Walpoles live at Mannington, and when we heard there were follies . . . but they are the tiniest scraps, removals of small columns, an arch, fragments of this and that, brought from Norwich *c.*1860 by the 4th Earl of Orford and clustered round the old ruined church. The only original structure seems to be a small, circular, red-brick building, once thatched but ruinous since at least 1902, as shown by an old photograph. It was too delicate to be a tower, and too small for a summer-house: perhaps a Gothic toolshed?

There is a splendid bath-house at Melton Hall in MELTON CONSTABLE, an estate which pops on and off the market with confusing rapidity. From the back it is a plain two-storey cottage in which an old couple have lived for the past 18 years, but from the front it is a wonderful celebration of Gothick, with a three-sided, three-storey tower as the centrepiece, giving the impression of a church from the big house. The windows were originally much larger, and the tower's top storey is sham; the sad thing is that the occupants aren't allowed into the park to see the front of their house – the tall gate giving access to the deer-park is permanently locked. A mile north, at BRININGHAM, is the fat, circular, five-storey Belle Vue Tower, probably built as a 16th-century look-out tower (described by Pevsner as a Standing), but chopped and changed over the years so that the octagonal bottom storey is dated 1721. It has been used as an observatory, a signalling tower and a cottage; this last seems to be where its future lies. From a distance it looks more like a stray grain silo than a folly.

A good mark of a folly is the delay between conception and completion, like the Jefferson Monument in Washington DC, the world's tallest obelisk. The longest delay imaginable, however, was that involved in the building of the Repton Temple at SHERINGHAM HALL, designed in 1812 and completed in 1975, 163 years later. The reason is that Abbot Upcher, who bought the estate in 1811 for 50,000 guineas (at the age of 26), died suddenly in 1819 before the house and grounds were properly finished, leaving his wife too heartbroken to carry on with the plans. The temple was finally built by the trustees of the estate as a 75th birthday present to Thomas Upcher, the direct descendant of the Abbot. The temple differs from the one planned by Repton in that it is hexagonal, not circular, and built of Portland stone rather than brick with flint infill.

Everyone has his own ideal of a folly, usually based on the first one seen; the tower at WESTWICK is close to ours. It seems purposeless — big, shabby, uncared for, mistakenly called an obelisk on the Ordnance map and by the locals. Clearly seen from the railway, it nevertheless tries to hide in a corner of a wood, shambling in the undergrowth. The tower stands on a square red-brick plinth with heavy flint rustications on the corners and round the now bricked up round-arch doorway. There is an Alice in Wonderland-type doorlet set into the brick, through which one can see the wooden spiral staircase — but here our wonderfully developed sense of self-preservation took over, and we refrained from exploring any higher. The tower itself is a heavy, round, brick-rendered column with porthole windows and a projecting octagonal flat metal roof. By the evidence lying on the ground it used to have a conical spire, but that was taken down because, according to an old lady living in one of the lodges, the top was unsafe. As the tower appears to be on the direct flightpath for the runway at Coltishall fighter base, we would imagine the Air Force had a say in the matter. The lodge the old lady lived in was once at the foot of an arch, formerly the entrance to Westwick Hall, which straddled the B1150 to North Walsham, but that too got in the way of the 20th century and had to go in 1981, much to the old lady's regret. The arch and the tower are preserved on the Westwick village sign, a nicely carved and painted piece of local pride which all Norfolk villages sport.

The exuberant early Victorian Gunton Tower, a sort of combination lodge/eyecatcher/observatory to GUNTON PARK, is a memorable building to discover in the rolling Norfolk countryside. It looks like no recognised style of architecture — 19th-century municipal or railway English is the nearest one can get. It has three storeys topped by a flagpole: the top storey is a glass-walled observatory room with two interior levels; the second storey a single large room with two tall round-arched windows in each wall (the staircase to the top floor meanders uncertainly through the air, ignoring the safety of the walls, before latching itself to the south side wall for the last few feet of the climb); and the ground floor a tall arch through which the drive to the main house runs. The accommodation on the ground floor is in the four wings, which curve out to front and back giving a symmetrical appearance. The tower is now being converted into three apartments, but although they were proud of the work they were doing, the builders were not envious of the prospective tenants. 'We've worked up here through two winters, and we know what it's like,' commented one. But the view, they admitted, was indeed superb. 'The only place in Norfolk where you can see the sea and Norwich Cathedral from the same room,' said the other proudly. When they started work, every pane of glass in the building had been smashed, and the floors were rotten. Now the tower looks brand new – an excellent preservation job for an excellent folly. It was built by Lord Suffield before 1835, and the local story is that he was convinced a popular uprising was imminent, and built this 100-foot tower so that he could watch the proceedings with a degree of detachment. In fact the Baron was a liberal, a vehement critic of the government's conduct after the Peterloo Massacre, and an outspoken abolitionist. A keen sportsman, he may well have envisaged the tower as some sort of grandstand.

To the west of Norwich itself is COLNEY HALL, with a 19th-century grotto conservatory attached. Grottoes are not common in Norfolk (strange for a county with such a long shore line) and we have come across only two others, one at DENTON near Bungay, a 1770 example with gables and arches, and the other at Shadwell Park in BRETTENHAM near Thetford. The Denton grotto is said to have been made with coral and shells from the Great Barrier Reef; not surprisingly it is the best in the county. Nearby is a re-erected church window forming a romantic Gothic ruin. 'Shadwell' is a corruption of St Chad's Well, and in the grounds is apparently a medieval spring, once a place of pilgrimage, which was beautified by one of the Buxton family to make a grotto with statues in niches and stone seats – but we weren't allowed to see it, getting a very cool reception indeed from a manservant when we asked for permission at the spick-and-span Teulon house. There is also a scrawny little distyle temple at the edge of the woods.

The 144-foot Norfolk Pillar at GREAT YARMOUTH, a monument to Norfolk-born Horatio Nelson, would not normally merit inclusion in a book such as this if it weren't for the fact that the Coade stone figure on the top is Britannia, not Nelson, and is looking inland rather than out to sea. It was built to the design of William Wilkins in 1817–20, and predates the 41-foot taller Trafalgar Square column by some 20 years. Unlike the Trafalgar Square column, the Norfolk Pillar is also a tower; closed for some years for restoration (Britannia is now glassfibre rather than Coade), it is open to the public in July and August. The sadness from a folly lover's point of view is that the competition for the Great Yarmouth monument was not won by Francis Chantrey, who proposed a 130-foot floodlit statue of Nelson at the end of a pier 'on a pedestal made of the bows of vessels taken from the enemy'. Still, the EEC would have made us take it down by now.

There is a curious cast-iron milestone on the edge of a field of gladioli at RAVENINGHAM, made by John Thomas Patience in 1831 (praise be to artists who sign their works!) for Sir Edmund Bacon. It is a 10-foot high octagonal Gothic turret, like a chimney, set on a crumbling plinth. Most of the distances and places have now disappeared, and all that is left on the three front faces is the enigmatic:

RAVENINGHAM

MILES   TC   4è

III

If the finest folly in the county is at Crimplesham, then the oddest must be the clock-tower at LITTLE ELLINGHAM. A tall square tower with one large clock-face (and three blank circles), it has a smaller top storey with louvred doors and a little domed roof. Clustered round the bottom like the wings of a Greek church are four once identical two-storey cottages with chimneys at the front. Pevsner speculates that it could be *c.*1855, and it certainly has the style of mid-Victorian industry – it is not a pretty sight, but undeniably a memorable one.

South-east of Norwich an eyecatcher pops up to the east of the A146 near LANGLEY. On closer inspection it becomes a small, elegant archway with two lodges attached: 'Designed by Sir John Soane 1784, Restored by Capt. & Mrs. R. D. Hutton 1980'. On top of the lodges are greyhounds rampant on shields above the motto 'TOVIOVRS FIDELE'. It is too small ever to have been used as a lodge; its function must simply have been to catch the eye.

Suffolk

Frederick Augustus Hervey (1730–1803), Bishop of Derry, 4th Earl of Bristol, 5th Baron Howard de Walden, was ambitious, enormously wealthy, keen on art, obsessed with building and, thankfully for us, as eccentric as all the Herveys. He was also that rare thing among 18th-century aristocrats, a man blessed with a strong social conscience and a highly developed sense of fair play. Unlike many of his predecessors, he took an active interest in the affairs of his large and prosperous diocese, building new roads and bridges, sponsoring coal-mining operations, even appointing an Irishman as his chaplain, an unheard of move for an Anglican bishop. While not going so far as to advocate an independent Ireland – such an attitude would have been rare indeed among the ruling classes – he did believe that the franchise should be extended to Roman Catholics. But it is his buildings that concern us here, and particularly those in Suffolk. An obelisk was erected to his memory, and surprisingly enough the glorious paean of praise inscribed upon it would seem to be largely true. What also surprises is that the only other folly on his estate would appear to be ICKWORTH HOUSE itself, the only oval stately home. It was begun in 1796 by the Irish architect Francis Sandys from a design by Mario Asprucci, but as the Earl Bishop had already started on a circular house in Ballyscullion, Co. Londonderry, in 1787 (which in turn was inspired by John Plaw's round house Belle Ile in Lake Windermere), the origin of the idea is evident. Even earlier, in 1785, Hervey had built the circular Mussenden Temple in Co. Londonderry on a magnificent coastal site. He attracted a certain degree of criticism by naming it after Mrs Mussenden, a notably attractive 22-year-old widow, but she conveniently alleviated any hint of scandal by dying before it was finished. The Earl Bishop demonstrated his untypical liberalism by allowing the local Catholics to celebrate Mass in the temple. But back to Suffolk again, where the only other interesting building on the estate is, not surprisingly, called 'The Round House'. This is a private house with a conical roof and central chimney, half-timbered under the eaves, well hidden from the main road. It looks too recent to have been the responsibility of the bishop, and we are left to ponder the ambiguity of the 18th-century comment on his eccentricity: 'God created men, women and Herveys'.

Suffolk has a fine variety of follies, some of the most famous in the country, and also boasts the one generally acknowledged to be the first. FRESTON Tower, on the banks of the Orwell, has an uncertain history. The date of its construction is given as 1549; some say it is by Edward Latimer, others by Hugh de Freston. Its purpose is equally obscure: whether it was part of a long forgotten house, or a symbolic representation of the Castle of Knowledge, a popular 16th-century motif, or simply a free-standing prospect tower is not known. One point in favour of the more prosaic first explanation is that the bottom three storeys on the south side are windowless, which of course they would be if this part of the tower had abutted another building. This side also has the only entrance, a miserable little affair compared with the sophistication of the rest of the building, fit only for an internal doorway (although a turn of the century postcard shows it with a brick-arched surround). Finally, there are traces on the brickwork of some other structure having been joined to the tower at some stage. Nevertheless, the only story one hears with any degree of regularity is that of the education of the lovely Ellen de Freston, for which the tower was built — even the curriculum has been handed down to us:

Monday (Ground floor): Charity
Tuesday (First floor): Tapestry
Wednesday (Second floor): Music
Thursday (Third floor): Painting
Friday (Fourth floor): Literature
Saturday (Fifth floor): Astronomy
Sunday (out of the tower): Church

It makes a good story; other versions have her ending up on the roof in the arms of the builder, furthering her education in a different manner.

But could Suffolk have another contender for the title of Britain's first folly? In the same year that Freston Tower was built, nearby ERWARTON HALL produced a gatehouse — but what a gatehouse. Bizarre in the extreme, it long predates any similar follies, but had it been built in the 18th century (it could have been built at any time) it would have been an inevitable inclusion. Architecturally it resembles nine brick Saturn V rockets in a square of three by three, with an archway cut through the centre three. The motive was purely decorative, an avenue of architecture which has remained unexplored.

The peninsula which separates the Orwell and the Stour is home to two other famous follies — 'The Cat House' and the Tattingstone Wonder. WOOLVERSTONE, a popular yachting centre and marina along the banks of the Orwell, is famous for 'The Cat House', a castellated red-brick Gothick cottage of 1793 on the riverside. The east wall is taken up almost entirely by an enormous Gothick window, only partly real, which formerly (until the trees grew up) overlooked the Orwell. In the bottom left-hand corner of this window sat a painted cat, and the local tale is that the cat was displayed to tell smugglers that the coast was clear. When we visited in the autumn of 1980 the cottage was in the process of being renovated and there was no cat to be seen, so evidently the revenue man was around. Another painted window in the county is at Mulberry House, the old vicarage in PAKENHAM, near Bury St Edmunds, where an upstairs window has an 18th-century parson in wig and bands looking out. We had hoped to hear that he was put in the window whenever the Devil was around to warn him that the coast was not clear, but there is no local legend here: it was painted by Rex Whistler when he was stationed nearby during the Second World War.

The rather cruel epithet 'Silly Suffolk' which has oppressed the county for years is claimed by Suffolk partisans to be a linguistic corruption of 'Selig Suffolk', 'selig' being the German for fortunate or blessed. Why the Germans should have chosen this particular word (which also means deceased) to describe an English county is not revealed; the English appellations for places such as Württemberg or Baden-Baden elude us for the moment. Certainly the blessed inhabitants of the village of TATTINGSTONE were silly enough in 1790 for the local squire, Edward White, to vow to give them something they could really gawp at. Thus came the Tattingstone Wonder, one of the most famous follies in Britain. Its fame stems largely from its euphonic name, because it is far from being the only one of its type and indeed there are several follies in Suffolk itself which are more bizarre. Nevertheless, the Wonder is a splendid example of a folly. It started life as a pair of cottages, until Squire White decided to enliven the view from Tattingstone Place. He built a third cottage on the end and topped it with a square flint church tower, omitting the southern wall because it wasn't visible from the house. The front of the cottages was replaced by a façade with two Gothick windows, and the crowning touch was a large rose window on the south-eastern wall. The last time we visited, the cottages were uninhabited, and work is currently in progress to flood the valley between the Wonder and the big house to make the Alton reservoir, thereby adding a touch of landscaping Squire White would surely have approved.

Suffolk must have the widest variety of follies in any county; except for a grotto there are good examples of every type. There are not enough in any one group to be able to list them stylistically, so they are best discussed by taking an anti-clockwise tour of the county, starting from Ipswich. Orwell Park stands on the north bank of the Orwell, in the village of NACTON. It used to be the home of Admiral Vernon, nicknamed 'Old Grogram' from his habit of wearing trousers in that material, and cursed by generations of sailors for decreeing that the naval issue of rum should be watered down – hence 'grog'. The house is now a prep school, and in the grounds are not one but three towers erected by George Tilman in the mid-19th century. One is an observatory tower attached to the house, another an Italianate water-tower, and the third a clock-tower with a circular stair turret, dated 1859.

East of Wickham Market, near BENTWATER in the flatlands known as the Sandlings, is the most amazing lodge in Britain. Rendlesham as a village no longer really exists, but 1,500 years ago it was the seat of the kings of East Anglia. Even Rendlesham Hall disappeared in 1950, but its lodges survive. Woodbridge Lodge is confusingly marked on the Ordnance map as a water-tower, but anything less like any form of water-tower is difficult to imagine. It looks like an insane chapter house from a madman's cathedral; from the outside it is impossible to divine the floor plan without the most detailed investigation, so cluttered up is the exterior with buttresses and pinnacles. As the column was promoted from a mere architectural artefact, a device for supporting other parts of a building, into a self-sufficient monumental column, so here at Rendlesham we see the same promotion of the far more exciting flying buttress into an end in itself; Woodbridge Lodge is little more than an exercise in flying buttresses and pinnacles with a little house crammed in among them. Four graceful and mighty buttresses, enough to hold up a good sized abbey, fly up to support only themselves; they are cleverly disguised chimneys. The building is variously dated between 1790 and 1820, and it was constructed for Peter Isaac Thellusson, son of Peter Thellusson, who was thought by many to be the richest man in England when he died in 1799. In 1801 Thellusson employed Henry Hakewill, an architect whose speciality was Tudor Gothick, to Gothicise Rendlesham Hall. The lodge could well be attributed to Hakewill; or it could have been built in 1806 to celebrate Thellusson's elevation to the peerage as Baron Rendlesham. Ivy Lodge, at the main entrance gate to Bentwater's RAF base, is so covered with ivy that it is difficult to discern its real shape, but it basically consists of a ruined tower joined by an elegant arch which spans the drive to a smaller tower. Through the gate the entrance to the lodge proper, which is in the larger ruined tower, is through a semi-circular arched doorway flanked by two matching windows, the whole set in a large infilled dropped arch. It may be that the ivy supports the building; certainly in the last five years it has grown to such an extent that the folly is currently more vegetation than construction.

The village of THORPENESS, north of Aldeburgh, is unusual in that it was built in its entirety as a speculative development holiday centre. The old fishing hamlet of Thorpe was acquired by G. Stuart Ogilvie, landowner, playwright and barrister, who proceeded to build what his copywriters variously described as 'the ideal holiday village' and 'the Home of Peter Pan'. One problem was how to supply expected amenities such as mains water without disfiguring the landscape with an obtrusive water-tower. The answer came with the removal of a windmill from Aldringham, the next village, to replace the American 'New Mill' in Thorpeness which pumped water into a rusty iron tank beside it. A system of lakes and waterways called 'The Meare', complete with a miniature sham fort, had been designed by Ogilvie in 1910, but the war intervened and it was not until 1923 that he installed the 'new' old post-mill and cast around for a suitable means of disguising the necessary water-tank. Now Ogilvie was very fond of dovecotes, and had already disguised his own water-tower at Sizewell Court, a mile up the coast, as a dovecote in 1908, using the bottom part as a carpenter's workshop. What more natural than to use the same idea at Thorpeness, but on a very much larger scale? So 'The Gazebo' was built, a five-storey house beneath the brilliantly concealed 30,000-gallon water-tank: the tank was disguised as an everyday clapboard house with pitched roof, chimneys and sham windows, perched incongruously on top of a 60-foot tower. 'Who on earth would want to live in it with all the water rushing up and down?' was the major objection to the scheme, but Ogilvie had no difficulty finding tenants. Mr and Mrs Malcolm Mason moved in, and Mrs Mason loved it. She wrote poems for children, and one, inspired by her house, was called 'The House in the Clouds':

> The fairies really own this house — or so the children say —
> In fact, they all of them moved in upon the self same day . . .

When she recited this to Ogilvie one evening at dinner he was enchanted, exclaiming, 'The name must be changed to The House in the Clouds — and you are my Lady of the Stairs and Starlight'. The name, like the Tattingstone Wonder, has helped make this one of the country's most famous follies. The success of Thorpeness meant that yet more water was needed, so a 40,000-gallon tank was built in 1929, camouflaged as a large, square, faintly Norman tower over an arch in a parade of mock Tudor houses. Thorpeness is now on mains water, and the huge tank in 'The House in the Clouds' has been dismantled. A recent owner put a bathroom in on each floor, overspending in the process, and when we last visited this unique house it was once again on the market.

The north-east corner of Suffolk is bare of follies, apart from a little temple by William Wyatt in the grounds of HEVENINGHAM HALL, a property in the throes of being restored 'regardless of expense by a furriner', and which also boasts a magnificent thatched ice-house with stepped gables at the entrance, very similar to the one at Holkham Hall in Norfolk; and what Pevsner describes as 'a nightmarish High Victorian house' called the Tower House in the Marina, LOWESTOFT, built in the ubiquitous yellow brick of the town in 1865.

Shrubland Park at CODDENHAM is now a well known health farm, but in 1849–54 Sir Charles Barry did magnificent work on the house and garden in an attempt to re-create the Villa d'Este in rural Suffolk. On the edge of one of the few hills in the county is a well preserved polygonal prospect tower of four storeys and a higher stair turret. It is heavily battlemented and very private, being surrounded by a high barbed-wire fence.

On the Norfolk border by Thetford is EUSTON HALL, built on land so thin-soiled that in the words of Robert Bloomfield, the poet and author of *The Farmer's Boy* (1800), 'whole fields hereabout get up and blow away'. It is surprising that the Dukes of Grafton had the time or money, while struggling to make a profit from these miserable acres, for architectural fripperies in the park; but there is a fine and elaborate Temple or Banqueting House by Kent dated 1746, an eyecatcher arch, also by Kent, and a watermill disguised as a church with battlemented tower. As at Holkham, Matthew Brettingham was involved with Kent, although he is not specifically credited with any of the buildings.

Over on the A11 the village of ELVEDEN is dominated by a folly-house in Elveden Hall, acceptably Italianate from the outside (including the essential mid-Victorian water-tower) but with a spectacularly oriental interior. Down the main road near ICKLINGHAM, at the junction of three parishes, is a gigantic war memorial, a Corinthian column tower 113 feet high, designed by Clyde Young and topped with an urn. It is no longer possible to climb the 148 steps to the top as the entrance has inevitably been blocked up. (The inclusion of a war memorial in a book on follies may reasonably be questioned; but a look-out tower on the A11 must rank fairly low when one considers the most fitting way of commemorating the valiant dead of three tiny Breckland parishes, especially if we can no longer look out of it. The same amount of money could have endowed a small cottage hospital for many years.)

BARTON MILLS, the next village, has a remarkable façade to the Vicarage. Pevsner describes it as *c.*1800, castellated, with a raised centre and a quatrefoil window, but extensive rebuilding has since taken place. The façade remains, much cleaned up, but the Vicarage behind is completely new, the battlements now cleanly defined in yellow brick, blending rather unhappily with the knapped flint façade, the quatrefoil window replaced by a simple round one while the four Gothic windows remain on the ground floor. The central arched doorway has been blocked up. It is a startling sight when approached from the main road.

At the back of 2 Benton Street, HADLEIGH, is an undated Gothic sham ruin, and just to the west of the town, on ALDHAM Common, is the 1819 monument to the memory of the giant Dr Rowland Taylor, sometime Parson of Hadleigh, who was burned to death in 1555 for being a Protestant. Suffolk's newest follies are at BRANTHAM, overlooking the Stour, where Mr and Mrs Birch built two obelisks and a Temple of Venus in the early 1970s. The brick obelisk, topped with a ball finial, is supposed to have Vestal Virgins dancing round the base, but they haven't quite got round to that yet.

North-West England

Cumbria

For most of us, Cumbria consists of the Lake District and little else. As regards follies, there are quite a few in that particular area, and also concentrations round Carlisle and Furness. In the Lake District, Wordsworth has become a major cottage industry and consequently we find his name linked with a number of follies of which in all probability he was totally innocent. Here as in Northumberland the folly tends to blend with its surroundings, so the favoured style is Gothic.

The first town in Cumbria as we arrive on the A6 from Lancashire is MILNTHORPE, a seaside resort of sorts in the 19th century. Here the folly is a small round tower, possibly designed by architect George Webster in the late 1830s when he worked on Milnthorpe church. Webster also built part of Dallam Tower, west of the village. The park, which is open to the public, has a rustic deer-house. Across the estuary of the river Kent is Castle Head, the residence of John Wilkinson, the eccentric engineer and inventor to whom many firsts in the iron trade can be credited, among them the launching of the first iron ship and the installation of the first large French steam engine. He was a personage of such wealth and importance that he had his own money coined, which circulated freely at the time. Tantalisingly, the *Dictionary of National Biography* notes that his 'domestic arrangements were of a very peculiar character', but does not elaborate. After his death in 1808 the great iron-master was buried as he directed, in an all-iron coffin. From then on a wearying time set in for the corpse; until it found a final resting place in LINDALE churchyard, near his extraordinary cast-iron obelisk, the body was moved no fewer than three times.

At HAMPSFIELD, near Grange-over-Sands, is a rustic open tower rather ambitiously called 'The Hospice'. Together with a now-vanished direction indicator, it was erected for the benefit of travellers by Thomas Remington, the vicar of Cartmel. Another little tower can be found south of ALLITHWAITE, the embattled early 19th-century Kirkhead Tower.

The train but not the car can cross the Leven viaduct, where Lake Windermere empties into Morecambe Bay, and on the other side is CONISHEAD Priory, built from 1821 onwards by the inefficient Philip Wyatt for Colonel T. R. Gale Braddyll. The house is one of the more astounding monuments of the Gothic revival, eventually costing the Colonel over £140,000; the estate had to be sold in order to meet the bill. During the 15 years it took to build Conishead, Braddyll diverted himself by building a few follies. A medieval chapel on Chapel Island, Cartmel Sands, was transformed into a sham ruined eyecatcher which, for its own part, has now fallen into genuine ruins after a storm in 1984. Nearer to the house is a tower on the top of Hermitage Hill, octagonal and machicolated, with cross arrowslits and a tiny bartizan turret. Roger Fisher, a local racehorse trainer, is currently restoring it. Braddyll's best conceit is his mausoleum on a hill near BARDSEA. It is triangular, set on a round base, with buttresses on the corners, corbels, little pyramids topping the corners and a cupola with a lantern light. In each side of the building is a pointed niche, and in one of these is a sepulchral urn. The weathered folly seems to be descended from the wilder Irish buildings of the 18th century, especially Thomas Wright's Tollymore follies.

North of ULVERSTON on Hoad Hill stands the monument commonly called 'The Hoade', which commemorates the Under Secretary to the Admiralty, geographer and miscellaneous writer Sir John Barrow, who had died in 1848, two years before the erection of this remarkable and striking folly. Designed by A. Trimen as a 100-foot high, landlocked copy of the Eddystone Lighthouse, and decked out with inscriptions and emblems relating to Sir John's career, it naturally has never served as a lighthouse, although Trinity House stipulated when it was built that it should be capable of being used as such should the need arise.

Sir John Pennington, 1st Baron Muncaster, erected *c.*1800 a tall

Gothick tower north of Muncaster Castle, near RAVENGLASS on the river Esk, to mark the spot where Henry VI, in flight from someone, encountered a shepherd who led him safely to his master's castle. The octagonal tower, set on a promontory overlooking the Esk valley, stands three storeys high and has a broad door, cross arrowslits and lancet windows all around the third storey, and a pyramidal roof. A wash drawing by Thomas Sunderland shows the tower topped by a slender needle. The stables at the castle are screened by a highly decorated Gothick wall, castellated and flanked by a turret.

In the woods near the village of FINSTHWAITE, on the shores of Lake Windermere, is a tower raised by James King of Finsthwaite House in 1799. An inscription declares that Pennington Tower was built, 'To honour the officers, seamen, and marines of the Royal Navy, whose matchless conduct and irresistible valour decisively defeated the fleets of France, Spain and Holland, and promoted and protected liberty and commerce . . . '. Perhaps Mr King, when pressed, would stress 'commerce'. Halfway up the lake is the ferry that runs between FAR SAWREY and Bowness. On the Far Sawrey side is the castellated Gothic Station Cottage. The more interesting folly is above it on Claife Heights, most of which is owned by the National Trust. Here 'The Station', a summer-house, was built *c.*1799 by the Rev. William Braithwaite, who originally named it 'Belle View'. Braithwaite planted about 40,000 trees on his newly acquired land, much to the chagrin of Wordsworth, who wrote in one of the Lake Guides:

> The Pleasure house is happily situated, and is well in its kind, but, without intending any harsh reflections on the contriver . . . it may be said that he, who remembers the spot on which this building stands, and the immediate surrounding grounds as they were less than thirty years ago, will sigh for the coming of that day when Art, through every rank of society, shall be taught to have more reverence for Nature.

Wordsworth may rest assured that presently Nature is busily engaged in getting her own back, for 'The Station' is dilapidating fast. The pavilion is made of different kinds of stone and built on an octagonal ground plan. Several towers are attached to the two-storey core: possibly this was done by its second owner, J. C. Curwen, who bought the place two years after Braithwaite built it. The window openings and the doors are rectangular, the towers castellated. Originally the upper windows contained stained glass, 'giving a good representation of the manner in which the landscape would be affected in different seasons . . . '. Apparently this worked like a giant Claude Lorraine glass. From the building, a short stretch of wall with an arch and cross arrowslits runs off into the rock.

In 1825 Wordsworth, together with Southey, Wilson and Canning, made up the party celebrating Sir Walter Scott's birthday by means of a regatta, a common event on Windermere. It started from Storrs Point, south of BOWNESS. In all probability the Lakers were watching the show from Storrs Temple, an octagonal building with four arches and four tablets remembering four Admirals of the Fleet: Duncan, St Vincent, Howe and Nelson. Joseph Gandy built this monument on the lake's edge at Storrs Hall, now an hotel, for Sir John Legard in 1804.

Although Wordsworth planted a tree in the grounds of WRAY Castle, he must have hated having to witness, in the final years of his life, the wealthy Liverpudlian surgeon James Dawson's arrival at the banks of Windermere and his building of a neo-Gothic pile, all arrowslits, corbels and battlements, to the designs of H. P. Horner. Adding insult to injury, Dawson erected, after felling a few trees to make room for an adequate park, a string of sham ruins in the grounds of the castle. Most have now been demolished. John Longmire's Folly is one of those remaining, a small, squat, embattled tower with arrowslits and quatrefoils. A fortress stands beside it. Longmire himself, an original from Troutbeck, did not have much to do with it, but the building incorporates some of the stones he used for carving his mottoes and poetry. One stone even carried an 'Ode to the National Debt'. H. P. Horner must have been the architect, for the tower echoes Wray Castle, and must have been built around the same time, 1840–7.

AMBLESIDE, on the northern end of the lake, has a vernacular cottage built on a bridge across a little beck. Bridge House is owned by the National Trust; its striking site has given rise to a baseless story — that it was built by a Scottish family in order to avoid paying ground rent. In fact it was a summer-house to Ambleside Hall, although in Victorian times a family was crammed into the tiny house, said to be the smallest in England.

The slopes of HELVELLYN sport several monuments to dramatic events. At Grisedale Tarn above THIRLMERE a rock is known as 'Brothers Parting'. Some lines by Wordsworth were inscribed on the rock at the suggestion of Canon H. D. Rawnsley, one of the founders of the National Trust, but most of the carving weathered away, so a new inscription took its place. 'Brothers Parting' was originally placed on the spot where in 1805 the brothers John and William Wordsworth took leave of each other, as John was on his way to join the East Indiaman *The Earl of Abergavenny*. The ship struck a rock on the Dorset coast and foundered with the loss of 200 men, John among them. Canon Rawnsley rescued the memorial, which had been dynamited to make way for a reservoir, and had it reassembled near the Straining Well above Legburthwaite. East of Helvellyn is Striding Edge where, in 1890, the Gough Memorial was erected. Gough was a Quaker who frequently visited the Lakes. In 1804, walking on Helvellyn with his dog, he fell to his death, and the following spring a shepherd found his body with the dog beside it, still guarding his master. Soon after the tragedy became known, Wordsworth, Scott and Humphry Davy climbed to the spot, and the verses written by Scott and Wordsworth about the faithful dog are quoted on the simple stone monument. Another, less affecting monument records the coming of the Machine Age by commemorating the landing of an aeroplane on Helvellyn's summit in 1926.

DERWENT WATER holds several islands: Derwent, St Herbert's, Lord's and Rampsholme. A disputed fifth, the Floating Island, appears now and then and consists of weeds floating on the lake's gases. On Derwent Island are the barely discernible ruins of the remarkable buildings Joseph Pocklington sprinkled about his territory. Like the other islands, it is now the property of the National Trust, but there is no public access. Pocklington was connected with Peter Crosthwaite, an early exploiter of Lakeland tourism; he bought the island in 1781, renamed it Pocklington Island, and proclaimed himself Governor. He built a boat-house in the guise of a picturesque chapel, a druids' circle, a proper chapel and, in order to defend the island's sovereignty, a fort and battery. Pocklington's crony Crosthwaite was not slow to capitalise on the venture. He had just settled at Keswick after a considerable time spent on the high seas, and installed himself as publisher of guides, curator of the Keswick Museum and general tourism officer, billing himself 'Admiral at Keswick Regatta; who keeps the Museum at Keswick, & is Guide, Pilot, Geographer and Hydrographer to the Nobility and Gentry, who make the Tour of the Lakes'. In connivance with Pocklington, who had published his own map with views of the follies under Crosthwaite's imprint, he organised a mock naval battle in 1781: 'The Storming of Pocklington's Island'.

The last of the follies associated with Wordsworth is Lyulph's Tower in the National Trust's Gowbarrow Park on the shores of ULLSWATER. Ullswater was the lake that found most favour with 18th-century amateurs of the picturesque, not least because of its sextuple echo — the Duke of Portland, who owned property locally, kept a vessel on the lake 'with brass guns, for the purpose of exciting ecchoes,' wrote Gilpin in 1772. The opening line of 'The Somnambulist' is 'List, ye who pass by Lyulph's Tower', while the Gowbarrow daffodils inspired Wordsworth's famous poem. The tower, a hunting box once lived in by the Duke of Norfolk's gamekeeper, is castellated with octagonal turrets on each corner and a trapezoidal ground plan. It dates from 1780, and stands on the site of the medieval tower of Baron de L'Ulf of Greystoke, the 1st Baron of Ullswater, who gave his name to both the lake and the present building.

The entry for GREYSTOKE in Hutchinson's *History of Cumberland* (1794) mentions that 'The farmholds near the castle have some ornamented buildings, and extensive plantations, made by his Grace the Duke of Norfolk, as objects from the road leading to the castle'. Hutchinson underrated the three first-grade follies at Greystoke. Like several other buildings of their type, these rural conceits referred in name to the American War of Independence. Their more specific purpose is said to have been to irritate the Duke's Tory neighbour, the Earl of Lonsdale. They are heralded from the south by an octagonal obelisk off the B5288, called the Greystoke Pillar. Mount Putnam (now Fort Putnam), named after General Israel 'Puffing' Putnam, is in the immediate vicinity, a screened farm with sturdy castellations, a turret, pointed arches and a tall Gothick window. The wall screening the byre is executed in a baffling manner. Pointed arches along the whole length are interspersed with pillars used as buttresses. The tops of the pillars are banded with stone leavage, and on some the top is extended with a round shaft with ball finial, like the minarets on the stable block at Hope End in Hereford. Bunker Hill is less well screened: only the centre part of the farm, in which pointed windows are set, is castellated on three sides. Another farm does without any decorations but is granted the name Jefferson. Spire House is a farm made into an eyecatcher in a rather off-hand but effective manner. Only part of the façade has a range of castellations, with two double-pointed and two round blind arches below. Between these are a rectangular and a pointed window. A third and much smaller polygonal storey supports the lead spire. The resemblance to a church spire is intentional: a local farmer had told the Duke that his creed did not necessitate church attendance for worship, and that his own house would suffice. The Duke took this dictum to its logical conclusion and built the farmer a house that looked like a church. The architect for these delightful follies is unknown, but Francis Hiorne was staying at Greystoke in 1787, to discuss with the Duke of Norfolk the projected repairs and alterations to Arundel Castle, which culminated in the triangular folly-tower known as Hiorne's Tower. The party made an expedition to Alnwick in Northumberland 'for Mr Hiorne's information', where they must have seen Robert Adam's Brizlee Tower, then only six years old. The 11th Duke's enthusiasm for building (and for an independent America) could well mean that he was the architect responsible, with Hiorne working in an advisory capacity. Whoever it was knew what he was doing; these follies wear their 200 years well.

The PENRITH Beacon, just outside the town on a high hill, doesn't really count as a folly as it was genuinely built as a warning tower, because of the threat to the town by Scottish troops in 1715, replacing an earlier beacon on the same spot. It was restored a second time in 1780, by which time the threat of a Scottish invasion surely must have receded. The tower is a plain square building with a pyramid roof and round-arched windows, and merits a Grade I listing. The beacon proved to be of unexpected use when in 1805 it flashed the warning of a Napoleonic invasion. This had Scott curtailing his tour of the Lakes and hurrying back to Scotland where he joined the volunteers, but it proved to be a false alarm. In Penrith itself is a small Victorian clock-tower commemorating Philip Musgrave of Eden Hall.

SHAP WELLS, some four miles south-east of Shap, enjoyed a brief spell as a spa in the 19th century, but a covered wellhead is all that remains to show for it. William Lowther, Earl of Lonsdale, took an interest in developing the possibilities of the mineral wells and it was he who paid for the monument celebrating Victoria's accession to the throne. According to *The Builder* of 1842, the sculpture of Britannia on top of the octagonal pillar and the symbolic bas reliefs on three sides of the base were done by Thomas Bland, a self-taught sculptor. A Mr Mawson from Lowther village was the architect. Lonsdale was enthusiastic about giving local talent a chance; Bland hailed from REAGILL, a hamlet three miles north-east of Shap where many of his efforts — those he wanted to keep to himself — can be seen in a large garden behind a farm building. They represent the expected output of a naive but able craftsman: fairy figures, monarchs, animals and quaint vases.

Another amateur, though on a far grander scale and rich enough to indulge all her architectural fantasies, was Lady Anne Clifford, Countess of Pembroke, Dorset and Montgomery (she was married twice, which accounts for her string of titles). After her second husband died in 1650 she set to work in earnest. Aged 59, her face mutilated by smallpox since she was 34, and with no further interest in the marriage game, this formidable woman rolled up her sleeves, put on a pair of stout boots, assembled a band of dedicated labourers and set to rebuilding, restoring and repairing the castles that belonged to her northern estates: Appleby, Barden Tower, Brough, Brougham, Pendragon and Skipton. Churches and chapels followed: Appleby, Barden, Bongate, Brougham, Maller-stang, Ninekirks and Skipton, as well as almshouses at Appleby and Bethmesley. Throwing in a few oddments, Anne Clifford erected the statue to Spenser in Westminster Abbey and that to her old tutor, the poet Samuel Daniel, in Beckington Church, Somerset. Among these trifles was also the Countess Pillar on the

A66, east of BROUGHAM CASTLE. It is octagonal with a cube on top, decorated with a sundial and an inscription. The pillar was erected in 1656 to commemorate the death of Lady Anne's mother, Margaret, in 1616, a woman of 'greate naturall wit and judgment, of a swete disposition, truly religious and virtuous, and endowed with a large share of those four moral virtues, prudence, justice, fortitude and temperance.'

At APPLEBY itself is the plain Bee House, and at Mallerstang, 14 miles south-east and some way from Pendragon Castle, are the remains of Lady's Pillar (1664), the purpose of which is unrecorded. Lady Anne went on building inexorably until her death at the age — remarkable for that time — of 86.

A mile or two north of Appleby is BRAMPTON Tower, a Victorian castellated tower-house worth seeing if one is in the area. RAVENSTONEDALE to the south has a more amusing sight in Lane Cottage, a chimeric collection of late Gothic elements. The idea of architecture as a joke is impressed upon it by the 'signature' the builders made, an inscription running 'T. Hewitson del. W. Hodgson sculp.' as on an 18th-century engraving. The name of Hodgson is well known around these parts, so the cottage is likely to be a local product.

Back towards the north of Cumbria, north-west of Penrith on the A5305, is SEBERGHAM, where Sir Henry Fletcher, like the Duke of Norfolk a Whig, converted a farmhouse into a castellated eyecatcher. The resemblance to the Greystoke follies is perhaps not accidental. The screened house was duly noted in Hutchinson's county history of 1794, some years after it was built.

St Mary's Church in WREAY, trapped between the M6 and the A6, is a freak in architectural chronology. Visually, both the exterior and the interior differ widely from their actual date — 1840–2. What is even more surprising for the time is that the architect was a woman, Miss Sarah Losh, granddaughter of John Losh, 'The Big Black Squire' from Woodside near Carlisle. Of his seven sons, John, the father of Sarah and her sister Katherine, inherited the house, while a younger son, William, went to Sweden, became consul for Sweden and Prussia in Newcastle, and managed John's iron works. Sarah was known for her beauty and intelligence, and in 1817 the two sisters and their uncle William went on the Grand Tour, travelling at least as far as Naples. In the early 19th century a woman's involvement with architecture would consist at the most of doodling plans for a model farm cottage. Sarah Losh, however, started practising architecture in earnest *c.*1830, and although no one would have dreamed of employing a female architect, as the squire's daughter she had the entire village at her disposal. Several of her houses can be found in Wreay and along the road to Brisco, and *c.*1830 she built the village school and provided the master with his own two-storey house. This is very simple and none too beautiful, yet it does have the distinction of being based on the measurements of an 1,800-year-old house Sarah had drawn and measured when she was in Pompeii. The Pompeiian Cottage is not the only result of her travels: the Sexton's cottage next to the churchyard appears to have the same provenance, although there are modern additions. The church is Miss Losh's masterpiece; although it is not a folly it is too unusual to omit. It seems to have been largely based on the basilicas she had seen in Italy, but the details and the carvings are indisputably Arts and Crafts — 50 years ahead of the movement. Much of it was done by Miss Losh and the local sculptor William Hindson, but her cousin William S. Losh also assisted, as well as supplying the stained glass from France. The death of Katherine in 1835 prompted Sarah to build St Mary's, and in the churchyard is her mausoleum, *c.*1850, built of huge stones assembled in the Cyclopean manner and containing a marble statue of Katherine by the professional sculptor David Dunbar the Younger. On the walls are medallions of Sarah's parents, John and Isabella Losh. The churchyard also houses a sun dial, a memorial cross and a Mortuary Chapel, now used as a shed. This is a replica of St Perran's Oratory, excavated near Perranporth, Cornwall, in 1835, of which Sarah had accurate measured drawings. Her styles varied; at Langarth, BRISCO, she built a Tudor house, and she also designed and decorated the sandstone wellhead at St Ninian's Well in Brisco. The inscription is no longer legible.

At Curthwaite, south of THURSBY near Carlisle, is a peculiar cottage of 1709, called Fiddleback. The house and a barn at the back merge into each other to form what seems to be the premeditated shape of a fiddle or a figure of 8. Nothing more is known about it.

The nicely nicely named Mr George Head Head of Rickerby

House (now Eden School) in STANWIX, Carlisle, is supposed to have had a fondness for folly-towers. The one near the old house looks like a dovecote; it has three storeys and is octagonal, with lancet windows. It was built *c.*1835 when dovecotes had gone out of fashion and culinary habits had changed as well, and the solution offered is that it was moved here from another site to serve as an ornament. One of Head's cottages was converted into a girls' school, and about this time he raised a classical lodge to Rickerby House, carving in the tympanum his arms and the motto 'STUDY QUIET'. An exhortation to the girls? George Head Head's predecessor at Rickerby House was 'Nabob' William Richardson, who towards the end of the 18th century built himself a belvedere tower on a tumulus next to Hadrian's Wall near OLDWALL, north of Carlisle Airport. Toppin Castle, a mile south-west of HAYTON, a farm converted into a tower-house, is another of Head's follies. The four-storey tower is battlemented with Gothic windows, Head's coat-of-arms and a smaller side turret.

LITTLE ORTON, west of Carlisle, has a later tower-farm, the well-named Tempest Tower of 1875, while DRUMBURGH HOUSE, overlooking the Solway Firth, has a plain and tiny Georgian folly-tower. Nearer the mouth of the Eden in SANDSFIELD, north of Burgh by Sands, a memorial column to Edward I, who died here on 7 July 1307 on his way to fight the Scots, was put up in 1685. A flood demolished the monument in 1795, but eight years later it was re-erected on the same site and in exactly the same manner as Thomas Langstaffe's original. The square pillar is about 20 feet high and has four arched openings on the top, from which a cone and a stone cross rise.

NETHERBY is virtually on the Scottish border, and many of the estate buildings have been screened with embattled walls. One solitary screen, consisting of a wall between two towers decorated with cross arrowslits, guards a salmon coop which was built for Sir Robert Graham in the mid-18th century. The difficulty is to decide whether or not they were purely ornamental: border lords did not remain border lords through their love of frivolity, and it was not long since castellations and machicolations really meant something.

From Netherby we return to CARLISLE, where the cathedral was quite radically restored in 1856. Most of the windows were renewed, and two of the old windows were incorporated into a small building in Nelson Road, demolished in 1967; two others survive in the grounds of Bunker Hill House (strong pro-American sentiment hereabouts) on the Orton road going west from the town.

A large number of follies can be found in the area immediately to the east of Carlisle – enough to make an enjoyable, if busy, day trip. At CORBY CASTLE, along the river Eden, the earlier garden buildings, many of them listed Grade I, appear to be the result of a Grand Tour made by their builder, Thomas Howard, for the Italian influence pervades the garden. First there is the cascade, looking like the waterworks in a minor Tuscan villa, its head crowned by a temple with carvings of Neptune, a lion and mermaids. The cascade itself spouts from a grotesque monster head, assisted at the flanks by two Hounds of Hades, each with the traditional three heads, while a ten-foot high amateur statue of Polyphemus the Cyclops near the cascade leads us to expect a Cyclopean Grotto. Thomas Howard wrote plays to be staged in this area; the suggested date is the early 18th century, as Buck engraved the cascade in 1739 and Sir John Clerk of Penicuik noticed the statue in 1734. The cascade now ends in a pond with a statue of Nelson, put there by Philip or Henry Howard. The River Walk starts here. Two square grotto rooms give views of the river and the village of Wetheral, and in one of the rooms there used to be a tablet bearing lines from *Paradise Lost*. Along the walk stood a Roman altar, as well as a tablet bearing quotations from Horace and Shakespeare, but as early as 1794 they were reported as having been 'much damaged by mischievous people'. The walk is terminated by a classical tempietto built for Thomas Howard, with a carved pediment outside, and inside some alpine scenes painted by Matthew Nutter in 1832. South-east of the castle is a dovecote converted at the front into a classical temple, an Ionic portico carrying a balustrade and pediment. It dates from the mid-18th century, and on the frieze is an inscription in Italian: 'A QUELLA CHI LO MERITA'. Philip Howard is credited with arranging the conversion of the dovecote, but his son, Henry, had the best motive, for his Italian fiancée Maria died in 1739, aged 23. Like grandfather Thomas, father and son were inveterate travellers, and accounts of their journeys would shed more light on the Corby garden.

In 1833 Henry Howard placed a statue of St Constantine on the river bank opposite St Constantine's Cells, medieval caves that served as hermitages, and in the same year the smithy was built in Corby village as an imaginative reconstruction of Vulcan's Forge. Horses were shod under the classical porch at the front; at the back is an arched doorway with medieval fragments.

The small town of WETHERAL on the other side of the river had a wonderful folly-house built by the Misses Waugh in 1790, but this has now been demolished. North-west on the A69 about a mile and a half away is Whoof House Folly, where a large church window was encased in brickwork and re-erected in the garden in 1868. The window is round-headed, with an oval in the tracery, and comes from Arthureth Church in Aglionby near Longtown; it is in fact a Gothic survival, as the church was built in the 17th century. At NEWBY EAST, near Newby Demesne farmhouse, are two circular gazebos, one of which has lost its roof, terminating a wall. These, and the adjoining Scottish Baronial farmhouse, probably belonged to Thomas Henry Graham of Edmond Castle, which was Tudorised by Smirke in 1824 and 1844; the gazebos probably date from the 1840s.

Between the hamlet of Faugh and CASTLE CARROCK, south of Brampton, is Tarn Lodge, dated 1807. On a hill overlooking the house is a small, two-storey tower, square, embattled and anonymous. In the centre of BRAMPTON is the Howard Memorial Shelter, an octagonal open building commemorating George James Howard of Naworth Park, 9th Earl of Carlisle, and his wife Rosalind Frances; they died, respectively, in 1911 and 1921. Whoever subscribed to erect this building did so without the support of the local publicans, for as soon as Howard inherited the earldom he closed all the public houses on his extensive Yorkshire and Cumberland estates. On this matter he was wholeheartedly supported by his wife, who had Radical as well as Temperance leanings.

Near the village of KIRKLINTON, off the A6071 north-west of Brampton, the Rev. G. E. Bell erected a couple of columns, taken from the medieval church of St Cuthbert when it was rebuilt in 1845, as an eyecatcher. East of the village, towards HETHERSGILL, is the biggest surprise of the region — a beautiful 18th-century dovecote with a coat-of-arms dated 1599 is found to contain a two-seater privy!

Lancashire

Strangely enough, Lancastrian follies tend to be concentrated in the industrial south rather than the rural north. In neither area is the quality of the highest, with the notable exception of Lord Leverhulme's replica of Liverpool Castle at Rivington. Towers are the predominant feature, and so are best grouped together.

After the 1889 Paris Exhibition imitations of the Eiffel Tower sprouted all over Europe, a tiny copy even finding its way into a public park in Prague. Of the few epigons to survive, the BLACKPOOL Tower is perhaps the best known, 2,500 tonnes of steel erected by Maxwell & Tuke in 1891–4, after sufficient time had elapsed for Eiffel's masterpiece to prove its safety. Blackpool Tower, at 568 feet, is only about half the height of its model, but it achieves a similar dominance over the landscape – for not even the most ardent Lancastrian would claim that Blackpool could rival Paris architecturally. But why include the tower here? After all, it was built as a strictly commercial undertaking and as such has been successful. Because of the megalomania of the undertaking; because to see it with a fresh pair of eyes is to see how bizarre is the very idea; because it is a wonderful, useless structure if one forgets the money motive. Additionally, the Tower Ballroom is one of the great sights of northern Europe, a must to see both for the decoration and for the ritual dancing. Currently the whole entertainment complex is undergoing a £1,300,000 facelift; Blackpool Tower will be with us for a long time to come.

A couple of towers have settled east of Ormskirk, among such delightfully named villages and hamlets as Dangerous Corner, Hunger Hill, Stormy Corner, Ring o' Bells and Robin Hood. Near

DALTON is Ashurst's Beacon, its pyramidal top seen from afar as a church steeple, built in 1798 during the Napoleonic Wars. It was followed 34 years later by the Parbold Bottle, erected on the A5209 outside PARBOLD, north of Dalton – a sugar-loaf to commemorate the Reform Act.

There is a 62-foot tower at Holymosside, BELMONT, along the A675, built during George III's reign. The usual crowd of stories has become attached to it, of which the claim made for it to have been an observatory seems the least far-fetched. It is supposed to be haunted, one of the few follies of which that can be said. Why aren't there more folly ghosts in this, the most haunted country in the world?

North of Belmont, on top of DARWEN Hill, is the Jubilee or Victoria Tower. Dating from 1887 and built from local stone, it has a buttressed octagon, decorated with shields above the open arched base, supporting the octagonal tower; the shaft is pierced by elongated windows and the embattled parapet serves for a crown. But royal sentiment was not the only reason for this tower. In 1878 five men were served with writs by the local squire after a Sunday afternoon stroll on Darwen Moor. He argued that they were trespassing on private property and frightening game; the men banded together, fought the case and won, thus opening the moors for public enjoyment. With good Lancastrian economy, the tower serves to celebrate both the Jubilee and the walkers' victory. In Darwen itself, visitors may be interested by the tower chimney at the India Mills on the south side of town. Built in 1859–67, the mill's tall tower is one of a variety of tower chimneys that came into being with the publication of several tracts on chimney building in the 1850s and 1860s. Leeds may have finer examples, but for sheer nerve of design and robustness the Darwen chimney holds its own.

There are two more Jubilee towers in the county: one is on the moorland south-east of QUERNMORE, near the hamlet of Upper Browtop, and the other is south of SILVERDALE, near Warton Sands. Silverdale, in the top north-western corner of the county, has yet another tower: the 1816 Lindeth Tower, square, three-storeyed and mildly Gothic, standing in the garden of Tower House, opposite Gibraltar Farm. Mrs Gaskell is supposed to have penned several of

141 A sham castle on a genuine medieval castle keep, Tutbury

142 Lyveden New Bield, Brigstock

143   Old John, Bradgate Park

144   The grotto entrance at Chatsworth

145 Speedwell·Castle, Brewood

146 Sanderson Miller's 'Castle Inn' on Edge Hill

147 The Chinese Pavilion at Shugborough Park, Milford

148   Classical windmill, Chesterton

149   The Quarters, Alresford

153   Belmount Tower, Belton

her works here. Inland again, at BLACKO, is Stansfield Tower, built
in the latter half of the 19th century by a businessman who wanted
to see the sea. A cottage at the seaside would certainly have cost
him less.

On the banks of the RIVINGTON reservoir in Lever Park is a sham
ruin replica of Liverpool Castle. The real castle used to stand where
Derby Square is now, but was demolished in 1720 for a very 20th-
century reason — to make way for the city's increasing traffic.
Sufficient detail must have survived to inspire Lord Leverhulme's
enthusiastic start on the full-size replica in 1916, but the noble
soapmaker's zeal flagged somewhat in later years, and the castle still
hadn't been completed by the time of his death, in 1925.
Nevertheless, the folly he concocted on the desolate moorland 20
miles from Liverpool is quite spectacular, amounting to something
much more than the common-or-garden sham castle. Castles by
their nature are seldom small, but this really does impress by its
sheer size. There are roofless rooms, corridors to explore, a very
solid spiral staircase, a little tower or two and excitingly unsafe
parapets. It is reached by long imposing avenues and, like the
surrounding countryside, is usually deserted. The architect is
thought to have been Thomas H. Mawson, the landscape gardener
responsible for laying out Roynton Gardens (now Lever Park),
who had a long and fruitful association with the then William
Hesketh Lever. The masonry and detailing are very similar in style
to the various garden buildings at Roynton, but by 1916 Mawson
was no longer working for Lever. As he makes no mention of the
replica in the list of works he undertook for Lever, and as he
commented in his autobiography that working for him merely
involved implementing detailed orders, the plans for the castle may
well have been drawn up by the energetic Viscount himself. The
last word on this amazing building has to be left to the 2nd Lord
Leverhulme, who in 1927 wrote, 'Already the newness is wearing
off . . . the uninitiated will not know that the replica is not a
genuine ruin. As a bold experiment in landscape design it has
certainly succeeded. Future generations will be grateful for this
careful reconstruction of a piece of bygone Liverpool.'

Roynton Gardens (or Lever Park) itself is wonderful, the ghost
of a grand garden. The Cottage, Leverhulme's bijou mansion

planned on the side of Rivington Pike, has long been demolished, but the plan of the garden, scored so hard into the inhospitable hillside, remains. Walks, lakes, seats, terraces, all are in a state of suspended decay, as if it needed only a team of enthusiastic gardeners for a couple of weeks to get things straight – but it is all an illusion; the garden is not yet beyond reclamation, but the cost is certainly beyond any private and most municipal pockets. The preservation of the Watch Tower at the top of the garden, built as recently as 1902 in the contemporary style – echoes of Webb, Voysey and Mackintosh – is essential, but already the interior is derelict and a new roof is needed. It is a square, three-storey tower with a steeply pitched roof and a chimney rising from the third floor; presumably the lower two floors, not affording such extensive views, were unheated. On top of the Pike, above the gardens, is a small square tower built by a Mr Andrews in 1733 as a shelter and belvedere. There is some mild early Gothic decoration, and of course all the windows and doors have been blocked up. Visible from miles around, the little 'tower' is only about 15 feet high.

There are miscellaneous Gothicisms all over the county: a castellated stable screen of 1819 at ELSWICK, sham castle dog kennels at GISBURN, a Gothic pigsty at Kirk House, OVER KELLETT, and, just north at Capernwray Hall, a Gothic keeper's tower dating from the Regency period. Spire Farm in BROWSHOLME has, as we hoped, a superfluous spire 'put up because it looked nice, I suppose', and at New High Riley, east of ACCRINGTON, is a Georgian eyecatcher tower with lower wings and quatrefoil windows, the ensemble serving as stables. Two abbey ruins have been improved by additions – at SAWLEY an arch was rebuilt from bits and pieces at the entrance to the abbey, and at WHALLEY the arches of Whalley Viaduct echo the scanty remains of Whalley Abbey.

North of Whalley is CLITHEROE, where in the public park below Clitheroe Castle a turret stands in a formal pond. It came from the parapet of the Houses of Parliament, and was given to the Borough of Clitheroe by Captain Sir William Brass, MP, to celebrate the Coronation. Another removal is at WHEELTON, where the top of Wheelton Church stands in the garden of Prospect House. Divested of its former function, it makes a good garden temple – a domed rotunda on a six-column base, dated 1776. Much more spectacular as a feat of architectural engineering was the removal of Claughton Hall, near Hornby in the LUNE VALLEY, from its original site to a hilltop a little way to the north along the A683. This was the idea of a Mr Esmond Morse, in the 1930s, and he did it for the view; but he forgot part of the building, and the lost property is now called Claughton Hill Farm.

To commemorate one of his wives, the thrice married linoleum manufacturer James Williamson, Lord Ashton, erected the Ashton Memorial as the *pièce de résistance* of Williamson Park in LANCASTER. This vast edifice, built in 1906 on the same principles as the American personal coupé in the 1950s (gigantic on the outside but with virtually no usable interior space), was obviously heavily influenced by St Paul's and St Peter's: it is reached by an elaborate flight of stairs, and is a confection of domes, cupolas and columns. It was designed by John Belcher Jr, whose hallmark was a resplendent neo-baroque style. The memorial cost Williamson the staggering sum of £87,000. The folly has now been boarded up, as it is in urgent need of repair and, among other things, the enormous dome has been declared unsafe. As we were going to press, we heard that a £600,000 grant has been made for the preservation of this astounding monument.

Another of Lancaster's exceptional buildings has already been saved. Until recently the Music Room, a summer-house built *c.*1730 for Dr Marton, Vicar of Lancaster, was in danger of being crushed between encroaching houses, sheds and garages. Then the Music Room was bought by the Landmark Trust, and the buildings in front of it were demolished, thereby providing much needed breathing space. The building is square, three storeys high, with a belvedere balustrade on the roof and a classical façade decorated with pilasters – but the best feature is the music room itself, which is chock full of intricate and highly detailed plaster-work, most of which has been saved and restored (only the Muse Terpsichore had to be replaced by a modern rendering). Considering the building's vicissitudes – at one time in the 19th century it formed part of a lighting and heating works – its survival is nothing short of a miracle.

We leave Lancashire with a living folly, a vegetable folly in fact.

At Barrowford, in order to commemorate his part in Napoleon's downfall, Colonel Clayton of Carr Hall planted an avenue of trees near the house in the shape of his regiment's formation on the eve of the battle of Waterloo. Trees standing away from the avenue represent the officers, but which one represents the gallant Col. Clayton has now been forgotten.

Greater Manchester

Bits of Cheshire and bits of Lancashire have been concreted over to make this urban county, dominated by grimy, smoky, rainy Manchester. The whole county is a shrine to industry; and it is muck and brass that give Mancunians their strong sense of self-awareness, reflected in a passionate adoration of their internationally famous soccer teams and of course the Lancashire Cricket Club, historically now a club from another county – but could anybody conceive of the idea of a rival Greater Manchester Cricket Club?

The continuing process of decay and regeneration common to all urban areas naturally means that any outlandish or derelict follies have been swept away, and no money is available for the restoration of the few that remain – at least, that's what we thought, but we underestimated the Mancunian capacity for sentiment. Sir Robert Peel was born near Bury, then in Lancashire but now in Greater Manchester. In 1850 he was killed in a riding accident in Hyde Park, and the following year the citizens of RAMSBOTTOM erected the Peel Tower, a monument on Holcombe Moor a few miles from his birthplace. The 128-foot tower was designed, in true northern fashion, by a committee (who wanted battlements), and it cost £10,000. Inevitably the square stone tower has suffered the usual depredations of vandals and the weather, and when it became clear that the internal staircase was no longer safe the tower was blocked up (stage three in the life of a folly) and people sat back to await its eventual collapse. But in 1984 Bury Council put forward a £50,000 scheme to restore it to its former glory, and with a £3,000 grant from Greater Manchester Council and anticipated grants from the North West Tourist Board and the

393

Countryside Commission, their plan to turn the landmark into a full-scale tourist attraction – the views from the top must be sensational – looks like succeeding. Another folly rescued? We hope so. Ramsbottom has another, lesser known monument in Grant's Tower, which commemorates the philanthropic Grant brothers who personified all the positive aspects of the Victorian era and who found their literary commemoration as the benevolent Ned and Charles Cheeryble in *Nicholas Nickleby*, although Dickens based them in London. It was through their industry that Ramsbottom developed from a small agricultural community into a thriving township.

Another important local family was the Nuttalls of Nuttall Hall, who erected a Gothick screen at their home farm in order to hide some ghastly barn or pigsty. The screen, with a large central arch and Wrightesque arrow-slits, deteriorated with the farm's conversion into a dyeworks and later return to its original use. This part of England was enthusiastic about screening disagreeable objects or turning them into eyecatchers; the influence of Cheshire with its many Gothic farm buildings is strong.

South-west of Ramsbottom is TOTTINGTON, where Joshua Knowles's industrial Tottington Mill of 1840 was later converted into a farm. It is now known as Tower Farm, because it incorporates an embattled 60-foot tower, the surviving part of the original calico print works. Hartshead, on the north-eastern periphery of Manchester near MOSSLEY, has a little tower on a big hill which, though small, makes an effective eyecatcher, in the distance looking like a nipple caught by surprise. What better reason for its construction than the Prince of Wales's marriage in 1863? Originally the tower was to have been 85 feet high, but when money or stamina ran out the edifice was declared finished and capped off with a conical roof.

At WORSLEY, on the other side of the county, is the Ellesmere Memorial of c.1870, a neo-Gothic shrine on a hill above the motorway. We have not managed to see this, although it is under threat of demolition. HEATON, in the northern reaches of Manchester itself, offers a good view of the city from its park. It was a beautiful, clear, sunny day when we were there, not a rain cloud in sight, but then when we went to Chicago it wasn't windy.

Rain is endemic to Manchester, but that day the portico of the old Manchester Town Hall, built by the pushy architect Francis Goodwin in 1822–5 and removed here in 1912, glowed yellow and dry in the sunset. Although what remains is but a snippet of the original colonnaded town-hall front, in its parkland setting it is positively huge. Four massive Ionic columns support the architrave between the two endbays, and it sits grandly in front of the lake, basking in the rare sunset.

Curiously, we could discover no follies in the southern half of the county, although there are plenty clustering along the Cheshire border. There is an eyecatcher at Windlehurst, but it was built for Wybersley Hall in Disley, Cheshire, so it is covered in that chapter. Obviously there are some to be found, but we hope to avoid the kind of wild goose chase we were taken on by Williamson's Folly, a remarkable object said to be in the centre of Manchester at the Museum. Upon enquiry, we discovered that the folly in question was not a building at all but a fossilized tree – 'a magnificent Sigillaria with stigmarian roots' – of such stupendous size that when it was presented by the Victorian naturalist William Cranford Williamson to the Manchester museum it was immediately dubbed 'Williamson's Folly'.

Ask a Mancunian to name a folly in Manchester and the chances are you will hear about Knolls House in SALFORD. It isn't a folly, except to its perspiring owner, who wants to demolish the thing and isn't allowed to; it is a substantial mock-Tudor house built in 1824 by William Yates, a wealthy antiquary, and one of the first examples of the Tudor revival which reached its apogee a century later in Surrey and similar satellite counties. The façade, however, is not a sham but a real Tudor frontage rescued from a building in Market Street and re-erected by Yates. For 75 years it served as the headquarters of a removal company, who now want to demolish it and replace it with an office block – 'This house began as a folly and is continuing as one,' complained the managing director. Nothing should stand in the way of commerce in Manchester.

Merseyside

Merseyside's *raison d'être* is Liverpool, wrenched out of Lancashire but given an added bit of breathing-space. To the north the coastline is littered with golf-courses and clubs, stretching past sleek chic Southport, the first garden city, and a Lancastrian hinterland, while to the south-west the prepuce of the Wirral has been sliced from Cheshire, joining Birkenhead to its spiritual home at last. Birkenhead itself is home to Port Sunlight, one of the earliest model industrial villages; and the world-famous Tranmere Rovers, who can boast more draws than any other team in the Football League; and BEBINGTON. Here used to be a wall, built by a Thomas Francis in the first years of the 19th century. Only fragments remain, as it served no useful purpose other than to carry the weight of Mr Francis's apparently unstoppable graffiti. The youth of Liverpool have snatched up the banner dropped by Mr Francis, and his influence can now be seen throughout the city, though it is doubtful whether his precious wall ever echoed emotions such as 'SKINS RULE!' or 'KOP PANSIES'.

INCE BLUNDELL is rural Merseyside, almost a village, threatened by Liverpool. The house belonged to Henry Blundell, who erected his Pantheon as a fitting depository for his famous collection of antique sculpture. In the garden are a Tuscan temple and a matching column crowned with an eagle, both by William Everard, whose portrait shows him with the design for the temple in his hands. The group was probably built in the 1780s.

KNOWSLEY HALL, home of the Earls of Derby, is even closer to the city, its house and park trapped alike in an urban pincer movement. Near the park's generous lake is an early 18th-century tower, remodelled from round to square. Another building features in a description of 1766, illustrating the finer points of park-breaking:

> At Knowsley-house, having by fair words and a small bribe, prevailed upon one of Lord Derby's grooms to get the keys to the gate, we passed through the park, thus making a short cut to Prescot, where we intended to dine . . . On top of the highest eminence in this delightful park is a very neat summer house with four arched windows opening on as many elegant and extensive prospects. These landscapes are painted in the arch of each respective window, but they are mouldering away and no care is taken to renew them.

The summer-house is still there, but the paintings, of course, are long gone.

Towers are useful in areas where space is limited (as Manhattan demonstrates so spectacularly), but so are tunnels, and in the 19th century Joseph Williamson, a man of initially ample means, engaged workmen to excavate a system of tunnels beneath his native city. There doesn't appear to have been any reason for the project, which must have cost a large fortune, and the tunnelling had to stop when the railway came to LIVERPOOL. Now most of the tunnels have caved in or been filled in, but there are still rumours of an entrance . . .

Redevelopment is endemic in Liverpool. Recent redevelopment has cost us the city's most famous building, the Cavern (perhaps once part of Williamson's tunnels?), and the essential redevelopment of the appallingly decayed dockland area is threatening the existence of the works of Jesse Hartley, surveyor to the Liverpool Dock Trustees from 1824 to 1860, a methodical, reliable, conscientious type of man who would have shuddered at the very thought of building follies. He approved of solidity and scale, but above all he liked building. He liked building a lot. Dockland is his memorial; the whole place is conceived on a massive plane with gigantic walls and piers, everything rather larger than necessary. Two individual pieces deserve special mention: at the entrance to Salisbury Dock looms the Victoria Tower of 1848, a many-sided clock-tower with a tapering base, machicolated and embattled, a giant guarding the docks. The low tower at the entrance to Wapping Dock dates from

1855 and resembles a Hun's hut — a conical shape with sides flattened towards the top. Hartley's follies deserve to survive.

There is a chance that Merseyside will be graced by a few new follies. What will happen to the palace erected by the People's Republic of China in 1984 for the Great Garden Exhibition? And a scheme has recently been proposed to encourage local people to erect whimsical buildings in Toxteth. It is difficult to resist visualising the outcome: a rusticated Memorial Arch to the Riots of 1982? the improvement of burnt-out shops into creeper-covered sham ruins?

North-East England

Cleveland

Collieries, moorlands, a few sleepy seaside towns, the Cleveland Hills and, above all, industry — such is the nature of the county fashioned out of parts of Durham and the North Riding of Yorkshire. There are few follies, and no remarkable ones, but most were built by remarkable men.

When Henry Pease, railway promoter, MP for South Durham and member of the Peace Society, brought the railway to the coast in the 1860s, SALTBURN-BY-THE-SEA was conceived. It had been Pease's idea to build the town out of white brick, 'so that the new resort would gleam like the celestial city'. It still has all the trappings of a successful seaside town — pier, ample hotels, a municipal park — but somehow it never caught on. The Albert Memorial in the Valley Gardens attempts to brighten a bleak holiday which even the best follies cannot save. This classical portico was the façade to Barnard Castle railway station; did Pease want to preserve a favourite building or was he merely economising?

A hundred years or so before its brief venture into tourism the Saltburn beach saw a helter-skelter chariot race. One chariot was driven by the Rev. Laurence Sterne, the other by John Hall-Stevenson, squire of SKELTON Castle, Sterne's cousin by choice and a lesser known writer of facetious books. In between beach races at Saltburn, sojourns at Scarborough and 'fact-finding' trips to London, Hall-Stevenson resided at Skelton Castle, a mile or two south of Saltburn. He had a fortune to spend and professed that his only aim in life was enjoyment, which he pursued so steadily that within a few years he had managed to turn himself into a drunkard and near bankrupt. He started his career as a rake by leaving

Cambridge without a degree, but not before first becoming Sterne's bosom pal. Hall-Stevenson set off on his Grand Tour in 1738, returning safe and spoilt, and some years later inherited Skelton Castle. South of the house he had a souvenir of his tour erected, a classical rusticated wellhead temple, supplying the mansion with water. Skelton Castle itself, heavily castellated, was used by the Hell Fire type 'club of demoniacks', founded by Hall-Stevenson, Sterne and other libertines, for convivial evenings. They probably also had the run of Hall-Stevenson's large pornographic library. The 'demoniacks' referred to Skelton as Crazy Castle, the name it also took in Hall-Stevenson's *Crazy Tales* of 1762. It is doubtful whether the club met also in the grotto situated in the bank of the castle's moat, for that appears to be 19th-century.

Hall-Stevenson's neighbour, Marwood Turner of KIRKLEATHAM HALL, died on the Grand Tour in 1739; he had probably been his companion. Another member of the family, Sir Charles Turner, had a couple of castellated round bastions erected, flanking the ha-ha near Kirkleatham Hall. These, and the crenellated Gothick gate, were possibly built by either John Carr or William Chambers, both of whom had also worked at Skelton. The bastions were built about the same time as the publication of *Crazy Tales* and later two more, this time square, were added to Turner's Hospital, the nearby almshouses. The remarkable Turner Mausoleum with its pyramidal roof, built by James Gibbs in 1740, stands attached to Kirkleatham Church.

In the grounds of Smirke's Wilton Castle of *c.*1800, south along the A174 from Kirkleatham, is the rubble of what Pevsner asserts to have been a folly-tower. But this is only a foretaste of what is to come: the column on ESTON NAB replaces a signal station which dated from the Napoleonic wars and had become a prominent local landmark. It was demolished by the chemical giant ICI, and could be read as just another example of rampant capitalism except that the company had honestly tried to maintain the building but lost the fight to vandalism. So the old ruin had to go, its function as an eyecatcher carried on by the new tapered column built, using stones from the original building, by ICI in 1956. This new eyecatcher is to commemorate the old signal station − one tries to imagine the shareholders' meeting where the ICI directors announced that they had built a folly.

At the other end of the scale is the folly garden at YARM, where David Doughty, a builder by profession, spent much of his time and capital in creating a miniature castle on the corner of a garden wall. Further down in the garden are a couple of churches, some sham fragments and two armoured knights made of concrete. They have survived since the 19th century, a rare longevity in gnomic circles.

The old Durham part of Cleveland has in WYNYARD PARK a small group of garden buildings and one folly. Charles William Stewart, 3rd Marquess of Londonderry (1788–1854), had Philip Wyatt build the Wynyard mansion in 1822–9. Wyatt was later sacked because of incompetence, and later the other Wyatts took over. The Marquess had £80,000 a year to spend because of his successful investments in Durham collieries and because of his undertaking of the development of Seaham, further north. The result was a house whose interior was generally agreed to be in rather vulgar taste. Some particular aspects shocked the Princess Lieven, who described in a letter the four-poster bed she had seen in Lady Londonderry's bedroom. Its posters were formed by 'large gilt figures of Hercules, nude and fashioned exactly like real men'.

However, the buildings in the grounds were not as daring or as original. The Greek and Roman temples were designed by Benjamin Wyatt, who also designed the classical Lion Bridge, and the only folly is the 127-foot high obelisk, erected in 1827 to commemorate the Duke of Wellington's visit to Wynyard. The Marquess considered himself a close friend of the Iron Duke, but Wellington's feelings towards Londonderry were ambivalent – some of his letters and despatches from the battlefield refer scathingly to him. Originally the obelisk bore the inscription 'Wellington Friend of Londonderry', but when the Marquess was refused a seat in Wellington's 1828 Cabinet the inscription was altered to plain 'Wellington'. His final revenge came in 1852, when the Order of the Garter which had become vacant with Wellington's death was bestowed upon him.

Durham

On the map, Durham promises to be a county well endowed with follies; around the city of Durham the names of several hamlets indicate an eccentric inventiveness that bodes well for our hunt. Battles (always a fertile loam for folly-growers) are commemorated by the villages of Quebec and Inkerman, while more personal fates are remembered in Pity Me and Unthank. Towards the east, Running Waters and Deaf Hill would seem more at home in an Indian reservation. The Durham follies are a continuation of the style set in North Yorkshire, a Gothick that is both quirky and imaginative yet looks sturdy enough to resist any' marauding hordes of Picts.

Shortly after the French Revolution a Polish dwarf visited the town of DURHAM, liked what he saw and decided to spend the remainder of his 99 years in these parts. 'Count' Joseph Boruwlaski, of noble birth but without any actual right to the title, had wandered around Europe for most of his life, displaying his stature in society where he became quite a success – Voltaire, Maria Theresia of Austria and George III all took an interest in him. But the novelty wore off, and Boruwlaski was obliged to keep himself alive by giving concerts, a poorly disguised means (given his musical talents) of begging for alms. In 1788 he wrote his memoirs in French; they were translated into English and German and were still in print as late as 1820. The Prebendary of Durham donated a residence called 'The Bank's Cottage' to the count, which was later demolished, but a small temple in South Bailey with Doric columns and two low-ceilinged rooms (the Count billed himself as three foot three) still carries the name 'The Count's House'.

Together with another extant building, an ice-house, it stood in the grounds of the cottage where he lived until his death in 1837.

BURN HALL, south of Durham, was originally planned as a dwelling for the banker George Smith by John Soane. Nothing came of it; the only buildings realised were an ice-house and a highly ambitious cow-shed. The cow-shed was erected by Soane in 1783 as a neo-classical, semi-circular pavilion with two pyramid-roofed side pavilions. Soane was Smith's principal architect; he had tried out the same design for a cow-house in Marlesford, Suffolk, another of Smith's estates, and later built the mansion at Piercefield in Gloucestershire near Chepstow, a place of pilgrimage for those in search of the Picturesque. In 1793 Smith's bank collapsed, but after the turn of the century his fortunes appear to have revived sufficiently for him to employ Soane in the redecoration of his London residence. The cow-house is now being converted into a human-house.

On the village green at WESTERTON, to the south, stands a simple circular tower with tiny buttresses, cruciform arrow-slits, a rather martial looking doorway and a plaque commemorating the bicentenary of the publication in 1750 of the *Original Theory . . . of the Universe* by the builder of the tower, Thomas Wright, astronomer and folly designer extraordinaire. The tower was intended as an observatory, but as it was started the year before Wright's death in 1786, he didn't have much occasion to use it. Totally without foundation is the local legend that a tunnel from the tower leads to Durham Cathedral, seven miles away. The observatory formed part of Wright's scheme, like Henry Holland's in Kent, to erect a copy of Pliny's famous villa together with vast and elaborate gardens at nearby Byers Green, his birthplace.

BISHOP AUCKLAND has another of the ecclesiastical follies so typical of northern England. In 1760 Bishop Richard Trevor had his palace embellished with a gatehouse designed by the dilettante architect Sir Thomas Robinson: a Gothick confection of battlements, finials and quatrefoils, part of it acting as a clock-tower. The more important building is, however, the deer-house, a few hundred yards to the north. It consists of an arcaded, square building with another square inside and pinnacles to mark the corners of the four walls, which carry the usual array of battlements. In the middle of the west wall rises a battlemented square tower, beautified with more pinnacles, cross arrowslits and quatrefoils. The deer-house was built seven years after the palace gatehouse, for which both Robinson and Richard Bentley had submitted designs — but one should always remember that the great Thomas Wright lived only a matter of three miles away.

The lodges to WITTON CASTLE, west of Bishop Auckland, are all castellated, with the south lodge given the full treatment as a gatehouse with turrets and arrowslits. In the same style, and probably of the same date (1811), is the Gothick three-storey tower, the top of which is used as a dovecote. The ground floor of the tower is arcaded and an embattled summer-house is attached.

The wild Dales start at HAMSTERLEY, a little to the west, where the last outpost of civilisation and democracy is represented by a tall pinnacle from the Houses of Parliament, brought over to Hamsterley Hall in the 1830s, together with a domed summer-house from Beaudesert in Staffordshire. R. S. Surtees, the sporting novelist, gothicised some of the surrounding buildings when he took over the Hall in the early 19th century.

The 1st and 2nd Earls of Darlington embraced the Gothick revival with great enthusiasm. In the architectural free-for-all that followed, the family seat of RABY CASTLE was gothicised by Daniel Garrett, James Paine, Sir Thomas Robinson and John Carr, who between them were responsible for submitting a remarkable number of designs, many of which were executed. Among these are Garrett's arcaded Gothick Seat, the Bath House (also ascribed to Robinson) and Paine's Raby Hill House and Park Farm, two of several castellated farm buildings in a severe but effective style. Near the house, Paine erected the Gothick Screen on a hill-top — five bays and a central gateway with battlements and arrowslits as prescribed by the art of military fortification. The screen is repeated, in a slightly different shape, as an eyecatcher façade on the top of a hill behind the castle. This differs only marginally from Paine's original design, the most noticeable deviation being that his battlements on the right-hand side are ruinated. The façade consists of a screen wall with square, low towers at the ends and a gateway with a Norman arch. Over the arch is a painted *trompe l'oeil* window, perhaps an afterthought as it does not appear in the original design. The archway is flanked by two towers ending in truncated obelisks. Battlements, quatrefoils and arrowslits are strewn liberally over the façade.

From the Gothick glory of Raby, the road leads past Streatlam Castle, Barnard Castle and the remains of Egglestone Abbey to GRETA BRIDGE and Rokeby. Rokeby Park and its romantic surroundings provided the setting for Sir Walter Scott's eponymous epic, although a remark in an old guide-book questions Scott's claim to be an admirer of nature: '. . . it will probably strike every visitor that the popular poet has somewhat erred in the direction usually taken by irresponsible writers: exaggeration'. 'Rokeby' was conceived on Scott's visits to the house between 1809 and 1812, and the actual writing of the poem is supposed to have taken place in a natural cave in the grounds, which was further excavated and roofed over in Scott's lifetime. A rustic table inside provides the hermit touch. Not far from the grotto near Mortham Tower, also part of the estate, is a sepulchral urn of stone with iron handles and an inscription:

> To the long try'd love of a sister
> J. B. S. M. inscribed this monument, July 5 1797

The initials are those of John Bacon Sawrey Morritt, owner of Rokeby and a friend of Scott's.

The column celebrating the Treaty of Aachen which ended the war between England and France in 1748 was brought over to GAINFORD, on the A67, in 1923, to stand in the grounds of Edleston Hall; with it came a classical summer-house from Stanwick Park in North Yorkshire, commissioned by Hugh Smithson Percy, 1st Duke of Northumberland, whose more famous follies were built at Alnwick. Stanwick, a William Kent house, was demolished in that year.

DARLINGTON's greatest claim to fame is as the world's first railway terminus, so it is fitting that its baronial clock-tower should have been built by a railway man, the Quaker promoter and industrialist Henry Pease. Designed by Alfred Waterhouse, the tower's shaft has double lancet windows, with a clock-face on the superstructure, on the corners of which are small turrets. A churchlike spire tops the lot and at the foot are the initials 'H. M. P.' and the date 1874. Tower Road together with the tower once formed part of the Pierrepoint estate, where only a grotto remains of the elaborate early Victorian gardens.

At COATHAM MUNDEVILLE's Hallgarth Hotel, on the northern approach to Darlington from the A1, is another of the Gothick deer-houses particular to the north country. It is quite small, with corner turrets decorated with the expected cruciform arrowslits, a double-arched Tudor entrance and a stepped gable.

Hardwick Hall near SEDGEFIELD, east of the next A1 junction, is one of those parks that shame county councils. A report in the *Northern Echo* in 1979 had the council justifying its decision to let the follies in the park fall to pieces, because 'to return the three existing monuments . . . to their original standards' would cost hundreds of thousands of pounds. Anything is possible when councils are spending money, but it cannot be necessary, if money is short, to restore them to a pristine, unromantic state. A few thousand pounds and some willing volunteers would at least consolidate the buildings, and these follies, the finest in Durham, need to be saved. John Burdon, who came into possession of the Hardwick estate in 1748, started by celebrating the Palladian style. The recently demolished Banqueting House was the showpiece, with busts of Vitruvius, Inigo Jones and Palladio himself. The Doric Bath House has also gone. The Temple of Minerva (1754–7) – a domed octagon with an Ionic square surround of which the major part has fallen down – is the only one of the classical buildings to survive, and then only just.

Strangely enough, the Gothick style was welcomed with equal fervour at Hardwick. Of these follies, a seat and a grotto have been destroyed. The Buon Retiro, a hermitage incorporating a sham library (the shelves were painted with dummy books) and two corner towers, is a virtual ruin. The sham ruined gateway, the threatened destruction of which prompted the newspaper article, is still crumbling away. Its arch is partly made out of fragments from the medieval Guisborough Priory and has a round towerette to one side. There is also a small bridge. All the buildings, Palladian and Gothick, were designed by James Paine between 1748 and 1764, and John Bell, a Durham builder who was Paine's chief assistant in the region, did the construction work. Now that Painshill in Surrey, not long ago thought to be past redemption, is being carefully and imaginatively restored, a similar undertaking to preserve the gardens and buildings at Hardwick should be considered.

Cleveland and Tyne & Wear have between them reduced Durham's coastline to a minimum. The short stretch remaining has a solitary folly to show for itself — a Gothick embattled tower standing north of HAWTHORN and built for Admiral Mark Milbanke who had built Sailor's Hall, his summer seat, nearby.

Humberside

This artificial county, fabricated by bureaucrats tearing a swathe from Yorkshire's East Riding and biting a chunk off north Lincolnshire, two counties eternally separated by the massive natural barrier of the Humber estuary, has a surprising number of good follies, the great majority being in the old East Riding. Hull – Kingston upon Hull, but nobody ever calls it that – is the reason for Humberside. A sprawling city of nearly 300,000, it spreads its fishy tentacles north, east and west, entwining the old villages and towns of Sutton, Hessle, Anlaby and Cottingham. In the grounds of Castle Hill Hospital at COTTINGHAM, a Gothic hexagonal tower of whitewashed brick was erected as an eyecatcher for Cottingham Castle, built 1814–15 but now demolished. Folly and castle were owned by the banker and MP Thomas Thompson, father of the Benthamite General Thomas Perrouet Thompson, whose real claim to fame was as the inventor of the 'Enharmonic Guitar'. Perhaps the folly was built as a music room to keep the noise of the inventor's creation at a civilised distance from the house?

HULL was the birthplace of the slave emancipator William Wilberforce, who is commemorated by the Doric 90-foot Wilberforce Column in Queen's Gardens, which was put up in 1834 with funds provided by public subscription the year after the great man's death. On the A63 leaving Hull there is a remarkable stretch of road bordered by four minor follies, from Hull to Market Weighton. ELLOUGHTON has one of those confusing edifices called 'The Castle', where a passing reference in an old guide-book can start a wild goose chase more often than not ending at a bungalow with flowerpots spaced along the roof. A 'castle' can range from a humble lodge to a megalomaniac pile of Fonthillian dimensions. This one is in between and late — an 1886 embattled villa which justifies its name with tiny turrets.

The old Town Hall in Hull was demolished in 1914, and the fragments were used in BRANTINGHAM to build a war memorial. Although the method is folly, the result is not. Further west at SOUTH CAVE is Cave Castle, concocted for B. Barnard by Henry Hakewill in 1804. Hakewill's forte was the Gothic, and especially Tudor Gothic, castle. Parts of the house were demolished in the 1930s, the building already having been tampered with in 1875, but it is to this period that we owe the bizarre gateway. The last of the string of follies on this road is at NORTH CAVE, where Castle Farm served as an eyecatcher to Hotham Hall. Now its castellations have been removed, and little folly feeling remains.

Humberside's only folly group is at SLEDMERE, home of the Sykes family. A century and a half of sustained folly building by that remarkable clan, stretching from the last quarter of the 18th century to the First World War, has left a confusion of monuments, memorials and eyecatchers; patience and a steady hand are required to discover which of the two Marks, two Tattons and two Christophers were responsible for what.

The first folly-building Sykes was Sir Christopher, the 2nd Baronet, a great agricultural improver, expressing an aptitude that runs in the family. Castle Farm, thought by many (but not by us) to be the best folly in the group, was put up as an eyecatcher in 'Capability' Brown's landscape after 1776, when the park was enclosed. The building was originally intended as a dower-house, but Mother preferred to stay where she was, in the main house. Although Sir Christopher designed many of the farm buildings himself, Castle Farm was almost certainly designed by John Carr. It was intended to resemble a gatehouse, and provides a competent façade for hiding the house itself; there is no record of it actually being used as a farm building until 1895. One highly personal architectural touch is given between the two sturdy towers flanking the 'gateway' by piercing the tall castellations alternately with arches and quatrefoils. The individuality of the architecture has led to its being attributed to Brown himself, or even to Joseph Rose, a plasterer who worked for the Wyatts. Another eyecatcher, a pedimented arch on a hilltop near the B1251, probably dates from around this time, but there is no record of the architect or of when it was built.

Sir Christopher eventually got his memorial 39 years after his death, in 1840, when the village well was given a classical rotunda as a canopy by Sir Tatton Sykes, a famous sportsman and stockbreeder. It was his son, another Tatton, who became the family's true eccentric. He inherited in 1863, and straightway donned the mantle of an autocrat.

Soon after his mother, who adored flowers and gardens, died, Sir Tatton had the lawns and flowerbeds ploughed up, forbidding the villagers to grow the 'nasty, untidy things' around their cottages. Another bewildering measure was to forbid his tenants the use of their front entrances; newly erected houses were given *trompe l'oeil* front doors. As a builder Sir Tatton was enthusiastic, to say the least. He decided to repair and restore the churches in this part of the East Riding and, together with the architect Temple Moore, tackled quite a number of them, developing the Tatton style as he went along and disbursing over £2,000,000 in the process. In 1865 there appeared on Garton Hill, three miles south of the house, the finest folly in Humberside and one of the best in Britain. The Sir Tatton Sykes Memorial Tower by J. Gibbs (not the famous one) probably had more to do with the warmth of local remembrance for the old squire than with the younger Tatton's not so very fond memories of his father, who habitually sent his son on long voyages so as not to have to endure him at home. 'Erected to the memory of Sir Tatton Sykes Bart by those who loved him as a friend and honoured as a landlord', the memorial consists of a 120-foot pyramidal Gothic tower with bas-relief plaques round the base – one showing old Sir Tatton on horseback, another decorated with agricultural emblems – and inscriptions such as 'THE MEMORY OF THE JUST IS BLESSED' running as a frieze round all four sides. The main features of this horrific and utterly compelling monument are indescribable: they constitute a full frontal attack on the rules of architecture and taste as anybody has ever known them. Nevertheless, it undeniably fulfils the primary function of a monument – to draw attention to itself – and it has remained standing in a very exposed position for 120 years.

Sir Tatton and Temple Moore later erected their own monument in 1895, the Eleanor Cross just outside the walls of the park, a copy of the Northampton Cross. Not surprisingly, there was no memorial for this Sir Tatton when he died in 1913, but there was to be another, the Wagonners' Memorial, a squat column decorated with rural and then battle scenes, the basic impression being that of the Trajan Column set inside a highly ornamented wine press and squeezed to the point of bursting. Sir Mark Sykes, Sir Tatton's heir, was something of a traveller, probably in his turn running away from a stifling parent. He went to the Middle East several times and installed a Turkish Room in the house. In 1912 he raised a company of Yorkshire Wagonners, and during the war occupied himself by designing their memorial. The monument was erected immediately after his own death in 1919, the last of a long line of memorials at Sledmere.

Just outside BRIDLINGTON is the other great Humberside folly, Carnaby Temple, an individualistic reworking by John Carr of the Temple of the Winds in Athens, splendidly sited in the open amid fields that stretch for miles until they disappear into the sea. We visited it on a hot breathless day in early summer — it is rare for there not to be a sharp little breeze, but that day the air was fat and humid. We had attacked the temple from the wrong side, having no map, and had walked for 20 minutes with hope diminishing before catching a glimpse of it two miles away. The descriptions of its condition were wrong; work has recently been done to preserve it from the whims of weather and the more determined vandal. Octagonal, brick-built, two-storeyed, an ogee roof with the motif repeated on the lantern above, it has had its roof tarred and its windows sealed up; there is also evidence of some repointing work on the bricks. Evidently it is intended to be preserved. An outhouse was stuck on a mound at the back when the tower was lived in, but curiously it does not detract from the elegance of the structure. Carnaby Temple was built in 1770 for Sir George Strickland of Boynton Hall, who had a late medieval summer-house Gothicised at the same time.

Further down the coast HORNSEA, now famous for its pottery, has Bettison's Folly, a 50-foot, castellated, round brick tower. It is supposed to have been erected in 1844 by Mr Bettison for the purpose of carriage-watching; the idea was that servants should try to sight the master's gig so they could serve dinner the moment he burst into the house demanding food. The story of how it got its name is so ordinary as to be almost certainly true: shortly after it was built a young sailor scrambled up it and hung a piece of cardboard from the top, proclaiming it to be Bettison's Folly.

At Wassand Hall, SEATON, a little inland from Hornsea, is Mushroom Cottage, a *cottage ornée* with just the right ingredients: thatched roof, supported by rustic pillars, and Gothick windows. It was built by Thomas Cundy in 1812–14, at the same time as the Hall. Back on the coast, but ten miles further south, is GRIMSTON Garth, a triangular house built by John Carr for Thomas Grimston in the 1780s, when the fashion for triangular buildings was at its height. A tall hexagonal tower stands surrounded by three lesser round towers forming the triangle; the centre tower is said to contain both a Gothick and a Chinese room. Attached are some lower buildings, also castellated, and *c.*1812 the Gatehouse was added, with battlements, turrets and a portcullis – a particularly true-to-history embellishment of the type that was to become so popular through J. C. Loudon's engravings of gateways. John Earle, a mason from Hull, worked on the gatehouse, but it is not clear whether he was the architect or not.

Across the Humber to South Humberside, and the follies fade. Only two scraps are worth mentioning – a sham ruin of 1885 on the promenade at CLEETHORPES, and a crenellated façade to a pigsty at the vicarage in WOOTTON. This part of Humberside is physically and spiritually Lincolnshire, and rather fine follies close by are described in that chapter.

Northumberland

Apart from the Seaton Delaval mausoleum, a handful of obelisks and a garden temple or two, England's northernmost county has almost no neo-classical follies. Moorish and Chinese conceits are unheard of. Peers and gentry alike have, as befits this weathered and sparsely populated area, embraced the only possible folly style – Gothick. It has been adapted for every type of building: towers, façades, sham castles, summer-houses, dovecotes and kennels. Strangely enough, no one seems to have bothered with coastal follies despite a romantic shore; most of the follies are inland, and are Georgian rather than Victorian.

The first exception is Seaton Sluice: it has a harbour. An embattled octagonal structure (called 'The Octagon') with faintly Gothick windows seems to date from the time the harbour was rebuilt in 1761–4. The delightfully named Starlight Castle is nearby. SEATON DELAVAL, a mile inland, forms together with Blenheim Palace and Castle Howard Vanbrugh's famous triad of country houses. The ringed shafts of the portico and the rustic centre block of the façade in Vanbrugh's original design give it a precocious, Ledoux-like tinge. The grounds contain an obelisk and a crouching black mausoleum like a squat seven-bayed country house in an overgrown wood. The lead or copper that once sheathed the dome has been stripped off, leaving the bare wooden framework rising above the portico as an Eiffel dome. It was built in 1766. Despite the menace pervading this gloomy structure, life at Seaton Delaval was not all despondency: John Delaval, one of the occupants of the mausoleum, died in 1775 at the age of 20, 'as a result of being kicked in a vital organ by a laundrymaid to whom he was paying his addresses'. Sir Francis Blake, one of the later owners, enjoyed an occasional practical joke: unsuspecting house guests were plunged into a cold bath by means of a mechanical device attached to their beds.

Blagdon Hall, set in a wooded area along the A1 near STANNINGTON, was built for the Ridley family, at least four generations of whom used the same name — Sir Matthew White Ridley. It was the 2nd Baronet who donated a conduit, the Cale Cross (also known as the Scale), built by David Stephenson in the early 1780s, to the Corporation of Newcastle. It was removed from its original site in 1807 and returned to Sir Matthew, who re-erected the open temple in the grounds of Blagdon House, where it still stands, an elaborate frieze with urns on top, resting on four columns and four pillars. Another open temple which has lost its dome came to Blagdon from another Ridley property, Heaton Hall in Newcastle, where it had been built by the local architect William Newton in 1783. An imposing 19th-century stone bridge with statuary on the parapets by J. G. Lough crosses the lake, and on the north bank is a small Gothick sham ruin.

West of Stannington, on the A696, is BELSAY HALL, the remarkable house built by Sir Charles Monck, who changed his name from Middleton in 1799. This very austere Greek Revival house was built in 1807–17, its owner acting as his own architect. Monck had received his inspiration from a two-year honeymoon in Athens spent with a third party, Sir William Gell of Hopton Hall in Derbyshire, an eminent dilettante. Monck transfigured the quarry that had yielded the stone for the building of Belsay into a garden, closely following Richard Payne Knight's and Uvedale Price's precepts on the Picturesque, and the valley walks and underpasses in particular seem to illustrate a passage in Price's *An Essay on the Picturesque* (1794):

> . . . such [i.e. Picturesque], for instance, are the rough banks that often inclose a bye-road or a hollow lane: Imagine the size of these banks and the space between them to be increased till the lane becomes a deep dell, — the coves large caverns, — the peeping stones hanging rocks, so that the whole may impress an idea of awe and grandeur . . .

A second journey of the classically minded Sir Charles, to Italy in the 1830s, prompted a row of curiously broad-arched cottages in the village, but for the village school in 1842 he finally chose Gothic.

Further away from Newcastle the Gothick style dominates. At BAVINGTON HALL, west of Belsay, is a dovecote in that mode, castellated like a fortress, the keep within the walls acting as the actual dovecote. South of Wark-on-Tyne, Lancelot Allgood goth-icised both his estates: SIMONBURN CASTLE and NUNWICK. The ruined medieval castle at Simonburn, of which only a small part still stands (it was razed by villagers convinced that a treasure lay buried in the ruins), was enhanced with Gothick fragments in 1766 to make a tolerable eyecatcher. Two years later the Gothick kennels were built in the grounds of Nunwick House on a rectangular plan, battlemented and with pointed windows, to serve as an eyecatcher to the house. Near the house is a spiral shaft originating from the 13th-century St Mungo's Church in Simonburn, which was restored and rebuilt by the architects William and Robert Newton in 1762–3. Perhaps they were also called in to design Allgood's eyecatchers.

Several miles west of Belsay along the A696, some villages and houses have connections with the famous Lancelot 'Capability' Brown. He was born in Kirkharle in 1715 or 1716, went to school in Cambo, and worked at Kirkharle Hall. A clump or two in the grounds of CAPHEATON HALL are said to have been planted by him, and it is tempting to think that the small Gothick sham-ruined church in the park may be one of his creations. In the 1760s Brown worked for Sir Walter Calverley Blackett, MP, of Wallington Hall, near CAMBO, a National Trust property. By the house are a standing stone pilfered from a nearby stone circle, and four griffins' heads which came from Aldersgate in London and were said to have been brought to the North as ballast on Blackett's coal barges. The heads were first set on top of Daniel Garrett's Rothley Castle, but were later removed to the immediate vicinity of the house. The mighty sham Rothley Castle was erected on its hilltop position *c.*1745, south of the serpentine lake designed by Brown. It is reputed to have been intended as a point of defence in the Jacobite troubles: a stretch of walling ending in two squat machicolated towers with a third tower in the centre. Its rather fancy decorations of cross arrowslits, pointed doors and windows, blind arches and whale-bones (these last have now disappeared) proclaim its perfunctory use. Thomas Wright's Codger's Fort of 1769 is not far off. More sparsely decorated, it repeats the Rothley Castle plan with some variations, mainly in roofing the end-bastions with pyramids of rough stone.

John Sharp, vicar of HARTBURN from 1749 to 1792, was a keen antiquarian, and it was to him that Bamburgh Castle owed its restoration in 1757. About this time Sharp built himself a tower-house at Hartburn, some three miles from Codger's Fort. The little house's most attractive feature is the façade, castellated, with crowstepped gables and ogee windows. A small grotto bridge spanned the brook by the side of the house; later the house was partly used as a school and eventually became one of Britain's more intriguing post offices. John Sharp's father was Thomas Sharp, Archdeacon of Northumberland, who lived in an old peel tower in ROTHBURY. Around 1720 he assembled the unemployed masons of the village and set them to build him an observatory — a round and castellated tower, with classical doorways and windows instead of Gothick, for which this was a decade or two too early. Considering its date, Sharp's Folly makes an early but not entirely convincing eyecatcher.

LEMMINGTON Hall, near the B6341 leading from Rothbury to Alnwick, has a Soane-designed column in the grounds. This tall Doric monument, brought to Northumberland shortly after the First World War, originally stood at Felbridge in Surrey, where it was erected in 1785 in memory of Edward and Julia Evelyn. An urn sits on top of the column and a snake, carved by Soane's sculptor Edward Foxhall, coils around its base. Nearby Lemmington Branch Farm has a very broad, Gothick façade and castellated centre gable, walls and end gables, with cross arrowslits and ogee windows. William Newton, who built the temple at Heaton Hall and may have been responsible for the Gothick work done at Simonburn and Nunwick, could also be credited with this superb eyecatcher: he designed the now demolished Lemmington Hall and that he was well versed in the Gothick idiom is apparent from his Kielder Castle, built for Lord Northumberland of Alnwick.

The town of ALNWICK itself can mean only one thing: the seat of the Percys. For nearly 1,000 years this family has dominated the north of England; where the Percys led, others followed. The impetus for the Gothick movement in northern England came from the rebuilding programme at Alnwick Castle, an undertaking that spanned most of the latter half of the 18th century. In the 1750s the immensely rich Hugh Percy Simpson, 1st Duke of Northumberland, started the restoration of Alnwick, until then a ramshackle collection of castle walls, towers and corridors, most of it in a more or less ruined state. James Paine started the tremendous task of redoing both the interior and exterior, but later the Adam brothers were called in. After some years the castle began to look presentable and the Duke had 'Capability' Brown fashion the park; as his labours took effect, the Duke turned his attention to the construction of a few follies.

Among the earliest ornaments was the Lion Bridge of 1773 – three embattled arches with arrowslits and quatrefoils and the lead statue of a lion on one side of the parapet. Denwick Bridge, leading to the north-east, also came in for the Gothick. treatment. The Percy lion formed the staple part of the decorations on the estate, and a quarter of a century later the Duke was lampooned in a pamphlet called *Wood and Stone: or a Dialogue between a Wooden Duke and a Stone Lion*. Another of the 1st Duke's buildings is quite a way from Alnwick, near Cumbria and the Scottish border. KIELDER CASTLE is a castellated hunting lodge built by William Newton in 1772–5. It is now the Forestry Commission headquarters for Kielder Forest.

Alnwick's finest and most famous folly stands on top of a hill to the north variously known as Brizlee, Brislaw and Briesley Hill. One of the County Histories has it that Brizlee Tower, a tall, fanciful construction, was the result of the Duke's admiration for the gaudy product of a pastrycook. Despite stories of the Duke being his own architect, the tower, a tremendously ornate architectural dessert, was almost certainly designed by the Adam brothers in 1777. The story of the pastrycook may not be entirely without foundation: the renowned chef Carême published *Le Pâtissier pittoresque* in 1815, designs for all sorts of follies to be executed in more or less edible materials.

The tower is about 80 feet high, starting from a broad base with pointed arches and canopied niches. Above this is a balustrade with fancy open-work battlements of an intricate design, and from here the shaft supplies three more storeys of pointed windows and niches. On the top is another balustrade and a battlemented octagon, on which is an iron cresset with little trefoils on the rim. A small plaque immodestly records the Duke's achievements in planting trees in the area:

> CIRCUMSPICE
> EGO OMNIA ISTA SUM DIMENSUS;
> MEI SUNT ORDINES,
> MEA DESCRIPTIO;
> MULTAE ETIAM ISTARUM ARBORUM
> MEA MANU SUNT SATAE

The haughty Duchess's interest in her family history was responsible for the restoration of the Malcolm Cross, recording the death of the Scottish king Malcolm II seven centuries earlier. A couple of miles north-east of the castle is Ratcheugh Cliff, on top of which sits the gazebo, built *c.*1784 by Adam and part of an uncompleted grand design. The windows all around the gazebo, poised above a long screen with pointed arches and battlements, earned it the name of Ratcheugh Observatory. In the town itself is Pottergate Tower, built in 1768 around a medieval core and paid for by the Borough, although the Duke must have had his say in the affair and the folly is obviously the product of the castle workmen and architects. North-west of the town are the ruins of Hulne Priory, where in 1776 both Adam and Brown improved the medieval ruins. Tradition has it that Adam did the interior of the summer-house, set amidst the ecclesiastical remains, and that Brown designed the exterior. The Gothick windows and door are indeed in Brown's style, except for a niche in the side wall which is more related in its ornamentation to Brizlee Tower. The façade has two white round portrait plaques of the Duke and Duchess, set in two quatrefoils made in 1773 by the relatively unknown George Davy.

Near the entrance to Hulne Park is the tiny monument to William the Lion, King of Scotland, erected *c.*1860 by Algernon

156 The chapel, Crimplesham
157 'The House in the Clouds', Thorpeness
158 One of the Rendlesham lodges, Bentwaters

163   The Repton Temple, built in 1975 at Sheringham
164   The Bonomi Mausoleum, Blickling

165 Gunton Park Tower

166 Church cottage façade, Barton Mills

167   The replica of Liverpool Castle on the shores of Rivington Reservoir

168   Freston Tower

169   Roynton Gardens watch-tower on the slopes of Rivington Pike

Percy, the 4th Duke. The arched square on a plinth commemorates the capture of William after an unsuccessful siege in 1174. It was Algernon who obliterated the old Adam interior of Alnwick Castle and had it redone according to his taste.

The Peace of 1814 was commemorated by the Peace Column, complete with small bell on top, a Tuscan column in the woods on the golf-course, built by the 2nd Duke. But this Duke's folly fame lies with a column he did not build, 'The Farmer's Folly' near the station, an impressive affair − Trafalgar Square rurally resettled. Amid four lions, a fluted column on a broad base rises 83 feet to a drum on which perches an aristocratic lion. Its official name is 'The Tenantry Column', and it was built in 1816 to the designs of David Stephenson, the architect shared by the Percys and Sir Matthew Ridley of Blagdon Hall. It was raised by the Duke's tenant farmers to express their gratitude for his reduction of their rents by 25 per cent after the catastrophic fall in agricultural prices after 1814. Pragmatically, the Duke felt that if they could afford to make such a tangible expression of their gratitude they could afford to pay higher rents, so he upped them to the old levels.

Along the A697 near Wooler are two small Gothick buildings: an octagonal dovecote with quatrefoils near the hamlet of HAUGH HEAD; and Homilton Tower, a ruined hilltop tower with pointed openings and blind arches, at HUMBLETON. Ewart Park, three miles north-west of WOOLER, is of more consequence. In the second half of the 18th century the house was owned by a Colonel Horace St Paul, who started alterations in 1787. One tower at Ewart Park, four storeys high with prominent quatrefoils and machicolations and battlements, is supposed to be medieval and to have come from the astonishing Twizel Castle on the Scottish border.

TWIZEL CASTLE virtually defines the folly. It is magnificent, huge and impossible, the product of a building mania never satisfied. Men worked on this house for nearly 50 years to no purpose − it was never finished, never inhabited. Sir Francis Blake was the onlie begetter, but little is known about Twizel except that work started *c.*1770 under James Nesbit and that George Wyatt was working there in 1812. It sits on the north bank of the river Till just before it flows into the Tweed, and reached the height of five storeys before work stopped.

FORD CASTLE has a pair of high quality Gothick gates of such sham-castle pretensions that they cry out to be classed as follies. The South Gate of 1773 is a creation of James Nesbit, the architect of ill-fated Twizel, and it consists of a thin, castellated arch with rustic archway and tiny quatrefoils. Alexander Gilkie's East Gate of 1801 is in the Sturdy style. A sham portcullis provides the centre, with the gateway flanked by two three-storey towers decorated with blind and open quatrefoils, blind niches and a clock-face in the right-hand tower. Walls with cross arrowslits and the inevitable castellations connect the embattled end-pavilions.

The final Northumbrian folly is, as might be expected, Gothick: a tall tower with a stair turret at HAGGERSTON, on the A1 just before Berwick. It was part of an 18th-century house left standing after the rest had been demolished, but its only real claim to fame is that of the most northerly folly in England.

Tyne and Wear

Tyne and Wear, a chunk taken out of Northumberland and Durham, is a largely monumental county. Rural buildings are usually first among the casualties in industrial areas, but monuments receive more consideration. Beyond the immediate Newcastle area, the old Durham part of the county seems to have all the follies.

The Grey Monument, a Doric column-tower with 164 steps standing at the end of Grey Street in NEWCASTLE, is one of the country's many memorials to Charles, 2nd Earl Grey, who put the Reform Bill through Parliament. It was erected in 1838, still in the Earl's lifetime although he had withdrawn from active politics, and the statue of Grey on top of the column was sculpted in 1837 by Edward Hodges Baily, RA. The column was built by the local architects John and Benjamin Green, a father-and-son team who specialised in churches, bridges and monuments. The PENSHAW Monument is another work by the Greens, a smaller copy of the Athenian Temple of Theseus, essentially a roofless, wall-less, longish Doric temple supported by pillars. One of the best known follies in the north-east, it is visible from miles around, blackened with industrial soot from the many surrounding collieries and factories, a satanic response to the pure white Hellenic ideal. It was erected in 1844 as a memorial to John George Lambton, 1st Earl of Durham and Governor of Canada, who had died in 1840. The honeycomb of mineworkings in the area has seriously undermined the foundations so that despite its apparent solidity the building is now extremely unsafe and the public are forbidden access; once a staircase inside one of the massive columns led up to the 70-foot high parapet walk to allow visitors to enjoy the view. Not far from the Penshaw Monument is the Victoria Viaduct spanning the river Wear at WASHINGTON. Another classical copy, this one was based on the Roman-built Alcántara viaduct in Spain.

At WHICKHAM, south of Newcastle, stands a monument to Long John English, a Victorian stone-mason and wrestler who is supposed to have sculpted his own bust, which graces the top of the column. South of Whickham, near Rowlands Gill, is the GIBSIDE estate, owned from 1721 to 1767 by George Bowes, a Whig MP and member of an old-established Durham family who made their fortune from coal. It was mining that paid for the glamorous estate, but the wheel turns, and it is mining subsidence that has caused the ruination of almost all the Gibside buildings. Gibside Chapel, the Palladian mausoleum built by James Paine in 1760–6, was rescued some 20 years ago, when it was given to the National Trust. The Column of British Liberty, representing 140 feet of Doric-columned whiggery, with a statue of the selfsame British Liberty by Richardson on top, seems never to have been threatened by the mining activities. This monument, facing the chapel, took £2,000, eight years (1750–7) and two architects (Daniel Garrett and James Paine) to build. The house and Palladian orangery, also by Paine, are now in ruins. Against all odds, however, Gibside's most important edifice has recently been saved: the Gothick Banqueting House, built in 1751 by Garrett, had already lost most of its interior decorations and a spire on top of the two-storey bow when restoration was started in 1980 by the Landmark Trust. It is an embattled and ogee-windowed affair, standing above a lake and overlooking the other buildings in the park, its most prominent feature being the bow, facing the lake with quatrefoils and topped by three gables, each ending in pinnacles. Somehow it manages to look like a bishop's mitre.

The seaside village of WHITBURN is pleasant enough, although there is a neighbouring colliery. In the back garden of a Victorian fancy, Whitburn House, stands a medieval window, originally part of St John's Church, Newcastle, which was demolished in 1848. The sham ruin was erected in 1867–9 when the house was built. Landward at CLEADON Park's Sunniside Lane is the Cleadon Pumping Station with yet another of the Italianate towers so dear to the Victorians, and to builders of pumping stations in particular. This one dates from the 1860s and was put up by Thomas Hawksley, the civil engineer who also worked at Rivington Pike in Lancashire.

North Yorkshire

Money attracts money; follies attract follies. Almost every county has a particular area studded with follies and others with great barren deserts. Sometimes this is because the thickly follied area was once fashionable, the views spectacular, or because mad squires were thick on the ground, but as often as not there seems to be no particular reason why everyone suddenly started building. North Yorkshire has by any standards the greatest number of follies in the centre and north of England, and it is possible to point to a concentration of them roughly following the river Ure, and centring on the cathedral town of Ripon.

John Aislabie was Chancellor of the Exchequer until he was implicated in the disastrous South Sea Bubble crash of the 1720s. Nationally he fell into disgrace, but locally the Aislabies remained honoured and respectable gentry. Aislabie used a large part of his fortune to create STUDLEY ROYAL, his estate a few miles from Ripon, now a National Trust property. The garden there, created over a period of 20 years by John Aislabie, his son William and their chief gardener William Fisher, acts as a link between the formal French style and the new romantic landscape movement. They made use of the undulating valley of the Skell to lay out a series of ornamental ponds leading from a large sheet of water at the garden entrance to the focal point, the grandest eyecatcher in Britain — the genuine ruins of Fountains Abbey.

John Aislabie's buildings, among them Campbell's Banqueting House of 1729, the Temple of Piety and the Octagon Tower, are all in the classical vein. After his father's death in 1742 William Aislabie finally took over, and from then on the Studley gardens were fitted out with follies. The craggy west side of the valley on which the Octagon Tower stands may represent a kind of political landscape, perhaps in reference to William Aislabie's unpublished 'Essay upon some Particulars of the Ancient and Modern Government, Conventions and Parliament of England', treating of politics from the Saxons to Edward I. The Octagon Tower stands on a hill known as Constitution Hill. Originally a classical pavilion, it was altered in 1738 by William into a Gothick belvedere that had to be approached by a tunnel cut into the hillside. It has all recently been most carefully restored. Next to the tower is a small construction which could well be England's first barbecue. Walking south along the ridge we come across the ruins of a pillar, referred to as a Column to Liberty. Next is the rotondo Temple of Fame and finally Anne Boleyn's Seat in carpenter's Gothick. This seat provides the famous Surprise View of Fountains Abbey. One is not supposed to cheat — the undergrowth along the side of the walk is meant to be a little thicker — so keep your eyes straight ahead. The surprise view is spectacular even when anticipated.

From here, a path through the back of the wood leads to Mackershaw Lodge, a Greek-fronted eyecatcher visible from the Pillar and the site of the now demolished house. The outer parts of Studley are follywise at least as interesting as the garden itself. A wooded walk leads from the Lodge to Mackershaw Trough and the Chinese Wood. By now one has entered what is known as the Valley of the Seven Bridges, or Mackershaw Valley, also a National Trust property. The rustic bridges are all in the same style and were built by William Aislabie when he made Mackershaw into a sub-Studley, the much rougher and less artificial site reflecting his avant-garde taste for the Picturesque and the Chinese. A view *c.*1750 by Balthasar Nebot, who painted most of Aislabie's possessions, shows an open Chinese building, more Tartar than Cantonese, on a steep cliff and, in the distance, a small white building, possibly the entrance to Mann's Cave. Only the circular foundations of the Chinese building remain, together with two rustic gateposts which give entrance to a small copse. According to a bill, work was carried out on 'ye Cheineys Building & . . . Pillars &c in South scrarr' from December 1744 until October 1745. The Belvedere, a few hundred yards from the site of the Chinese building, has also disappeared, but a little further off the Roman Pill Box guards the valley's proper entrance from Studley. This simple, square building was dedicated to the Roman legend of the three Horatii, another political reference.

From here one can return to Studley or have a look at the double ice-houses and the Gothick Studley Lodge at the park's main entrance. Above Studley the drive, aligned with Ripon Cathedral, starts at solitary St Mary's Church. Behind this Burges church the obelisk is hidden, built in 1815 in place of William Aislabie's Stowe-inspired pyramid. On re-entering Studley and following the High Walk along the west ridge, past a small, neglected, Greek seat, one arrives, finally, in the valley again, at the area called Quebec. This encompasses a rustic bridge and a pond with the Quebec Monument in the middle, in memory of General Wolfe, who died in the battle for the Heights of Abraham in 1759. Through the woods on the east crag can be seen the Temple of Fame, intended as a celebration of Wolfe's fame, and opposite the monument a small rustic grotto has been cut into the hillside. Some yards south of Quebec is Tent Hill, where an oriental building formerly stood, and round the corner in Bank Wood, towards the ruins of Fountains Abbey, is the rubble of the Gothic Rustic Lodge.

To the south of the park, superbly placed on How Hill like St Michael's on Glastonbury Tor, is the Chapel of St Michael de Monte, built on a site associated with the court of a Saxon king. The medieval chapel that stood here fell into ruins after the Dissolution, and in 1718, two years after he inherited Studley Royal, John Aislabie rebuilt it, making it into a quasi-chapel, classical, but with a cross on top and incorporating the original gothic inscription, 'SOLI DEO HONOR ET GLORIA'. Politically inspired Studley and its surroundings may have been, but the religious aspect should not be overestimated: in 1737 gaming tables were installed in the How Hill 'chapel'.

Although William Aislabie had Mackershaw Valley to experiment with, he was surely torn by the dichotomy faced by all planners with a respect for the past: on the one hand, the need to conserve his father's garden at Studley, which he properly realised to be a masterpiece although hopelessly old-fashioned by 1750; on the other, the desire to implement his own schemes and designs. While on the lookout for new terrain, he came across the steep and remote Ure valley near GREWELTHORPE, another Aislabie property, and in 1750 planting and building started in the woods at Hackfall.

Hackfall became one of the first, and perhaps the greatest, 'romantick' gardens in England. With its hanging woods, wild river and rocky cliffs, only Hawkstone in Shropshire can rival it. The centrepiece at Hackfall was, however, formed by the Fountain Plain, a formal arrangement reminiscent of designs in Batty Langley's *New Principles of Gardening* (1728). The garden became a Yorkshire showcase for the next century and a half; even early in this century charabancs from Harrogate arrived at the entrance, tourists paying a small fee and proceeding on foot, stopping to take tea in the Graeco-Roman folly at Mowbray Point. The gardens at Hackfall have now fallen completely into decay; most of the trees were felled in the 1930s, and the buildings have been set fire to or otherwise slighted. Restoration would be a massive and costly operation, but enough information can be gleaned from the contemporary accounts of such distinguished 18th-century travellers as William Gilpin, Arthur Young and Thomas Pennant to make it feasible.

Near the entrance are the ruins of what must have been a covered stone and a tufa seat, reverently called Kent's Seat (Kent was a hero of Aislabie), facing the Alumn Cascade, which still trickles feebly down the mossy stones. A little further on is Fisher's Hall, named after John Aislabie's chief gardener, who died in 1743 and who also worked for William. The roof of this octagonal lancet-windowed grotto room set on a little mount came down long ago, but the inside walls still show the remains of shells and pieces of glass. Above the door is a tablet inscribed 'W.A. 1750'. Fisher's Hall seems to owe something to a design of Robert Morris in his *Architectural Remembrancer* — but as this was not published until 1751, perhaps the reverse applies. Walking down the slippery steps to the River Ure, one comes to the scanty remains of what must have been a store-room for fishing tackle and/or wine, or perhaps it was a barbecue like the one at Studley Royal.

To the north is the Fountain Plain, where the formal layout has disappeared into the undergrowth, the pond now a stagnant sheet of water with a small peninsula on which was formerly a 'Fountain throwing Water to a great height'. Near the pond are the ruins of a grotto 'situated in front of a cascade which falls forty feet', and the Rustic Temple, a simple enough folly made of huge boulders, with a niche for a statuette in one of its walls. Still further to the north are the remains of the Sand Bed Hut and a small obelisk, broken in two and probably dating from Victorian times, when Lord Ripon owned Hackfall.

The two most important follies are on the edge of the cliffs that form the natural boundary of the estate. Mowbray Castle towers high above the river to the south, and is visible from the other side of the garden (the view towards Mowbray Castle was painted by Turner in 1816). The castle is a sham-ruin tower, to be seen from both sides, and great care has been taken with the detail, even on the inside. It takes its name from the De Mowbrays, fierce medieval knights who lived near here, and the romance is enhanced by the fact that almost all of them died violent deaths. Above Fountain Plain stands the Mowbray Point Banqueting House, with a ruined Gothic servants' hall not far away. Mowbray Point has two distinct façades, one turned towards the fields and showing an elysian Greek front (or back), the other facing the great expanse of land beyond Hackfall itself and representing a fake Roman ruin — three arches of crumbling sandstone, like a minor edition of the Caracalla Baths in Rome, and perhaps inspired by Langley's engravings of sham Roman ruins.

It took us five separate visits to check all the sites of the follies at Hackfall — or perhaps we were just looking for excuses to revisit the place; desolate as it now is, it still retains a powerful fascination, especially on a bleak winter's morning with the ghost of Aislabie inspecting the grounds. The writer of an 1822 guide-book caught the place at a happier moment:

> To Hackfall's calm retreats, where Nature reigns
> In rural pride, transported fancy flies.
> Oh! Bear me, Goddess to these sylvan plains,
> Where all around unlaboured beauties rise.

Not far from Grewelthorpe, in KIRKBY MALZEARD, is Mowbray House. The heavily overgrown Victorian gardens here have only folly bits and pieces — a small obelisk with ball finial and a crest on a two-stepped base marking the site of the original Mowbray Castle, and a rough stone called the Mushroom Stone which looks nothing like a mushroom — while down in the shallow valley with its equally shallow rivulet are the literal bits and pieces: a heap of pillars, stones and pieces of pediment, the mossy remains of a collapsed Greek seat. By the time we left, in the deepening twilight, the place was beginning to look like the setting for an M. R. James story. We didn't wait for the werewolves and hobgoblins.

A tour of the remaining follies in North Yorkshire can best be started back at RIPON. In the garden at the back of No. 9 Park Street is a pair of exceptionally large 18th-century gazebos built into the garden wall, one ruined, one less ruined but still in a precarious state of health. It is astonishing that nothing has been done to preserve them. Halfway between Ripon and Grewelthorpe a tall tower appears on the skyline. This should be approached from the hamlet of AZERLEY, parking the car at a roadside lodge with amateur roughstone castellations. The astonished visitor will notice when crossing the fields that Azerley Tower gets smaller and smaller, like something out of *Alice*, until all that remains is a slender castellated tower rising from a petite Victorian house, now uninhabited. The story behind it is the oft-repeated one of the landowner surveying his labour forces from the top of the tower. The tower stands like a jewel among the corrugated iron debris of what appears to have been a failed agricultural enterprise.

The road continues past Grewelthorpe and Hackfall to MASHAM, home of the famous 'Old Peculier' beer, named after the Peculier of Masham, a medieval official. Just before Masham a signpost on the right points to Nutwith Cote Farm, a small mansion also known as Old Swinton Hall which until recently contained a Chinese wallpapered room. One of the outbuildings stands on a base with niches for beeboles, one of only two such arrangements in the country, and past the house is a ruined classical dovecote on a little knoll, still looking austere and dignified. Nutwith in former times was a resting place for monks on their way from Rievaulx to Fountains, and there is local talk of an ancient tunnel used by the monks in order to pass beneath the river Ure.

New Swinton Hall is only a mile or so to the west, near ILTON. It was built by the owner himself, William Danby (1752–1833), with a little help from James Wyatt, John Foss and Robert Lugar, the work taking a remarkable 50 years, continuing well into the 1820s. Swinton's central tower, by Lugar, can almost be counted as a folly in its own right. Danby was a good example of the English eccentric. His literary works, mostly written in old age, consist of four illuminating volumes of thoughts: *Travelling Thoughts*, *Thoughts chiefly on Serious Subjects*, *Thoughts on Various Subjects* and *Ideas and Realities*, with an additional *Extracts from Young's Night Thoughts, with Observations upon them* published a year before his death. At the same time as this late literary flowering Danby took to crenellating his mansion and to relieving the unemployment in the area.

His first project was the labour-intensive work of creating another Stonehenge, with a shilling a day paid to the workers. No common-or-garden stone circle this; Mr Danby, like a true Yorkshireman, believed that a job had to be done properly if it was to be done at all, and the result was an enormous oval of altars, menhirs, dolmens, sarsens and other phallic and neo-Druidical paraphernalia standing amidst the Yorkshire moors. Several solitary standing stones lined a ceremonial avenue leading to the temple. It is well preserved in the middle of Forestry Commission land, an unnatural object unnaturally surrounded by gloomy evergreens, and popular with picnickers. Vandals come off second best against these massive monoliths, but make their presence known in other ways: to take a photograph we had to remove over 40 empty lager cans tastefully scattered throughout the folly. A guide to the district, dated 1910, repeats the old hermit story, claiming that 'the builder of the temple offered to provide any individual with food, and a subsequent annuity, providing he would reside in the temple seven years, living the primitive life, speaking to no one and allowing his beard and hair to grow. It is said that one man underwent this self-imposed infliction for four-and-a-half years, at the end of which he was compelled to admit defeat. Several others made the attempt, but had to relinquish it.' If this is true, it is the longest tenure we have come across in any of the hermit stories. Visiting the Druids' Temple on a windy January afternoon we were astonished that anyone could have lasted four and a half minutes, let alone four and a half years. Towards the west through the trees a view has been left open towards Leighton Reservoir, lying far below in the valley.

While writing his observations upon Young's *Night Thoughts* Danby undertook another enterprise, the building of Quarry Gill Bridge, south of SWINTON. This Gothic bridge, designed by Foss, forms an ensemble with the nearby rustic stone seat, from which Danby could watch the deer sauntering in the lowlands, left to his own night thoughts as the sun set and the damp filtered through the blankets covering his body. A year later he was dead, aged 81. Robert Southey, who visited him some time before his death, thought much of Danby, and so did his villagers. They lost a benevolent employer and a considerate landlord who would open his private grounds 'for public inspection'.

South of the Druids' Temple on MASHAM MOOR is a tiny sham ruined tower, another Gothic mood piece. It is dated 1824; no further information is available, but the date and situation do suggest William Danby as the builder. Not far away is Dallowgill Moor, near the hamlet of GREYGARTH. On top of a hillock stands the Greygarth Monument, a roughstone tower now in ruins, but two storeys high in the days that the Aislabie family owned a coalfield here.

Slobbering Sal is not a North Yorkshire original but the name of a female head, rather like the heads on medieval capitals, attached to a large structure like a grotto entrance and spouting a gentle but never-ending stream of water from her mouth, even in the dryest summers. High in the woods above EAST WITTON, on Witton Fell, it can be found marked on older maps as Tilsey Folly. The arch above the newly re-roofed grotto entrance is inscribed 'M$^{q/s}$ of A / 1821' for the Marquess of Ailesbury.

From East Witton the A6108 leads to Leyburn, crossing the Ure by means of a converted suspension bridge at MIDDLEHAM. The original suspension bridge was built in 1829, but when it was converted to an ordinary bridge the pylons were medievalised by the addition of castellations and blind arrowslits. Another example of this style is the sham castle at the back of Thornborough Hall, near LEYBURN, now the Rural District Offices. The Hall was built in 1863 by Joseph Aloysius Hansom, inventor of the hansom-cab and builder of Middleham Bridge, in partnership with Edward Welch.

The sham castle, hard against a cliff in its Victorian garden with a small rustic bridge, looks several score years earlier than the mansion, perhaps nearer the date of the bridge, and consists of a centre block guarded by two round towers with another shorter tower on the upper level. The back of the little castle, just big enough to house the rusting remains of a Leyburn-built hand mangle, is the cliff face, and to reach the next storey one has to walk to the end of the garden and turn back along an upper path.

Towards the east of Leyburn, between CONSTABLE BURTON and Patrick Brompton (two villages that sound more like a charge sheet), is the Akebar Caravan Park, with a shop which takes the unexpected form of a castle farm and has just been finished. It consists mainly of its own façade, leaving the tourists little space for squeezing their rain-tanned bodies through the turnstiles. The façade is about 100 yards long and faces Constable Burton. It is superbly asymmetrical; one end has a vernacular house, the other a sham ruined tower with a small corner outcrop. In between is a rough wall, partly ruined, with an ogee gate with pediment and finials. The façade looked like the fulfilment of a long-held dream. The construction workers told us that the owner doesn't like it to be called a folly because he just wanted it to blend with the surroundings, but as its immediate surroundings consist of acres of parked caravans, the shop is a prime example of what a modern-day folly can be, as opposed to the studied retrospection of Quinlan Terry and Peter Foster.

Wensleydale is famous far beyond Yorkshire for its beauty and its cheese. Little enough cheese can be found there now, but the beauty remains. Beyond SWINITHWAITE on the A684 to Aysgarth lies Temple Farm, and on the north side of the road, hidden among the trees behind a high wall, is a dilapidated but still beautiful temple of 1792 by John Foss. It consists of a rusticated octagonal base with blocked arches and the bas-relief of a dog above the door. The staircase runs between the outer and inner walls, leading to a balcony around a smaller domed octagonal room on the first floor, still with most of its delicate plasterwork intact. It was built for nearby Swinithwaite Hall, together with a belvedere which we failed to find. Near the famous AYSGARTH Falls is Sorrell Sykes

Park, the home of a particularly quaint set of follies. As an entrée, a tall chimney stands in the garden of a farmhouse to the east of Sorrell Sykes Farm; it was bought by a Major some years ago and transported from the Home Counties to Yorkshire in two army trucks. The Farm is a weird amalgam of building styles. The façade towards the road has only a series of farmhouses to show for itself, except for a west wing of 1921 with huge classical windows, but the park façade is that of a Palladian mansion of *c.*1750. The park is essentially a lawn bounded by a steep ridge, with a great variation of heights in between. On the lawn stood a column with an eagle on top, until in 1980 a tractor accidentally knocked it down. The base is still there, as is the eagle, regretfully eyeing the rubble of its perch. Halfway along the ridge stands a sham ruin, built to hide the site where earlier in the 18th century there had been a lead mine. An old gully still leads down to the lawn where lead deposits form a few hillocks. The centre of the ruin consists of a blank arch, above which is an *oeil-de-boeuf* window and a small pediment. The flanking walls have small pointed arches and windows, and are in danger of becoming genuine ruins. To the east the sham-ruin screen is mirrored on the other side of the valley by Bolton Castle. From the screen one walks down to a field with a strictly vernacular barn, but along the edge are three follies in a neat row: first a cone like a spinning top, a large smoke-hole, constructed from rough-stone in 1921; then a tiny gate consisting of two cones with a bend stone for an arch, too small for anyone to enter the field through; and finally the Rocket Ship, as it is locally known, a cone rising from a square base with a room inside. Buttresses are placed against the base, probably because the local builder was afraid the cone wouldn't stand on its own, and it is the buttresses that give the folly a startling resemblance to Dan Dare style rockets from 1950s' comic strips.

SETTLE is quite a way from Aysgarth, but the traveller with time to spare and an eye for a beautiful landscape will find the drive through the moors rewarding. Train enthusiasts agree that the Settle–Carlisle line is the loveliest in England, so catch it quick before British Rail closes it down. This small market town has a remarkable town-house called 'The Folly', or Folly Hall. The lintel bears the date 1679, and the three-storey house shows the characteristics of 'Gothic Survival' architecture, with the entrance as the most astonishing feature: double Gothic arches of an uneasy design above a doorway flanked by Gaudíesque pillars. The house deserves to be called a folly on the strength of its highly individual decoration alone, but it seems the main reason for its name was that Thomas Preston, the builder, ran out of capital and had to leave his knick-knack unfinished.

En route to Pateley Bridge we pass SKIPTON CASTLE where Lady Anne Clifford, an indefatigable builder and restorer of six castles and a dozen or so churches and chapels, made herself a grotto-room lined with shells. As it is actually inside the castle it can scarcely be counted as a folly, no matter how shell-covered. On the moor south of PATELEY BRIDGE are two tall ruined pillars which upon closer inspection look like the arches for a cathedral nave. Yorke's Folly, or 'The Stoops', was built for John Yorke of Bewerly Hall. Originally there were three Stoops, dating from 1800 and built, naturally, by unemployed workmen, but one fell down in 1893. As Bewerly Hall was originally owned by Fountains Abbey monks, Fountains may have been the inspiration. The old chapel at Bewerly still has an inscription reading 'SOLI DEO HONOR ET GLORIA', like the chapel on How Hill.

Between Pateley and Studley is SAWLEY HALL, where Earl de Grey was busy restoring Sawley Abbey in 1848. Some of the old material was used to make a rustic bridge over a road, while another bridge seems to have remained at a fragmentary stage, perhaps deliberately making a sham ruin. The house on the left as the road continues to Fountains Abbey is also built from remnants, making for a very peculiar but lovingly tended dwelling. Immediately south of Sawley is Ripley Castle, in the valley of the Nidd. Here the estate village has deliberately been rebuilt by the Ingleby family to resemble an Alsatian community, with the result that a typically English village has its largest house labelled 'Hôtel de Ville' and a sentry-box by the castle bearing the legend 'Parlez au Suisse'. The owners used to call Ripley Castle 'das Schloss' — the only similarity between Ripley and Alsace seems to be the inability to distinguish German from French.

HARROGATE as a spa is a mainly Edwardian invention. When John Thompson built his observatory on Harlow Hill, on the edge of

Harlow Moor, the first Pump Room had yet to be built. The 90-foot tower is without any decoration whatsoever – no battlements, finials or other frills; its sole purpose was to serve as an observatory. However, not until 1933 was it turned into a proper observatory, complete with telescope and everything. It was open to the public by 1900; people paid sixpence to enter, although a guide had to admit, 'that Helvellyn is visible in clear weather is a local superstition'. KNARESBOROUGH, on the banks of the river Nidd, is a planet to Harrogate's sun. The riverscape, with houses and churches strewn along the river banks, gives the town a foreign look. In other ways it resembles parts of Derbyshire, not least because of the large numbers of hermits' caves. The Chapel of Our Lady of the Crag, sometimes mistakenly called St Robert's Chapel, is a medieval wayside shrine with beautiful gothic decorations; immediately above it is Fort Montagu. Langdale's *The Tourist's Companion* of 1822 has a description:

> Fort Montagu is three storeys high, inhabited by a family who live beneath the rock, which has nothing artificial but part of the front. It was the work of sixteen years, performed by a poor weaver and his son, which since its completion has been called Fort Montagu, from this poor man's kind patroness, the Duchess of Buccleugh [Lady Elizabeth Montagu]; having on the top a fort with cannon, a flag waving and other military appearances. The same ingenious artificer has cut a solid rock in such a way as to form a garden, with terraces, on the very acme of the cliffe. And by the labour of many years he has formed in the garden . . . pleasant walks, ornamented with a profusion of shrubs and flowers. Here is also a green-house and tea-room, which are much frequented by the visitors from Harrogate, &c.

Ribston Hall, at LITTLE RIBSTON, home of the Ribston Pippin, is south-east of Knaresborough. A Gothick arch of the late 18th century standing in the park may have been designed by John Carr of York. The keystone in the gate to the kitchen garden shows a Janus face, smiling on one side, sticking his tongue out on the other – very apt, as Janus is the god of doors, of opening and closing, of beginning and end. Local tradition says the face is that of a former butler shown while receiving and having received an order.

Allerton Park, near ALLERTON MAULEVERER at the junction of the A1 and the A59, has a large round Doric temple surrounded by a colonnade. It is possibly by Henry Holland, and is a very large garden ornament or a mausoleum rather than a folly, but it is a pity to see the temple in such a ruinous state. South of York lies BISHOPTHORPE, where the Archbishop of York's palace and the gatehouse are built in Batty Langley-style Gothick. Thomas Atkinson had them built in 1763–9 for Robert Hay Drummond. Archbishop Drummond was no conscious builder of follies, yet there is an unintentional folly in Bishopthorpe: when St Andrew's Church was demolished in 1899 the west front was left standing to make a superb eyecatcher, now lost in a green lane leading down by the side of the palace to the river Ouse.

Near TADCASTER is Grimston Park, the 19th-century house of Sir John Hobart Caradoc, 2nd Baron Howden, and his wife Catherina Skravonsky. Howden was a diplomat whose appointments carried him all over the world, never allowing him a long stay at Grimston. He must have set his mind on a beautiful home, however, for as soon as his father died in 1839 building started under Decimus Burton, and Grimston was created while Howden was in South America. The tapering tower near the house reflects Howden's (and Burton's) cosmopolitanism: it is of the type loosely called Italianate, a style which never succeeds in suppressing other influences. On top of the balustrade is an open hexagonal tempietto, somewhat resembling the Choragic Monument at Alton Towers, and the dome bears a rustic flagpole. Hazlewood Castle, a mile west of Grimston, was built in the 1760s and 1770s. The small octagonal towerlet, looking rather ramshackle, probably dates from this period. It is castellated, with round windows on the second floor and arches at ground level. Too small to have served as a belvedere, it was perhaps considered a fine spot for picnicking. There is another octagonal tower in HOWSHAM Woods. Its lack of stature is the result of having had a storey or two lopped off 'for safety's sake'. There is also a Gothic water-mill, possibly late 18th-century, but it is in a bad state of repair.

Howsham is the best vantage point for the south approach to CASTLE HOWARD, the spectacular palace built for the rather nondescript but obviously uncontrollably wealthy 3rd Earl of

Carlisle, Charles Howard, by the soldier and playwright Sir John Vanbrugh. Vanbrugh gave the Earl the sumptuous baroque palace he so desperately wanted, but indulged his own preferences for battlements in the walls and outbuildings. The extraordinary thing about this commission is that when Vanbrugh was approached by Howard he was a military man just embarking on a remarkably successful second career as a popular playwright, and so far as is known he had never before shown the slightest inclination towards architecture. Yet he was incontrovertibly appointed the architect for Castle Howard, and even if he was aided by Nicholas Hawksmoor it seems that the design was his.

Before reaching Vanbrugh's fortified walls, the visitor encounters at the extreme edge of the Howard estate, on Bulmer Hill near Welburn, the column to the memory of George William Frederick Howard, the 7th Earl. The column was designed by F. P. Cockerell. The Carrmire Gate of *c.*1725, a rusticated arch with broken pediment and six tiny pyramids on piers, running off into castellated walls, is actually by Hawksmoor. After some 2,000 feet of wall a tall gate of 1719, with side pavilions and a pyramid roof, provides the main entrance to the estate. The gate was designed by Vanbrugh, but it is the castellated wall with a total of 11 different Gothick bastions that shows his hand at its best. Some of the bastions are square, others round or hexagonal, all harking back to Vanbrugh's Blackheath Castle and the Claremont Belvedere which he had built since first starting on Castle Howard in 1699. Further north, on the crossing of the two drives, stands a 100-foot obelisk, dating from 1714 and thus Vanbrugh's first folly here.

East of the great house is Vanbrugh's Temple of the Four Winds, an offshoot of Palladio's Villa Rotonda at Vicenza and the viewing point for the carefully composed, Claude-like picture of Sion Wood to the left, the New River bridge in the middle distance and, as a focal point, Hawksmoor's gigantic mausoleum, the burial place of the 3rd Earl of Carlisle. The mausoleum is shaped like a Greek tholos, round, with pillars carrying a frieze. Around it Daniel Garrett later added the fortified wall, square with semicircular projections on each side. To the south-west of the mausoleum is the tall Hawksmoor pyramid of 1728, and further to the south-east is Pretty Wood, hiding another pyramid and a column called the

Four Face; the same name serves the large vase with four heads, one on each side, at Bramham Park.

SCAMPSTON HALL is on the A64 leading towards the coast. 'Capability' Brown worked here in 1772–3 for Sir William St Quintin, and the classical bridge with pavilion, near the house at the edge of the lake, was built to his specifications. At the back of the pavilion is a tiny cascade spanned by a wooden rustic bridge, probably of the same period. Further to the south is the deer-house, a cottage done up with a castellated façade, Gothick in style, as most deer-houses are for some reason.

Near the coast is HUNMANBY, where the sporting squire Humphrey Osbaldeston lived in Hunmanby Hall; his more famous brother George lived a few miles away at Hutton Bushel. Humphrey built himself an 'Early English' gateway to the hall, using stones from Filey Brigg, paying no heed when people protested against his pillaging of natural resources but continuing his work until the ruined gateway was complete; inevitably, coastal erosion was greatly accelerated and continues to this day. Nevertheless, this parasitical folly makes a pretty sham ruin, with the pointed windows on both sides of the arch covered in creeper. Hunmanby Gate is supposed to have been erected in 1809, although Thomas Allen in his *History of the County of York* (1831) gives the date as 1829.

SCARBOROUGH has a folly or two, not counting the 75-foot war memorial obelisk on the summit of Oliver's Mount with its spectacular views over the sea and surrounding countryside. South of the town is Baron Albert's Tower of 1842, a ruin, though never intended as such. The tower takes its name from the builder, Albert Denison, 1st Baron Londesborough, who as President of the British Archaeological Association was very much interested in Saxon tumuli. Just inland from North Bay is one of Scarborough's many public gardens, the Japanesque Peasholme Park which was begun at the height of the fashion, in Edwardian times. It has everything – a glen, miniature lakes, a cascade and two islands in the main lake – and the buildings, a floating bandstand, a café and the *pièce de résistance*, the Pagoda, are all in the Japanese style. The two-storey, 30-foot high pagoda was designed by George W. Alderson as late as 1929. Normally at night during the season the large waterfall is illuminated, and, to add to all these pleasures, mock naval battles are fought on the lake twice a week — a pleasant revival of a popular folly pastime. In 1984, however, the park was closed and the grand cascade silent — we hope this is only temporary.

Further north along the coast is the romantically named ROBIN HOOD'S BAY, where the outlaw is supposed to have had some ships ready for any necessary escapes. Here Fyling Old Hall has a pigsty screened by a classical façade with Egyptian details, built for the eccentric Squire Barry *c.*1883. Directly west is the 45-foot FALLING FORCE (or Foss) on Sneaton Moor, where in nearby Newton Woods a hermitage has been hollowed out of the solid rock. A pointed entrance leads into a room which can seat up to 20 people. The rock itself is inscribed 'The Hermitage' and 'G + C 1790'. Newton Hall, not far off, has an obelisk to the memory of James Brown, who made the moor 'blossom like a rose'.

Near Colen Campbell's tiny, elegant EBBERSTON Lodge, inland on the A170, is King Aelfrid's Cave where the Northumbrian King is supposed to have succumbed to mortal wounds received in battle. Above the cave towers a sham tumulus, erected as a memorial to King Aelfrid in 1790. West of HELMSLEY is Duncombe Park, with Duncombe Terrace, a drive flanked by two temples: an Ionic Temple of *c.*1730 which has been attributed to Vanbrugh, and a slightly later Tuscan Temple. Like the Aislabies, the Duncombes were fortunate in having the ruins of a genuine abbey, Rievaulx, in their grounds. In about 1758 a second terrace was made, directly overlooking the abbey ruins, and at intervals trees on the steep bank were cut away so that a series of carefully composed views revealed themselves to promenaders. This beautiful half-mile walk along Rievaulx Terrace (a National Trust property) starts from the Tuscan Temple and moves towards the Ionic Temple, which contains some startlingly ugly furniture by William Kent. There have been plans to link both terraces, so that the resulting drive would be about three miles in length.

Just north of the ruins of nearby BYLAND ABBEY is a belvedere tower, built by J. Dodds for John Wormald, a partner in Child's Bank and father of the famous surgeon Thomas Wormald, in the year Victoria ascended to the throne. The square tower is rather plain, topped by iron railings, with only cruciform windows as a nod to the Middle Ages. Wormald was optimistic about the young Queen's forthcoming reign. A poem above the door to the tower reads:

See rich industry smiling on the plains
And peace and plenty tell Victoria reigns!

In the northern part of the beautiful country town of RICHMOND is Temple Lodge, a Gothick castellated mansion built in 1769 for another John Yorke. In the grounds is a Gothick contraption, an octagonal tower on a square base, with an outside staircase, pinnacles and Gothick windows. The Culloden Tower was built in 1747, immediately after the battle, and commemorated the strong involvement of the Yorke family. Joseph Yorke, John's son, fought at Culloden, while Charles and Philip Yorke were both responsible for legislation concerning the Pretender and his fellow travellers. Unlike the great majority of follies, the interior of Culloden Tower is sumptuously decorated in the rococo style; even more unlike most follies, the decoration is in excellent repair and is likely to remain so, since the tower has been bought by the Landmark Trust. The architect is thought to be Daniel Garrett, and the same goes for the Temple at Aske Hall, a mile or so north of the Culloden Tower. Aske Hall Temple is one of the largest Gothick follies in Britain, and was probably used as a banqueting house. The base is formed by an arcade with a central projecting entrance and half-round endbays. On top of this is a two-storey central block, castellated, with two half-round turrets at the flanks, also castellated. This is typical façade architecture, with only a staircase at the back, supposedly to allow bawds from the town to enter unobserved. Bawds? In Richmond, Yorkshire? In all probability the staircase was put at the back so as not to interfere with the over-all concept of the design.

Another even more intriguing, though less grand, folly is Oliver Duckett, on the other side of the road and further south. This was once the site of the home of Mr Oliver Duckett, and the folly is one of the few to have been named after a person. Sir Conyers Darcy took the building, a medieval pillbox and once an outpost for Richmond Castle, and 'restored' it into a thoroughly martial folly, with a high projecting and virtually unassailable base and a round bastion tower with ample gunports and a pointed door and window. As there is absolutely no entrance in the base, the only access could have been by ladder.

A mile to the north is SEDBURY Hall at Gilling West, which has a little watch-tower exquisitely sited on an outcrop of rock, built at the beginning of the 19th century by John Foss for Sir Robert D'Arcy Hildyard. The splendidly castellated farm buildings on the same estate are earlier, and could well have been designed by John Carr *c.* 1770; they make a bold and lively eyecatcher from across the valley. Also in the vicinity are an embattled cottage and an archway to HARTFORTH HALL, assembled out of the bric-à-brac of a demolished medieval church.

South Yorkshire

South Yorkshire is as poor in follies as North Yorkshire is rich. The urban expanses of Sheffield, Rotherham, Doncaster and dozens of industrial villages leave little space for follies, and the few that do appear are dominated in quantity and quality by the buildings at Wentworth Woodhouse and Wentworth Castle.

A small, squat structure is the first building on the A1 as we cross the county boundary from West Yorkshire. Near the signpost to BURGHWALLIS the arched, square little building suddenly pops up on the left. Robin Hood's Well, as it is called, was carefully moved to this site when the A1 was widened, and now it sits at the end of the lorry-filled lay-by. This unassuming object has been preserved when so many others are lost because it is thought to have been designed by Vanbrugh in 1711. The original site marked the spot where the Bishop of Hereford was said to have been forced to dance after being robbed by Robin Hood.

On SUTTON MOOR, a mile or two east of Burghwallis, a square castellated tower and a companion obelisk hide their history from the interested folly-hunter. We could not discover date, builder, architect or reason for their existence. We know more about Locke Park Tower in BARNSLEY, a typical Victorian idiocy comprising a 70-foot belvedere tower with a round wooden hut on top of a punctiliously correct Italianate drum, built in 1877. Locke Park had been donated to the people of Barnsley by Phoebe Locke in memory of her husband Joseph, a prosperous railway engineer. Phoebe died in 1866, and 11 years later her sister, Miss McCreary, erected the tower as a memorial to her, a memorial within a memorial. The initials 'S. M. C.' are still visible on the weather-

444

vane. The obelisk and statue on top of Kendray Hill, a mile to the east of Locke Park, is not a folly but a monument to the 361 men and boys killed in the underground explosion at the Oaks colliery in 1866.

BIRDWELL, south of Barnsley, muddled us. We looked for a hermitage because of a steep hill called Hermit's Hill; we found that Lady's Folly at nearby Tankersley had been demolished; and we fruitlessly tried to hunt down the reported 'Boston Castle' — but all we found was an obelisk standing like a mene tekel and declaring 'Wentworth Castle 3 miles/1775'. But Wentworth Castle must wait a little longer. 'Boston Castle' was said to have been demolished when the M1 was built, but there were unconfirmed reports that it had been reprieved. It turned out to be a case of mistaken identity — a pity, for to judge from an old photograph it was a remarkable eyecatcher in a curious asymmetrical design. The story that it had been erected by the 3rd Earl of Effingham to celebrate the Boston Tea Party was grafted on to this building — there was great sympathy for the American colonies' struggle against the Crown among the Whig aristocracy — but the story actually belongs to the *real* Boston Castle, a square, castellated shooting-box standing over the Rother valley, a mile south of ROTHERHAM. Tea is said to have been forbidden at the house-warming in 1775, a doubtful sacrifice, as one cannot imagine the assembled lords to have been seriously incommoded by the prohibition. Both follies could well have been built by the same architect, and for the same patron, for the castellations of both fake and genuine had the same hard edge. Near Birdwell in HOYLAND NETHER is another hunting-tower or folly, Hoyland Lowe Stand, again a tower with little history. Two storeys high, with a higher turret, it seems to date from the 18th century.

On quite a different level from the Boston Castle vagaries is the mystery concerning dates and the builder of Hartcliffe Tower at Thurlstone, near PENISTONE. The tower itself is simple enough: round, roughstone and plain, though we do not know what the roof was like since it was blown off in a gale. The architect, or rather the head mason, was a Mr Askham from Thurlstone. 'About 1851' is the nearest we can get to a date, while a Captain Ramsden is said to have been the builder. But John Ramsden, a local man who was a captain in the East India Company's mercantile fleet, died in 1841. A puzzle. Not far away, towards Cubley, is a square, battered gazebo with pointed windows on all sides and an oriental looking roof, topped by a pike.

In SHEFFIELD, monuments, rather than follies, are thick on the ground. The Cholera Monument is a Gothic spire just east of the Midland station in a public park off Norfolk Road. It commemorates the 400 cholera victims buried there in 1832, the year the monument was built. The Crimean War Monument, which cost £1,000 to build, has now been moved from its old mid-town site to the Botanical Gardens in the south-west of the town. However, some relief from worthy monuments was provided by Mr Charles Simmons, who between the wars built a castellated sham castle in Longford Road.

That rivalry has sometimes been a cause for the building of follies is well illustrated in the case of the Wentworth Castle and Wentworth Woodhouse estates. When William Wentworth died in 1695 he made Thomas Watson his heir, rather than, as expected, Thomas Wentworth. Understandably irritated, and in a permanent fit of pique, Wentworth, later the 1st Earl of Strafford of the second creation, built Wentworth Castle at Hood Green, seven miles away from his kinsman's Wentworth Woodhouse residence. The first folly Strafford erected was a sham castle set on a hill west of Wentworth Castle, called Stainborough Castle. According to Horace Walpole, it was built 'in the true style' — in other words, conforming to contemporary ideals. The four round corner towers were named after Strafford himself and his three daughters (why not his wife?), but only the south-east tower still stands, the others having collapsed in 1962, after a storm that also destroyed most of the trees in Bramham Park. Stainborough must have been built before 1730, very early for a fully-fledged sham castle.

Near the entrance to the house is Steeple Lodge, probably also built by the 1st Earl (a copy of this folly was erected by the 2nd Earl at Boughton in Northamptonshire). Steeple Lodge is a fake church, the main feature of which is a Gothick tower with four obelisk-like pinnacles on each corner. The adjacent castellated cottage is inhabited, so the folly is well looked after. When the 1st Earl died in 1739 William Wentworth inherited, and the first thing he seems to have done was to erect, near Stainborough Castle, another obelisk, dedicated to Mary Wortley Montagu, one of his neighbours and the introducer, in 1720, of smallpox inoculations into England.

At Wentworth as well as Boughton the new Earl's building fever resulted in a great number of often very elaborate follies, spurred on by Walpole's ever favourable comments. In 1743 a Column to Minerva, in the Corinthian order, was put up to commemorate the death of Wentworth's father-in-law, the 2nd Duke of Argyll, and in 1756 Rockley Woodhouse followed, a classical building with a tower, of which no trace remains. Three years later a copy of the famous Chichester market cross was completed in Menagerie Wood. It had taken a long time to evolve: Walpole had written in 1752 to Richard Bentley, his architect-protégé, that he would bring him 'a ground plot for a Gothic building which I have proposed you should draw for a little wood, but in the manner of an ancient market cross'. Now the cross is in ruins, and restoration is urgently needed if we are not to lose every trace of one of Bentley's best efforts. A folly that has totally disappeared deserves a mention here, as it is often confused with Stainborough Castle, and even now people persist in quoting Walpole's 'the ruins of a large imaginary City' with regard to the sham castle. The 'City' was, however, the ruins of fortifications built in 1765–6 on the edge of a hill on Worsborough Common, about two miles east of Wentworth. On nearby Blacker Common another string of fortifications was added a year later, together with a pyramid known as the Smoothing Iron. All this, including a Chinese Temple, has gone, leaving Wentworth Woodhouse the leader in South Yorkshire follies.

It had not always been this way. Walpole, after lauding Strafford ('Nobody has a better taste than this Lord'), continued with a description of the rival follies at WENTWORTH WOODHOUSE: 'Now contrast all this, and you may have some idea of Lord Rockingham's . . . There are temples in cornfields; and in the little wood, a windowframe mounted on a bunch of laurels, and intended for a hermitage.' Despite Walpole's comments the follies at Wentworth Woodhouse have outlived, and bettered, their neighbours. Thomas Watson, 1st Marquess of Rockingham, built only one of the Wentworth 'specials' – the impressive Hoober Stand, designed by

Henry Flitcroft and erected in 1748 to celebrate the Pretender's defeat at Culloden, where Watson had also fought. Hoober Stand is as strange as its name, over 100 feet of smoke-blackened yellowstone, triangular, with rounded corners tapering towards the top and lucarne windows to light the now inaccessible staircase. From a distance it hovers over the horizon like the apparition of a crazy factory chimney, but the iron railings at the top proclaim its true function as a belvedere tower. It is a unique structure, an appendix in the history of architecture — we know of no other like it in the world — but its enchanting name turns out to have a prosaic meaning: Hoober is a nearby hamlet, while Stand is the local name for a tower.

The 2nd Marquess of Rockingham matched his neighbour's *folie de bâtir*. In 1776–81 John Carr built a huge, solitary Tuscan column for him, 15 feet higher than Hoober Stand, as a monument to Viscount Keppel, Rockingham's First Lord of the Admiralty, who had earlier achieved immense public popularity when he was acquitted in a court martial on five charges including 'scandalous haste in quitting the scene of a naval engagement'. Keppel's Column stands south of the house, beside the A629. Again, it was built as a belvedere. The enlargement *ad absurdum* of what is after all only an architectural element carries Keppel's Column beyond the boundaries of mere monument and makes it into a perfect folly. Coincidentally, a young naval officer who, under pressure from Sir Hugh Palliser, falsified his log and testified against Admiral Keppel had a column built to *his* memory near Street in Somerset — 50 years later, when he had become Admiral Sir Samuel Hood.

Around 1780 another unique structure appeared on the estate, north of the house in a small wood. The Needle's Eye, a slender pyramid with a tall ogee arch through it and a flamboyant urn on top, was probably designed by Carr, but the most important factor behind this beautiful folly is the story of how it came to be, a story at once ridiculous and credible. One night the Marquess, like Tommy Osborne an excellent coach-and-four man, accepted a flattering wager that he could 'drive a carriage through the eye of a needle'. The sober dawn brought home the monstrosity of the bet, and also the impossibility of failure; hence the construction of this elegant wager winner, a narrow arch just wide enough to allow a coach through, and called 'The Needle's Eye'. We will never really know the truth of these wager/folly stories (see the tales about Mad Jack Fuller in Sussex) but the Marquess was known to favour the odd bet: he once staked £500 on a race between five turkeys and five geese from Norwich to London.

Rockingham died in 1782 and was interred in a three-storey mausoleum near Nether Haugh, built by John Carr in 1785–91. There are yet more follies at Wentworth Woodhouse: first, the Round House, a castellated ex-windmill not far from the Needle's Eye, with neither date nor architect; and over the road from the Round House, close by a garden centre set within the remains of an early 19th-century Japanese garden, the Bearpit, an underground tunnel with barred niches where the bears had their quarters. The two entrances to the Bearpit are highly decorated with festoons, volutes and shields, all in the mannerist style of the early 17th century. A couple of free-standing, ill-proportioned statues probably date from the same time.

West Yorkshire

Despite the collieries and textile mills, West Yorkshire still has quite a few follies. There is a preference for Gothick towers, most of them in the area round Bradford, which is J. B. Priestley and John Braine territory. A scene in Braine's *Room at the Top* is set in a fictional Gothick folly:

> The Folly was an artificial ruin in the Gothic style. There were three turrets, sawn off, as it were, obliquely, and far too small ever to have been much use as turrets. The tallest even had two window slits. One side of the main building had a door and an aurora of stone around it, and the other had three windows ending a little too abruptly half way up. It was very solidly built . . . 'My great-great-great-grandpa built this,' Susan said. 'He was called Peregrine St Clair and he was terribly dissipated and used to be a friend of Byron's. Mummy told me a bit about it; he had orgies here. All of Warley practically was St Clair and he could do just what he liked.'

After this splendid introduction the first folly in the county is a disappointment. At WETHERBY in the north-eastern tip of West Yorkshire is a garden containing a gazebo brought over in the 1930s from Ferriby Hall in Humberside. It is simply a square room with a pyramidal roof topped by an urn, dating from the second half of the 18th century.

BRAMHAM PARK, due south of Wetherby, has more buildings but again nothing particularly distinguished, save the Gothick Temple. Most of the Bramham buildings were raised for George Fox, Lord Bingley. The provenance of the Gothick Temple, in the southern part of the park near the graves of the family's dogs, can be traced through two design books. The temple dates from 1750 and has been attributed to James Paine, in which case Paine lifted it straight out of Batty Langley's plate number 57 in *Gothic Architecture Improved* (1747). This in turn was based on plates 70 and 71 in James Gibbs's 1729 *A Book of Architecture*. Langley expanded on Gibbs's classical design: the pilasters were changed to buttresses and the round windows became Wankel pistons, while the round-arched door and windows on the ground floor grew pointed and on top of the structure a band of ogee gables with trefoils and finials was added. As it now stands, only very minor details were changed in Paine's final version. A classical temple near the entrance, originally an orangery designed by Paine, has been converted into a chapel. The other temples are also classical, except for a rustic house, once thatched, and an 1845 Gothic summer-house to the south. Richard Pococke's *Travels Through England*, a manuscript account of his visits to parks and country houses, contains a description of Bramham. Apparently Pococke found the number and variety of temples bewildering:

> One comes round to a Dorick building like the front of a temple & then to a Gothick building not quite finished [the Langley copy] & so one descends to the water, from which there is an avenue to the house, & another up to a round Ionick Temple, something in imitation of the Temple of Hercules at Tivoli . . . & from [the ascent to the temple] are three or four visto's cut, one of which is terminated by a Dorick building, something like the Portico of Covent garden Church: — & to the west of the garden in the Park is a thatched house, to which the family sometimes go for variety & take some refreshments . . .

Pococke visited Bramham in 1750, so would not have seen the obelisk behind the 'Ionick Temple', erected in 1763. In the northern part of the garden is 'The Four Faces', an urn on a pedestal with four faces representing the four seasons.

On the outskirts of ABERFORD are the remains of Parlington Park, with the Triumphal or Victory Arch, a rickety three-arched conceit proclaiming 'LIBERTY . IN . N . AMERICA . TRIUMPHANT . MDCCLXXXIII'. It was designed by Thomas Leverton for Sir Thomas Gascoigne in

1781, when Cornwallis's surrender brought a successful end to the American Revolution. The arch was not completed until the 1783 Treaty of Versailles. Gascoigne was an MP, and he was not alone in his pro-Republican stance, or in going so far as to commit himself in stone to honour a rebellion against the Crown — the Duke of Norfolk built his follies at Greystoke in Cumbria for the same reason. Obviously not everyone was like-minded. In 1806 the Prince of Wales came to visit Parlington, got as far as the arch, read the inscription and immediately turned back. Also in the park is the crumbling base of a round tower — the main house was demolished in 1950, and the follies suffer from neglect as a result.

The boat-house at Kettlethorpe Hall in NEWMILLERDAM is now incongruously set with its back to 20th-century housing. It is the medieval façade of the old Bridge Chapel in Wakefield, consisting of five pointed arches and gables and a ruined second storey. The façade was re-erected here in 1847 when it was decided to renovate the chapel. Behind it a room has been made. The whole building is rather battered, as befits a building in a public park, but this is one of its main charms. The park also contains the ruin of a Gothic cattleshed.

Two miles to the east is WALTON HALL, now a sports club and once the residence of one of Britain's greatest eccentrics, the traveller, naturalist, taxidermist and devout Catholic Squire Charles Waterton (1782–1865). Waterton was far too practical to bother with any deliberate follies, but in the course of his long life enough ornamentation was added to his house and grounds to be considered as such. Early on, Waterton turned his estate into a nature reserve, keeping out poachers by means of a three-mile wall. Most of his buildings reflected his concern for animals — a couple of stone pigsties, an intrusion-proof tower for the birds — but he was also no stranger to mottomania, placing a millstone round a tree and inscribing it 'The National Debt'. The smaller buildings at Walton Hall were designed and erected by Jack Ogden, a former mason and poacher turned keeper. Unlike many animal lovers, Waterton quite liked humans as well, and he regularly opened the grounds and even the house to visitors. According to *Charles Waterton: His Home, Habits and Handiwork*, written by his friend Richard Hobson, he even constructed a 'Chair-swing, of truly

170 Carnaby Temple, Bridlington

171   The Ashton Memorial, Lancaster

172 Mowbray Castle, Hackfall, Grewelthorpe

173 Tatton Sykes Memorial, Sledmere

178 Mowbray Point in Hackfall Gardens, Grewelthorpe

179 Akebar caravan shop, Constable Burton

180   Folly Gate, Hunmanby

181   Druids' temple, Ilton Moor

182   The Octagon, Studley Royal

183 Craigiehall Temple, Cramond Bridge

184 Kinkell Pyramid, Cononbridge

185   The Choragic Monument of Lysicrates, Calton Hill, Edinburgh

186   The National Monument, Calton Hill, Edinburgh

noble dimensions and of extensive sweep, in which many a buxom country girl has joyously received the swinging attentions of her devoted swain . . . '.

The entrance to the house still surprises visitors with its two door-knockers; the one in the form of a welcoming face is a fake, while the other works, and makes a face appropriate to the occasion. In the grounds is a roughstone grotto, sometimes put to good use:

> . . . the hundred lunatics, from the Wakefield Asylum, who were wont to be kindly permitted by Mr Waterton to have their harmless and frolicsome merriment — their dancing, and their dinner, within the grotto — were always delighted, and even tranquillised, so as to temporarily forget their pitiable and frequently unhappy condition, and one and all to declare the grotto to be an elysium.

An old Water Gate, which together with a swivel cannon had once held off Cromwell's troops, was embellished by Waterton with a cross. Some years earlier a cross had been erected on top of a temple near the grotto, and this was held by Waterton to have been the first to be erected in public view in England since the Reformation.

Nostell Priory in WRAGBY is a National Trust property three miles east of Walton. It was built for the Winn family by James Paine, with Robert Adam adding a wing in 1766. Adam would also seem to have been responsible for the remarkable Pyramid Lodge pierced by an arch and otherwise known as 'The Needle's Eye' — the much more famous Needle's Eye at Wentworth Woodhouse in South Yorkshire is only 25 miles away. In the park are several Gothick fabrics, among them an arched seat and the Menagerie, which was the keeper's cottage. This too has been ascribed to Adam, but if so it is not one of his finer works. It is polygonal, with pointed windows and doors and rather weak castellations.

HUDDERSFIELD itself has two folly-towers. The Victoria Jubilee Tower of 1897, south of the town on the 900-foot Castle Hill at Almondbury, is a grim, grey, square, tapering tower with a higher corner turret and a spectacular view from the top. It is a popular local tourist attraction, not least because of the pub on the opposite hill. The author of an Edwardian guide-book, hardened to the claims made on behalf of various belvedere towers, pointed out that 'The Victoria Tower commands a wide view, in which, *of course*, York Minster is *sometimes* visible'. The second tower is in the north-west perimeter of the town, in LINDLEY. It is a square clock-tower with an octagonal pagoda roof of copper, originally built for the Sykes family by the arts and crafts architect Edgar Wood, and with sculptures by T. Stirling Lee: 'This tower was erected by James Neild Sykes Esq JP of Field Head, Lindley for the benefit of his native village in 1902'. A desire for beauty more than folly seems to have conjured up this delectable tower, an important contribution to the architectural mood at the turn of this century. The survivals in Ravensknowle Park are perhaps more congruous with the word folly. The park, a mile and a half to the east of the town centre, was donated to Huddersfield as a First World War memorial. After the Huddersfield Cloth Hall was demolished in 1929, parts of it were removed to Ravensknowle, where the old clock-tower was re-erected on top of a shelter made of stones from the old Hall.

Kirklees Park in BRIGHOUSE has the most improbable epitaph we have discovered on our travels affixed to Robin Hood's Grave, an enclosure with railings. While there seems to be no reason why this should not be the site of Robin's grave, the inscription is wonderfully bogus:

> Hear Underneath dis laitl stean
> Laz robert earl of Huntingtun
> Ne'er arcir ver az hie sa geud
> An pipl Kauld im robin heud
> Sick utlawz az hi an iz men
> Vil england nivr si agen

> Obiit 24 Kal Dekembris 1247

Bierley, on the outskirts of BRADFORD, has a dilapidated grotto — a jumble of rocks which could be described as cavelets — and the remains of a fake stone circle in the park where Bierley Hall once stood, now the hospital. No dates, no builder. There is nothing special to see in Bradford except its answer to Highgate: Undercliffe Cemetery has some remarkably fine monuments.

HALIFAX can boast the best folly in the county, one of the finest in the whole country: Wainhouse's Tower, also known as Wainhouse's Folly or the Octagon Tower. The preoccupations of John Edward Wainhouse (1817–83) resemble those of R. H. Watt in Knutsford, Cheshire. Both started their building activities late in life; both built a remarkable factory tower (although the Wainhouse one stands supreme); and both threw into the bargain some quaintly decorated cottages. It all started with the Smoke Abatement Act of 1870. Wainhouse owned, together with a large fortune from an inheritance, the Washer Lane Dye Works in southern Halifax, which was run by a manager. After the Act came into force, it became necessary to build a tall chimney to carry the smoke out of the valley in which the works were built. In 1871 plans were drawn up by the architect Isaac Booth for a chimney that would be fed with the smoke from the factory by means of a pipeline. In 1874 Wainhouse sold the works to his manager, who refused to bear the tremendous costs incurred in finishing the chimney. Wainhouse decided to keep it himself and convert it into a tower which he proposed to use as 'a general astronomical and physical observatory'. The tower was finally completed in 1875 by the architect Richard Swarbrick Dugdale at a total cost of £14,000, and in such an elaborate style that not even a pocket telescope could have been fitted in between the orgy of finials, pillars, buttresses and balustrades. The very slender tower rises 275 feet high, its shaft decorated with Gothicisms, and the ornate top is in a perverted but well-proportioned neo-renaissance style. The result of four years' work is a belvedere tower by a medieval watch-tower out of Château Chambord.

Wainhouse's Tower is naturally linked with its owner's feud with Sir Harry Edwards, a parvenu industrialist, Freemason and Justice of the Peace. From 1873 onwards one small incident quickly provoked another, and within a few months the two men were at each other's throats. After Edwards misused his position as JP things went from bad to worse and Wainhouse became afflicted, like so many Victorians, with the pamphleteering mania. From 1876 until he died he penned a flood of pamphlets, unanswered by Edwards, as the JP seems to have been a weak correspondent. It has been suggested that Wainhouse built the tower so that he could keep a constant eye on Edwards's activities. Another alternative is that Wainhouse was goading Edwards, who abhorred chimneys – but he also abhorred white cattle and white linen hanging out to dry (strange man) and there is no record of Wainhouse taunting him in this manner.

Wainhouse placed mottoes referring to his row with Edwards wherever he could. West Air, his eccentric house (no two windows are the same), was built in 1877, also by Dugdale, and has, among others, an inscription quoting the *Aeneid*: 'Parcere subjectis et debellare superbos': 'Spare the lowly and make war upon the proud'. Wainhouse not only spared the lowly, he also took to embellishing their humble abodes. In Scarr Bottom a row of cottages was fitted out with mottoes and ornate Gothic porches, while the houses in Wainhouse Terrace had their balconies renewed and supported by a colonnade like a Mediterranean stoa. The balcony can be reached by two bridges projecting from squat, machicolated towers; sadly the houses have now been demolished, but the gallery remains.

Another conspicuous folly in the area is the obelisk called Stoodley Pike, two miles east of TODMORDEN. In 1814, after Paris had surrendered, it was decided by the local gentry to erect a commemorative obelisk to be paid for by public subscription. Building was stopped when word reached Todmorden that Napoleon had escaped from Elba, but started again when word reached Todmorden of the triumph at Waterloo. The finished result was a weird structure, a base with a fat column on it topped by a tall cone. On 8 February 1854, however, the obelisk collapsed, and the *Halifax Guardian* commented on this as an 'evil omen', since on the same day word reached Todmorden that the Russian Ambassador had left England prior to the outbreak of the Crimean War. The prominent burgesses of the town decided to build a new obelisk, and by 1 June plans were submitted. The new monument, the same height (120 feet) as the old one but built to a different design, was ready in time to celebrate the peace treaty between Britain and Russia. The architect was a local man, James Green, and the building contractor a Mr Lewis Crabtree. Wise after the event, they prudently surrounded the new obelisk with eight heavy buttresses upon which a balustrade was erected, with the obelisk proper towering above. It cost £812, and the momentous occasion was fêted by the Todmorden poet J. Barnes:

> . . . like the fabled Phoenix, thou
> From thy ashes rose
> Thy friends were firmer, greater, now,
> Than had been all thy foes . . .

The inscription on the obelisk reads:

STOODLEY PIKE

A PEACE MONUMENT

ERECTED BY PUBLIC SUBSCRIPTION

Commenced in 1814 to commemorate the surrender of Paris to the Allies and finished after the Battle of Waterloo when peace was established in 1815. By a strange coincidence the Pike fell on the day the Russian Ambassador left London before the declaration of war with Russia in 1854, and it was rebuilt when peace was proclaimed in 1856.

Repaired and lightning conductor fixed 1889.

Curiously, the obelisk has remained standing, despite 1914, 1939 and even 1982. It is so solid that probably only a nuclear blast would topple it.

Every English county has its share of splendid place-names, and West Yorkshire is no exception, with Goose Eye, Scapegoat Hill, Triangle, California, Krumlin, Canada, Toot Hill, Catherine Slack and many others. West of Bradford is a hamlet called EGYPT where some former quarreymen built grit walls along the road, earning the stretch the rather grandiose title of 'The Walls of Jericho'.

South of KEIGHLEY in the Worth Valley is Oakworth Park, now Oakworth Municipal Park. The mansion, of which only the portico has been left standing, belonged to Sir Isaac Holden (1807–97), inventor and textile millionaire. Holden was something of a health crank, though he redeemed himself by smoking a couple of cigars a day and having the occasional drink. His mind was rather fixed on the outdoor life, but to shelter his wife on rainy days he attached a winter garden to the house. This alone was reputed to have cost him £120,000, a preposterous sum, although other sources go as low as £30,000 – still not cheap, but including a Turkish bath. The winter garden has been lost, but the park itself has deteriorated only slightly. Work was carried out between 1864 and 1874 by specially imported Italian and French labourers, who made the gardens into a twilight world of caves, grottoes and underpasses. Most of the paraphernalia is still there: the summer-house, the grand cascade, the grottoes and, the star attraction, the sham fossil tree which, on closer inspection, reveals a flight of steps leading to the hanging gardens.

Although it differs from his description, St David's Ruin, overlooking the B6429 at HARDEN Banks, near the 'Malt Shovel', was the inspiration for John Braine's fictional St Clair folly. It was built for Benjamin Ferrand in 1796 (the initials and date are carved in the pointed door arch) and served as an eyecatcher to his now demolished St Ives, built in 1759 by James Paine. The ruin was tidied up in the 1950s, when the artfully damaged tower, which left one Gothick window-frame intact though surrounded by crumbling masonry, was truncated into a neat cylinder with a band delineating the start of the second storey. A piece of ruined wall with a pointed arch through it stands on its own; once it was probably connected. St David's Ruin is a superb example of the Mow Cop genre of folly – more precise and controlled than its predecessors Mow Cop and Old John, more Georgian in atmosphere, but certainly one of the three best interpretations of this style in the country.

The Old Tower, off the A6034 above CRINGLES on Rombalds Moor, seems to have lost its credentials; it was probably a hunting stand. The part of the moors near Ilkley to the east used to have another hunting tower by the Thimble Stones, on the highest point of the moor. Elam's Tower, in the grounds of Woodhouse Grove School in APPERLEY BRIDGE, still survives in reasonable condition, although a degree of vandalism has inevitably occurred. Robert Elam bought Lower Wortley Manor, as it was then known, in 1799, and on the hill where the tower now stands was a pagoda, probably built by the previous owners. The village unemployed were set to work to pull down the pagoda and erect the tower in its stead, and it was completed in 1804. The locals refer to it as the Old Water Tower, but it is doubtful if it was used as such.

In OTLEY churchyard is a replica of the northern entrance of the

Bramhope Railway Tunnel – a tunnel folly as grand as Clayton in West Sussex – built as a memorial to the navvies who died driving the two and a quarter mile tunnel under Bramhope Moor. Its façade, with one polygonal turret and a higher, round turret flanking the arched entrance, has been repeated at the other end of the monument to give two matching façades with a short length of tunnel in between. The structure, which looks like a large toy fort, is only about six feet high, and it was paid for by the contractors, sub-contractors and those who survived. Appropriate biblical texts adorn the monument, which curiously doesn't mention how many men were killed – probably between 18 and 30. The tunnel itself was built in 1845–9, and the larger turret was used to house railway staff before becoming a store; now it is derelict and the floors have fallen in. As far as British Rail is concerned, this is not the age of the folly.

ADEL is a village on the verge of being swallowed by Leeds. In Back Church Lane, at York Gate, a small garden has been created; it is quite recent, and plants and tiny buildings are still being added. Several pieces from demolished buildings have found a refuge here, and some were used in the three garden buildings: an arbour with a slate roof; a stone classical tempietto; and an open, rustic construction rather grandly called 'The Folly'. It is good to see tradition carried on. LEEDS itself has a surprising diversity of follies. Weetwood Hall, north of the town centre, has a good Victorian grotto, looking older, and in Cardigan Road is a bear-pit which was once part of the Leeds Zoological and Botanical Gardens, opened in 1840. Now it stands forlornly among modern houses in the north-western quarter of the city. The bear-pit has a sham castle façade of two castellated turrets and a wall in between, with three barred entrances for the bears' lairs. The walls and towers are crumbling, inadvertently turning the sham castle into a sham ruin.

Roundhay Park, on the north-eastern edge of Leeds, has a more substantial ruin. The 800-acre park was laid out for Thomas Nicholson in the 1820s; in 1872 it was bought by Leeds Corporation for the large sum of £140,000 and opened to the public by Prince Arthur. Only a few amenities for visitors had to be added, since there was already a rustic hermitage on the upper lake and a sham castle, curiously unnamed, near Waterloo Lake. The castle is square, with round corner towers, the tallest at the front, and a pointed entrance and cruciform arrowslits in between. The folly is very well done, built out of roughstone, which catches just the right flavour. The same material was used for Cobble Hall, a large lodge to the east of the castle, also castellated and with pointed windows. The 'tasteful, circular Corinthian temple presented to the borough in 1882 by the late Sir John Barran, Bart', described in the 1909 edition of *Baddeley's Yorkshire*, is now known simply as 'The Fountain'. Another sham castle in the Stonegate Road, King Alfred's Castle, was demolished some years ago.

Southern Leeds is the more industrialised part of town; there is little call for surburban sham castles. Yet the area contains buildings stranger than cardboard Camelots — an Egyptian mill, an Italian chimney and a Moorish warehouse. The Temple Mills in Marshall Street were built for John Marshall in 1842 by Joseph Bonomi Jr, brother of the more famous Ignatius, and James Combe, a local architect. The whole Temple Mills project is alleged to have cost around £250,000. It was worth it. It was a matter of course to build the chimneys in the shape of obelisks, but the façade is the real wonder — trapeziform, with winged emblems above the entrance and a portico with huge lotus-flower capitals. The grime on the building and the ignorant lettering of the firm that took over the premises are the only non-Egyptian motifs. Bonomi drew his inspiration from the temples at Dendera, Edfu and Philae after spending eight years in Egypt. On his return he set up practice with an almost unrivalled knowledge of Egyptian architecture, confident that it was to be the next fashionable style — but apart from the spring at Hartwell House in Buckinghamshire, the Egyptian Court at the Crystal Palace and this wonderful mill, commissions were virtually non-existent.

An enlightened and considerate employer, John Marshall had his mill equipped with 66 glass domes on the flat roof in order to let daylight percolate to the factory floor. Then he conceived the idea of allowing his workers somewhere to relax, so he had the rest of the roof grassed over to provide a spacious lawn. Mowing was a problem, with all the domes in the way, but Marshall hit on a brilliant solution: he hoisted up a flock of sheep which had the dual benefit of keeping the grass cropped and providing extra wool for the mill. Unfortunately one of the more adventurous sheep clambered on to a glass dome and hurtled through to its death, killing one of Mr Marshall's employees in the process. Few factory workers meet Nemesis in the shape of a flying sheep nowadays; despite this sad accident Marshall appears to have had his workers' interests foremost.

It was through the influence of Sir Robert Rawlinson, civil engineer and pamphleteer, that the Tower Works in Globe Road acquired its towers. In 1857 Sir Robert complained to *The Builder* about the ugliness of the average factory chimney, and in 1858 he published *Designs of Factory Shafts*, followed some time later by *Designs for Factory, Furnace and Other Tall Chimneys*, in which the medieval and Italian renaissance styles of tower were favourably discussed. Rawlinson found an ally in the battle against the Dull Chimney in J. C. Loudon, the leader of contemporary opinion on matters such as landscape gardening and architecture. As a direct result of the campaign Thomas Shaw, a Yorkshire architect, built the first of the Globe Road chimneys in 1864, inspired by the Lamberti tower in Verona. When a second tower was needed, a very tall copy of the gothic campanile in Florence by Giotto was built. It was finished in 1899, together with a boiler-house which serves as a monument to those who furthered the cause of the textile industry. The campanile still makes a welcome contribution to the Leeds skyline.

In St Paul's Street is a brick and terracotta Spanish/Moorish fantasy, a warehouse built in 1878 for John Barran, a clothes manufacturer, by L. Ambler. It even used to have minarets on the roof, but these have now gone.

The final folly in West Yorkshire is small and difficult to find. In RAWDON, on the way to the Leeds/Bradford airport, is a simple domed retreat, a kind of elaborate summer-house, hidden deep against a wall in Cragg Woods. Built of stone and steel, it is still in good condition, but we do not know who built it, or when.

Scotland

Borders

Nobody needs to be told that Scotland is different from England or Wales, least of all the Scots, who have their own national folly style centred on the Gothic, mostly of a sturdy, rustic variety. That there are relatively few good follies around must be blamed on the landscape, which needs no improvement, and on the dramatic changes in national history that took place during the 18th century. The Pineapple, the Lanrick Tree (both in Central) and McCaig's Folly (Strathclyde) are astounding exceptions. In quantity, the Scots equivalent of the obelisk is the dovecote, which we have sometimes included in England because of its rarity; in Scotland the ornamental dovecote bordering on follydom is such a common commodity that we have not been able to refer to any but the finest here. Lothian is a particularly rich hunting ground. We have, however, included many steadings (Scottish farm buildings), though by no means all: the Gothicised steading is peculiar to Scotland, and good examples can be found everywhere. With so large and wild a country we feel sure that many an undiscovered folly must lurk in a lonely glen or by the shore of a remote loch. We look forward to being told of them.

The first folly to be encountered as we enter Scotland on the A7 is quite an appropriate one: the hilltop cone near TEVIOTHEAD commemorating a shepherd poet, Henry Scott Riddell. Sugar-loaves are particularly Georgian ornaments, but this one was erected as late as 1874. A short, but not too short, résumé of the poet's life is inscribed on a tablet which was fixed above the cone's entrance in 1894. Another memorial is on top of the 777-foot high PENIEL HEUGH — a round column 150 feet tall with a balustrade surrounding a conical top, celebrating the Battle of Waterloo. Further to the north, at Pirnie, is FAIRNINGTON HOUSE with a little Gothic pavilion in the grounds. The most romantic thing about it is its name, Baron's Folly.

In ECKFORD churchyard a small folly seems to have lost its way and found itself among the graves. This 12-foot high, round towerette, castellated with arrowslit windows and three steps leading to a door, was built as a watch-house, and there was to be a guard inside to scare off any body-snatchers trying to dig up a freshish cadaver for the ever-demanding dissection rooms of the medical faculties. Even in the days of cheap labour it would have been expensive to maintain a permanent watch in what is only a small village, so perhaps the watch-tower functioned like the fake alarm systems on the walls of suburban bungalows.

John Smith, father of the bridge-building John and Thomas Smith, was responsible for the sculpting of the huge naive statue of Sir William Wallace in Roman garb, towering 22 feet high on his plinth above DRYBURGH. This first monument to Scotland's national hero was erected in 1814 by the Earl of Buchan, and the plinth, showing a gay disregard for capitalisation, proclaims:

WALLACE
Great patriot hero
Ill-requited Chief

while an urn in front is inscribed:

The peerless knight of Ellerslie
Who waved on Ayr's romantic shore
The beamy torch of liberty
And roaming round from sea to sea
From glad obscure or gloomy rock
His bold compatriots called to free
This realm from Edward's iron yoke.

Wallace's counterpart is a statue at HALLYARDS, south-west of Peebles. David Ritchie, the model for Sir Walter Scott's *The Black Dwarf* (1816), is represented in a woodman's tunic, dagger in belt and leaning negligently on a tall stick. The statue was sculpted by Robert Forrest, an autodidact famous for his carvings of Scott's heroes and for the Wallace Monument in Lanark. Ritchie's cottage is to the south of Hallyards; it was expressly erected for the dwarf by Sir James Nasmyth in 1802 and has normal doors and windows except on one side, where the dwarf's special entrance is about three feet high. David Ritchie lived in this cottage until his death in 1811.

Castellations and screens on proletarian buildings achieved popularity in the Scottish Borders equal to that in the English border counties. North of Dryburgh in former Berwickshire is WESTRUTHER, where some cottages were done up with battlements to serve as eyecatchers to Spottiswood House, built in 1832 by William Burn but now demolished, while at Rosetta, a manor a mile north-west of PEEBLES, the stable block is effectively hidden behind a castellated screen. Rosetta was built in 1807 for Dr Thomas Young, physician and Egyptologist, and the house owes its name to the fact that Young helped to decipher the Rosetta Stone.

East of Peebles is TRAQUAIR House, where the unused main gates are known as the Bear Gates. They were finished in 1745 and according to one story the Earl of Traquair kept them shut after Culloden, when the last person to pass through them was Bonnie Prince Charlie. This story is perpetuated on every bottle of Traquair House Ale, a blisteringly strong beer brewed at the house and occasionally obtainable elsewhere. Implicit in this summary is approbation of the Stuart cause, but the Jacobite earl was not a wholehearted supporter of the Bonnie Prince himself at the time, and the extent of his succour lay in a promise that the Bear Gates should not be opened until the Stuarts reigned. A promise made is a promise kept, and the gates have stayed shut ever since. A less exciting story tells that the 7th Earl of Traquair closed them on the day the last Countess died, in 1796, refusing to have them opened until a new Countess came to Traquair. The brick gate piers were built in 1737–8, but it was only in 1745 that the two bears carrying the Traquair shield and the motto 'IUDGE NOUGHT' were carved by George Jamieson from stone quarried at Penicuik. Near the house are two pavilions with ogee roofs; the south pavilion has a painting of the Toilet of Venus on its ceiling.

There are two Whims in Scotland (there is a Whimsey in

Gloucestershire), and it would be pleasant had whim been adopted as the Scottish word for folly; it has the right feel. Despite the attempt at Blair Atholl in Tayside, though, the name did not catch on. WHIM House on the borders of Lothian acquired its name through the siting of the estate by Archibald Campbell, 3rd Duke of Argyll, and here again whim is used in the same context as folly would have been in England. Argyll bought the terrain, ominously called Blair Bogg, in 1729, from his friend Thomas Cochrane. The transaction was treated as a joke between the two men – 'a Comical Bargain' – but the duke was bent on making the estate arable and after 30 years of hard work and a vast outlay there were nurseries, pleasure grounds and gardens at Whim. Formerly there was a castellated dovecote designed by Lord Milton, the Duke's associate, but this was truncated years ago. The story of Milton designing the dovecote sheds some interesting light on the practice of folly building: he apparently searched contemporary architectural pattern books for a Gothick tower as a model; not finding what he wanted, he had to resort to his own inventiveness.

At BLYTH BRIDGE's Netherurd House is an entrance arch made of two whalebones fixed to folly-style gate piers. The house itself was built in 1791–4 for William Lawson by Robert Burn. Burn was enough of a folly architect to grasp this opportunity for creating a small conceit, which had to be rebuilt in 1959. A little further down the A72 towards Biggar is the village of SKIRLING, the seat of Baron Carmichael of Skirling, first Governor of Bengal. He was a pleasant though diffident man with a quixotic sense of humour, which manifested itself in his gift to the village – around the green is a collection of bizarre painted wrought-iron figures, including pigs, lizards, flowers, birds and other whimsies. The work was done after the First World War by Thomas Hadden of Edinburgh, who decorated the grounds of Carmichael's house in similar fashion.

Central

There are few follies here, because Central is one of the smaller new Scottish counties, but two of them, the Lanrick Tree and the Pineapple, are among the finest in the British Isles.

At the end of the walled garden in DUNMORE PARK is the Pineapple, a folly *par excellence* and a stone fruit to revitalise the most jaded palate — gigantic, dwarfing the surrounding trees, it is the most singular monument to come out of the little practised art of fruit architecture. In 1761 the 29-year-old John Murray, 4th Earl of Dunmore, had been married two years. Perhaps it was his marriage going sour that prompted the enormous fruit; or it was a belated wedding present; or the result of a frivolous wager; or to commemorate the growing of a pineapple (not the first; they had been grown in hothouses in Scotland for nearly 30 years) . . . whatever the reason, this extraordinary building never fails to astonish. From a range of side pavilions rises an octagon with Gothick windows, the arches of which culminate in carved stone foliage. Then the actual pineapple starts, 53 feet high and brilliantly carved from stone. There is no need to describe it, since it is a remarkably accurate rendering, but two centuries ago the fruit was so rare, luxurious and desirable that it made today's luxuries such as caviar, smoked salmon and champagne mundane by comparison, and since the pineapple was scarcely seen except by the very rich the stone copy must have astounded the locals.

The building was planned and designed with the utmost care, each of the gently curving leaves being drained separately in order to prevent frost from damaging the delicate masonry. There are two entrances, a classical loggia to the south and a Gothick doorway to the north on the upper level, leading into the second storey. The keystone above the south entrance carries the date 1761, and above this is a carved heart and the inscription 'FIDELIS IN ADVERSIS', commemorating the marriage in 1803 of George Murray, the 5th Earl of Dunmore, to the daughter of the Duke of Hamilton. Some years ago the Landmark Trust took the building on a long lease from the National Trust for Scotland and carefully restored it for letting as a holiday home. Sadly, the name of the designer of this wonderful structure has not been recorded — it is a work of genius, certainly unique and probably impossible to duplicate nowadays. Tradition ascribes it to Sir William Chambers, but he was working in London at the time it was built and it is not mentioned in his writings, as such a remarkable building surely would have been. A hermit's cave has been reported nearby, so perhaps the Pineapple was not the only Dunmore folly. A little way to the north, going back to the main road, is a ruined and very dilapidated stone tower mantled with ivy and with a tiny bartizan turret poking out of the side.

The enormous 220-foot high Wallace Monument dominating the town of STIRLING from its site above the bridge — where in 1297 Sir William Wallace, Scotland's national hero, wreaked havoc on the English — was designed by J. T. Rochead and took ten years from 1859 to build. It is a splendid, confident, exuberant celebration of a tower, with bartizans, pinnacles, rough harling, boles, buttresses and an impressive open-worked spire. The 15-foot statue of Wallace by D. W. Stephenson on a niche in the wall must, such is the hero's renown in these parts, be lifesize. A friend who first visited the monument whetted our appetite by describing it and adding, 'If you think *that's* weird, wait until you see the custodians!'

Up the river Teith is LANRICK CASTLE, where Lieutenant-General Sir John Murray MacGregor erected a stone tree in the woods, possibly a memorial. Although it is over 50 feet high and at least 10 feet in diameter, the bottom half of the tree, mossy and lichen-covered on the north side and complete with stumpy branches and pollarded limbs, merges into the woods with all the other trees; one can almost pass it without noticing — a case of not being able to see the tree for the woods. Then, 30 feet up, everything goes awry, naturalism vanishes and the stone tree is truncated and bears a crown (of all the trees that are in the wood?). From here a weird structure rises: slender columns supporting a circular base on which is another column and a couple of flambeaux and palmettes on square supports. The reason for the construction of this disturbing building may lie in the history of the MacGregor family. The *Dictionary of National Biography* tells how in the 17th and 18th centuries the clan was under a ban which, among other things, prohibited them from using the name MacGregor, the General being given the name of Murray. In 1774 the ban was lifted and the General was called out to be the chief of the MacGregors, although he did not assume the name until the year of his death in 1822. The folly may well commemorate either of these events.

A tiny folly-tower, almost too small to be noticed by anyone but village children playing, hides on the side of a hill in the hamlet of MUGDOCK. Trimmed to half its height, it is strenuously guarded by loose alsatians from the neighbouring cottage.

Dumfries and Galloway

The southernmost Scottish county is big and sparsely follied. For the tightest definition of the word only one would qualify – the rest are monuments, such as a column of 1714 at THORNHILL, dedicated to the memory of the 2nd Duke of Queensberry who died in 1711, and a monument at MOFFAT to the sheep that turned much of the Scottish farmland into wasteland.

A more interesting memorial is the grave of the shepherd Johnny Turner, sited on remote Bishop Forest Hill above the GLENKILN reservoir. Old Johnny was terrified of the Resurrectionists and determined not to let them get his dead body, so he hacked his own grave out of the solid rock. An inscription marks the spot. Stranger still are the sculptures that stand on the hillside, the last place one would expect to find an open-air art gallery, with works by Epstein, Moore, Renoir and Rodin, erected by the local landowner.

GATEHOUSE OF FLEET is a quaintly named village at the head of Fleet Bay. The Jubilee Clock-tower is a typical Scottish harled tower, a gently battered base rising to a bartizaned upper storey surmounted by the most improbable castellations, curling like phoenix flames. Just south of the town in Fleet Forest is Cally House, where the architect and landscape gardener James Ramsey laid out the gardens in the 1780s. About 1789 he must have designed the Gothick temple, hidden between newly planted trees, and originally housing a 'farm-servant'. Now the two-storey tower is dilapidated, but it was sturdily built so it may yet survive. It is square, with corner buttresses and a flight of steps leading to a door with an uncouth arch. The castellations are quite heavy, a course of open slabs of stone filled in with rubble.

About five miles south of Gatehouse of Fleet is BORGUE, famed for 'The Cow Palace', a model dairy farm built *c.*1901 for James Brown. The Gothic buildings were designed with great care and put up at great expense, so much so that local rumour still has it that Brown's dozen cows were held in the stables by chains of silver. The central Corseyard Tower was to have been the farm's grandest feature, a water-tower built as a baronial castle, but upon completion the tower was found to be utterly useless as a means of water supply.

The Queensberrys were diligent in commemorating themselves. In DUMFRIES there is a column designed by Robert Adam to honour the 3rd Duke; it was built in 1780 in Queensberry Square and moved to the County Buildings in 1934.

Fife

For some reason (perhaps because it is a kingdom rather than a county) Fife was left untouched when the other Scottish counties were packed into huge administrative bundles. The best folly is at Balcarres House in Colinsburgh; meanwhile a study of the map yields some interesting names, such as Wormit, Cult Hill, the *Sunday Express*'s favourite town Auchtermuchty, Coaltown of Burnturk and, like something out of Thomas Love Peacock, Gowkhall.

Woodhead Farm at LOW VALLEYFIELD, east of the immaculate medieval town of Culross, is very much a seaside frivolity. There is nothing exceptional about the building's structure; it is the grace notes that turn it into a pretty little musical box of a house. The doorway and windows are in the Gothic mode, surrounded by rustication, and the side walls have blind windows in the same style. Above the entrance is a large quatrefoil light — all probably the work of a local builder who used his pattern book over-enthusiastically.

Nairn's Folly at KIRKCALDY is little more than a name. The Nairn involved made his fortune through his famous floor coverings, and the 'folly' is merely a strip of wall to keep the public off a particular stretch of beach. Further along the coast WEMYSS CASTLE has a home farm castellated and ornamented with cross arrowslits. James Wyatt's nephew Lewis designed a Gothic gateway and lodge here for William Wemyss, but they were never built — perhaps the farmhouse was also his work.

Still travelling west we reach LEVEN. Mr Walter Bissett of that town is now dead, and his cottage garden, covered in shells from top to bottom and side to side, has disappeared, but his triumphant Shell Bus remains: every square inch of it is covered in shells, except the windows. This being Scotland, there is also a shell picture of Robbie Burns. The only other shell bus we have heard of is at Buailedubh on South Uist in the Western Isles — perhaps this is a peculiarly Scottish pastime.

After a spell of 21 years in India, the Hon. Robert Lindsey bought part of the Balcarres estate in COLINSBURGH from his elder brother, and built himself a very visible eyecatcher on Balcarres Crag. It is one of the most elegant, archetypal follies in Scotland: a neat sham castle with ruined arch and walls, carefully worked in the local grey stone with startling white for the bold castellations and as a highlight for the windows and doors. There is a flagpole, arrowslits, pointed arches, a round window — everything the folly lover could want. Lindsey must have built it between 1790 and 1820, most probably at the very end of the 18th century. South of BALCARRES, on the coast at Elie, is 'The Lady's Tower', a two-storey bath-house built especially for Lady Janet Anstruther of Elie House, to enable her to bathe unobserved; loungers were shooed away by a servant ringing handbells. The Gothicky structure may have been built by William Adam, who worked at the house in the 1740s, when he also helped to popularise the Gothick style in Scotland by supervising the building of Inveraray Castle.

Inland at KINGLASSIE stands a late Georgian tower called Blythe's Folly, on top of Redwells Hill. A rough-harled, square, four-storey building with fancy battlements, it served the Home Guard as a look-out tower in the Second World War, but old buildings are treated like old soldiers and it is now in danger of collapsing through neglect.

We have not seen the column to the Earl of Hopetoun on MOUNT HILL, north-west of Cupar, nor the Waterloo Tower between Newport-on-Tay and TAYPORT. No doubt readers will tell us if they are worthy of inclusion in subsequent editions.

Grampian

A practice peculiar to the North is the building of elaborate garden pavilions in walled gardens; a good example is the Gothick summer-house in the garden at FASQUE. It consists of a centre pavilion, pyramid-roofed with tiny quatrefoil windows, and two flanking hexagonal towers that carry pointed windows and blind quatrefoils for decoration. Like Fasque, the summer-house was probably built between 1809 and 1820 and is attributed to John Paterson. There is a world of difference between Paterson's worthy but rather dull mansion and summer-house and his FETTERESSO Church near Stonehaven with its air of frivolity. The eccentric groundplan, whitewashed exterior, gay turrets and overall cardboardy quality all suggest to the visitor that the church's primary function was that of an eyecatcher from Fetteresso Castle rather than a place of worship.

At HARLAW is a hexagonal monument with a pyramidal roof put up in 1911 to commemorate the Battle of Harlaw 500 years before. The dairy at Castle Forbes, three miles north of WHITEHOUSE, was probably built by Archibald Simpson in the second decade of the 19th century. The dairy seems to have been intended as a serious agricultural establishment, and instead of the rustic bijoux or Chinese trinkets most dairies of the period turned out to be, it consists of a squat round tower with castellations and three crowstepped, gabled side pavilions tacked on, resembling the side pavilions at the Culzean Home Farm.

The old county of Aberdeenshire has place names to conjure with: Loanend, Egypt, Old Deer, and the Prop of Ythsie. This last named has a small Gothic tower built on the highest point of the

Haddo estate, now in the care of the National Trust for Scotland. Overlooking the village of TARVES with a fine view over central Aberdeenshire, the plain, square tower was built as a tribute to the 4th Earl of Aberdeen, an able Foreign Secretary who became a victim of the Peter Principle by being promoted beyond his level of competence to Prime Minister, where the tribulations of the Crimean War brought about his downfall.

The Culsh Memorial on the Hill of Culsh at NEW DEER should by rights be called the Fordyce Memorial, as it was built in 1876 to the memory of William Dingwall Fordyce of Brucklay Castle, which is now a picturesque ruin. It is a fine tower, square for the first two storeys then octagonal, with tall arched windows at the top, the whole edifice capped by an extremely tall spire. Fordyce was the local laird, a man untypical of his time. He was elected Liberal MP for East Aberdeenshire in 1866, and although he was himself a large landowner he quickly aroused the anger of his neighbouring landlords by championing the rights of farmworkers and labourers. He died early, at the age of 39, and the memorial plaque on the tower is unaffectedly simple and, for once, genuine in its sentiments:

> This Tower was erected by Tenants and friends in token of their sorrow for his early death and their warm remembrance of him as a just and liberal landlord, a trustworthy Member of Parliament, and an exemplary Christian gentleman. 'No Man Liveth To Himself.'

The architect John Smith, who roamed these parts in the first half of the last century, was responsible for Pitfour House at OLD DEER, about seven miles from New Deer. In a recent article on Pitfour, A. A. Tait characterises Smith as 'a notable Greek Revival architect, with a moment of crisis in mid-life which turned him into Gothic Johnny of later life'; another source refers to him as 'Tudor Johnny'. He may have been responsible for some of the follies at Pitfour. In 1816 James Ferguson, the owner of the estate, had the Memorial Gates erected, pillars topped with urns commemorating William Pitt and Lord Melville, who were much revered by Ferguson. But the real changes at Pitfour started when old Ferguson died in 1820 and his son the Admiral took over. The sailor centred the landscape on the large Pitfour Lake, naturally enough considering his profession; on the shore is a Temple of Theseus, a miniature copy of the Temple of Theseus in Greece, a rather morbid choice for an admiral considering that the Athenian hero was killed by being thrown into the sea. The lake was intended to be the start of a most ambitious project: a canal to the sea at Peterhead, ten miles away. Unsurprisingly, insufficient funds led to the cancellation of the project, but not before a tower had been erected in the Forest of Deer as a lookout point down the canal. Another reason given for the building of the tower is that it was used as an observatory grandstand for the racecourse (which still exists, though it is no longer in use) laid out by the Fergusons in the middle of the forest. The story goes that Admiral Ferguson used to take cold baths here in order to keep his body shipshape. Also on the lake is the ruined Gothic boat-house, its ragged outlines enhancing the beauty of decay at Pitfour. Together with the house and some other buildings, Admiral Ferguson's mausoleum was demolished this century. Only the mausoleum's portico survives as a bus shelter, a pedestrian end for an admiral's last resting place.

Duff House near BANFF suffered the same fate as Pitfour. Here the ravages of time have left only one building standing, a ruined classical temple on Downhill, the work of William Adam. Another temple and a triumphal arch on an island in the river Deveron have gone, and so has a circular Gothick tower at the Bridge of Alva, south of the house. The temples were built for William Duff, 1st Earl of Fife, and the tower was erected by the 2nd Earl, who was keen on agricultural reform.

Between Elgin and the CROOK OF ALVES, off the A96, stands York Tower, said to have been raised on the spot where Macbeth met the three witches, although the tower merely commemorates the Duke of York; it was built in 1827 by Alexander Forteath and is three storeys high, embattled, machicolated and decorated with blind cruciform arrow slits. Further west, just before FORRES, is the Nelson Monument, octagonal like York Tower but earlier, dating from 1806, and designed by a local architect, Charles Stuart. If the date is correct, this would appear to be the first Nelson monument in Britain. England was to wait a further 14 years before honouring her native son.

Highland

After the '45 and Bonnie Prince Charlie's flight to France the Highlanders became inveterate monument builders, putting up scores of memorials referring to Culloden and its aftermath, and a similar number of caves, cottages and cairns where Charles Edward or one of his supporters is supposed to have hidden. We have ignored most of them, but the real enthusiast can chase cairn after cairn, spotted across the countryside like obelisks in southerly regions, all commemorating the same thing.

GLENFINNAN is another Stuart rallying point, for it was here that the Prince's standard was raised and the long road leading to Derby and back to nemesis at Culloden began. The monument is accordingly substantial; enclosed by an octagonal wall is a tall round tower with palmette battlements, surmounted by a statue of the luckless Prince. The Glenfinnan Monument, the property of the National Trust for Scotland, was put up in 1815 by Alexander Macdonald, and carries inscriptions in Gaelic, English and Latin. On the Invergarry side of LOCH OICH, next to the A82, stands an obelisk topped by seven heads and a hand holding a sword. The monument was raised in 1812 above the Well of the Seven Heads, and came by its name in the wake of a clanland killing when seven brothers were brought to justice by having their heads chopped off. The heads were washed in the well before being put on public display. With admirable internationalism, the inscription is written in French as well as in the three languages used at Glenfinnan. Near Glencoe at BALLACHULISH is the Steward o' the Glens monument, marking the spot where the Steward was hanged on the false accusation of shooting a Campbell.

479

Sir Hector Munro built a folly to commemorate his own heroism: a replica of the Gates of Negapatam, an Indian stronghold he had captured from the Dutch. After 20 years of service in the Indian army, he retired in the 1780s to Novar House near EVANTON in Cromarty, during the last years of his life finding time to develop Novar into a model estate and to share some of his fortune by paying the unemployed to build this eyecatcher of three battlemented arches, the centre one taller, with a ruined pillar standing to one side. Heavy and oppressive – very Scottish rather than Indian – it is reminiscent of Yorke's Folly in North Yorkshire in its situation.

Above GOLSPIE a road winds to the top of the 1,300-foot Beinn na Bragie, on which stands the enormous statue of the 1st Duke of Sutherland, who was responsible for the controversial Highland Clearances. He died in 1833. William Burn designed the pedestal in 1887 and the statue itself is by Chantrey. There is an obelisk on the bridge at Golspie to the Sutherland clan and another monument to the Duke at Lilleshall in Shropshire, where he also had land. At DUNROBIN Castle, the family seat, a summer-house of 1732 is so packed with big-game trophies that it has become known as 'The Hunting House'.

On the north coast of Scotland near THURSO Castle is Harald's Tower, erected for Sir John Sinclair (1754–1835), sometime President of the Board of Agriculture and champion of James Macpherson's claim that Ossian, the medieval Scottish poet, really existed. Harald, an Earl of Caithness, was killed here at the end of the 12th century, and Sinclair believed he was descended from him. But the most extraordinary piece of architecture in this region is the wildly fantastic Gothick of Sinclair's Thurso Castle Lodge. It is basically a square embattled block, but the south-west corner has a taller three-storey, square tower built out of it; each corner of the lodge has a thin, elongated bartizan turret with massively oversized crenellations, three with chimneys and the fourth, jutting out of the taller tower, a statue. The gate arch is massively top heavy, with two spidery legs supporting yet another pair of bartizan turrets separated by extremely ornate battlements above machicolations with no fewer than five steps. This is a truly manic piece of Gothic revival architecture, and although the prolific architect William

Burn worked here in 1834 it is doubtful whether he had the undisciplined imagination to produce such a folly.

Colvin notes an 1801 engraving by the architect A. McInnes of a proposed Washington Monument, a round castellated tower, near Thurso, but we do not know whether it was ever realised. Thurso now has Britain's most northerly follies, but this was not always the case: in the 16th century a Dutch farmer, Johan de Groot, settled about ten miles along the coast with his seven sons. The brothers continually disputed precedence, so de Groot had an octagonal table made to settle the issue. Unfortunately it was too large for the farmhouse, so the farmhouse was rebuilt in an octagon shape to take the table. The Scotticisation of de Groot's name has given him posthumous world-wide fame, and now the JOHN O'GROATS Hotel continues the tradition by having an octagonal room.

Scotland's newest folly, dating from 1970, is at Kinkell Castle near CONONBRIDGE; although some would claim it to be merely a large garden sculpture, the owner (and builder) avers that it was built in pure folly spirit. Only time will tell, but it has a good start, as it is a half-familiar yet purposeless structure taking the form of a pyramid topped with the inside of a round-headed arch, a giant, upside-down tuning-fork passing through the structure to allow a gap through which one can watch the moon rising.

Lothian

Lothian has a surprising number of major follies, with Edinburgh and its outskirts boasting more per square mile than any other urban district in Britain outside London. Coming in from the east on the A1 there is a small Victorian embattled octagonal tower with side turret on the Broxmouth House estate, between BROXBURN and East Barns. At TYNINGHAME HOUSE to the north-west the 1960s have left some unexpected traces about the house and grounds: the house contains several *trompe l'oeil* murals, while the garden harbours knick-knacks now coming back into fashion – a battlemented Gothick pavilion and an off-the-peg Gothick arbour. A century earlier is the 1856 obelisk with a laudatory inscription to Thomas Hamilton, 6th Earl of Haddington, 'who at a period of the greatest national depression had foresight and energy to set the example of planting on an extensive scale and to be an active and successful promoter of agricultural improvement . . . ', and to his wife, 'of whose valued suggestions and assistance her husband has left an ample record'. A contemporary of the Earl, who died in 1735, judged him differently: 'hot, proud, vain and ambitious'.

The gardens of Gosford House, near ABERLADY on the shores of the Firth of Forth, two miles from Luffness, were landscaped by Alan Ramsay and now contain a caravan park. On a knoll in the woods stands the mausoleum of the Earls of Wemyss, classical of course, with a pyramidal roof. It may have been designed by Robert Adam, who started work on the house in 1790. Ramsay was planting the area surrounding the mausoleum in about 1796, and he was probably responsible for the nearby ice-house, with its Gothick ante-room.

Amisfield House, a mile or so north-east of HADDINGTON, has been demolished, but the outbuildings remain. John Henderson built the four Doric pavilions, one of which doubles as a dovecote, in the corners of the large walled garden in 1783–5. Beside the Tyne is a classical temple, presumed to have been designed by Isaac Ware, but the best feature is Amisfield Mains ('mains' derives from demesne, and is the Scottish term for a home farm). This farm was given the full screen treatment – pyramidal gables with slim castellations and pointed arches – and in all probability this is the 'Castle' that Robert Mylne noted in his diary in 1766 as being built for the Earl of Wemyss; it is therefore contemporary with Mylne's tower for Thomas Farr at Blaise Castle in Avon. Another, lesser, screened farm can be seen at Gilmerton House opposite the Museum of Flight at EAST FORTUNE, north-east of Amisfield. On the Garleton Hills north of Haddington is a monument to General John Hope, 4th Earl of Hopetoun, who soldiered in the West Indies, Egypt and the Iberian peninsula. The monument, a slim brick tower, was erected shortly after his death in 1823.

The garden volcano is an all too rare treat in the folly canon. Chambers enlarged on its supposed use as a garden ornament by the Chinese in his *Dissertation on Oriental Gardening* (1772), but the mainspring for the slight popularity of the volcano must be sought in those Grand Tours that reached Vesuvius: the 18th- and 19th-century traveller to Naples usually brought back with him one of the numerous paintings, prints and painted boxes depicting the eruptions of Vesuvius. Volcanoes mainly remained a manifestation of the *jardin anglo-chinois*; as a result, they are almost entirely restricted to the Continent. The Tivoli Gardens in Paris boasted an erupting volcano; near Doorn in the Netherlands an entire cottage poses as a lump of volcanic rock; and the most famous of them all, the 'Stein', still exists at Wörlitz near Dessau in East Germany. The Cadells, iron founders and coal merchants from COCKENZIE AND PORT SETON, aptly managed a small volcano (albeit only in name) in their Cockenhouse garden. Behind a whale arch is a small grotto with a shell interior and tufa-covered walls, presumably intended to simulate a recent eruption. It cannot be said to be a successful imitation. The builder, aware of this, reinforced the point by inscribing 'HECLA' above the entrance, referring to the Icelandic volcano of that name, and the tufa is said to have come from that same mountain — but another, closer Hecla on South Uist in the Hebrides is the more likely source.

Further along the coast, a mile or so west of MUSSELBURGH, is Newhailes, where another shell-lined grotto stands in the gardens of Newhailes House. This was perhaps erected when Miss Dalrymple inherited the house in 1792, shell grottoes being particularly feminine follies. Also in the gardens is an obelisk to the memory of poor John Dalrymple, 2nd Earl of Stair, whose life started on the wrong foot when he was rejected by his parents at the age of eight after accidentally shooting his brother. He died in 1747.

Day and night the ogre of demolition hovers over Lothian's most gimcrack folly, PORTOBELLO Tower. From 1763 onwards a certain William Jamieson energetically developed a stretch of land along the coast west of Edinburgh until it became a popular watering-place. He named it Portobello. The tower is the sole survivor of a series of early buildings there and originally served as a belvedere. Several details are genuinely medieval, most of them originating from demolished medieval churches and houses in Edinburgh. The octagonal main tower is rusticated, with battlements and pointed arches, some now blank. A higher, square turret in the same Gothick style is attached.

South of Edinburgh is Dryden Tower at BILSTON. This is a proper folly, no adapted dovecote but a straightforward, otiose, folly-tower, tall, lonely and irrelevant. It stands uncertainly in a semi-rural, semi-industrial landscape surrounded by concrete posts and fencing to keep out the inquisitive, reinforced by 'DANGER – KEEP OUT' notices. For once these are fully justified: the two remaining pinnacles of the four that once graced its graceless roof are poised to penetrate the foolhardy climber. It appears to date from the mid-19th century and was presumably built by a fan of the poet Dryden, or by a man called Dryden. It would be good to find out more.

Rosebery, on the B6372 a mile east of YORKSTON, has lost its house, but the steading is still working. Its architect couldn't or wouldn't take sides in the Battle of Styles still raging in the early 19th century, and accordingly crenelled the walls of the steading but hit upon rogue classicism for the structure's centrepiece, the

190   Nelson's Tower, Calton Hill, Edinburgh

191 McCaig's Folly, Oban

192 The folly-tower at Penicuik

193 Belvedere steading, Rosneath

194   Dryden Tower, Bilston

clock-tower. Two storeys of round arches and bizarre pointed windows are surmounted by a single, pointed, blank window leading up to the clock-face and finally culminating in an octagonal church spire with oval lights and a weather-vane. Across the road are the gate piers to the house, clustered pillars with stiletto pyramids on top. The architect must have been an amateur – a likely candidate is Archibald John Primrose, 4th Earl of Rosebery, who, if capable of publishing a book entitled *An Address to the Middle Classes on the Subject of Gymnastic Exercises* (1848), was certainly capable of designing this monstrosity.

Sir John Clerk of PENICUIK was the Scottish answer to Lord Burlington. He thoroughly influenced early 18th-century building and gardening in Scotland, and his manuscript poem 'The Country Seat' (1727) bears witness to his Palladian leanings and prescribes the siting of mansions and gardens. Clerk took a premature dislike to the Gothick style, which at this date had scarcely begun. At the end of his epistle he exhorts:

> From your gen'ral Rules instruction take,
> What Edifice to raise or Gardens make:
> But other are, on whom those Rules you waste,
> For Goths will always have a Gothic taste.

This did not prevent Sir John from erecting a few follies at Penicuik; he invariably chose the Roman style – obviously none was in the Gothick. Opposite the house on a hill called Knight's Law stands the well turned-out Roman look-out tower of 1748–51, a tall, circular, battlemented tower with open machicolations and blank windows, a very smooth building that could have been lifted out of a Poussin painting. Aligned with the house is Ramsay's Monument, reached by crossing the Esk over the Centurion's Bridge of 1738. The monument is an obelisk-cum-archway, built by Sir John's son James a year after Ramsay's death in 1758. To the west, on the south bank of the river, is the Hurley Grotto, a 40-foot long tunnel with a military-style rusticated entrance and, inside, a room with the inscription 'TENEBROSA OCCULTAQUE CARA' (Beware of dark and secret things). Clerk called the grotto 'a frightful cave . . . To those who enter, first occurs the memory of the Cuman Sybil, for the ruinous aperture, blocked up with stones and briars, strikes the eye.' After some yards visitors 'stand in doubt whether they are among the living or the dead . . . there comes upon the visitor a shudder'.

The tunnel had another, rather unexpected function: that of a telescope. According to Sir John it was possible, standing at one end and looking through the tunnel, to determine the sun's diameter. James Clerk carried on where his father left off, and in the 1760s he designed the stables back at the house. On top of the rear entrance to the stable block is a replica of a Roman building, commonly known as Arthur's Oven, which had been demolished in 1743 in Stirlingshire. As in so many Scottish steadings, part of the stable block doubles as a dovecote.

Sir James Hall of Dunglass in the far east of the county also held strong architectural opinions, though he tended towards the theoretical rather than the practical. In 1813 he published his notorious *Essay on Gothic Architecture*, in which he sought to prove that the gothic style derived directly from prehistoric hut-dwellers, who found, so Sir James claimed, that reeds and willows could most easily be bent into common gothic motifs. In pursuing this theory he had constructed a Willow Cathedral in 1794, a painting of which makes his case pleasantly convincing. The detached spire in the picture is uncannily reminiscent of the Cone at Barwick Park in Somerset, or even Watts Towers in Los Angeles, but as might be expected nothing now remains of this prodigy of basket-weaving.

Near Edinburgh Airport, at TURNHOUSE on Corstophine Hill, stands a tall monument. Clermiston or Cammo Tower was built in 1871 by William MacFie to celebrate Sir Walter Scott's centenary, and is clearly visible from aeroplanes coming in to land. The tower is also claimed to have been the inspiration for Robert Louis Stevenson's *Kidnapped*. The folly is round, four storeys high, topped with a corbelled and embattled parapet. For openings there are slit windows and a round-headed entrance doorway. Further to the west, at QUEENSFERRY on top of Binns Hill, is another tall, circular building, an eyecatcher called Midhope Tower, built in 1826 to a design by Alexander Allen for Sir James Dalyell.

We came across the Craigiehall Temple at CRAMOND BRIDGE while lost in the country lanes behind the airport, looking for Clermiston Tower. Suddenly a squat, round building poked its head over a ridge, and a dash across a field revealed this forgotten basilica. Inside are two beautiful stone fireplaces; once there were two floors. The majestically carved coat-of-arms on the semi-circular pediment carries the motto 'NEMO ME IMPUNE LACESSIT', and a plaque set in the wall to the right of the entrance reads:

DUM LICET IN REBUS IUCUNDIS

VIVE BEATUS

VIVE MEMOR QUAM SIS AEVI BREVIS

C : H : W : 1759

Halfway between the coast and LINLITHGOW is the Hope Monument, an elaborate Victorian cross to commemorate Brigadier-General Adrian Hope, who died at the Siege of Lucknow in 1858. There is another Hope monument on a golf-course south of the town, a tall cone on a plinth, erected to commemorate the General's father, John Hope.

A mysterious early 19th-century tower, octagonal with castellations, stands to the north-east of TORPHICHEN – mysterious because we can't find out anything about it. We would love to hear from any reader who can enlighten us.

Finally we move to EDINBURGH. The gate lodge to Redford House was assembled out of the spare parts of William Adam's Royal Infirmary of 1738–48, most of which was demolished in 1884. The most noticeable pieces of the lodge's preposterous ornamentation are the enormous volutes set against the wall and reaching to the top of the structure, and these give it (somewhat obscurely) its name, 'The Drummond Scrolls'. Prestonfield House, originally built in 1687 by Robert Mylne, is now a smart restaurant. The design of the once famous Ace of Clubs gardens – supposed to have been laid out in this pattern to celebrate a famous triumph in a card game – has been overplanted, but the story lingers. In LEITH on the banks of the Forth, near Moray Place, stands St Bernard's Well, a circular, domed, classical temple designed in 1789 by the landscape painter Alexander Nasmyth and sheltering a statue of Hygeia by D. W. Stephenson. The mineral spa had been discovered in about 1760, but when Francis Garden, Lord Gardenstone, partook of the waters he was so gratified by the imagined effect that he had the temple erected. Sadly, Gardenstone, a slightly eccentric bachelor who kept pigs in his bedroom and insisted on being buried in an unmarked grave, died a mere four years later at the unremarkable age of 72. The entrance to Moray House in the centre of Edinburgh has a pair of stiletto piers not unlike those at Rosebery. At the back of the house is a rectangular summer-house with rusticated doors and windows. On the façade corners are small lions holding shields in their claws, one of the shields being monogrammed 'MH'. The 1707 Act of Union between Scotland and England is said to have been signed inside the pavilion.

The city's famous Scott Monument in elegant Princes Street serves as a prelude to the equally august follies on Calton Hill – but here we are treading on dangerous ground, for few Scotsmen will enjoy seeing these national monuments classed as follies. In 1836 a competition was held to choose the best design for a Scott memorial. George Meikle Kemp, an unknown architect who was nevertheless thoroughly versed in the Gothic idiom, came third, but for some reason the competition was held again and this time Kemp carried off the first prize. His design showed a stage spire nearly 200 feet high, worked open, with the whole gamut of pointed arches and pinnacles being used. The building of the monument took seven years, from 1840 to 1846, but in 1844 Kemp was accidentally drowned in the Union Canal, bereaving us of a potentially great folly architect.

In the early 19th century Calton Hill, which dominates the city, was designated as a Scottish Valhalla, but the first monument erected on the hill was to Nelson, the all-England hero. The Gothick observatory had already been sited there before the rest of the monuments were built, exploiting the hill's picturesque characteristics to maximum effect. In a bid for consistency the Nelson Monument, designed by Robert Burn and built in 1807–16, was also in the Gothick style. The monument was built on a trapezoid ground plan. The walls connect four corner towers and out of the midst of what was originally intended to be a restaurant rises a tall tower, staged and embattled and expressly made to look like an upside down telescope. Above the entrance is the date, 1805, and an inscription which dedicates the building to Nelson, and to 'the great victory of Trafalgar':

TOO DEARLY PURCHASED WITH HIS BLOOD.
THE GRATEFUL CITIZENS OF EDINBURGH
HAVE ERECTED THIS MONUMENT:
NOT TO EXPRESS THEIR UNAVAILING SORROW FOR HIS DEATH:
NOR YET TO CELEBRATE THE MATCHLESS GLORIES OF HIS LIFE:
BUT, BY HIS NOBLE EXAMPLE, TO TEACH THEIR SONS
TO EMULATE WHAT THEY ADMIRE AND, LIKE HIM, WHEN DUTY
REQUIRES IT,
TO DIE FOR THEIR COUNTRY.

Sprayed in paint on the wall below is another sentiment: 'ENGLISH OUT OF SCOTLAND'. Still, the good citizens of Edinburgh did not tire of their patriotism and in 1822 embarked on another project, a monument to commemorate Scottish soldiers killed in the Napoleonic Wars. The architects C. R. Cockerell and William Playfair came up with a rather bizarre idea, a replica of the Parthenon, harking back to Edinburgh's self-bestowed sobriquet of the Athens of the North. The designs were approved and an appeal was launched for £42,000 to realise the building. Eventually only £16,000 was subscribed, but the building work had already started. By 1829 Playfair had to admit defeat, and he spoke of the National Monument as 'the pride and the poverty of Scotland'. When it was evident that no more money was forthcoming the project was abandoned and the half-finished sham temple consolidated and proclaimed as the National Monument. Just 12 massive Doric columns supporting an ornamental frieze were built, a *memento mori* as poignant in its ruined state as the broken pillars to be seen in graveyards. At roughly the same time the Playfair Monument was built, a scholarly mix of the Tomb of Theron at Agrigento and the Lion Tomb at Cuidos: a base with a tomb surrounded by heavy Doric pillars designed by William Playfair to commemorate his uncle, Professor Playfair. Naturally by 1830 it was time for Robert Burns to be immortalised. Thomas Hamilton designed him a tholos-style temple on a base, supporting a sculpture group. A year later the philosopher Dugald Stewart, who died in 1828, was honoured with a copy of the Choragic monument of Lysicrates, again by Playfair.

Strathclyde

The southern part of this huge and varied amalgam of Lowlands and Highlands contains a few dull monuments together with some unexpected pleasures, particularly in Glasgow. The best follies are to be found in the old Argyllshire, with the Inveraray estate acting as a kind of time capsule.

CULZEAN (Cullane to the Sassenachs) is a National Trust for Scotland property spectacularly sited on the Ayrshire coast. Its conversion by Robert Adam into a sham medieval castle for the 10th Earl of Cassillis during the last quarter of the 18th century is, in hindsight, a matter of course, dictated by the *genius loci*. As at Alnwick Castle, Adam took great care in shaping the castle's surroundings. For the approach from Morriston he devised a striking design – a Romano-Gothick viaduct spanning the glen in front of the castle. In the end he had to tone down his plans, but the effect as realised is still remarkable. The entrance archway has been erected as a sham ruin with crumbling side towers, and the fabric of the viaduct has also been given a ruinous appearance. The visitor finally enters the forecourt through a castellated classical archway, and the forecourt and some of the gardens are enclosed by cardboardy embattled walls, towers and turrets. Adam took the idea for the viaduct from the approach to Hadrian's Villa near Rome. In the gardens stands an early 19th-century Camellia House, with ogee windows, battlements and corner pinnacles, and on the edge of Swan Pond are a Gothick aviary and the octagonal Swan Cottage, both designed by Robert Lugar about half a century after Adam. A design for the Pheasantry at Culzean appeared in Lugar's 1823 *Plans and Views of Buildings Executed in*

England and Scotland in the Castellated and Other Styles.

Further along the coast the Home Farm, the most elegant steading in Scotland, was built to Adam's designs in 1775–7. The buildings are on a canted square plan, with four archways connecting the four rectangular stables that make up the square. Four churchlike buildings, with crosses and embattled gables, stand at 90° to the stables. The Home Farm has been extensively restored and was converted into a Park Centre in 1973.

In 1778 Robert Adam added a tea house to Richard Oswald's estate at Auchincruive, near ST QUIVOX outside Ayr. The setting of the folly is almost as dramatic as that of Culzean, disturbed only by the aeroplanes landing at Prestwick. It stands on a circular base which has four turrets attached to it. The second storey is the actual tea house, circular with a course of blind arches and battlements hiding a low pyramidal roof. The structure is a concoction out of Theodoric's Mausoleum at Ravenna by the Tomb of Caecilia Metella in Rome.

Opposite the church in ALLOWAY and overlooking the River Doon and its 'Auld Brig' is the tall Burns Monument, the result of a competition won by Thomas Hamilton in 1818. This version of the Lysicrates Monument, here mounted on an Egyptian base, was built in 1820–3. Some years later Hamilton was to build another Burns Monument, on Edinburgh's Calton Hill. Although Hamilton used a different design, his colleague William Playfair came up with yet another Lysicratic Monument for the Calton Hill site a year later. At FAILFORD a globe on top of a pillar marks the spot where Burns took leave of Highland Mary – Mary Campbell, the recipient of his 'Will ye go to the Indies, my Mary?' The reason for the parting was Burns's intended emigration to Jamaica, but the financial success of his first collection of poems, printed at Kilmarnock, made the journey unnecessary. As KILMARNOCK played such a crucial role in the poet's life, the town has its own 80-foot Burns Monument, standing in Kay Park.

Burns, Scott, Wallace and Robert the Bruce would together have topped the Most Popular Scotsman award in any 19th-century poll. In Ayrshire Wallace vies with Burns for first place, but at least at TARBOLTON – which also has connections with Burns – Wallace is represented by the Gothick pinnacled and battlemented Barnweil

Tower, which commemorates his burning of the Barns of Ayr. It was in Ayr that the Hammer and Scourge of England began his fight for Scottish independence. The Burns faction struck back with the Burns Tower at MAUCHLINE, another top-heavy little tower in the favoured Scots Baronial style, with crow-stepped gables and the customary bartizan turrets.

On the coast south of the seaside resort of LARGS stands a tall, slim tower rather like an Irish round tower, which commemorates the battle of Largs in 1263 when the Norwegian King Haakon was beaten and the Hebrides were finally brought under Scottish rule.

Near the village of DUNSYRE about two miles west of the Peebles–Lanark border is Stonypath, a bogland garden developed from 1967 onwards by the poet Ian Hamilton Finlay. It is a fine and justly famed new garden, but although there is an Apollo Temple, a broken column or two and an avalanche of poetic mottoes and inscriptions, the insistent namedropping of pastoral painters and writers and garden theorists tends to get on one's nerves. Everything in Stonypath is on such a small and fragile scale that one starts hankering after something more manly, like a Wallace monument or a sturdy Gothick eyecatcher. But before we return to the more macho Scottish follies, there is another small monument commemorating someone without whom this book could never have existed: Major-General William Roy, the Father of the Ordnance Survey, who started his career in 1747 by mapping Scotland, is remembered by a triangulation stone at Milton Head, near CARLUKE.

On the outskirts of Glasgow a poet not Burns is honoured – a Gothic monument in NEWTON MEARNS commemorates Robert Pollok, who wrote the mighty, flawed and now almost forgotten minor masterpiece 'The Course of Time'. In industrial HAMILTON a huge drum rises high above a colonnaded square base, forming the vast and impressive mausoleum of the Dukes of Hamilton. But the folly here is Chatelherault, an immensely long screen with four pavilions inset, built in 1731–43 for the 10th Duke of Hamilton. The pavilions, rusticated and with vases on the roof, are connected to each other by a classical screen with a centre archway. The building was to be used as stabling but also allowed a degree of ducal leisure use: the absurdly small rooms in the pavilions still retain traces of fine plasterwork and grand fireplaces among the shattered windows and rotting floors. By 1979 the bowling green in front of the screen had been turned into a gravel pit, and the whole massive façade seemed inclined to follow it, but the honey-pink decay strengthens its romanticism and its role as a superb eyecatcher from Hamilton Park. It is now being comprehensively restored.

Like any large city, GLASGOW is well endowed with monuments: there is the Scott Monument in George Square, the Battle of Langside Memorial in Queen's Park and the Nelson obelisk in Glasgow Green, designed in 1806 by David Hamilton. But there are more exciting buildings in Glasgow than are dreamed of in a monumental philosophy — for example those by the native architect Alexander Thomson, better known as 'Greek' Thomson although he had an equal right to the epithet 'Egyptian', on the strength of his persistent use of Egyptian motifs in his works (his churches, of which the best was the now demolished Queen's Park Church, contained many examples, and in Union Street a warehouse of his design goes by the name of Egyptian Halls, although only the upper storeys show the characteristic bulging pillars). Thomson struck a more oriental chord in his design for a dwelling at 200 Nithsdale Road, where in 1871–3 he built a residence suitable for a minor official in the court of Rameses II. The portico pillars and the chimneypots on the flat roof are among the house's more conspicuous details.

Much 19th-century Glaswegian commercial architecture favoured the exotic. One of its most explicit examples is Templeton's Carpet Factory in Templeton Street, Glasgow Green, built in 1889 by William Leiper and often threatened with demolition, but now finally saved and subdivided into small offices and workshops. It is quite simply spectacular, medieval Italian architecture carried far beyond anything the Guelphs or the Ghibellines could aspire to, with a polychromatic façade beggaring description. See it — and see too its rival, the ICI warehouse in Tradeston Street, with its pointed windows, crenellations and, on its corner, a dominant tower, designed in 1900 by W. F. McGibbon who was inspired by the Bargello in Florence.

North of Glasgow we enter a different Strathclyde — this huge administrative area comprises no fewer than six old counties — and come into the old Dunbartonshire and a column, complete with a Latin inscription by Dr Johnson, to the memory of Tobias Smollett, author of *Humphrey Clinker*, at RENTON near his birthplace. On the other side of Gare Loch is ROSNEATH. Here the landscape painter Alexander Nasmyth designed a Gothick eye-catcher steading for the Duke of Argyll around 1802. The belvedere tower in the centre of the fabric is the most prominent feature, rising high above the farm roofs. Tall, blind, pointed arches decorate the façade, together with a fancy balustrade and bartizans. Two octagonal towers with pyramid roofs echo the main tower, while the round towers ending the steading on both sides give the impression of belonging to an earlier date.

On the golf-course on the outskirts of fashionable MILNGAVIE stands a quiet little hexagonal tower reminiscent, with its blind windows, of the Pepperbox in Wiltshire. It is known locally as 'The Folly', but could just as easily have been built as yet another dovecote.

In faraway Kintyre are some more Gothicisms. The cardboard Gothick of the entrance arch to Torrisdale Castle, south-west of CARRADALE, is nudged towards follydom by dint of its decorations: lancet windows pierce the walls either side of a Tudor arch, above which is a tablet with what are probably the MacAlister arms; the bartizan turrets carry arrowslits. Torrisdale was built *c.*1815 by James Gillespie Graham for General MacAlister. In the garden of Oatfield House near CAMPBELTOWN, towards the Mull of Kintyre, stands a peculiar small grotto, in fact little more than a large niche. It has a Georgian air, but the façade consists of pointed double arches and a large open quatrefoil, all said to have been taken from Dunblane Cathedral in 1890.

North of the peninsula, seven miles from KILNINVER overlooking Seil Sound, is Armaddy Castle. South of the house is an 18th-century boat-house, or rather the remains of one. The façade still stands, a pointed entrance arch and cruciform arrowslits making it into an excellent eyecatcher. Nearby, in the same vein of overgrown decay, is a rustic bridge with six obelisks for pylons.

Rather late in life Archibald Campbell, 3rd Duke of Argyll, started turning his estates at INVERARAY into a pleasance. From 1745 onwards Roger Morris built the castle that became the first major Gothick work in Scotland. The same architect drew up a contract on 2 October 1747 for 'a pidgeon house to be built at the end of the back walk being a Circular building 20 f^t Diam.^{r} & 42 f^t high . . . for which he is to be paid Fourty Eight pounds Ster.' Morris was also to 'build a Tower upon Duniquaick 20 f^t Sq & 45 f^t high . . . for the sum of Fourty Six pounds Ster.' The whitewashed dovecote still stands in a meadow. It is circular with a rusticated entrance and a conical roof with ornamental chimney. The Watch Tower on Duniquoick Hill is also lasting well, providing a prominent landmark. The tower is built of rubble, with a pointed and rusticated entrance and window, and a pyramidal roof from which the original staging has now almost totally weathered away after nearly two and a half centuries of harsh Scottish winters. At the same time a grotto was built at nearby Bealachanuaran, serving as a wellhead. It is a classical building, set into the hillside, with a pediment and ball on top and a large and heavily rusticated arch as an entrance. Sadly, the Gothick dairy of 1752 has been demolished. Under the 5th Duke, John Campbell, the ornamentation of the policies (to use the Scottish word) was resumed. A small domed ice-house was built in 1785, probably to Robert Mylne's design, north of a plot called Cherry Park. In the late 18th and early 19th centuries several Gothick lodges and cottages were built on the estate, one of the prettiest being 'The Hexagon', a summer-house beside the river Aray and possibly designed by Nasmyth, who at this time was also building Rosneath steading. It is a pity that one of Nasmyth's more far-flung designs was never built: a drawing shows a Gothick lighthouse tower for Inveraray harbour with battlemented parapets and machicolations rising from a castellated and buttressed base. On top of the tower a small Chinese pavilion was planned.

Towards the north-east of the estate, in Glen Shira, are several Gothick farm buildings, almost all decked out as eyecatchers with pointed arches, battlements and quatrefoils. Maam Steading, designed by Mylne in 1787–9, stands out from its companions. It was originally planned as a circle, not uncommon for Scottish farms, but eventually only a half-circle was realised, with blank castellated white walls to end both sides. In the centre the barns have been given the screen treatment; castellations and pointed arches abound.

The Duke of Argyll occasionally employed the poet Duncan Ban MacIntyre, born 1726, who jobbed as a forester. MacIntyre neither spoke nor wrote English, but his Gaelic poetry proved popular enough for him to live off the proceeds and his fame survived into the 19th century, when in 1859 Freemasons and Scottish Nationalists erected a monument to his memory on Beacon Hill, south of DALMALLY. The massive circular granite temple commands superb views over the mountains and glens.

North of Oban near NEW SELMA, overlooking Ardmucknish Bay, is Lady Margaret's Tower, erected by Lady Campbell 'anno 1754'. She was the second wife of Sir Duncan Campbell, who built the house on the estate. The tower is square, with a tall blind arch in which is set a door with a classical pediment, and at the top is a battlemented parapet with bartizan turrets and a domed elevation.

John Stewart McCaig adhered to the Victorian philosophy that wealth obliged the holder to better the education of the less fortunate. As a banker, philosophical essayist and art critic (self-styled), McCaig strove to improve the fishermen of OBAN. In order to share the experiences of his tours in Italy, he lectured on several occasions to the Oban Young Men's Free Church Mutual Improvement Society (OYMFCMIS), and to accustom the Obanians to a free and casual communion with Great Art he built in 1890–1900 a badly remembered copy of the Colosseum (the arches are Gothic!), giving work to the unemployed masons of the area into the bargain. The enormous blackened cylinder with its two courses of open arches dominates the town and harbour. It is known as McCaig's Folly or McCaig's Tower, after the tower he intended to build in the centre. The original plan was that the building should serve as museum, art gallery and McCaig family memorial, but none of this came about and the huge hollow shell now encloses a prettily landscaped public garden. As a philosophical essayist and art critic McCaig may not have achieved national prominence, but as a folly builder he ranks among the finest. McCaig's magnificent mad folly, unique in Britain, is unforgettable.

Tayside

Most European countries have a few spots called Little Switzerland, but topographical names inspired by German scenery are quite rare. Britain does have some instances: the area round Alton Towers is known as the Staffordshire Rhineland, and the 729-foot Kinnoull Hill at Bridgend in PERTH is surmounted by a sham ruin said to have been built in conscious emulation of the many romantic ruins that stud the steep banks of the Rhine between Cologne and Coblenz. Prince Albert ceaselessly remarked on the similarities between parts of Scotland and parts of Germany. This sequel to Lorelei consists of a round tower, set between bits and pieces of wall, battlements and pointed arches, overlooking the Tay; the tower was built by Robert Auriol Hay, 9th Earl of Kinnoull. The situation reminded him of the panorama of the Rhine he had enjoyed on his grand tour with his neighbour the Earl Gray of Kinfauns, and he held picnics by the tower, bringing back fond memories of 'Vater Rhein'.

Queen Victoria's discovery of Scotland left a spoor of memorials, usually arches, in the Highlands. Many were temporary; the finest of them all was Queen Victoria's Arch in DUNDEE, lost in the 1960s when it was demolished to make way for the Tay road bridge. It was built by J. T. Rochead in 1848, a pinnacled riot of Norman Gothicism, rising twin-turreted to a height of 88 feet. Excited contemporary observers noted that the Prince Consort, on first seeing it, remarked 'Good morning, gentlemen', while the Queen wrote in her diary merely that 'a staircase, covered with red cloth, was arranged for us to land upon'. She did notice the arch at Camperdown House, probably a temporary structure, and commented on the number of triumphal arches in Perth (which reminded Albert of Basle). One by William Mackenzie remains from 1842. An 1877 arch stands at EDZELL (pronounced Aigle), at the entrance to the town, but this is not Victorian; it was erected to the memory of the 11th Earl Dalhousie.

Dalhousie's father, William Ramsay Maule, 1st Baron Panmure, erected Camus's Cross on Camustane Hill on the Panmure estate south of CRAIGTON. It was designed in 1839 by John Henderson to commemorate the 17th-century 1st Earl of Panmure, Patrick Maule. That Maule found time to build it is remarkable in itself, for his life was devoted, to the exclusion of virtually everything else, to becoming as dissipated a roué as possible. Like the Marquess of Queensberry, he survived 'thanks to a constitution of extraordinary strength and a fortune of vast resources', but on the other hand he was also credited with performing many 'unostentatious acts of charity'. Also on the estate is the Marriage Column, celebrating the marriage of James Maule to a daughter of the Duke of Hamilton in 1687, a year after Maule became the 4th Earl of Panmure. The monument was built by Sir William Bruce as an elongated gate post with the names of the lovers inscribed in gold. Another date for the column is given as 1672, in which case the names were added later.

Around 1850 Patrick Allen Fraser considerably enlarged Hospital-field House, just outside ARBROATH. Twenty-five years later he built a mortuary chapel at the house, and as he was an amateur architect he enthusiastically included all the latest architectural tricks and fashions. The end result is wildly out of control, a Scottish baron's nightmare. Much saner is the castellated steading at Langley Park, near the MONTROSE Basin, square with a screen front consisting of a crenellated entrance arch and corner towers, or rather screens pretending to be towers, and decorated all over with cruciform arrowslits and pointed windows. It is probably late Georgian.

Living follies generally exclude themselves from a work such as this, being possibly too contentious for an innocuous guide. An exception has to be made in the case of the MEIKLEOUR Hedge, a remarkable affair planted in 1746, the tallest hedge in the world. It spans 586 yards and in places tops 100 feet; unlike well-known tourist disappointments like the Hampton Court Maze this really is something to see, a beech hedge to gawp at. Trimming is a major operation — the A984 has to be closed to traffic — and the best time to see it is in high summer. It was raining when we saw it one August; only the bottom 12 feet had been trimmed and the rest loured shaggily over the wet road.

One fine day in 1757 John Murray took his uncle James, 2nd Duke of Atholl, for a stroll through the woods near DUNKELD House. The Duke's reaction when he reached the banks of the river Braan is not known, but what he saw was a brand new building, the Hermitage, overlooking Black Lynn Fall. It was his nephew and heir's surprise gift to his favourite uncle, adding to the already existing corpus of follies at Dunkeld, among them a Chinese Temple of 1753 and a Temple of Fame, both now destroyed. A similar fate lay in store for the Hermitage, but it rose like a phoenix from its fire to survive, though in a somewhat simplified version. Caught up in the fashionable enthusiasm for the 2nd-century Gaelic bard Ossian, perpetrated by James Macpherson's spurious trans-lation of 'Fingal', the 4th Duke decided to reshape the Hermitage in 1785. He employed the young architect James Playfair to do the work, copying designs by the Duke's court painter Charles Steuart; the decorations included scenes from the life of Ossian, and the Hermitage was renamed Ossian's Hall. The Dukes of Atholl do not seem to have been popular with their tenantry in the 19th century; Ossian's Hall was fired in 1821, with only minor damage, but the vandals were more successful in 1869, this time resorting to dynamite. Eventually it was rebuilt, and it is now in the care of the National Trust for Scotland; the folly is but a shadow of its former self but the scenery alone merits a detour. Ossian's Cave, about half a mile away, probably also dates from the 4th Duke's reign; there used to be an inscription from 'Fingal' above the entrance, but whether it was removed in embarrassment when it was discovered that the author was Macpherson or whether it has simply disappeared, we cannot tell.

En route to another of the Duke of Atholl's estates, BLAIR ATHOLL, we pass through PITLOCHRY, where stands a younger brother of Yorkshire's Bramhope Tunnel Monument. The horseshoe-shaped Clunie Arch was erected partly to the memory of the men killed driving the Clunie Tunnel for the Tummel hydro-electric scheme that also created the new reservoir of Loch Faskally, and partly to the greater glory of the directors, contractors and architects of the scheme. The horseshoe shape is a replica of the cross-section of the tunnel. 'The Whim' is the Atholls' folly at Blair Castle. Based on a drawing (or a doodle) by the 2nd Duke of Atholl, it was built around 1761; sadly the name is more promising than the actual building, although during construction it was referred to as 'The Ruin'. It stands as an eyecatcher at the end of a lawn and is, though Gothick, severely symmetrical. A high wall couples two end pavilions with round-arched windows, pyramid roofs and crosses on top. On the raised level back from the top of the wall stands a screen, narrow but quite high; a centre arch and two smaller side arches are topped by token battlements. The intended use of the building other than as an eyecatcher is unimaginable; it is purely a whim.

Another eight miles along the A9 will bring you to DALNACAR-DOCH, where General Wade erected a pillar to mark the completion of another section of his highland roads. The story has it that he placed a penny on the flat top of the finished pillar and returned a year later to find it was still there, proving that the local inhabitants were either short or honest.

The keyword to Taymouth Castle, near KENMORE, is 'rustic' although there is a considerable amount of work of an earlier date than the 19th century, when rusticity was all the rage. The later buildings at Taymouth would seem to date from around 1806, when Alexander Nasmyth was called in, or from the late 1830s, when James Gillespie Graham worked at the castle. The rustic lodges fall into two categories: those with irregular eaves, slate roofs and entire trees as supports, such as Rustic Lodge and Fort Lodge; or those which counterfeit miniature castles, like Delarbe Lodge and Rock Lodge. These are rubble-built towers with additional wings, all embattled and with the root and branch work more subdued. The latter buildings possibly belong to the early 19th century, as does the hermitage by Loch Tay, near the Falls of Acharn, now a dilapidated octagonal ruin with a grotto-tunnel, much like the Octagon Tower and tunnel at Studley Royal in Yorkshire. The dairy at Taymouth is in keeping with the other buildings, and dates from the mid-18th century. It is in a mixed Swiss-Balkan style, square with tree-trunks all around, added in the 19th century, and offset by the white quartz walls. There is a second storey with a balustrade and inside is some rustic furniture, the best pieces reminiscent of Edwards and Darly's *A New Book of Chinese Designs* (1754). Near the castle, across the river, is an earlier tower, three storeys high, Gothick, with a battlemented wall running off from it. To the east is the Star Battery, a small bastion, a motif repeated by the Fort in the west near Kenmore, built in 1774 by John Baxter and replacing an earlier fort by John Patterson of 1764 (although a map of 1754 shows the site already marked as 'The Fort'). Again near the castle is the Cross, also known as Maxwell's Temple after the 18th-century agricultural improver Robert Maxwell (no relation). This elaborate Gothic cross was built in 1831 by William Atkinson. The rustication extends to the estate village of Kenmore, with tree-root fencing painted a cheerful red.

COMRIE, east of St Fillans on the end of Loch Earn, has an 1811 monument to Viscount Melville on Dunmore Hill in Glen Lednock – not as fascinating as the surrounding countryside, but it makes an excellent excuse to include a beautiful part of Tayside otherwise bare of follies.

Western Isles

On the northernmost tip of NORTH UIST the wind howling in from the Atlantic is so strong that it is often impossible for a man to stand up. In 1961 the 5th Earl Granville crawled to within 50 yards of the raging sea with his architect, Sir Martyn Beckett, and shrieked 'Build me a fourteen bedroom, eight bathroom house HERE!' It was agreed that the house had to be on one floor – anything higher would have blown down in a remarkably short space of time – and so Sir Martyn devised a wind-cheating ring-shaped house like the Hertfordshire model dairies at Driver's End and Kings Langley. It isn't a folly, because shooting parties are probably the biggest growth industry in the Hebrides, but it is undeniably eccentric.

As might be expected on these now increasingly popular but once subsistence level islands, there are no real follies to speak of. However, to pass away the time of day on South Uist, Mrs Flora Johnson has covered a bus standing in her BUAILEDUBH garden with shells. Through the years she has managed to cover almost every inch of metal with beautiful patterns of the different shells found in abundance on the nearby beaches. From a distance the bus looks as if it could have risen from the sea encrusted with shells after an eternity as Neptune's coach.

LEVERBURGH on South Harris was built as a model village by Lord Leverhulme, who also features in Lancashire with his superb replica of Liverpool Castle at Rivington. As the owner of vast tracts of Harris and Lewis, Leverhulme had great plans to better the lot of the islanders. But the islanders showed very little interest in having their lots bettered by a foreigner, and after his attempts to build a port to rival Stornaway in the north had met with mind-numbing apathy, the usually indomitable soap baron conceded defeat and abandoned the project. Fragments of the glory that might have been remain.

Gazetteer

FOLLIES

ENGLAND

Avon

BADMINTON, Ragged Castle
BANWELL, bone caves and tower;
Banwell Castle
BATH, Ralph Allen's sham castle;
Pinch's Folly; 20 Lansdown
Crescent, Moorish summer-
house
BRISLINGTON, Black Castle
BRISTOL, Cabot's Tower; Goldney
House tower and grotto
CLEVEDON, Walton Castle
COMPTON GREENFIELD, Hollywood
Park Tower
CROMHALL, Priest's Hill Tower
DODINGTON, cascade
HAWKESBURY, Somerset Monument
HENBURY, Blaise Castle
HUNSTRETE, arches
LANSDOWN, Beckford's Tower
LONG ASHTON, 'The Observatory'
MARSHFIELD, pillar, Three Shires
MIDFORD, Roebuck's Folly; 'The
Priory'

STOKE GIFFORD, sarcophagus
WARMLEY, Neptune
WICK, Tracy Park columns
WORLE, observatory

Bedfordshire

AMPTHILL, Catherine's Cross;
Queen Catherine's Summer-
house
APSLEY GUISE, Henry VII Lodge
BUSHMEAD, 'The Grotto'
FLITWICK, sham bridge
GREAT BARFORD, dummy archway
HEATH AND REACH, wellhouse
clock-tower
LINSLADE, gazebo; railway tunnel
LUTON, water-towers
OLD WARDEN, Swiss Garden
PERTENHALL, octagonal summer-
house
ROXTON, rustic congregational
chapel
SOUTHILL, fishing temple
TURVEY, Jonah and his Wife

WOBURN, follies
WREST PARK, pavilion and columns

Berkshire

ASCOT PLACE, grotto
ASHAMPSTEAD, Blorenge House
  tower
BASILDON, Peacock Place garden
HAPPY VALLEY, Cyclopic Bridge
MONKEY ISLAND, follies
PURLEY, flint pavilion
REMENHAM, spire; ice-house;
  Wyatt's Temple (NT)
SULHAM, tower
SUNNINGHILL, Tittenhurst Park,
  Ringo's folly
TEMPLE COMBE, Druids' Circle
WINDSOR, Frogmore sham ruin
WINTERBOURNE, Hop Castle

Buckinghamshire

ASTON CLINTON, Aston Hill Chalet
ASTWOOD, dovecote
AYLESBURY, rose window; Fred's
  Folly
BEACONSFIELD, Hall Barn follies
BOURNE END, Lord Boston's Folly
BUCKINGHAM, Lord Cobham's gaol
BULSTRODE PARK, tower and Swiss
  Cottage
BURNHAM, Lodge and Dairy
CHALFONT ST GILES, 'The Vache'
CHICHELEY, Grange Farm
  eyecatcher
CLIVEDEN, iron pagoda (NT)
COLESHILL, dairy
DINTON, sham castle
DORNEY, hermitage
DROPMORE, aviary

ELLESBOROUGH, Chequers grotto
FAWLEY, sham ruin
FILGRAVE, Coronation Clock-tower
GAYHURST, circular lavatory and
  others
GREAT MISSENDEN, Gothic summer-
  house
HADDENHAM, 'The Bone House'
HARTWELL, follies
HUGHENDEN, column (NT)
IVER, cascade
LANGLEY PARK, grotto
LITTLE HORWOOD, Manor House
MEDMENHAM, screen and tower
MIDDLE CLAYDON, Claydon House
  (NT)
MILTON KEYNES, Bradwell cows;
  Neath Hill clock-tower; Willen
  peace pagoda
PENN STREET, Woodrow High
  House grotto
STOKE MANDEVILLE, Elm Cottage
STOKE POGES, column; Gray's
  monument (NT) and alcove
STOWE, follies (NT)
TYRINGHAM, Lutyens pavilions
WADDESDON, aviary (NT)
WESTON UNDERWOOD, alcove and
  temple
WEST WYCOMBE, follies (NT)
WOTTON UNDERWOOD, Turkish
  temple

Cambridgeshire

ABBOTS RIPTON, Lord de Ramsey's
  follies
CAMBRIDGE, Hobson's Conduit;
  Laundry Farm
CASTOR, Milton Hall kennels

GAMLINGAY CINQUES, Full Moon
Gate
HEMINGFORD GREY, Pompeiian
grotto and temple
MADINGLEY, Madingley Hall sham
bridge
NORMAN CROSS, column
STAMFORD, Burghley House Bath
House
WIMPOLE HALL, sham castle (NT)
WISBECH, flint house; grotto (NT)

Cheshire

ADLINGTON HALL, shell-room and
mock castle
ALDERLEY EDGE, stone circle
BOLLINGTON, Clayton's Chimney;
White Nancy
COMBERMERE, Brankelow Folly
DISLEY, Woodbank Garden tower;
Wybersley Hall eyecatcher
HARTHILL, Mickerdale Cottage
KNUTSFORD, Mrs Gaskell's Tower;
Watt's follies
LYME PARK, Lyme Cage and Lantern
(NT)
MOW COP, castle (NT)
RUNCORN, Halton Castle
SANDIWAY, toll-booth tower
STYAL, stone circle
TATTON PARK, Sheep-stealer's
Tower (NT)
TILSTONE FEARNALL, gatehouse

Cleveland

ESTON NAB, ICI beacon
KIRKLEATHAM HALL, pavilions
SALTBURN-BY-THE-SEA, Albert
Memorial
SKELTON, grotto and wellhead

WYNYARD PARK, follies
YARM, folly garden

Cornwall

COTEHELE, tower
HELSTON, Grylls' Gate
LAUNCESTON, Werrington Park
sugar-loaves
LISKEARD, Treworgey clock-tower
MENABILLY, grotto
MORWENSTOW, Hawker's vicarage
MOUNT ARARAT, tower
MOUNT EDGCUMBE, 'The Ruin'
NEWQUAY, Huers' House
PENZANCE, Roger's Tower; Legrice
Folly
POLPERRO, shell-house
PORT ISAAC, 'The Birdcage' (NT)
PORTQUIN, Doyden Point tower
(NT)
REDRUTH, Carn Brea Castle and
Monument
ST IVES, Knill Monument
STRATTON, Civil War Monument
TRELISSICK, Tower (NT)
TRURO, Lander Column
VERYAN, round houses
WHITESAND BAY, Lugger's Cave
(NT)

Cumbria

ALLITHWAITE, Kirkhead Tower
AMBLESIDE, Bridge House (NT)
APPLEBY, Lady Anne Clifford's
follies
BARDSEA, Braddyll Mausoleum
BOWNESS, Storrs Hall Temple (NT)
BRAMPTON, Howard Memorial
Shelter; Brampton Tower
BRISCO, St Ninian's Well

BROUGHAM CASTLE, pillar
CARLISLE, Bunker Hill church window folly
CASTLE CARROCK, Tarn Tower folly
CONISHEAD, Priory Tower
CORBY CASTLE, cascade, summer-house and tempietto; Vulcan's Forge
DERWENT WATER, Derwent or Pocklington Island (NT)
DRUMBURGH HOUSE, tower
FAR SAWREY, 'The Station'
FINSTHWAITE, Pennington Tower
GREYSTOKE, follies
HAMPSFIELD, 'The Hospice'
HAYTON, Toppin Castle
HELVELLYN, two monuments
HETHERSGILL, dovecote privy
KIRKLINTON, Vicarage garden columns
LINDALE, cast-iron obelisk
LITTLE ORTON, Tempest Tower
MILNTHORPE, tower
NETHERBY, sham castle
NEWBY EAST, Newby Demesne gazebos
OLDWALL, Richardson's Folly
PENRITH, Beacon Tower; Musgrave Clock-tower
RAVENGLASS, Muncaster Tower
RAVENSTONEDALE, Lane Cottage
REAGILL, folly garden
SANDSFIELD, Edward I Monument
SEBERGHAM, eyecatcher
SHAP WELLS, Queen Victoria Monument
STANWIX, Rickerby Tower
THIRLMERE, Brothers Parting
THURSBY, Curthwaite Fiddleback
ULLSWATER, Lyulph's Tower
ULVERSTON, Hoad Hill Monument

WETHERAL, caves, statue; Whoof House folly; Vulcan's Forge
WRAY, John Longmire's Folly
WREAY, Sarah Losh's Church and Pompeiian Cottage

Derbyshire

BIRCHOVER, Rowter Rocks
BUXTON, Solomon's Temple
CHATSWORTH, gardens
CODNOR, Jessop Memorial
CRICH, Derby Assembly Rooms façade
DALE, rock hermitage
ECCLES PIKE, gateway
ELVASTON, Moorish Temple
FOREMARK, rock hermitage
HOPTON, Hopton Hall follies
MATLOCK, Victoria Tower; Riber Castle
NEWTON SOLNEY, Bladon Castle
OSMASTON, chimney
QUARNDON, Spa House
RAMSLEY MOOR, Nelson and Wellington monuments
RENISHAW, Gothic arch
STANTON MOOR, tower
SUDBURY, deercote (NT)
SWARKESTONE, grandstand
TWO DALES, Sydnope Stand

Devon

ASHBURTON, House of Cards
ASHFORD, Upcott folly gate-house
BABBACOMBE BAY, grotto
BERRYNARBOR, Watermouth sham ruin
BIDEFORD, 'The Old Folly'

BLACKAWTON, Oldstone's follies
BRAUNTON, Mortimer's Folly
BUCKLAND BEACON, Ten Commandments Tablets
BURRATOR RESERVOIR, Sheepstor arches
CHAGFORD, Rushford Tower
CHUDLEIGH KNIGHTON, Pitt House tower
CLOVELLY COURT, ornamental seats
COLATON RALEIGH, Bicton China Tower
COMBE MARTIN, 'Pack o' Cards' Inn
DARTMOOR, Rev. Bray's inscribed rocks
DEVONPORT, Civic Centre tower and column; H.M.S. Drake Tower
DODDISCOMBSLEIGH, Haldon Belvedere
EXETER, Bishops' Palace folly
EXMOUTH, 'A La Ronde' and 'Point in View'
FILLEIGH, Castle Hill arch
GIDLEIGH TOR, Prinsep's folly
GREAT TORRINGTON, pyramid
HARFORD, Hall Pleasure House
HARTLAND, gates and arch; Pleasure House
HATHERLEIGH, Pearce Belvedere
IVYBRIDGE, Filham House tower
KENTON, Oxton Hermitage
KINGSWEAR, Daymark Tower
LEE ABBEY, Duty Point Tower
LYMPSTONE, Mrs Peters's Clock
LYNMOUTH, Rhenish Tower
MAMHEAD, Castle
MILTON ABBOTT, Endsleigh Cottage grotto
OFFWELL, Bishop Copleston's Tower

PAIGNTON, Little Oldway Tower
PLYMSTOCK, Radford gatehouse
POWDERHAM CASTLE, belvedere
SALTRAM, Gothic belvedere (NT)
SHOBROOKE PARK, gazebo
SIDMOUTH, Knowle Grange grotto
STICKLEPATH, card cottage
TEIGNMOUTH, miniature lighthouse
WATER, tower
WESTLEIGH, Tapeley Park grotto
WIDECOMBE IN THE MOOR, Scobitor Round House
WOODFORD, Triumphal Arch Cottage

Dorset

BOURNEMOUTH, Upper Gardens Tower; Seafield Gardens Tower, Tucton Rd
CHARBOROUGH PARK, tower
COOMBE KEYNES, eyecatcher lodges
ENCOMBE, rock arch
HORTON, Sturt's Tower
KIMMERIDGE, Clavel Tower
MELBURY SAMPFORD, prospect tower
MILTON ABBAS, sham chapel
PORTESHAM, Hardy Monument (NT)
STEEPLE, Creech Grange Arch (NT)
SWANAGE, Burt's follies
WIMBORNE ST GILES, rustic arch; grotto

Durham

BISHOP AUCKLAND, deer-house
BURN HALL, cow-house
COATHAM MUNDEVILLE, deer-house
DARLINGTON, clock-tower; grotto
DURHAM, 'The Count's House'
GAINFORD, Gainford Hall column
GRETA BRIDGE, Rokeby cave and urn

HAMSTERLEY, pinnacle and summer-house
HAWTHORN, Sailor's Hall tower
RABY CASTLE, eyecatchers
SEDGEFIELD, Gothic ruin
WESTERTON, observatory
WITTON CASTLE, lodges

East Sussex

BRIGHTLING, Mad Jack Fuller's follies
BRIGHTON, Royal Pavilion; Carn Court Monument
ERIDGE, Saxonbury Tower
FIRLE, tower
HEATHFIELD, Gibraltar Tower
HOVE, garden chapel
RINGMER, Willingham House grotto
STANMER, Stanmer House monument

Essex

ALRESFORD, Chinese fishing pavilion
AUDLEY END, folly group
BAYTHORN END, Whitleys Hermitage
BELCHAMP WALTER HALL, gateway
BRAXTED PARK, hermitage
BRIGHTLINGSEA, Bateman's Folly
CHELMSFORD, conduit; Hylands Park Gothick cottage; water-tower
CLACTON, Moot Hall
COLCHESTER, Berechurch Hall Folly; Castle arch and temple; Jumbo water-tower; 'The Minories' summer-house
COLNE ENGAINE, column
EPPING, Copped Hall pavilions; High Street water-tower

FINGRINGHOE, Fingringhoe Hall bear-pit
GREAT DUNMOW, Stone Hall
HARLOW, Sir Frederick Gibberd's follies
HATFIELD GREAT PARK, shell-house (NT)
HEYBRIDGE, Heybridge Towers
HIGH BEACH, catacombs
HOCKLEY, spa
LAYER MARNEY, tower
LITTLE WALDEN, Cinder Hall
MIDDLETON, arch
MISTLEY, Adam swan; Mistley Towers
PENTLOW, Bull's Tower
RAYLEIGH, old windmill
SAFFRON WALDEN, castellated laundry; Elm Grove garden folly
SOUTH WEALD, Weald Hall belvedere tower
SOUTHEND, pier
THEYDON GARNON, Hill Hall lake temple
THORNDON HALL, folly group
TOLLESHUNT MAJOR, Beckingham Hall gatehouse
UPSHIRE, Warlies Park rotunda

Gloucestershire

AMBERLEY, St Chloe Eyecatcher
BARNSLEY, alcove and temple
BATSFORD, Batsford Park Japanese house
BERKELEY, Berkeley Castle eyecatcher
CHALFORD, gazebo
CHIPPING CAMPDEN, Kingcomb sham castle

CIRENCESTER, Cirencester Park follies

COATES, 'The Thames Head'

COLEFORD, 'The Rock House'

DRYBROOK, Euroclydon Hotel

FAIRFORD, Fairford Park column

FRAMPTON ON SEVERN, orangery

LOWER SWELL, Moorish cottage

NORTH NIBLEY, Tyndale Monument

PAINSWICK, folly garden and Red Stables

PRESTBURY, Grotto Tea Gardens

RUARDEAN, tower-house

SELSLEY, Ionic column

SEZINCOTE, Sezincote House

SIDDINGTON, 'The Round House' tower

STANCOMBE PARK, folly garden

STANWAY, pyramid

STAUNTON, Ionic columns

STROUD, Rodborough Fort sham castle; Woodchester Park tower

TUTSHILL, look-out tower

WINCHCOMBE, Bleby House grotto

Greater London

ABERDEEN PLACE, NW8, Crocker's Folly

BALLANCE ROAD, E9, Carroll Stone

BATTERSEA PARK, Peace Pagoda

BELVEDERE ROAD, SE19, castle house

BUCK LANE, NW9, castle house

CASTLEWOOD PARK, SE18, Severndroog Castle

CHISWICK HOUSE, W4, cascade

CLOCK TOWER PLACE, N7, clock-tower

CRYSTAL PALACE, SE19, dinosaurs

DUCK'S HILL ROAD, NORTHWOOD, rotunda

FITZGERALD AVENUE, SW14, coach-house

FRIERN BARNET ROAD, N11, 'The Turrets'

GEORGE GREEN, E11, Jubilee Fountain

GREEN LANES, N4, Stoke Newington Pumping Station

GROSVENOR GARDENS, SW1, shell-houses

GROTTO ROAD, TWICKENHAM, Pope's Grotto

GUNNERSBURY PARK, W3, tower

HAMPSTEAD LANE, NW3, 'The Logs'

HAMPTON COURT, Hampton Court House grotto; Huck's Chalet

HAMPTON COURT ROAD, Shakespeare Temple

HOLLY VILLAGE, NW5

IMPERIAL INSTITUTE ROAD, SW7, Collcutt Tower

ISLEWORTH, Osterley Park grotto

KENSINGTON GORE, SW7, Albert Memorial

KENWOOD, NW3, sham bridge

KEW GARDENS, pagoda and arch

LANGFORD PLACE, NW8, house

LEINSTER GARDENS, W2, sham façade

LINCOLNS INN FIELDS, WC2, toolshed

LINSCOTT ROAD, E5, Greek façade

LIPHOOK CRESCENT, SE23, tower

LORDSHIP LANE, N17, Bruce Castle Tower

MARBLE HILL PARK, Countess of Suffolk's grotto

MARKHOUSE ROAD, E17, 'The Lighthouse'

MEATH GARDENS, E2, arch

MORTLAKE HIGH STREET, SW14, Sir Richard Burton's tent

PAGODA GARDENS, SE3, Chinese house

PHIPPS BRIDGE ROAD, SW19, castle house

PINNER HILL ROAD, HARROW, Tooke's Folly

QUAKER'S WALK, N21, tower-house

REPOSITORY ROAD, SE18, 'The Rotunda'

ROUND HILL, SE26, St Antholin's Spire

RYLETT ROAD, W12, Gothic stables

SOHO SQUARE, W1, Tudor toolshed

SOUTHALL, water-tower

SOUTH BANK, SE1, Oxo tower

STAMFORD BROOK ROAD, W6, Grotto Cottage

STRAWBERRY HILL, TWICKENHAM, 'The Chapel in the Woods'

STREATHAM, SW16, St Michael's Convent tower

SUTTON, Carshalton House grotto and water-house; Carshalton Park grotto

SWISS COTTAGE, NW3, 'The Swiss Cottage'

TOWER COURT, N16, sham ruin

TRAFALGAR SQUARE, WC2, 40 faceted lamps

TWICKENHAM, York House grotto fountain

THE VALE, SW3, Russian izba

VICTORIA EMBANKMENT, WC2, Cleopatra's Needle

VICTORIA PARK, E9, Victoria Fountain

WANSTEAD PARK, E11, grotto

WATERTOWER HILL, CROYDON, Norman water-tower

WICKHAM ROAD, BECKENHAM, Siamese garage

WOODFORD GREEN, Harts Hospital sham abbey

WOODSIDE PARK, N22, round house

Greater Manchester

HEATON PARK, colonnade

MOSSLEY, Hartshead Tower

RAMSBOTTOM, Grant's Tower; Nuttall Farm screen; Peel Tower

SALFORD, Knolls House

TOTTINGTON, Tower Farm

WORSLEY, Ellesmere Memorial

Hampshire

AVINGTON, Avington House pavilion

BOLDRE, Walhampton House grotto

BRAMSHOTT, Bird's Folly

DROXFORD, Studwell Lodge tunnel

EAGLEHURST, Luttrell's Tower

EAST TISTED, Rotherfield Park towers

FARLEY MOUNT, pyramid

FARRINGDON, Massey's Folly

GOSPORT, Hermitage follies

HAMBLEDON, Hopton House tower

HARTLEY WINTNEY, West Green House follies (NT)

HAVANT, Leigh Park follies

HAWLEY, Minley Manor gazebo

HEADLEY, Headley Park folly

HIGHCLERE, Heaven's Gate; Grotto Lodge; Jackdaw's Castle

HOUGHTON, sham ruin

HURSLEY, Cranbury Park ruins

HURSTBOURNE PARK, monument

HYTHE, Chinese pavilion; Knightons

MEDSTEAD, Jonathan's Folly

MOTTISFONT, Abbey summer-house

NETHER WALLOP, pyramid

NORTHINGTON, castle cottage

ODIHAM, King John's Hunting Lodge (NT)
PETERSFIELD, Grange Farm House
PORTCHESTER, Nelson Monument
PORTSMOUTH, Naval Monuments
ROCKBOURNE, Eyre Coote Monument
SHAWFORD, Cromwell's House and belvedere
SHERBORNE ST JOHN, 'The Vyne' garden pavilion (NT)
STRATFIELD SAYE, summer-house
SWAY, Peterson's Folly
WARNFORD, grotto and dower house
WEST MEON HUT, tetralithon

Hereford and Worcester

ABBERLEY, clock-tower
BREDON HILL, tower
BROADWAY, tower
CLENT GROVE, sham ruin
CROOME D'ABITOT, garden buildings
DEFFORD, Dunstall Castle
DINMORE, grotto
DOWNTON CASTLE, hermit's cave and library tower
GREAT WITLEY, giant fountains
HAGLEY, Hagley Park sham ruin
HEREFORD, Castle column
LEDBURY, Hope End stables
LEINTHALL EARLS, Gatley Park, 'The Folly'
LUGWARDINE, Longworth Pillar
MORTIMER'S CROSS, sham castle gate (NT)
ROSS-ON-WYE, Kyrle's follies; Chinese kiosk of 1975
ROUS LENCH, Chafy Tower
SHOBDON, arches

SPETCHLEY, root-house
STOURPORT, Redstone Rock
TENBURY WELLS, pagoda
WHITCHURCH, memorial clock

Hertfordshire

ABBOT'S LANGLEY, Ovaltine dairy
ALDENHAM, sham ruin
ASHRIDGE, Bridgewater Monument (NT)
AYOT ST LAWRENCE, church
BARNET, Hadley Highstone Memorial
BENINGTON, sham castle
BROOKMANS PARK, folly arch
COTTERED, Japanese garden
DRIVER'S END, Node Dairy
GILSTON, Gilston Park porch
GREAT AMWELL, Myddleton Monument; Flint House column, garden temple
HATFIELD HOUSE, small tower
HEMEL HEMPSTEAD, Gadebridge Park tower
KNEBWORTH, Queen Anne's Chapel
LITTLE BERKHAMSTED, Stratton's Observatory
NEWGATE STREET, Greek dairy
ST ALBANS, Prospect Road arch
ST PAUL'S WALDEN, temples
SOUTH MIMMS, Clare Hall, St Antholin's Church
STANSTEAD ABBOTS, Briggens eyecatcher and tower
WALTHAM CROSS, Temple Bar (NT)
WARE, Scott's Grotto

Humberside

BRIDLINGTON, Carnaby Temple
BROUGH, tower

CLEETHORPES, sham ruin
COTTINGHAM, Castle Hill Tower
GRIMSTON, Grimston Garth Tower
HORNSEA, Bettison's Folly
HULL, Wilberforce Column
NORTH CAVE, Castle Farm
SEATON, Mushroom Cottage
SLEDMERE, folly group
SOUTH CAVE, Cave Castle gateway
WOOTTON, pigsty

Isle of Wight

BLACKGANG, South View,
   Shakespeare Memorial
CALBOURNE, Swainston Temple
CHALE, Hoy's Monument and The
   Salt Cellar
EAST COWES, Royal follies at
   Osborne; shell-house
KINGSTON, Billingham gazebo
RYDE, Appley Tower
TOTLAND, Tennyson Monument

Kent

BIRCHINGTON, Quex Park Waterloo
   Tower
CANTERBURY, Dane John
DUNKIRK, tower
FARNINGHAM, screen; Mill House
   folly
GILLINGHAM, Shogun clock-tower
GREATSTONE-ON-SEA, listening
   device
HADLOW, May's Folly
KEARSNEY, Abbey ruin
KINGSGATE, Lord Holland's follies
KNOLE, 'The Birdhouse' (NT)
LITTLESTONE-ON-SEA, tower
MAIDSTONE, Mote Park rotunda
MARGATE, grotto

MEREWORTH, Castle arch
ROLVENDEN, gnome garden
SHEERNESS, 'Ship On Shore'
TENTERDEN, Hales Place turrets
THROWLEY, Belmont sham church
   and grotto
TONBRIDGE, 'The Cedars' grotto
WALDERSHARE PARK, belvedere
WESTERHAM, belvedere

Lancashire

ACCRINGTON, New High Riley
   eyecatcher
BELMONT, tower
BLACKO, Stansfield Tower
BLACKPOOL, Blackpool Tower
BROWSHOLME, Spire Farm
CLITHEROE, turret
DALTON, Ashurst's Beacon
DARWEN, India Mill Chimney;
   Jubilee Tower
ELSWICK, stable screen
GISBURN, dog kennels
LANCASTER, Ashton Memorial;
   Music Room
LUNE VALLEY, Claughton Hall
OVER KELLET, Capernwray Hall
   gamekeeper's lodge; Kirk House
   Gothic pigsty
PARBOLD, Parbold Bottle
QUERNMORE, Jubilee Tower
RIVINGTON PIKE, Liverpool Castle;
   Roynton Gdns
SAWLEY, rebuilt arch; abbey ruins
SILVERDALE, Lindeth Tower;
   Warton Sands Tower
WHALLEY, Whalley Viaduct Gothic
   arches
WHEELTON, Prospect House
   rotunda

Leicestershire

BARSBY, Godson's Folly
BELVOIR, Belvoir Castle grotto
BRADGATE PARK, Old John
BURTON ON THE WOLDS, shell room
CLIPSHAM, Mr Wheatley's folly (not yet built)
EXTON, Bark Temple and Fort Henry
LONG WHATTON, Whatton House gardens
LOUGHBOROUGH, Garendon Park follies
MEASHAM, Mr Talbot's Gothic Cathedrals
NORMANTON, church tower
RAVENSTONE, sham windowed almshouse
SCRAPTOFT, grotto

Lincolnshire

ASHBY PUERORUM, arch
ASWARBY, columns
BELTON HOUSE, Belmount Tower and Sham Ruin (NT)
BOSTON, Freemasons' Hall
BOULTHAM, Hartsholme Hall column
BRANSTON, Mr Lovely's gates
BROCKLESBY, Hermitage and Newsham dry bridge
CAISTOR, Pelham's Pillar
COLEBY HALL, temples
DENTON MANOR, grotto
DUNSTON, Dunston Pillar
EAGLE, 'The Jungle'
FILLINGHAM, gateway
GATE BURTON, 'Shatoo'
GREATFORD, folly garden
LONDONTHORPE, bus shelter

LOUTH, Brackenborough Hall sham ruin; Vicarage spire; 'The Priory'; Broadbank folly
MARSTON HALL, gazebo
SLEAFORD, Westgate walling
SOMERBY HALL, pillar
SWINSTEAD, Vanbrugh pavilion
TEALBY, Castle Farm
WOODHALL SPA, Wellington Memorial

Merseyside

BEBINGTON, graffiti wall
INCE BLUNDELL, column
KNOWSLEY HALL, tower and summer-house
LIVERPOOL, Hartley's Dockland follies; tunnels; tower

Norfolk

BLICKLING HALL, pyramid and racecourse stand (NT)
BRETTENHAM, grotto
BRININGHAM, Belle Vue Tower
COLNEY HALL, grotto
CRIMPLESHAM HALL, chapel
DENTON, grotto
GREAT YARMOUTH, Norfolk Pillar
GUNTON PARK, tower
HEYDON HALL, tower
HOLKHAM HALL, column
LANGLEY, eyecatcher gatehouse
LITTLE ELLINGHAM, clock-tower
MELTON CONSTABLE, Melton bathhouse
RAVENINGHAM, cast-iron turret
SAXTHORPE, Mannington Hall follies
SHERINGHAM HALL, Repton-style temple
WESTWICK, tower

Northamptonshire

BADBY, Lantern House
BRIGSTOCK, Lyveden New Bield (NT)
CASTLE ASHBY, folly group
DEENE, Kirby Hall
FINEDON, Exmill Cottage; Woodford Wellington Tower
GEDDINGTON, Boughton House Chinese Tent
HOLDENBY, arches
HORTON HALL, eyecatcher and menagerie
NASEBY, Monument
NEWNHAM, sham ruins
NORTHAMPTON, Boughton follies
PRESTON CAPES, eyecatcher
RUSHTON, Triangular Lodge

Northumberland

ALNWICK, folly group
BAVINGTON HALL, dovecote
BELSAY HALL, gardens
CAMBO, Wallington, Rothley Castle, Codger's Fort (NT)
CAPHEATON HALL, sham ruin; Littleharle Tower
FORD, Castle gates
HAGGERSTON, tower
HARTBURN, Gothic façade
HAUGH HEAD, dovecote
HUMBLETON, Homilton Tower
KIELDER, Castle
LEMMINGTON, column and façade
NUNWICK HOUSE, kennels
OTTERBURN, Percy Cross
ROTHBURY, Sharp's Folly, Whitton
SEATON DELAVAL, mausoleum
SIMONBURN CASTLE, eyecatcher
STANNINGTON, Blagdon Hall follies

TWIZEL, Castle
WOOLER, Ewart Park Tower

North Yorkshire

ALLERTON MAULEVERER, rotunda
AYSGARTH, Sorrell Sykes follies
AZERLEY, tower
BISHOPTHORPE, Church façade
BYLAND ABBEY, Oldstead Tower
CASTLE HOWARD, follies
CONSTABLE BURTON, Akebar caravan shop
EAST WITTON, Slobbering Sal
EBBERSTON, Aelfrid's Memorial
FALLING FORCE, hermitage
GREWELTHORPE, Hackfall Woods
GREYGARTH, Greygarth Monument
HARROGATE, Harlow Hill Tower
HARTFORTH HALL, arch
HELMSLEY, Duncombe Park
HOWSHAM, Howsham Woods Castle
HUNMANBY, gate
ILTON, Druids' temple
KIRKBY MALZEARD, Mowbray House follies
KNARESBOROUGH, Fort Montagu
LEYBURN, sham castle
LITTLE RIBSTON, Arch and Butler
MASHAM, Nutwith classical dovecote
MASHAM MOOR, tower
MIDDLEHAM, castellated bridge
PATELY BRIDGE, Yorke's Folly
RICHMOND, Oliver Duckett, Aske Hall; Culloden Tower
RIPON, gazebos
ROBIN HOOD'S BAY, pigsty
SAWLEY HALL, bridge arch; Ripley Castle Alsatian village

SCAMPSTON HALL, deer-house
SCARBOROUGH, pagoda; Baron
   Albert's Tower
SEDBURY, watch-tower and
   castellated farm buildings
SETTLE, 'The Folly'
SKIPTON CASTLE, grotto room
STUDLEY ROYAL, follies
SWINITHWAITE, temple
SWINTON, Gothic bridge
TADCASTER, Grimston Park Tower,
   Hazlewood Castle Tower

Nottinghamshire

BESTWOOD, Pumping Station
CLIPSTONE, Duke's Folly
CLUMBER PARK, temples (NT)
ELSTON, Middleton's Folly
LINBY, Castle Mill
NEWSTEAD, sham forts
NOTTINGHAM, pagoda; Rope Walk
   tunnel and pagoda
NUTHALL, summer-house
SCARRINGTON, horseshoe pile
THORESBY, Budby Village
WELBECK ABBEY, underground
   rooms

Oxfordshire

ABINGDON, sham ruin
BLENHEIM, column and arch
BUCKLAND, ice-house and rotunda
CHIPPING NORTON, Mr Bliss's
   Tweed Mill
COKETHORPE, Fish House Mill
COLESHILL, Strattenborough Castle
   Farm
DITCHLEY PARK, grotto and temples
FARINGDON, Lord Berners' Folly
HENLEY DEER PARK, mound

HENLEY-ON-THAMES, Friar Park
   grotto
HIGHMOOR, US Army model house
HOLTON, folly mound
IPSDEN, druids' circle and
   monument
MAPLEDURHAM, eyecatcher
MIDDLETON STONEY, Gothic barn
NUNEHAM COURTENAY, Carfax
   Conduit
OXFORD, Cauldwell's Castle;
   Judge's Lodging House;
   Madden's pyramid
ROTHERFIELD GREYS, Chinese Bridge
ROUSHAM, eyecatcher
SHIPLAKE, Crowsley Park grotto
STOKE ROW, Maharajah's Well
STONOR PARK, stone circle
WHEATLEY, Shotover sham façade
WOODCOTE, 'The Folly'
WOOLSTONE, tower
WROXTON, eyecatcher

Shropshire

ACTON BURNELL, grotto
ATCHAM, Attingham eyecatcher
   (NT)
CALLOW HILL, Flounders Folly
HADNALL, Waterloo Windmill
HAWKSTONE, folly group
HODNET, columns
IRONBRIDGE, Gothic warehous
PITCHFORD, tree-house
QUATFORD, tower and castl
SHREWSBURY, Shoemaker'
   Gateway etc.
TONG, pyramid hen-ho
UFFINGTON, Haughmo
WESTON RHYN, Quin

Somerset

ATHELNEY, King Alfred's Monument
BURROW BRIDGE, sham church (NT)
BUTLEIGH, Hood Monument
CHEDDON FITZPAINE, Hestercombe House temples
CHILTON POLDEN, Stradling's Folly
COMBE FLOREY, Winter's Folly
COTHELSTONE, sham ruin
CROWCOMBE, sham ruins
CURRY RIVEL, Burton Steeple
DUNSTER, Conygar Hill Tower (NT); Spear's Cross Garden
EAST CRANMORE, Paget's Tower
ELWORTHY, Willett's Tower
GOATHURST, folly group
ILCHESTER, 'Bell Tower'
KILMERSDON, Ammerdown Park lighthouse
KNOWLE HALL, eyecatcher
MONTACUTE, St Michael's Tower (NT)
WEST HORRINGTON, Romulus and Remus
WEST QUANTOXHEAD, St Audries' shell grotto
WIVELISCOMBE, pinnacle
WRANGWAY, Wellington Monument (NT)
YEOVIL, Barwick Park follies; Brympton D'Evercy alcove

South Yorkshire

BARNSLEY, Locke Park Tower
BIRDWELL, Boston Castle eyecatcher
BURGHWALLIS, Robin Hood's Well
HOOD GREEN, Wentworth Castle; Steeple Lodge
HOYLAND NETHER, Hoyland Lowe Stand
PENISTONE, Hartcliffe Tower and gazebo
SHEFFIELD, monuments; sham castle
SUTTON MOOR, tower
WENTWORTH WOODHOUSE, follies

Staffordshire

ADBASTON, Batchacre porch and tower
ALMASTON, Blithfield Goat Lodge
ALTON TOWERS, folly group
BIDDULPH, Biddulph Grange Chinese Garden
BREWOOD, Speedwell Castle
BROCTON, dovecote and sham ruin
CHEDDLETON, Basford Hall bathhouse
CODSALL, Chillington Hall façades and temples
ECTON, mock castle
ENVILLE, Chinese pavilion and eyecatcher
FAZELEY, castellated bridge
FORTON, Sutton Monument
GAILEY, round house
HALES, Pell Wall Lodge
ILAM, tower
IPSTONES, Belmont sham church
KIDSGROVE, round tower
LICHFIELD, observation pavilion
MERETOWN, Aqualate Hall, 'The Castle'
MUCKLESTONE, Oakley Folly
OKEOVER, classical closet
SANDON, Lord Harrowby's follies
SEIGHFORD, sham church
SHARESHILL, tower
SHUGBOROUGH PARK, follies (NT)

SOMERFORD, eyecatcher
STAFFORD, Castle
TIXALL, Bottle Lodge, rotunda
TRENTHAM, Sutherland Monument
TUTBURY, sham castle
WESTON-UNDER-LIZARD, tower
WILLOUGHBRIDGE, Wells bath-house
WOMBOURN, Bratch Cottage;
    Bearnett House tower

Suffolk

ALDHAM, Taylor Monument
BARTON MILLS, Church Cottage
BENTWATER, Rendlesham lodges
BRANTHAM, Brantham Glebe Birch
    follies
CODDENHAM, Shrubland follies
ELVEDEN, Hall
ERWARTON HALL, gatehouse
EUSTON HALL, Euston Mill
FRESTON, tower
HADLEIGH, Gothic ruin
HEVENINGHAM HALL, temple
ICKLINGHAM, monument
ICKWORTH, oval house, round
    house, obelisk
LOWESTOFT, 'The Tower House'
NACTON, Orwell Park towers
PAKENHAM, parson painting
TATTINGSTONE, Tattingstone
    Wonder
THORPENESS, 'The House in the
    Clouds'
WOOLVERSTONE, 'The Cat House'

Surrey

ADDLESTONE, Woburn Park Garden
BOX HILL, tower (NT)
CATERHAM, Whitehill folly-tower,
    War Coppice Rd

CHALDON, Willey Farm tower
CHERTSEY, St Anne's Hill, gazebo
CHOBHAM, Westcroft Park bell-
    tower
CLANDON, Maori House (NT)
CLAREMONT, Vanbrugh belvedere,
    temple, grotto (NT)
CLAYGATE, semaphore house
COBHAM, Foxwarren Watch-tower;
    Painshill Park follies; Semaphore
    Tower
DORKING, Tower Cottage
EPSOM, 'The Durdans', horse tomb
ESHER, Waynflete Tower; garden
    temple; Travellers' Rest
GATTON, Town Hall
GODALMING, Busbridge follies
LEITH HILL, Hull's Tower (NT)
LINGFIELD, Starborough Castle
MERSTHAM, tower
NUTFIELD, Wellhouse Tower;
    Redwood
PEPER HAROW, sham ruin; Bonville
    Fount
PRINCE'S COVERTS, Jessop's Well
REIGATE, Chapel Windmill; sham
    castle gateway
SHERE, Albury Park tunnels;
    wellhead
VIRGINIA WATER, classical ruin; Fort
    Belvedere
WITLEY, Whitaker Wright's follies
WOTTON, Tortoise House; temple

Tyne and Wear

CLEADON, Pumping Station
NEWCASTLE, Grey Monument
PENSHAW, Penshaw Monument
    (NT)

ROWLANDS GILL, Gibside Column (NT)
WASHINGTON, Victoria Viaduct
WHICKHAM, Long John Monument
WHITBURN, sham ruin

Warwickshire

ALCESTER, Oversley Castle Tower
ARLESCOTE, pavilions
BURTON DASSETT, 'The Beacon'
CHARLECOTE PARK, west entrance (NT)
CHESTERTON, classical windmill
COMPTON WYNYATES, Compton Pike
EDGE HILL, 'Castle Inn'
FARNBOROUGH, Farnborough Hall gardens (NT)
HALFORD, 'The Folly'
IDLICOTE, dovecote/water-tower
SOUTHAM, monument
STRATFORD UPON AVON, Clopton House Tower

West Midlands

COVENTRY, cemetery gazebo
EDGBASTON, George Road bothy; Perrot's Folly
HALESOWEN, 'The Leasowes'
LIFFORD, watch-tower
SUTTON COLDFIELD, Ashfurlong Hall pavilion
WALSALL, Skidmore Observatory

West Sussex

ARUNDEL, Hiorn Tower
CASTLE GORING, Rat's Castle
CLAYTON, tunnel entrance
COLGATE, Holmbush Tower

GOODWOOD, shell-house
HICKSTEAD, sham castle
LORDINGTON, Racton Monument
NORTHCHAPEL, Shillinglee Deer Tower
PATCHING, Michelgrove Ruins
PETWORTH, Upperton Monument
PULBOROUGH, Toat Monument
SLINDON, Nore Folly (NT)
STEYNING, Wappingthorne water-tower
TILLINGTON, Pitshill Tower
UPPARK, Vandalian Tower (NT)

West Yorkshire

ABERFORD, Parlington Park arch
ADEL, folly garden
APPERLEY BRIDGE, Elam's Tower
BRADFORD, Bierley Hall grotto
BRAMHAM PARK, Gothick Temple
BRIGHOUSE, Robin Hood's Grave
CRINGLES, tower
EGYPT, The Walls of Jericho
HALIFAX, Wainhouse's Tower
HARDEN, St David's Ruin
HUDDERSFIELD, Ravensknowle Park; Victoria Tower
KEIGHLEY, Oakworth Park Gardens
LEEDS, bearpit; Moorish warehouse; Roundhay Park sham castle; Temple Mills; Tower Works, Globe Rd; Weetwood Hall grotto
LINDLEY, clock-tower
MIRFIELD, Dumb Steeple
NEWMILLERDAM, Kettlethorpe Hall boat-house
OTLEY, Bramhope Tunnel Monument
RAWDON, domed retreat

TODMORDEN, Stoodley Pike
WALTON HALL, sham ruin
WETHERBY, ex-Ferriby Hall gazebo
WRAGBY, Nostell Priory pyramid
(NT)

Wiltshire

AMESBURY, grotto
BOWDEN PARK, gatehouse and
grotto
BOWOOD, Bowood House cascade
and Golden Gate
COMPTON CHAMBERLAYNE, arch
CORSHAM, Corsham Court folly
wall
DEVIZES, Castle; Market Cross;
Shane's Castle
ETCHILHAMPTON HILL, Lydeway
Monument
FONTHILL GIFFORD, remnants of
Fonthill Abbey
LACOCK, columns (NT)

MONKTON FARLEIGH, Brown's Folly
NEWTON TONEY, grotto; Benson's
Folly
ODSTOCK, Longford Castle
ROOD ASHTON, lodges
SALISBURY, Bourne Hill porch
SANDRIDGE, tower
SAVERNAKE FOREST, Ailesbury
Column; Tottenham Park
summer-house
SPYE PARK HOUSE, gateway
STOURHEAD, Follies (NT)
TOLLARD ROYAL, Larmer Gardens
TROWLE COMMON, Longscroft Farm
WANBOROUGH, church with spire
and tower
WARDOUR CASTLE, grotto
WEXCOMBE, pineapple
WHITEPARISH, 'The Pepperbox'
(NT)
WICK HILL, Maud Heath's Column
WILTON, Wilton House Old
Schoolhouse

WALES

Clwyd

ABERGELE, Gwyrch Castle
DENBIGH, castellated farm
HAWARDEN, sham castle
HENLLAN, New Foxhalls
LLANBEDR DYFFRYN CLWYD, Castell
Gyrn
MARFORD, village
MOEL FAMAU, Jubilee Tower
MOSTYN, Dry Bridge Lodge
NERCWYS, sham castle
PEN-Y-STRYT, Sir Watkin's Tower
RUABON, column and Nant-y-Belan

Tower
WREXHAM, Acton Park screen

Dyfed

ABERYSTWYTH, Pen Dinas Column
CILWENDEG, shell-house
DEVIL'S BRIDGE, Johnes's arch
LAMPETER, Derry Ormond Tower
LLANARTHNEY, Paxton's Tower
PENALLY, Tower of the Winds
PENTRE-BACH, Mail Coach Pillar

Glamorgan

ABERDULAIS, aqueduct
BLACK PILL, column, tower and
  eyecatcher cottage
CARDIFF, Castle
JERSEY MARINE, pleasure park
KITTLE, Kilvrough Tower
NEATH, Ivy Tower
PENRICE, Penrice Wall
PONTYPRIDD, Glyntaff druid towers
REYNOLDSTON, stone circle
TONGWYNLAIS, Castell Coch

Gwent

KEMEYS COMMANDER, folly house
LLANGATTOCK NIGH USK, Clytha
  Castle
MONMOUTH, Kymin Naval Temple
  and Round House
PONTYPOOL, shell grotto

Gwynedd

AMLWCH, Bull Bay Roman baths
DOLBENMAEN, Bryncir Tower
GLYNLLIFON PARK, Fort
  Williamsbourg
LLANFACHRETH, arches
LLANFAIRPWLLGWYN, Marquess of
  Anglesey's Column; Nelson
  statue
LLANFROTHEN, Plas Brondanw
  Watch-tower
LLANRWST, Maenan Tower
PORTMEIRION, village
RHIWLAS, Price mausoleum

Powys

CRIGGION, Rodney's Pillar
MACHYNLLETH, forge
NEW RADNOR, Cornewall Lewis
  Monument

SCOTLAND

Borders

BLYTH BRIDGE, whalebone arch
DRYBURGH, Wallace on the Hill
ECKFORD, watch-tower
FAIRNINGTON HOUSE, Baron's Folly
HALLYARDS, Black Dwarf
PEEBLES, Rosetta castellated stables
PENIEL HEUGH, Waterloo Column
SKIRLING, Lord Carmichael's figures
TEVIOTHEAD, Riddell Cone
TRAQUAIR, folly gates
WESTRUTHER, castellated cottages
WHIM, dovecote

Central

DUNMORE PARK, pineapple
LANRICK CASTLE, tree
MUGDOCK, folly-tower
STIRLING, Wallace Monument

Dumfries and Galloway

BORGUE, 'The Cow Palace'
DUMFRIES, Queensbury Column
GATEHOUSE OF FLEET, Cally House
  Gothick temple; Jubilee clock-
  tower

GLENKILN, Johnny Turner's
Monument; modern sculptures
MOFFAT, ram on fountain
THORNHILL, column

Fife

BALCARRES, Lady's Folly
COLINSBURGH, Balcarres Crag
KINGLASSIE, Blythe's Folly
KIRKCALDY, Nairn's Folly
LEVEN, shell bus
LOW VALLEYFIELD, Woodhead Farm
MOUNT HILL, Hopetoun Monument
TAYPORT, Waterloo Tower
WEST WEMYSS, home farm

Grampian

BANFF, Downhill Temple
CROOK OF ALVES, York Tower
FASQUE, Gothick pavilion
FETTERESSO, church
FORRES, Nelson Tower
HARLAW, monument
NEW DEER, Culsh Memorial
OLD DEER, Pitfour follies
TARVES, Prop of Ythsie Tower
WHITEHOUSE, Castle Forbes Dairy

Highland

BALLACHULISH, Steward o' the
Glens Monument
CONONBRIDGE, Kinkell Pyramid
DUNROBIN, 'The Hunting House'
EVANTON, Gates of Negapatam
GLENFINNAN, tower
GOLSPIE, Sutherland statue
JOHN O'GROATS, octagonal room
LOCH OICH, Well of Seven Heads
THURSO, Castle lodge; Harald's
Tower; Washington Monument

Lothian

ABERLADY, Gosford mausoleum
BILSTON, Dryden Tower
BROXBURN, Broxmouth Pillar
COCKENZIE AND PORT SETON,
Cockenhouse Volcano
CRAMOND BRIDGE, Craigiehall
Temple
EAST FORTUNE, Gilmerton screen
EDINBURGH, Calton Hill follies;
'The Drummond Scrolls';
Moray House pavilion;
Prestonfield Ace of Clubs
House; Scott Monument
HADDINGTON, Amisfield Mains;
Hopetoun Monument
LEITH, St Bernard's Well
LINLITHGOW, Hope Monuments
MUSSELBURGH, Newhailes grotto
PENICUIK, Arthur's Oven; Clerk's
follies
PORTOBELLO, tower
QUEENSFERRY, Midhope Tower
TORPHICHEN, tower
TURNHOUSE, Clermiston Tower
TYNINGHAME HOUSE, pavilion
YORKSTON, Rosebery steading

Strathclyde

ALLOWAY, Burns Monument
CAMPBELTOWN, Oatfield grotto
CARLUKE, Milton Head Memorial
CARRADALE, Torrisdale Castle arch
CULZEAN, follies
DALMALLY, monument
DUNSYRE, Stonypath garden
FAILFORD, Burns Pillar
GLASGOW, Scott Column; Glasgow
Green Battle Column;
Templeton and ICI warehouse;

GLASGOW *cont'd*
  200 Nithsdale Road
HAMILTON, Chatelherault;
  mausoleum
INVERARAY, folly group
KILMARNOCK, Burns Monument
KILNINVER, Armaddy Castle boat-
  house
LARGS, tower
MAUCHLINE, Burns Tower
MILNGAVIE, 'The Folly'
NEW SELMA, Lady Margaret's
  Tower
NEWTON MEARNS, Pollok
  Monument
OBAN, McCaig's Folly
RENTON, Smollett's Column
REST AND BE THANKFUL, stone
ROSNEATH, Belvedere steading
ST QUIVOX, Auchincruive Tea
  House
TARBOLTON, Barnweil Tower

Tayside

ARBROATH, Hospitalfield Mortuary

BLAIR ATHOLL, 'The Whim', Blair
  Castle
COMRIE, Melville Monument
CRAIGTON, Panmure Monument
DALNACARDOCH, Wade Stone
DUNDEE, Triumphal Arch
DUNKELD, Dunkeld House,
  Ossian's Hall and Hermitage
EDZELL, Dalhousie Arch
KENMORE, Taymouth Castle
  rustication
MEIKLEOUR, hedge
MONTROSE, Langley Park steading
PANBRIDE, Camustane Hill Tower
PERTH, Kinnoull Hill Tower;
  Triumphal Arch
PITLOCHRY, Clunie Memorial
  Arch

Western Isles

BUAILEDUBH, shell bus
LEVERBURGH, folly village
NORTH UIST, Callernich House

NOTABLE OBELISKS

ENGLAND

Avon

NEMPNETT THRUBWELL, Nempnett
  Needle

Bedfordshire

AMPTHILL, obelisk
CHICKSANDS, obelisks
SOUTHILL, obelisk

Buckinghamshire

CHALFONT ST PETER, obelisk
ELLESBOROUGH, Coombe Hill
  obelisk

Cambridgeshire

HARSTON, Wale obelisk

Cheshire

APPLETON, obelisk

COMBERMERE, Brankelow Folly; obelisk
EATON PARK, obelisk
FARNDON, obelisk
KNUTSFORD, Legh obelisk
NETHER ALDERLEY, Stanley obelisk

Cornwall

BOCONNOC, Lyttelton obelisk
BODMIN, Gilbert obelisk
BOTUS FLEMING, Dr Martyn's tomb
FALMOUTH, Killigrew obelisk
FOWEY, Victoria & Albert obelisk
PADSTOW, Victoria obelisk

Cumbria

BROUGHTON-IN-FURNESS, obelisk
KENDAL, Castle Howe obelisk; Tolson Hall obelisk
LINDALE, obelisk

Derbyshire

OAKERTHORPE, obelisk

Devon

ARLINGTON, Arlington Court Obelisk (NT)
HATHERLEIGH, Morris obelisk
MAMHEAD, Castle and obelisk

Dorset

ENCOMBE, rock arch; obelisk
MILBORNE ST ANDREW, obelisk
MORETON HOUSE, obelisk
PORTLAND BILL, obelisk
STALBRIDGE, Thornhill House obelisk

WIMBORNE MINSTER, Kingston Lacy obelisks (NT)

Durham

BARNINGHAM, Grouse obelisk
DURHAM, Salvin obelisk

East Sussex

BALDSLOW, Beauport Park obelisk

Essex

LOUGHTON, 'The Warren'; horse obelisk
SOUTHEND, Crowstone obelisk

Gloucestershire

BISLEY, Nether Lypiatt obelisk

Greater London

BOUNDS GREEN ROAD, N11, obelisk
EAST CHURCHFIELD ROAD, W3, obelisk
MANOR HALL AVENUE, NW4, obelisk
SANDY LANE, HAMPTON WICK, Brown obelisk
STANMORE, obelisk
TIBBET'S CORNER, SW19, Fire Plates obelisk

Greater Manchester

DUNHAM MASSEY, obelisk (NT)

Hereford and Worcester

EASTNOR, obelisk
LICKEY, obelisk

Hertfordshire

BARKWAY, obelisk
TRING, Nell Gwynne obelisk
WADESMILL, obelisk

Humberside

BELTON, obelisk

Isle of Wight

CULVER DOWN, Yarborough obelisk

Kent

BILSINGTON, obelisk
HIGHAM, obelisk
RAMSGATE, obelisk

Lincolnshire

STOKE ROCHFORD, obelisk

Merseyside

LIVERPOOL, obelisk

Northumberland

BEDLINGTON, obelisk
LANTON, obelisk
OGLE, obelisk
SEATON DELAVAL, obelisk
SWARLAND, Nelson obelisk

North Yorkshire

RICHMOND, obelisk
RIPON, obelisk
WEST HESLERTON, Newton Hall
    obelisk

Oxfordshire

STOKE LYNE, Foxhound obelisk

Shropshire

LILLESHALL, Sutherland obelisk
WILLEY, Shirlett Hall obelisk

Somerset

COPLEY WOOD, Roundway obelisk

South Yorkshire

HOOD GREEN, obelisk
NORTON, obelisk
SUTTON MOOR, obelisk

Staffordshire

TIXALL, obelisk

Suffolk

HELMINGHAM, obelisk
ICKWORTH, obelisk

Warwickshire

EDGE HILL, obelisk
STRATFORD ON AVON, Welcombe
    obelisk
STRETTON-ON-DUNSMORE,
    Departure Monument

West Midlands

MERIDEN, Cyclist's obelisk

West Sussex

COCKING CAUSEWAY, Cobden
    obelisk

West Yorkshire

TODMORDEN, Stoodley Pike obelisk

Wiltshire

CHERHILL, Lansdown obelisk

WALES

Dyfed

CARMARTHEN, Picton obelisk

Powys

NORTON, Green Price obelisk
PEN-Y-FAN, Tommy Jones's obelisk

SOME SCOTTISH OBELISKS AND DOVECOTES

Borders

DUNS, Nisbet pentagonal dovecote
EDNAM, Thomson obelisk
WHIM, dovecote

Central

FALKIRK, Carron House dovecote
KILLEARN, Buchanan obelisk

Dumfries and Galloway

ANWOTH, Rutherford obelisk
CARSPHAIN, Deer obelisk
WIGTOWN, Murray obelisk

Fife

DUNFERMLINE, Pittencrieff dovecote

Grampian

INVEREY, Lamont obelisk

Highland

BALMACARA, Murchison obelisk

CORPACH, Cameron obelisk
MOY, Mackintosh obelisk

Lothian

ABERLADY, Luffness dovecote
CARLOPS, Newhal obelisks
GLADSMUIR, Trabroun dovecote
HADDINGTON, Huntington
    dovecote; Nungate dovecote
HARBURNHEAD, column and
    dovecote
WEST SALTOUN, Saltoun dovecote

Strathclyde

CRAWFORD, obelisk
ERSKINE FERRY, Blantyre obelisk
HELENSBURGH, Bell's obelisk

Tayside

ABERNYTE, Megginch dovecote
NEW SCONE, obelisk

Bibliography

The following is a comprehensive listing of reference material consulted in the preparation of this volume, but we should point out that we do not include the numerous 18th- and 19th-century county histories, old tourist guides and guidebooks to gardens and/or follies, or articles and books concerning one specific folly or architect. Because of the bulk of material in *Country Life*, articles from that magazine have not been specified here either. Extensively used were the volumes of *The Royal Commission on Historical Monuments*, *The Victoria County Histories*, *The Shell County Guides*, Arthur Mee's *The King's England* series, *Garden History: the journal of the Garden History Society* and *The Journal of Garden History*. We should like also to acknowledge our special debt to Barbara Jones's *Follies and Grottoes*, Nikolaus Pevsner's *The Buildings of England* series, the many volumes of the *Dictionary of National Biography* and Howard Colvin's *Biographical Dictionary of British Architects: 1600–1840*.

J. J. C. Andrews, *The Well-Built Elephant and Other Roadside Attractions*, New York, 1984

Anon., *Decorations for Parks and Gardens*, London, 1790

Anon., *The Rise and Progress of the Present Taste in Planting Parks, Pleasure Grounds, Gardens, & c.*, London, 1767 (reprinted Newcastle-upon-Tyne, 1970)

J. Alexander, 'Follies', *Lincolnshire & Humberside Arts Diary*, 1977

B. J. Archer, *Follies: architecture for the late twentieth-century landscape*, New York, 1983

M. Archer, *Indian Architecture and the British*, Feltham, 1968

C. Aslet, 'Pavilioned in Extravagant Splendour', *The Times*, 1983

W. A. Bagley, 'Some Sussex Follies', *Sussex County Magazine*, 1937

R. C. Bald, 'Sir William Chambers and the Chinese Garden', *Journal of the History of Ideas*, 1950

J. Baltrusaitis, *Aberrations: quatre essais sur la légende des formes*, Paris, 1957

—— 'Jardins et pays d'illusion', *Traverses*, 1976

F. Barker and R. Hyde, *London As It Might Have Been*, London, 1982

W. Beckford (ed. Boyd Alexander), *Life at Fonthill*, London, 1957

J. S. Berrall, *The Garden: an illustrated history*, Harmondsworth, 1978

P. Bicknell, *Beauty, Horror and Immensity: picturesque landscapes in Britain, 1750–1850*, Cambridge, 1981

M. Binney and A. Hills, *Elysian Gardens*, London, 1979

E. Burke, *A Philosophical Enquiry into the Origin of Our Ideas of the Sublime and the Beautiful*, London, 1773 (*ed. princ.*, 1756)

A. Burton, *The Shell Book of Curious Britain*, Newton Abbot, 1982

R. G. Carrott, *The Egyptian Revival: its sources, monuments and meanings, 1808–1858*, Berkeley, Calif., 1979

G. Carter, P. Goode and L. Kedrun, *Humphrey Repton: landscape gardener, 1752–1818*, London, 1982

Sir Hugh Casson (ed.), *Follies*, London, 1963

—— *Monuments*, London, 1963

W. Chambers, *Designs of Chinese Buildings*, London, 1757

—— *Dissertation on Oriental Gardening*, London, 1772

H. F. Clark, 'Eighteenth-century Elysiums: the role of association in the landscape movement', *Journal of the Warburg and Courtauld Institutes*, 1943

—— *The English Landscape Garden*, Gloucester, 1980 (*ed. princ.*, London, 1948)

K. Clark, *The Gothic Revival*, London, 1975 (*ed. princ.*, 1928)

D. Clifford, *A History of Garden Design*, London, 1962

T. H. Cocke, 'Pre-Nineteenth-century Attitudes in England to Romanesque Architecture', *Journal of the British Archaeological Association*, 1973

H. Colvin, *A Biographical Dictionary of British Architects: 1600–1840*, London, 1978 (*ed. princ.*, 1954)

H. Colvin and J. Harris (eds), *The English Country Seat*, London, 1970

P. Conner, *Oriental Architecture in the West*, London, 1979

N. Cooper, 'Indian Influence in England: 1780–1830', *Apollo*, 1970

D. Cox, *Odd & Unusual Bedfordshire*, s.l., 1982

J. S. Curl, *The Egyptian Revival*, London, 1982

J. Curling, 'Castles in the Air', *Lilliput*, 1948

R. A. Curtis (ed.), *Monumental Follies*, Worthing, 1972

A. Dale, *James Wyatt*, Oxford, 1956

T. Davis, *John Nash: the Prince Regent's architect*, Newton Abbot, 1973

—— *The Gothick Taste*, Norwich, 1974

T. D. W. Dearn, *Designs for Lodges and Entrances to Parks, Paddocks, and*

Pleasure-Grounds, in the Gothic, Cottage and Fancy Styles, London, 1823 (*ed. princ.*, 1811)

P. Decker, *Chinese Architecture*, London, 1759 (reprinted Farnborough, 1968)

—— *Gothic Architecture Decorated*, London, 1759 (reprinted Farnborough, 1968)

R. Desmond, *Bibliography of British Gardens*, Winchester, 1984

R. Dixon and S. Muthesius, *Victorian Architecture*, London, 1978

J. Dobai, *Die Kunstliteratur des Klassizismus und der Romantik in England*, Bern, 1974–7

R. Dutton, *The English Garden*, London, 1945

J. Elffers and M. Schuyt, *Fantastic Architecture*, London, 1980

R. Elsam, *An Essay on Rural Architecture*, London, 1803 (reprinted Farnborough, 1972)

E. Erdberg, *Chinese Influence on European Garden Structures*, Cambridge, Mass., 1936

D. Erwin, 'A Picturesque Experience: the hermitage at Dunkeld', *The Connoisseur*, 1974

K. A. Esdaile, 'The Small House and its Amenities in the Architectural Handbooks: 1749–1847', *Transactions of the Bibliographical Society*, 1917–19

P. Eyres (ed.), *Mr. Aislabie's Gardens*, Bradford, 1981

R. Fedden and R. Joekes (eds), *The National Trust Guide*, London, 1984 (3rd edn)

M. Felmingham and R. Graham, *Ruins*, Feltham, 1972

H. Fenwick, 'Features and Follies', *Scots Magazine*, 1965

F. D. Fergusson, *The Neo-Classical Architecture of James Wyatt*, unpublished PhD thesis, Harvard, 1973

M. Fischer, *Katalog der Architektur- und Ornamentstichsammlung der Kunstbibliothek Berlin*, i, *Baukunst England*, Berlin, 1977

J. Fleming, *Robert Adam and his Circle*, London, 1962

—— 'Adam Gothick', *The Connoisseur*, 1968

L. Fleming and A. Gore, *The English Garden*, London, 1979

P. Frankl, *The Gothic: literary sources and interpretations through eight centuries*, Princeton, NJ, 1960

G. E. Fussell, 'Natural Ice', *Architectural Review*, 1952

J. Gandy, *The Rural Architect*, London, 1805

J. Gaus, 'Die Urhütte: über ein Model der Baukunst und ein Motiv in der bildenden Kunst', *Wallraf-Richartz Jahrbuch*, 1971

G. Germann, *Gothic Revival in Europe and Britain: sources, influences and ideas*, London, 1972

W. Gilpin, *Essays on Picturesque Beauty; on picturesque travel and on sketching landscape*, London, 1794

M. Girouard, *The Victorian Country House*, London, 1978

—— *Life in the English Country House*, London, 1979

J. Gloag, *Georgian Grace: a social history of design, 1660–1830*, London, 1956

—— *Mr. Loudon's England*, Newcastle-upon-Tyne, 1970

R. H. Goodsall, 'Follies and Gazebos', *A Second Kentish Patchwork*, 1968

M. Grant, 'Full Circle at the Folly', *Country Fair*, 1967

L. Greeves (ed.), *The National Trust Atlas*, London, 1981

Mrs D. Guinness, 'The Deliberate Follies of Ireland', *Ireland of the Welcomes*, 1972

R. Gunnis, *Dictionary of British Sculptors: 1660–1851*, London, 1968 (*ed. princ.*, 1953)

J. Hadfield (ed.), *The Shell Guide to England*, London, 1977

M. Hadfield, *The English Landscape Garden*, Aylesbury, 1977

M. Hadfield, R. Harling and L. Highton, *British Gardeners: a biographical dictionary*, London, 1980

W. Halfpenny, *New Designs for Chinese Temples, etc.*, London, 1750

W. and J. Halfpenny, *Rural Architecture in the Chinese Taste*, London, 1752

—— *Rural Architecture in the Gothic Taste*, London, 1752

J. Hall, *Essay on the Origin, History and Principles of Gothic Architecture*, London, 1813

R. Harbison, *Eccentric Spaces*, New York, 1977

E. Harris, 'Burke and Chambers on the Sublime and Beautiful', *Essays in the History of Architecture presented to Rudolf Wittkower*, London, 1967

—— 'False speranze e vani desideri: progetti di Thomas Wright', *Arte illustrata*, 1973

—— 'Batty Langley: a tutor to freemasons (1696–1751)', *The Burlington Magazine*, 1977

J. Harris, 'Exotism at Kew', *Apollo*, 1963

—— 'The Dundas Empire', *Apollo*, 1967

—— *Sir William Chambers: Knight of the Polar Star*, London, 1970

—— *The Artist and the Country House: a history of country house and garden view painting in Britain, 1540–1870*, London, 1979

—— 'William Kent's Gothick', *A Gothick Symposium*, London, 1983

G. F. Hartlaub, *Der Gartenzwerg und seine Ahnen*, Heidelberg, 1962

G. Hartmann, *Die Ruine im Landschaftsgarten*, Worms, 1981

W. Hawkes, 'The Gothic Architectural Work of Sanderson Miller', *A Gothick Symposium*, London, 1983

L. R. G. Headley, 'The Follies of Dorset', *Dorset Arts Magazine*, 1984

J. Heeley, *Letters on the Beauties of Hagley, Envil and The Leasowes*, London, 1777

A. Hellyer, *The Shell Guide to Gardens*, London, 1977

R. Hewlings, 'Ripon's Forum Populi', *Architectural History*, 1981

W. Hipple, *The Beautiful, the Sublime and the Picturesque in Eighteenth-century British Aesthetic Theory*, Carbondale, 1957

G. Hogg, *Odd Aspects of England*, Newton Abbott, 1968

A. M. Holcomb, 'The Bridge in the Middle Distance: symbolic elements in the Romantic landscape', *The Art Quarterly*, 1974

H. Honour, *Chinoiserie: the vision of Cathay*, London, 1961

J. D. Hunt, 'Emblem and Expression in the Eighteenth-century Landscape Garden', *Eighteenth-century Studies*, 1971

—— *The Figure in the Landscape: poetry, painting and gardening during the eighteenth century*, Baltimore, Md, 1976

J. D. Hunt and P. Willis (eds), *The Genius of the Place: the English landscape garden, 1620–1820*, London, 1975

P. Hunt, *The Book of Garden Ornament*, London, 1974

C. Hussey, *The Picturesque*, London, 1927

—— *English Gardens and Landscapes: 1700–1750*, London, 1970

E. Hyams, *Capability Brown and Humphrey Repton*, London, 1971

O. Impey, *Chinoiserie: the impact of Oriental styles on Western art and decoration*, London, 1977

D. Jaques, *Georgian Gardens: the reign of nature*, London, 1983

E. Jameson, *1,000 Curiosities of Britain*, London, 1947

D. Jarrett, *The English Landscape Garden*, London, 1978

C. Jencks, *Bizarre Architecture*, London, 1979

F. I. Jenkins, 'Harbingers of the Eiffel Tower', *Journal of the Society of Architectural Historians*, 1957

—— 'Some Nineteenth-century Towers', *RIBA Journal*, 1958

—— 'John Foulston and his Public Buildings in Plymouth, Stonehouse and Devonport', *Journal of the Society of Architectural Historians*, 1968

G. W. Johnson, *A History of English Gardening*, London, 1829 (reprinted New York, 1982)

B. Jones, 'Beside the Sea', *Architectural Review*, 1947

—— *Follies and Grottoes*, London, 1953

—— *Follies and Grottoes*, London, 1974 (new edn)

M. Jourdain, *The Work of William Kent*, London, 1948

E. Kaufmann, *Architecture in the Age of Reason*, New York, 1968 (*ed. princ.*, 1955)

A. Kelly, 'Coade Stone at National Trust Houses', *National Trust Studies 1980*, London, 1979

P. Kidson, P. Murray and P. Thompson, *A History of English Architecture*, Harmondsworth, 1979

R. A. Kindler, 'Periodical Criticism 1815–1840: originality in architecture', *Architectural History*, 1974

N. and B. Kitz, *Painshill Park: Hamilton and his picturesque landscape*, London, 1984

R. P. Knight, *The Landscape: a didactic poem*, London, 1794
—— *An Analytical Inquiry into the Principles of Taste*, London, 1805

D. Lambin, 'Notes on Space and Space Perception in Eighteenth-century Parks and Gardens', *Kunst und Kunsttheorie des XVIII. Jahrhunderts in England*, Hildesheim, 1979

L. Lambton, *Beastly Buildings: the National Trust book of architecture for animals*, London, 1985

C. Lancaster, *Architectural Follies in America or Hammer, Saw, Tooth and Nail*, Rutland, Vt, 1960

S. Lang, 'The Principles of the Gothic Revival in England', *Journal of the Society of Architectural Historians*, 1966

S. Lang and N. Pevsner, 'Sir William Temple and Sharawaggi', *Architectural Review*, 1949

B. and T. Langley, *New Principles of Gardening*, London, 1728
—— *Gothic Architecture Improved*, London, 1747 (reprinted Farnborough, 1967)

F. Laske, *Der Ostasiatische Einfluss auf die Baukunst des Abendlandes*, Berlin, 1909

B. Lassus, *Jardins imaginaires*, Paris, 1977

J. Lees-Milne, *The National Trust: a record of fifty years' achievement*, London, 1945
—— *Earls of Creation*, London, 1962
—— *William Beckford*, Tisbury, 1976

T. Lightoler, *The Gentleman and Farmer's Architect*, London, 1774 (*ed. princ.*, 1762; reprinted Farnborough, 1968)

C. J. E. Prince de Ligne, *Coup d'oeil sur Beloeil; et sur une grande partie de l'Europe*, Paris, 1922 (*ed. princ.*, 1781)

I. G. Lindsay and M. Cosh, *Inveraray and the Dukes of Argyll*, Edinburgh, 1973

J. C. Loudon, *An Encyclopaedia of Gardening*, London, 1822
—— *An Encyclopaedia of Cottage, Farm and Villa Architecture and Furniture*, London, 1833

A. O. Lovejoy, *Essays in the History of Ideas*, Baltimore, Md, 1961

J. Macaulay, *The Gothic Revival 1745–1845*, Glasgow, 1975

R. Macaulay, *Pleasure of Ruins*, London, 1953

Bibliography

M. McCarthy, 'Sir Thomas Robinson: an original English Palladian', *Architectura*, 1980

—— 'Thomas Wright's Designs for Gothic Garden Buildings'; 'Thomas Wright's Designs for Temples and Related Drawings for Garden Buildings', *Journal of Garden History*, 1981

R. F. Maccubin and P. Martin (eds), 'Special issue: British and American gardens', *Eighteenth-century Life*, 1983

M. McMordie, 'Picturesque Patternbooks and Pre-Victorian Designers', *Architectural History*, 1975

E. Malins, *English Landscaping and Literature: 1660–1840*, London, 1966

—— 'Indian Influences on English Houses and Gardens at the Beginning of the Nineteenth Century', *Garden History*, 1980

E. Malins and the Knight of Glin, *Lost Demesnes: Irish landscape gardening, 1660–1845*, London, 1976

E. Manwaring, *Italian Landscape in Eighteenth-century England*, New York, 1925

C. Marriott, 'The Necessity of Follies', *Architectural Review*, 1950

S. Marsden and D. McLaren, *In Ruins: the once great homes of Ireland*, London, 1980

J. P. Martinon, 'Les espaces corrigés', *Traverses*, 1976

G. Mason, *An Essay on Design in Gardening*, London, 1795

W. Mason, *The English Garden*, London, 1777–81

C. Meeks, 'Picturesque Eclecticism', *Art Bulletin*, 1950

—— 'Creative Eclecticism', *Journal of the Society of Architectural Historians*, 1953

U. M. Mehrtens, *Folly in Groot-Brittannië aanzet en ordening aan de hand van een bronnenonderzoek*, unpublished PhD thesis, Utrecht, 1980

H. C. Mettin, *Fürst Pückler reist nach England*, Berlin, 1938

W. G. J. M. Meulenkamp, 'Portfolio Follies: journaal van een reis naar Engeland, etc.', *Maatstaf*, 1978

—— *'Fuller hath done a very great thing': 'Mad Jack' Fuller and his follies*, unpublished PhD thesis, Utrecht, 1980

C. Middleton, *Decorations in Parks and Gardens*, London, 1800

N. Miller, *Heavenly Caves: reflections on the garden grotto*, London, 1982

S. H. Monk, *The Sublime*, Ann Arbor, Mich., 1960 (*ed. princ.*, 1935)

J. Mordaunt Crook, *The Greek Revival*, Feltham, 1968

—— 'The Pre-Victorian Architect: professionalism and patronage', *Architectural History*, 1969

—— Introduction to C. Eastlake, *A History of the Gothic Revival*, London, 1872 (reprinted New York, 1970)

Bibliography

—— *The Greek Revival: neo-classical attitudes in British architecture, 1760–1870*, London, 1972

R. Morris, *The Art of Architecture: a poem*, London, 1742

—— *Rural Architecture*, London, 1750

—— *The Architectural Remembrancer*, London, 1752 (reprinted Farnborough, 1971)

T. Mowl, 'The Case of the Enville Museum', *Journal of Garden History*, 1983

—— 'The Evolution of the Park Gate Lodge as a Building Type', *Architectural History*, 1984

K. Murawska, 'An Image of Mysterious Wisdom Won by Toil: the tower as symbol of thoughtful isolation in English art and literature from Milton to Yeats', *Artibus et historiae: rivista internazionale di arti visive e cinema*, 1982

C. W. Nachmani, 'The Early English Cottage Book', *Marsyas*, 1968

P. J. Neville Havins, *The Spas of England*, London, 1976

E. Newby and D. Petry, *Wonders of Britain*, London, 1968

A. Nuijten, *Op de valreep beschouwd: Hackfall, een tuin en zijn gebouwen*, unpublished PhD thesis, Utrecht, 1983

P. Oppé, 'Robert Adam's Picturesque Compositions', *The Burlington Magazine*, 1942

C. Over, *Ornamental Architecture in the Gothic, Chinese and Modern Taste*, London, 1758

T. C. Overton, *Original Designs of Temples (The Temple Builder's Most Useful Companion)*, London, 1766

J. B. Papworth, *Rural Residences*, London, 1818 (reprinted Farnborough, 1971)

A. Parreaux and M. Plaisant (eds), *Jardins et paysages: le style anglais*, Lille, 1977

R. Paulson, *Emblem and Expression: meaning in English art of the eighteenth century*, London, 1975

N. Pevsner, 'The Other Chambers', *Architectural Review*, 1947

—— 'Good King James's Gothic', *Architectural Review*, 1950

—— (ed.), *The Picturesque Garden and its Influence Outside the British Isles*, Dumbarton Oaks, 1974

N. Pevsner and S. Lang, 'The Egyptian Revival', *Architectural Review*, 1956

J. Piper, 'Pleasing Decay', *Architectural Review*, 1947

J. Plaw, *Ferme ornée; or Rural Improvements*, London, 1795

W. F. Pocock, *Architectural Designs for Rustic Cottages*, London, 1807 (reprinted Farnborough, 1972)

M. Praz, 'Costume 14: Follies', *Bellezza e bizzarria*, Milan, 1960

E. Preston, *Curious England*, Aylesbury, 1977

U. Price, *An Essay on the Picturesque*, London, 1794

A. W. Reinink and J. Vermeulen, *Ijskelders*, Nieuwkoop, 1981

H. Repton, *Observations on the Theory and Practice of Landscape Gardening*, London, 1803

O. Reutensvard, *The Neo-Classic Temple of Virility and the Buildings with a Phallic-shaped Ground Plan*, Lund, 1971

M. Revesz-Alexander, *Der Turm als Symbol und Erlebnis*, The Hague, 1953

RIBA, *Catalogue of the Drawings Collection of the Royal Institute of British Architects*, London, 1969–76

A. E. Richardson, *Robert Mylne*, London, 1955

D. S. Richardson, *Gothic Revival Architecture in Ireland*, unpublished PhD thesis, Yale, 1971

P. A. Robb, 'The Temple of Pan at Halswell Park, Somerset', *Garden History*, 1977

J. M. Robinson, 'Model Farm Buildings of the Age of Improvement', *Architectural History*, 1976

—— *The Wyatts: an architectural dynasty*, Oxford, 1979

—— *Georgian Model Farms*, Oxford, 1983

—— *The Latest Country Houses*, London, 1984

J. Rory (ed.), *Adam de la Halle: le jeu de la feuillée*, Paris, 1977

G. le Rouge, *Détails des nouveaux jardins à la mode (Jardins anglo-chinoise à la mode)*, Paris, 1776–88

A. Rowan, *Garden Buildings*, Feltham, 1968

—— 'Gothick Restoration at Raby Castle', *Architectural History*, 1972

—— 'Batty Langley's Gothic', *Studies in Memory of David Talbot Rice*, Edinburgh, 1975

P. de la Ruffinière du Prey, 'John Soane, Philip Yorke and their Quest for Primitive Architecture', *National Trust Studies 1979*, London, 1978

—— *John Soane: the making of an architect*, Chicago, 1982

J. Rykwert, *On Adam's House in Paradise: the idea of the primitive hut in architectural history*, New York, 1972

—— *The First Moderns: the architects of the eighteenth century*, Cambridge, Mass., 1980

W. Shenstone, *The Works in Verse and Prose*, London, 1766 (*ed. princ.*, 1764)

J. Simmen, *Ruinen-Faszination in der Graphik vom 16. Jahrhundert bis in die Gegenwart*, Dortmund, 1980

D. Simpson, *Gothick: 1720–1840*, Brighton, 1975

O. Sirén, *China and the Gardens of Europe*, New York, 1950

J. Smith (ed.), *The Landmark Handbook*, Shottesbrooke, 1977

South Yorkshire County Council, *Follies & Monuments of South Yorkshire*, Gainsborough, 1977

P. Stanton, *Pugin*, London, 1971

J. Steegman, *The Rule of Taste from George I to George IV*, London, 1968 (*ed. princ.*, 1936)

K. Stempel, *Geschichtsbilder im frühen englischen Garten*, Münster, 1982

S. H. Stephenson, *Rustic Furniture*, New York, 1979

K. Stromberg, 'Von Göttern und Gartenzwergen: die bewohnte Natur als Kunst und Kunstkammer', *Kunst & Antiquitäten*, 1981

D. Stroud, *Humphrey Repton*, London, 1963

—— *Capability Brown*, London, 1975

D. C. Stuart, *Georgian Gardens*, London, 1979

R. Sühnel, *Der Park als Gesamtkunstwerk des englischen Klassizismus am Beispiel von Stourhead*, Heidelberg, 1977

J. Summerson, 'The Vision of J. M. Gandy', *Heavenly Mansions*, New York, 1963

—— *Architecture in Britain: 1530–1830*, Harmondsworth, 1970 (*ed. princ.*, 1953)

D. Sutton (ed.), 'The Splendours of Stowe', *Apollo*, 1973

A. A. Tait, *The Landscape Garden in Scotland: 1735–1835*, Edinburgh, 1980

—— 'The Landscape Garden and Neoclassicism', *Journal of Garden History*, 1983

N. Temple, *John Nash and the Village Picturesque*, Gloucester, 1979

C. Thacker, *Masters of the Grotto: Joseph and Josiah Lane*, Tisbury, 1976

G. S. Thomas, *Gardens of the National Trust*, London, 1979

P. Toynbee (ed.), 'Horace Walpole's Journals of Visits to Country Seats, &c.', *Walpole Society*, 1928

A. Vidler, 'The Architecture of Lodges: ritual form and associational life in the late Enlightenment', *Oppositions*, 1976

H. Vogel, 'Ägyptisierende Baukunst des Klassizismus', *Zeitschrift für bildende Kunst*, 1928–9

H. Walpole, *Works*, London, 1798–1825

D. Watkin, *Thomas Hope and the Neo-Classical Idea*, London, 1968

—— *The English Vision*, London, 1982

I. Weibezahn, *Geschichte und Funktion des Monopteros*, Hildesheim, 1975

R. White, 'The Influence of Batty Langley', *A Gothick Symposium*, London, 1983

R. White and T. Mowl, 'Thomas Robins at Painswick', *Journal of Garden History*, 1984

J. Whitelaw, *Follies*, Aylesbury, 1982

D. Wiebenson, 'Greek, Gothic and Nature: 1750–1820', *Essays in Honour of*

Walter Friedlaender, Glückstadt, 1965

—— *Sources of Greek Revival Architecture*, London, 1969

Sir Clough Williams-Ellis, *Architect errant*, London, 1971

P. Willis, 'Capability Brown in Northumberland', *Garden History*, 1981

—— (ed.), *Furor hortensis: essays on the history of the English landscape garden in memory of H. F. Clark*, Edinburgh, 1974

M. I. Wilson, *William Kent: architect, designer, painter, gardener: 1685–1748*, London, 1984

J. Wilton-Ely, 'Beckford the Builder', *William Beckford Exhibition 1976*, Tisbury, 1976

R. Wittkower, 'English Neo-Palladianism, the Landscape Garden, China, and the Enlightenment', *L'arte*, 1969

C. Wolsdorff, 'Englische Publikationen des 18. Jahrhunderts zu "Architecture" und "Building"', *Kunst und Kunsttheorie des XVIII. Jahrhunderts in England*, Hildesheim, 1979

T. E. B. Wood, *The Word 'Sublime' and its Context*, The Hague/Paris, 1972

K. Woodbridge, *Landscape and Antiquity*, Oxford, 1971

—— 'Kent's Gardening: the Rousham letters', *Apollo*, 1974

—— *The Stourhead Landscape*, s.l., 1974

T. Wright, *Arbours and Grottos: a facsimile of the two parts of 'Universal architecture' (1755 and 1758)*, London, 1979

W. Wrighte, *Grotesque Architecture*, London, 1790 (*ed. princ.*, 1767)

P. Wrightson, *The Small English House*, London, 1977

B. Zijlstra, *De folly en haar ontwerp in de 18e en vroeg 19e architectonische handboeken*, unpublished PhD thesis, Utrecht, 1980

Index

Index

Index

Index

Index

Index